Communications
in Computer and Information Science 435

Constantine Stephanidis (Ed.)

HCI International 2014 – Posters' Extended Abstracts

International Conference, HCI International 2014
Heraklion, Crete, Greece, June 22-27, 2014
Proceedings, Part II

 Springer

Volume Editor

Constantine Stephanidis
Foundation for Research and Technology - Hellas (FORTH)
Institute of Computer Science
N. Plastira 100, Vassilika Vouton
70013 Heraklion, Crete, Greece
and
University of Crete
Department of Computer Science
Heraklion, Crete, Greece
E-mail: cs@ics.forth.gr

ISSN 1865-0929   e-ISSN 1865-0937
ISBN 978-3-319-07853-3   e-ISBN 978-3-319-07854-0
DOI 10.1007/978-3-319-07854-0
Springer Cham Heidelberg New York Dordrecht London

Library of Congress Control Number: 2014940387

Typesetting: Camera-ready by author, data conversion by Scientific Publishing Services, Chennai, India

Printed on acid-free paper

Springer is part of Springer Science+Business Media (www.springer.com)

Foreword

The 16th International Conference on Human–Computer Interaction, HCI International 2014, was held in Heraklion, Crete, Greece, during June 22–27, 2014, incorporating 14 conferences/thematic areas:

Thematic areas:

- Human–Computer Interaction
- Human Interface and the Management of Information

Affiliated conferences:

- 11th International Conference on Engineering Psychology and Cognitive Ergonomics
- 8th International Conference on Universal Access in Human–Computer Interaction
- 6th International Conference on Virtual, Augmented and Mixed Reality
- 6th International Conference on Cross-Cultural Design
- 6th International Conference on Social Computing and Social Media
- 8th International Conference on Augmented Cognition
- 5th International Conference on Digital Human Modeling and Applications in Health, Safety, Ergonomics and Risk Management
- Third International Conference on Design, User Experience and Usability
- Second International Conference on Distributed, Ambient and Pervasive Interactions
- Second International Conference on Human Aspects of Information Security, Privacy and Trust
- First International Conference on HCI in Business
- First International Conference on Learning and Collaboration Technologies

A total of 4,766 individuals from academia, research institutes, industry, and governmental agencies from 78 countries submitted contributions, and 1,476 papers and 225 posters were included in the proceedings. These papers address the latest research and development efforts and highlight the human aspects of design and use of computing systems. The papers thoroughly cover the entire field of human–computer interaction, addressing major advances in knowledge and effective use of computers in a variety of application areas.

This volume, edited by Constantine Stephanidis, contains extended abstracts of posters addressing the following major topics:

- Social Media and Social Networks
- Learning and education
- Design for All, accessibility and assistive environments

- Design for aging
- Games and Exergames
- Health and well-being
- Ergonomics and Safety
- HCI in business, tourism and trasport
- Human-human and human-agent communication
- User experience case studies

The remaining volumes of the HCI International 2014 proceedings are:

- Volume 1, LNCS 8510, Human–Computer Interaction: HCI Theories, Methods and Tools (Part I), edited by Masaaki Kurosu
- Volume 2, LNCS 8511, Human–Computer Interaction: Advanced Interaction Modalities and Techniques (Part II), edited by Masaaki Kurosu
- Volume 3, LNCS 8512, Human–Computer Interaction: Applications and Services (Part III), edited by Masaaki Kurosu
- Volume 4, LNCS 8513, Universal Access in Human–Computer Interaction: Design and Development Methods for Universal Access (Part I), edited by Constantine Stephanidis and Margherita Antona
- Volume 5, LNCS 8514, Universal Access in Human–Computer Interaction: Universal Access to Information and Knowledge (Part II), edited by Constantine Stephanidis and Margherita Antona
- Volume 6, LNCS 8515, Universal Access in Human–Computer Interaction: Aging and Assistive Environments (Part III), edited by Constantine Stephanidis and Margherita Antona
- Volume 7, LNCS 8516, Universal Access in Human–Computer Interaction: Design for All and Accessibility Practice (Part IV), edited by Constantine Stephanidis and Margherita Antona
- Volume 8, LNCS 8517, Design, User Experience, and Usability: Theories, Methods and Tools for Designing the User Experience (Part I), edited by Aaron Marcus
- Volume 9, LNCS 8518, Design, User Experience, and Usability: User Experience Design for Diverse Interaction Platforms and Environments (Part II), edited by Aaron Marcus
- Volume 10, LNCS 8519, Design, User Experience, and Usability: User Experience Design for Everyday Life Applications and Services (Part III), edited by Aaron Marcus
- Volume 11, LNCS 8520, Design, User Experience, and Usability: User Experience Design Practice (Part IV), edited by Aaron Marcus
- Volume 12, LNCS 8521, Human Interface and the Management of Information: Information and Knowledge Design and Evaluation (Part I), edited by Sakae Yamamoto
- Volume 13, LNCS 8522, Human Interface and the Management of Information: Information and Knowledge in Applications and Services (Part II), edited by Sakae Yamamoto

- Volume 14, LNCS 8523, Learning and Collaboration Technologies: Designing and Developing Novel Learning Experiences (Part I), edited by Panayiotis Zaphiris and Andri Ioannou
- Volume 15, LNCS 8524, Learning and Collaboration Technologies: Technology-rich Environments for Learning and Collaboration (Part II), edited by Panayiotis Zaphiris and Andri Ioannou
- Volume 16, LNCS 8525, Virtual, Augmented and Mixed Reality: Designing and Developing Virtual and Augmented Environments (Part I), edited by Randall Shumaker and Stephanie Lackey
- Volume 17, LNCS 8526, Virtual, Augmented and Mixed Reality: Applications of Virtual and Augmented Reality (Part II), edited by Randall Shumaker and Stephanie Lackey
- Volume 18, LNCS 8527, HCI in Business, edited by Fiona Fui-Hoon Nah
- Volume 19, LNCS 8528, Cross-Cultural Design, edited by P.L. Patrick Rau
- Volume 20, LNCS 8529, Digital Human Modeling and Applications in Health, Safety, Ergonomics and Risk Management, edited by Vincent G. Duffy
- Volume 21, LNCS 8530, Distributed, Ambient, and Pervasive Interactions, edited by Norbert Streitz and Panos Markopoulos
- Volume 22, LNCS 8531, Social Computing and Social Media, edited by Gabriele Meiselwitz
- Volume 23, LNAI 8532, Engineering Psychology and Cognitive Ergonomics, edited by Don Harris
- Volume 24, LNCS 8533, Human Aspects of Information Security, Privacy and Trust, edited by Theo Tryfonas and Ioannis Askoxylakis
- Volume 25, LNAI 8534, Foundations of Augmented Cognition, edited by Dylan D. Schmorrow and Cali M. Fidopiastis
- Volume 26, CCIS 434, HCI International 2014 Posters Proceedings (Part I), edited by Constantine Stephanidis

I would like to thank the Program Chairs and the members of the Program Boards of all affiliated conferences and thematic areas, listed below, for their contribution to the highest scientific quality and the overall success of the HCI International 2014 Conference.

This conference could not have been possible without the continuous support and advice of the founding chair and conference scientific advisor, Prof. Gavriel Salvendy, as well as the dedicated work and outstanding efforts of the communications chair and editor of *HCI International News*, Dr. Abbas Moallem.

I would also like to thank for their contribution towards the smooth organization of the HCI International 2014 Conference the members of the Human–Computer Interaction Laboratory of ICS-FORTH, and in particular George Paparoulis, Maria Pitsoulaki, Maria Bouhli, and George Kapnas.

April 2014   Constantine Stephanidis
                                                 General Chair, HCI International 2014

Organization

Human–Computer Interaction

Program Chair: Masaaki Kurosu, Japan

Jose Abdelnour-Nocera, UK

Sebastiano Bagnara, Italy

Simone Barbosa, Brazil

Adriana Betiol, Brazil

Simone Borsci, UK

Henry Duh, Australia

Xiaowen Fang, USA

Vicki Hanson, UK

Wonil Hwang, Korea

Minna Isomursu, Finland

Yong Gu Ji, Korea

Anirudha Joshi, India

Esther Jun, USA

Kyungdoh Kim, Korea

Heidi Krömker, Germany

Chen Ling, USA

Chang S. Nam, USA

Naoko Okuizumi, Japan

Philippe Palanque, France

Ling Rothrock, USA

Naoki Sakakibara, Japan

Dominique Scapin, France

Guangfeng Song, USA

Sanjay Tripathi, India

Chui Yin Wong, Malaysia

Toshiki Yamaoka, Japan

Kazuhiko Yamazaki, Japan

Ryoji Yoshitake, Japan

Human Interface and the Management of Information

Program Chair: Sakae Yamamoto, Japan

Alan Chan, Hong Kong

Denis A. Coelho, Portugal

Linda Elliott, USA

Shin'ichi Fukuzumi, Japan

Michitaka Hirose, Japan

Makoto Itoh, Japan

Yen-Yu Kang, Taiwan

Koji Kimita, Japan

Daiji Kobayashi, Japan

Hiroyuki Miki, Japan

Hirohiko Mori, Japan

Shogo Nishida, Japan

Robert Proctor, USA

Youngho Rhee, Korea

Ryosuke Saga, Japan

Katsunori Shimohara, Japan

Kim-Phuong Vu, USA

Tomio Watanabe, Japan

Engineering Psychology and Cognitive Ergonomics

Program Chair: Don Harris, UK

Guy Andre Boy, USA
Shan Fu, P.R. China
Hung-Sying Jing, Taiwan
Wen-Chin Li, Taiwan
Mark Neerincx, The Netherlands
Jan Noyes, UK
Paul Salmon, Australia

Axel Schulte, Germany
Siraj Shaikh, UK
Sarah Sharples, UK
Anthony Smoker, UK
Neville Stanton, UK
Alex Stedmon, UK
Andrew Thatcher, South Africa

Universal Access in Human–Computer Interaction

**Program Chairs: Constantine Stephanidis, Greece,
and Margherita Antona, Greece**

Julio Abascal, Spain
Gisela Susanne Bahr, USA
João Barroso, Portugal
Margrit Betke, USA
Anthony Brooks, Denmark
Christian Bühler, Germany
Stefan Carmien, Spain
Hua Dong, P.R. China
Carlos Duarte, Portugal
Pier Luigi Emiliani, Italy
Qin Gao, P.R. China
Andrina Granić, Croatia
Andreas Holzinger, Austria
Josette Jones, USA
Simeon Keates, UK

Georgios Kouroupetroglou, Greece
Patrick Langdon, UK
Barbara Leporini, Italy
Eugene Loos, The Netherlands
Ana Isabel Paraguay, Brazil
Helen Petrie, UK
Michael Pieper, Germany
Enrico Pontelli, USA
Jaime Sanchez, Chile
Alberto Sanna, Italy
Anthony Savidis, Greece
Christian Stary, Austria
Hirotada Ueda, Japan
Gerhard Weber, Germany
Harald Weber, Germany

Virtual, Augmented and Mixed Reality

**Program Chairs: Randall Shumaker, USA,
and Stephanie Lackey, USA**

Roland Blach, Germany
Sheryl Brahnam, USA
Juan Cendan, USA
Jessie Chen, USA
Panagiotis D. Kaklis, UK

Hirokazu Kato, Japan
Denis Laurendeau, Canada
Fotis Liarokapis, UK
Michael Macedonia, USA
Gordon Mair, UK

Jose San Martin, Spain
Tabitha Peck, USA
Christian Sandor, Australia

Christopher Stapleton, USA
Gregory Welch, USA

Cross-Cultural Design

Program Chair: P.L. Patrick Rau, P.R. China

Yee-Yin Choong, USA
Paul Fu, USA
Zhiyong Fu, P.R. China
Pin-Chao Liao, P.R. China
Dyi-Yih Michael Lin, Taiwan
Rungtai Lin, Taiwan
Ta-Ping (Robert) Lu, Taiwan
Liang Ma, P.R. China
Alexander Mädche, Germany

Sheau-Farn Max Liang, Taiwan
Katsuhiko Ogawa, Japan
Tom Plocher, USA
Huatong Sun, USA
Emil Tso, P.R. China
Hsiu-Ping Yueh, Taiwan
Liang (Leon) Zeng, USA
Jia Zhou, P.R. China

Online Communities and Social Media

Program Chair: Gabriele Meiselwitz, USA

Leonelo Almeida, Brazil
Chee Siang Ang, UK
Aneesha Bakharia, Australia
Ania Bobrowicz, UK
James Braman, USA
Farzin Deravi, UK
Carsten Kleiner, Germany
Niki Lambropoulos, Greece
Soo Ling Lim, UK

Anthony Norcio, USA
Portia Pusey, USA
Panote Siriaraya, UK
Stefan Stieglitz, Germany
Giovanni Vincenti, USA
Yuanqiong (Kathy) Wang, USA
June Wei, USA
Brian Wentz, USA

Augmented Cognition

Program Chairs: Dylan D. Schmorrow, USA,
and Cali M. Fidopiastis, USA

Ahmed Abdelkhalek, USA
Robert Atkinson, USA
Monique Beaudoin, USA
John Blitch, USA
Alenka Brown, USA

Rosario Cannavò, Italy
Joseph Cohn, USA
Andrew J. Cowell, USA
Martha Crosby, USA
Wai-Tat Fu, USA

Rodolphe Gentili, USA
Frederick Gregory, USA
Michael W. Hail, USA
Monte Hancock, USA
Fei Hu, USA
Ion Juvina, USA
Joe Keebler, USA
Philip Mangos, USA
Rao Mannepalli, USA
David Martinez, USA
Yvonne R. Masakowski, USA
Santosh Mathan, USA
Ranjeev Mittu, USA

Keith Niall, USA
Tatana Olson, USA
Debra Patton, USA
June Pilcher, USA
Robinson Pino, USA
Tiffany Poeppelman, USA
Victoria Romero, USA
Amela Sadagic, USA
Anna Skinner, USA
Ann Speed, USA
Robert Sottilare, USA
Peter Walker, USA

Digital Human Modeling and Applications in Health, Safety, Ergonomics and Risk Management

Program Chair: Vincent G. Duffy, USA

Giuseppe Andreoni, Italy
Daniel Carruth, USA
Elsbeth De Korte, The Netherlands
Afzal A. Godil, USA
Ravindra Goonetilleke, Hong Kong
Noriaki Kuwahara, Japan
Kang Li, USA
Zhizhong Li, P.R. China

Tim Marler, USA
Jianwei Niu, P.R. China
Michelle Robertson, USA
Matthias Rötting, Germany
Mao-Jiun Wang, Taiwan
Xuguang Wang, France
James Yang, USA

Design, User Experience, and Usability

Program Chair: Aaron Marcus, USA

Sisira Adikari, Australia
Claire Ancient, USA
Arne Berger, Germany
Jamie Blustein, Canada
Ana Boa-Ventura, USA
Jan Brejcha, Czech Republic
Lorenzo Cantoni, Switzerland
Marc Fabri, UK
Luciane Maria Fadel, Brazil
Tricia Flanagan, Hong Kong
Jorge Frascara, Mexico

Federico Gobbo, Italy
Emilie Gould, USA
Rüdiger Heimgärtner, Germany
Brigitte Herrmann, Germany
Steffen Hess, Germany
Nouf Khashman, Canada
Fabiola Guillermina Noël, Mexico
Francisco Rebelo, Portugal
Kerem Rızvanoğlu, Turkey
Marcelo Soares, Brazil
Carla Spinillo, Brazil

Distributed, Ambient and Pervasive Interactions

**Program Chairs: Norbert Streitz, Germany,
and Panos Markopoulos, The Netherlands**

Juan Carlos Augusto, UK
Jose Bravo, Spain
Adrian Cheok, UK
Boris de Ruyter, The Netherlands
Anind Dey, USA
Dimitris Grammenos, Greece
Nuno Guimaraes, Portugal
Achilles Kameas, Greece
Javed Vassilis Khan, The Netherlands
Shin'ichi Konomi, Japan
Carsten Magerkurth, Switzerland

Ingrid Mulder, The Netherlands
Anton Nijholt, The Netherlands
Fabio Paternó, Italy
Carsten Röcker, Germany
Teresa Romao, Portugal
Albert Ali Salah, Turkey
Manfred Tscheligi, Austria
Reiner Wichert, Germany
Woontack Woo, Korea
Xenophon Zabulis, Greece

Human Aspects of Information Security, Privacy and Trust

**Program Chairs: Theo Tryfonas, UK,
and Ioannis Askoxylakis, Greece**

Claudio Agostino Ardagna, Italy
Zinaida Benenson, Germany
Daniele Catteddu, Italy
Raoul Chiesa, Italy
Bryan Cline, USA
Sadie Creese, UK
Jorge Cuellar, Germany
Marc Dacier, USA
Dieter Gollmann, Germany
Kirstie Hawkey, Canada
Jaap-Henk Hoepman, The Netherlands
Cagatay Karabat, Turkey
Angelos Keromytis, USA
Ayako Komatsu, Japan
Ronald Leenes, The Netherlands
Javier Lopez, Spain
Steve Marsh, Canada

Gregorio Martinez, Spain
Emilio Mordini, Italy
Yuko Murayama, Japan
Masakatsu Nishigaki, Japan
Aljosa Pasic, Spain
Milan Petković, The Netherlands
Joachim Posegga, Germany
Jean-Jacques Quisquater, Belgium
Damien Sauveron, France
George Spanoudakis, UK
Kerry-Lynn Thomson, South Africa
Julien Touzeau, France
Theo Tryfonas, UK
João Vilela, Portugal
Claire Vishik, UK
Melanie Volkamer, Germany

HCI in Business

Program Chair: Fiona Fui-Hoon Nah, USA

Andreas Auinger, Austria
Michel Avital, Denmark
Traci Carte, USA
Hock Chuan Chan, Singapore
Constantinos Coursaris, USA
Soussan Djamasbi, USA
Brenda Eschenbrenner, USA
Nobuyuki Fukawa, USA
Khaled Hassanein, Canada
Milena Head, Canada
Susanna (Shuk Ying) Ho, Australia
Jack Zhenhui Jiang, Singapore
Jinwoo Kim, Korea
Zoonky Lee, Korea
Honglei Li, UK
Nicholas Lockwood, USA
Eleanor T. Loiacono, USA
Mei Lu, USA

Scott McCoy, USA
Brian Mennecke, USA
Robin Poston, USA
Lingyun Qiu, P.R. China
Rene Riedl, Austria
Matti Rossi, Finland
April Savoy, USA
Shu Schiller, USA
Hong Sheng, USA
Choon Ling Sia, Hong Kong
Chee-Wee Tan, Denmark
Chuan Hoo Tan, Hong Kong
Noam Tractinsky, Israel
Horst Treiblmaier, Austria
Virpi Tuunainen, Finland
Dezhi Wu, USA
I-Chin Wu, Taiwan

Learning and Collaboration Technologies

**Program Chairs: Panayiotis Zaphiris, Cyprus,
and Andri Ioannou, Cyprus**

Ruthi Aladjem, Israel
Abdulaziz Aldaej, UK
John M. Carroll, USA
Maka Eradze, Estonia
Mikhail Fominykh, Norway
Denis Gillet, Switzerland
Mustafa Murat Inceoglu, Turkey
Pernilla Josefsson, Sweden
Marie Joubert, UK
Sauli Kiviranta, Finland
Tomaž Klobučar, Slovenia
Elena Kyza, Cyprus
Maarten de Laat, The Netherlands
David Lamas, Estonia

Edmund Laugasson, Estonia
Ana Loureiro, Portugal
Katherine Maillet, France
Nadia Pantidi, UK
Antigoni Parmaxi, Cyprus
Borzoo Pourabdollahian, Italy
Janet C. Read, UK
Christophe Reffay, France
Nicos Souleles, Cyprus
Ana Luísa Torres, Portugal
Stefan Trausan-Matu, Romania
Aimilia Tzanavari, Cyprus
Johnny Yuen, Hong Kong
Carmen Zahn, Switzerland

External Reviewers

Ilia Adami, Greece
Iosif Klironomos, Greece
Maria Korozi, Greece
Vassilis Kouroumalis, Greece

Asterios Leonidis, Greece
George Margetis, Greece
Stavroula Ntoa, Greece
Nikolaos Partarakis, Greece

HCI International 2015

The 15th International Conference on Human–Computer Interaction, HCI International 2015, will be held jointly with the affiliated conferences in Los Angeles, CA, USA, in the Westin Bonaventure Hotel, August 2–7, 2015. It will cover a broad spectrum of themes related to HCI, including theoretical issues, methods, tools, processes, and case studies in HCI design, as well as novel interaction techniques, interfaces, and applications. The proceedings will be published by Springer. More information will be available on the conference website: http://www.hcii2015.org/

General Chair
Professor Constantine Stephanidis
University of Crete and ICS-FORTH
Heraklion, Crete, Greece
E-mail: cs@ics.forth.gr

Table of Contents – Part II

Social Media and Social Networks

Learning and Education

Design for All, Accessibility and Assistive Environments

Design for Aging

Games and Exergames

Health and Well-Being

Ergonomics and Safety

HCI in Business, Tourism and Trasport

Human-human and Human-Agent Communication

User Experience Case Studies

Table of Contents – Part I

Design Methods, Techniques and Knowledge

The Design of Everyday Things

Interacting with Information and Knowledge

Cognitive, Perceptual and Emotional Issues in HCI

Multimodal and Natural Interaction

Algorithms and Machine Learning Methods in HCI

Virtual and Augmented Environments

Social Media and Social Networks

Ent-it-UP

A Sentiment Analysis System Based on OpeNER Cloud Services

Sara Pupi, Giulia Di Pietro, and Carlo Aliprandi

Synthema Srl Via Malasoma 24 56121 Ospedaletto (Pisa) – Italy
{sara.pupi,giulia.dipietro,carlo.aliprandi}@synthema.it

Abstract. In this paper we present a web application that exploits OpeNER Cloud Services. Ent-it-UP monitors Social Media and traditional Mass Media contents, performing multilingual Named Entity Recognition and Sentiment Analysis. Since consumers tend to trust the opinion of other consumers, reviews and ratings on the internet are increasingly important. Given the huge amount of data flowing in the web, it has become necessary to adopt an automatic data analysis strategy, in order to understand what people think about a certain product, brand or topic. The goal of Ent-it-Up is to carry out statistics about retrieved entities and display results in a communicative, intuitive and user friendly interface. In this way the final user can easily have a hint about people opinions without wasting too much time in analyzing the huge amount of User-Generated Content.

Keywords: Reference Application, OpeNER, Named Entity Recognition and Classification, Sentiment Analysis, Social Media, User-Generated Content.

1 Introduction

Customer reviews and ratings on the internet are increasingly important in the evaluation of products and services by potential customers. In certain sectors, it is even becoming a fundamental variable in the purchase decision. Consumers tend to trust the opinion of other consumers, especially those with prior experience of a product or service, rather than trust company marketing opinions which are usually business oriented. Given the huge amount of data flowing in the web, it has become necessary to adopt an automatic data analysis strategy. It gives the possibility to understand what people think about a certain product, brand or topic without wasting too much time in exploring User-Generated Contents.

On the other hand, traditional Mass Media still play an important role in the way people get information. Opinion Mining in Media is a pretty new – but already consolidated - field of research. People operating in this sector aims to know *who* is speaking, about *what*, *when* and in *what sense*. **Named Entity Recognition and Classification** (NERC) are important in determining roles (*who, what* and *when*) while **Sentiment Analysis** (SA) is necessary to determine the attitude of a writer with respect to the overall contextual polarity of the text (*what sense*).

C. Stephanidis (Ed.): HCII 2014 Posters, Part II, CCIS 435, pp. 3–8, 2014.

OpeNER has created base technologies for Crosslingual NERC and Sentiment Analysis that are enabling industry users both to implement and contribute to a basic set of core technologies that all require and allow them to focus their efforts on providing tailored and innovative solutions at the rules and analysis levels. OpeNER aims to provide enterprise and society with online services for Crosslingual Named Entity Recognition and Classification and Sentiment Analysis.

In the paper we will present a new multimedia web application, **Ent-It-UP**, developed leveraging on OpeNER Cloud Services[1]. This application is a media monitoring solution for live analytics on User-Generated Contents (UGCs) and video contents.

2   Ent-it-UP Design

Ent-it-UP is an application accessible from the Web that provides users with a clear and effective visualization of the knowledge extracted from two different sources: User-Generated Contents and the transcriptions of videos. In the following sections we describe the necessary steps which will lead from the collected data to their communicative and intuitive visualization through the Ent-it-UP interface.

2.1   Data Harvesting

The first thing that has to be done is to collect the data and store them into a database. The data are taken from two different sources, in order to have the possibility to look at the same thing from two different point of view. In fact, the first source we take our data from are Social Media (such as blogs, forums, Online Travelling Agencies and so on) - which can be taken into account to know *what people think* -, and the second one are international news programs – which can be taken into consideration to know *what news say*. The first dataset needs to be pre-processed in order to delete noise and get clean text. On the other hand the news programs, needs to be processed by the SAVAS Speech Recognition Engine[2] in order to get transcriptions of the recorded videos. The system returns both an XML file and a plain text file. The XML contains information about words' timestamp and will be used to link transcribed text to the video itself. The raw text will be taken as input by OpeNER tools. The same happens to the UGC text previously cleaned.

All the data retrieved so far are stored on a MongoDB management system.

2.2   Data Annotation

The raw text files obtained are processed by the OpeNER Cloud Services which consist of a series of NLP tools, listed below.

- Language Identifier
- Tokenizer

---

[1] http://opener.olery.com/
[2] http://voiceinteraction.pt

- Tree Tagger
- Part-of-Speech Tagger
- Polarity Tagger
- Property Tagger
- Constituent Parser
- Kaf-Naf Parser
- Named Entity Recognition
- Scorer
- Named Entity Detection
- Opinion Detector

It is possible to use only some of the NLP tools or all of them. Of course, some basic analysis is required to provide implementation of Named Entity Recognition and Sentiment Analysis. This basic analysis can be performed by only two NLP tools, which are the Tokenizer (as far as the language of the text is known, otherwise the Language Identifier is required too) and the Part-of-Speech Tagger.

Thus, in order to implement Ent-it-UP functionalities, these are the four NLP tools that have been used:

- Tokenizer
- Part-of-Speech Tagger
- Named Entity Recognition
- Polarity Tagger

The result is a KAF (Knowledge Annotation Framework) [1][2] file which has an XML-like structure. It consists of several linguistic layers (Figure 1).

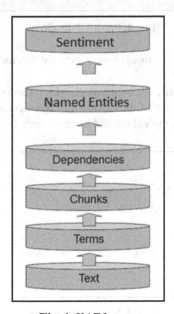

Fig. 1. KAF Layers

The annotated levels of the KAF that will be taken into account from the Ent-it-UP system are the *terms* level (from which it gets the word polarity) and the *named entities* level. These data are also added to the MongoDB database.

2.3   Data Processing

Once the raw texts have been transformed into KAF, they can be elaborated. Some PHP scripts perform queries to the MongoDB collections and return quantitative results such as entity frequency, entity occurrences and other metrics.

2.4   Data Visualization

The above mentioned results have now to be shown. Some of the functionalities offered by Ent-it-UP are the following.

Fig. 2. Ent-it-UP tagcloud

The user has the possibility to explore a general interactive tagcloud of the most frequent entities (Figure 2).

He can also explore an entity-focused report, which can be obtained by searching for a specific entity or choosing one of those shown in the tagcloud. The report includes the occurrences of the entity into the videos and its cross time frequency (Figure 3).

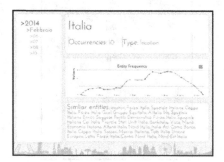

Fig. 3. Ent-it-UP timeline

If the user decide to focus his search on transcriptions of videos he can also explore a video-focused report choosing one specific video among those present in the collection. The report includes statistics about the entities composition (percentage of entities recognized in the video transcription that has been identified as `people`, percentage of entities identified as `organization`, and so on). This report also provides a tagcloud of those entities found in the video. The user can further choose to narrow down the tagcloud selecting the only category of entities he is interested in (Figure 4).

Fig. 4. Ent-it-UP statistics   **Fig. 5.** Ent-it-UP transcription

The user can also explore the transcription in which entities are marked with different colors according to their type (i.e. entities identified as `people` are colored in orange, entities identified as `location` are colored in green and so on). Terms with polarity (positive, negative or neutral) are also highlighted (respectively green, red and grey). The user can choose to highlight only entities (all types or just some), only sentiment, or both. Next to the transcription there is a player of the video. If the user wants to listen to the point in which a certain word is spoken he can just click that word in the text and the video will jump to that point (Figure 5).

3 Usage Case

In this section is presented a usage case in which both data sources are exploited. In the following case, in fact, UGC and video contents are both useful to the user, who can look at the same thing from two different point of view.

Suppose that the end user is interested in investigating what people think about a certain city. For example he wants to know how Paris is perceived by people. He could be interested in knowing what areas or features are the most mentioned and whether people love them or do not. On the other hand, he could be interested in having an overall insight of the city news events.

The user can access Ent-it-UP, search for the keyword *Paris* using one or the other dataset. In this way, he can get two different kind of information about Paris. In fact, choosing to use the UGC source he would probably get every-day-life information about Paris (*what people think*). On the other hand, choosing the video source, the user would probably get information about the facts happening in Paris (*what news say*).

4   Conclusions

This paper has presented Ent-it-UP as reference application of the OpeNER project. We have presented how Ent-it-UP monitors Media contents, performing multilingual Named Entity Recognition and Sentiment Analysis on User-Generated Content and video transcriptions. After a short introduction we have described the Ent-it-UP design, identifying the main steps that leads from raw texts to some kind of knowledge. We have reported a usage case in which Ent-it-UP could be used to have an overall insight of a place. However it could be used to discover information also about a certain brand, person, organization and so on.

Ent-it-UP allows the user to focus on other activities rather than spend time analyzing the raw language resources.

Acknowledgment. This work is part of the OpeNER project which is funded by the European Commission 7th Framework Programme (FP7), grant agreement no 296451.

References

1. Tesconi, M., Ronzano, F., Minutoli, S., Aliprandi, C., Marchetti, A.: KAFnotator: a multilingual semantic text annotation tool. In: Proceedings of the 5th Joint ISO-ACL/SIGSEM Workshop on Interoperable Semantic Annotation, in Conjunction with the Second International Conference on Global Interoperability for Language Resources (ICGL 2010), Hong Kong, January 15-17 (2010)
2. Bosma, W., Vossen, P., Soroa, A., Rigau, G., Tesconi, M., Marchetti, A., Monachini, M., Aliprandi, C.: KAF: a generic semantic annotation format. In: Proceedings of the 5th International Conference on Generative Approaches to the Lexicon GL 2009, Pisa, Italy, September 17-19 (2009)
3. Aliprandi, C., Scudellari, C., Gallucci, I., Piccinini, N., Raffaelli, M.,, A., Álvarez, A., Arzelus, H., Cassaca, R., Luis, T., Neto, J., Mendes, C., Paulo, S., Viveiros, M.: Automatic Live Subtitling: state of the art, expectations and current trends. In: NAB Broadcasting Conference, Las Vegas, Nevada, United States (April 2014) (forthcoming)

Heuristic Evaluation of a MMORPG: Guild Wars 2

Zafer Bozyer[1] and Pınar Onay Durdu[2]

[1] Department of Management Information Systems, Bartin University,
Bartin, Turkey
zaferbozyer@bartin.edu.tr
[2] Department of Computer Engineering, Kocaeli University, Izmit, Kocaeli, Turkey
pinaronaydurdu@kocaeli.edu.tr

Abstract. Usability of computer games is essential for the competitive game development market. Heuristic evaluation is one of the frequently used methods for this purpose. In this study, heuristic evaluation of Guild Wars 2 was conducted. Heuristics that were specifically developed for computer games from the literature were extracted for the evaluation under five categories. These were ease of playability and learnability, decent visual design and adequate interaction with the player, adequate satisfaction level of game content, game play and game mechanics, adequate fictionalized and supportive game narrative and adequate communication components and socializing opportunities. Six evaluators evaluated the game based on the given heuristics. The participants reported some usability issues which should be resolved.

Keywords: HCI, heuristic evaluation, game, MMORPG.

1 Introduction

Recent data show that the revenue gathered form the game market was 70,4 billion dollar in 2013 and it was expected to be 86,1 billion dollar in 2016 [1]. Massively multiplayer online role playing games (MMORPGs) are the one of the computer game genre that attracts millions of gamers and defined as the fast growing game genre [2]. The reason for the success of these games is based on the emerging technologies that provide more realistic virtual environments and socialization opportunities to its users [3].

Applying usability evaluation methods in software development since 80s had a positive effect on the productivity and profitability of software [4]. Heuristic evaluation method is the one that is generally used in the evaluation of computer games. It is an expert-based inspection method based on the investigation of the system according to design heuristics [5].

In this study, one of the MMORPGs, Guild Wars 2, has been selected to implement a heuristic evaluation based on a heuristic set extracted from the computer games literature to reveal the usability problems. This MMORPG was selected because it had the highest market share in 2012 [6] and it has been claimed that it did not have the shortcomings of the previous MMOPRPGs [7].

C. Stephanidis (Ed.): HCII 2014 Posters, Part II, CCIS 435, pp. 9–14, 2014.

2   Related Work

MMORPG genre is different since it provides an interactive social environment to its users. They are somewhat difficult to learn since intense knowledge related to the game narrative and fantastic items should be transferred to the players and interaction which is too many, takes place through different combinations of keyboard commands. Therefore, it is not easy to enable sufficient level of player-game interaction.

Use of heuristic evaluation in games has been increased since Malone's [8] study on developing heuristics specific to computer games. Afterwards some researchers had studied on the usability of games and game heuristics development [9-15].

There are also some specific usability studies related to MMORPG genre. Cornett [2] conducted a study with nineteen participants who were inexperienced with MMORPGs and revealed that they ran into difficulties due to usability issues. Another study was conducted by Song and Lee [16] on a popular MMORPG called World of Warcraft and they determined eighteen problems. They defined fifty four key factors for heuristic evaluation in four areas which were game play, game interface, game narrative and game mechanic. Turkay and Adinolf [17] studied whether different forms of customization would affect the user enjoyment or motivation to play in MMORPGs.

3   Method

3.1   Participants

The study was conducted with six participants who were experienced in MMORPGs because inexperienced users will not be able to assess the game according to the given heuristics since they will not be able to learn the game in a short time. However, these six participants were grouped as experienced Guild Wars 2 players and inexperienced Guild Wars 2 players in order to determine whether experience level would affect their assessments. MMORPG experiences of the participants were between 8 to 10 years. All participants were male and graduate students of engineering or information systems. The ages of the participants range from 21 to 27.

3.2   Data Collection Tools and Procedures

Heuristics from the game usability literature were extracted for the evaluation. Forty items were determined and grouped under five categories as can be seen in Table 2 in Appendix. Only one heuristic "Provide adequate localization and language support" (Heuristic 10) was added based on the detailed narrative that needed to be understood by the players. The categories were ease of playability and learnability, decent visual design and adequate interaction with the player, adequate satisfaction level of game content, game play and game mechanics, adequate fictionalized and supportive game narrative and adequate communication components and socializing opportunities.

Participants were required to evaluate Guild Wars 2 game based on the given heuristics in two phases. In the first phase they were required to determine whether there was a usability problem related with the heuristics. In the second phase they defined the severity of the usability problems based on the severity rating determined by Nielsen [18]. Inexperienced Guild Wars 2 players were allowed to play the game 12-24 hours before the evaluation in order to explore and learn the game.

4   Findings

In the study, heuristics that were rated as 2 to 4 were considered as having a usability problem based on the Nielsen's [18] 0-4 scale. Usability problems found in the 15 of the 40 determined heuristics as can be seen in Table 1. Nine of the problems were determined by experienced Guild Wars 2 players while 2 of the problems were determined by inexperienced Guild Wars 2 players. In addition, four problems were determined by both experienced and inexperienced Guild Wars 2 players.

Table 1. Heuristics that were rated as having usability problems

ID	Heuristics	Participants (given rates)
1	Provide adequate help content and interesting and absorbing tutorial	Exp3 (2), NExp2 (2)
4	Allow customization of user interface	Exp1 (3), Exp2 (2), NExp1 (2), NExp2 (2), NExp3 (2)
5	Allow customization of the functions of control elements such as keyboard buttons	NExp3 (2)
7	Game atmosphere do not enhance cognitive/mental load	Exp2 (2), NExp2 (2),
10	Provide adequate localization and language support	Exp1 (4), Exp3 (3), NExp1 (3), NExp3(3)
11	Well-organized hierarchical structure and proper depth and breadth of menu layers	Exp1 (2), Exp3 (2)
16	Provide adequate (neither more or less) audible feedback	Exp3 (2)
24	Provide fair reward system and satisfying reward contents	Exp1 (3), Exp2 (2), Exp3 (2)
26	Different game modes (PvP, PvE, WvW) have been included in a balanced manner	Exp1 (3), Exp2 (2), Exp3 (2)
27	Pace to apply adequate pressure to the gamer without discouraging them	Exp2 (2)
29	Provide the fair play between all gamers, different classes and races	Exp1 (3), Exp2 (3), Exp3 (2)
30	The player has a sense of control over game and there are no limitations to restrict player.	NExp2 (3)
32	The story should be great and adequately laid into the game	Exp1 (2)
37	The game story reaffirm gamer interest after they have become bored with general gameplay	Exp2 (2)
38	Easy to communicate with other players in the game	Exp1 (2), Exp3 (2)

Inexperienced players defined that players were limited since it was difficult to increase level without accomplishing a task and it was difficult to move the avatar just by using keyboard. However, experienced players did not mention these as problems. Some players from both groups found the tutorial or help feature of the game inadequate and mentioned that the game increased the cognitive load since it had too many details. Serious usability problems were related with the issues of "customization of the interface" (4,5), "the need of adequate language support" (10), "fair reward system" (24), "balanced game modes" (26), "balance between classes" (29), "player's sense of control" (30).

5   Conclusion

This study reports on a heuristic evaluation of the game Guild Wars 2. Forty heuristics which were grouped in five categories were used for the evaluation. Evaluation results show that game did not comply 15 of the heuristics. Among these problems the customization of the interface and language support were rated above the average of two points in evaluations. Therefore these two issues should be dealt primarily.

Experienced Guild Wars 2 players revealed more problems than inexperienced players since MMORPGs are complex and hard to learn. Experience and knowledge about the game becomes essential during the evaluation. On the other hand, inexperienced players revealed some problems which were missed by experienced players since they might have internalized them.

One of the important findings of this study was that localization and language support was essential in MMORPGs. Because they include a detailed narrative [10], [12] and if there is no language support, players can lose focus of the game and can not follow the story. Although some studies [19] mentioned about the comprehension difficulties due to being in other language, there was not any heuristic specifically defined for the language support. In addition, the features of games, especially MMORPGs, are enhancing rapidly due to technological advances in game industry. Therefore, new heuristic sets that will cover the current usability requirements of MMORPGs should be developed in future studies.

References

1. Newzoo: Global Games Market Report Infographics, Global Games Market 2012 -2016, http://www.newzoo.com/infographics/global-games-market-report-infographics/
2. Cornett, S.: The usability of Massively Multigamer Online Roleplaying Games: Designing for New Users. In: Proceedings of the Conference on CHI 2004, pp. 703–710 (2004)
3. Tang, T.Y., Cheung, Y.M., Chu, P.H., Lam, S.C., Chan, W.K., Yiu, C.C., Ho, K.F., Sit, K.: A Study of Interaction Patterns and Awareness Design Elements in a Massively Multiplayer Online Game. Int. J. Computer Games Technology, 1–8 (2008)
4. Bias, R.G., Mayhew, D.J.: Cost-justifying usability: An update for the Internet age, 2nd edn. Morgan Kaufmann, San Francisco (2005)
5. Nielsen, J.: Heuristic evaluation. In: Nielsen, J., Molich, R.L. (eds.) Usability Inspection Methods, pp. 25–62. John Wiley & Sons, New York (1994)
6. ESA: Essential Facts About the Computer and Video Game Industry, http://www.theesa.com/facts/pdfs/ESA_EF_2013.pdf
7. O'Brien, M.: Guild Wars 2 Design Manifesto, https://www.guildwars2.com/en/news/guild-wars-2-design-manifesto/
8. Malone, T.W.: Heuristics for designing enjoyable user interfaces: Lessons from Computer Games. In: Proceedings Human Factors in Computer Systems, Washington, D.C., pp. 63–68. ACM, New York (1982)
9. Clanton, C.: An Interpreted Demonstration of Computer Game Design. In: Proceedings of the Conference on CHI 1998, pp. 1–2 (1998)

10. Jenkins, H.: Game design as a narrative architecture. In: Wardip-Fruin, N., Harrigan, P. (eds.) First Person: New Media as Story, Performance, and Game. The MIT Press, Cambridge (2002)
11. Federoff, M.: Heuristic and Usability Guidelines for the Creation and Evaluation of Fun Video Games. Master Thesis, Department of Telecommunications, Indiana University (2002)
12. Desurvire, H., Caplan, M., Toth, J.A.: Using Heuristics to Evaluate the Playability of Games. In: Proceedings of the Conference on CHI 2004, pp. 1509–1512 (2004)
13. Korhonen, H., Koivisto, E.M.I.: Playability heuristics for mobile games. In: Procedings MobileHCI, pp. 9–16 (2006)
14. Williams, D., Ducheneaut, N., Xiong, L., Zhang, Y., Yee, N., Nickell, E.: From tree house to barracks: The social life of guilds in World of Warcraft. Games and Culture 1, 338–361 (2006)
15. Pinelle, D., Wong, N.: Heuristic evaluation for games: usability principles for video game design. In: Proceedings of the Conference on CHI 2008, pp. 1453–1462 (2008)
16. Song, S., Lee, J., Hwang, I.: A New Framework of Usability Evaluation for Massively Multi-player Online Game: Case Study of "World of Warcraft" Game. In: Jacko, J.A. (ed.) HCI 2007. LNCS, vol. 4553, pp. 341–350. Springer, Heidelberg (2007)
17. Turkay, S., Adinolf, S.: Free to be me: a survey study on customization with World of Warcraft and City Of Heroes/Villains players. Procedia-Social and Behavioral Sciences 2, 1840–1845 (2010)
18. Nielsen, J.: Severity Ratings for Usability Problems (1998), http://www.nngroup.com/articles/how-to-rate-the-severity-of-usability-problems/
19. Omar, H.M., Jaafar, A.: Heuristics Evaluation in Computer Games. In: 2010 International Conference on Information Retrieval & Knowledge Management, pp. 188–193 (2010)
20. Shim, K.J., Hsu, K.-W., Srivastava, J.: An Exploratory Study of Player Performance, Motivation, and Enjoyment in Massively Multiplayer Online Role-Playing Games. In: SocialCom/PASSAT, pp. 135–140 (2011)

Appendix

Table 2. Heuristics list extracted for usability evaluation of Guild Wars 2

Heuristics	Source
A. Ease of playability and learnability	
1. Provide adequate help content and interesting and absorbing tutorial	[5], [11], [12], [15]
2. Easy to learn and easy to manage in game character, but hard to master.	[8],[12], [16]
3. Easy to comprehend the functions of user interface components	[15]
4. Allow customization of the user interface	[16], [17]
5. Allow customization of the functions of control elements such as keyboard but-	[11], [15], [16]
6. There are similarities between game and real world (metaphors)	[5], [8], [16]
7. Game atmosphere does not enhance cognitive/mental load	[5], [12], [15], [16]
8. Provide sufficient and perceptible visual representations such as icons, signs and descriptions	[15], [16]
9. Provide standardized key combinations, shortcuts that are used in MMORPGs	[11], [12]
10. Provide adequate localization and language support	

Table 2. *(continued)*

B. Decent visual design and adequate interaction with the player	
11. Well-organized hierarchical structure and proper depth and breadth of menu layers	[5], [11], [12], [16]
12. The game design is aesthetically satisfactory	[5], [16]
13. Provide minimalist on-screen interface that comprise only necessary elements	[12], [15]
14. Provide consistent interface in control, color, typography, and dialog design	[11], [12]
15. Provide adequate (neither more or less) visual feedback	[8], [11], [15]
16. Provide adequate (neither more or less) audible feedback	[8], [11], [12], [15]
17. Provide consistent, clear and immediate responses to the user's actions	[8], [12], [15], [17]
18. Allow to customize video and audio settings	[5], [15]
19. Game atmosphere and visual elements provide recognition rather than recall	[5], [12]
C. Adequate satisfaction level of game content	
20. The gamer empathizes through game play and game character (avatar)	[12], [16], [17]
21. Provide clear tasks and overriding goals	[12]
22. Provide the opportunity to choose a task or a goal within the multiple tasks and goals.	[8], [9]
23. Provide multiple ways to win	[9], [12]
24. Provide fair reward system and satisfying reward contents	[9], [12]
25. Provide various difficulty level according to each gamer's level	[8], [9]
26. Different game modes (PvP, PvE) have been included in a balanced manner	[14], [20]
27. Pace to apply adequate pressure to the gamer without discouraging them.	[9], [11], [12]
28. Provide game content re-playable	[11], [12]
29. Provide the fair play between all gamers, different classes and races	[9], [16]
30. Provide sense of control over game and there are no limitations to restrict player	[5], [12]
31. The game's AI provide reasonable yet unpredictable outcomes	[8], [12], [15],[16]
D. Adequate fictionalized and supportive game narrative	
32. The story should be great and adequately laid into the game	[10], [11], [16]
33. Provide the players create, control their own story content	[10], [11], [16]
34. The game story evokes famous tales, mythology and other works	[10], [16]
35. Discovering the story as part of game play	[12], [16]
36. The game contain intriguing and interesting game story	[11], [12], [16]
37. The game story reaffirm gamer interest after they have become bored with general gameplay	[10], [16]
E. Adequate communication components and socializing opportunities	
38. Easy to communicate with other players in the game.	[14], [20]
39. Provide adequate game content to ensure being part of a team.	[14], [20]
40. Provide to access community pages to players for exchange ideas and procure information	[14], [20]

Developing Sustainable Process in Water Economy Using Social Media

Karim E. Fraoua[1,3], Christian Bourret[1,3], and Eric Sotto[2,3]

[1] Université Paris-Est, 77454 Marne-la-Vallée, France
{Karim.Fraoua,Christian.Bourret}@u-pem.fr
[2] Novancia Business School Paris
Eric.Sotto@novancia.fr
[3] Equipe Dispositifs d'Information et de Communication à l'Ere Numérique (DICEN),
Conservatoire national des arts et métiers

Abstract. The main idea developed here is how to involve people to promote a new behavior to economize water as supported by the local authorities process. Usually, the population is affected by the cities policies when they are subject to fines related to high water use during times of crisis. Then the local authorities impose solutions without consultations of concerned communities. This top-down process is often considered as imposed by the mayor or the local authority and may lead to bad feeling by the population and is not corresponding to a new societal behavior in the social web era. We will suggest a new way to involve the population using the social media as a new approach to imply them in this process. This information can be conveyed and shared with the public in such way to support mayor or authorities policies. In other way we will propose a new approach using social media processes as a node in the first hand to encourage the population to participate to the debate and to fit a new solution encouraging all population to get part of the policies adopted based on a bayesian approach.

Keywords: Sustainability, social media, Bayesian recommender system.

1 Introduction

Social networks are scrambling more decision-making processes, particularly in France, heavily influenced by the Colbert model and hierarchical relationships between all actors. The Colbertism, corresponds to the state interventionism in the economy and in all social relationships. This politics remains valid in France, although the role of citizens in decision-making has emerged. Everywhere we see flowering social networks as a means of dissemination of information. The structure of the social web can be a great asset in the development of new public policies. This "bottom-up" approach allows to create acceptable, realistic and desirable policies, especially in the case of sustainable development. A particular interesting case concerns issues which concern citizens who are directly affected by phenomena due to climate change. The "Bottom-Up" policy is now possible, due to the emergence of various

C. Stephanidis (Ed.): HCII 2014 Posters, Part II, CCIS 435, pp. 15–20, 2014.
© Springer International Publishing Switzerland 2014

participative tools where the community manager of the animation starts over perceptions and initiatives at the level of the citizen who is on the ground where the policy will be in place. So these messages can be published and taken into account by the "decision makers".

2   Citizen Social Network : A Participatory Place for Local Democracy

We can consider now that social networks are territories or organizational forms which include enough participants, which have a critical size for the formation of groups [1] on which it can build links and operate forms of collaboration between people connected and interconnected in a virtual social space. Social networks are "a relational advanced technology" [2] as collaborative form and conversational device available are 2.0 services to promote link building. In this digital territory, participants act independently and publish across hierarchies, resulting egalitarian relationships between all actors, and thus rebalancing the power between experts, decisions-makers and "amateurs" that are common [3] citizens.

These exchanges are similar to conversations "face to face", improvised, non-profit and pleasant. [4] Thus, we believe that citizens have a platform for reproducing usual conversations, in public, neighborhood. In addition, we see the introduction of "moments of discussion" [5]. In other words, it is a form comparable to the agora or the forum, where each citizen can debate any topics of general interest. What is also interesting on social networks? It is also an opportunity to build links without the need for a real involvement of the participant. We hold that a social network is a form of urban sociability characterized by small research links [6]. We believe that social networking is a space to perform a specific activity, collective and unifying, but without commitment.

3   Forum about Water Economy Practices

In the theoretical framework of social interactionism and mobilizing floating concepts of conversational interactions and usual one [7,8,9], we highlight the specific and salient features of exchange occurring in this spatiotemporal framework diffused in a wide audience. The interpretation of the results suggests that in a public forum, participants evolve rapidly towards egalitarian relationships, proximity and show a cooperative behavior and caring, especially in ensuring auto regulation inside the forum in case of conflict. A participative platform as the forum dedicated to the citizens, requires few resources or technical skills and work without supervision. As such, it contributes to the reduction of costs associated with the operation of a neighborhood committee especially for the less endowed municipalities. Within the Public forums, we identify "lead users" [10]. These suppliers of innovation appropriate a product, service, or project topic and suggest ways to original improvement, based on an individual experimentation with imagination and small means. To conclude, the lack of supervision of forum is considered as a source of "surprises" from the part of citizens [11]. These innovative practices match those identified by Michel de Certeau [12] when he considers individuals as "poachers" in search of flaws and shortcomings of a product to act in unexpected way. Taking this as read, our point of view is that the citizen forum is a reservoir of ideas and practical uses encountered in different contexts of achievements likely to improve the supply of "water saving practices" proposed by the municipality [13]. We can conclude that the forum of discussion shows clearly and formalizes the popular knowledge, this little everyday actions related to water economy and allows to legitimize the actions of the municipality

4   How to Assess Proposals, a Bayesian Approach

Kahneman et al. [14] demonstrated that many mistakes are made by people in the judging process as mental operation during the estimation of a probability of an event. Systematic errors related to the Bayesian standard, highlighted by their experiences are explained by mental shortcuts, more accessible, less costly in time and concentration. When the cost of normative Bayesian computation is important, the agent tends to use examples of the problem that have marked his experience which enable him to make approximations. Therefore, the decision is made via arbitration of the payoff between these shortcuts and more rigorous calculation [15]. The information system will aim in our work to help user to better define our rational capabilities reasoning in uncertain situations, as in water consumption and its impact on our future. Although we believe that climate change is perceptible, our behaviors are often irrational in view of the advent of the crisis yet present. . Public perception is mainly driven by climate change science, still considered with uncertainty about the timing of future warming

The Bayesian theory allows us to define two approaches [16]. The first one assumes perfect knowledge of the specific and unique probabilities of the event and the second assumes that probability is the result of a dependent human judgment based on his own knowledge. The issue of the social web and the contribution of experts who will address at this level of knowledge are often imperfect and thereby improve the degree of belief in the coming of climatic change. In this regard, Bayesian standard is defined according to three criteria [17,18, 19], the first epistemic, consider our capacity to define a probability of realization of an event according to predefined scheme depending of each individual and obtained or calculated in subjective priori way that can vary from one individual to another. Thus, a probability represents the degree of belief in the event of an H level with individual having a level of knowledge K, at a given time. We note:

$$P = \left(\frac{H}{K}\right) \qquad (1)$$

When a person acquires a new complementary information partition D, he is able to revise its degree of belief H and then estimated probability will be

$$P = \left(\frac{H}{D}\right) \qquad (2)$$

It is also possible that the degree of knowledge K at a given time is low or the degree of belief H is limited. From this point of view, the social web goal will have a dual purpose, an informational component capable of raising the level of knowledge K and a raising impact on the component related to a beneficial future result. The role of the social web and experts is to increase the probability related to the dynamic consistency as a result of new information D that would influence Bayes formula, knowing that the information would be given a priori to evaluate a correct probability, is given subsequently to revise this probability. The main problem that arises when we offer a service, is how to properly evaluate it and in our case how to reach a consensus. More and more tools now allow e-commerce websites to anticipate the needs of potential buyers and provide them services or products that match their needs [20]. What are the right choices in our case and how to evaluate it? We see that with these societal changes that are combined with use of increasingly intense social networks, every citizen can propose an idea or evaluate it, previously validated by the technical services or at expert level. When an idea is rejected, it must be explained why. This obstacle overtaken, we see that this web space locally sponsored at the political level will enable every citizen to express themselves.

In order to construct an efficient system, we can use evaluation models and make them close of e-commerce model, here it is a policy proposal at the service of citizens. Recommender systems are generally classified into three categories [21]: the content-based models, collaborative filtering and hybrid models. System based on the content descriptions use to match the need or at least the user preferences. In general, the model uses the opinion of the group to predict the interest of another user or to generate interest. This approach will allow each user to be sure that its proposal will be viewed and evaluated by other users. In the case of management of water consumption, where the needs and behaviors are not the same, it should appear groups according to the customs and then headlights and ideas can so be born. The consensus issue from these exchanges will create a normative law or rule accepted by all citizens. The profile of the citizen is an important parameter to consider. A preliminary questionnaire can place citizens in the context of its proposal. Every informed citizen and subject to prior exchange with others is able to accept a coherent proposal. Users define a relationship of trust and thus we can eliminate the so-called psychological biases.

There are rules that could help define the reliability and support of an idea but it will be based on a general rule of thumb and not of consensus. Indeed the relevance is based on the number of recommendations a mixed idea on the total number of recommendation. The reliability is the number of recommendations of one idea on the number of total recommendations. It is the mining rule [22], so we see that the level of information is essential so the individual may be in a Bayesian normative approach and considers that the collective interest as essential in the light of the group's interest

5   Conclusion

We see through this presentation that the political process has really changed in the field of decisions that involve active participation of citizens, Colbert and the hierarchical model has lived. This participation can be controlled through social web which have become an accepted practice and used by citizens. The difficulty of evaluating an idea is increasingly mastered as incentives for participation. Better information through the use of social web can lead to concrete proposals and which may correspond to the policy due a strong involvement of citizens in processes that affect them. This dual acceptance will lead to better control choices that do not compromise the future of the citizens in situation previously considered as uncertain.

References

1. Balagué, C., Fayon, D.: Facebook, Twitter et les autres..., 2nd edn. Pearson Village Mondial, Paris (2012)
2. Stiegler, B.: Le bien le plus précieux à l'époque des sociotechnologies. In: Réseaux sociaux: Culture politique et ingénierie des réseaux sociaux. FYP éditions, Paris (2012)
3. Flichy, P.: Le sacre de l'amateur. Sociologie des passions ordinaires à l'ère numérique. Editions du Seuil et La République des Idées, Paris (2010)
4. Tarde, G.: Ecrits de psychologie sociale. Editions Privat, Toulouse (1973); Goffman, E.: La mise en scène de la vie quotidienne. 1. La présentation de soi. Les Editions de Minuit, Paris (1973)
5. Gaudin, J.P.: La démocratie participative. Armand Colin, Paris (2007)
6. Moulier-Boutang, Y.: Les réseaux sociaux numériques: une application de la force des liens faibles. In: Réseaux sociaux: Culture politique et ingénierie des réseaux sociaux. FYP éditions, Paris (2012)
7. Goffman, E., Winkin, Y.: Des moments et des hommes. Seuil/ Minuit, Paris (1988); Goffman, E.: Les cadres de l'expérience. Les Editions de Minuit, Paris (1991)
8. Kerbrat-Orecchioni, C.: Les interactions verbales, tome 2. Armand Colin, Paris (1992); Kerbrat-Orecchioni, C.: Le discours en interaction. Armand Colin, Paris (2005)
9. Traverso, V.: La conversation familière. Presses universitaires de Lyon, Lyon (1996); Traverso, V.: L'Analyse des conversations. Armand Colin, Paris (2004)
10. Von Hippel, E.: Democratizing Innovation. The MIT Press, Cambridge (2005)
11. Crepon, M., Stiegler, B.: De la démocratie participative: fondements et limites. Mille et une nuits, Paris (2007)
12. De Certeau M.: L'invention du quotidien, t. 1. Art de faire. Gallimard (Folio / Essais), Paris (1980, 1990)
13. Moati P.: L'économie des bouquets, le marché des solutions dans le nouveau capitalisme. Editions de l'aube, Paris (2008)
14. Tversky, A., Kahneman, D.: Availability: A heuristic for judging frequency and probability. Cognitive Psychology 5(2), 207–232 (1974)
15. Tversky, A., Kahneman, D.: Judgment under Uncertainty: Heuristics and Biases. Science, New Series 185(4157), 1124–1131 (1974)
16. Baratgin, J., Politzer, G.: Is the mind Bayesian? The case for agnosticism. Mind & Society 5(1), 1–38 (2006)
17. Hacking, I.: Slightly more realistic personal probability. Philosophy of Science 34(4), 311 (1967)
18. Hacking, I.: The emergence of probability. Cambridge University Press (1975)

19. Seidenfeld, T.: Why I am not an objective Bayesian; Some reflections prompted by Rosenkrantz. Theory and Decision 11(4), 413–440 (1979)
20. Schafer, J.B., Konstan, J.A., Riedl, J.: E-commerce recommendation applications. In: Applications of Data Mining to Electronic Commerce, pp. 115–153. Springer US (2001)
21. Burke, R.: Hybrid recommender systems: Survey and experiments. User Modeling and User-Adapted Interaction 12(4), 331–370 (2002)
22. Tan, P.N., Steinbach, M., Kumar, V.: Introduction to data mining. Addison-Wesley, Cloth (2006)

Photo Polling Wall: Expressing and Sharing Ideas on Public Display

Ah young Han, Jung min Kim, Eun ah Park,
Ji hyung Kang, Hyung jae Cho, and Seyeon Lee

Korea Advanced Institute of Science, Guseong-dong, Yuseong-gu, Daejeon, Korea 305701
{ahyounghan,kj0821,eunah_park,jh.kang,
drzovil,birdkite}@kaist.ac.kr

Abstract. Photo Polling (PP) Wall is an interactive polling system in which community members can express and share their ideas on certain subjects through public displays, mobile devices, and social network services. The PP wall system will be a combination of multimedia services (sound effect), public display, mobile web service and client & server. With these features, we propose the PP wall system as an experimental platform for developing other interactive contents.

Keywords: Public displays, Social Network Services, interaction design, mobile devices, Unity engine.

1 Introduction

We are witnessing a proliferation of displays in public spaces, such as advertising billboards, information boards and simple screens for showing television or video contents [1]. These displays typically suffered from the lack of user interaction. In the regard we designed "Photo Polling Wall", an interactive polling system in which community members can express and share their ideas on certain subjects through public displays, mobile devices, and social network services. This system is expected to be a fun and effective platform for communication in a relatively intimate community such as schools and workplaces [2, 5].

2 System Design

"Photo Polling Wall" is a photo-based polling system with mobile accessibility and SNS characteristics. The PP Wall is designed with the following three basic ideas.

First, the PP Wall is composed of the profile photos by users and chosen examples by an administrator for visualization. Lots of people are willing to reveal their identity to the other people [3].

The second idea is that it is polling system in response to the designated topic from an administrator. Because people can express their opinion as well as voting, the PP

C. Stephanidis (Ed.): HCII 2014 Posters, Part II, CCIS 435, pp. 21–25, 2014.
© Springer International Publishing Switzerland 2014

Wall has to be designed for people to write down comment. They can use mobile devices such as smart phone [4].

Third, the PP Wall takes advantage of Facebook. With the already popular SNS, accessibility and usability problems can be relieved, and the system can be extended into an alternative social media.

2.1 Polling Procedure

The user first connects to the PP Wall web page through the QR codes, which are placed around public displays and logs in to the Facebook account. The page shows the ongoing poll's items set by the polling administrator and other users who have already participated. The user selects an item, makes a comment, and supports other user's opinions.

Fig. 1. Stepwise sequence to the PP Wall access

2.2 Display

The display client of the PP Wall is implemented with Unity Engine (http://unity3d.com/) [5]. Display clients are connected to a PHP server which receives necessary data from the Facebook and sends processed data back to the clients.

2.3 Visualization

In designing the PP Wall, there are two main goals. The first is to intuitively represent the ongoing situation of the polling. The second is to give the user proper visual feedback to encourage participation.

The client shows items with respective photos, names and colors by the administrator. The items freely move around on the screen. They push back each other, changing their courses continuously. When the user selects an item in the mobile device, the item gets larger in size. Since the camera is programmed to focus on the largest item, the most popular item is placed at the center of the screen. When the user joins the polling, his/her Facebook profile image is zoomed in and the choice and comment are displayed at the bottom of the screen. Consequently, the competitive nature of the polling is intuitively conveyed.

The profile image is attached to the selected item by a spring-like string. It periodically bounced against the selected item back and forth pushing other items away. When the participant makes an additional comment or agreed with other participant's comments, the profile image gets larger. Besides, a colored speech bubble with emoticons is attached to the profile image. As a result, active users are rewarded by being more visible than others.

Fig. 2. Displaying the PP Wall

2.4 Development Details

On the mobile client side, mobile web pages with PHP are the main interface. On server side, the database saves whole data from users' devices. Based on data form the database, this system prepares the necessary resources for the web pages and public displays. Finally, to get user information from Facebook and post back the polling result on Facebook, this system is registered as a Facebook app.

3   Evaluation

We activated the PP Wall through 3 community-based displays for 5 days. We installed a screen with projector in KAIST library. We gave the four topics for 5 days. The first topic was the plan of this vacation. We changed the topic next day which was the career after graduating, and we operated the PP Wall all night. The participants increased gradually from the second day. The topic on the third day was about favorite idol groups. For the last, we chose the topic, which late-meal do you want to have for tonight.

4   Results

4.1   Data Analysis

We got total 170 comments. Except comments by the same participants, we found out that 114 students took part in this experiment. We found that some friends of the participants reacted on Facebook walls about some popular and simple topics such as favorite Idol groups. We didn't expect this kind of further participation in Facebook. Because the topic of voting were designed to be posted on Facebook walls when the participants joined in the polling. In other words, even those who could not see the display were informed about the ongoing voting from Facebook.

Furthermore, we discovered several friends of the participants clicked 'Like' in Facebook about the posted topics of the PP Wall. They left meaningful opinion about the topic.

4.2   Continuous Participation

'Continuous Participation' is defined as joining or clicking more than once within 5 days. In case of the PP Wall, log-in state is maintained until intentionally logging-out. About 20 percentages of all participants had a tendency of Continuous Participation. It showed a possibility to develop a new kind of Social Networks Service using public displays. If the experiment period is longer than 5 days, much data might be collected for more accurate results.

4.3   Place for Communication

The participants can leave comments up to 80 letters. Because this experiment was conducted in a particular community, the participations tended to discuss about community-based topics. For instance, some campus couple uploaded comments like a love letter. Moreover, even though the participants didn't know each other, they freely expressed themselves as to the topics as they seemed close friends. We can forecast that PP Wall can be an interesting system for gathering data or sharing opinions.

5   Conclusion and Future Works

The PP wall system is a combination of multimedia contents (sound effect), public display, mobile web service and client & server. In this regard, the PP wall system as a good platform for developing other interactive contents.

However, this study had limitations regarding accessibility to the system. We designed the PP Wall to be accessed with Q.R code but many users were not familiar with the Q.R code. We also found a problem in Facebook log-in process. Since 'allow' button is located at the bottom of the display on some smart phone, going to the next page is difficult.

In our current version, the voting scene was not broadcasted to the user's personal devices due to some technical difficulties. If the broadcasting feature is implemented in the next version, users will be able to play the PP wall remotely as well as in front of the large displays with friends. It means that the PP wall can be a unique combination of a mobile game and a SNS-based social game. This will make the PP wall a new kind of group participatory game in which people share opinions and comments and have game experience at the same time.

References

1. Tang, A., Finke, M., Blackstock, M., Leung, R., Deutscher, M., Lea, R.: Designing for bystanders: reflections on building a public digital forum. In: Proceedings of the Twenty-Sixth Annual SIGCHI Conference on Human Factors in Computing Systems (CHI 2008), pp. 879–882. ACM, New York (2008)
2. Huang, E.M., Russell, D.M., Sue, A.E.: IM here: public instant messaging on large, shared displays for workgroup interactions. In: Proceedings of the SIGCHI Conference on Human Factors in Computing Systems (CHI 2004), pp. 279–286. ACM, New York (2004)
3. Scheible, J., Ojala, T.: MobiLenin combining a multi-track music video, personal mobile phones and a public display into multi-user interactive entertainment. In: Proceedings of the 13th Annual ACM International Conference on Multimedia (MULTIMEDIA 2005), pp. 199–208. ACM, New York (2005)
4. Kubitza, T., et al.: Using mobile devices to personalize pervasive displays. ACM SIGMOBILE Mobile Computing and Communications Review 16(4), 26 (2013)
5. Greenberg, S., Rounding, M.: The notification collage: posting information to public and personal displays. In: Proceedings of the SIGCHI Conference on Human Factors in Computing Systems (CHI 2001), pp. 514–521. ACM, New York (2001)
6. Unity Engine, http://unity3d.com/

Are Bitcoin Users Less Sociable? An Analysis of Users' Language and Social Connections on Twitter

Ivan Hernandez, Masooda Bashir, Gahyun Jeon, and Jeremiah Bohr

University of Illinois, Urbana-Champaign, Illinois, USA.
{hernan27,mnb,jeon29,jbohr2}@illinois.edu

Abstract. Bitcoin, a peer-to-peer payment system and digital currency, has seen much growth and controversy in the four years since its introduction. Yet, despite Bitcoin's growing importance, little is known about its users. Our research explores what type of people use this domain and what concepts they tend to emphasize in their language. We analyzed over 50,000 messages from over 6,000 users of the social networking community, Twitter. Our analyses show a consistent pattern that people interested in Bitcoin are far less likely to emphasize social relations than typical users of the site. Specifically, Bitcoin followers (1) are less likely to mention family, friends, religion, sex, and emotion related words in their tweets and (2) have significantly less social connection to other users on the site. These findings offer the first empirical look at what exactly makes Bitcoin users distinct from others and can have implications for the future of the currency.

Keywords: Bitcoin, Twitter, LIWC, Relationships, Text Analysis, Virtual Currency, Social Network Sites.

1 Introduction

Bitcoin, a peer-to-to-peer payment system and decentralized digital currency, has gained an increasing amount of public interest since its inception in 2009. The currency is represented as data within a shared network, and generated by anyone running a Bitcoin mining application over the internet, which can then be transferred directly to people in the network. Over the last four years, its price has fluctuated wildly, going through various cycles of appreciation and depreciation, reaching valuations as high as $1,000 USD per coin to lows of less than a dollar. The trend though has steadily continued upwards, and the currency is receiving more mainstream attention. Popular retailers such as Overstock, Zynga, Wordpress, Baidu, and TigerDirect all accept Bitcoins as a form of payment. Politically, governments across the world have also acknowledged its growing importance. Chinese, Finnish, German, and Canadian governments have all established policies for Bitcoin use, and most other major world governments have issued statements concerning their position on regulation [1]. Yet, despite the currency's growth and potential to impact major markets, we still know very little about the people using Bitcoin. However, it is the users who promote and

C. Stephanidis (Ed.): HCII 2014 Posters, Part II, CCIS 435, pp. 26–31, 2014.
© Springer International Publishing Switzerland 2014

affect the value of the currency. Therefore, understanding their thoughts, feelings, and values may inform us about the future of Bitcoin.

2   Language Analysis

The present research seeks to examine what Bitcoin users think more/less about compared to the typical person. One way to address this question is to study the content of their speech. Psychological research on language finds that the words we use mirror our thoughts and feelings at that moment [2]. Traditionally, analyzing language content involved performing a case-by-case coding of conversations by a trained expert. While this qualitative approach allows for an in-depth understanding of a small sample of conversations, the method was not designed to get a comprehensive picture of an entire culture or group. However, over the past decade, computer-based methods of text-analysis have addressed these issues handling larger amount of text in a faster, broader, and more cost-efficient way.

One of the most widely used text analysis computer programs is the Linguistic Inquiry and Word Count (LIWC) [3]. LIWC analyzes text samples (e.g. a news story, a blog post, an e-mail) on a word-by-word basis and compares each word to an internal dictionary of over 2,000 words divided into different linguistic categories (e.g. positive emotions, personal pronouns, money-related). For every text sample, it outputs the percentage of total words in the text that reflect each linguistic category. For example, if the four-word text sample, "I am happy, today," is given to LIWC, the it would output a value of .25 for positive emotion (i.e. "happy"), and .25 for 1st person pronoun (i.e. "I"), and would give a value of 0 for categories like "money."

While LIWC contains dictionaries that measures traditional linguistic content such as parts-of-speech, one of its greatest benefits is that it also contains dictionaries that measure psychological processes (e.g. anger, cognitive mechanisms, social engagement) in text. These dictionaries were developed using methods similar to those used for traditional psychological scales. First, the developers created a list of emotional and cognitive dimensions often studied in social, health, and personality psychology. Then, using reference books, past psychological scales, and personal opinion, they created an initial list of words that matched each dimension. Independent judges then rated their acceptability, with majority agreement deciding what words remained. These remaining words formed the preliminary dictionaries. To evaluate the dictionaries' psychometric properties, the authors cross-validated them against a corpus of 24,000 text samples totaling over 168 million words. Words were excluded if they were used less than .005 percent of the time or not mentioned in English word frequency reference manuals. The internal consistencies for binary ($\alpha = .83$, $\sigma = .15$) and percentage codings of the words ($\alpha = .40$, $\sigma = .16$) are in ranges common to the field. Further, most dictionaries have a correlations of .40 or greater with judges' ratings of text on the dimension they represent, establishing the dictionaries' predictive validity. Although a non-contextual word count strategy such as LIWC will be more prone to errors than a human coder would, the amount of influence an error has on the results diminishes with larger data. Thus, LIWC has the potential to provide insight into the thoughts and values of people, and its disadvantages are minimized as the data it is given increases.

3   Twitter Data

In the present research we use the microblogging website, Twitter, as our source of daily language. Twitter is currently the 11th most popular website in the world [4] and allows users to post short form messages ("tweets") that describe their thoughts, sentiments, and concerns at a given moment. Studying Twitter data offers several methodological advantages for this project. By using Twitter, instead of survey questions, we lower the risk of demand characteristics and observer effects in people's responses. Rather, this data is more representative of a user's mindset as it occurs over a longer period of time and in an unprompted, casual setting. Therefore, Twitter data is more suited for studying a person's state of mind on a day-to-day basis, and recent research finds convergent results between data collected on Twitter and psychological studies [5,6]. Additionally, Twitter's popularity allows researchers to study populations that would be difficult to access through university participant pools or field surveys. Users interested in certain people/topics (e.g. Barack Obama, Pope Francis, Apple) subscribe ("follow") to updates from those figures/companies/topics. Therefore, the followers from those account provide a sample of the desired population to study. Lastly, the magnitude of the data is significantly greater than in traditional contexts, allowing for a more comprehensive analysis of a population. Twitter thus provides a unique opportunity to study psychological constructs on a large scale that is not possible through traditional survey and laboratory methods.

4   Method

4.1   Data Collection

Data collection began on February 1st, 2014 and ended on February 4th, 2014. Using the Twitter Advanced Programming Interface (API) via the Twython package for Python [7], we obtained a list of the of the followers to the most popular Bitcoin exchange at the time, MTGOX (@MTGOX), which had approximately 25,000 followers. To increase the likelihood the users in our sample were human and not automated accounts, we only included users who posted to Twitter from a web browser or a mobile application. From this list, we randomly sampled 14,956 users. Of those users, 34%, (5,101) made their information publically available. We then accessed their entire message history on Twitter since the creation of their account. Additionally, we recorded the number of accounts the user followed, and that followed the user.

We also collected the tweets of 4,988 randomly sampled users who posted from a browser or mobile device. This sample came from the Twitter Streaming API, which provides a real-time sample of all tweets posted publicly at a given moment. Upon connecting to the API, we compiled a list of the users in stream. Therefore, this sample of users serves as a representation of a typical person who posts on Twitter and as a control group to the users interested in Bitcoin.

4.2 Data Preparation and Cleaning

Due the noise that non-English and non-active accounts introduce into text analysis, we followed the exact data cleaning procedures that similar research has used [6]. Because the LIWC dictionaries are based on the English language, we removed all timelines that were not in English. We filtered users by coding the percentage of words in a user's timeline that matched the stop words (e.g. prepositions, articles, pronouns) of 14 European languages. The collection of stop words came from the natural language toolkit (NLTK) package for Python. We removed any user that had a higher percentage of stop words in any non-English language than the percentage of English stop words. Because shorter text may not be as reliable and some accounts may not be active, we only included timelines that contained at least 20 tweets in their history. Lastly, we removed all numbers, special characters, hyperlinks, and punctuation from the text and converted each letter to lowercase. After data cleaning, our dataset contained 2,673 MTGOX followers, and 4,180 control users.

4.3 Measures

The current research took an exploratory approach to examine what psychological terms/categories/identifiers Bitcoin Twitter users differ on compared to the average Twitter user. We used the Linguistic Inquiry and Word Count (LIWC) program to measure how much their language emphasizes a variety of psychological processes. The internal dictionary contains six categories of psychological processes: "social," "affective," "cognitive," "perceptual," and "biological." Those conceptual dictionaries contain various subdictionaries that capture the different facets of the general domain. For example, the "social" dictionary is a collection of subdictionaries relating to "friends," "family," and "humans" in general. LIWC also contains dictionaries relating to personal concerns including: "work," "achievement," "leisure," "home," "money," "sex," and "religion." (see Pennebaker et al for a full list of the LIWC dictionaries and sample words[3]).

5 Results and Discussion

Due to the large sample size (N = 6,853 users), all tests of mean differences were significant at the conventional .05 level. Therefore, for the results, we discuss the pattern of effect size differences (*Cohen's d* and confidence intervals of the effect) between Bitcoin followers on Twitter and the typical user. Our results show a clear and consistent pattern, where Bitcoin users are less likely to emphasize concepts pertaining to relationships with others.

Compared to the typical site user, Bitcoin users were far less likely to talk about content in LIWC's "social" dictionary (d = -1.34, 95% CI = [-1.40, -1.29]). This dictionary contains all of the words found in the subdictionaries for family (e.g. brother, mother), friends (e.g. buddy friend), and humans (e.g. adult, baby) as well as all non-first-person-singular personal pronouns and verbs that suggest human interaction (e.g. talking, sharing). Additionally, the subdictionaries for family ($d = -.92$, 95% CI = [-.97, -.87]), friends ($d = -1.0$, 95% CI = [-1.05, -.95]), and humans ($d = -.69$, 95% CI = [-.74, -.64]) reflected the same pattern, indicating that the differences are not restricted to one specific social aspect. Related dictionaries show a similar trend. Bitcoin users are less likely to talk about sexual topics ($d = -1.28$, 95% CI = [-1.33, -1.23]), religion ($d = -.48$, 95% CI = [-.53, -.43]), and the home ($d = -0.35$, 95% CI = [-.4, -.31]. As a further examination, we calculated the 50 words that Bitcoin users say more often relative to typical users, and did the same for the typical users. These differences also suggest a lower social emphasis in what Bitcoin users say (figure 1).

Fig. 1. Words that showed the biggest positive difference in frequency between typical site users compared to Bitcoin users (left) and Bitcoin users compared to typical site users (right). Font size indicates the relative magnitude of the difference between groups for that word.

We also examined differences in language for concepts related to social processes, such as emotions (both positive and negative). Past research finds that emotions serve social functions and arise in response to social issues [8]. Their presence in speech may therefore serve as another indicator of social connection. Bitcoin followers were much less likely to have emotional content ($d = -1.13$, 95% CI = [-1.18, -1.08]) in their tweets. In addition to examining overall emotion differences, we found the same trend for the emotional subdictionaries. Bitcoin followers were less likely to mention both positive ($d = -.93$, 95% CI=[-.98, -.88]) and negative emotion words ($d = -1.33$, 95% CI=[-1.39 , -1.28]). The negative emotion dictionary is composed of subdictionaries relating anxiety, anger, and sadness. Bitcoin users were less likely to mention sadness ($d = -.66$, 95% CI=[-.71, -.61]) and anger ($d = -1.16$, 95% CI=[-1.21, -1.11]), but were equal on anxiety ($d = .003$, 95% CI=[-.08, .09]). The swearing dictionary shows a similar trend, where Bitcoin users are less likely to use expletives ($d = -1.10$, 95% CI=[-1.15, -1.05]) Therefore, Bitcoin users' tweets contained generally less emotional content, with the exception of anxiety.

This lack of social focus was also reflected in the users' connection with other users on the site. We compiled a list containing the number of people the Bitcoin followers/control users followed as well as how many people followed them. Due to the strong left skew in the distribution of each, the log-transformed the number of people each user followed and that followed them. We again found a strong difference between Bitcoin enthusiasts and typical users. People interested in Bitcoin on Twitter followed less people ($d = -1.04$, 95% CI = [-1.06, -1.02]) and had less people following them as well ($d = -.58$, 95% CI = [-.60, -.57]).

6   Conclusion

Our results show that people interested in Bitcoin on Twitter are much less likely to emphasize socially related dimensions in their daily language. Concepts pertaining to family, friends, humans, home, religion, sex, swearing, and emotions were mentioned less frequently, compared to a typical site user. We also found that they were less engaged with others on the site compared our control sample. This research is the first to suggest what psychological differences exist between Bitcoin users and the average person. Based on our findings, one possibility is that people interested in Bitcoin are distinctively less socially involved and emotionally expressive. Future research may seek to examine these differences further in different contexts as well as the implications less social connection may have. While Bitcoin has become increasingly more popular, the public may still be largely unaware of its details. This lack of information may be due in part to its users' lower social connectedness. Further, the adoption of the currency may be slowed if its users' social networks are less dense compared to others'. Collectively, our findings suggest many new possible avenues for research on Bitcoin users, and offer insight into how this currency may develop in the future.

References

1. BitLegal Index, http://bitlegal.io/list.php
2. Pennebaker, J.W.: The Secret Life of Pronouns: What Our Words Say About Us. Bloomsbury Press, New York (2013)
3. Pennebaker, J.W., et al.: The Development and Psychometric Properties of LIWC 2007. LIWC. Net, Austin (2007)
4. Twitter.com – Site Info, http://alexa.com/siteinfo/twitter.com
5. Golder, S.A., Macy, M.W.: Diurnal and Seasonal Mood Vary with Work, Sleep, and Daylength Across Diverse Cultures. Science 333(6051), 1878–1881 (2011)
6. Ritter, R.S., et al.: Happy Tweets: Christians Are Happier, More Socially Connected, and Less Analytical Than Atheists on Twitter. Social Psychological and Personality Science 5(2), 243–249 (2014)
7. Twython 3.1.1, http://pypi.python.org/pypi/twython
8. Keltner, D., Haidt, J.: Social Functions of Emotions at Four Levels of Analysis. Cognition & Emotion 13(5), 505–521 (1999)

Public Media on the Web for Everyone – An Evaluation of the Norwegian Broadcasting Cooperation's Website

Siri Kessel, Norun Sanderson, and Weiqin Chen

Oslo and Akershus University College of Applied Sciences
Post box 4 St. Olavs plass, 0130 Oslo, Norway
{Siri.Kessel,Norun.Sanderson,Weiqin.Chen}@hioa.no

Abstract. Media plays a key role in ensuring freedom of expression which is an essential foundation for democracy. The emerging e-society poses pressing challenges for accessibility to public media on the Web. In this project we focus on The Norwegian Broadcasting Cooperation's Website, NRK.no and study the possible accessibility issues and solutions using heuristic evaluation and focus group interviews with users.

Keywords: Accessibility, universal design, public media, heuristic evaluation, focus group.

1 Introduction

Media is a most important arena for general education and public debate. It plays a key role in ensuring freedom of expression, which is an essential foundation for democracy [1]. In the emerging e-society more and more of media content and public debate takes place on the Internet. Ensuring accessibility for all to these new arenas is therefore essential for equal participation.

In Norway the rights to access Internet services are stated in the Discrimination and Accessibility Act (DAA) [2], the regulation for section 14 in DAA [3] and in governmental ICT policy. The goal is to give all citizens equal access to the e-society. The government has allocated large amount of funding to expand broadband constructions and to increase digital knowledge. In 2012, 99.9 % of Norwegian households had possibilities for broadband access and ICT competence has been implemented as basic skills in the curriculum in primary schools. However, little attention has been paid to accessibility concerns in spite of many citizens having difficulties in accessing websites.

This project aims to gain knowledge on how complex web-based media services can be more universally designed through identifying accessibility issues and testing solutions with users. As a first step, we focus on The Norwegian Broadcasting Cooperation's Website, NRK.no, and conduct heuristic evaluations and focus group interviews to collect data on the content creation and management tool, Polopoly, and selected web pages in NRK.no.

C. Stephanidis (Ed.): HCII 2014 Posters, Part II, CCIS 435, pp. 32–36, 2014.
© Springer International Publishing Switzerland 2014

2   NRK.no and Polopoly

The Norwegian Broadcasting Corporation (NRK) is Norway's largest media house. It is mainly financed by annual broadcasting licence fee. Everyday almost nine out of ten Norwegians use one or more of NRK's services [4]. NRK.no is the website for NRK and it provides online news, TV, radio and a number of other services. According to NRK, there are 400 journalists working with the news portal at NRK.no, publishing about 250 articles daily.

Polopoly is a content creation and management tool used by NRK journalists to prepare content to the NRK.no news web pages. The Panorama rendering system, developed in-house at NRK, is used for rendering the web pages for NRK.no. Polopoly stores articles and other content together with metadata in a database and Panorama retrieves metadata and content when rendering web pages according to predefined templates. Journalists have a number of optional settings for creating metadata concerning the type of article and describing the different elements comprising the article.

3   Method

We have conducted heuristic evaluation on Polopoly. Two accessibility experts evaluated Polopoly based on the WAI guidelines ATAG (Authoring Tool Accessibility Guidelines) 2.0 part B [5]. The evaluations have been conducted in cooperation with NRK, the department of New Media (Nye Medier), who set up a test environment for the researchers.

The focus group interviews focus on selected web pages in NRK.no including news notices, domestic news, culture and entertainment, science, and opinions and debate.

The focus group interviews were semi-structured. The participants were from the following groups: 1) visually impaired, including blind and partially sighted, 2) hearing impaired, including sign language users, 3) cognitively impaired, 4) people with foreign language background, 5) elderly, and 6) volunteers in an organisation for underprivileged people. In total 19 users participated in the five group interviews.

The interview included questions concerning devices and experience using the Web and NRK.no as well as personal preferences. More specifically, the interview focused on their experience with different functions and design of NRK.no, including general design, structure, layout, navigation, text content, language, multimedia, and discussion. In addition, the participants were asked to discuss challenges in using NRK.no and give suggestions on future improvement.

4   Findings

In this section we summarise the results from the heuristic evaluations and the focus group interviews.

4.1   Heuristic Evaluation of Polopoly

The heuristic evaluation focused on to what extent Polopoly allows the creation of accessible content in compliance with the ATAG 2.0 B guidelines. Table 1 shows the compliance of Polopoly with the criteria.

Table 1. Compliance of Polopoly with ATAG 2.0 B

Criteria	Level A	Level AA	Level AAA
B.1. Fully automatic processes produce accessible content	Pending	Pending	Pending
B.2. Authors are supported in producing accessible content	No	No	No
B.3. Authors are supported in improving the accessibility of existing content	No	No	No
B.4. Authoring tools promote and integrate their accessibility features	No	No	No

We have completed the evaluation of Polopoly concerning criteria in B.2, B.3, and B.4 and found that either Polopoly is not compliant, or the criteria are not applicable. It shows that Polopoly does not provide enough support for journalists to create accessible content. Since B.1 involves the evaluation of both Polopoly and Panorama, the evaluation is currently not completed. Nevertheless, the results clearly indicate that much work needs to be done in order for Polopoly to help journalists create accessible content. It is likely that the rendering tool Panorama plays an important role in the process of publishing accessible content in NRK.no. This role should be further clarified in future work.

4.2   Focus Group Interviews

The users experience many challenges when using NRK.no. Table 2 shows a list of common issues that more than one group has identified. These issues cover what the groups think important, as well as barriers, challenges, and missing functions. The group numbers are presented in Section 3.

Many other important issues were also identified by individual groups. For example, Three out of four in the elderly group preferred Arial font. Some of the articles were found using inconsistent font or text style (e.g. Italics or " " for direct quotation). The elderly users found that some icons were not easily recognizable and that the names in some menus and their corresponding page titles were not consistent with each other.

The visually impaired group missed the keyboard navigation support in some occasions such as menu items and videos where the play button was not accessible through keyboard. They also found that some of the text for pictures were unnecessarily long and sometime irrelevant for the content of the pictures.

Table 2. Issues identified by more than one user groups

Component	Issues	Groups
Structure, layout and design	• Background and foreground contrast including both text and pictures (Missing text and buttons when using high contrast)	1, 4, 5
	• Size and position of picture (title of articles under picture(s))	1, 2, 4, 5, 6
	• Recognisable structure throughout the pages	All groups
	• Strong colour for highlighting (Missing)	1-5
	• Highlight or alert of important information (missing)	2, 5
Multimedia	• Subtitle for videos	2-6
Content/language	• Easy accessible explanation for foreign, domain-specific, and difficult words	2, 4
	• High quality of article content	1-5
Discussion	• Moderation is necessary	2, 4, 5, 6

The hearing impaired group thought that it was important to show whether a video has subtitle or not so that they could decide whether to download and open the video. A subtitle icon would save a hearing impaired person from the frustration of using time to download a video before finding out that the subtitle is missing. They also found some mismatches between article titles and the accessible content. For example, an article text was not consistent with the article title. The video content was, but it had no subtitle. The hearing impaired group found this frustrating.

Some groups gave different or even conflicting opinions concerning certain aspects on the webpages. For example, different persons preferred different font style and font size setting for different levels of headings and texts. Some preferred long sentences while other preferred short ones. Some preferred difficult terms while others needed easily accessible explanations for them.

Several groups expressed the importance of personal settings where they could specify their preferences. Some visually impaired users were dependent on such settings.

Another common feedback is that the discussion opportunities were not widely used by the groups. Most people we interviewed had never posted any comments, although some had read other's posts. Users with foreign language background were afraid that posts by person with foreign names and not perfect language would cause unpleasant experiences. Hearing impaired users highlighted that making an impairment visible could cause negative experiences. Both, therefore, preferred that NRK moderates their comments.

Although some of the issues identified do not prevent the individual persons in the groups from using NRK.no, they result in low efficiency and sometimes create confusion, frustration and irritation. User experiences could be improved greatly if these issues are addressed.

5 Discussion and Future Work

This paper presents the preliminary results from an ongoing project concerning universal design of public media on the Web. The heuristic evaluations of the content creation and management tool Polopoly and the focus group interviews on NRK.no have provided us with very interesting results. The participants were in general positive towards NRK.no and they experienced high quality contents and recognisable structure. In addition, NRK.no is free from advertisement, which they thought is a very positive feature.

Some of the issues identified in NRK.no can be caused by Polopoly and Panorama. For example, Polopoly does not have an option to add alternative text to pictures. Instead, Panorama combines caption and title of the picture, name of photographer and bureau as the alternative text for the picture. This creates an unnecessarily long and seldom relevant description, which has been pointed out by the visually impaired group.

Currently we are starting the heuristic evaluation of selected pages in NRK.no. Further we are planning user testing of NRK.no with different users who could face challenges on the Web due to either digital gap, Norwegian as second language, low income, cognitive, sensory or motor impairments. We are also in close collaboration with NRK for immediate improvements of NRK.no based on the results so far.

One of our foci in future work is plain language in online public media [6, 7]. We will study whether general public, especially people with cognitive difficulties, language barriers and little/lower education can easily understand and use the information provided by NRK.no.

Acknowledgement. This project is funded by The Delta Centre on behalf of the Norwegian Ministry of Children, Equality and Social Inclusion. We would like to thank Helge Kaasin and NRK for their collaboration and support. We would also like to thank all the anonymous participants for their valuable feedback.

References

1. European Convention on Human Rights. Article 10
2. LOV-2013-06-21-61, Barne-, Likestillings- og Inkluderingsdepartementet (in Norwegian)
3. FOR-2013-06-21-732, Kommunal- og moderniseringsdepartementet (in Norwegian)
4. NRK.no., http://nrk.no/ (last visited March 7, 2014)
5. ATAG 2.0 Part B, http://www.w3.org/TR/ATAG20/ (last visited March 7, 2014)
6. Steinberg, E., Bowen, B., Duffy, T.: Plain Language: Principles and Practice. Wayne State University Press (1991)
7. Miesenberger, K., Petz, A.: Easy to Read on the Web – State of the Art and Research Directions. Procedia Computer Science 27, 318–326 (2014)

A Study on Private SNS (Social Networking Service) Usage of Seniors

Cheongah Kim and Younghwan Pan

Graduate School of Techno Design, Kookmin University, Seoul, Korea
rewindvirus@gmail.com, peterpan@kookmin.ac.kr

Abstract. As online SNS market has rapidly grown in recent years, the user preference has shifted from open SNS to private SNS which provides closer, more private communication space. Also, the age group of users has expanded to those in their 50s and above, forming a network with real-names and social relationships on a daily basis. Based on various ties, achievement, and social status built offline, the seniors are integrating their online and offline identity. Thus, this study has examined their private SNS usage patterns to explore how the SNS influences their interpersonal and social relationships, in terms of adding new characteristics. The ultimate goal of this study is to improve and enhance the social relationships of seniors offline through private SNS to boost their life satisfaction by expanding their social ties.

Keywords: SNS (Social networking service), Private SNS, Senior, Smart senior, BAND.

1 Introduction

According to UN, the definition of 'aging society,' 'aged society' and 'super-aging' society is when the population aged 65 and over is at least 7%, 14%, and 20% of the entire population respectively. According to data from National Statistical Office in Korea, the country has around 6.1 million seniors aged 65 and over, representing 12.2% of the entire population in 2013. The percentage could exceed 20.0% in 2030, indicating that Korea will rapidly become a super-aging society.

When the middle-aged smart device users become seniors, the number of seniors using smart devices is expected to skyrocket. As a result, their online activities and roles will have a major impact on their social relationships. In this thesis, 'smart seniors' refer to those in their later middle-aged years right before and after retirement. In other words, they are in the latter period of 2nd to third stage of life(Table 1) and familiar with smart devices. The term was used by Asahi Shimbun in Japan on September 15, 1999. [2]

As the number of smart seniors is on the rise and smart phones have become popular among all age groups, the number of seniors in their 50s and above using smart phones has substantially risen. When it was surveyed, 1 out of 4 respondents (25.3%) in their 50s and above responded they had used SNS before.(Fig.1)

C. Stephanidis (Ed.): HCII 2014 Posters, Part II, CCIS 435, pp. 37–42, 2014.
© Springer International Publishing Switzerland 2014

Table 1. Three Stages of Life of 30,000 Days [1]

1st	2nd	3rd
childhood, young adult years	middle-aged years early senior years	mid-to-late senior years
- 7,500 days	- 15,000 days	-7,500 days (20.5 years)

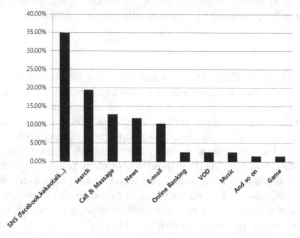

Fig. 1. Utilization of Smartphone Functions among Seniors (Source: Senior Portal 'Your stage', www.yourstage.com, 2012)

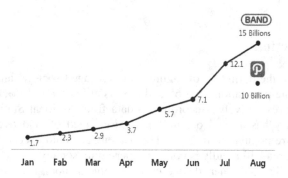

Fig. 2. Number of Monthly App Operation for BAND (Source: www.Flurry.com, 2013)

As online SNS market has rapidly grown, the user preference has shifted from open SNS to private SNS which provides closer, more private space; it reflects the issues with open SNS such as invasion of privacy and flood of ads. As a result, the age group of private SNS users has expanded to those in their 50s and above, forming a network with real-names and social relationships on a daily basis. Also, the private SNS has led to increased offline interactions and is being used actively. In particular,

---

[1] Hakuhodo Institute of Life and Living & Hakuhodo INC (2009).

'BAND' in Korea has established itself as a top, sustainable private SNS, as it allows users in their 40s and above to easily build their own network with friends and family members online.(Fig.2) Based on such phenomenon, this study has analyzed the private SNS usage of retired, alienated seniors, along with things they pursue, to boost their quality of life and satisfaction by enhancing their offline relationships through private SNS.

2   Features and UI of Private SNS

2.1   Classification of SNS

SNS is defined as a platform for establishing social networks of people who share the same or similar interests, activities, background or ties.[7] Also, SNS is a new communication mode with two-way functions that encompass virtual reality such as Second Life.[5] In a narrow sense, SNS refers to services aimed at forming and maintaining interpersonal networks. There are two types of SNS: open SNS and private SNS.

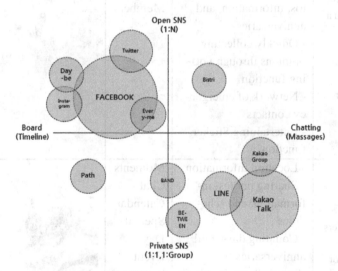

Fig. 3. SNS Positioning Map by Type

Open SNS revolved around online networking, which can lead to offline interactions, and the major ones are Facebook, Twitter, and KaKao Story. Users with similar interests can get closer to each other by posting comments and photos on a theme of their interest through the system of forming ties through online search.

Private SNS allows users to get closer to people they already know, and major ones are BAND, Daybe, and Between. Private SNS revolves around communication and ties, instead of contents.(FIG.3)

2.2   Classification of Private SNS

In this thesis, there are two types of private SNS: 1:1 SNS that offers a reserved space for only two people such as a couple and close friends; 1:n SNS that is smaller than open SNS and offers a space for the following individuals: friends; people with similar interests; parents and teachers; teachers and students; neighbors; people who went to the same school. Examples of 1:1 SNS are Between(Table 2) and Couple, and those of 1:n SNS include Path, BAND(Table 2), Kakao Group, Kakao Agit, With, and Daybe.

Table 2. Features and Main Functions of BAND and Between

	Features	Main Functions	Screen
BAND SNS that allows users to form a small group with people they are close to and share various information.	- Easy and quick registration and invitation - Sharing schedules, announcements, photos, information, and anniversaries - Quickly collecting opinions through voting function - Network of emergency contacts - Entertaining Sticker function	Board Photo Chat Calendar Members	
Between SNS that offers an exclusive space only for couples and close friends.	- Location information - Sharing photos, information, and schedules - Counting days until anniversaries -Photo album function	Moments Chat Calendar Special-Day Event box	

3   Private SNS User Behavior

3.1   Scope and Method of Research

Through an online pre-survey, in-depth interviews were conducted with diverse SNS users residing in Seoul, 10 for each of the following 3 age groups (A-people in 20s and 30s/ B- people in 40s and 50s/ C- people in 60s and above). To identify the SNS usage of smart seniors and compare it with other age groups, two different age groups (A, B) were selected and they were asked the same questions. Group A had members who use both open SNS Facebook, and private SNS, BAND and Between. Group B and C had members whose mainly use Facebook and BAND.

3.2   Analysis

SNS activities have the following 7 characteristics: 'identity,' expressing oneself differently from other people online; 'presence,' allowing users to recognize the status of themselves and others; 'relationships,' forming ties with family members and friends and retaining them through the system; 'conversation,' communicating with others through chatting, Messenger and other methods; 'reputation,' allowing users to identify whether someone is good or bad; 'sharing,' forming a network through sharing, recommending, or distributing a content or information among users; 'groups,' a form of community created among people with similar interests or specific purposes.

The 7 characteristics of SNS organized by Gene Smith[3] were applied to the results of in-depth interviews to indicate the different characteristic of each SNS. The darker the color is, the stronger the characteristic is in each service. (Fig.4)

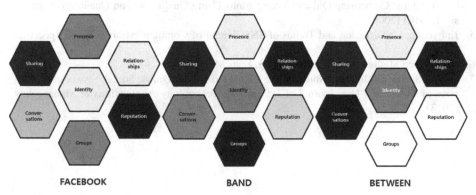

Fig. 4. Comparative Analysis of SNS with 7 Characteristics

4   Conclusion

The purpose of this study is to boost the life satisfaction of seniors through private SNS that is more developed for current and future seniors by strengthening and expanding their social ties, especially among smart seniors. To accomplish the objective, people who use both open SNS and private SNS were selected among different age groups for comparison with seniors in terms of user behavior. Open SNS has the following problems: invasion of privacy due to leakage of personal information; excessive exposure to unnecessary information. As a result, more and more users opted for private SNS. In particular, seniors had the most complaints about the problems of open SNS, leading to the highest popularity of private SNS among seniors. In terms of age group, the following characteristics were identified. First, the younger the users were, the more they valued the ties and exchanges with current friends. The older the users were, the more they valued maintaining ties with old and long-time friends. Second, seniors who are more used to offline interactions had a tendency to get involved in both online and offline interactions. In other words, their online interactions often led to offline interactions. Third, seniors preferred UI that displays all main functions on one screen, instead of simple UI with functions hidden on the screen, due to their lower familiarity with devices and physical conditions than those of young people. It is worthwhile to develop a new UI that facilitates the interaction of seniors with old friends, based on the characteristics of seniors.

References

1. Hakuhodo Institute of Life and Living & Hakuhodo INC: Kyodai Shijo 'Elder' No Tanjo (2003)
2. Murata, H.: Senior Shift No Shougeki, Diamond (2012)
3. Kietzmann, J.H., Hermkens, K., McCarthy, I.P., Silvestre, B.S.: Social media? Get serious! Understanding the functional building blocks of social media. Business Horizons (2011)
4. Kang, J., Kim, S., Lee, I., Kim, J.: Social Network Service Research for Quality of Life of Older Adults: Comparing Old and Young adults Using Qualitative and Quantitative Analysis. In: HCI (2009)
5. Jinhyeong, L.: Diffusion and Trends of SNS. Jounal of Communication & Radio Specetrun (2012)
6. Meta Trend Media Group: Trend Syncing, Hans Media (2011)
7. Bomil, S.: An Exploratory Study on the Characteristics of Online Social Network and Purpose of Custimer's Use. Journal of Information Technology Applications & Management (2013)

Towards a Micro-Contribution Platform That Meshes with Urban Activities

Shin'ichi Konomi[1], Wataru Ohno[2], Kenta Shoji[2], and Tomoyo Sasao[2]

[1] Center for Spatial Information Science, The University of Tokyo,
5-1-5, Kashiwanoha, Kashiwa, Chiba 277-8568, Japan
[2] Graduate School of Frontier Sciences, The University of Tokyo,
5-1-5, Kashiwanoha, Kashiwa, Chiba 277-8563, Japan

Abstract. In this paper, we discuss a mobile, context-aware platform for people to request and/or carry out microtasks in urban spaces. The proposed platform is based on our analysis of the activities of people in urban spaces including public transport environments, and considers various contextual factors to recommend relevant microtasks to citizens.

1 Introduction

Crowdsourcing provides a service platform for harnessing the skills of the large, network-connected crowd [1]. Integrating it with ubiquitous computing would allow for capture, sharing and validation of a massive amount of data [2], and development of a pervasive participatory system.

A key challenge in mobile crowdsourcing is the provision of the right task requests to the right people at the right time, at the right place, and in the right way. One of the approaches to tackle this challenge is task recommendation. Recent proposals to recommend tasks to crowdworkers exploit different approaches to match users and tasks [3,4,5] although they do not consider mobile contexts.

In this paper, we discuss a mobile, context-aware platform for people to request and/or carry out microtasks in urban spaces. The proposed platform is based on our analysis of the activities of people in urban spaces including public transport environments, and considers various contextual factors to recommend relevant microtasks to citizens.

2 The Urban Context

To develop a micro-contribution platform that can be integrated with urban spaces effectively, we investigated two types of prominent activities in a city: (1) using public transportation and (2) visiting food venues.

Firstly, we examined the activities of public transit users, focusing on their use of *spare time* while on the move, based on informal field observation at 20 train stations of a Japanese railroad line as well as a survey which we have carried out by using a Japanese online crowdsourcing service called Lancers [6].

C. Stephanidis (Ed.): HCII 2014 Posters, Part II, CCIS 435, pp. 43–47, 2014.

Table 1. Activity Choice

(1) Reading	(8) Using an alternative means of travel
(2) Shopping	(9) Going back to work / going home
(3) Snacking	(10) Smoking
(4) Taking a walk	(11) Visiting an amusement spot
(5) Dining	(12) Staying at a hotel
(6) Playing games	(13) Others
(7) Working / studying	

A key result from this investigation reveals different patterns of activities for different lengths of spare time. Respondents of the survey answered multiple choice questions by selecting the preferred activities at train stations, for different spare-time lengths, i.e., 0–5, 5–10, 10–20, 20–30, 30–60, and more than 60 minutes. They chose from the 13 activities that are shown in Table 1[1].

We received responses from 151 citizens in total. Figure 1 shows the number of respondents who preferred each activity for different lengths of spare time. Reading is the most popular activity to kill time in public transit environments, and it is particularly popular for shorter spare time of less than 30 minutes. We can see that some activities are skewed towards the shorter time length, and other activities towards longer time length. If people use a mobile application that recommends these activities (e.g., [7]), the length of upcoming spare time could be inferred based on chosen activities. The length of spare time is an important contextual information for a system that asks people to perform a small task while on the move. We also found that demographic information such as age groups and occupation is correlated with activity choices for spare time.

Secondly, we examined the activities of people who eat out based on a survey, focusing on the influence of social context over the choice of restaurants. We carried out the survey by using Lancers. We received responses from 193 citizens, and 32 percent of them had compromised on the choice of a food venue in the last 7 days. Interestingly, they are more likely to compromise when they eat out with many people. Figure 2 shows that when they eat out with more than 5 people, less than 10 percent of them decide by themselves which food venue to visit. We also found that people who eat out frequently are more likely to decide by themselves where to visit in social eat-out situations.

What this implies is that social context affects people's discretionary movement and behaviors. This can be a critical aspect when people in a social situation may carry out a microtask.

---

[1] The survey was conducted in Japanese. Items in this table have been translated from Japanese into English by the authors.

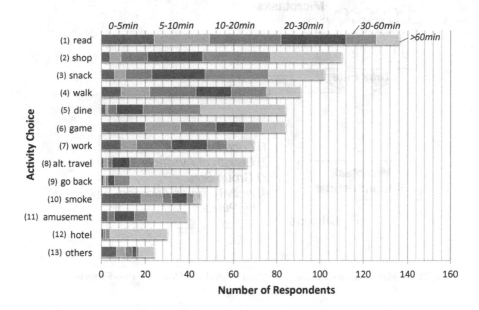

Fig. 1. Number of Respondents by Activity Choice for Different Length of Spare Time

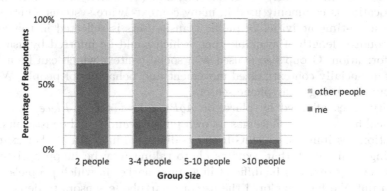

Fig. 2. Patterns of Compromise in Selecting Place to Eat Out

3   Micro-contribution Platform

We have designed a micro-contribution platform based on the studies presented in the previous section. As shown in Fig. 3, the platform recommends microtasks to citizens by using context-based task filtering, which is based on the pre-filtering model of contex-aware recommendation [8].

This platform represents users, tasks and contexts based on a hierarchical model of generalization so as to remedy the problem of data sparseness, which is a major issue in context-aware collaborative filtering systems.

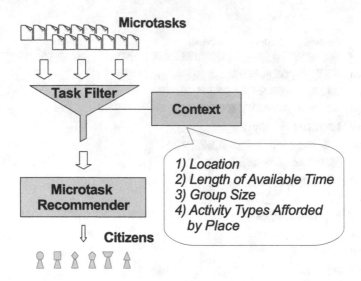

Fig. 3. A Micro-Contribution Platform Based on Context Pre-Filtering

The platform considers the four types of contextual information: (1) location, (2) length of available time, (3) group size, and (4) activity types afforded by place. Location is commonly used in many context-aware systems. Our discussions on spare-time activities of public transit users is reflected in the second type of context: length of available time, which could be inferred by using implicit information. Group size is used as a social context which can be used to incorporate socially contextualized movement and behaviors of people. We can infer group size using smartphone sensors.

Activity types afforded by place, or *AoP (Affordance of Place) context* is also critical because each place has its own physical and social constraints. It is about action possibilities, which Gibson has discussed in depth [9]. For example, performing a microtask that requires photo taking may be inappropriate in a museum. Typing text can be difficult in a supermarket in which people's hands are often full. We have explored the use of smartphone sensors to detect high-level AoP contexts in some areas at a public park.

4   Concluding Remarks

We have examined the urban contexts that are familiar to many, i.e., public transport environments and eat-out activities, and proposed a micro-contribution platform. We acknowledge that the proposed platform not only create opportunities but also introduce risks related to privacy violation as well as potential intensification of mobile cocooning. Working everywhere on mobile phones could potentially deprive citizens of the opportunities to interact with the 'real' world. Although there are no easy solutions to these issues, appropriate integration of microtasking and the urban contexts should focus on the improvement of quality of life as a whole.

Acknowledgments. This research was supported by the Environmental Information project under the Green Network of Excellence (GRENE) program of MEXT, Japan.

References

1. Hoßfeld, T., Tran-Gia, P., Vucovic, M.: Crowdsourcing: From Theory to Practice and Long-Term Perspectives (Dagstuhl Seminar 13361). Dagstuhl Reports 3(9), 1–33 (2013)
2. Vukovic, M., Kumara, S., Greenshpan, O.: Ubiquitous crowdsourcing. In: Proceedings of Ubicomp 2010, p. 523. ACM Press, New York (2010)
3. Ambati, V., Vogel, S., Carbonell, J.: Towards Task Recommendation in Micro-Task Markets. In: Human Computation, pp. 1–4 (2011)
4. Difallah, D.E., Demartini, G., Cudré-mauroux, P.: Pick-A-Crowd: Tell Me What You Like, and I'll Tell You What to Do. In: Proceedings of WWW 2013, pp. 367–374 (2013)
5. Yuen, M.C., King, I., Leung, K.S.: TaskRec: A Task Recommendation Framework in Crowdsourcing Systems. Neural Processing Letters II, 516–525 (February 2014)
6. Lancers (2014), http://www.lancers.jp
7. Bellotti, V., Price, B., Rasmussen, P., Roberts, M., Schiano, D.J., Walendowski, A., Begole, B., Chi, E.H., Ducheneaut, N., Fang, J., Isaacs, E., King, T., Newman, M.W., Partridge, K.: Activity-based serendipitous recommendations with the Magitti mobile leisure guide. In: Proceedings of CHI 2008, pp. 1157–1166. ACM Press, New York (2008)
8. Adomavicius, G., Tuzhilin, A.: Context-aware recommender systems. In: Recommender Systems Handbook, pp. 217–253 (2011)
9. Gibson, J.J.: The Ecological Approach To Visual Perception. Houghton Mifflin Harcourt (1979)

SOPHIE: Social, Open Pro-active Hub for Information Exchange to Support Intelligence Communities

Jan Willem Streefkerk, Aletta Eikelboom, Rosie Paulissen, Ingrid van Bemmel, Anne-Fleur Hemmer, Ward Venrooij, and Kees den Hollander

TNO, The Netherlands
{j.w.streefkerk,aletta.eikelboom,rosie.paulissen,
ingrid.vanbemmel,anne-fleur.hemmer,ward.venrooij,
kees.denhollander}@tno.nl

Abstract. Military intelligence communities need to collect, process and disseminate information as quickly and efficiently as possible, for example in answering requests for information by commanders. Currently, the flow of information between the field and intelligence communities is hampered by disparities in the integration of the various components of the information chain. We propose to create a hub for information exchange called SOPHIE, where information from heterogeneous sources comes together. This hub proactively notifies military users to relevant information based on their profile. In addition, users can search or browse available information products and consult experts to receive quick answers to their information requests.

Keywords: intelligence community, collaboration, context-awareness, military.

1 Introduction

The primary task of military intelligence communities is to collect, process and disseminate information to support missions of commanders on all levels. Commanders and staffs request specific information relevant to their mission. Intelligence analysts compile and send information products in response to these requests. However, currently information does not reach recipients timely and efficiently, thereby making military missions less effective. A number of problems can be identified. Due to time constraints, information requests go unanswered, or receive only a generic answer. Especially when information requests are not specific enough, the context of the mission is not considered and quality criteria for the product are lacking. On a general level, differences in goals, prioritization and mindset limit effective understanding and collaboration between intelligence and command and control communities.

Military organizations should strive towards a tight coupling between Command & Control (C2), Intelligence (I) en Surveillance & Reconnaissance (S&R) [1], [2]. These three processes are currently not synchronized into one chain of information: the C2ISR-chain. Due to the scarcity of resources (sensors, UAVs) and the

C. Stephanidis (Ed.): HCII 2014 Posters, Part II, CCIS 435, pp. 48–54, 2014.

increasingly complex operational environment, an efficient integration of this chain is required to allow commanders to benefit from information obtained from ISR sensors [3]. In this chain, the Environment Cell is a pivotal point; analysts in this cell are responsible for gathering information and answering Requests for Information (RFIs) from commanders. As pointed out above, clear information requests, insight into available information and speedy information processing are vital requirements to allow information to flow efficiently through this whole chain. Catalysts for this process are improved technological means of information exchange, such as mobile devices and big data analysis.

This project builds on innovative technologies to strengthen the C2ISR chain. First, we provide insight into current functioning of the intelligence chain, focusing on the interaction between the Environment Cell (EC) and the commanders in the field. Then, we propose the concept of SOPHIE: a Social, Pro-active Hub for Information Exchange between the EC and commanders. We present the functionality illustrated by a use case and point out future directions. As this is work in progress, we plan to host a first evaluation session with end-users in April 2014.

2   Domain Analysis: Current Practices and Bottlenecks

This domain analysis is based on results from three research activities: 1) observations of the functioning of the Environment Cell during a military exercise (feb/march 2013), 2) interviews with three platoon commanders with expeditionary experience and 3) a workshop where military experts and human factors experts were brought together to identify current practices and bottlenecks.

In all these activities, the focus of research was on the processing of an 'request for information' (RFI) into a finished information product and the interactions between commanders and experts in the Environment Cell in this process. At a global level, the process is as follows; an information request from a commander is sent to the EC digitally (e-mail) or on paper using standard forms. Information requests originating from the field (near real-time) are done by radio via the mission manager in the operations room. Depending on the priority of the request and the available knowledge and expertise, a request can be answered directly by an analyst. Alternatively, information needs to be gathered by sensors to answer this request. When information becomes available to answer this request, depends again on the priority and the available resources. The analysts in the EC gather the available information into an information product, and make it available to the commander (either digitally or on paper).

What can be concluded is that at this moment, the intelligence gathered and processed in the EC is insufficiently contributing to Command & Control, mainly due to low quality and accessibility of information, insufficiently flexible technological resources and misunderstandings or cultural differences between the actors. To start with the first point; it is currently hard to keep track of available information and where this is stored. In the EC, a number of databases are used for the analysts, but commanders have no direct access to EC databases. They do have access to a large number of generic information products, but these are stored in a very user-unfriendly way and are hard to search or browse even for analysts. Moreover, the standard information forms are not helping commanders to ask specific and context-dependent questions, resulting in insufficient or standard answers or no answer at all. In fact, very little feedback is provided as to the status of a request. In the case of radio requests, the mission manager in the operations room is not trained in handling intelligence information requests.

Concerning the technological resources, a lot of the interaction is done by phone or in face-to-face contacts, which are not recorded and cannot be reproduced. E-mail is also increasingly used, but this is only efficient from one person to another, not to groups. Products are stored in a secured data folder, in a standard, pre-determined folder structure which cannot be changed ad-hoc. Over periods of months, these folders can become very extensive and hard to search. Finally, the differences between actors are hampering efficient communication and understanding between the EC and commanders in the field. This has mainly to do with different opinions on what information should be made available and for what reasons, resulting in discussions on the priority of a request. But also insufficient insight into each other's work practices, differences in rank and differences in security focus are not contributing.

3   Technological Innovations

Based on our domain analysis and relevant literature on military information exchange, we identified three global directions for solutions.

1. Make information products better available through intelligent access and better documentation. For example using smart technologies such as reasoning based on user-defined document tags, ontologies or information fusion technologies [4]. Also increase accessibility of information where and when it is needed, using innovative hardware such as mobile or head-mounted devices and augmented reality. Support of the RFI process should provide feedback on the status of a request.
2. During initiation of a request, the context, boundary definitions and possible impacts ("what happens when you do not receive this information") of the request should be made much more explicit, instead of filling out a standardized, generic form. This should be partly done by a digital e-partner ("Intelbuddy"), who keeps a profile of your information needs and wishes [5]. Also, by strengthening the informal human-human communication, for example by bringing commanders into direct contact with the necessary experts or analysts based on their profiles [6].
3. The amount of available information and the speed of availability should be increased. Primarily by quick documentation in the field of mission-relevant observations and findings, using categorized annotations and tags. Smart algorithms should facilitate the matching between information elements and user profiles [4].

4   SOPHIE Concept

Following the directions outlined above to improve the interaction and collaboration between intelligence communities and commanders, we propose the concept of SOPHIE: a Social, Open Pro-active Hub for Information Exchange. Using SOPHIE, commanders can access existing information products and initiate new information requests, even in the field. SOPHIE builds up a user profile (including interests, role and context factors) by monitoring mission planning, execution and mission reports. Based on the profile, SOPHIE helps to make information requests more specific, with

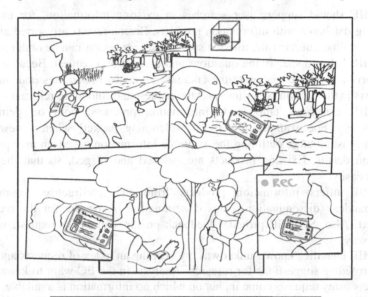

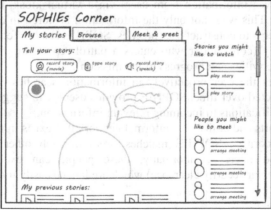

Fig. 1. Illustrations showing SOPHIE monitoring mission execution in real time (top) and an impression of SOPHIEs corner where the informal knowledge network is maintained (bottom)

emphasis on quality criteria: what do users need to do with the information? In addition, SOPHIE notifies users to relevant new information and makes suggestions to consult other experts or documentation. All personnel including intelligence analysts connect and maintain an informal knowledge network using SOPHIE [6].

As Fig. 1 illustrates, SOPHIE takes many forms, from an e-partner that monitors mission execution to a virtual kiosk where users can record implicit knowledge, share experiences and consult other experts. Specifically, we define eight functionalities that should be included in SOPHIE to address the current bottlenecks in the process and provide added benefit to end-users.

1. SOPHIE should support user searches in existing information, for example in existing databases with information products. Search results are sorted and orderd based on time, source, role, mission so that relevant results can be obtained.
2. SOPHIE helps to specify the questions and context of a request. Because SOPHIE supports the user to elaborate the context, demands, boundaries and impact, the analysts in the EC can better interpret the request and find more relevant results.
3. SOPHIE constructs tailor-made information products, both on demand and proactively. For example, a sort of 'welcoming packet' when a new mission planning is initiated, outlining the available information based on user profile and mission details. Existing products are indexed and tagged, so that they can be found easily.
4. SOPHIE offers information products from the intelligence community to commanders (dissemination). This dissemination is specific for the request and context. Also, SOPHIE provides feedback on the status of a request, while it is underway.
5. SOPHIE identifies known-unknowns, by keeping an index of requests and answers and providing suggestions for research. Analysts in the EC want to know on what subjects many requests come in, but on which no information is available.
6. SOPHIE receives information from users via a virtual kiosk, either manually or autonomously. This way, not only the information is stored in a retrievable place, but this also helps to construct user profiles. SOPHIE can be 'fed' with information either explicitly (commander who enters a patrol report) or implicitly (SOPHIE monitors the activities and progress of the mission).
7. SOPHIE guides the user proactively in information searches. Based on the user profile constructed over time, SOPHIE provides users with suggestions for 'further reading' or notifications to incoming relevant information.
8. SOPHIE supports and utilizes the informal network that exists in military operations. In a 'coffee corner', SOPHIE matches users to each other based on profile similarities and interests. Informally, these people can exchange information (depending on their security clearance) which are logged easily for later retrieval.

5   Future Directions

This poster presents the concept of SOPHIE, a social, open pro-active hub for information exchange to support interactions between intelligence communities and military commanders. In our domain analysis, we found evidence to suggest the process of initiating and answering an information request can be improved in military operations. Specifically, low availability of information, inflexible technological resources and misunderstanding of work activities between the user groups hamper efficient use of intelligence in the C2 chain [3]. This is not merely a technological challenge, but requires an integrated approach [1]. Our hub employs innovative technologies to address current bottlenecks, not only on a technological level (improved dissemination, better retrieval and tagging, matching of information relevance to user profiles) but also on an interpersonal level (increasing and maintaining an informal network, fostering collaboration). In our workshop, the validity of this integrated approach was confirmed by both the military and the human factors experts. In fact, in ongoing research, our team strives towards a technical demonstrator within a relevant military scenario by the end of 2014. In addition, the main functionalities and underlying assumptions are further checked with military end-users in a workshop evaluation.

Importantly, SOPHIE does not improve the *quality* of information itself. Investment in smarter and better sensor capability is a sine qua non to provide the commanders in the field with better information. In addition, if SOPHIE is to succeed, organizational and security aspects of military intelligence need to be reconsidered: who has the responsibility for following up on notifications? Who can control what is stored in the user profiles and which matches are made? Who has access to information and to what level? For technical implementation, challenges on reasoning structures, matching algorithms and information fusion tools must be overcome.

In the future, we see SOPHIE positioned not as the next best analysts' tool, nor as a Battlefield Management System for platoon commanders. We see SOPHIE as the pivotal point in making information better available, through helping those who need the information to ask for it in the right way. Only stronger integration of the various components of the C2ISR chain can truly contribute to an information-guided approach to military operations.

Acknowledgements. This research is supported by the Dutch Ministry of Defense within the C2ISR program (V1334).

References

1. Boury-Brisset, A.C., Frini, A., Lebrun, R.: All-source Information Management and Integration for Improved Collective Intelligence Production. Defence Research And Development Canada Valcartier, Quebec (2011)
2. Hershey, P., Wang, M.C., Graham, C., Davidson, S., Sica, M., Dudash, J.: A policy-based approach to automated data reduction for intelligence, surveillance, and reconnaissance systems. In: MILCOM 2012, pp. 1–6. IEEE Press (2012)
3. Moore, R., Schermerhorn, J., Oonk, H., Morrison, J.: Understanding and Improving Knowledge Transactions in Command and Control. In: ICCRTS Conference (2003)

4. Lerouvreur, X., Dambreville, F., Dragos, V.: Principles of a unified framework for heterogeneous information fusion and assessment. In: Military Communications and Information Systems Conference. IEEE (2013)
5. Neerincx, M.A.: Modelling cognitive and affective load for the design of human-machine collaboration. In: Harris, D. (ed.) HCII 2007 and EPCE 2007. LNCS (LNAI), vol. 4562, pp. 568–574. Springer, Heidelberg (2007)
6. Wollocko, A.B., Farry, M.P., Stark, R.F.: Supporting tactical intelligence using collaborative environments and social networking. In: SPIE Defense, Security, and Sensing. International Society for Optics and Photonics (2013)

To Catch a Thief: Practical Methods of Using Social Networks as a Mechanism for Identifying Corporate Insider Threats

Martyn Styles

University of South Wales, United Kingdom
03157210@glam.ac.uk

Abstract. Is it possible to utilize psychological profiling through social network analysis to identify potential corporate insider threats? This research will aim to provide corporate information security teams with techniques capable of recognizing the signs of an insider threat.

Keywords: Cyber security, social networking, information security, crime.

1   Introduction

The insider threat to organizations is bigger than ever before, thanks in part to the growing trend amongst certain individuals who believe that terms such as "confidential", "non-disclosure" and "private" no longer apply to any piece of data which, for reasons of ethics, conscience or organization profit should normally remain safeguarded within the boundary of the office walls. This research will attempt to illustrate the possibilities for identifying corporate insider threats through analyzing social networks, with the aim of identifying internal individuals who are potential data security threats through keyword analysis of popular social and professional networks such as Facebook, Twitter and LinkedIn.

2   Insider Definition

An insider is generally defined as any person within an organization who accesses data which may be regarded as useful by external persons if extracted from the organization, without the full knowledge of that organization. The oxymoron of the 'insider threat' is such that information security teams find it challenging to even countenance the thought that the typical employee has the capability to 'go rogue'. Information security teams are generally primed to detect threats from the outside trying to get in, rather than identify employees trying to egress data out of the organization.

Following the precedent of trust-betrayal by highly privileged serial-leakers; such as Chelsea/Bradley Manning and Edward Snowden, corporate employees may be tempted to release business secrets for amusement or financial gain. Although recent research

C. Stephanidis (Ed.): HCII 2014 Posters, Part II, CCIS 435, pp. 55–58, 2014.
© Springer International Publishing Switzerland 2014

has been performed to help identify insider threats (Claycomb W.R. et al., 2011) (Greitzer and Hohimer, 2011) (Greitzer et al., 2010), very little has been accomplished by using social network data pertaining to an organization. A recent model for understanding insider threats was proposed by Legg P. et al. (2013), which builds on earlier work by Magklaras and Furnell (2002) and Anderson (1980) to help describe a system capable of identifying indicators of misuse in IT systems. Anderson (1980)describes three categories of internal abuse: 1. Masqueraders – insiders that exploit security weaknesses in systems 2. Misfeasors – an insider who abuses legitimate privileges 3. Clandestine users – insiders with significant privileges that enable them to hide from audit logs. For the purposes of this research, we are looking for indications of a Misfeasor (in law, the abuse of lawful authority in order to achieve a desired result.) – a user of a system who exercises their legitimate access to data to remove it from the organization. Although Small (2009) says "If systems are compromised, does it matter if the cause was malice, misuse or mistake?", I believe that mistakes are a necessary risk in any business, however malice and misuse are avoidable.

Both masqueraders and clandestine users are typically I.T. employees, but the methods used to extract information from the organization are often similar to the misfeasor – typical egress mechanisms being through the use of email, web page uploads, file sharing sites or USB memory stick.

3   Privacy and Ethical Issues

Evidently there are a number of privacy and ethical issues raised with researching social networking data. In Europe, the EU Privacy Directive governs the rights of individuals for their personal data behavior to remain un-monitored, however in a corporate environment there are exceptions given a reasonable suspicion of wrongdoing and where the data movement between the individual and a social networking site involves corporate data. Ethical considerations for social media research will determine the extent to which investigations into end-user social networks can be exploited, using guidelines published by British Psychological Society (2010), Moreno et al. (2013), Henderson et al. (2012) and Zimmer (2010), and it is expected that for the purposes of the research paper, all personal details will be anonymized.

4   Insider Detection Process Flow

The process flow of insider detection is based on the following:

- *Egress Detection:* Detect unauthorized outgoing corporate data streams
- *Social Net Analysis*: Assess social network content related to the perpetrator
- *Behavioral Profiling:* Inaugurate behavioral profiling of the individual
- *Threat Identification:* Identify these activities as potential insider threat

Egress Detection: To initially aid in the identification of corporate data theft, we use commercial Data Leak Prevention (DLP) tools to flag emails with attachments containing potentially confidential data, sent from internal users to GoogleDocs, Gmail, Yahoo!Mail and other personal file sharing websites, since this method of data egress can be a strong indication of an insider threat. However useful this method is, using it to identify insiders may be limited because quite often false positives incorrectly trigger as DLP alerts through misguided users sending documents to home computers as a short-cut means of completing work or they are simply personal files such as photographs.

Social Net Analysis: Commercial tools such as IBM i2 Analyst's Notebook and Paterva Maltego facilitate the analysis of multiple social network streams in a visual manner. For this research project we are using Maltego and a selected number of online tools for social network analysis. To test the capability of using social networks to indicate potential insiders, a taxonomy of key words associated with the business activities carried out by an organization was refined for use in the social networking searches, and a list of current users was imported into Maltego to facilitate a search of social networks for keywords. The software has the ability to search a variety of different social networks as well as sites like pastebin.com, which is commonly used to leak information. With Maltego we search for interesting files found on social media sites that relate to the list of users.

Behavioral Profiling: Psychological profiling for potential insider threats is suggested by Shaw (2006), Stanton et al. (2005) and Crossler et al. (2013). When verifiable confidential corporate data is egressed through email attachments to personal email domains or file sharing website uploads, DLP alert data can be passed into Maltego and linked to the user's 'Person' item, so that a diagram can be formed of the relationships. In this way we can begin to understand confidential data movement beyond the corporate firewall.

Threat Identification: A combination of corporate data egress detection and social network analysis are used in the identification of insider threats. We use Maltego to visualize the insider threat.

5   Conclusion

The experiments we have undertaken thus far indicate that social network analysis is a valid method of detecting potential insider threats. Further work needs to be performed to validate our findings, however early indications are encouraging that the use of social network analysis is a useful mechanism for detection of an insider threat.

References

1. Anderson, J.P.: Computer security threat monitoring and surveillance. James P. Anderson Co. (1980)
2. British Psychological Society, Code of Ethics and Conduct (2010)

3. Claycomb, W.R., Huth, C.L., Flynn, L., Mcintire, D.M., Todd, B.: Chronological Examination of Insider Threat Sabotage: Preliminary Observations. CERT Insider Threat Center, Carnegie Mellon (2011)
4. Crossler, R.E., Johnston, A.C., Lowry, P.B., Hu, Q., Warkentin, M., Baskerville, R.: Future directions for behavioral information security research. Computers & Security 32, 90–101 (2013)
5. Greitzer, F., Kangas, L., Noonan, C., Dalton, A.: Identifying at-Risk Employees: A Behavioral Model for Predicting Potential Insider Threats (2010)
6. Greitzer, F.L., Hohimer, R.E.: Modeling Human Behavior to Anticipate Insider Attacks. Journal of Strategic Security 4(2), Article 3 (2011)
7. Henderson, T., Hutton, L., Mcneilly, S.: Ethics and online social network research – developing best practices. In: BCS HCI Workshop on HCI Research in Sensitive Contexts: Ethical Considerations, Birmingham, UK (2012)
8. Legg, P., Moffat, N., Nurse, J.R.C., Happa, J., Agrafiotis, I., Goldsmith, M., Creese, S.: Towards a Conceptual Model and Reasoning Structure for Insider Threat Detection (2013)
9. Magklaras, G.B., Furnell, S.M.: Insider Threat Prediction Tool: Evaluating the probability of IT misuse. Computers & Security 21, 62–73 (2002)
10. Moreno, M.A., Goniu, N., Moreno, P.S., Diekema, D.: Ethics of social media research: common concerns and practical considerations. Cyberpsychol Behav. Soc. Netw. 16, 708–713 (2013)
11. Shaw, E.D.: The role of behavioral research and profiling in malicious cyber insider investigations. Digital Investigation 3, 20–31 (2006)
12. Small, M.: The root of the problem – malice misuse or mistake. Computer Fraud & Security, 6–9 (2009)
13. Stanton, J., Stam, K., Mastrangelo, P., Jolton, J.: Analysis of end user security behaviors. Computers & Security 24, 124–133 (2005)
14. Zimmer, M.: 'But the data is already public": on the ethics of research in Facebook. Ethics and Information Technology 12, 313–325 (2010)

Social Networking Keyword Monitoring:

1. http://backtweets.com/
2. http://google.com/alerts
3. http://www.icerocket.com/
4. http://www.netvibes.com
5. http://tweetdeck.twitter.com/
6. http://www.paterva.com/web6/products/maltego.php
7. http://www-03.ibm.com/software/products/en/analysts-notebook/

Automatic Estimation of Influence of Acquaintances in a Social Group and Its Key Influencers from Their Communication and Location History

Junichi Suzuki[1,*], Yasuhiro Kawahara[2], Hiroshi Yoshida[2], Yosuke Bando[3], Konosuke Watanabe[3], Daniel J. Dubois[3], and Nobuhiko Watanabe[1]

[1] Open Innovation Laboratory, Information Services International - Dentsu, Ltd., Tokyo, Japan
junichi@isid.co.jp
[2] Open University of Japan, Graduate School of Arts and Sciences, Chiba, Japan
kawahara2@ouj.ac.jp
[3] Media Lab, Massachusetts Institute of Technology, Massachusetts, United States
bandy@media.mit.edu

Abstract. Information can be delivered to a target person with maximum efficacy via a specific information transferer. We developed a compass system that established an anonymous method to analogize in-city acquaintances and used location information and each visitor's smartphone to detect analogically the significant influencers of a target person. Based on the data regarding information transferred between group members and their location history, we derived a model for estimating how acquaintances influence each other in a social group and for locating influencers.

Keywords: Social city, Social graph, O2O, LBS, location based services, Area differentiation, Ambient communication, Spatial marketing, Behavioral marketing, Human communication, Positioning, Mobile system.

1 Introduction

Fundamentally, human beings are social and their desire to connect with others is universally acknowledged. A reason behind this nature is that we confirm our existence through mutual support and participation in the society [1]. However, social networking services (SNSs), which we use daily, do not completely satisfy our desire for an organic relation with others in real spaces. Foursquare, which puts "colocation," "co-encounter," and "co-activity" into practical use and helps people to connect with others, does not provide comprehensive attention to connections already established by people.

The social media revolution was ignited by the emergence of Facebook in 2004. Since then, the tidal wave of social media has fascinated people and completely changed the perspective of how they share information and communicate with each

---

* Corresponding author.

C. Stephanidis (Ed.): HCII 2014 Posters, Part II, CCIS 435, pp. 59–64, 2014.

other. Alvin Chin's and Daqing Zhang's comprehensive review of a sequence of these movements indicates [2] that there is no room to doubt the business opportunity and market scale in the field of social media, especially for online-to-offline (O2O) and location-based social networking (LBS) services such as Facebook and Foursquare. And social network analysis using information transmission in online SNS was reported [3].

Today, there are thousands of useful services making our communication simple and easy, and to socialize with others, we no longer have to depend on being in the same place and at the same time as them. Thus, the main purpose for our physical visit to certain places has shifted from being communication-oriented to being material-oriented, and physical spaces such as cities and shopping complexes are evaluated by their practical functions, which lead to the fading away of our belonging to spaces. Most people do not pay attention to the differences between cities for the purpose of shopping, working, or even residing there. We have been studying spatial and behavioral marketing along with the so-called "commoditization of real spaces" and the changes caused by it from the perspectives of area-differentiation strategy and ambient-communication strategy.

In addition to the problem of commoditizing real spaces, there is a need to resolve deep-rooted problems over online and offline communication against the background of the drastic growth in e-commerce and mobile computing. The situation around O2O and LBS sheds light on challenges that current SNSs present. For example, users start disliking an information source, such as a shop or a shopping complex for promoting information, perceiving its announcements like spam. In addition, real spaces are suffering from so-called "showrooming," where the consumption process does not complete within the offline environments and shop spaces function merely as showrooms [4][5].

Standing on the understanding of the challenges as described, we developed a system to analyze an intra-city social graph to enable visitors access local content through their friends in Grand Front Osaka (GFO), a large-scale complex facility, via the latest social network service, the compass system. This communication ecosystem not only provides reliable information or amplifies the reasons behind a visit but also lets users become a hub for their friends and others within their intra-city social graph. From this viewpoint, our approach is different from other SNSs in terms of its success in making fans of real spaces and satisfying their desire for mutual support and social participation.

We conducted an experiment in November 2013 to evaluate the validation of information shared via a user's friends (intra-city social graph). This article summarizes the experiment outcomes and analyzes the relationship between shared information and behavioral changes.

2   Grasp of Visitor Position by Compass System

GFO offers a compass system that aims to anonymously guess the interpersonal relationships of the person who visited the town. This compass system presumes the mobile terminal position by using wireless LAN access points and the user's smart-phone terminal by referring to the radio field strength the terminal receives and the position of the access point [6]. Moreover, this system has the ability to perform a check-in when visitors stop by each spot in town. It was observed that the compass system required only 60 minutes or less to differentiate two people from among un-specified town visitors after the two had succeeded in checking-in to a target spot [7].

In this study, the function of the compass system has been enhanced to make poss-ible its use outdoors, to analogize the interpersonal relationship of a traveling group. The GPS function of the terminal was used together with the positioning system, and the function that allows checking in at an arbitrary point was installed. In addition, a smartphone application that achieves photograph sharing using proximity communi-cation was developed as a tool to examine how information received from a specific acquaintance influenced the addressee. The information transmission situation in a travel group and the moving pathway of everybody can be grasped by using positional GPS logs and the information added to each photograph. Moreover, the experiment tested the design of a method for grasping the influence level in the group by using these pieces of information.

3   Information Propagation via Proximity-Based Photo Sharing

We provided the participants with a smartphone application for sharing pictures, built on top of a mobile resource sharing platform called ShAir [8]. Owing to the ad hoc peer-to-peer wireless communication capability of the platform, pictures were auto-matically shared whenever the participants moved close to each other. Capturing pic-tures was the only operation the participants performed in the application, which avoided an additional burden on the participants for sharing operations. Proximity-based sharing naturally limited recipients of pictures to a subgroup of the participants traveling together. Pictures were gradually and eventually shared with other partici-pants, as people from different subgroups met and as subgroups' members changed over time. Subsequently, pictures were shared between participants; thus, permitting us to witness information propagation among the participants. To keep a track of this, when a user captured a picture, the application attached an auxiliary header to the picture file and stored the user ID as well as a timestamp. The header was shared along with the picture, and whenever another user received the picture, the application added their user ID and another timestamp to the header. Fig. 1 shows a screenshot of the application with a picture and a list of the user IDs and timestamps associated with the picture.

4   Grasping the Foreign Tourist's Action

To investigate this idea (grasping the influence level in the group), the information flow and individual loci of a group of 15 incoming tourists was recorded. All travelers possessed smartphones with our Android application installed, which obtained GPS positional information at one-minute intervals and shared photographs captured by individuals within the group. The travelers were based in an Osaka hotel and they interacted throughout the eight days. As illustrated in Fig. 2, received information appeared to trigger an action among the travelers. The plot exhibits the temporal progression of the traveler's distance from the spot where the photograph was captured. The pattern in which the person who received a photograph captured in a certain place moved to that place was frequently observed through the experiment period.

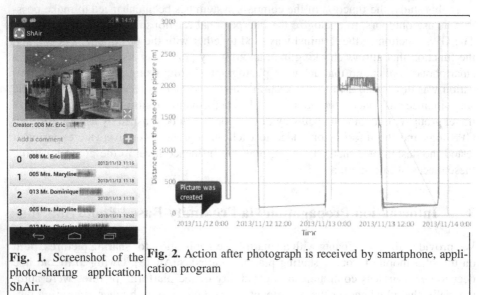

Fig. 1. Screenshot of the photo-sharing application. ShAir.

Fig. 2. Action after photograph is received by smartphone, application program

5   Interpersonal Influence Levels in a Travel Group

To elucidate how group members are influenced by photograph exchange at a place P taken by other members, we constructed a model that explains how pictures travel and influence the behaviors of members. In this model, how pictures travel is explained by the Markov model of state vectors of logical values, each representing whether a member has received or not received a photograph of place A from member B. Assume that members A, B, and C in the group send pictures to member D. The state vector of D then contains three logical values. Initially, D's state vector is (0,0,0), implying that D has acquired none of the pictures sent from members A, B, and C. When member D receives a photograph from A, the state vector changes to (1,0,0).

The output of this process alters from Has not visited place P to Has visited place P. These two states are assumed to depend on the state vector, which contains information on the photographs sent from other members. The whole model is illustrated in Fig. 3.

Table 1. Probability of reaching an outcome from different state vectors.

State vector			Probability of reaching state Has visited place P
0	0	0	0.1
0	1	0	0.1
0	0	1	0.3
0	1	1	0.7
1	0	0	0.5
1	1	0	0.6
1	0	1	0.8
1	1	1	0.9

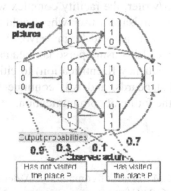

Fig. 3. Model of photograph exchange and behavior influence

The Markov model progresses from left to right. In this figure, the numbers beside the arrows pointing from the state vector to the output are probabilities. For example, the arrow from (0,0,0) to the state *Has not visited place P* is accompanied by 0.9, implying that when member D has acquired no pictures of place P, the probability that member D has not visited P is 0.9. These probabilities from the state vector to the output can be computed from GPS records and logs of picture-sharing via ShAir. We then perform regression analysis between the state vectors and probabilities of reaching the state *Has visited place P*. For example, assume that the probabilities of reaching this state are as listed in Table 1.

Regression analysis yields the following results:

1st element: 0.4
2nd element: 0.15
3rd element: 0.35
y-intercept: 0.05

Here, the 1st element is a logical value indicating whether or not member D receives a photograph of place P from member A. The slope of the 1st element appears to explain the influence of member A on member D. In this algorithm, all steps for elucidating the influences of a member can be processed automatically from the given GPS and ShAir log data. Furthermore, models can be extended to more members easily.

6   Summary and Discussion

We made a customization of the GFO's official location-based smartphone application "compass system" to enable users to use it not only inside the GFO but also in other areas, including outdoor spaces. Then we conducted an experiment with the cooperation of 15 French tourists visiting Japan as a group in November 2013 to create intra-city social graph anonymously, to evaluate validation of information shared by a user's friends (intra-city social graph) in a physical space, and to estimate a person's influence over the group. This paper summarizes the experiment outcomes and analysis of the relationship between shared information and behavioral changes. Considering GFO's leading hardware and software, such as its 36 touch panel-operated digital signs that are capable of individual certification by an NFC (Near Field Communication) reader/writer, the facility complex will contribute to advanced and flexible studies. We now envisage a user who would like to use the facility via biometric information, e.g., heart rate and brain wave. We define our next tasks to study the growth opportunity of LBS using personal data and to examine the application of NFC/RFID (Radio Frequency IDentification) to cities along with activities to make them of international standards, and will continue to conduct further experiments and researches about the future of communication.

References

1. McMillan, D.W., Chavis, D.M.: Sense of community: A definition and theory. Journal of Community Psychology 14, 6–23 (1986)
2. Chin, A., Zhang, D.: Mobile Social Networking, pp. 2–3. Springer (2014)
3. Vinciarelli, A., Favre, S.: Broadcast news story segmentation using social network analysis and hidden Markov models. In: Proceedings of the 15th International Conference on Multimedia, pp. 261–264 (2007)
4. Chen, C.-W., Cheng, C.-Y.: How online and offline behavior processes affect each other: customer behavior in a cyber-enhanced bookstore. Quality & Quantity 47(5), 2539–2555 (2013)
5. Friedkin, N.E., Johnsen, E.C.: Social Influence Network Theory. Cambridge University Press (2011)
6. Kawahara, Y., Yokoi, N., Yoshida, H., Hosaka, H., Sakata, K.: Positioning System Using RSSI from PHS Cell Stations. In: 5th Int. Conf. on Networked Sensing Systems, p. 227 (2008)
7. Suzuki, J., Kawahara, Y., Yoshida, H., Watanabe, N.: Social City Development and Analogy of Location Based Social Graph (Within-City Human Relations). Applied Social Science 51, 593–599
8. Dubois, D.J., Bando, Y., Watanabe, K., Holtzman, H.: ShAir: Extensible Middleware for Mobile Peer-to-Peer Resource Sharing. In: Proceedings of the 9th Joint Meeting of the European Software Engineering Conference and the ACM Symposium on the Foundations of Software Engineering (Industrial Track), pp. 687–690 (2013)

Learning and Education

Virtually Augmented Classroom Curriculum

Kevin Ambrose

Graduate Center, CUNY, New York, USA
kambrose@gc.cuny.edu

Abstract. This poster will detail step-by-step instructions for building a virtually augmented classroom curriculum for an undergraduate college course. Information will be provided on choosing a virtual environment, defining the parameters of a virtual course assignment, training students and instructors on using a virtual environment, setting up the virtual environment (e.g., installing applications, running a private or public server, hosting solutions, etc.), and grading a virtual assignment. Best practices will be discussed and the results of a qualitative study using undergraduate students and a virtual course assignment will be presented.

Keywords: Second Life, OpenSimulator, virtual environment, curriculum.

1 Why Virtual Environments are Great Teaching Tools

Virtual Environments (VEs) allow for the creation of realistic 3d representations of real world environments which can be interacted with and explored in real time (Cobb et al., 2002). Virtual environments serve as unparalleled teaching and learning tools for a number of reasons. According to Smokowski and Hartung (2003) virtual environments allow the instructor to personalize the content and user experience of an assignment; VEs enable students to learn from potentially unlimited repetitions of a target skill; VEs promote internalization of knowledge and application of key skills; VEs emphasize responsibility; and VEs allow the instructor to collect and record process and outcome data in real-time. Additionally, virtual environments allow students to become a community of learners where they can learn together, collaborate on tasks, and share knowledge. Finally, virtual environments as well as other electronic screen media, foster student engagement and increase motivation during tasks.

2 Determine the Virtual Environment to Use

A number of virtual environments are available to choose from for building a classroom curriculum. The environment chosen depends on the scope of the course assignment; the technological expertise and willingness to learn of the instructor and students; and the time and monetary investment that one can make. Two major virtual environments used in higher education are Second Life® (SL) and OpenSimulator.

C. Stephanidis (Ed.): HCII 2014 Posters, Part II, CCIS 435, pp. 67–71, 2014.
© Springer International Publishing Switzerland 2014

2.1   Second Life

Second Life® is a multi-user virtual world created by a company called Linden Lab. Second Life® is free to use, does not require a large amount of technical expertise, and there are over 100 educational institutions (i.e., colleges, universities, and K-12 schools http://wiki.secondlife.com/wiki/Second_Life_Education_Directory) with a presence in Second Life. SL is easy to set-up; simply visit the download webpage (Fig 1. http://secondlife.com/support/downloads/) download and install the Second Life Viewer, which will allow you to view and interact with other users and objects within Second Life. After installation, you will be asked to create a username and choose an avatar that you can later customize (see Fig. 2). In SL you will be able to simulate anything that is possible in real life and a myriad of additional things only limited by your imagination, building (creating objects), and scripting (programming) skills.

Pros and Cons. Advantages of using SL include support from Linden Labs for academic institutions; a large user base with many support groups, forums, and wikis; a number of marketplaces and individuals to purchase pre-made objects, buildings, etc. from; ease of installation, set-up, and use. Drawbacks to using Second Life include the cost of buying and maintaining land; issues regarding ownership of intellectual property; little support for 3rd party 3D viewers; and the need for an internet connection to access the environment.

Fig. 1.

2.2   OpenSimulator

OpenSimulator (OS) is a free, open-source multiuser 3D virtual world platform. OpenSim can be used as a standalone virtual environment and run off of a single computer or a "grid" which can be used to connect to other public OpenSim virtual

Fig. 2.

spaces. In standalone mode, you can have a single user or a limited amount of multiple users access your virtual space through your computer's address. In grid mode, you can set-up a MySQL server or use a variety of other hosting options to have multiple users access your virtual space. To download OpenSim simply select the appropriate binary package from http://opensimulator.org/wiki/Download (see Fig 3) and make sure that you have the appropriate dependencies (required software) installed for your operating system by checking the list at this link: http://opensimulator.org/wiki/Dependencies Be sure to keep track of your username and password for your local account. After installing OS and running the application (see Fig 4), you will need to download a viewer to view the 3D environment. The most popular viewers are Firestorm, Eclipse, and Imprudence; a list of viewers can be found here: http://opensimulator.org/wiki/Connecting When the viewer is installed, you must launch it and then choose whether you will be accessing OS locally or connecting to a public grid. You have the option of setting up your own server to make your grid accessible to multiple users and hold a large amount of regions (virtual space). One good guide for a MySQL install can be found here: http://opensimuser.wordpress.com/2008/07/16/opensim-mysql-install-guide/

Pros and Cons. Advantages of using OpenSim is that it is free to use; OS can be modified if you download the source code; you own everything that you create and there is no cost to import or export your creations; you can run a virtual world without the need for an internet connection; OS can be run off of a thumb drive (http://becunningandfulloftricks.com/2010/10/07/a-virtual-world-in-my-hands-running-opensim-and-imprudence-on-a-usb-key/); and there are low-cost hosting options available. Disadvantages of using OpenSim include the large amount of documentation required to understand how to set-up and use the program and a 3D viewer; the large amount of technical expertise required to run your own grid that can accommodate multiple regions and users; conflicting sources of information or a lack of documentation for issues within the OS community; and difficulty of finding support or troubleshooting help for issues.

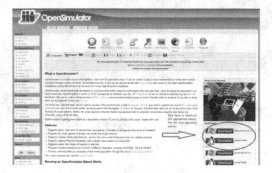

Fig. 3.

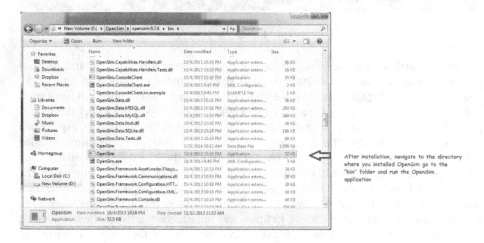

Fig. 4.

3   Curriculum Best Practices

It is important to know the scope of the class assignment; your student's comfort level and experience with virtual spaces; what student work will be required; and how you will grade students on their work. Instructors should survey their students on their prior experience and comfort level with using similar environments and using technology in their academic and personal lives. It may be helpful to pair experienced students with inexperienced ones to ensure completion of the course assignments. Students should be given a tutorial on how to navigate the virtual environment and how to complete simple tasks such as walking, running, flying, using chat, and using gestures. One best practice to facilitate student work is to create a group both within and outside of the virtual environment for students to discuss issues, ask for help, and share tips. Another best practice is to have class sessions dedicated to tutorials on skills required to complete the class assignment. Even though OpenSim and Second Life are two separate environments the skills needed in both (building and scripting) are the same. There are many resources within SL to learn building and scripting that you and your students can use such as Builder's Brewery; The College of Scripting, Music, and Science; and the Ivory Tower Library of Primitives. It is important to check in with students periodically and have them report on their progress on the course assignment. Lastly, as with all courses, it is important that students are aware of what is required of them of the assignment and how they will be graded (e.g., paper, inworld project, etc.).

4   Conclusion

Using virtual environments in the classroom is not difficult; Second Life and Open-Simulator are two virtual world options for instructors to consider when they are interested in including a virtual component to their courses. While these environments do have some drawbacks, the number of advantages greatly outweighs the costs and they have the potential to enhance and improve instruction for any course.

References

1. Cobb, S., Beardon, L., Eastgate, R., Glover, T., Kerr, S., Neale, H., Parsons, S., Benford, S., Hopkins, E., Mitchell, P., Reynard, G., Wilson, J.: Applied virtual environments to support learning of social interaction skills in users with Asperger's Syndrome. Digital Creativity 13(1), 11 (2002)
2. Smokowski, P.R., Hartung, K.: Computer Simulation and Virtual Reality: Enhancing the Practice of School Social Work. Journal of Technology in Human Services 21(1/2), 5 (2003)

A Case Study about Detailed Reports of the Asynchronized e-Learning Management System Applied by Elginkan Foundation

Cihat Okan Arikan[1], Orkun Mersinogullari[2], and Mustafa Murat Inceoglu[3]

[1] Ege University, Emel Akın Vocational School, Turkey
cihat.arikan@ege.edu.tr
[2] Ege University, Information Systems Research Center (ISRC), Turkey
orkun.mersinogullari@ege.edu.tr
[3] Ege University, Faculty of Education,
Dept. of Computer Education and Instructional Technologies, Turkey
mustafa.inceoglu@ege.edu.tr

Abstract. In this study which was carried out by Ege University, it was evaluated mass distance learning activities, both calitatively and cantitatively.

Keywords: Elginkan Foundation, e-Learning, MOODLE, results of assessments.

1 The Role of e-Learning in Vocational and Technical Education

The development and progress of countries requires the fundamental elements of industrialization i.e. qualified human resources having knowledge, skill and work ethics to achieve a high level of efficiency. The improvement of knowledge and skill level of qualified personnel would create a consistent base for economic success. Vocational education is supposed to be designed as being oriented to directions namely, preparing a successful carrier path for young individuals and training qualified personnel for the economy. Nowadays, the great contribution of vocational and technical education in the realization of rapid technological change is a conceded fact by everybody; especially the educators and the employers are being the leading ranks [1, 2].

When the Turkish job market is observed, it is easily noticed despite the increasing employment rates, the demand for vocational and technical educated qualified work force is rolling up every day [3]. Whereas Turkey has offered various local educational programs [4, 5, 6], a massive initiative was failed to be enacted. Especially, broadcasting vocational and technical distance education to a vast audience via Internet has great potential in this aspect. The distance education allows housewives, new graduates and prisoners which have limited or no access to the job market for being able to be trained for a profession. The distance education does not enable the individuals to achieve an extended range of knowledge but also offers the chance of getting new capabilities and skills. The distance education especially is effective for skill development at vocational and technical training. The learner is being bestowed via

C. Stephanidis (Ed.): HCII 2014 Posters, Part II, CCIS 435, pp. 72–77, 2014.

distance education especially the advantage of participating to the lectures of distinguished academic staff that have the latest level of academic know-how. Upon achievement of international vocational competencies and standards, any student residing at any part of world might be able to awarded international certification via international examinations through distance education. Such certificated students may get employed easily at any country which they like [7].

From the other side of the scenery, there is also a group in Turkey (actually at worldwide), whose members already have attended to vocational education in the field of informatics, demanding to refresh their professional knowledge. For this group of individuals, distance learning may be regarded as a lifelong learning activity. In this respect, distance learning would evolve as a lifelong vocational and technical learning activity. Such educational examples are given at [8, 9].

2   Material and Method

In recent years, the Universities in Turkey have started the e-learning sector and the first graduations had been made. Ege University is also providing e-learning programs both in synchronized and asynchronies platforms which are supported by Ege University Information Systems Research Center (ISRC). As the number of educational institutions offering distance education rises e-learning became the trend. One of the most effective users of this trend in Turkey is Elginkan Education Foundation. The Elginkan Education Foundation had been founded in 1985 and center was located in Manisa, Turkey. Elginkan Foundation's Education Center (EFEC) provides free learning materials to their participants and makes this teaching process completely free for years. Usually teaching is made by e-learning style instead of physical classrooms. In this stage, remote e-learning platform is used as MOODLE (Modular Object-Oriented Dynamic Learning Environment). This platform provides the users could participate to the courses from all over the country. All the users have a unique username and password to login to the system. After a successfully login, all the user activities in his/her course pages are logged and these logs are used in this study for calculating the results statistically.

EFEC has open several courses for the participants for different areas. The opened courses are follows: Computer Operator, Pre-Accounting, Computer Aided Design (Unigraphics NX CAD), Computer Aided Design (AutoCAD), Project Management, Web page design, Basic training in occupational health and safety, Advanced Excel, Digital photograph processing (Photoshop), Communication skills seminar, Dynamic web programming with PHP.

All the course's contents are prepared by ISRC for e-Learning materials such as Adobe Flash Professional, Adobe Presenter, Adobe Captivate, Adobe Premiere, Camtasia Studio and iSpring Pro Suite software. These software are the e-learning preparation tools that are the leaders of this sector. Some of the courses include several video files that briefly describing the topics. All the prepared materials packed as SCORM based e-Learning standards. SCORM provides all the actions in these packed materials should be logged (such as viewed or not or how many percent of the content has viewed etc.).

EFEC gives great importance to the views of the students involved in classes. Because of this purposes, they make several surveys for getting feedbacks from their users. These surveys evaluate the adequacy of the course content, teacher abilities, learning materials and the used e-Learning system background. According to the results of these surveys, managers of the Foundation can make changes for the content and conduct of the courses.

These surveys applied to the participants as soon as the course finished. These surveys are made before the graduation exam. The graduation exam applied only to the students who want to apply and under the authority of the Ministry of Education is just making the graduation exam for participants whether they can attend by paying the examination fee. The EFEC never takes this payment.

In this study case, all the EFEC courses examined and participants' logs are determined if they are acceptable or not. If all the parts of a course completed by the participants, these results are accepted and if user had abandoned the course and not finished as uncompleted state, it is not accepted. Log values are directly taken from the MOODLE system's reporting abilities (logs, activity reports, course participations and statistics) and also used for 3rd party plugins for the grouping these values, for example, MocLog Gismo (a graphical interactive student monitoring and tracking system that extracts tracking data from an online course maintained with MOODLE, and generates graphical representations that can be explored by course instructors) and Progress Bar Block (The block provides a color coded display of the required actions of a learner in a course. Each box represents an activity or resource that the student must read/complete. There is also an expected date aspect, so that a student can quickly see whether they have completed something or not and on time or not).

EFEC's e-Learning materials and participants are examined and detailed reports have been documented for the finished courses by ISRC. Due to continuing courses available, it is not yet fully completed but to develop the courses for participants, a qualitative study will be carried out for this case and the results will be presented in the full text paper for this study.

3   Results

During 2013, Ege University MOODLE Distance Learning System offered total 15 courses in which the users were monitored by Elginkan Foundation Distance Learning Unit. A total of 15,000 trainees were registered to the aforementioned courses however, only a certain number of the registered trainees were able to complete the courses and some of them were fail to follow the whole course program because of various reasons. For being able to assess the completed courses from the view point of trainees, an "Education Assessment Survey" was introduced to the participant trainees upon completion of 2nd group of courses just before the commencing of 3rd and 4th group courses. The survey was consisting of total 6 questions, as displayed in Table 1. The answers for these questions were classified between the range of 1 – 5 numbers as, 5=VERY GOOD, 4=GOOD, 3=MEDIOCRE, 2=POOR, 1=VERY POOR.

Only the volunteers were subjected to the survey upon completion of the related course. Consequently, the number of the registered trainees and the number of trainees which filled out the survey forms were happened to be different, and the percentages of survey participation are revealed in Table.1. The assessments were based on the average values (1 – 5) of answers which were given by trainees for each question. By applying average values for each average within themselves for all courses, it was aimed to display a general overview about all of the courses. Reviewing the survey outcomes would reveal that the number of trainees and the number of survey participants were different for each course. Hence, each course was assessed on an individual basis.

A general evaluation of the results would display, for total 7 courses, the number of 953 survey respondents out of total 5879 trainees that revealing approximately 25% of the participants had completed the courses. On this basis, a general evaluation of the points which were compiled from the answers of the addressed questions showed an average of 3.75 – 3.82 range. The range suggests that the Distance Learning system was perceived by the participants as having a medium level viability which was able to offer sufficient know-how regarding educational setting within a good enough training platform.

Within the context of this survey also, an open ended question were addressed to respondents, namely, "Would you please share your ideas about the course that you were attended". This question was answered by 593 individuals. Here below, 5 examples compiled from the answers for each having negative and positive reflections.

3.1   Examples of Answers with Positive Reflections

- (Web Page Design) "I regard the education as highly useful and efficient"
- (Photoshop) "Your institution is offering really a successful education. I would like to present my sincere thanks to everyone those who contributed."
- (Advanced Excel) "I have previous experience and knowledge on Excel. Actually, I can say that this education enabled me to get expert knowledge. I was really good. Thanks."
- (Computer Operator) "I have achieved effective learning and gained explicit knowledge about many aspects which were obscure to me previously."
- (AutoCAD) "I think, it was beneficial for my personal development."

3.2   Examples of Answers with Negative Reflections

- (Web Page Design) "In my idea, it was not sufficient for transferring info to users. It was necessary to call the office for getting info about the examination time and setting whereas it was quite possible to resolve by an online notification within distance learning system."
- (Photoshop) "The volume level of video presentation was considerably poor but on the other hand, it was a useful education, I would like to present my thanks to Elginkan team, they offer very useful training courses.."
- (Advanced Excel) "It was a very gray course by means of material supply."
- (Computer Operator) "Although a highly functional system, it was hard to comprehend for the trainees having a slim background."
- (AutoCAD) "The video image quality was not sharp. In my idea, this should have been smooth out."

Table 1. Ege University - Elginkan Foundation 2013 Courses, Outcomes of Educational Assessment Survey

Course Designation	Number of Trainees	Number of Survey Respondents	Participipation (%)
Computer Aided Design - AutoCad	989	140	14,16 %
Computer Aided Design - SolidWorks	989	198	20,02 %
Computer Operator - 8	323	85	26,32 %
Advanced Excel	1.557	215	13,81 %
Digital Photographing (PhotoShop)	841	135	16,05 %
Web Programming with PHP	609	68	11,17 %
Web Page Design	571	112	19,61 %
General Sum/Average	5.879	953	16,21 %

Course Designation	5=VERY GOOD, 4=GOOD, 3=MEDIOCRE, 2=POOR, 1=VERY POOR				
	The level of meeting your expectations for training	Training content newsworthy	The interactivty of the training by means of effectivity	The contribution of the training to your personal development	The sufficiency of distance training
Computer Aided Design - AutoCad	3,73	3,83	3,56	3,91	3,79
Computer Aided Design - SolidWorks	3,49	3,49	3,48	3,54	3,47
Computer Operator - 8	3,95	4,02	3,81	4,09	3,92
Advanced Excel	3,61	3,74	3,38	3,68	3,53
Digital Photographing (PhotoShop)	4,19	4,27	4,10	4,24	4,27
Web Programming with PHP	3,47	3,54	3,49	3,47	3,46
Web Page Design	4,01	4,05	3,79	4,00	3,87
General Sum/Average	3,75	3,82	3,62	3,82	3,73

4   Conclusions

As a result of the distance learning program which has been carried out by Ege University in collaboration with EFEC, 11,109 students were registered to the system and in alignment with the outcomes of the qualitative and quantitative studies which were enacted via compiled data from student respondents, it is already commenced the improvement process for being able to achieve a more effective system.

References

1. Ramlee, B.M.: The role of vocational and technical education in the industrialization of Malaysia as perceived by educators and employers. PhD Thesis, Purdue Univ., http://docs.lib.purdue.edu/dissertations/AAI9952000/ (last accessed: March 2, 2014)
2. Seng, L.S.: Vocational technical education and economic development – the Singapore experience. Institute of Technical Education (ITE) Paper, no: 9, https://www.ite.edu.sg/ (last accessed: March 2, 2014)
3. Republic of Turkey, Turkish Labor Agency, http://www.iskur.gov.tr/ (last accessed: March 2, 2014)

4. Inceoglu, M.M.: International standards based information technology courses: A case study from Turkey. In: Gervasi, O., Gavrilova, M.L., Kumar, V., Laganá, A., Lee, H.P., Mun, Y., Taniar, D., Tan, C.J.K., et al. (eds.) ICCSA 2005. LNCS, vol. 3483, pp. 56–61. Springer, Heidelberg (2005)
5. Uzunboylu, H., Cavus, N.: A case study of technical and vocational education in Turkey. In: Uzunboylu, H., Cavus, N. (eds.) World Conference on Educational Sciences: New Trends and Issues in Educational Sciences, Procedia Social and Behavioral Sciences, vol. 1(1), pp. 160–167. Elsevier (2009)
6. Kizgin, Y., Karaosmanoglu, K.: The importance of computer based education in vocational and technical training: A field study on accounting programs in vocational and technical training in Turkey. In: 3rd International Conference on Education and Information Systems: Technologies and Applications, vol. 2, pp. 80–84 (2005)
7. Simonson, M.: What the accreditation community is saying about quality in distance education. The Quarterly Review of Distance Education 8(2), 7–9 (2007)
8. Akoojee, S., Mcgrath, S.: Vocational education and training through open and distance learning, Routledge Falmer and the commonwealth of learning. International Journal of Educational Development 25(5), 586–587 (2005)
9. Uhomoibhi, J., Ross, M.: Globalisation and e-Learning: Integrating University and Professional Qualifications for Employability and Lifelong Learning. In: Proceedings of the 8th International Conference on E-Learning. Book Series: Proceedings of the International Conference on e-Learning, pp. 404–408 (2013)

HCI Aspects to Teaching Primary School Children the Islamic Prayer

Mohammed Farsi

School of Engineering and Computing Sciences, Durham University, England, UK
moahmmed.farsi1980@gmail.com

Abstract. A fundamental objective of Human-Computer Interaction (HCI) is to design a system that provides the user with a positive experience. This is achieved by matching the experience with the user's personal aims and goals. This study adopts a Virtual Environment setting for teaching the Islamic prayer to primary school children.

Keywords: Human-Computer Interaction, Virtual Environments, Islamic prayer, Kinesthetical learning, X-Box 360 Kinect, Learning preferences.

1 Background and Objectives

A fundamental objective of Human-Computer Interaction (HCI) is to design a system that provides the user with a positive experience. This is achieved by matching the experience with the user's personal aims and goals. This study adopts a Virtual Environment setting for teaching the Islamic prayer to primary school children. The iIP software (Interactive Islamic Prayer) has been designed for the Xbox 360 Kinect, covering the various movements of the prayer in sequence without the use of a controller. The Microsoft's Kinect for XBox 360 is a more recent and progressive form of VE, which employs markers to recognise, capture, track and decipher a user's movement through infrared technology (DePriest & Barilovits, 2011). This has been described as a "revolution in the making" as the method of interaction between human and computers is no longer bound by tangible objects like a controller, mouse or keyboard (Hsu, 2011). In doing so, the objective is to focus on specific HCI elements within the iIP software that would facilitate a "user-friendly" experience for the students, through direct interaction of mimicking the displayed movements during the prayer.

2 Method

30 primary school children and 3 teachers were asked to evaluate their overall experience of the iIP software from an HCI perspective. Through a quantitative analysis of the participants' learning experience, this study investigates the importance of HCI in the design and development of the training software, particularly in relation to those

C. Stephanidis (Ed.): HCII 2014 Posters, Part II, CCIS 435, pp. 78–83, 2014.

that adopt a Virtual Environment setting. As part of the data analysis, questionnaires were given to the participants to evaluate the usability, usefulness and overall learning experience of the iIP software.

2.1   iIP Software

The iIP software consists of various screens and levels, which guide the user through the Islamic Prayer.

Start Screen

Users begin with the start screen to enter the training software. The user must place and keep their right hand over the "Start" button for approximately 3-5 seconds until the loading bar is complete.

The Main Screen

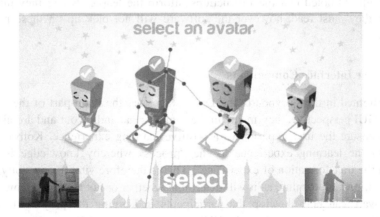

The main screen introduces the user to the iIP where learners can first choose their instructional avatar. They do so by placing and keeping their right hand over the character until the loading bar has completed.

Level Examples

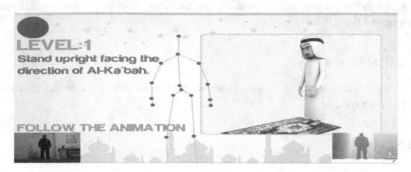

Level 1 is the first position of the Islamic prayer, where the user must stand upright. The user is given instructions on what to do, as well as watching their instructional avatar.

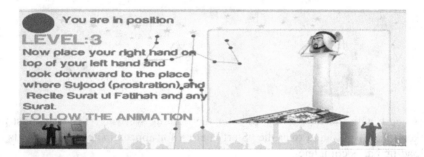

Level 3 is the third movement of the prayer – placing the hands on the chest

It should be noted that the instructions inform the learner where they must look or what they must read, however the software will not pick up on these particular aspects.

2.2   User Interface Components

As highlighted in the storyboard, the Level stages are the main part of the software. From a GUI perspective, they maintain the same format and layout and are ultimately used to ensure the user experiences a positive learning experience. Kolb (1984:38) refers to the learning experience as the "process whereby knowledge is created through the transformation of experience". This is therefore vital to any study involving education and learning, as it will determine whether or not the HCI element of the iIP software can help develop the participants in learning the prayer. Figure 4.3 demonstrates key components of the GUI for the Level screens:

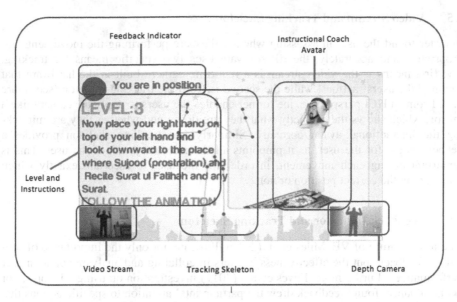

Fig. 1. Main components of the GUI for the Level screens

2.3   Instructional Coach Avatar

To aid the users in how to perform the various prayer components correctly, an instructional avatar is positioned on the screen throughout the Level screen from the beginning to the end of the prayer (Figure 4.3). In the Main Screen, a selection of avatars has been designed, so user has the option to select their preference. The choices have been designed to suit all audiences including younger or older males/females. Similar to the design used in Charbonneau, Miller and LaViola (2011), the procedure for each specific movement of the prayer will be achieved by splitting the display screen into two halves; one showing a detailed instructional tutorial video of the desired movement. The other half will be the user's avatar that will track and display the movements of the user. The goal will be for the participant to follow and complete the movement as shown on the instructional tutorial. Utilising the constructivism approach described by Benson (2011), the participant will continue to build upon previous knowledge and movements until the whole prayer is complete. This makes the user feel that they are a part of the software, which in turn elevates their learning experience. The remaining screens show the movements that the users will be instructed to complete in order to complete one unit of prayer.

2.4   Levels and Instructions

Upon selection, the instructional avatar will then begin to perform the prayer movements. The user can also read the instructions, which reinforces the visual aid from the avatar. The instructions are both clear and concise for easy comprehension. Moreover, the Arabic phrases that are used throughout the prayer have been transliterated for English speaking audiences in case they are unfamiliar with Arabic.

2.5　Video Stream and Tracking Skeleton

In order to aid the user in assessing whether they are performing the movements appropriately and accurately, the iIP software uses two specific means for tracking. The first means is the video stream is a real-time camera built-in the hardware that captures the users' actions, while the second is from the tracking skeleton (see figure 4.3). From an HCI perspective, the former enables the users to apply the camera like a mirror, which shows them exactly what they are doing and whether they are mimicking the interactional avatar correctly. Similarly, the tracking skeleton provides a deeper insight for the user, as it pinpoints all the relevant joints of the user. This is important during each movement, in order for the user to ascertain exactly which joints are in the correct position or not.

2.6　Feedback Indicator and Tracking Skeleton

Due to the nature of VE, Miles et al, (2012) illustrate not only the importance of providing feedback, but the effectiveness it offers in collating and analysing data on user performance. Furthermore, Eaves et al's (2011) investigation on using VE for motor skills in dance, found feedback drew the participants' attention to specific actions that were required to be learnt. In terms of formative assessment, this will occur in real-time when the participant attempts to perform each prayer component. The participant will receive immediate feedback, whereby the software will inform them if they have succeeded in the movement, focusing attention on accuracy and timings. This is done through the use of visual and auditory aids, in the form of a green or red light in the corner of the screen and a sound to indicate the movement has been performed correctly (Figure 4.5). Furthermore, if the participant has not fulfilled the appropriate requirements, the program will ask them to repeat the movement; hence, it will not continue until the user has completed each task. Miles et al (2012) refer to this as guidance and informative feedback, which guides users to the correct body movement and provides statistical information on performance respectively. Kelly et al (2010) also used informative feedback in VE in a difference context, namely for training and improving golf swings. The design was similar to that mentioned above, whereby a "coach" avatar displayed guided movements that the user could mimic and compare.

Fig. 2. Red and Green indicator (and caption)

Moreover, if a joint is not recognized or is in an incorrect position, it will turn red to notify the user. This can however be a limitation of the software, because it occurs when joints overlap one another or are interconnected, which are necessary during the prayer (i.e. placing the hands on the knees or placing one hand over the other).

3 Conclusion

From a preliminary study, the results revealed positive feedback from the participants, who indicated they were extremely satisfied with their overall experience in using the iIP software. The students found it fun, educational and easy to use, whilst the teacher felt it was a valuable alternative in teaching the prayer.

Acknowledgement. I would like to express my gratitude to the Ministry of Higher Education in Saudi Arabia for sponsoring my scholarship for this research, and also to my PhD supervisor, Malcolm Munro for his continuous support.

References

1. Benson, J.B.: Advances in Child Development and Behavior. Elsevier Science, Academic Press (2011)
2. Charbonneau, E., Miller, A., LaViola, J.: Teach Me to Dance: Exploring Player Experience and Performance in Full Body Dance Games. In: Proceedings of the Eighth International Conference on Advances in Computer Entertainment Technology (ACE 2011), Article 43(8) (November 2011)
3. DePriest, D., Barilovits, K.: LIVE: Xbox Kinect's Virtual Realities to Learning Games. In: TCC 2011 Proceedings (2011)
4. Eaves, D.L., Breslin, G., van Schaik, P., Robinson, E., Spears, I.R.: The short-term effects of real-time virtual reality feedback on motor learning in dance. Presence: Teleoperators and Virtual Environments, Special Issue: Virtual Reality and Sports 20(1), 62–77 (2011)
5. Hsu, J.H.-M.: The Potential of Kinect in Education. International Journal of Information and Education Technology 1(5) (2011)
6. Kelly, P., Healy, A., Moran, K., O'Connor, N.E.: A virtual coaching environment for improving golf swing technique. In: Proceedings of the ACM Workshop on Surreal Media and Virtual Cloning (SMVC 2010), pp. 51–52. ACM Press, NewYork (2010)
7. Kolb, D.A.: Experiential learning: experience as the source of learning and development. Prentice Hall, Englewood Cliffs (1984)
8. Miles, H., Pop, S., Watt, S., Lawrence, G., John, N.: A review of virtual environments for training in ball sports. Computers & Graphics 36(6), 714–726 (2012)

An Automatic and Innovative Approach for Converting Pedagogical Text Documents to Visual Learning Object

Ali Shariq Imran[1], Atif Mansoor[2], and ABM Tariqul Islam[3]

[1] Faculty of Comp. Science and Media Technology,
Gjøvik University College, Norway
{ali.imran}@hig.no
[2] Institute of Avionics and Aeronautics, Air University, Islamabad, Pakistan
{atif.mansoor}@gmail.com
[3] Visual Computing Lab, Dept. of Comp. Science, University of Rostock, Germany
{tariqul.islam}@uni-rostock.de

Abstract. In this paper, we present a novel idea of converting pedagogical text documents to visual learning objects by automatically extracting nouns and semantic keywords from the text documents, and representing these keywords as a word cloud. A word cloud contains words that are weighted based on frequency, time, appearance, etc., depending on the concept they are used for. Each word in the word cloud would correspond to a visual representation of that word. A visual representation may contain drawings, figures, images, etc. that explains the given concept. The extracted keywords are used to query the Internet to find the corresponding visual representation of a given word. The idea is to bring text documents to life by creating a visual representation of the important concepts from the text documents. This paper is a work in progress.

Keywords: pedagogic, text documents, visual learning object, word cloud.

1 Introduction

Burmark, in his book [1] stated that the visual aids such as images, drawings, graphics, videos, etc. can improve learning by up to 400%, as they actively incorporate all the human senses into learning experience. It is also a well-established fact that about approximately 65% of the world population are visual learners and the rest of 35% of the world population consist of textual, auditory and kinesthetic learners [2]. Furthermore, 90 percent of information that comes to the brain is visual [3]. Thereby, turning the important concepts in text documents to their visual representation can improve the learning experience of the users, and to some extent the learning outcome.

The complex ideas are better retainable and implementable as depicted in graphical manner. In computer science, flow chart gives more understandable depiction of complex relations and dependencies. The spatial representation of

C. Stephanidis (Ed.): HCII 2014 Posters, Part II, CCIS 435, pp. 84–88, 2014.

information coupled with images carry much more meaning and also helps the learner to identify and associate similar ideas. Along with improvement in retention ability, it also aids in critical thinking by developing the associability aspect.

The human brain consists of different areas that work together to translate the viewed images into retained information. In human brain, the visual information is processed in the visual cortex. It is positioned in occipital cortex, situated at the rear side of human brain. As an image is formed at the retina, the different information like shape, orientation, color etc. are transported by different neurons to the occipital cortex. The human brain is divided into two hemispheres, each containing one visual cortex. The left hemisphere collects the view from right eye and the right hemisphere receives the view from left eye through respective visual cortex. The occipital cortex consists of subparts that play an important role in detection, classification and learning. The object location and identification is performed here. The signal from occipital cortex is transmitted to temporal cortex that performs recognition, forming memory and understanding different reactions. The signals are also transferred to parietal cortex that cohesively forms the view from various signals received from senses. It performs spatial attention and spatial mapping. The cerebellum located in the rear lower part of the brain is responsible for cognitive activity like learning. Cerebellum though having a weight just 10% of total weight of the brain contains higher number of neurons compared to total sum of neurons in other part of brain. The whole biological action in the brain with respect to visual learning demonstrates a lot of activity that in turn result in overall better retention and memory.

2   Methodology

In this work, we aim to automatically turn the educational text document into a visual learning object (VLO) (an image) by extracting and finding important words from the document using natural language processing (NLP) techniques, including statistical measures such as frequency count or term frequency inverse document frequency (TF-IDF) [4]. The proposed algorithm reads the pedagogical documents consisting of text files and performs the semantic analysis on them as shown in Figure 1. In the semantic analysis a text document is analyzed automatically to extract important words, known as keywords. A preprocessing step is required before performing the semantic analysis on the potential keywords. The preprocessing steps required to extract potential keywords from the pedagogical text documents are described as follows:

1. In the first step, the text document file is read and all punctuation and capitalization is removed.
2. A tokenizer is then used to separate the text into individual words.
3. Next, all the stop words are removed. Stop words consists of those words in English language which do not convey any significant meaning on their own, such as 'and', 'is', etc [4].

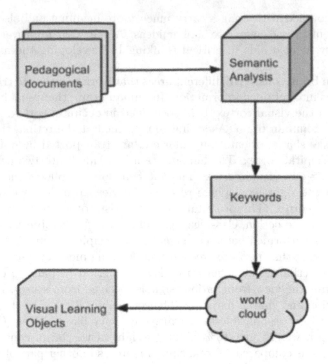

Fig. 1. A block process diagram representing how the pedagogical documents are converted into visual learning objects

4. The duplicate words are removed afterwards.
5. The last step is to apply stemming [5]. Stemming is the process of bringing words to its root form. For example, the word 'stemming' can be converted to its root form as 'stem'.

At this stage, statistical measure such as frequency count or TF-IDF can be employed on the candidate keywords to further short-list the potential keywords. The potential keywords obtained as a result can either be a noun, a verb, an adverb or an adjective. These are different parts-of-speech (POS) of a language. Generally, the nouns POS are used to represent real world entities and concepts, so the nouns are further processed in the semantic analysis. At the end of pre-processing steps, the algorithm analyzes all the nouns POS candidate keywords semantically.

The semantic analysis consist of two steps. In the first step the importance of short-listed candidate keywords is calculated based on the visual similarity concept [6]. Visual similarity measures the visualness of a given word, which in fact defines how important a word is in the given context. It is measured by computing a similarity of a given candidate word and visual seed words. The seed words are the ground truth against which the visualness of a candidate word is determined. The seed words can be defined manually or they can be extracted automatically from the document's corpus, metadata, and/or title. Visualness is calculated using semantic similarity metric between words. There are many different metrics to compute the visualness [7]. For any given word w, It is defined as:

$$vis(w) = \sum_{i=1}^{n} vis(s_i) \frac{sim(w, s_i)}{\sum sim(w, s_i)}, \tag{1}$$

where $i = 1, 2, ...n$, for the whole set of n seed words $s_1, s_2, ...s_n$, and $sim(w, s_i)$ is the semantic similarity between the word w and a seed word s_i. The visualness of a given seed word s_i is denoted by $vis(s_i)$. The resulting visualness score $vis(w)$ is in the range of 0 to 1.

Calculating visualness will give us a refined set of potential candidate keywords. We may however still need to refine the words further to have better semantic meaning. For example, the refined keywords might contain few words with dual meanings. For instance, if 'cancer' is one of the short-listed keyword, then it can either refer to a zodiac sign or a disease. The algorithm then needs to disambiguate the correct sense of a word in order to fetch the right image from the Internet. This can be addressed using a word sense disambiguation (WSD) process [8], given as:

$$Disambiguation(s_i) = |context(s) \cap gloss(s_i)|, \tag{2}$$

Where s is a seed word, $context(s)$ represents the whole set of all seed words, and $gloss$ defines all possible sense i of s. The assigned sense of s is the ith where s_i maximizes the $Disambiguation$ value.

In short, the score is calculated by counting the number of overlapping words between the gloss of each sense s_i and the word's context. Visualness and WSD will give us the refined set of semantically accurate keywords.

The keywords are then be depicted as a word cloud. The word cloud is pasted onto various objects like a globe or other objects, chosen on the basis of interest it infuses in the intended learner group. Further, using 'Microsoft Kinect gestures' the users are able to interact with the word cloud. For example, they can rotate the globe or the object and see different words appear on it from the extracted document with variable font size, color and appearance etc. The choice of font size, color, appearance etc. depends upon the number of word occurrence in the text or importance ascertained by semantic analysis, along with the target group like children, students, adults from specific profession etc.

By interacting with the word cloud, the users can see corresponding visual objects associated with the words. Users may further be directed to relevant information at Wikipedia, PowerPoint presentations, and videos over the Internet corresponding to chosen keywords. This will allow an interactive learning experience, and it could be a fun and interesting tool to teach young children.

3 Conclusion

In this paper, we propose an innovative and novel approach to convert text documents to visual learning objects by automatically extracting semantic nouns from the document. The proposed algorithm reads the text document files, do the tokenization of words, shortlist nouns, remove duplicates, and extract semantically accurate and meaningful keywords. Semantically accurate keywords are extracted using visualness and word sense disambiguation process. The keywords are represented as a word cloud. The algorithm then query the search engines with extracted keywords to find correspondence images from the Internet. It then associates the appropriate image to the extracted keyword. This paper is a work in progress and we are evaluating the outcome and the results. We believe that creating a visual representation of the important words in a text documents will improve the learning outcome, especially for teaching young kids.

References

1. Burmark, L.: Visual Literacy: Learn to See, See to Learn. Association for Supervision and Curriculum Development, p. 115 (2002) ISBN 0871206404, ISSN 978087120640
2. David, H.J., Carr, C., Yueh, H.-P.: Computers as Mindtools for Engaging Learners in Critical Thinking. TechTrends 43(2), 24–32 (1998)
3. Hyerle, D.: Visual Tools for Transforming Information into Knowledge, 2nd edn., Corwin (2009)
4. Manning, C.D., Raghavan, P., Schutze, H.: Introduction to Information Retrieval. Cambridge University Press, Cambridge (2008)
5. Sharma, D.: Stemming Algorithms: A Comparative Study and Their Analysis. International Journal of Applied Information Systems 4(3), 7–12 (2012)
6. Qiu, Y., Guan, G., Zhiyong, W., Feng, D.A.: Improving News Video Annotation with Semantic Context. In: Proceedings of the 2010 International Conference on Digital Image Computing: Techniques and Applications, DICTA 2010, pp. 214–219. IEEE Computer Society, Washington, DC (2010)
7. Li, H., Tian, Y., Ye, B., Cai, Q.: Comparison of Current Semantic Similarity Methods in WordNet. In: International Conference on Computer Application and System Modeling (ICCASM), October 22-24, vol. 4, pp. V4-408–V4-411 (2010)
8. Agirre, E., Edmonds, P.: Word Sense Disambiguation: Algorithms and Applications. Text, Speech and Language Technology, vol. 33, XXII (2006) ISBN 978-1-4020-4809-8

Computer-Supported Training System
for Clinical Engineer

Ren Kanehira[1], Hideo Hori[1], Kazinori Kawaguchi[1], and Hideo Fujimoto[2]

[1] FUJITA Health University, 1-98 Dengakugakubo, Kutsukake-cho, Toyoake,
Aichi, 470-1192, Japan,
kanehira@fujita-hu.ac.jp
[2] Nagoya Institute of technology, Nagoya, Japan,
fujimoto@vier.mech.nitech.ac.jp

Abstract. It is required for a clinic engineer to have highly professional know-ledge as well as skills for the operation of medical machines. Such knowledge and skills are normally difficult to master only by teaching and practicing at universities with limited time. Therefore, it is expected to have new training system supported by advanced computer system using the information and communication technology (ICT). In this study, a training system with ICT for clinical engineer was constructed. With the system, several problems in operating medical machines were made clear, and solutions and proposals for such problems were given with examples.

Keywords: Information communication technology, Computer training system, Clinic engineer, E-learning system, Skill science, Medical equipment.

1   Introduction

The term of "Clinical engineers" (CEs) means such a person who deals with the operation and maintenance of medical machines for saving the life or curing the disease of patients under the guidance of doctors.

There is a closer relationship in the modern society between medical and engineering, as the result of the fact that high-tech medical machines have been more and more applied in therapy. At the same time, any mistake or misuse of such machines would be closely related to the state of disease of patient or even a human life. The responsibility of the clinical engineer is ever high, and his job contents may change a lot with time. While a clinical engineer is a technician to control medical machines using knowledge on electronics and mechanics, he is also one that with the task to improve the science and technology on clinic engineering [1].

However, it is very difficult for a student to become a qualified CE who has to master so many techniques within so limited period of time. As the results, the CEs feel quite often the lack of knowledge and skill after graduated and start to work in a hospital. Therefore, it is expected to have a new computer-supported training system, better with the use of ICT, for clinical engineers.

C. Stephanidis (Ed.): HCII 2014 Posters, Part II, CCIS 435, pp. 89–94, 2014.
© Springer International Publishing Switzerland 2014

In fact, it has been attracting much attention to apply computer technologies in several e-learning systems [2]-[4]. Similarly, it has been considered possible to apply such technologies also in the field of clinic medicine [5] [6], though, there has not yet developed a satisfactory total training system using at the same time both operating information and visual information for CEs.

In this study, aiming the goal of an advanced computer-supported training system being low cost, rich in simulated experiences, and with good repeatability, we proposed one using the up-to-date technologies in our sequential research results on computer-added skill-up training systems [7]-[12]. The system was applied practically upon undergraduates in a medical university to demonstrate its effect.

2   Investigation Research

2.1   Investigation Research on Clinical Engineers

A preliminary investigation on the research subject was done on experienced teaching professors and 4-year students by a questionnaire to ask what they most want to teach or to know.

Questionnaire was first done on highly experienced professors or teachers. On the question of whether or not a computer-supported training system is necessary, all persons answered yes, which confirmed the necessity of such system.

And next questionnaire was done on students. On the question of whether or not you have enough time for practice, the answers are 25% for yes against 75% for no (Fig.1 (a)). On the question of the necessity of such system, 100% is yes (Fig.1 (b)).

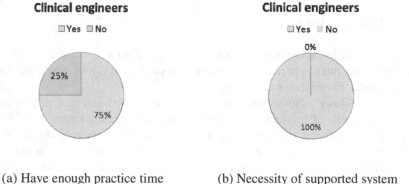

(a) Have enough practice time   (b) Necessity of supported system

Fig. 1. Questionnaire results on clinical engineers

Further questionnaire was done upon professors from different departments on different medical machines of heart-lung machines, artificial cardiac pacemaker, continuous renal replacement therapy, mechanical ventilator, respectively, and answers were obtained as the following:

- Heart-lung machines: such system is necessary, better with training on mastering different treatments for different diseases and trouble-shooting.
- Artificial cardiac pacemaker: it is necessary, better with training on the confirmation of the mode of artificial cardiac pacemaker, e.g., the simulation of confirmation of such modes used in third degree complete atrioventricular block.
- Continuous Renal Replacement Therapy: simulation system need is particularly high for new students, e.g., simulator can give signs by colors to show if the operations are suitable. It is required also for trouble-shooting during operations.
- Mechanical ventilator: a system capable of measuring the ventilation volume, ventilation number, and circuit the internal pressure, the relationship between O_2 and CO_2, and simulation of blood pressure.

2.2   Investigation Research on Students of Clinical Engineer

Furthermore, we did a questionnaire on the 4th grade students in our university by "did you forget the operation sequence of heart-lung machines after you have become the 4th grade student (before hospital practice). Surprisingly, all 31 students regardless of gender answered with "yes, I forgot"! The reasons may be multiple, but "fewer chances to touch and operate the equipment" becomes the dominant.

Another questionnaire was pout upon the 4th grade students by a question "do you want to use a computer simulation system capable of simulated experience in preparation and review of your text. The answers divided into different training items, in which 90% of students answered "yes".

It is confirmed through preliminary investigation that such a training system with simulation paying attention operation method and practice skills is very necessary. Based on the results, this study takes the multimedia training as main research subject to solve problems in clinic engineering education, and a total computer-supported training system capable of knowledge learning and skill-up was studied.

3   Propose of Education and Training System

3.1   Learning Support by Questionnaire

The mode selection and trouble shooting in mechanical ventilator operations were selected as research subjects in the construction of education system.

Electronic textbook for learning was prepared from the materials investigated on above two subjects. Ask and answer method was used, which are further connected to explanations by voice, animations and sounds, operated and displayed with the personal computer or mobile phones. A training system was then constructed.

To support knowledge learning, questions and answers and explanations was filed into"ask and answer" textbook using software (Q & A mode question set). An example was demonstrated in Fig.2 on the training term of "mechanical ventilator: modes and trouble-shooting". It can be understood that simple and repeatable training, with real-time response, is obtained (Fig. 3).

If clicking the①"Challenge a question" term in Fig. 2, questions and selections, and selected answers are demonstrated as shown in Fig. 4. Explanation can be referred by selecting ②"View the answer" after the answer. To Select the③O button if recorded by personal report, or the ④X one, so one can even know his ⑤correct answer rate and ⑥challenge number, and therefore is evaluated.

Fig. 2. Display of Q & A mode question set

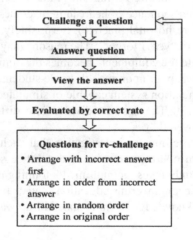

Fig. 3. Learning support by Q & A mode

The above training using the system shows that a student obtains knowledge not only from reading the textbook, but looking for answers to a selected question with real-time evaluation. The effect was confirmed by practice.

Fig. 4. Real-time evaluation

3.2 Teaching of Troubleshooting

How to treat medical troubles or how to do operations without trouble is one of the main subjects for a clinical engineer. However, a textbook cannot answer all questions for trouble shooting because of the complexity and variety in different operations, different systems and even different hospitals by shipment time and manufacturers of medical equipment. Recently due to some medical accidents reported, safety education has been taken into considerable account in CE education. In this study for first of all, accidents from system troubles or operation mistakes most popularly related to CEs are confirmed, with related education and training methods provides.

Here we take the trouble shooting case on mechanical ventilator such as water condensation, too dry or too wet in respiratory tract, etc. Proper steps and check-points were set, and learning was progressed by confirming such check-points. Alarm sound, lighting images, and animation on operations were prepared for efficiency.

Way of example, the checkpoints, countermeasures, and operations of trouble shooting in mechanical ventilator are listed as following.

- Reconfirm the connection to breathing circuit
- Check the heated humidifier for any damage
- Drain off water in water trap
- Check the warmness of heated humidifier
- Co-use with artificial nose is prohibited

A clinic engineer works on the operation and maintenance of medical machines which needs both knowledge and skill. It is important for him to become skilled by repeated practice. For developing a more effective training method for clinic engineer, we proposed a computer-supported system including the learning of textbook knowledge, operation method and trouble-shooting with the use of multimedia.

4 Conclusions

In this study, a training system for the knowledge and skill required for a clinical engineer was constructed. A preliminary investigation was firstly carried out to clarify the research subject and problems in conventional training. Based on the investigation, the mode selection and trouble shooting in mechanical ventilator operations were selected as research subjects. An Ask-and-answer method was used, which are further connected to explanations by multimedia such as voice, animations and sounds, operated and displayed with the personal computer or mobile phones. The effect was confirmed by practical training on medical university students.

Because it is understood that the most important training for a clinic engineer is with closely and repeated touch to the operation machines, and real-time response, the next step of this study is to increase the operation ability of the system. Further, it is considered to introduce more animation elements and game factors (e.g., well point and competition system) to develop better training system interesting the yang students.

Acknowledgments. This study was supported by JSPE KAKENHI Grant Number 25350304. I would like to thank clinical engineers and 4th grade students for cooperation of research studies.

References

1. Japan Association for Clinical Engineers (2014), http://www.ja-ces.or.jp/ce/
2. Journal of Japan Association for Simulation-based Education in Healthcare Professionals, vol. 1 (2013), http://square.umin.ac.jp/model/
3. Japan e-learning, Education IT Solutions EXPO, http://www.edix-expo.jp/en/Home/
4. Watanabe, K., Kashihara, A.: A View of Learning Support Research Issues Based on ICT Genealogy. J. Educ. Technol. 34(3), 143–152 (2010)
5. Noh, Y., Segawa, M., Shimomura, A., Ishii, H., Solis, J., Hatake, K., Takanishi, A.: Development of the Evaluation System for the Airway Management Training System WKA--1R. In: Proceedings of the Second IEEE RAS/EMBS International Conference on Biomedical Robotics and Bio Mechatronics (2008)
6. Sueda, T.: Development of a Training Simulator for Extracorporeal Circulation with a Heart-Lung Machine, Hiroshima University (2010), http://hutdb.hiroshima-u.ac.jp/seeds/view/3/en
7. Kanehira, R., et al.: Development of an Acupuncture Training System using Virtual Reality Technology. In: Proceedings of 5th FSKD, pp. 665–668. IEEE Press (2008)
8. Chen, L.Y., et al.: Basic experiment for analysis of acupuncture technique. In: Proceedings of 6th EUROSIM, pp. 1–6 (2007)
9. Kanehira, R., Yang, W., Narita, H., Fujimoto, H.: Insertion Force of Acupuncture for a Computer Training System. In: Wang, F.L., Deng, H., Gao, Y., Lei, J. (eds.) AICI 2010, Part II. LNCS, vol. 6320, pp. 64–70. Springer, Heidelberg (2010)
10. Kanehira, R., Yang, W.P., Narita, H., Fujimoto, H.: Acupuncture Education System with Technique-oriented Training. In: Proceedings of FSKD 2011, pp. 2524–2528. IEEE (2011)
11. Kanehira, R., Yang, W., Fujimoto, H.: Education and training environments for skill mastery. In: Wang, F.L., Lei, J., Lau, R.W.H., Zhang, J. (eds.) CMSP 2012. CCIS, vol. 346, pp. 451–458. Springer, Heidelberg (2012)
12. Kanehira, R., Narita, H., Kawaguchi, K., Hori, H., Fujimoto, H.: A training system for operating medical equipment. In: Information Technology in Medicine and Education. LNEE, vol. 269, pp. 2259–2265. Springer, Heidelberg (2013)

Building Domain Ontologies for Hyperlinked Multimedia Pedagogical Platforms

Zenun Kastrati, Ali Shariq Imran, and Sule Yildirim Yayilgan

Department of Computer Science and Media Technology Gjøvik University College, Norway
{zenun.kastrati,ali.imran,sule.yayilgan}@hig.no

Abstract. This paper examines building of the course ontology for describing and organizing hyperlinked pedagogical content. The ontology is used to structure and classify multimedia learning objects (MLO) in hyperlinked pedagogical platform called HIP, and to assist students to search for lectures and other teaching materials in a reasonable time and more efficiently. In addition, this paper proposes a new approach to improve the classification performance by enhancing the information representation model using concepts from the pedagogical course domain ontology. The model will automatically estimate weight of concepts within the ontology, and it will combine the weight with concepts' importance which is calculated using Term Frequency Inverse Document Frequency – $tf*idf$ algorithm. This paper is a work in progress. We are in process of creating and implementing the course ontology and an experiment will be conducted to evaluate the classification performance in terms of efficiency and effectiveness for the approach proposed in this paper.

Keywords: Ontology, concept vector space, Markov chain model, HIP.

1 Introduction

Recently, the rapid developments in technology and the increasing usage of computer and other electronic devices have made other forms of education possible, which are different from the traditional ones. The distance learning is one amongst them where students can access the information without being present in class. To improve distance learning process, new means of communication and studying were introduced and new frameworks were created [1]. One such eLearning platform is Hyper Interactive Presenter – HIP [2].

HIP is a technology-rich pedagogical platform that uses combination of media elements to deliver the learning objects. The elements comprise of electronic documents such as wiki pages and PDF documents, presentations, lecture videos, an intelligent pedagogical chat bot. In addition, it also provides navigational links, tagged keywords, and frequently asked questions (FAQ).

A huge amount of information in HIP platform comes from different media modalities that need to be organized, structured and hyperlinked. Structuring and organizing such a wealth of information is labor intensive, prone to errors and a cumbersome task. Structuring information is required due to the need for classifying various

C. Stephanidis (Ed.): HCII 2014 Posters, Part II, CCIS 435, pp. 95–100, 2014.

learning objects with different content into certain predefined classes. In this regards, an automatic classification plays a key role in organizing these massive sources of unstructured information into a structured format. Therefore, we propose a new approach to automatically organize the pedagogical multimedia content using an automatic classification based on the pedagogical course domain ontology.

The course domain ontology consists of a set of concepts in the domain of teaching and associated relations. Concepts are generally expressed through natural languages and most concepts in ontology will be represented as clusters of relevant terms. Specifically, each concept in the ontology will be formed by a list of synonym terms. This ontology development process is known as bottom-up approach ontology learning [3]. This representation is important for the use of the ontology, as it will make it easier to link the concepts in the ontology to the learning objects in actual HIP platform.

Ontology based classification approach represents semantic aspects of information coming from different media modalities through entities defined within the course domain ontology. The learning object using the domain ontology is represented as a vector where the vector components represent concepts. Concepts are extracted from ontology and their importance is calculated from the corpus using statistical measures used in traditional information retrieval tf*idf.

The contribution of ontology concepts in classification process depends on the position where they are depicted in the hierarchy and this contribution is indicated by weight. The hierarchy consists of concepts such as classes, subclasses and instances that may have different weights to represent the concepts' importance.

Furthermore, this paper also proposes a new model to enhance the information representation by automatically estimating the weights of the concepts in the ontology. Thus, in addition to enhancing the representation model, we will improve the classification performance in terms of efficiency and effectiveness.

In the rest of this paper, an overview of previous research work with respect to implementation of course domain ontology on eLearning platforms is given, followed by a section which describes the new proposed approach. A short description of implementation is given in section 4. The paper will conclude with a short section describing the conclusions and future work.

2   Related Work

This section describes research that has been carried out by researchers in the area of domain ontologies for intelligent eLearning architectures and systems, and it examines the key difference between our work and other research.

Course domain ontology, as a knowledge for certain course domain, can be utilized at development time to clarify the meaning of the concepts and their properties for a specific domain of interest, particularly to aid understanding, communicating and facilitating system integration. This can be accomplished during the requirements engineering phase. Also, generating an eLearning course using course ontology could assist in defining a systematic approach in developing eLearning course [3], [4].

In the light of above, several researchers analyze and develop domain ontologies for specific topics in eLearning. Researchers in [5] conducted a research on designing and developing an ontology in an area of databases that could be used in the provision of an eLearning course. They created an ontology for database systems course and a textbook was used as the initial corpus for building this ontology.

An ontology for C Programming language course was developed and presented in [6]. The authors analyze the problems in developing an ontology for a course domain and demonstrate the applicability of their proposed approach for the development of eLearning course ontology. Since developing an ontology is an engineering process, they proposed to use the same standard which is used for developing the software project life cycle processes. Moreover, an example of how the course ontology can be utilized in developing the Algorithms Design and Analysis course was presented in [7].

Our work is different from others in terms of its usage and its application to HIP. Besides building course domain ontology, we will also use it as a means to structure and organize the semantic content in HIP pedagogical platform. The others work described uses the ontology engineering process approach for creating a vocabulary for a certain course domain.

Furthermore, our ontology will be implemented in a real pedagogical platform and it will be employed to enhance the information representation model using its concepts' importance and weight.

3   Proposed Model and Methodology

The following section gives an elaboration of the representational model proposed in this paper which is inspired from [8]. The proposed model consist of three subtasks; mapping the domain ontology into a Markov chain model, calculation of transition probability matrix for Markov chain model and calculation of information content for each concept in ontology. The final step is building a concept vector space as an information representation model.

3.1   Modeling of Markov Model by a Domain Ontology

Following the formal definition of the domain ontology, we will adopt a model where the course domain ontology will be presented as a directed acyclic graph in which concepts such as classes and their instances are structured in a hierarchy. This definition will be represented by the tuple $O = (C, H, I, type(i), rel(i))$ [8], where:

- C is a non-empty set class identifiers
- H is a set of taxonomy relationship of C
- I is a potentially empty set I of instance identifiers
- $type(i)$ is an instance type relation that maps each instance in I to a set of one or more classes in C
- $rel(i)$ is an inter-instance relation that maps each instance in I to a set of zero or more other related instances in I.

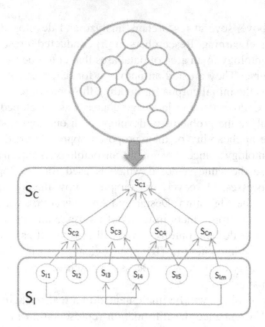

Fig. 1. Mapping of ontology into a Markov chain model

The graphical representation of the ontology will be implemented using the Markov chain model.

The Markov chain model is an equivalent mapping which means that classes in the ontology and the instances of those classes are mapped to states in the Markov chain model and all instance-to-class relations and hierarchical relations between classes are mapped to state transitions. This mapping is illustrated in Fig. 1, where the ontology is represented as a circle at the top and the Markov chain model is below. The latter is partitioned in two disjoined subsets, SC that indicates states of classes and SI indicates states of instances.

3.2 Calculation of Transition Probability Matrix and Information Content

The probability matrix for Markov chain model will be calculated based on the Page Rank algorithm [9]. We will employ this algorithm because our Markov graph owns a feature called irreducible which guarantees the convergence of the algorithm. A graph is irreducible when it is finite and, from every state it is possible to go to every other state, and the probability of transition from a state u to a state v is only dependent on the state u and not on the path to arrive at state v.

The page rank algorithm will be adjusted with two other parameters presented in [8], which are as follows:

- A probability distribution weight, ω, which determines how probabilities are distributed between states representing classes, S_C, and states representing instances, S_I.

- Weighting factor of instance *weight(i)* that maps each instance in *I* to a normalized weight between 0 and 1, and it is calculated as:

$$weight(i) = \sum_{i=1}^{n} edge\,(i)/totalEdges$$

Once we get the transition probability matrix, we can calculate the Information content which will give us the importance of each concept relative to other concepts.

3.3   Building the Information Representation Model

The final step of proposed model is building the information representation model using concept vector space. The information representation model will be created using the importance and the weight of concepts. Importance of concepts is calculated using *tf*idf* algorithm while weight of concepts is calculated as described in section 3.2.

4   Proposed Implementation

The main goal of using ontology is to organize MLO objects. Every new unlabeled learning object will be assigned to a predefined category in HIP. This will be done by calculating the similarity between the extracted terms from the learning object and the ontology concepts. The learning object will be assigned to a category having the highest similarity value with respect to that learning object.

5   Conclusion and Future Work

HIP is an eLearning platform that provides different types of media elements to deliver the learning objects. Structuring and organizing huge amount of learning objects comprising of multiple media elements is labor intensive, prone to errors and a cumbersome task. Therefore, the organization of the pedagogical multimedia content using an automatic classification approach based on ontology is described in this paper.

Ontology represents semantic aspects of the learning objects through entities defined within the domain ontology. Each learning object that uses ontology is represented as a vector, whose components indicate the importance of a concept. These concepts vectors are created by concepts extracted from the pedagogical course ontology and their importance and weight. Concepts' importance is calculated from the corpus by using statistical measures from information retrieval while concepts' weight is calculated using the model proposed in section 3.2. The new approach we are proposing, besides keeping information on importance of concepts, it will enrich the representation model by estimating weight of concepts automatically within the ontology.

Further research is required to implement the proposed model in order to have a reliable comparison and to evaluate the performance of the proposed model with the existing classification methods.

References

1. Imran, A.S., Cheikh, F.A.: Multimedia Learning Objects Framework for E-Learning. In: The International Conference on E-Learning and E-Technologies in Education (2012)
2. Imran, A.S., Kowalski, S.J.: HIP - A Technology-Rich and Interactive Multimedia Pedagogical Platform. Accepted in HCII (2014)
3. Happel, H.-J., Seedorf, S.: Applications of Ontologies in Software Engineering. In: Semantic Web Enabled Software Engineering, SWESE 2006 (2006)
4. De Nicola, A., Missikoff, M., Schiappelli, F.: Towards an ontological support for eLearning courses. In: Meersman, R., Tari, Z., Corsaro, A. (eds.) OTM-WS 2004. LNCS, vol. 3292, pp. 773–777. Springer, Heidelberg (2004)
5. Boyce, S., Pahl, C.: Developing Domain Ontologies for Course Content. Educational Technology & Society, 275–288 (2007)
6. Yun, H.-Y., Xu, J.-L., Wei, M.-J., Xiong, J.: Development of Domain Ontology for E-learning Course. In: IT in Medicine & Education, ITIME 2009 (2009)
7. El-Ghalayini, H.: E-Course Ontology for Developing E-Learning Courses. Developments in E-systems Engineering (2011)
8. Frost, H.R., McCray, A.T.: Markov Chain Ontology Analysis (MCOA). BMC Bioinformatics 13(14), 23 (2012)
9. Brin, S., Page, L.: The anatomy of a large-scale hypertextual Web search engine. In: Proceedings of the Seventh International Conference on World Wide Web (1998)

Learning Support Interface for Arithmetic Word Problem Based on Eye Movements Reduction

Tomoko Kojiri[1], Kento Nakamura[1], and Yuki Hayashi[2]

[1] Faculty of Engineering Science, Kansai University
3-3-35, Yamate-cho, Suita, Osaka, 564-8680, Japan
[2] Faculty of Science and Technology, Seikei University
kojiri@kansai-u.ac.jp

Abstract. Learning process in arithmetic word problem consists of three learning steps; extracting key numbers from problem text, creating equations, and deriving the answers of equations. When learning with computer using digital learning tools, learners sometimes are not able to concentrate on the learning since they have to move their eyes frequently between several learning tools, such as a tool that displays problem text and a memo tool. This research aims at developing a learning interface that consists of textbook window and memo window and a support functions that realize smooth learning with minimum eye movements between them. In the textbook window, learners can select key numbers by selecting them using a mouse. Selected numbers are copied to the memo window automatically. After learners create equations and derive answers in memo window, descriptions in memo window are copied to the textbook window automatically. Based on these functions, learners' unnecessary eye movements between two windows can be reduced.

Keywords: learning support interface, eye movement, arithmetic word problem.

1   Background and Objective

With the development of the e-Learning, learners are given learning materials from new learning devices, such as web browser and smart phones, while considering their ideas on memo tools. Under such learning environment, learners sometimes are not able to concentrate on the learning since they have to move their eyes frequently between two different tools. Such learners can be seen especially when they solve problems that consist of several solving processes and that need learning materials to be checked repeatedly in order to derive their answer.

Many traditional researches try to create real world-like learning interfaces [1-3]. Most of them develop tools that learners can manipulate as the same way as how they do in the real world, such as digital pens. These researches support only specific learning activity, such as writing. A few researches consider drawbacks that are caused by the eye movements between plural learning activities with different learning tools, such as reading text in browsing tool and creating ideas in memo tool.

C. Stephanidis (Ed.): HCII 2014 Posters, Part II, CCIS 435, pp. 101–105, 2014.
© Springer International Publishing Switzerland 2014 2014

This research focuses on the arithmetic word problems and aims at developing the learning interface that realizes smooth learning between different learning tools. This research firstly analyzes the eye movements that occur during the learning activities in arithmetic word problems. Then, we develop the learning support interface which can reduce unnecessary eye movements between a tool that displays text and a memo tool.

2   Learning Support Interface for Arithmetic Word Problems

Learning process in arithmetic word problem consists of three learning steps; extracting key numbers, creating equations, and deriving answers of the equations. During the learning, learners tend to use two learning tools, such as a textbook which describes the problem text and a memo in which their ideas can be written down freely. We have conducted the preliminary experiment in order to analyze which learning tools are used during which learning steps and in which steps eye movements occur frequently. In the experiment, three undergraduates in our university were asked to solve problems while wearing special glasses with camera (Figure 1). Problem texts were shown in a computer and paper memo is prepared on the desk. By analyzing the eye direction and descriptions in memo, applied tools for each learning step are determined.

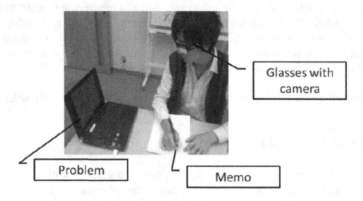

Fig. 1. Environment of preliminary experiment

As a result, learners tended to extract key numbers/words by observing problem text and write them in the memo. The equations were created by combining the extracted key numbers from problem text and were solved in memo. The answers of the equations became candidates of the next key numbers and sometimes are written in the memo again as next key numbers. The eye movements between problem text and memo can be seen during the key number extraction and creation of equation.

Based on the result, we have designed the interface which reduces unnecessary eye movements between problem text and memo (Figure 2). Our interface consists of two windows: textbook window and memo window. Problem texts are shown in the textbook window, and creation of equations and derivation of their answers are available in the memo window. In addition, in the textbook window, key numbers can be selected from the problem text by selecting them using mouse and selected numbers are copied to the memo window automatically. Also, created equations and answers in memo window are copied to the textbook window so as to make learner select next key numbers easily.

Figure 3 shows developed textbook window and memo window as a prototype. In the textbook window, problem text and equations that are derived by learner in the memo window are appeared. Learners can select key numbers/words from text by selecting them using mouse. Selected key numbers/words are allocated as texts on the buttons in the memo window. By clicking these buttons, texts on the buttons are inputted to equation creation area so that learners can create the equation easily. Learners are also able to modify texts and add answers of equations in the equation creation area. When equations are created and equation completion buttons are pushed, texts in the equation creation areas are copied to the end of the problem text in the textbook window.

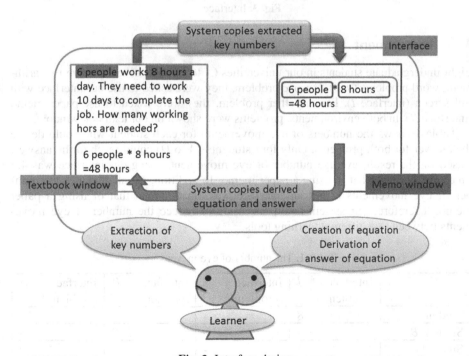

Fig. 2. Interface design

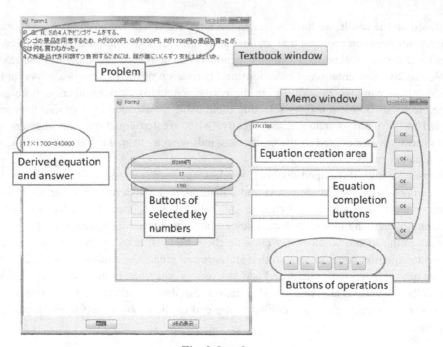

Fig. 3. Interface

3   Experiment

Eight undergraduate students in our universities (*A* to *H*) were asked to solve two arithmetic word problems (*a*, *b*). For one problem, they were asked to use our interface with full screen (interface *I*). For the other problem, they were asked to use paper memo (interface *II*). In both environments, problems were shown on our textbook window.

Table 1 shows the numbers of eye movements for each student who could derive the answer for both problems. Only four students (*A* to *D*) could reach to the answer. Based on the result, average number of eye movements using our interface was 4.5 times smaller than that of using a paper memo. In addition, for all students, the number of eye movements using our interface was smaller than that of using a paper memo. Therefore, our system could successfully reduce the number of eye movements between two different learning tools.

Table 1. The number of eye movement

	Interface *I* /problem *a*	Interface *I* /problem *b*	Interface *II* /problem *a*	Interface *II* /problem *b*
Student *A*	8	-	-	10
Student *B*	-	6	8	-
Student *C*	4	-	-	12
Student *D*	-	7	13	-
Average	6.3		10.8	

Our interface restricts the type of learning activities that can execute in each window. We have asked if their solving processes were changed by using our interface. Some students commented positively that they could execute each learning activity carefully by using our interface. However, some other students told us that they were uncomfortable with the restriction. So, in future, we need to investigate the effect of our interface from viewpoints of the learning performances.

4   Conclusion

In this paper, we have developed learning support interface for arithmetic word problem. In our interface, key numbers selected from a textbook window are automatically copied to a memo window, and equations that are derived in a memo window are added to the problem text in the textbook window. Based on these functions, the number of eye movements during the learning has been reduced.

Currently, in order to utilize our interface, texts of word problems should be embedded into the system beforehand. If learners can select problems that are provided in the web and can input them into the system by themselves, our interface can be used more widely. Therefore, we need to develop the mechanism which can obtain texts from indicated web site and set them as a problem text in the textbook window.

References

1. Miura, M., Kunifuji, S., Shizuki, B., Tanaka, J.: AirTransNote: augmented classrooms with digital pen devices and RFID tags. In: IEEE International Workshop on Wireless and Mobile Technologies in Education 2005 (WMTE 2005), pp. 56–58 (2005)
2. Holman, D., Vertegaal, R., Altosaar, M., Troje, T., Johns, D.: Paper windows: interaction techniques for digital paper. In: Proceedings of the SIGCHI Conference on Human Factors in Computing Systems, pp. 591–599 (2005)
3. Lai, W.C., Chao, P.Y., Chen, G.D.: The Interactive Multimedia Textbook: Using A digital Pen to Support Learning for Computer Programming. In: Proceedings of the 7th International Conference on Advanced Learning Technologies (ICALT 2007), pp. 742–746 (2007)

Designing an Interactive Tutoring Tool for Improving Mathematical Skills

Despina Lepenioti[1], Stella Vosniadou[1], and Christina Alexandris[2]

[1] Department of Philosophy and History of Science,
National and Kapodistrian University of Athens, Athens, Greece
des_lepenioti@hotmail.com, svosniad@phs.uoa.gr
[2] Department of German Language and Literature, School of Philosophy National
and Kapodistrian University of Athens, Athens, Greece
calexandris@gs.uoa.gr

Abstract. Based on the developmental transitions proposed by Stafylidou and Vosniadou (2004), three training sessions were created using the Cognitive Tutor Authoring Tools. The purpose was to compare the effects of two external representations on fraction understanding and interpretation, compared to a control group that received no training. The participants in the experimental groups were trained in creating external and symbolic representations for fractions using pies or number lines. Results indicated that participants in the experimental groups had greater improvement from pretest to post-test than the control group. The number line experimental group had greater improvement in tasks testing fraction equivalence and fraction interpretation as measure than the pie experimental group. Based on the results of the classroom experiment and the resulting User Requirements, the proposed interface was further reinforced with various sessions concerning fraction operations, including addition and subtraction. Special emphasis was placed on user-friendly and ergonomic interaction.

1   Introduction

Students' knowledge of fractions in elementary school has been shown to predict students' overall mathematical ability in high school [1], [2]. This finding indicates that fractions are important. However, fractions have been shown to be difficult for students to understand. Vosniadou and her colleagues [3] have explained these difficulties to result from negative transfer of natural number knowledge and operations.

Stafylidou and Vosniadou [4] described three developmental transitions in the development of the fraction concept. First, students see the fraction as two independent natural numbers. Second, students consider fractions to be always smaller than the unit. Only in the third developmental transition students see fractions as a relation between the numerator and the denominator, but they still face problems understanding the density of the rational numbers [5].

In order to test the effects of training using interactive external representations for fractions on fraction understanding we designed an interactive tutoring tool that included three training sessions where students would create external and symbolic representations for fractions.

C. Stephanidis (Ed.): HCII 2014 Posters, Part II, CCIS 435, pp. 106–111, 2014.
© Springer International Publishing Switzerland 2014

The effectiveness of the tool was tested with a training classroom experiment. We expected that the students who practiced with the tool would demonstrate better learning gains in the post-test compared to the pretest, than the students in the control group, who received no training. We also expected that the students who practiced for fractions with the number line external representation would have larger pretest – post-test differences than the students who practiced using the pie external representation because of the different properties of pies and number lines [6],[7].

We finally hypothesized that different external representations would promote different interpretations of fraction, as has been shown in previous research [8],[9]. The pie would promote the interpretation of fraction as part of a whole and the number line would promote the interpretation of fraction as a measure.

2   Data Collection and User Requirements

For the design and evaluation of the Tutoring Tool, data was collected from input by students participating in experimental interactive training sessions involving a set of tasks determined by a pretest – post-test instrument.

The participants were 80 6th graders, 45 boys and 35 girls, with mean age 12.2 years and they attended three middle class elementary schools in a suburban area of Athens. The participants were randomly assigned to one of two experimental groups (pies vs. number lines) or to the control group. The experimental groups practiced in creating external and symbolic representations for fractions using the Interactive Tutoring Tool. The pretest and post-test were given to all the participants in the school classroom and lasted no more than a school hour each.   The training took place in the school computer lab, in three sessions and every session lasted for less than a school hour.

The pretest – post-test instrument, included two equivalent forms of the fraction understanding assessment instrument. The assessment instrument included tasks testing conceptual understanding of fractions and procedural understanding of fractions. Four problems that tested the interpretation of fractions as part-whole relationship or as a measure were also added [6].

For the training sessions we designed our tutoring tool using Cognitive Tutor Authoring Tools [10]. The tool included web based problem sets in three sessions, namely "Choose Symbolic", "Write Symbolic" and "Make External". The problems embedded interactive representations of pies or number lines and students could provide answers, get feedback and help and manipulate the representations while the students were interacting with the external and the symbolic representation for the fraction.   In the beginning of the "Choose Symbolic" session, the experimental groups were presented with an introduction which created the context for the corresponding representation. In the pie experimental group (a) fractions were introduced as pieces of pizza and in the number line experimental group (b) fractions were introduced as measures of distance. In the beginning of every session, students worked with two examples-trials where they received instructions in bubbles while they tested their answers and manipulations: partitioning and selecting parts on pies (a) and partitioning and selecting points of distance

on number lines (b). In the middle and in the end of every session students were presented with a short video of the sequence of fractions they worked on. In every session,
fraction sequences were created based on the developmental transitions described by
Stafylidou and Vosniadou [4], in order to help students understand that some properties
of natural numbers cannot be applied on rational numbers. As a first step, students
worked on mathematical problems involving creating representations for unit fractions,
followed by problems involving simple fractions that had the same denominator. In
addition, students worked on problems for fractions that had the same numerator. As a
second step, students worked on problems with fractions consistent with natural number
ordering, namely: (1a) fractions that have large components as natural numbers and
large numerical magnitude as fractions or (1b) fractions that have small components as
natural numbers and small numerical magnitude as fractions. Additionally, students
worked with fractions inconsistent with natural number ordering: (2a) fractions that
have large components as natural numbers and small numerical magnitude, or (2b) fractions that have small components as natural numbers and large numerical magnitude.
Finally, the third step included problems with fractions equal to the unit followed by
improper fractions.

2.1   Results

No differences on pretest were found by a two – way ANOVA for Group,
[$F(2,71)=2.755$, $p=0.070$, $\eta^2=0.072$], or School, [$F(2,71)=0.756$, $p=0.473$, $\eta^2=0.021$].
A 3 Group (pies-number lines-control) × 2 Time (pretest-post-test) repeated measures
ANOVA on final score tested the effects of training and revealed main effects for
Group, [$F(2,77)=5.255$, $p=0.007$, $\eta^2=0.120$], due to the fact that the participants who
practiced using the tool had a greater mean score on all tasks than the participants in
the control condition. Post hoc analysis revealed significant differences only between
the group that practiced using the number line and the control group, ($p=0.005$). The
same analysis revealed the same main effect for Group, [$F(2,77)=5.432$, $p=0.006$,
$\eta^2=0.124$], regarding only tasks testing conceptual understanding of fractions, where
post-hoc analysis revealed again significant differences only between the group that
practiced using the number line and the control group, ($p=0.004$). Group performance
from pretest to post-test was tested for every task. The number line group had significantly better scores from pretest to post-test in more tasks than the pie group, especially in the tasks Fraction Equivalence and Fraction Interpretation as measure, where
the pie group demonstrated no significant improvement.

3   Design Parameters for Fraction Operations

In order to test more hypotheses concerning how external representations can support
conceptual and procedural fraction understanding, the tool was redesigned to address
also fraction operations such as fraction addition and fraction subtraction.

3.1 Tutoring Tool Content

The determination of the content of the Tutoring Tool involves the handling of two issues, the Symbolic and External Representation for fractions (1) and the Order of Problem Sets (2).

Symbolic and External Representation for Fractions. In every problem in the existing training sessions, either the symbolic or the external representation for fractions were presented to students and students had to choose, insert or create the corresponding one. The sixth graders that participated in the classroom experiment had little prior experience in interacting with an educational tool. These Users were familiar with the pie external representation and they were able to perform simple actions after being instructed to, for example, inserting numbers, choosing from multiple choice items, pressing buttons for help or submit and test their answers. Students had no prior experience with the number line for representing fractions. In the beginning of the training sessions, students indicated that using and manipulating the number line external representation was a difficult task for them.

After the students became familiar with the representations, they were presented with sessions designed for fraction addition and fraction subtraction involving both the symbolic and the external representation for fractions. Students had to change both representations at every step in order to proceed and find the resulting fractions.

Order of Problem Sets. The sequence of the problem sets is based on Stafylidou and Vosniadou, [4].

Set-1 To help students test their perceptions in the first developmental transition, in fraction operations, the first problem sets include operations with a unit fraction and a simple fraction with same denominators, followed by operations with two simple fractions with same denominators. Students then solve problems for operations involving fractions with equal numerators.

Set-2 In the second step, students solve fraction operations with fractions that are both consistent with natural number ordering, followed by problems with a consistent and an inconsistent with natural number ordering fraction. These problems target to help students comprehend that some properties of natural numbers cannot be applied to rational numbers.

Set-3 To challenge students to a more advanced perception of fractions, the last problem set includes operations with one equal to the unit fraction and a simple fraction, followed by operations with one or two improper fractions. Students may thus perceive that fractions can represent a quantity greater than the unit.

Set 2 and 3 aim at helping students see the fraction as a relation between the numerator and the denominator, which is described in the third developmental transition, where students have gained a better understanding of the fraction concept.

3.2 Interface Design

The User Interface design is aimed to address the above-presented issues in respect to User requirements. The interaction with the Tutoring Tool is targeted to young students and should, therefore, be easy to use, without too many additional features which may tire and discourage the User or may not be easily understood. Strategies such as verification questions are used and clarifying and explanatory elements should be present or directly available for a successful interaction. Keeping the interface features consistent throughout the interaction can help avoiding distractors or any additional cognitive load on Users which may result to an unsuccessful interaction.

Ergonomic Features of Interface (a). Specifically, the external representations, namely, pies or number lines, were presented on the left side of the screen and the symbolic representations, the fraction numerical components, were presented on the right side of the screen. The Interaction – Dialogue framework on the bottom of the screen and the Help button on the top right side of the screen were constantly presented. Feedback and help are available and consistent throughout the interaction. Students are able to move to the next problem only after the problem they are working on is solved. Every step is assessed and immediate feedback is provided. The "Done" button tests final answers and, if correct, moving to the next problem is enabled.

Verification Questions and Explanatory Elements (in Form of Bubbles) (b). The example-trials aimed at guiding students on the way of interacting with the tool such as the manipulation of the representations and the actions required to provide answers. The example trials had the purpose also of showing to the users the way of thinking using the external representations in the corresponding to the fraction interpretation context. In fraction operations, explanatory elements are added in order to explain to students the required procedural steps in order to find the result of the operation and the corresponding fraction conceptual aspects: For example, in steps required to make equivalent fractions, two fractions can represent the same magnitude.

3.3   User Feedback

In the end of the training the users stated that they were satisfied with their performance and that they would like to use the tool again in the future. They could use the tool and the representations with ease and they completed with success more than 95% of the problems right after the example-trials. The results from the classroom experiment confirm the learning gains for the students that practiced using the tool.

4   Conclusion and Future Work

The purpose of the designed tool is to support students understand the conceptual aspects of the fraction concept while avoiding misconceptions emerging from their prior knowledge about natural numbers. The tool is designed to avoid any distractors or additional cognitive costs. Furthermore, the proposed tool can be used to test hypotheses about fraction understanding and the effect of external representations on the fraction concept development. Creating representations for fractions helps students understand the properties of external and symbolic representations and build a mental model for the representation where they can test their perceptions for the fraction concept. Future work and increased application of the tool includes extending its application to address natural number representation on the number line for younger users and supporting the transition from natural numbers to rational numbers.

References

1. Siegler, R.S., Thompson, C.A., Schneider, M.: An integrated theory of whole number and fractions development. Cognitive Psychology 62, 273–296 (2011)
2. Siegler, R.S., Duncan, G.J., Davis-Kean, P.E., Duckworth, K., Claessens, A., Engel, M., Ines, M.: Early predictors of high school mathematics achievement. Psychological Science 23 (2012)
3. Vosniadou, S.: Conceptual change in learning and instruction: The framework theory approach. In: Vosniadou, S. (ed.) The International Handbook of Conceptual Change, 2nd edn., pp. 11–30. Routledge, New York (2013)
4. Stafylidou, S., Vosniadou, S.: The development of students' understanding of the numerical value of fractions. In: Verschaffel, L., Vosniadou, S. (eds.) Conceptual Change in Mathematics Learning and Teaching, Special Issue of Learning and Instruction 14(5), 503–518 (2004)
5. Vamvakoussi, X., Vosniadou, S.: How many decimals are there between two fractions? Aspects of secondary school students' reasoning about rational numbers and their notation. Cognition and Instruction 28(2), 181–209 (2010)
6. Lamon, S.J.: Teaching fractions and ratios for understanding: Essential content knowledge and instructional strategies for teachers. Routledge, New York (2012)
7. Bright, G.W., Behr, M.J., Post, T.R., Wachsmuth, I.: Identifying fractions on number - lines. Journal of Research in Mathematics Education 19(3), 215–233 (1988)
8. Kieren, T.E.: On the mathematical, cognitive, and instructional foundations of rational numbers. In: Lesh, R. (ed.) Number and Measurement: Papers from a Research Workshop, pp. 101–144. ERIC/SMEAC, Columbus (1976)
9. Charalambous, C.Y., Pitta-Pantazi, D.: Drawing on a theoretical model to study students' understandings of fractions. Educational Studies in Mathematics 64(3), 293–316 (2007)
10. Aleven, V., McLaren, B.M., Sewall, J., Koedinger, K.R.: The Cognitive Tutor Authoring Tools (CTAT): Preliminary Evaluation of Efficiency Gains. In: Ikeda, M., Ashley, K.D., Chan, T.-W. (eds.) ITS 2006. LNCS, vol. 4053, pp. 61–70. Springer, Heidelberg (2006)

Instructional Activities in a Discussion Board Forum of an e-Leaning Management System

Yanfei Ma, Cathryn Friel, and Wanli Xing

School of Information Science and Learning Technologies, University of Missouri
Columbia, MO, USA
{ymyp6,wxdg5}@mail.missouri.edu,
FrielC@missouri.edu

Abstract. This study was primarily interested in dynamic interactions between instructors and an e-learning Management System (Blackboard) with specific focus on the discussion board forum. We examined how instructors seek information to assess students' input in an e-learning discussion board forum and determined which pedagogical features need to be improved to facilitate instructional activities. The findings suggest that the ability to easily track and respond to students' post is the most important instructional activity to instructors while reading student posts and replying to students are the most frequent instructional activities. Interacting with students and facilitating group discussion are the most difficult instructional activities. Therefore, this study indicated that Blackboard discussion board designers may need to improve discussion board pedagogical features to make interaction with students and facilitating group discussion more convenient and accessible for instructors who must now forage for the information they need to assess student contributions.

Keywords: E-learning management system, Blackboard, discussion board, information foraging theory, instructional activities, pedagogical features.

1 Introduction

As learning management systems become more popular at higher education institutions, online discussion forums are being more widely used. Online discussion forums have found their way into traditional, face-to-face, hybrid and online courses. Learning management systems often facilitate different types of interaction. In the context of e-learning, Moore (1989) divided this interaction into three categories: (a) learner-instructor; (b) learner-learner; and (c) learner-content (as cited in Bouhnik & Marcus, 2006). A fourth category of interaction (Hillman, Willis, Gunawardena, 1994; Bouhnik & Marcus 2006), learner-system or student-system interaction, has been identified and refers to the technologies, platforms and applications individuals use to interact with instructors, fellow students and the content. According to Arbaugh and Benbunan-Fich (2007), "Learner-system interaction facilitates or constraints the quantity and quality of the other three types of interactions". Students and faculty are

C. Stephanidis (Ed.): HCII 2014 Posters, Part II, CCIS 435, pp. 112–116, 2014.
© Springer International Publishing Switzerland 2014

in agreement that the quality and quantity of interaction in a discussion board can increase their satisfaction in the course (Picciano, 2002). Instructor responsiveness is one of the most important elements to successfully achieve meaningful interaction in a distance-education course (Blignaut & Trollip, 2003).

2   Purpose of Study

The primary focus of this study was to reveal instructor-system interaction by investigating instructional activities within a discussion board forum in an e-learning management system (Blackboard). Learning activities entail complex processes of interactions, and the benefits of learning management systems, like Blackboard, can easily be lost if that complexity is not appreciated, understood, and dealt with in a satisfactory manner by users (Bouhnik & Marcus 2006). While investigating discussion board forums in online learning environments, great care needs to be exercised to ensure that the discussion board itself remains transparent and does not create a psychological or functional barrier to instructors. Thus, information Foraging theory (Pirolli & Card, 1999; Trepess, 2006) was applied to investigate how instructors perceive their instructional activities in a learning management system (e.g., Blackboard discussion forum) to determine their preferences and strategies to obtain valuable information needed for assessing students' input.

3   Method

3.1   Context

This study conducted an online survey and a follow-up interview using the same pool of participants at a Midwestern university. All participants were selected from a pool of faculty and graduate instructors in the College of Education. The online survey was distributed to faculty members and graduate instructors who had experience using the Blackboard discussion board in their online courses. Eighteen participants responded to the online survey and nine of them participated in follow-up interviews. All participants were actively using Blackboard discussion boards with experience ranging from less than six months to more than six years. Of the participants who indicated they checked the discussion board, 56% of them check the boards daily with 40% of those respondents checking the boards two to three times a day.

3.2   Procedures

Seven instructional activities in Blackboard discussion boards were proposed for participants to evaluate and discuss:

- Creating a forum in a discussion board
- Creating group discussions

- Facilitating group discussions
- Reading students' post
- Replying and interacting with students
- Viewing discussion board statistics
- Grading discussion board participation

The online survey was created in Qualtrics and sent out via email. The collected data was exported from Qualtrics for analysis. Interview participants were recruited through the distributed survey. Interview data were recorded and coded into main themes.

4   Results

4.1   What Instructional Activities in the Blackboard Discussion Board Are Important to Instructors?

Respondents reported that the ability to easily track student posts (83%) and respond to posts (78%) was ranked as the most important activity. Of particular interest to the researchers was the importance of the ease of grading students' posts. The researchers expected that the ease of tracking students' posts to be positively correlated with grading. The results indicated that tracking student posts goes beyond just grading and may be important for other aspects of teaching.

4.2   What Instructional Activities in the Blackboard Discussion Board Do Instructors Perform Most Often?

When asked which activity instructors performed most frequently, 33% indicated reading student posts. Replying to students, creating forums and facilitating group discussions were ranked immediately after that. Other activities such as viewing discussion board statistics and grading were not performed as often. This makes sense as discussions usually last for a week or more within a course.

4.3   What Instructional Activities Are Difficult for Instructors to Perform?

While using the Blackboard discussion board, 53% of the instructors stated that they experienced some difficulty. According to the results, replying and interacting with the students and facilitating group discussions were chosen as the most difficult tasks. This may have been a reflection of the students' participation and involvement in the discussion board did not meet instructors' expectations. As one participant stated, "It's hard to enforce 'norms' of behavior on some students" and another stated "It took several years to create a workable way to structure small group discussions." At this point, pedagogical features of the discussion board forum regarding instructor-student interaction were not satisfactory.

5   Conclusion

This study contributes to generalizable knowledge in the human-computer interaction field, particularly in e-learning instructor-system interaction. From the instructor's perspective, the convenience and accessibility of the online course delivery model of a discussion board forum guides and encourages students' questions, postings and dialogue (Harris & Sandor, 2007). The most frequent instructional activities performed by instructors were reading and replying to students' posts. This indicates that discussion board designers may need to improve pedagogical features to make reading and replying to students more convenient and accessible for instructors who must otherwise forage for the information needed to assess student contributions. Considering the utility of discussion boards, pedagogical usability (Nokelainen, 2006) should be assessed to promote instructors' experience in implementing instructional activities. The biggest issue facing instructors is how to encourage students to participate more in discussions and provide meaningful input, which supports other research findings (Cheung and Hew 2004; Dennen, 2005; Lee et al. 2011). These findings indicate that designers should consider adding features to assist instructors' interaction with students and facilitate group discussions. Overall, findings of this study indicate that Blackboard Discussion board designers need to consider refining pedagogical objectives and adding value to support instructor-student interaction in a discussion board forum.

6   Discussion

Regardless of the online environment, whether it is a website, social media environment or learning environment, information is continuously being sought. Information foraging theory asserts that people will modify their searching strategies for the environment to make seeking information more effective and efficient. It was a change in environment that aided instructors in finding the valuable information they needed to access student participation in a discussion board. There are still aspects that ought to be changed to assist instructors' information foraging and instructional activities. Many learning management systems fall short in their design evaluations, and as such do a disservice to instructors and students alike. As Nokelainen (2006) indicates, usability evaluation within a learning system is not enough; it is essential to evaluate the pedagogical design of the system. Further research is needed to fully explore the design elements within learning systems' discussion board forums that support pedagogical usability within the system.

Acknowledgements. We would like to express our greatest gratitude to the people who have helped and supported us throughout this study. We are grateful to Dr. Joi Moore and Dr. Holly Henry for their initial support and continuous suggestions to the study. We would like to express a heartfelt thanks to Robert Wadholm for his insightful comments. We also would like to express our gratitude to Dr. David Reid, the Blackboard Administrators and Support Staff for providing us access to the environment of Blackboard.

References

1. Arbaugh, J.B., Benbunan-Fich, R.: The importance of participant interaction in online environments. Decision Support Systems 43(3), 853–865 (2007)
2. Blignaut, A.S., Trollip, S.R.: Measuring Faculty Participation in Asynchronous Discussion Forums. Journal of Education for Business 78(6), 347–353 (2003)
3. Bouhnik, D., Marcus, T.: Interaction in distance-learning courses. Journal of the American Society Information Science and Technology 57(3), 299–305 (2006)
4. Cheung, W.S., Hew, K.F.: Evaluating the Extent of Ill-Structured Problem Solving Process among Pre-Service Teachers in an Asynchronous Online Discussion and Reflection Log Learning Environment. Journal of Educational Computing Research 30(3), 197–227 (2004)
5. Harris, N., Sandor, M.: Developing online discussion forums as student centred peer e-learning environments. In: ICT: Providing Choices for Learners and Learning. Proceedings Ascilite Singapore 2007, pp. 383–387 (2007)
6. Dennen, V.P.: From message posting to learning dialogues; Factors affecting learner participation in asynchronous discussion. Distance Education 26(1), 127–148 (2005)
7. Hillman, D.C., Willis, D.J., Gunawardena, C.N.: Learner interface interaction in distance education; an extension of contemporary models and strategies for practitioners. American Journal of Distance Education 8(2), 30–42 (1994)
8. Lee, H., Kim, J.W., Hackney, R.: Knowledge hoarding and user acceptance of online discussion board systems in eLearning: A case study. Computers in Human Behavior 27, 1431–1437 (2011)
9. Nokelainen, P.: An empirical assessment of pedagogical usability criteria for digital learning material with elementary school students. Educational Technology & Society 9(2), 178–197 (2006)
10. Picciano, A.G.: Beyond student perceptions: Issues of interaction, presence, and performance in an online course. Journal of Asynchronous learning networks 6(1), 21–40 (2002)
11. Pirolli, P., Card, S.K.: Information foraging (1999), http://act-r.psy.cmu.edu/papers/280/uir-1999-05-pirolli.pdf (retrieved March 28, 2013)
12. Trepess, D.: Information Foraging Theory (2006), http://www.interactiondesign.org/encyclopedia/information_foraging_theory.html (retrieved March 28, 2013)
13. Silius, K., Tervakari, A.M., Pohjolainen, S.: A multidisciplinary tool for the evaluation of usability, pedagogical usability, accessibility and informational quality of web-based courses. In: The Eleventh International PEG Conference: Powerful ICT for Teaching and Learning, vol. 28 (2003)

Integration of Technology into Classrooms:
Role of Knowledge and Teacher Beliefs

Neda Najdabbasi and Margus Pedaste

University of Tartu, Salme 1a, 50103 Tartu, Estonia
najdabbasi@gmail.com, margus.pedaste@ut.ee

Abstract. One of the most promising recent advancements in education has been the extensive inclusion of technology. Educational technology focuses profoundly on how to encourage teachers to integrate technology in the curriculum; however, teachers do not often apply technology as it should be according to its affordability. Two of the teachers' reasons for not using technology in the class are typically related to their beliefs and knowledge. The aim of the present review was to understand the relationship between teachers' pedagogical beliefs and knowledge with the integration of technology to improve technology use in education. We developed a model to support the integration of technology and students in classrooms by focusing on teachers' pedagogical beliefs and knowledge. According to this study, the roles of teachers are facilitating students in acquiring technology-related knowledge, motivating them for using technology, and creating situation where students should integrate technology in learning.

Keywords: technology integration, pedagogical beliefs, knowledge, education.

1 Introduction

In the recent decades, one of the most important advancements in education could be dedicated to an extensive spread and inclusion of technology in educational settings. Educational technology can provide valuable information and knowledge for students to have a related career as a subject of interest position in the future [1]. Many researchers agree that technology can be used effectively as a cognitive tool as well as an instructional media [2]. Bruce and Levin [3] pointed that technology can be helpful in classroom settings by helping communication, encouraging inquiry, assisting students' self-expression, and constructing teaching products. Also, Bransford et al. [4] indicated that the role of technology includes being able to bring the real-world experiences into the classroom, providing framework that allows learners to participate in complex cognitive tasks, increasing opportunities to receive sophisticated and individualized feedback, expanding opportunities for teacher development, and building interaction between teachers and students. These findings show that the factors affecting the use of technology are more complicated than researchers initially assume [1]. Undoubtedly, technology makes the learning process more interactive and, consequently, more exciting and memorable. Recently, educational standards often expect

C. Stephanidis (Ed.): HCII 2014 Posters, Part II, CCIS 435, pp. 117–122, 2014.

teachers to use information and communication technology (ICT) to enhance learning and teaching in the classrooms [1, 5, 6]. Furthermore, there are some challenges such as inadequate infrastructure, lack of training and personal expertise, and weak technical supports that frequently prevent teachers from using technology in the classroom [7]. Also, recent assessments show that technology has not been effectively used for learning facilitation in the schools yet. Hence, technology performance needs fundamental changes in the roles of teachers and students, instructional strategies, and educational setting [8]. Teachers' knowledge and pedagogical beliefs are two sets of barriers that are often discussed to understand why technology is differently integrated into teaching among teachers who are prepared with relevant knowledge [9, 10].

It is important to examine the best way to enhance student learning with technology. Hence, it is essential to first consider the factors affecting teachers' decision to use technology in their classrooms before discussing the different instructional applications to maximize the effectiveness of technology [1, 11]. Hence, the present study attempts to provide a model to support the integration of technology and student by focusing on teachers' pedagogical beliefs and knowledge. Our guiding research was "How teachers' beliefs and knowledge should be considered in a model for integrating technology into classrooms."

2   Integration of Technology in Education

Many studies have focused on the benefits of technology integration for using technology in educational settings [1, 5, 9]. Often, the use of technology in education is important to motivate student learning [12]. However, it also helps students to improve several general skills such as problem solving and self-regulation or ICT skills [12, 13]. In other words, technology integration has found about how teachers use technology to convey familiar activities more reliably and productively [9, 14]. Although a few teachers have used technology as a learning device or asked students to use, most teachers do not integrate technology effectively into teaching and learning and just use it to design instructional materials or provide lectures [1, 15, 16]. Because education of technology is important, the integration of technology in teacher training and professional growth has been significantly highlighted [10]. Hence, many countries have focused on the application of ICT in their communities to develop students' thinking skills. For instance, the development of the ICT in Europe between 2000 and 2011 has been quite dynamic [17]. Also, the integration of technology in classrooms in the United States and Japan reached 100% in 1993 and 2003, respectively [18].

3   Teacher Pedagogical Beliefs

Beliefs are a collection of attitudes and values [12]. Hence, beliefs have a tendency to influence practice in terms of value [8, 15]. Beliefs about the value of something comprise the realized importance of specific goals and choices [19]. Understanding teachers' beliefs that make technologies integrated into teaching would be supportive in improving technology integration trainings [10]. Teachers' beliefs in relation to technology are fundamental about whether technology can help them to achieve the instructional aims that they perceive to be most important [12, 20]. Teacher beliefs about teaching and learning are called pedagogical beliefs [21]. Hence, each teacher holds a set of beliefs that specify priorities for pedagogical knowledge and facilitates acquiring knowledge by students [16, 21]. Also, there has been a growing research interest in exploring teachers' beliefs about pedagogy or education, value, and self-efficacy that underlies how they apply technology [5, 12, 21]. In research on teacher beliefs in technology integration contexts, Kima et al. [10] noticed a difference that researchers study beliefs only associated with technology, although there should be basic beliefs that are associated with teacher beliefs in relation to technology.

Because belief systems influence how teachers use technology in the classroom, teacher pedagogical beliefs are considered even more influential than teacher knowledge in technology integration.

4   Teacher Knowledge

Inasmuch as the teacher plays a main role in the educational process, it is important to have some developed knowledge [22]. Basically, teachers need to have the basic technology skills to prepare their students to be technologically capable [8]. According to Lawless and Pellegrino [23], technological literacy has fast become one of the basic skills of teaching. Although most teachers believe that technology helps them accomplish professional and personal tasks more efficiently, they are reluctant to incorporate the same tools into the classroom. Lack of relevant knowledge and also lack of specific technology knowledge and skills are the common reasons given by teachers for not using technology in the classroom [8, 23].

According to Shulman [24], teachers' knowledge includes knowledge of the subject (content knowledge), knowledge of teaching methods and classroom management strategies (pedagogical knowledge), and knowledge of how to teach specific content to learners in specific contexts (pedagogical content knowledge [PCK]). The technological pedagogical content knowledge (TPCK) framework builds on Shulman's descriptions of PCK to describe how teachers' understanding of educational technologies and PCK interact with one another to produce effective teaching with technology [25]. Because focusing on technology knowledge and skills is important, technology integration cannot occur if the teacher lacks the knowledge or skills. Hence, the TPCK facilitates teacher professional development and teachers' use of technology.

5   Discussion

In our review, we identified that teachers' pedagogical beliefs and different types of knowledge belong to the important elements of a model for supporting the integration of technology into classrooms. However, according to the models of Hew and Brush [9] and Bate [26], the roles of school principals and local authorities, government policies and resources, leadership, school culture, equipment, and infrastructure should also be considered. As a synthesis of our review and other models, we propose an integrated model that is open for further justifications and discussions. This model is presented on Figure 1. According to our model of integrating technology and students, there are two stakeholders (teachers and school leaders) and five activities (teachers' beliefs, teachers' knowledge, students' behavior, governmental policies, and financial support) that should be taken into account in planning on change in the use of technologies in educational settings. School leaders should act according to the governmental policies that should enable the application of educational technologies by financial support and by encouraging the change of teachers' beliefs and the improvement of teachers' knowledge needed in this process. Teachers have "positive pedagogical beliefs" and knowledge needed to effectively use the tools in changing students' behavior (so that they are encouraged to learn using technology), and technology will be "organically" integrated into the classroom—there are more often designed situations where students and technology are integrated in a classroom.

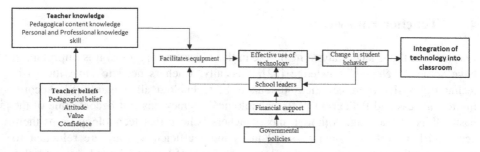

Fig. 1. Model of the integration of technology into classroom

According to this model, teachers should have beliefs that technology is valuable in students' learning. Next, they need particular knowledge and skills to support students in learning with technology. Liu [16] also pointed that the integration of technology includes opinions and applications related to the use of technology during education, and it relies on teachers' pedagogical beliefs to practice. Hence, it can affect procedures of teaching. Mumtaz [27] highlighted that the role of pedagogy and teachers' beliefs about teaching and learning with ICT are central to integration. However, in addition, there are several factors that influence teachers' decisions to use ICT in the classroom: access to resources, support in their school, and school and national policies. In this respect, school leaders or owners can increase their sense of confidence by making technical and pedagogical support to teachers to examine new applications [28].

Hence, to improve the pedagogical beliefs to adopt the concept of good teaching and also to obtain the knowledge, teachers still need confidence to perform it within their particular contexts. In fact, in the context of technology integration, teachers' beliefs and knowledge toward technology may be conceptualized as their interest in the use of technology. In other words, teachers' beliefs and knowledge are strongly connected to the teaching application.

6   Conclusion

In this research, beliefs and knowledge of instructional practices were the most important issues related to teacher changes that are required to facilitate technology and student integration into classroom. To achieve this purpose, it is critical to motivate teachers to understand how they must use technology for the facilitation of meaningful learning, which enables students to construct connected knowledge.

According to the subjects described in this review, three recommendations for future studies about the role of teacher and school activities are suggested: promoting and changing pedagogical beliefs and knowledge about the benefits of using technology for teachers, providing new educational models for encouraging students for performing new technology in schools, and creating more situations for integrating students with technology in their classrooms.

References

1. Baek, Y., Jung, J., Kim, B.: What makes teachers use technology in the classroom? Exploring the factors affecting facilitation of technology with a Korean sample. Computers and Education 50(1), 224–234 (2008)
2. Kleiman, G.M.: Myths and realities about technology in K-12 schools: Five years later. Contemporary Issues in Technology and Teacher Education 4, 248–253 (2004)
3. Bruce, B., Levin, J.: Roles for new technologies in language arts: Inquiry, communication, construction, and expression. In: Jenson, J., Flood, J., Lapp, D., Squire, J. (eds.) The Handbook for Research on Teaching the Language Arts. Macmillan, New York (2001)
4. Bransford, J.D., Brown, A.L., Cocking, R.R.: How people learn: Brain, mind, experience, and school. National Academy Press, Washington, DC (2000)
5. Koc, K.: Student teachers' conceptions of technology: A metaphor analysis. Computers and Education 68, 1–8 (2013)
6. Teo, T.: Factors influencing teachers' intention to use technology: Model development and test. Computers and Education 57(4), 2432–2440 (2011)
7. Mehlinger, H.D., Powers, S.M.: Technology & teacher education: A guide for educators and policymakers. Houghton Mifflin Company, Boston (2002)
8. Ertmer, P.A., Ottenbreit-Leftwich, A.T.: Teacher technology change: How knowledge, confidence, beliefs, and culture intersect. Journal of Research on Technology in Education 42(3), 255–284 (2010)
9. Hew, K.F., Brush, T.H.: Integrating technology into K-12 teaching and learning: Current knowledge gaps and recommendations for future research. Educational Technology Research and Development 55(3), 223–252 (2007)
10. Kima, C.M., Kima, M.K., Lee, C.H., Spector, J.M., DeMeester, K.: Teacher beliefs and technology integration. Teaching and Teacher Education 29, 76–85 (2013)
11. Inan, F.A., Lowther, D.L.: Factors affecting technology integration in K–12 classrooms: A path model. Educational Technology Research and Development 58(2), 137–154 (2010)
12. Ottenbreit-Leftwich, A.T., Glazewskib, K.D., Newby, T.J., Ertmer, P.A.: Teacher value beliefs associated with using technology: Addressing professional and student needs. Computers and Education 55(3), 1321–1335 (2010)

13. Ereiter, C., Scardamalia, M.: Education for the knowledge age: Design-centered models of teaching and instruction. In: Alexander, P.A., Winne, P.H. (eds.) Handbook of Educational Psychology, 2nd edn., pp. 695–713. Erlbaum, Mahwah (2006)

14. Hennessy, S., Ruthven, K., Brindley, S.: Teacher perspectives on integrating ICT into subject teaching: Commitment, constraints, caution, and change. Journal of Curriculum Studies 37(2), 155–192 (2005)

15. Hermans, R., Tondeur, J., van Braak, J., Valcke, M.: The impact of primary school teachers' educational beliefs on the classroom use of computers. Computers and Education 51(4), 1499–1509 (2008)

16. Liu, S.H.: Factors related to pedagogical beliefs of teachers and technology integration. Computers and Education 56(4), 1012–1022 (2011)

17. Hüsing, T., Korte, W.B., Fonstad, N., Lanvin, B., Welsum, D.V., Cattaneo, G., Kolding, M., Lifonti, R.: E-skills for competitiveness and innovation vision, roadmap and foresight scenarios. Final report, European Commission (2013)

18. ICT in Education in the world, http://www.ake.blogfa.com/ (retrieved)

19. Anderson, S.E., Maninger, R.M.: Pre-service teachers' abilities, beliefs, and intentions regarding technology integration. Journal of Educational Computing Research 37(2), 151–172 (2007)

20. Watson, G.: Technology professional development: Long-term effects on teacher self-efficacy. Journal of Technology and Teacher Education 14(1), 151–165 (2006)

21. Ertmer, P.A.: Teacher pedagogical beliefs: The final frontier in our quest for technology integration? Educational Technology Research and Development 53(4), 25–39 (2005)

22. Van Dijka, E.A., Kattmannb, M.U.: A research model for the study of science teachers' PCK and improving teacher education. Teaching and Teacher Education 23(6), 885–897 (2007)

23. Lawless, K.A., Pellegrino, J.W.: Professional development in integrating technology into teaching and learning: Known, unknowns, and ways to pursue better questions and answers. Review of Educational Research 77, 575–614 (2007)

24. Shulman, L.S.: Those who understand: Knowledge growth in teaching. Educational Researcher 15(2), 4–14 (1986)

25. Koehler, M.J., Mishra, P.: What happens when teachers design educational technology? The development of technological pedagogical content knowledge. Journal of Educational Computing Research 32, 131–152 (2005)

26. Bate, F.: A bridge too far? Explaining beginning teachers' use of ICT in Australian schools. Australasian Journal of Educational Technology 26(7), 1042–1061 (2010)

27. Mumtaz, S.H.: Factors affecting teachers' use of information and communications technology: A review of the literature. Journal of Information Technology for Teacher Education 9(3), 319–341 (2000)

28. Somekh, B.: Factors affecting teachers' pedagogical adoption of ICT. In: Voogt, J., Knezek, G. (eds.) International Handbook of Information Technology in Primary and Secondary. Springer International Handbooks of Education, vol. 20. Springer, New York (2008)

A Proposal of Measurement Levels of Acculturation among International Students in Japan

Hyunjoo Judy Oh[1] and Katsuhiko Ogawa[2]

[1] Graduate School of Media and Governance, Keio University,
Fujisawa-shi, Kanagawa, Japan
lilyzip@sfc.keio.ac.jp
[2] Faculty of Environment and Information Studies, Keio University,
Fujisawa-shi, Kanagawa, Japan
ogw@sfc.keio.ac.jp

Abstract. The term acculturation refers to the result of the processes of adopting the cultural traits or social patterns of another group. Although not all groups undergo acculturation in the same method, the underlying hypothesis is that there will be two main components to how acculturation takes places. It is projected that attitudes and behaviors are the two main components that determine the level of acculturation (Berry, 2005). Using this principle, there will be multiple trials of experimentation to prove or disapprove this hypothesis. Ultimately, this paper will focus on defining a measure of acculturation and reporting how our experimentation methods will affect international students with acculturation.

Keywords: Acculturation, culture, guidelines, culture shock, adaptation, assimilation, and cultural groups.

1   Introduction

There are different patterns as to how an individual acculturate, integrate, and assimilate into new cultures both psychologically and socioculturally. More recently, there are studies that involve ethno-cultural groups and how each relate to each other and change as a result of attempting to live together in culturally different societies (Berry, 2005).

For this project, the first step is was to conduct interviews with random international students and ask about the types of changes that they have had to make in order to acculturate into Japanese society. After gaining background information through the in-person interviews, an online survey was launched to assess specific thought processes about the entire acculturation process. The responses from the in-person interviews provided important insights as to how the questions for the online survey were to be constructed. Individuals with lower scores on the survey revealed that the level of acculturation into Japanese culture and society was estimated to be low.

C. Stephanidis (Ed.): HCII 2014 Posters, Part II, CCIS 435, pp. 123–127, 2014.
© Springer International Publishing Switzerland 2014

2   Measurement

2.1   Experimentation Method and Concept

After surveying 25 individuals who have reportedly spent time abroad or were foreign to Japan, I have discovered that there were roughly six main areas that were related to acculturation and adaptation to new lifestyles. The following section outlines the six main areas that I have identified for this study.

Language Usage and Media Preference
Language usage refers to the level of Japanese usage when it comes to speaking, reading, and writing. Media preference is determined by how much an individual chooses to watch or listen to Japanese media over any type of entertainment source that comes from their home country.

Cultural Identity and Balance of Cultures
Cultural identity requires an individual to identify the culture that they are the most comfortable with. If an individual is a foreigner to Japan, it is essential to balance between cultures and to embrace all differences in cultural beliefs, values, and behaviours to fit in to a new society.

Relationships
Relationships refer to an individual's social life in Japan. It assesses how well an individual makes acquaintances and friends even with differences in languages, beliefs, cultures, and customs.

Health, Well-Being, and Mobility
Health and well-being refers to both the physical and mental wellness of an individual. Mobility refers to how much an individual may feel comfortable with using the public transportation system in Japan.

Food and Diet
Food and diet refers to how much an individual's diet may have changed after moving to Japan. This section also assess whether an individual prefers Japanese diets over the meals from their country of origin.

Personal Hygiene
Personal hygiene assesses whether an individual feels more obligated to care about their physical aesthetics. For instance, it examines if an individual spends more time and effort to follow the latest Japanese fashion trends.

Because this experiment requires both the pre-experiment and post-experiment thought process of each participant, the same survey will be distributed numerous times compare the changes. To visually examine the before and after differences in the survey outcomes, I have decided to use a 6-dimension diagram to present my data outcomes.

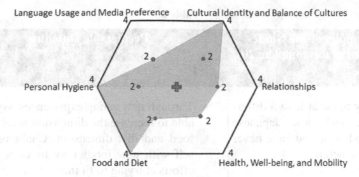

Fig. 1. An example of a 6-dimension diagram that present 1 respondent's survey results in a visual format

Table 1.

Scores – Definition on Survey			
1	2	3	4
Strongly Disagree	Disagree	Agree	Strongly Agree

2.2   Usage

By utilizing the six main areas as the main dimensions of the hexagon, each response can be visually represented. For example, if the blue area inside the hexagon is shown to be smaller in size, the respondent has chosen answers that connect to lower scores. Ideally, the blue area inside the hexagon should increase in size after the experiment as higher scores tend to reveal that an individual is more likely to be comfortable in their new settings and culture.

3   Guidelines

Based on the responses of these participants, I have developed a lifestyle guideline. To justify and rationalize the ideas behind each guideline, I referred to the responses of the survey. For instance, if the survey answers have revealed that watching Japanese TV has improved language skills, I would create a guideline that may require a participant to watch TV.

Only a selected number of individuals from the pool of 25 foreigner/Japanese students participated in a one-week experiment. The experimentation consisted of following a tool that was consisting of guidelines.

When the experimentation had started, each participant needed to choose 7 of the 20 guidelines. These guidelines ordered a person to act a certain way and be designed to help and facilitate easier acculturation. Once the experimentation was over, each participant wrote a statement about each change made.

Table 2.

Few examples of the Guideline (3 out of the complete 20).	Predictable Outcome
• Try to eat at least 5 different and new Japanese foods that you have never tried before.	• Through new eating experiences, you will be able to increase the dimension level from the food and diet dimension. Challenging oneself with new foods may translate to one's efforts at trying to fit in.
• Replace showers with baths at least 3 times during this experimentation timeframe.	• This guideline was testing the participant's willingness towards changes in lifestyle. It is expected that the personal hygiene dimension's dimension level may increase.
• Try to follow the current fashion style by trying different hair styles or trying on new styles of clothing that is out of your comfort zone.	• This guideline is expected to increase the personal hygiene and cultural identity dimension level. If one is trying to fit in to another culture through certain actions, it can be translated as one's efforts toward acculturation.

Using the results of the survey and the actual thought processes of each individual, acculturation will be measured using two components: attitude and behaviour. For example, if a participant dislikes seafood due to its texture, this can be considered an "attitude" as there is no action involved. If the same participant makes changes to their diet by adding seafood once the experiment starts, this can be considered a "behavioural" change. As one set of experimentation outcome may not be sufficient in drawing conclusions, it may be necessary to repeat the experimentation a number of times to ensure data integrity.

4   Conclusion and Further Work

During the initial stage of the project, in-person interviews have been conducted to discover the drastic lifestyle changes that international students have experienced in order to acculturate successfully into the society. Apart from the obvious issues that come from language barriers, there were some interesting changes that were found insightful. Subsequently, the approach concentrated on translating these small examples or episodes into questions for the survey and guideline.

According to the results of the experimentation, there were three main dimensions that the participants focused on following. First, majority of participants attempted to change or alter their diets to be more Japanese-oriented. Second, because all of the foreign participants regularly took showers, it was a new experience for them to change their hygiene regime to regular baths. Third, majority of the participants took attempts to improve their Japanese language skills by engaging in more social activities and conversations or by simply studying through reading or listening exercises. The most frequently followed guidelines were identified to be:

- Try to eat pre-made foods or convenience store foods and leave a note of whether you like it or dislike it.
- Replace showers with baths at least 3 times during this experimentation timeframe.
- Watch at 7 or more hours of Japanese TV during the week to improve your listening/speaking skills.

As for the continuation of this study, literature reviews and further experimentation is essential in setting clear parameters on defining "acculturation." Specifically, I plan to videotape an outing with two foreign individuals. This particular filming experiment will allow me to observe and record the different types of components of Japanese culture that will be new, different, and even shocking to the two foreign individuals have experienced throughout their lives. All of the participants will then be required to give feedback on the film. Based on the feedback of the participants, there will ideally be two more rounds of experimentation where the participants follow 7 of the 20 guidelines. To ensure a certain level of data integrity, multiple repeats of experimentation may be required to yield usable data.

References

1. Berry, J.W.: Acculturation as varieties of adaptation. In: Padilla, A.M. (ed.) Acculturation: Theory, Models, and Some New Findings, pp. 9–25. Westview, Boulder (1980)
2. Berry, J.W.: Acculturation: Living successfully in two cultures. International Journal of Intercultural Relations 29, 697–712 (2005)
3. Berry, J.W.: Contexts of acculturation. In: Sam, D.L., Berry, J.W. (eds.) Cambridge Handbook of Acculturation Psychology, pp. 27–42. Cambridge University Press, New York (2006a)
4. Unger, J.B., Reynolds, K., Shakib, S., Spruijt-Metz, D., Sun, P., Johnson, C.A.: Acculturation, physical activity and fast-food consumption among Asian-American and Hispanic adolescents. Journal of Community Health 29, 467–481 (2004)

Construction of Wireless Tablet-PC Classroom
for Computer-Assisted Language Learning in Japan

Yuichi Ono[1], Manabu Ishihara[2], and Mitsuo Yamashiro[3]

[1] University of Tsukuba, Foreign Language Center, Ibaraki, Japan
`ono.yuichi.ga@u.tsukuba.ac.jp`
[2] Oyama National College of Technology, Electrical and Computer Engineering, Tochigi, Japan
`ishihara@oyama-ct.ac.jp`
[3] Ashikaga Institute of Technology, Electrical and Computer Engineering, Tochigi, Japan
`yamashiro@ashitech.ac.jp`

Abstract. This paper describes our project to construct wireless Comput-er-Assisted Language Learning (CALL) classroom under non-wired settings in Japan. In 1990s, so-called CALL system began to be introduced into Japanese educational settings. The system was mainly wired desktop-based system. After two decades, administrators of the system have to decide what to do with the system; replace or abolish. It is needless to say that it costs extremely a lot for replacement. In the current paper, a new possibility is suggested: change into the wireless CALL classroom, where tablet computers will be used under wireless circumstances. We would like to describe out system model and point out some issues on login.

Keywords: computer-assisted language learning (CALL), tablet computer, second language acquisition, log-in, upload and download.

1 Introduction

The desktop-based wired PC room has been a standard model of Comput-er-Assisted Language Learning (CALL) for many years in foreign language teaching. The CALL classroom has provided various solutions to some of the challenges around English as a Japanese Foreign Language (EFL) field; lack of input, fewer opportunities for interaction, less motivated learners to use English, and so on. Tablet PC has some benefits in the foreign language classroom due to its mobile nature with wireless en-vironment; that is, the CALL system can be realized in non-wired traditional class-rooms. This study reports on our construction and touches on some issues to be dis-cussed with a focus on login.

2 Construction Backgrounds

The general desktop-based CALL system that is introduced in Japan is illustrated in Table 1 below, where two basic functions are available; class support function and communication function [1][2].

C. Stephanidis (Ed.): HCII 2014 Posters, Part II, CCIS 435, pp. 128–132, 2014.
© Springer International Publishing Switzerland 2014

Table 1. Standardized desktop-based CALL functions in Japan

Class support function	· Attendance/Absence · Follow up for late comers · On-demand function · Pair-lesson function · Group-lesson function · Automatic delivery / collection of materials · Collection of recorded sounded materials · Analyzer · Materials creation · Portfolio (Materials, achievements)
Communication function	· Monitoring · Inter-come · Modeling · Auto-call · Call-response

Since students' tables and chairs in a wired desktop PC room are physically fixed, the traditional CALL room can be considered as an individual learning model. The wireless tablet-CALL system allows free layout of the desks and chairs depending on the situation or tasks. For example, pair- or group- work with headphone is unnecessary in this new classroom, because they can do it face to face. Similarly, much of collab-orative work in the traditional CALL rooms, which is an essential pedagogy in the field of foreign language teaching, can be carried out face-to-face. For this reason, we can say that the communication and pair- or group- lesson functions are unnecessary for the wireless classrooms.

Then, the issues of choosing a proper tablet PC for pur purpose started to be discussed. The use of iPad is a kind of the trend in Japan recently. It seems that there are four reasons why iPad is so popular in educational settings in Japan; (1)Security, (2)Usability, (3) Management, and (4) Battery [2]. Each of these four reasons is convincing. We need to have one essential viewpoint to consider this issue, however. The point is concerning how tablets were utilized in the Instructional Design (ID) [3]. In our case, one of the purposes of our course is to improve the skill to use the computer for academic purpose. Our decision was Windows 8 tablet PC, with the picture given in Fig.1 and the specification in Table 2 below.

Fig. 1. Question items on impression

Table 2. Details on students' tablet PC

OS	Windows 8
Processor	Intel Atom, Z2760, 1.80 GHz, 2core
Memory	2GB
Storage	64GB
Display	25.7cm(10.1"), HD, Resolution: 1366 x 768
Communications	Broadcom IEEE 802.11a/b/g/n
Battery	2 cells (Li-Polymer) 3540 mAh Video mode : 9 hours
Others	Height : 18.7 mm Width : 167.5 mm Depth : 258.5 mm Weight : 1.26 kg

3   Construction

Next, we constructed basic hardware. In order to control 50 tablet computers in a single classroom, we set up two access points (AP) with different ranges. Servers, UPS, and PoE switches were set up as described in Fig. 2 below. Software were also installed. The packages are composed of by base system, server, web service, database, desktop, applications, and so on. An LMS (Learning Management System) server was also set up. Glexa and CaLabo Bridge were adopted in our study.

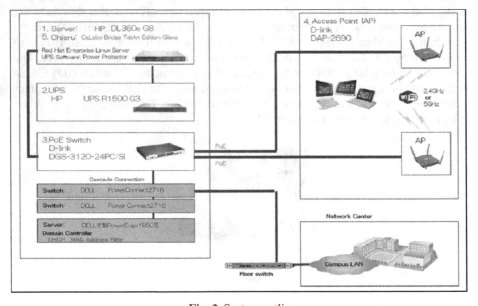

Fig. 2. System outline

4   Research

Needless to say, wireless processing capacity is a big issue for tablet CALL system. Various analysis might be possible to standardize the amount of communications to a comfortable level for learners. As a first preliminary study, we carried out a research on login. The instructor called the instruction of "start logging in" and everybody started to log in at the same time. Here is the table below to show the result of access logs into the LMS server.There are 42 participants in this experiments.

Table 3. Result of access log

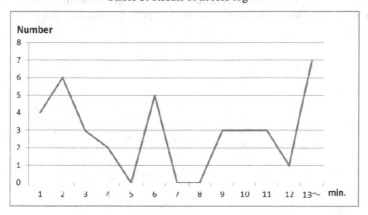

5   Discussion

The graph shows that not all the participants were able to login smoothly. Ac-tually, some participants were not able to do it in 15 minutes and changes their devices. It seems that there seems to be a level for the system to cover the number of tablets. When the amount of communications reaches to the maximum of its capacity, the system rejects being logged in further. Thus, three peaks of the graph appear to indicate its maximum. If correct, we need to try to reduce the chance of the net-related activity as much as possible. In sum, we need to customize the settings of every tablet PC. For this purpose we customize the following points:

- Manual mode of windows update
- Association of media files with Windows Media Player
- Manual mode of security software
- Change the timing of "Sleep" mode

Other reasons for the delay involve unfamiliarity of participants to use tablets; mis-typing of URL. So, we created every icon on the desktop. After these improvements, every tablet was successful in logging in.

There are more issues to be considered; the relationship of traffic with file size, each function of LMS, the use of video and recorded sound, Bluetooth coonection, and so on. We would like to report on these issues for the next opportunity.

References

1. Mikami, A., Nishibori, Y., Nakano, M.: Media use in English Education: from CALL to NBLT, Taishukan, Tokyo (2009)
2. Ono, Y., Ishihara, M., Yamashiro, M.: Construction of tablet-based CALL system and its issues, Research reports, Ashikaga Institute of Technology, No.48 (in press)
3. Keller, J.M.: Motivational design for learning and performance. Springer (2010)

The Role of Affective Factors in Computer-Aided Musical Learning for Non-musician Adults

Saebyul Park, Chung-Kon Shi, and Jeounghoon Kim[*]

Graduate School of Culture Technology (GSCT)
Korea Advanced Institute of Science and Technology, Korea Republic
{Saebyul_Park,chungkon,miru}@kaist.ac.kr

Abstract. The objective of this study is to reveal the relationship between affective factors and musical learning in computer-aided learning situation. Musical learning is a dynamic, integrated process which encompasses cognitive, psychomotor, and affective learning domains. While most studies on computer-aided musical learning tend to highlight cognitive and psychomotor factors, this study focuses on affective factors and experimentally investigates how these factors can influence visual, auditory, and audiovisual learning efficiency. This study contributes to computer-aided musical learning research by focusing on affective factors, which have been previously neglected in this field of study, proposing a new model of computer-aided musical learning systems. Additionally, by adopting affective computing methods to a platform specially optimized to create interactive sound, this study provides a new possibility of quantification of emotional changes when experiencing and learning music.

Keywords: Computer-Aided Affective Learning, Affective Computing, Musical Learning, Facial Recognition, Affective Agent.

1 Introduction

Alongside technological advance, there has been significant progress in the computer-aided instruction (CAI) field for musical learning over the last half-century. There have been numerous attempts to use computers in music education with high interdisciplinary approaches in various aspects of musical learning, which include music theories, listening skills, musical performances, and so on. A Number of studies have found that the use of computer can bring up positive effect on musical learning [1] [2] [3].

Musical learning is a dynamic, integrated process which encompasses cognitive, psychomotor, and affective learning domains. However, musical learning with computers has a tendency of highlighting cognitive and psychomotor factors, overlooking affective factors. This seems to result from the historical flow that behavioral and cognitive psychology have been major roots of music education since the 1960s [4]. In fact, development of computer-aided musical learning systems is more related with

---

[*] Corresponding author.

C. Stephanidis (Ed.): HCII 2014 Posters, Part II, CCIS 435, pp. 133–138, 2014.

the advancement of music "technology", rather than psychological consideration. The fact that CAI in music can be categorized into five generations, depending on the advent of new technology, such as personal computers, MIDI, and the internet [5] shows that CAI in the music education has been focusing more on applying new technology, rather than considering the intrinsic aspect of the human learning process.

This study aims to focus on the affective domain in computer-aided musical learning. The objective of this study is to reveal the relationship between affective factors and musical learning in computer-aided learning situation; specifically, how these factors can influence the learner's visual, auditory learning performances. To achieve this goal, a literature review on affective computing is conducted in order to design a method that can activate the learner's emotional state. Based on previous research, two prototypes of computer-aided music learning systems are developed on Max/MSP. An experiment is devised and carried out on how affective factors can influence auditory, visual and visual-auditory learning.

2   Affective Computing and Learning

An accelerated flow of findings in neuroscience, psychology, and cognitive science point out that the human brain is not a purely cognitive information processing system, but a system in which affective and cognitive functions are inextricably integrated. Over a decade ago, a movement to develop theories and technologies to integrate these two into computerized learning environments. The progress of affective computing area, which is referred as "computing that relates to, arises from or deliberately influences emotions [6]", has enabled computers to recognize the learner's emotional state and provide appropriate feedback. According to Picard [7], the major issues on affective computing and learning are 1) how to build tools and technologies that elicit, sense, communicate, measure, and respond appropriately to affective factors, 2) how to build new models and learning systems that incorporate affect, as a foundation for both new approaches to education and more effective machine learning, and 3) how to developing affectively vocative materials, things-to learn, and learning environments.

Table 1. Overall framework of computer-aided affective learning system studies

Categories	Goals	Methods
Affect Recognition	Development of Tools and Technology	Personal Preference Information
		Facial Expressions
		Physiological Data
		Speech Recognition
		Use of Questionnaire
Emotional Instruction System)	Building Systems and Models	Designing Emotional Agents
		Designing the Interface
	Evocative materials and learning	Designing Emotional Instructional Strategies

Computer-aided affective learning systems aim to enhance learning effectiveness through the activation of an emotional state, which is beneficial to learning [8]. A number of theoretical, technological, and practical studies on computer-aided affective learning systems have been carried in many different ways over the recent years. The studies of such systems can be categorized into two issues: a) how to develop tools to "recognize" the learner's affective state (Affect Recognition), and b) how to develop the system to "respond" to this emotional state to enhance the learning process (Emotional Instruction System). Table 1 shows the overall framework of the researches on learning and affective computing, based on Moridis' review [8].

3   Materials and Methods

3.1   Experimental System Design

Two prototype computer-aided music learning systems are developed: one for affective learning condition and the other for cognitive learning condition. The system is developed using MAX/MSP, developed by Cycling'74, a graphical environment optimized to create sound and multimedia interfaces. While both systems deliver learning sessions by playing sounds and enabling users to interactively play notes on an onscreen instrument, the affective system implements additional features based on affective computing studies.

Figure 1 shows the system diagram of the computer-aided affective musical learning system for the affective condition. The system has two parts: (1) course learning mechanism, which enables learners to access the course database of music theories; (2) affective learning mechanism, which is expected to enhance the learner's emotional states by emotional recognition and feedback.

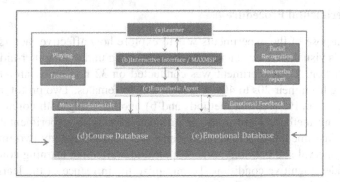

Fig. 1. System diagram for prototype of the computer-aided affective musical learning system

As discussed in chapter 2, a computer-aided affective learning system must be capable of 1) recognizing the learner's emotional states and 2) providing appropriate feedback to enhance the learning process. In order to fulfill these requirements, two different emotional methods were employed: 1) facial recognition and 2) emotional feedback through empathetic agent. For facial recognition, the idea of facial animation parameter normalization introduced by Pandzic and Forchheime [9], which can be used for 3D analysis of facial expressions with a set of facial parameters for expression with average recognition rate up to 91.3 % [10], was applied. With this approach, the implemented learning system can measure a quantified amount of emotional state by calculating ratios of learner's facial features during musical learning. The empathetic agent system is based on Moridis [11], which could be effectively used as emotional feedback to improve emotional state and brainwave activity toward learning. Figure 2 illustrates the results of the proposed and implemented system. (a) Emotional state bar is changed interactively based on learner's facial expression, while (b) the Empathetic agent provides verbal, non-verbal empathetic feedback through (c) Dialog Box during learning session. Learners can also hear the sound by clicking (d) Sound Button and playing an (e) Instrument. On the instrument, visual information is provided with different colors of the keys depending on the sound learners are currently studying.

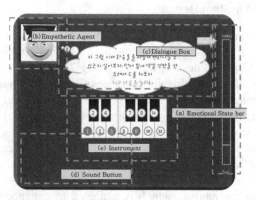

Fig. 2. System Interface

3.2   Experimental Procedure

The main purpose of the experiments was to explore how affective factors can influence learner's visual, auditory and audiovisual learning under computer-aided musical learning situation. The experiment was conducted on 32 non-musician adult participants ranging from their 20s to 40s, 17 males and 15 females. Two prototype systems, a) one using cognitive learning methods and b) another using both cognitive and affective learning methods were used for musical learning as experimental materials. During the experimental sessions, participants were asked to study two music theory chapters on interval and harmony: one chapter under affective learning condition, and the other under cognitive condition. To minimize the influence of the learning topics and tasks, participants were divided into 2 groups; 1) 'Group A' studied the topic 'interval' under affective conditions and the topic 'harmony' under cognitive conditions, and 2) 'Group B' studied the same topics under opposite conditions.

After studying for thirty minutes, participants were asked to solve tasks based on the learning materials studied during experimental session. For the tasks, participants were asked to decide which interval or chords they were looking (visual) or listening (auditory), and both looking and listening (audiovisual). To assess the effect of affective learning factors, the tasks were given in three different types. For the visual tasks, participants were not allowed to listen to the sound of the instruments, but could "see" the keys of piano to decide the answer. For the auditory test, participants couldn't see the keys, while they could hear sound. Lastly, for audiovisual, participants could both hear and see the information to decide the answer. Each task was composed of 5 questions, 15 in total.

3.3   Results

Figure 3 illustrates the descriptive statistics of participant task scores of visual, auditory, and audiovisual tasks under affective and cognitive conditions. Accuracy is highest when participants solved the task under audiovisual conditions, and lowest when only auditory information was provided.

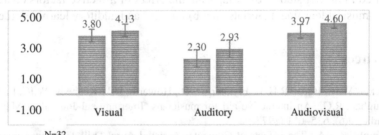

N=32

Task Condition	Average		Standard deviation		t-value	p-value
	Cognitive	Affective	Cognitive	Affective		
Visual	3.80	4.13	0.83	0.76	-.1589	.117
Auditory	2.30	2.93	1.16	1.06	-.2169	.034*
audiovisual	3.97	4.28	1.08	0.66	-.2692	.009*

*p<0.05

Fig. 3. Result of descriptive statistics and T-test analysis

A T-test between the scores of cognitive and affective tasks has been conducted on the three different types of study: visual, auditory, and audiovisual studies. Figure 4 summarizes the task accuracy results. In auditory and audiovisual tasks, affective learning models exhibit higher scores, and the difference is statistically significant. However, visual tasks fail to show significance. This result suggests that affective factors might be more related with auditory learning than visual learning, showing that affective factors might have a different influence level on visual, auditory learning efficiency during studying music.

4   Conclusion and Discussion

This study contributes to computer-aided musical learning research by showing the positive effects of affective factors, which have been neglected by most studies, and thereby highlighting the importance of them. The new model of computer-aided affective musical learning systems proposed in this study can provide learners an enhanced learning experience with greater learning efficiency. Additionally, by adopting affective computing methods to a platform specially optimized to create interactive sound and multimedia, this study provides a new possibility of quantification of emotional changes when especially experiencing music. We expect that this type of affective computing methods can be applied to many fields of studies: not limited to musical learning, but also musical expression and performances.

However, a challenging issue yet remains, regarding the true role of affective factors in learning. The result that affective factors can enhance auditory musical learning effectiveness has two possible explanations: 1) as auditory learning processes are not widely used compared to visual learning, affective factors might enhance learning experience when using relatively unfamiliar media, and 2) auditory learning processes benefitted from affective factors due to the audial nature of music. This question is to be verified in further studies by comparing the effect of affective factors on a) musical and non-musical learning materials, and b) musical and auditory learning processes.

References

1. Tucker, W.H., Bates, R.H.T., Frykberg, S.D., Howarth, R.J., Kennedy, W.K., Lamb, M.R., Vaughan, R.G.: An interactive aid for musicians. International Journal of Man-Machine Studies 9(6), 635–651 (1977)
2. Humphries, J.A.: The Effects of Computer-Assisted Aural Drill Time on Achievement in Musical Interval Identification. Journal of Computer-Based Instruction 6(3), 91–98 (1980)
3. Kulik, C.L.C., Kulik, J.A.: Effectiveness of computer-based instruction: An updated analysis. Computers in Human Behavior 7(1), 75–94 (1991)
4. Taetle, L., Cutietta, R.: Learning theories as roots of current musical practice and research. In: The New Handbook of Research on Music Teaching and Learning, pp. 279–298 (2002)
5. Peters, G.: Music Software and Emerging Technology. Music Educators Journal 79(3), 22–25+63 (1992)
6. Picard, R.: Affective computing. MIT Press, Cambridge (1997)
7. Picard, R.W., Papert, S., Bender, W., Blumberg, B., Breazeal, C., Cavallo, D., Strohecker, C.: Affective learning—a manifesto. BT Technology Journal 22(4), 253–269 (2004)
8. Moridis, C.N., Economides, A.A.: Toward computer-aided affective learning systems: A literature review. Journal of Educational Computing Research 39(4), 313–337 (2008)
9. Pandzic, I.S., Forchheimer, R.: MPEG-4 facial animation. The standard, implementation and applications. John Wiley&Sons, Chichester (2002)
10. Soyel, H., Demirel, H.: Facial expression recognition using 3D facial feature distances. In: Kamel, M.S., Campilho, A. (eds.) ICIAR 2007. LNCS, vol. 4633, pp. 831–838. Springer, Heidelberg (2007)
11. Moridis, C., Economides, A.: Affective Learning: Empathetic Agents with Emotional Facial and Tone of Voice Expressions. IEEE Transactions on Affective Computing 3(3), 260–272 (2012)

When Students Benefit from Analyzing Their Inquiry

Margus Pedaste and Külli Kori

University of Tartu, Salme 1a, 50103 Tartu, Estonia
{margus.pedaste,kulli.kori}@ut.ee

Abstract. There is a need to find out how to enhance the effect of a generally successful inquiry approach in schools. In our study, we hypothesized that supporting students' reflection could have a positive effect on their general inquiry knowledge, transformative inquiry skills, and domain-related knowledge. A scenario-based complex technology-enhanced learning environment called Science Created by You was used by 54 students (age, 14–18 years). The results demonstrated that students' general inquiry knowledge, transformative inquiry skills, and domain-related knowledge all improved statistically significantly; however, no changes were found in reflective activities—in analyzing inquiry, in assessing the value of analysis, and in considering alternative solutions. Indeed, students' domain-related skills were associated with reflection. The students with a higher level of knowledge analyzed their inquiry more often, and they considered more often alternative solutions of inquiry. No associations were found between domain-related knowledge and inquiry knowledge or skills.

Keywords: domain knowledge, inquiry learning, reflection, technology-enhanced learning environments.

1 Introduction

Inquiry learning is more effective than many other "traditional" learning approaches. Alfieri, Brooks, Aldrich, and Tenenbaum [1] have demonstrated in a meta-analysis that inquiry has a mean effect size of 0.30 against other forms of instruction (e.g., direct instruction or unassisted discovery). Furtak, Seidel, Iverson, and Briggs [2] found in their meta-analysis that the effect size could even be 0.50 in favor of the inquiry approach over traditional instruction. However, despite the proven value of inquiry, it is not often widely applied in schools, and therefore, there is a need to find out how to enhance the role of inquiry in teachers' everyday practice.

In our study, we hypothesized that supporting students' reflection in a complex technology-enhanced learning environment could have a positive effect on their general inquiry knowledge [3], transformative inquiry skills [4], and domain-related knowledge. If it would be so, then it is an important sign to the teacher to apply inquiry more often.

Reflection is a cognitive process of learning from the learner's own experience [5], and it supports students in analyzing their learning experience in order to change their

C. Stephanidis (Ed.): HCII 2014 Posters, Part II, CCIS 435, pp. 139–144, 2014.
© Springer International Publishing Switzerland 2014

behavior during the learning process or restructuring of knowledge structures if needed. In the context of science education, it is important that reflection could support inconsistencies between the student's initial understanding and scientific explanations [6]. However, the associations could even be two-directional. Baird and White [7] and Davis [8] showed that inquiry learning also improves reflection skills.

In order to find the relations between the level and improvement of reflective activities, general inquiry knowledge, transformative inquiry skills, and domain-related knowledge, a specific study was conducted in the SCY-Lab using a "learning mission" in ecology. SCY-Lab (http://www.scy-net.eu/) is a technology-enhanced learning environment designed for design-based inquiry learning through creating "products" [9,10]. Three research questions were formulated:

1. To what extent do students' general inquiry knowledge, transformative inquiry skills, and domain-related knowledge improve in using the complex technology-enhanced learning environment SCY-Lab?
2. What kind of changes appear in students' reflective activities if they practice reflection during inquiry in the SCY-Lab?
3. How can the level of reflective activities be associated with students' general inquiry knowledge, transformative inquiry skills, and domain-related knowledge?

2   Methods

Four voluntary teachers from four different schools asked their students (age, 14–18 years) to participate in the study. They all had to fill in a prequestionnaire and post-questionnaire that contained four parts. First, students' general inquiry knowledge was evaluated by two types of questions: students had to sequence the stages of inquiry and to explain why each of the stages is important in the inquiry process. Second, students had to formulate two research questions, hypotheses, and inferences. Research questions and hypotheses were formed on the basis of a story, and inferences were made on the basis of a figure presenting results of a study. The level of general inquiry knowledge and transformative inquiry skills was assessed according to a scale developed by Pedaste and Sarapuu [11]. Third, students' domain-related knowledge was assessed by asking two open-ended questions about why an ecosystem needs light and what the importance of photosynthesis is (questions related to the topic discovered in the SCY-Lab). In both cases, every correct aspect mentioned in the student's answer increased the final score. Fourth, students' reflective activities were described through three questions: *How often did you analyze your learning process? How important is analysis of the inquiry process and why? Will you do something differently next time in the inquiry process, and what would it be?*

The learning process was conducted in a scenario-based complex technology-enhanced learning environment Science Created by You (SCY) [9]. In this learning environment, a complex "mission" of learning ecological principles was completed. On this "mission," students combined hands-on data collection and working in the

Internet-based SCY-Lab learning environment. In the SCY ECO mission, students are asked to solve four problems [10]. In the current study, they had to solve only the problem to discover the role of light in the level on photosynthesis. In their learning process, students formulated research questions and hypotheses, planned and conducted an experiment, collected and analyzed data, and made inferences in order to draw conclusions. During this process, they were asked to reflect their learning by asking supportive questions as suggested by Kori et al. [6] and Runnel et al. [12]. They were asked to discuss their experiences of the whole inquiry cycle, to describe limitations of their inferences, and to explain what in their learning process should be done next time in the same/different way.

Only results of the students who completed both prequestionnaires and postquestionnaires were included to the analysis of the current study. In the cases where some students did not complete all four parts of the questionnaire, only the incomplete parts were excluded. In total, 54 students were involved in the analyses. Students' improvement in general inquiry knowledge, transformative inquiry skills, and domain-related knowledge was analyzed by t test, whereas their answers were distributed normally. The changes in categorical variables about reflective activities (distribution of categories before and after intervention) were tested with chi-square tests that were also used for finding associations of reflective activities with the level and changes of inquiry knowledge, inquiry skills, and domain-related knowledge. In this case, median split was used to differentiate the students who had a higher or lower level or change in knowledge or skills in comparison with the median.

3   Results and Discussion

According to the first research question of the study, students' improvement in general inquiry knowledge, transformative inquiry skills, and domain-related knowledge was clarified. t test results showed that all these improved statistically significantly in using the technology-enhanced learning environment SCY-Lab and, in particular, the ECO mission (Table 1).

Table 1. Comparison of students' general inquiry knowledge, transformative inquiry skills, and domain-related knowledge in the prequestionnaires and postquestionnaires.

Knowledge/skill (maximum score)	Prequestionnaire		Postquestionnaire		t test	p value
	Mean	St. Dev.	Mean	St. Dev.		
General inquiry knowledge (35)	27.3	3.8	30.3	2.9	−6.58	<0.01
Transformative inquiry skills (46)	24.6	9.4	30.6	8.2	−8.27	<0.01
Domain-related knowledge (8)	2.6	1.4	3.5	1.4	−6.35	<0.01

No statistically significant changes were found in students' reflective activities as a result of using SCY-Lab. Thus, the answer to the second research question is that learning in SCY-Lab does not initiate changes in students' reflective activities. The reason for this could be that reflection skills were not specifically supported in the learning environment. Reflective questions only guided students in analyzing their inquiry process. However, it was still possible to discover how reflective activities could be associated with students' knowledge and skills.

Our third research question was about the relations between the level of reflection activities, knowledge, and skills. The outcomes of chi-square analysis showed that the characteristics of reflection do not associate statistically significantly with the general inquiry knowledge and transformative inquiry skills. However, interesting associations were found with domain-related knowledge. The students who had lower knowledge gain would do something differently next time in the inquiry process ($\chi^2 = 4.4$, $p < 0.05$). It could show that reflective activities guided students toward understanding about their difficulties—if their knowledge gain was lower than average, then they started to think with higher probability on alternative approaches for learning.

It was also found that the students with a higher level of domain-related knowledge are more often analyzing their inquiry activities (in prequestionnaire, $\chi^2 = 7.8$, $p < 0.05$; in postquestionnaire, $\chi^2 = 5.8$, $p = 0.056$) and are most likely considering changes needed in their inquiry ($\chi^2 = 3.9$, $p < 0.05$). A possible explanation here is that a particular level of domain-related knowledge is needed in order to activate students' reflective thinking. This finding is in accordance with the studies of Pedaste and Sarapuu [13,14], who found that in acquiring problem solving skills in complex Web-based learning environments, students should be divided into groups and supported according to their personal needs in order to achieve maximum improvement. They detected five different groups, and two of them applied different learning strategies but were both successful without any support, whereas the three other groups all needed different types of cognitive or metacognitive support. In the context of supporting reflection for enhancing inquiry learning, further studies are needed to specify effective guidance strategies.

4   Conclusion

In the current study, we hypothesized that supporting students' reflection could have a positive effect on their general inquiry knowledge, transformative inquiry skills, and domain-related knowledge. However, we found that at least in complex technology-enhanced learning environments, such as the SCY-Lab, a higher level of reflection can be associated only with domain-related knowledge, but not with general inquiry knowledge or transformative inquiry skills. This finding is important in designing learning processes and students' support in complex learning environments. According to our findings, we recommend first to focus on developing reflection skills in the context of gaining domain-related knowledge. The students with a higher level of knowledge in pretests and posttests analyzed their inquiry more often than the others, and the students with a higher level of domain-related knowledge in the end of the learning processes considered more often alternative solutions of inquiry. However, even in this case, the students with a higher level of domain-related knowledge will benefit more. It could be hypothesized that students' general inquiry knowledge and transformative inquiry skills would be enhanced in use of reflection more if the reflective skills and domain-related knowledge are already improved to a specific level. This would be an interesting topic of further studies.

Acknowledgments. The SCY ECO mission was developed in the context of the SCY project, which was funded by the European Union (EU) under the Information and Communication Technologies theme of the 7th Framework Programme for R&D (grant agreement 212814). This document does not represent the opinion of the EU, and the EU is not responsible for any use that might be made of its content. We would like to acknowledge the SCY project members as well as teachers and students who participated in the study for their contributions.

References

1. Alfieri, L., Brooks, P.J., Aldrich, N.J., Tenenbaum, H.R.: Does discovery-based instruction enhance learning? Journal of Educational Psychology 103, 1–18 (2011), doi:10.1037/a0021017
2. Furtak, E.M., Seidel, T., Iverson, H., Briggs, D.C.: Experimental and quasi-experimental studies of inquiry-based science teaching. Review of Educational Research 82, 300–329 (2012), doi:10.3102/0034654312457206
3. Mäeots, M., Pedaste, M.: The role of general inquiry knowledge in enhancing students' transformative inquiry processes in a Web-based learning environment. Journal of Baltic Science Education 13(1), 19–31 (2014)
4. De Jong, T., Njoo, M.: Learning and instruction with computer simulations: Learning processes involved. In: de Corte, E., Linn, M., Mandl, H., Verschaffel, L. (eds.) Computer-Based Learning Environments and Problem Solving, pp. 411–429. Springer, Berlin (1992)
5. Moon, J.A.: A Handbook of Reflective and Experiential Learning: Theory and Practice. Routledge Falmer, London (2004)
6. Kori, K., Pedaste, M., Leijen, Ä., Mäeots, M.: Supporting reflection in technology-enhanced learning. Educational Research Review 11, 45–55 (2014)
7. Baird, J.R., White, R.T.: Metacognitive strategies in the classroom. In: Treagust, D.F., Duit, R., Fraser, B.J. (eds.) Improving Teaching and Learning in Science and Mathematics, pp. 190–200. Teachers College Press, New York (1996)
8. Davis, E.A.: Prompting middle school science students for productive reflection: Generic and directed prompts. The Journal of the Learning Sciences 12, 91–142 (2003)
9. de Jong, T., Weinberger, A., Girault, I., Kluge, A., Lazonder, A.W., Pedaste, M., Ludvigsen, S., Ney, M., Wasson, B., Wichmann, A., Geraedts, C., Giemza, A., Hovardas, A., Julien, R., van Joolingen, W.R., Lejeune, A., Manoli, C., Matteman, Y., Sarapuu, T., Verkade, A., Vold, V., Wanders, B., Zacharia, Z.C.: Using scenarios to design complex technology-enhanced learning environments. Educational Technology Research & Development 60(5), 883–901 (2012)
10. Pedaste, M., de Jong, T., Sarapuu, T., Piksööt, J., van Joolingen, W.R., Giemza, A.: Investigating ecosystems as a blended learning experience. Science 340(6140), 1537–1538 (2013)

11. Pedaste, M., Sarapuu, T.: Uurimuslike oskuste kujundamine ja hindamine. In: Koppel, L. (Toim.) GüMnaasiumi Valdkonnaraamat Loodusained. Bioloogia, pp. 68–81. Riiklik Eksami- ja Kvalifikatsioonikeskus, Tallinn (2012)
12. Runnel, M.I., Pedaste, M., Leijen, Ä.: Model for guiding reflection in the context of inquiry-based science education. Journal of Baltic Science Education 12(1), 107–118 (2013)
13. Pedaste, M., Sarapuu, T.: Developing an effective support system for inquiry learning in a Web-based environment. Journal of Computer Assisted Learning 22(1), 47–62 (2006)
14. Pedaste, M., Sarapuu, T.: The factors influencing the outcome of solving story-problems in a Web-based learning environment. Interactive Learning Environments 14(2), 153–176 (2006)

Self-educate Function Added on Gakuzai System

Haruya Shiba[1], Kousei Ueta[1], Yoshino Ohishi[1], Atuya Takedani[1], Takahiko Mendori[2], Yusuke Nishiuchi[1], Masanobu Yoshida[1], Hironobu Satoh, and Takumi Yamaguchi[1]

[1] Dept. of Electrical Engineering and Information Science,
Kochi National College of Technology, 200-1 Monobe-Otsu, Nankoku-city, Kochi, Japan
{e4702,e4707}@gm.kochi-ct.jp,
{shiba,nishiuchi,myoshida,satoh,yama}@ee.kochi-ct.ac.jp
[2] School of Information, Kochi University of Technology,
185 Miyanokuchi, Tosayamda, Kami-city, Kochi, Japan
mendori.takahiko@kochi-tech.ac.jp

Abstract. We give the electronic textbook (e-textbook) that the student can edit. When the student understands hearing the teacher's explanation, leaving only an important term, and obscuring the part where it explains it on the e-textbook, they remakes the textbook into them notebook. Because work to copy the content of the blackboard disappears and the teacher's explanation can be heard enough, the student can be expected to acquire knowledge in a short time. The WEB application that remakes the e-textbook into the notebook has developed. Now added the function of self-study work at home. The function makes problem-solving exercise automatically with reduced e-textbook content. The marked up items on e-textbook collect for selector that use in exercise. The student keep trying problem-solving exercise by new problem. The function provides learning opportunities for self-study work.

Keywords: ICT-based learning, e-textbook, reduction edit, learning style.

1 Introduction

In recent years, it becomes the spread of the portable information device, and familiar the computer book. There is a project that starts introducing the electronic equipment and the computer book into school lessons [1] and evaluate the educational effect [2], [3]. However, it is difficult to dramatic improve the education effect only by learning environment computerization. It is thought that a new education method to obtain a high education effect and a new learning method are needed.

In Japanese classrooms, teacher talks one-sidedly and write the aid of explanatory notes on blackboard that is similar to the content of the textbook. The students just listen to them and copy the content that the teacher wrote on the blackboard. The copied information has had a student, though work to copy it during the lesson should be useless in time and the labor, and be reduced.

We give the electronic textbook (e-textbook) that the student can edit. When the student understood hearing the teacher's explanation, leaving only an important term,

C. Stephanidis (Ed.): HCII 2014 Posters, Part II, CCIS 435, pp. 145–149, 2014.

hide the understood part on the e-textbook. The student remakes the textbook into them notebook. Because work to copy the content of the blackboard deletes and the teacher's explanation can be heard enough, the student can be expected to acquire knowledge in a short time. The e-textbook is rewritten by an electronic operation. The part that understood and became needless is not deleted but is only obscured. Therefore, even degrees of the cancellation and the edit of work how many can be done.

In the classrooms, an important word and the equation will be able to markup in the electronically. They can be easily achieved to make the wordbook by extract the markup word, and to make the problem-solving exercise preparing void sentences of the markup term. These functions might be useful so that the student may review or homework. When the learning method that uses the electronic textbook is used, it will be supported to be able to take note more easily than the current, and to memorization study and to solving the problem exercise. As a result, the education might be improved.

The WEB application that remakes the e-textbook into the notebook has developed. We call this framework "Gakuzai system". "Gakuzai" is a compound word of two Japanese words. The word of "gaku" same as "manabi", manabi means all the learning processes until knowledge is acquired and the word of "zai" is the material. The Gakuzai system offers the environment to support all process of study from a class by teacher to homework by student. This paper proposes a suitable next generation learning method in the e-textbook generation, and aims at system preparation that doesn't depend on Operating System and the browser.

2   Gakuzai System Overview

The Gakuzai system should have the following functions.

1. The e- textbook should be able to edit quickly during the lesson.
   (a) Function that the unnecessary part is hidden or replaced a short word.
   (b) Function that the markup an important word (text color, under line, bold-faced type, highlight).
2. The content of 1) must be reproduced in next classroom time.
3. The content of 1)   is required to be able to learn at home.
4. Two or more learners are able to edit jointly.
5. The collaborative learning that shares the edit result among learners.

All processes from individual study to the group study can be supported by these functions. The EPUB and the PDF are formats of a general computer book, which doesn't adopt, though there depends on software/hardware for specific inspection large, number of degrees of freedom of customizing low. We adopted HTML from depended on Operating System and the devices low, customized easy.

The server computer was prepared to distribute the e-textbooks and to keep the edited data. The Gakuzai system was constructed by using the PHP language and JavaScript on this server computer. Now implemented functions are 1st and 2nd function of the Gakuzai system in above.

2.1   Classroom Phase

Sentences that could be understood enough are hidden on the e-textbook or replaced by a short key word. The e-textbook makes is changed the formulary or the wordbook by this function. To explain study that uses the Gkuzai system, Kirchhoff's current law is made an example. [Text from Wikipedia: Kirchhoff's current law, (2014)]

```
This law is also called Kirchhoff's first law, Kir-
chhoff's point rule, or Kirchhoff's junction rule (or
nodal rule).
    The principle of conservation of electric charge im-
plies that:
    At any node (junction) in an electrical circuit,
the sum of currents flowing into that node is equal to
the sum of currents flowing out of that node, or:
    The algebraic sum of currents in a network of conduc-
tors meeting at a point is zero.
Recalling that current is a signed (positive or nega-
tive) quantity reflecting direction towards or away
from a node, this principle can be stated as:
```

$$\sum_{k=1}^{n} I_k = 0$$

```
n is the total number of branches with currents flowing
towards or away from the node.
```

Only a formula summation of I is left because the chapter of the explanation will only have to record only the name and the expression of the law that becomes not necessary for the student who understood this content, and the rest will be concealed.

2.2   Home Study Phase

If the under line is pulled during the lesson importantly, - in the example above, the under line has already pulled -, the exercise that removes this term from the explanation can be made from the automatic operation. The automatic generated exercise can help the self-learning. Therefore, the education effect can be expected to rise.

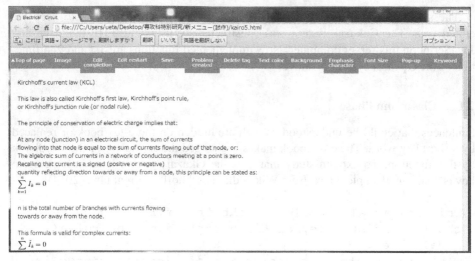

Fig. 1. The e-textbook edits form in Gakuzai sytem. The content of the textbook is displayed left side. User selects the strings for edit on this screen and edits with the top menu.

It responds to the fact of adding words because the replacement of the character only doesn't shorten the long one. Moreover, the image can be added same as words though the Gakuzai system can use taking the note with traditional style.

It did not implement the function to be used for self-learning. The results are shown below was prototyped a function of automatically generating the problem.

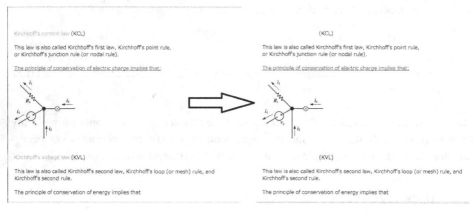

Fig. 2. Was withdrawn terms that you edited in class. This form can support the rote learning. State after editing (left). After creating a practice exercise (right).

This function was implemented as the ability to create automatic a practice question using the e-book that individuals are editing. Is used to create a practice question of a specific color text after editing. The rote learning, can be performed by pressing the button"creating problem". Text of a specific color is converted to white.

Unlike the above-mentioned functions, we implemented the ability to automatically create alternative practice exercise in terms that are registered with pop-up function. The contents of the statement blowoff with the input string that is chosen by pop-up function is stored in the database by pressing the pop-up Add button. How to create a Practice question, select a question from the words that are stored in the database. Then, the random arrangement can be extracted three words and correct answers. Practice question is changed each time you make an update.

3   Conclusions and Future Work

It was possible to implement the rote learning support functions and a practice question creation function. Therefore, iterative learning that could not be performed conventional has become supportable. We proposed a new education / learning method with the e-textbook. The WEB application software wear to practice this method was developed. Using this system practices the classroom, and the education effect will be evaluated in the future.

Acknowledgments. This study was supported by JSPS KAKENHI Grant Number 25330431 and 24501236.

References

1. Japan Ministry of Internal Affairs and Communications: Future School Promotion Research Society
2. http://www.soumu.go.jp/main_sosiki/joho_tsusin/eng/Releases/Telecommunications/110720_a.html
3. Rockinson-Szapkiw, A.J., Courduff, J., et al.: Electronic versus traditional print textbooks: A comparison study on the influence of university student's learning. Computers & Education 63, 259–266 (2013)
4. Matsuuchi, N., Nishiuchi, Y., et al.: TERAKOYA Learning System Linking Multipoint Remote Users for Supplementary Lessons. The Journal of Information and Systems in Education 9, 35–44 (2011)
5. Shiba, H., Ueta, K., Ohishi, Y., Mendori, T., Nishiuchi, Y., Yoshida, M., Satoh, H., Yamatuchi, T.: Implementation of a Learning Style by E-Textbook Contents Reduction Processing. In: Stephanidis, C. (ed.) HCII 2013, Part II. CCIS, vol. 374, pp. 94–97. Springer, Heidelberg (2013)

Developing an Interactive Learning Environment with Kinect

Serdar Şimşek[1,2] and Pınar Onay Durdu[2]

[1] NETAS Telecommunication Company,
34912, Kurtkoy, Pendik, Istanbul, Turkey
ssimsek@outlook.com
[2] Human Computer Interaction Research Laboratory,
Kocaeli University, Izmit, Kocaeli, Turkey
pinar.onaydurdu@kocaeli.edu.tr

Abstract. The use of interactive white boards has become more and more popular in educational settings. Despite their superior features to traditional counterparts, it is known that they are very expensive. Therefore, in this study, a lower cost interactive whiteboard application is developed by using Microsoft's Kinect which provides a natural interaction mechanism that eliminates the need of various interaction devices. However it has some problems in transforming the real world coordinates into virtual environment in addition to its robustness problem in detection and recognition. A solution is developed for fixing the transformation of the coordinates and robustness of the image processing issues and implemented to provide a lower cost interactive whiteboard in this research.

Keywords: Interactive whiteboard, interactive learning environment, Kinect.

1 Introduction

Interactive whiteboards (IWB) are interactive tools that are begun to be used widely in educational settings currently. This technology gained popularity based on its promising benefits to the quality of education [1-2]. According to the data of Decision Tree Consulting, IWB technology had one billion dollar part of the market at 2008 [3].

IWBs can be defined as touch-sensitive boards operated through a computer with the aid of digital overhead projectors [4]. They commonly include four main components; computers, digital projectors, an electronic board and a software package that is compatible with the hardware [5]. Interaction can be provided with different ways such as resistive, electromagnetic, capacitive, ultrasonic and optical based technologies [6]. In addition, these different techniques are mainly divided in two categories as active marker or a passive marker based on the signal source. Active markers are the source of signals and have better stability while passive markers are reflectors and they are unstable for signal detection. The former is mostly expensive while the latter has a low cost [7].

C. Stephanidis (Ed.): HCII 2014 Posters, Part II, CCIS 435, pp. 150–155, 2014.

Most of the commercial IWBs are controlled by the use of pen, finger, stylus or other device. However, new techniques are developed for the interaction such as Natural Interaction. Natural Interaction can be defined as the capture of body movements or sounds by natural interaction devices such as Kinect or Wavi X-tion in order to interact with computers [8]. This can be adapted to the IWB domain easily.

Recently, there are some studies that implemented Kinect in educational environments. Avancini [9] emulated an IWB using Kinect in his study. He applied nine point calibration technique for matching hand and mouse coordinates and enhanced the hand detection with finger detection.   Zhang et al. [5] proposed a low-cost IWB by the use of Kinect by applying machine vision theory with infrared scan technology by using an infrared LED pen. Cheong et al [10] developed a multi-touch IWB and its teaching module. Smorkalov et al [11] used Kinect to provide interaction with a virtual IWB found in an educational 3D virtual environment. Özcelik and Sengul [12] used Kinect for the interaction in a 3D virtual learning environment for the teaching of physics concept.

This paper presents an interactive learning environment that aimed to gather the benefits of enhanced learning opportunities provided by natural interaction [12]. The proposed system consists of three parts. These are IWB hardware, IWB software and interactive learning application (ILA).

2   The Proposed IWB

The interactive learning environment proposed in this study consists of three components. IWB hardware part was developed with the use of Kinect. IWB software was developed for the detection of human body and recognition of hand for matching the real world hand coordinates with the virtual mouse coordinates. Finally ILA software was developed for the organization and presentation of the educational materials.

2.1   IWB Hardware

IWB hardware of the proposed system depends on the use of Kinect. It is a motion sensing input device to control and interact with a computer through a natural user interface using gestures and spoken commands [13]. Kinect environment was chosen since it had an easy setup and could be controlled the IWB without the need of any other devices like a pen, mouse or gloves.

Kinect consists of four main components. The depth sensor consists of an infrared laser projector combined with a monochrome CMOS sensor. Kinect applications commonly depend on the passive markers for capturing an object or a moving person with depth sensor which can emit and receive infrared light simultaneously. The sensing range of this sensor is adjustable and Kinect software is capable of automatically calibrating the sensor. Kinect also includes a regular 8 bit VGA camera, multi-array microphone for sound recognition and motorized tilt for positioning.

For the effective use of Kinect, practical ranging limit is 1.2–3.5 m distance while using it in roughly 6 m2 area. The horizontal field of the Kinect sensor at the minimum viewing distance of ~0.8 m and the vertical field is ~63 cm [13].

2.2   IWB Software

Software was developed to interpret Kinect sensor data for real and virtual coordinates matching in Java. This software detects the human body and recognizes the human hand. Afterwards it provides to control mouse events with hand in front of the projected display. This software provides solutions to below issues;

- Matching the real world hand coordinates with virtual mouse coordinates.
- Stabilization of unstable hand coordinates.
- Handling mouse events with hand.
- Incapability of Kinect to detect the turn of the user.

Matching Algorithm. Kinect provides 3D virtual coordinates of the hand. These coordinates can be used to match the hand movements with mouse movements. In order to do this matching a coordinate transformation algorithm was designed. This algorithm uses four point touch calibration to find the projected display's origination point (O2) and bounds (P1, P2, P3) as in Figure 1. Than human hand coordinates were converted to the mouse coordinates with the Equations 1 and 2.

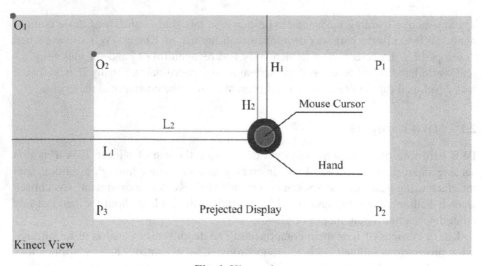

Fig. 1. Kinect view

CurrentMouseX = (((joint(hand).position.depth.x – O2.X) / (P1.X-O2.X)))* ProjectionArea.WIDTH(Virtual World);   (1)

CurrentMouseY = (((joint(hand).position.depth.y - O2.Y) / (P2.Y-O2.Y)))* ProjectionArea.HEIGHT(Virtual World);   (2)

After the matching, it was possible to move the mouse cursor wherever on the projected display. Least squares (LS) technique was applied to prevent the random movement of the cursor in the projected display. With this technique hand coordinates are used. These coordinates are taken from the hand click period.

Handling Mouse Events. Another issue to be solved was enabling mouse click events by hand. Therefore, another algorithm was developed as follows;

```
begin
  repeat
    StoredDepth := getZfromCalibration();
    CurrentDepth := joint(hand).depth.z;
    if CurrentDepth < StoredDepth
    then
      if MouseDown := 1;
      then
        MouseDown := 0;
        ApplyLS();
        RepositionMouse();
        Click();
    else
      MouseDown := 1;
      StoreCoordinateForLS();
  until program end;
end.
```

Turn Around Detection. Kinect cannot recognize the turn of the user. When the user turns in front of the device, the current position of hands are missed. Kinect confuses the left and right hand positions. In order to overcome this, a face tracking mechanism via OpenCV was applied to the system. When face tracking fails, this means a turnaround is occurred and left and right hand positions are switched.

2.3   Interactive Learning Application (ILA)

The final part of the learning environment is interactive learning application. The application was written with the Actionscript 3.0 on Adobe AIR® platform. Actionscript is a programming language to develop interactive application while Adobe AIR® provides to develop cross platform applications

ILA provides a solution for the lecturers to manage and handle their learning materials such as images, videos, flash animations, 3D objects, power point presentations, PDF documents and access to the YouTube and Flickr. It provides a direct access to all of these materials over this environment as can be seen in Figure 2.

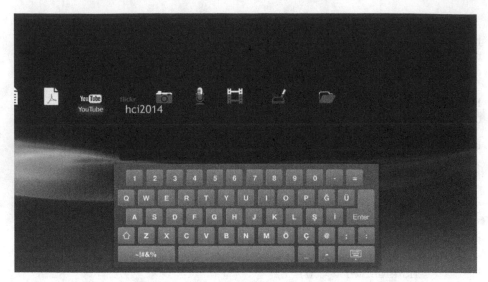

Fig. 2. ILA application

2.4   Cost of the Proposed Solution

In order to set up this proposed interactive learning environment three hardware components are needed. These are a projector, standard computer and a Kinect senor. Considering that a projector costs about 400 $, a standard computer costs about 600 $ and a Kinect sensor costs about 80 $, the total hardware cost of the proposed system is approximately 1080 $ which is about half the price of the commercial IWBs.

3   Conclusion

In this paper, an interactive learning environment developed with Kinect was proposed. Some approaches were offered to solve critical Kinect restrictions. The purpose of this system can be listed as low cost, natural interaction mechanism and ease of use.

However, environment still needs some enhancements such as enabling multi touch. In addition, usability evaluation of this learning environment was not conducted. Therefore, as future works these enhancements as well as the usability assessment of the system is planned to be done.

References

1. BECTA.: What the research says about Interactive Whiteboards (2003),
   http://dera.ioe.ac.uk/5318/1/wtrs_whiteboards.pdf
2. Smith, H.J., Higgins, S., Wall, K., Miller, J.: Interactive whiteboards: boon or bandwagon? A critical review of the literature. Journal of Computer Assisted Learning 21(2), 91–101 (2005)

3. Education   Week,   http://www.edweek.org/dd/articles/2007/09/12/ 02board.h01.html
4. Saltan, F., Arslan, K.: A new teacher tool, interactive white boards: A meta-analysis. In: Proceedings of Society for Information Technology & Teacher Education International Conference. AACE, Charleston (2009)
5. Zhang, S., He, W., Yu, Q., Zheng, X.: Low-cost interactive whiteboard using the Kinect. In: International Conference on Image Analysis and Signal Processing (IASP), pp. 1–5 (2012)
6. Simsek, S., Onay Durdu, P.: Interactive Learning Environment with Whiteboard Technology. In: Proceedings of the 5th International Computer & Instructional Technologies Symposium, pp. 1137–1143 (2011)
7. Lee, W.C., Merino-Schettino, D.A., López-Martínez, I., Posada-Gómez, R., Juárez-Martínez, U.: Virtual Board: A low cost Multi Touch Human Computer Interaction System. Procedia Technology 3, 178–186 (2012)
8. OpenNI, http://en.wikipedia.org/wiki/OpenNI
9. Avancini, M.: Using Kinect to emulate an interactive whiteboard. Unpublished Dissertation (2012)
10. Cheong, S.N., Yap, W.J., Logeswaran, R., Chai, I.: Design and Development of Kinect-Based Technology-Enhanced Teaching Classroom. In: Park, J.J.(J.H.), Jeong, Y.-S., Park, S.O., Chen, H.-C. (eds.) EMC Technology and Service. LNEE, vol. 181, pp. 179–186. Springer, Heidelberg (2012)
11. Smorkalov, A., Fominykh, M., Prasolova-Forland, E.: Virtualizing real-life lectures with vAcademia and Kinect. In: 2nd Workshop Off-The-Shelf Virtual Reality at the International Conference on Virtual Reality, VR (2013)
12. Özcelik, E., Sengul, G.: Gesture-based interaction for learning: time to make dream a reality. British Journal of Educational Technology 43(3), E86–E89 (2012)
13. Kinect, http://en.wikipedia.org/wiki/Kinect

Virtualizing Real-Life Lectures with vAcademia, Kinect, and iPad

Andrey Smorkalov[1], Mikhail Morozov[1],
Mikhail Fominykh[2], and Ekaterina Prasolova-Førland[2]

[1] Multimedia Systems Laboratory, Volga State University of Technology, Russia
{smorkalovay,morozovmn}@volgatech.net
[2] Program for Learning with ICT, Norwegian University of Science and Technology, Norway
{mikhail.fominykh,ekaterip}@ntnu.no

Abstract. In this paper, we present a project aiming at designing a low-cost technological setup for translating real-life lectures into a 3D virtual world. We present the design of the first prototype where we record the voice of a lecturer, presentation slides, and use a motion-capture technique to grasp gestures. Based on these data, we create a scene in a 3D virtual world, display the slides, play the recorded sound, and animate the lecturer's avatar. We discuss evaluation results and discovered limitations, and outline solutions. In addition, we propose the major types of learning scenarios for the use of the designed system.

Keywords: 3D virtual worlds, motion capture, vAcademia, Kinect, iPad.

1 Introduction

Various advanced Virtual Reality (VR) technologies are being developed or adapted for educational purposes, mostly in industry, military, and healthcare [1]. However, a broader deployment requires the development of low-cost and off-the-shelf solutions.

Many studies report the potential of three-dimensional virtual worlds (3D VWs) for educational activities [2]. In this work, we explore new ways of using 3D VWs for creating asynchronous content out of synchronous learning activities. Several techniques were adapted by educators for getting content out of traditional classes, such as video recording of face-to-face lectures and recording of webinars. Such recordings change the context of learning and do not provide a possibility for collaborative work or for further developing the content, except for annotating. 3D VWs are also used for generating educational content. However, activities there are usually recorded as 'flat' 2D video, eliminating many advantages of the technology.

Low-cost motion-sensing technologies such as Microsoft Kinect, Nintendo Wii Remote, and Playstation Move provide researchers and educators with new opportunities for improving learning. Multiple examples include a low-cost alternative for interactive whiteboards and multi-touch teaching stations designed based on Kinect [3]. Tablets, like iPad, and other mobile devices found various applications, among them –

C. Stephanidis (Ed.): HCII 2014 Posters, Part II, CCIS 435, pp. 156–161, 2014.

augmenting 3D VWs [4]. A tablet provides a more convenient interface for a VR application than mouse and keyboard, especially if the user wants to stand and move.

This paper introduces a project aiming at designing a low-cost technological setup for translating real-life presentations and lectures into a 3D VW. We record sound, use a motion-capture technique to grasp the gestures of a lecturer, and a hand-held tablet device for additional control of the media content. Based on these data, we create a scene in a 3D VW, playing the recorded sound, animating the lecturer's avatar and displaying the media content.

2   Virtualizing Real-Life Lectures

2.1   Technological Setup

We use three available technologies to implement the proposed system, vAcademia, Kinect, and iPad. Kinect is used for capturing the movement of a lecturer, while vAcademia is used for creating and recording the virtual replica of a lecture. In addition, the lecturer can use an iPad to control the environment and media content, such as drawing, switching slides, pointing, viewing the environment, and streaming in 2D.

Microsoft Kinect (http://www.microsoft.com/en-us/kinectforwindows/) is a low-cost motion sensing input device that is able to capture one or two humans. Apple iPad is a hand-help tablet device that has a touch screen can recognize finger gestures (http://www.apple.com/ipad/). vAcademia is an educational 3D VW (http://vacademia.com/). Its most distinctive feature is 3D recording. It allows capturing everything in a given location in the VW in process, including positions of the objects, appearance and movement of the avatars, media contents, text and voice chat messages [5]. 3D recording is often treated as an embedded screen capture mechanism. However, it is conceptually different from the video recording or screen capturing. A replayed 3D recording contains the entire 3D scene with all 3D objects, avatars, and all their actions. In addition to the virtual recording, vAcademia has a special set of tools to work with large amounts of media content [6].

2.2   First Prototype

System Implementation. The virtualizing real-life lectures mode interface is implemented using vAcademia Scripts. The Scripts initiate the beginning and the end of this mode. They provide Kinect-related information, including the skeleton in 2D and the recognition status of body parts. They interact with the Animation library of the graphic engine through the Script Executing Library. The Animation library controls the lecturer's avatar using Cal3D based on the data from Kinect plugin (Fig. 1).

vAcademia uses Cal3D library for implementing the skeleton avatar animation [7]. It allows to control the skeleton of an avatar by constantly and automatically recalculating its polygonal 3D model to match the current state of the skeleton. In the first prototype of the system, the Animation library of vAcademia requested a set of key points of the lecturer's body from the Kinect-support plugin (Fig. 1). If the lecturer was recognized by Kinect, Cal3D bones of the vAcademia avatar are oriented according to the key points. The system supported a 'sitting mode', when the motion-capture data were used for orientating arms and head and a 'standing mode' for all body parts.

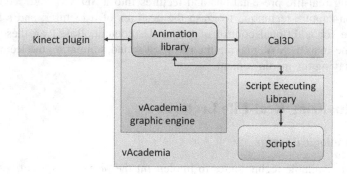

Fig. 1. Virtualizing real-life lectures mode interface of vAcademia

In addition, Kinect provides the status of each key point of the lecturer's body (not recognized, presumably recognized or recognized) as well as indicates if the body is cut in one of four directions by the camera visibility area. In order to eliminate unnatural poses, we divided the skeleton into five major parts (arms, legs, and head) and processed Kinect data for them separately. If a part of the skeleton remains unrecognized adequately for 0.2–0.5 seconds, the system sets it into the default state.

System Performance. vAcademia requires and actively uses one CPU core. Other cores may be also used, but less actively (10–30%), except for the process of the first load of the VW data. Kinect requires a dual-core CPU, but uses only one core, as the second is reserved for the application that uses Kinect data. These settings define the requirements for the computer to run the system designed.

System Evaluation Summary. Although the evaluation has not been systematic so far, it allowed us to improve many characteristics of the system. We conducted several evaluation sessions in several auditoriums with different configurations and lightning. The major evaluation data source is an interview with the lecturer. The following feedback on the technological setup is the most common:

The system applies too many restrictions on the lecturer's movements. First, the lecturer has to stay in the area in front of the Kinect device, and the space between them should be clear. Second, the lecturer has to face the device and not turn. Third, the lecturer has to use only one hand for pointing at the screen. Fourth, the lecturer has to avoid gestures that are difficult to recognize by the users of the 3D VW. In addition, we received suggestions on increasing the educational value of the system.

2.3   Applying Kinect for Motion Capture in vAcademia

The evaluation of the first prototype revealed three major limitations of Kinect in the given context and three corresponding challenges for the system implementation.

- C1: Kinect does not capture the gestures accurately enough. Therefore, we could not build a reliable avatar model and exclude unnatural poses.
- C2: Kinect does not recognize the turn of the lecturer. If the lecturer turns away from the device, it mixes up the left and the right.
- C3: An obvious, but serious challenge for applying Kinect is its inability to capture parts of the body that are covered by other body parts or foreign objects.

We addressed C1 by introducing several mechanisms. We limited the distance between the Kinect device and the lecturer. In addition, we fixed the Kinect device at a 0.5 meters distance from the floor. We introduced an additional filtration mechanism for sorting out unnatural positions, separating hands as distinct body parts. We addressed C2 by implementing the following algorithm. The turn is recognized relatively as a function of the position of the pelvis end points. The resultant value is valid within the range from -110 to 110 degrees against the "facing Kinect device" direction. We introduced colored markers for better recognition of the turns (Fig. 2).

Fig. 2. Lecture capturing process   **Fig. 3.** Lecture streaming process

Challenge C3 may be addressed by applying multiple Kinect devices. At the same time, new challenges may appear, such as the increase of the price, complexity in setting up the system, and complexity in merging the data from multiple sources.

2.4   Applying Kinect and iPad for Controlling Whiteboards in vAcademia

Based on the results of the system's first prototype evaluation, we have identified the following challenges for controlling virtual whiteboards and their contents.

- C4: The position and movement of the lecturer against the physical whiteboard should match the position and movement of his/her avatar against the virtual one.
- C5: A physical pointer needs to be captured and represented in the 3D VW, where it is often even more important. However, Kinect cannot capture a physical pointer.
- C6: Switching the slides requires interaction with the computer or a remote control, which does not convey any meaning when captured and translated into the 3D VW.

Addressing C4, we introduced a Setup mode for achieving the precise match between the physical and the virtual whiteboard (horizontally) and installing Kinect at 0.5 meters from the floor (vertically). Instead of trying to capture the physical pointer, we direct the virtual pointer based on the position of the lecturer's hand, addressing C5. If the half line that extends from the lecturer's hand crosses the physical whiteboard, the avatar in the 3D VW directs a virtual pointer to the same point (Fig. 3). In order to keep the lecturer aware of his or her hand being captured, we display a semi-transparent yellow area on the physical whiteboard on top of the slides (Fig. 2).

Addressing C6, we have been developing the switching slides functionality by recognizing standard Kinect gestures Swipe Left and Swipe Right. In addition, we decided to employ iPad for extending the possibilities of controlling media contents. Using vAcademia Presentation Remote app, the lecturer can stream handwriting and drawing to a virtual whiteboard and control other content on it without going back to the computer. The tablet is connected to the vAcademia client software through the vAcademia communication server using access code.

3   Learning Scenarios

We can identify several major learning scenarios for the systems we have been designing based on the evaluation results and user feedback.

Scenario 1: Lecturing as a Mixed Reality Activity. In this scenario, a live lecture could be attended simultaneously by the learners in real and virtual classrooms. As opposed to some existing solutions where distant learners watch the video of the lecturer, this setting has a number of advantages. This includes the possibility to design the virtual classroom recreating the physical one, thus providing distant learners with a greater sense of presence at the lecture. Additional advantages include possibilities for interactions between students in the physical and virtual classrooms (as the former might be logged in as avatars in the virtual classroom and perform activities there during the lecture) and recording student and lecturer activities in the same context.

Scenario 2: Round-Table Discussion as a Mixed Reality Activity. The system designed can be used for supporting round-table discussions. Some of the participants can join such an activity through the 3D VW, while some other can be captured from the real world through multiple Kinect-based systems. Each of them can capture two participants. Gestures are a very important component of round-table discussion, and the designed system provides a significant advantage over pure 3D VWs.

Scenario 3: Mixed Reality Educational Role Plays. In this scenario, the participants from the physical and the virtual classroom could engage in an educational role play, e.g. simulating a conflict management situation. The limitation in this context is that only one or two users could be captured by Kinect at a time, which could be dealt with by people from the physical classroom taking turns or by letting the users captured by Kinect play the roles of facilitators. The advantage of this approach is the possibility to create and record a shared virtual scene for the role play.

Scenario 4: Immersive 3D Recordings of Lectures. In this scenario motion capture is used for easy and low-cost creation of educational content for later (asynchronous) use, such as lectures and simulations. Using the vAcademia 3D recording functionality, any activity, including streaming Kinect-captured lectures, in the 3D VW can be easily saved and revisited later. The realization of this scenario can provide an advanced alternative to the video-recorded lectures, as the resultant 3D recordings combine the convenience of video and immersive qualities of 3D VWs. In this case, the limitation of 1–2 users being captured at a time is less important as several captured sessions with different avatars could be superimposed into one recording.

4   Conclusion and Future Work

The evaluation of the system for translating real-life lectures into a 3D VW demonstrated that the system functions as intended and has practical value. We also present the challenges we outlined for the system, including ways to address them.

Future development of the system will include support for interactive whiteboards that can replace the projector in the current setup. We plan to implement and evaluate emotion capture functionality using Kinect and Face Tracking SDK that will be important for supporting role-plays and creation of training simulations.

References

1. Rajaei, H., Aldhalaan, A.: Advances in virtual learning environments and classrooms. In: Abhari, A. (ed.) 14th Communications and Networking Symposium (CNS), Boston, MA, USA, April 3-7, pp. 133–142. Curran Associates, Inc. (2011)
2. de Freitas, S., Rebolledo-Mendez, G., Liarokapis, F., Magoulas, G., Poulovassilis, A.: Developing an Evaluation Methodology for Immersive Learning Experiences in a Virtual World. In: 1st International Conference in Games and Virtual Worlds for Serious Applications (VS-GAMES), Coventry, UK, March 23-24, pp. 43–50. IEEE (2009)
3. Cheong, S.N., Yap, W.J., Logeswaran, R., Chai, I.: Design and Development of Kinect-Based Technology-Enhanced Teaching Classroom. In: Park, J.J.(J.H.), Jeong, Y.-S., Park, S.O., Chen, H.-C. (eds.) EMC Technology and Service. LNEE, vol. 181, pp. 179–186. Springer, Heidelberg (2012)
4. Pakanen, M., Arhippainen, L., Hickey, S.: Studying Four 3D GUI Metaphors in Virtual Environment in Tablet Context. Visual Design and Early Phase User Experience Evaluation. In: 6th International Conference on Advances in Computer-Human Interactions (ACHI), Nice, France, February 24-March 1, pp. 41–46 (2013)
5. Morozov, M., Gerasimov, A., Fominykh, M., Smorkalov, A.: Asynchronous Immersive Classes in a 3D Virtual World: Extended Description of vAcademia. In: Gavrilova, M.L., Tan, C.J.K., Kuijper, A. (eds.) Trans. on Comput. Sci. XVIII. LNCS, vol. 7848, pp. 81–100. Springer, Heidelberg (2013)
6. Smorkalov, A., Fominykh, M., Morozov, M.: Stream Processors Texture Generation Model for 3D Virtual Worlds: Learning Tools in vAcademia. In: Lin, Q., Muhlhauser, M., Sheu, P. (eds.) 9th International Symposium on Multimedia (ISM), Anaheim, CA, USA, December 9-11, pp. 17–24. IEEE (2013)
7. Jingtang, L., Gang, Z., Dunming, T., Junjie, X.: Research of skeletal-based virtual human animation using Cal3D. In: 3rd International Conference on System Science, Engineering Design and Manufacturing Informatization (ICSEM), Chengdu, China, October 20-21, pp. 269–273. IEEE (2012)

Pilot Scenario Design for Evaluating
a Metacognitive Skills Learning Dialogue System

Dimitris Spiliotopoulos[1], Olga Petukhova[2], Dimitris Koryzis[3], and Maria Aretoulaki[4]

[1] Interaction Design Lab, University of Peloponnese, Greece
dspiliot@uop.gr
[2] University of Saarland, Germany
Olga.Petukhova@lsv.uni-saarland.de
[3] Hellenic Parliament, Greece
dkoryzis@parliament.gr
[4] DialogConnection, UK
maria@dialogconnection.com

Abstract. This work describes the experimentation on the application of evaluation methodologies for creating metrics that evaluate the experience of the users of the Metalogue system as they learn and using them to validate the effective ability of the system to assess them. Pilot scenarios were formulated in order to effectively train the system to train the users on metacognitive skills learning. Usability design common approaches, such as focus groups and user experience needfinding sessions were used to collect the data.

Keywords: TEL; multimodal interaction, usability evaluation.

1   Introduction

Metacognition has been studied and presented as strongly linked to learning approaches for several targets in learning [1]. Metacognitive strategies have been examined and evaluated on key aspects, such as in language learning and predicting leadership potential [2, 3]. The Metalogue[1] project approach is working towards creating a multimodal dialogue system that utilizes meta-cognitive abilities in a qualitative manner so that it can reason and explore dialogue behavior as well as adapt and predict behavioral patterns in conversations. The main objective is to use multimodal dialogue to interact with human participants during specific tasks during instructional scaffolding.

The selection of appropriate interaction scenarios is critical to the success of this experimentation. The system-human interaction should produce concrete results so that the system becomes more natural, with better understanding of the human behaviour. Additionally, the system should eventually come to exhibit sufficient metacognitive skills so that it may:

---

[1] Metalogue – Multiperspective Multimodal Dialogue: Dialogue System with Metacognitive Abilities, www.metalogue.eu

C. Stephanidis (Ed.): HCII 2014 Posters, Part II, CCIS 435, pp. 162–166, 2014.
© Springer International Publishing Switzerland 2014

- enable adaptation of the dialogue behaviour over time according to the dialogue partners' knowledge, attitude and confidence, and
- predict other dialogue partners' intentions and show proactive dialogue behaviour.

The following paragraphs present the use cases and requirements for this task and the rationale behind the interaction scenarios that were designed to create the environment for the experimentation.

2 Use Case 1: Call Centre Agents

The Metalogue dialogue system will be used by Call Centre agents in the UK to learn negotiation skills in dealing with customers / callers. Due to the nature of their work, Call Centre agents have got a really high attrition rate. Call Centres spend thousands of pounds a year to train new employees, only to lose them a couple of months later due to constant exposure to high stress situations over the phone. The Metalogue system will automate some of the training process and make it cost-effective, efficient, reusable, adaptable and extensible.

The system is designed to deliver a realistic training experience and to make it possible to give quantitative evaluations of how well a given call went. Initially, the user will select a given training exercise, whereupon the standard dialogue system (the one without metacognitive abilities) will simulate a service call, itself impersonating a "customer / caller" character with a given issue and the user will try to resolve the issue. The system keeps track of variables such as number of interactions, type of interaction (question, statement, acknowledgement, refusal, etc.), misunderstandings and conflict, and task-specific requirements, such as degree of politeness and formality degree of self-control, degree of firmness, argument clarity, product cross- and up-selling, etc.

If the interaction does not go well, a second participant, the "coach" system interrupts and gives tips to the trainee. In an initial pilot, the system may just react with a "negative" beep and / or display a red flag / light, which does not involve an interruption or intervention of the interaction. In later pilots, the system will be more "disruptive", in that it will actually interrupt the conversation and more or less actively intervene with pointers to what went wrong and with alternatives for better self-monitoring, self-control, and goal fulfillment. Hence the system feedback / intervention will be both online and real-time in future stages of its development. Since the system is modular, new scenarios can be added incrementally, as well as new features, such as support for additional sub-dialogue extensions adding new standard situations.

The system can also simulate different meta-cognitive skills, such as "aggressive" (the call centre agent remains stubborn about relinquishing a free service / product) or "defensive" (the call centre agent is flexible and gives in to the customer request for free service / product), depending on the corresponding business rules defined by the end user organisation. The system will be able to switch its learning / simulation strategy between the two modes and dynamically adapt its associated behaviour (communication style: turn wording, voice tone and speed, etc.). Again, this crude classification of meta-cognitive skills will be both based on existing established meta-cognitive research and on a "translation" of the research into concrete call centre terms relevant to business goals and business logic rules and agent training.

The system focus is more on modelling and simulating / exhibiting realistic behaviour based on real-world (logical from the call centre perspective) goals, and less on simulating the behaviour of irate and frustrated (and hence "illogical") customers / callers. Nevertheless, the simulated training scenarios will involve both frustrated but cooperative and irate and illogical customers to a certain degree. This is in order to model different types of communication situations and different meta-cognitive goals and skills.

3   Use Case 2: Youth Parliament and Debate

For this use case, the Metalogue system will be used to train young parliamentarians in Greece. It will observe and improve the metacognitive abilities of the trainees, creating societal abilities and skills of the new generation, introducing them into the modern world issues, such as rules, obligations, rights, social behaviour and responsibility. The setting is the Hellenic Youth Parliament that has an annual session where 300 students (ages 15-17) discuss several current affair issues, simulating the environment of the Hellenic Parliament's plenary sessions. To date, more than 4.000 participants have been part of this interesting simulation community.

After identifying a suitable public policy framework, two selected students will debate on it, in the presence of their tutor. The students will have a face-to-face debate on the selected policy presenting different opinions with justified arguments. It must be noted that, contrary to the previous use case where spoken dialogue was the main mode of interaction, in this case all the modalities are available, such as speech (verbal analysis, tone and intensity of voice), facial expression, gestures, body language. The minimum number of participants would be three, two students and one tutor.

There are several user-specific requirements such as the formal language, the need for additional training of students and tutors on the new technological environment of Metalogue pilots, the system adaptability to legal and policy language, and the participants' ability to debate in scripted and unscripted scenarios and vice versa. Finally the impact on system functionality is largely defined by the clarity of speech and the simultaneous speaking by the users.

4   Pilot Scenario Design

The domains of application are the Hellenic Youth Parliament for training youngsters in democratic debate and training of call centre agents in dealing with customer complaints and in up- / cross-selling additional products and services. There are two types of scenario for both domains:

- Scenario Type 1: Solve issue / disagreement (and try to sell something in case of call centre scenario). The goal is to win the argument (aggressive)

- Scenario Type 2:   Empathize, appease, give in (give something for free in case of call centre scenario). The goal is to achieve consensus (passive)

The system should be able to pick its strategy on the fly, or adapt its strategy depending on the business / organisation rules and the meta-cognitive learning goals being illustrated.

Learning design starts with telephone conversations (call centre domain) between the two interlocutors (caller and agent) who are monitoring themselves and the conversation. Then come the face-to-face debates (youth parliament domain) between the two interlocutors who are also monitoring themselves and the conversation. Additionally, for both domains, two or more observers (tutor and trainee) can join. They are monitoring the two interlocutors and also discuss among themselves the intentions, plans, strategies and dialogue behaviour of the interlocutors, as well as how they adapt to the current situation and the changes in the other interlocutor's behaviour. The original two interlocutors can act as the control group. The interaction is always between 2-4 participants each time, that is the two interlocutors as a minimum, plus one or more observers, tutor and trainee.

The system itself can be the Experiencer and the Observer, with dynamic feedback on self and interlocutor and later adaptive behaviour as a result. It may also be the Tutor with dynamic feedback and later intervention in interaction, plus metacognition analysis to the trainee.

5   Conclusion

This work reported on the considerations for creating interaction scenarios between a multimodal dialogue system with metacognitive abilities and human participants. Two cases were presented and analysed from the dialogue perspective as well as on the learning design. Through those scenarios, this experimentation aims to design, develop and test a real time interactive multimodal system that will be able to exhibit certain metacognitive skills while used to engage in interaction with human actors in order to train them. The training itself is an issue that is still under investigation. The metacognitive skills and the way to train students has been a focus in research. Critical thinking [4], decision making [5] and problem solving [6] are but a few metacognitive skill related abilities that could be of interest to this study. A critical factor will be the evaluation of the level of success of the dialogue system in such endeavor.

Acknowledgements. The work described here was partially supported by the EU ICT research project METALOGUE, FP7-ICT-611073.

References

1. Paris, S.G., Winograd, P.: How metacognition can promote academic learning and instruction. Dimensions of Thinking and Cognitive Instruction 1, 15–51 (1990)
2. Magaldi, L.G.: Metacognitive Strategies Based Instruction to Support Learner Autonomy in Language Learning. Revistacanaria de Estudiosingleses (61), 73–86 (2010)

3. Marshall-Mies, J.C., Fleishman, E.A., Martin, J.A., Zaccaro, S.J., Baughman, W.A., McGee, M.L.: Development and evaluation of cognitive and metacognitive measures for predicting leadership potential. The Leadership Quarterly 11(1), 135–153 (2000)
4. Magno, C.: The role of metacognitive skills in developing critical thinking. Metacognition and Learning 5(2), 137–156 (2010)
5. Cohen, M.S., Freeman, J.T., Thompson, B.: Critical thinking skills in tactical decision making: A model and a training strategy. In: Making Decisions Under Stress: Implications for Individual and Team Training, pp. 155–190 (1998)
6. McLoughlin, C., Hollingworth, R.: The weakest link: Is web-based learning capable of supporting problem-solving and metacognition. In: 18th Annual Conference of the Australasian Society for Computers in Learning in Tertiary Education, pp. 9–12 (December 2001)

Analysis on ICT Skills Present in Teachers in Active in Nine Spanish Territories

Inmaculada Tello Díaz-Maroto[1] and Antonia Cascales Martínez[2]

[1] Universidad Autónoma de Madrid, Spain
[2] Universidad de Murcia, Spain
inmaculada.tello@uam.es, antonia.cascales@um.es

Abstract. At the present time, it exists a debate about neutrality of the resources, but far from this controversy, what is clear is that people who employ them, give them value and meaning in the context in which it is used. The use that teachers give them, are not exempt from neutrality, so we have to practice them in the proper use thereof. This reflection leads us to consider the initial teacher education and with it, the continuous learning, both of them necessary and essential so that their educational work can be of quality. As can be gleaned from the skills mentioned by several authors, in the application of ICT in education is necessary a technical training and a pedagogical training. We must accompany the accessibility of such resources with the educational use of them. We will be then really using an education that uses ICT in their methodology in teaching and learning. ICT opens a new way to access information and a great communicative bridge for contact and learning. But for the teachers being able to carry out this work properly, they must first know the procedure, so they should be one of the leading figures involved in the process of teaching and learning, therefore it can be updated in the knowledge that the ICT demands, a proper use to it. To check the level of ICT training of teachers in service, we have applied a questionnaire on several dimensions related to ICT in the classroom: knowledge of these resources, teaching methodology, resource selection, evaluation and training received. The study sample consists of 147 teachers from four regions and 9 Spanish provinces. The sample used has been a purposive sampling, selecting teachers who have attended a training course on the use of ICT. The results show several differences in the knowledge of the ICT in the Spanish territory and a high demand for specific training adapted to the reality of each center.

Keywords: ICT Skills, Teachers, support, social justice.

1 Introduction

If we understand education as the basis for the development of any society, we must also seek to develop the Social Justice in the classroom , in order to create an egalitarian society and work towards building the society we long . "The yearning for greater social justice arises, first, by the clear perception of the many and growing injustices that surround us , but also in search of a better society ". In this sense, "the question of

C. Stephanidis (Ed.): HCII 2014 Posters, Part II, CCIS 435, pp. 167–170, 2014.
© Springer International Publishing Switzerland 2014

the kind of society that we care and that we want to work, to the question above ob-jectives, meaning or purpose of education" [1].

The accessibility and use of information technology and communication (ICT) open other gaps that may have effects on integration and social cohesion. That is why decisions about ICT are now related to issues that promote equity and social justice [2].That is why the current rules, states that one of the principles of education ensuring access for all to ICTs, fostering social justice. In this line, makes explicit reference to the responsible use of ICT as a pedagogical principle and as an educational goal, recognizing the need for centers with the necessary infrastructure to promote the use of information technologies and communication, as well as the necessary teacher training in this field.

We observe two important areas to be analyzed to improve the quality and equity in the classroom, the appropriate use of ICT and promoting Curricular Justice are evident. Therefore, the proper selection and use of ICT in the classroom is so necessary to promote more than a digital divide in schools, we achieve the opposite, strengthen and promote social justice in all classrooms.

Prado (2011) as Deputy Executive Secretary of ECLAC, considered the digital divide in the access and the use of ICT, emerging issues of inequality and welfare. However, for once the previous requirements of accessibility and connectivity technology , the basic processes of digital literacy training , and practical use of the tools of elementary information and communication technologies (ICT) for the operation of the mass media (mass media) , it is necessary to transcend the technical and technological approach that has been taken of ICT and mediational and interactional explore their role in the formation, which contribute to fair social conditions.

The potential of ICT for the educational process is proposed, which is required to reformulate education and empower " ... peer collaboration , active participation of students in their own learning process and increasing individualization processes through greater promotion of creativity and autonomy " [3] [4].This is achieved when the subjects constructed in relation to others, when the spaces for participation, etc. are provided. , As expressed [5], ICT backbone , political, social , economic, cultural development.

2   Design Process, Methods and Results

After reviewing the literature and be aware of the need for teacher training in the various stages of education in the knowledge society, we have carried out the data collection of the knowledge about claiming to have teachers through the implementation of a questionnaire.

To train teachers in the appropriate use of ICT, we must first know the reality of training teachers in service. For this reason, we have applied a questionnaire to analyze the knowledge that teachers have to attend a training course on "Teacher Training in the use of ICT in the field of inclusive schools and grade schools." The questionnaire was administered to a sample of 147 teachers from various regions of the Spanish territory.

The sample was selected through an intentional non-probability sampling, it was applied to those teachers who attended a training course related to the appropriate use of ICT. Attendees of the course teachers, 100 % of them responded. The questionnaire consists of 29 items , 7 questions related to the characteristics of the sample for subsequent contrasts , a second part in which printing is to know that teachers have about their level of knowledge with respect to ICT , the third part relating to the appraisal of teachers regarding the methodology they use ICT ; quarter related to the selection of appropriate resources, one-fifth to assess the use of ICT in the evaluation , and a final part to refer to teacher training in the appropriate use of ICT. The aim of the study was to perform an analysis of the degree of knowledge and perspectives that teachers in different regions of Spain have regarding the appropriate use of ICT in education. Based on the results, the goal is to offer training tailored to the needs of each locality.

The results indicate several differences respect to various aspects assessed (level of knowledge, methodology, resource selection, evaluation and training) in function of the locality from which teachers; we found statistically significant differences in all aspects except for the selection of ICT resources (no significant differences). There have done Scheffé tests to detect the groups among which those differences exist, for example, we detected differences in some cases in the evaluation of the chosen methodology, highlighting Cáceres above Sevilla and Granada. (Table 1)

Table 1. ANOVA results of a factor between different aspects and locality

	F	Sig.
Level of knowledge	2,650	0,010
Methodology	4,974	0,000
Selecting resources	1,721	0,099
Evaluation	4,126	0,000
Training	3,547	0,001

A variable that also could show us a interesting contrast was the age, in base the speech that sometimes is used about that older teachers are more reluctant to incorporating ICT in their classroom. But strikingly, they found no statistically significant relationships between the various aspects and age. Also, we haven´t obtained relationships between the various aspects and years of teaching experience. However, it has been statistically significant relationships between the aspect concerning the methodology and terms of training with respect to the educational level at which he teaches teachers. Thus, it is observed in both respects a statistically significant and positive, which indicates that the higher the educational level of teachers, they value most the methodology used with ICT and the formation in values, which indicate greater use of ICT in the classroom at higher levels.

Finally we asked them the type of school in which they imparted their teaching, by also study if there are differences in different aspects evaluated, depending on the type of facility in which they exercise their professional work. As we have analyzed the characteristics of the sample, we have saw there is a higher proportion of teachers in public school in contrast to private schools or rural schools, to private schools or rural schools, yet we have proceeded to perform ANOVA to analyze the results. In this sense, we can see in Table 2 that there are no statistically significant differences in the assessment of aspects of the study, depending on the type of school in which teachers work.

Table 2. Student t test results between different aspects and type of organization

	F	Sig.
Level of knowledge	0,668	0,514
Methodology	0,961	0,385
Selecting resources	0,170	0,844
Evaluation	1,747	0,178
Training	1,030	0,360

3   Conclusions

Based on the results obtained and the bibliographic analysis regarding the issue at hand, it has been possible to note some observations that allow us to design a training plan to accomplish with future teachers, at least through the Master Teacher Training for Secondary Education. We can highlight among the main conclusions:

- Generally schools do not promote Education for Development, Social Justice and Active Citizenship.
- It seems that future teachers of secondary respondents are aware that those concepts are not identical, but have no clear differences between them.
- We have to promote this concept in all the educational levels using news methodologies.

References

1. Murillo, F.J., Hernández-Castilla, R.: Hacia un Concepto de Justicia Social. REICE. Revista Iberoamericana sobre Calidad, Eficacia y Cambio en Educación 9(4), 7–23 (2011)
2. Duro, E.: Programa Desafío. La inclusión de adolescentes a la escuela en municipios de la provincia de Buenos Aires. UNICEF, Mime (2007)
3. Pérez, A.I. (ed.): Reinventar la profesión docente. Nuevas perspectivas y escenarios en la era de la formación y de la incertidumbre (Tema monográfico). Revista Interuniversitaria de Formación del Profesorado, vol. 68(24, 2) (2010)
4. Pérez, A.: Escuela 2.0. Educación para el mundo digital (2010), [En Red] Disponible en, http://www.injuve.es/sites/default/files/RJ92-06.pdf
5. Queraltó, R.: Ética y sociedad tecnológica: pirámide y retícula. Universidad de Sevilla, Sevilla (2002) [En Red] Disponible en, http://institucional.us.es/revistas/argumentos/5/art_2.pdf

Opportunities and Challenges of Using Technology in Mathematics Education of Creative Engineering Studies

Evangelia Triantafyllou and Olga Timcenko

Department of Architecture, Design and Media Technology Aalborg University Copenhagen
Copenhagen, Denmark
{evt,ot}@create.aau.dk

Abstract. This paper explores the opportunities and challenges of integrating technology to support mathematics teaching and learning in creative engineering disciplines. We base our discussion on data from our research in the Media Technology department of Aalborg University Copenhagen, Denmark. Our analysis proposes that unlike in other engineering disciplines, technology in these disciplines should be used for contextualizing mathematics rather than introducing and exploring mathematical concepts.

1 Introduction

Over the past years, changes in the engineering profession and engineering education have followed changes in technology and society (1). Disciplines were added and curricula were created to meet the critical challenges in society and to provide the workforce required to integrate new developments into our economy. To this end, a number of creative engineering educational programs have arisen (e.g. Architecture and Design, Media Technology, Sustainable Design). Such programs transcend the division between technical, scientific and creative disciplines. By focusing on innovation and new technologies, they aim at fostering creative thinking ability in their students (2).

In relation to mathematics education, this new development means that we experience a transposition from an industrial use of mathematics, where it is employed intensively by mechanical and construction engineers as a tool in order to develop products and build constructions, towards a situation where mathematics is increasingly used as the actual building blocks in various new digital products and creative expressions. This transposition has implications on how mathematics should be taught in more creative engineering disciplines.

The teaching of mathematics to students of such disciplines represents a challenge to the educational system; typically these disciplines are more related to arts and humanities, and constructed in specific opposition to the technology and science. The typical student lacks basic skills in mathematics and does not relate to the standard applications of mathematics (for example in science and economy) mentioned in textbooks (3). Those students often do not approach or perceive the mathematics the same

C. Stephanidis (Ed.): HCII 2014 Posters, Part II, CCIS 435, pp. 171–176, 2014.

way as mathematics students do, and moreover mathematics is used in a different way in creative disciplines than in science.

This paper emerges from our research set out to explore the opportunities and challenges of integrating technology to support mathematics education in creative engineering disciplines. In order to better inform our research, we conducted a study at Media Technology Department of Aalborg University Copenhagen, Denmark. This study focused on investigating different ways of introducing technology in mathematics education. Our results proposed that unlike in other engineering disciplines, technology in these disciplines should be used for contextualizing mathematics rather than introducing and exploring mathematical concepts.

2   Background Work

In the last decades, the rapid development in ICT has provided new possibilities for education to integrate digital technologies into schooling, and thus enhance teaching and learning. Such technologies have been widely used to face challenges in mathematics education both in primary and secondary schools, and in a lesser extent in universities (4). However, the use of such technologies has not met yet the initial expectations on reforming teaching and learning (5).

The use of technology for mathematics teaching and learning can be classified in two dimensions: 1) design and evaluation of theoretical frames that are used in technology-related research in the domain of mathematics education (6) and 2) the introduction of domain-specific technological tools. In the following, we cite some research approaches related to both dimensions.

In the field of theoretical frames, some researchers proposed the use of technology to develop applications of mathematics to the specific tasks required in the profession or towards a domain understanding of mathematics that resembles the understanding in the target profession. Within engineering education Shaffer has developed a framework designed to support the didactical transposition in terms of a relation between an epistemic frame (describing professional knowledge), and an epistemic game – a didactical design aiming at re-creating this professional knowledge in a school situation (7).

Other researchers favored blended learning designs that combine online and face-to-face instruction. Kashefi et al. designed a blended learning environment based on computer-based mathematical thinking and creative problem solving aimed at improving generic mathematics skills (such as communication, teamwork, problem solving, and technology skills) in a group of undergraduate engineering students (8).

Regarding the introduction of technological tools in university mathematics education, Matlab, GeoGebra and Computer Algebra Systems (CAS) have been the most popular choices. Matlab, which is an environment for numerical computation, visualization, and programming, has been particularly popular in mathematics courses intended for engineering students. It has been used by Chang for in-class activities that demonstrate linear algebra concepts (9), and by Pennell et. al for designing illustrative examples of differential equations in an engineering mathematics course (10).

Based on a threefold learning concept comprising mathematical methods, Matlab programming, and practical engineering, Behrens et al. developed a laboratory course for engineering students where mathematical basics were transferred to algorithms in Matlab in order to control Lego Mindstorms robots (11).

GeoGebra is open source dynamic mathematics software that combines the ease-of-use of dynamic geometry software with some basic features of computer algebra systems (Hohenwarter & Preiner, 2007). Diković has used GeoGebra to reform a part of a calculus course for undergraduate students in Business-Technology (Diković, 2009). Jaworski has used it to promote inquiry and facilitate conceptual understanding of students in a first year university mathematics course for engineering students (Jaworski, 2010).

CAS are software programs that support manipulation of mathematical expressions in symbolic form. During the past decades, a number of studies examined various educational uses of CAS (Brito et al., 2009), students' learning in CAS-equipped environments (Connors & Snook, 2001), and innovative teaching practices with CAS in university classrooms (Thomas & Holton, 2003).

However, little is known about the emerging field of technology for mathematics education in creative engineering. In the literature, it has not been discussed how technology could support the different (and more constructive) modes of application of mathematics and how it could influence the creative students' conception and attitude towards mathematics. Getting inspiration from the aforementioned research approaches, we conducted research in order to identify what kind of approach would best fit these creative disciplines. We attempt to answer these questions in the following sections.

3   Methods

With the aim of investigating how technology can support mathematics education in creative engineering, we conducted research, based on qualitative and quantitative methods. Our research was carried out at the Media Technology (MT) department of Aalborg University Copenhagen, Denmark in the 2012 – 2013 and 2013 – 2014 academic years. Aalborg University is unique in a Danish context because it has a portfolio of trans-disciplinary educational programs where the division between the "creative" designer or architect and the "scientific" engineer is increasingly challenged and transcended. The program in MT is one example of such educational programs.

The MT bachelor and master programs link many areas within film and media science, animation, sound design, computer science and psychology together to meet the growing need to understand new applications and to develop technology and program design that speaks to people's needs and taste (12). Thus, MT is an education that focuses on research, which combines technology and creativity.

We have been gathering data during three semesters in MT, in order to get insight in the process of mathematics teaching and learning in this department. During the first semester of our research, we introduced GeoGebra applets in the "Mathematics for Multimedia Applications" course, which is taught during the second semester of the bachelor study. During the second semester, we organized a math brush-up workshop, which used technological tools for putting mathematics into context (13). During the third semester, we organized a math brush-up workshop, which used a blended learning approach. During this workshop, students were given solved exercises as pencasts and online material for self-studying before each lecture. Lectures were dedicated to solving assignments.

Data were collected by combining quantitative methods (pre- and post-tests before and after the workshops), qualitative methods (questionnaires and interviews) and ethnographic methods (lesson and exercise solving observations).

Based on this data, we draw conclusions on which approach is better suited for creative engineers and discuss opportunities and challenges of introducing technology in creative engineers in the next section.

4   Results

Based on the methods described in the previous section, we were able to collect data on students' performance and preferences on technology in mathematics education in MT. Regarding performance, MT students are low achievers in mathematics and show low retention.   This is mainly due to lack of basic skills and conceptual understanding.

The analysis of our data also revealed that although MT students are technology oriented and prefer visual methods in many of their courses, they are reluctant to use technology for mathematics education. More specifically, 34.6% of the students do not like to use a computer for doing mathematics, while only 30.4% of them would like to do mathematics on a computer (the rest are responded neutrally). Our qualitative data showed that this is because of lack of confidence with mathematics. Students are afraid that the introduction of technological tools will result to added complexity. For the same reasons, students often prefer not to use visual methods when attempting to solve mathematical problems and therefore showed little interest in using GeoGebra applets for visualization of mathematics.

The blended learning approach was not successful either, because students were not diligent enough. Many of students did not perform the self-study required before the lectures, and therefore were unable to solve their assignments or to ask relevant questions. Our data shows that students accept their lack of knowledge in mathematics but at the same time they are not willing to work for getting this knowledge.

MT students favored the approach, which focused on using technology for putting mathematics into context. They stated that contextualization makes mathematics more interesting and improves their motivation to learn mathematics. Moreover, our data show that students' reported increased confidence on mathematics after they followed the workshop with mathematics into context.

5   Discussion

The results of our research showed that the introduction of technology in mathematics education presents both opportunities and challenges for creative engineering students. On one hand, technology could discourage these students, because they often have difficulties in mathematics due to lack of basic skills and conceptual understanding or due to an inability to perform deductive reasoning. Technological tools can provide visualizations and methods to interact with mathematical concepts, but they also require a basic understanding of these concepts. Therefore, students with low understanding in mathematics cannot take advantage of such tools, and they feel frustrated if they are obliged to use them. Moreover, students lack motivation and therefore they are not willing to invest time on studying mathematics. Therefore, methods that require extra effort by their side tend not to be successful.

On the other hand, technology could be used for connecting mathematics to its applications in professional or academic practices. Creative engineering students reported that they are aware of the importance of mathematics and would like to see its application aspects in their studies. Therefore, we believe that the introduction of technology in mathematics education for these students contributes to increase motivation and interest, when it offers new possibilities for creating contextualization of mathematics

References

1. Spinks, N., Silburn, N.L., Birchall, D.W.: Making it all work: The engineering graduate of the future, A UK perspective. European Journal of Engineering Education 32(3), 325–335 (2007)
2. Jørgensen, F., Busk Kofoed, L.: Integrating the development of continuous improvement and innovation capabilities into engineering education. European Journal of Engineering Education 32(2), 181–191 (2007)
3. Andersson, A., Ravn, O.: A critical perspective on contextualisations in mathematics education. Opening the cage: Critique and politics of mathematics education. Sense Publishers, Rotterdam (2012)
4. Lavicza, Z.: Integrating technology into mathematics teaching at the university level. ZDM 42(1), 105–119 (2010)
5. Reynolds, D., Treharne, D., Tripp, H.: ICT—the hopes and the reality. British Journal of Educational Technology 34(2), 151–167 (2003)
6. Drijvers, P., Kieran, C., Mariotti, M., Ainley, J., Andresen, M., Chan, Y.C., et al.: Integrating technology into mathematics education: Theoretical perspectives. In: Mathematics Education and Technology-Rethinking the Terrain, pp. 89–132. Springer (2010)
7. Shaffer, D.W.: How computer games help children learn. Macmillan (2006)
8. Kashefi, H., Ismail, Z., Mohammadyusof, Y., Mirzaei, F.: Generic skills in engineering mathematics through blended learning: A mathematical thinking approach. International Journal of Engineering Education 29(5), 1222–1237 (2013)
9. Chang, J.: A practical approach to inquiry-based learning in linear algebra. International Journal of Mathematical Education in Science and Technology 42(2), 245–259 (2011, 2013)

10. Pennell, S., Avitabile, P., White, J.: An engineering-oriented approach to the introductory differential equations course. PRIMUS 19(1), 88–99 (2009)
11. Behrens, A., Atorf, L., Schwann, R., Neumann, B., Schnitzler, R., Balle, J., et al.: MATLAB meets LEGO Mindstorms—A freshman introduction course into practical engineering. IEEE Transactions on Education 53(2), 306–317 (2010)
12. Medialogy study guide [Internet] (2014), http://www.studyguide.aau.dk/programmes/undergraduate/53181/academic-content/
13. Meyer, M.R., Dekker, T., Querelle, N.: Innovations in: Context in mathematics curricula. Mathematics Teaching in the Middle School 6(9), 522–527 (2001)

Development of Augmented Reality Teaching Materials with Projection Mapping on Real Experimental Settings

Shohei Tsuchida, Narumi Yumoto, and Shu Matsuura

Tokyo Gakugei University, Faculty of Education, 4-1-1 Nukuikita,
Koganei, Tokyo 184-8501, Japan
{tucchy040405,shumats0}@gmail.com, a100368k@st.u-gakugei.ac.jp

Abstract. An augmented reality (AR) technology was applied in connection with a method of projection mapping to display physical quantities on real experimental settings. Physical quantities such as force and velocity were visualized by AR objects and projected onto real objects in an experiment. This image projection onto real objects was found to be effective in such a case where a user manipulates the real object resulting in changes of the magnitudes of physical quantities and the object position. The time delay between the motion of projected AR objects and the video images of real objects was measured on a simple rotating bar object. It was found that the phase delay between the AR objects and the projected image of the real object increased with the angular velocity of the object. The present method seems to be most relevant to static or quasi-static content in which user manipulation is included.

1   Introduction

Augmented reality (AR) provides an extension of the real physical world by adding virtual elements [1]. AR technology has also been applied to the development of educational materials. Learners can interact with real objects and phenomena through virtual components that bridge between real things and abstract information [2]. The possibilities and limitations afforded by AR for a collaborative and immersive learning environment have been discussed [3].

A fundamental problem of science education is that the visible world is explained on the basis of physical elements that are invisible, such as forces exerted on an object in dynamical systems and electric current and voltage in an electric circuit.

In this study, AR is applied to visualize physical quantities in real experiments. In addition, AR components are projected directly onto the real objects of an experimental setting. The projection of digital images onto the surface of real objects is called projection mapping or video mapping [4]. The addition of visualized AR elements onto real objects is expected to make the explanation of physical phenomena more effective.

In this report, based on an example of the vector sum of forces, we discuss a method of constructing a real experiment supplemented with AR elements. In the method, AR objects are used to avoid video feedback as well as represent physical

C. Stephanidis (Ed.): HCII 2014 Posters, Part II, CCIS 435, pp. 177–182, 2014.
© Springer International Publishing Switzerland 2014

quantities. Inquiries on the educational benefits of the content were conducted using students within a graduate school of teacher education. Finally, measurements of the delay time between the image display and the real moving object were conducted to evaluate the possibility of applying the AR projection mapping method to moving objects.

2   Method

2.1   AR Projection Mapping Method

AR contents were created using the ARToolkit [5] with OpenGL. Images of objects were captured by a C615 Logicool Webcam into a Panasonic Let's note CF-S10 laptop PC in which ARToolkit was installed. An EPSON EB-1760W 3LCD projector was used to project the generated AR images onto the real objects in the experimental setting.

Video image projection onto a target object causes a video feedback [6]. The video feedback typically occurs when a video camera captures its monitor images. Under conditions of video feedback, the marker images are replicated and the generation of AR objects based on the marker images becomes extremely unstable.

To avoid marker replication, an AR object as a mask was located on the video image of every AR marker, as schematically shown in Fig. 1. In the projected images, the projected AR objects masked the patterns of the AR markers. At the same time, the images of the mask AR objects illuminated the real AR markers, so that the video camera can capture the AR marker pattern to generate the AR objects.

In addition, the entire scene captured by the camera was masked with a large dark colored plane in order to not replicate the real images. With this overall masking, only the experimental instruments should be illuminated. This is required when the room illumination is lowered to make the projected image of AR objects clearly perceptible.

A common procedure to set up AR projection is as follows (Fig. 1)

1. A base marker is placed within the camera view but outside of the projection area.
2. A screen mask AR that masks the entire view of the scene is generated on the basis of the base marker. The screen mask AR is dark colored and avoids the occurrence of video feedback.
3. The base marker also provides a reference frame for other markers.
4. AR elements (AR objects that correspond to physical quantities, such as force vector arrows) are generated from the corresponding element markers. At the same time, an illumination AR (an AR object that illuminates the real marker pattern by projection) is generated for each marker. The color of the illumination AR is made changeable from black to white. When the room lighting is lowered to exhibit the AR elements better, the color of the illumination AR needs to be brighter to illuminate the marker pattern.

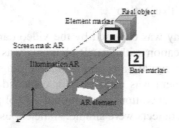

Fig. 1. Schematic representation of AR projection mapping. The entire projected area is masked by a Sscreen mask AR that has been generated from the base marker masks entire projected area. Illumination AR and AR element objects are generated from the element marker attached to the real object.

2.2   An Example of Teaching Material

In this section, an example of the content entitled "Force Vectors and Equilibrium" is briefly described. This content shows the vector summation of forces at equilibrium enabling the visualization of the tactile sensation of force.

As shown in Fig. 2a, a target weight was connected with two suspended weights of the same mass by means of strings hanging on pulleys. The target weight is in a state of equilibrium with the gravitational force directly on the weights and the tension of the strings in two directions. This system was set on the surface of a whiteboard using magnets to attach the pulleys. Two element markers (markers 1 and 2) were attached on the pulleys, and another element marker (marker 3) was fixed on the target weight. These markers provided the positions of the real objects, and three force vectors were calculated. Then, two tension vectors were generated from markers 1 and 2, and the gravitational vector was generated from marker 3. If one of the three markers were removed, two vectors appear in equilibrium.

A string connected to the target weight can be pulled by hand, as shown in Fig. 2b. If the user pulls the string, the summation of the above three forces becomes non-zero, and a net force acts on the system, causing reconfiguration to a new equilibrium state. The user can learn about the summation of force vectors through repetitions of predictions and experiments using this content.

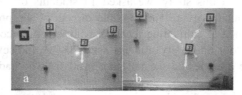

Fig. 2. Snapshots of the content entitled "Force Vectors and Equilibrium." content. a: 2 two string tensions (upward) and 1 one gravitational force (verticaldownward) are in an equilibrium state. The markers associated with figure elements 1 and 2 correspond to tensions, while the marker associated with a figure element 3 shows a plumb. b: aAnother string tension of sting (left downwards and right) are is added by hand, and the former vectors change their direction. The Mmagnitude of the additional tension changes with the position of the hand.

2.3   Time Delay of AR Projection

First, a digital timer display was captured by the video camera, and its image output from the ARToolkit application without AR elements was projected onto the screen. Side-by-side display of the digital timer and its output image were videotaped, and the time difference between them was measured for each video frame. The time differences associated with the generation of additional AR objects were similarly measured. These additional AR objects were simple, static cubes of the same size.

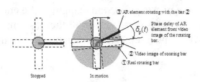

Fig. 3. Measurement of the phase delay of an AR object from the video image of a real bar configuration. Left: The AR bar (black bar) rotates with the video image of the bar configuration (broken line). Right: The video image and the AR bar was projected on the real bar rotating clockwise. Due to the delay times, the video image and the rendering of the AR object demonstrated a phase delay δ.

Second, a configuration comprising two crossed bars of 24 cm length was rotated along its center with a constant angular velocity. This simple apparatus was made using a LEGO EV3 robotic kit. A marker was placed at the center of rotation to generate a rotating AR object. By this marker, an AR bar was added and fixed on the video image of the bar. As the bar rotated, the marker and AR bar also rotated. The time delay was found between the real rotating body and the video image generated through the AR application. We measured the phase delay δ between the rotating AR object and the video image of the rotating body in the state of AR projection mapping, as shown in Fig. 3, for various constant angular velocities.

3   Results and Discussions

Our example content entitled "Force Vectors and Equilibrium" is designed for both learners and teachers. In this study, we asked 11 students of a graduate school of teacher education about the usage and possible effects of the present content. This graduate school is aimed at cultivating teachers who will play core roles at schools. Participants included four university students aged 20–29, and seven school teachers aged 20–60. Also, we interviewed six males aged 60–69 who had studied physics in their school days.

Fig. 4 shows histograms of participants' responses to the two questions: "Did you feel the change of force by moving the target point?" (left), and "Do you think manipulation of the object and force in this content is effective for understanding force?" (right). As a whole, we received positive responses on these questions. However, only one in seven schoolteachers chose "strongly agree" for the first question, and two in seven teachers chose "strongly agree" for the second question.

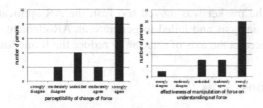

Fig. 4. Histograms of participants' response in using a 5- component Likert scales. Left: rResponses to the question, "Did you feel the change of force by moving the target point?" Right: rResponses to the question, "Do you think manipulation of the object and force in this content is effective on for understanding force?"

In the free comments of the teachers questioned, most of them admitted it was effective for learners to visualize the invisible physical quantity in the real experiment. However, they pointed out that it should be possible to change the original force (gravitational force) by adjusting the mass of the weights, and that quantitative expressions should be included. In this content, although the vector summation of forces changes with the position of the target weight, the extent of that change is not so impressively clear.

With respect to the other free comments, the participants particularly pointed out the disagreement between the motion of real objects and that of the AR elements. Figure 5a shows the measured time differences between the real clock and the video image of the clock with 0 to 3 additional AR objects. Without the rendering of additional AR objects, the time delay was 0.2 s. The delay time increased with an increasing number of simple cubic AR objects. Thus, perfect agreement between the motion of real objects and virtual images cannot be obtained by our system.

The above time delay study was for static content. For dynamical contents, the time delay between the video image and the change of the AR element should be considered. Figure 5b shows an increase in phase delay between the video image and the AR element for the apparatus described in Fig. 3 with increasing constant angular velocity. As the angular velocity was increased, the phase shift became extremely large, even for the case where only a single AR element was added. This delay of events has to be calibrated both in the interactive function of the content and in the motion content.

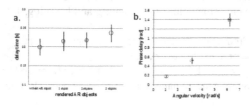

Fig. 5. Delay times of between an AR object display from and the motion of real objects. a: The difference between a real clock and the image of the clock in AR display with the rendering of 0 to 3 additional AR objects. b: The phase delay between the video image of a rotating object and the AR element object that rotates with the object at for various constant angular velocities.

In addition, if the marker was moved too fast, the AR application was unable to succeed in pattern analysis and failed to generate an AR element. In the above case, the marker was placed at the axis of rotation to reduce the frame loss.

4   Conclusions

In this study, an interactive teaching material on force vectors was created using a combination of AR technology and projection mapping. To avoid video feedback, both the real objects and the marker patterns were masked using AR mask objects. At the same time, the superposition of the screen mask AR and the local illumination AR controlled the brightness of projection illumination of the marker patterns.

This method enabled a visualization of invisible physical quantities on the actual experimental equipment. It also enabled a coupling of haptic sensing and visual perception in the content.

However, the process of image capture and projection was accompanied by a time delay. Furthermore, the time delay due to updating the positions of AR images increased with the velocity of marker motions. This may represent a strong restraint on the design method of contents that are based on AR projection mapping. An effective design method has to be developed in order to avoid creating misconception and confusion due to the time delay.

Acknowledgments. A part of this study has been funded by a Grant-in-Aid for Scientific Research (C) 21500842 from the Ministry of Education, Culture, Sports, Science and Technology, Japan. The authors would like to thank Enago (www.enago.jp) for the English language review.

References

1. Kato, H., Billinghurst, M.: Marker Tracking and HMD Calibration fro a Video-based Augmented Reality Conference System. In: Proceedings of the 2nd IEEE and ACM International Workshop on Augmented Reality, pp. 85–94 (1999)
2. Trindade, J.E.: Improving Physics learning with virtual environments: an example on the phases of water. Interactive Educational Multimedia 11, 212–236 (2005)
3. Dunleavy, M., Dede, C., Mitchell, R.: Affordances and Limitations of Immersive Participatory Augmented Reality Simulations for Teaching and Learning. J. Sci. Educ. Technol. 18, 7–22 (2009)
4. Integrated Visions Productions Video Projection Mapping,
   http://videomapping.tumblr.com
5. ARToolKit, http://www.hitl.washington.edu/artoolkit/
6. Crutchfield, J.P.: Space-time dynamics in video feedback. Physica D 10(1-2), 229–245 (1984)

Diagramming Mathematical Proofs Based on Logical Structures for Learners

Takayuki Watabe[1] and Yoshinori Miyazaki[2]

[1] Graduate School of Science and Technology, Shizuoka University, Shizuoka, Japan
`dgs13012@s.inf.shizuoka.ac.jp`
[2] Graduate School of Informatics, Shizuoka University, Shizuoka, Japan
`yoshi@inf.shizuoka.ac.jp`

Abstract. This study aims to help learners read mathematical proofs. Mathematical proofs consist of propositions and are logically structured. The structure is based on inferences, i.e., a proposition as consequence is derived from propositions as premises. However, the structure is not always represented explicitly in proofs written in natural language, which prevents learners from understanding the proofs. Therefore, we develop a system that allows mathematics teachers or content providers to create diagrams illustrating logical structures of proofs based on natural deduction to provide learners a visual aid that improves their understanding. The diagrams created by our system display natural deduction and arrange additional information (e.g., symbol definitions or explanation to assist understanding) as comments. Further, the system has a function to add buttons to show/hide parts of the proof based on individual learners' requirements. Further, we introduce the basic components of a diagram and the method to create it.

Keywords: Mathematics education, proof, diagramming, natural deduction.

1 Introduction

Mathematical proofs play a significant role in mathematics education, because proofs allow learners to confirm that theorems or propositions are logically true. However, proofs are usually written in natural language, occasionally causing learners difficulty when attempting to understand the logical structure of proofs. Proofs consist of propositions; further, propositions as consequences are derived from other propositions as premises by inference. If inference in proofs is represented intuitively, the learners' understanding of proofs is likely to be enhanced. Therefore, we propose a framework of diagrams for visualizing the process of applying inferences in proofs and a method that mathematics teachers and learning material developers can use to create such diagrams. Our system visualizes inference between propositions, each of which is represented in natural language.

Our diagram is based on proof diagrams used in natural deduction [1]. In proof diagrams, each proposition is separated explicitly, and the inference is represented as tandem propositions (i.e., lower propositions are derived from upper propositions).

C. Stephanidis (Ed.): HCII 2014 Posters, Part II, CCIS 435, pp. 183–188, 2014.

Because novice learners might find representation in proof diagrams difficult, we propose to change two components of proof diagrams. Although proof diagrams represent only the structure of inference, proofs written in natural language include additional information (e.g., definitions of symbols or explanations). Such additional content is important for learners to understand the proofs. Hence, we provide a function to arrange the content in diagrams as comments. Further, our system also provides support to include inferences that are used frequently in proofs, such as mathematical induction, the law of contraposition, or proof by exhaustion.

Software called a proof assistant was developed to help users produce proofs [2]. A proof assistant is used to interactively build a formal proof. The software can enhance learners' skills to write proofs. However, learning to write proofs is different from learning to read proofs, and reading is an important and necessary learning activity [3]. Moreover, learners who cannot grasp the structure of proofs should learn to read the proof, not write it. Our system aims to help learners read proofs. Previously, we proposed a framework for visualizing proofs [4]. In this paper, new functions are added to show comments and to adjust the content displayed; in addition, a method to create diagrams is discussed.

The remainder of this paper is organized as follows. In Section 2, we describe the basic components of our diagram and the relationship between components and natural deduction. Section 3 discusses the method to create diagrams, which includes constructing the inference structures, inserting comments in proofs, and applying templates (which correspond to inferences that appear frequently in proofs). In Section 4, our diagram of a proof is presented with an example. Section 5 presents concluding remarks and future works.

2   Diagram Components

Our diagram is based on the proof diagrams used in natural deduction. Proofs are represented as a tandem sequence that consists of premises and consequences. If all the premises situated above are true, the derived consequence situated below must be true. In our diagram, each proposition (i.e., a premise or a consequence) is enclosed by a rectangle, and premises and their consequence are connected with a line. Fig. 1 shows a diagram for the derivation B from A_1 and A_2 (or $A_1, A_2 \vdash B$).

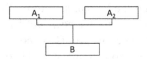

Fig. 1. Diagram of *the derivation B from A_1 and A_2*

The appropriate content of proofs depends on the learners' proficiency. If certain content is obvious to a learner, he/she will find them uninteresting (e.g., showing a proposition B in $A \vdash B \vdash C$ to a learner who knows $A \vdash C$). Therefore, a function to show/hide parts of proofs aids in determining the best content to display.

We adopt two different representations of proof diagrams in natural deduction for the intuitive understanding of learners. First, the derivation of multiple consequences from one premise is described. In natural deduction, because proof diagrams are structured as a tree, one premise must correspond to one consequence. For example, when we derive A from A *and* B and B from A *and* B, the premise A *and* B appears twice in the diagram. This notation might cause difficulties in understanding for the learners. In our diagram, when multiple consequences are derived from a single premise, the inference is represented as a single upper rectangle and multiple lower rectangles connected with lines. Fig. 2 shows a diagram of the inference.

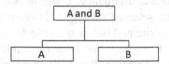

Fig. 2. Derivation of multiple consequences from a single premise

The second representation is a nested structure of proofs. In natural deduction, a consequence *if A then B* is derived from *derivation of A from B*. We consider that this inference constructs a nested structure, because the inference itself (which is the inner proof of the nest) serves as a premise. In natural deduction, a representation called *discharging A* is used to clarify that A is not a premise of *if A then B*, but such a representation might be challenging for novice learners. In our diagram, the inner proof of a nested structure (i.e., $A_1 \vdash A_2 \vdash \cdots \vdash A_n$) is enclosed by a rectangle, and the deriving proposition (i.e., *if A_1 then A_n*) is placed under said rectangle. Fig. 3 shows an example of a nested structure. The symbol "$\cdots$" shown in Fig. 3 represents a sequence of rectangles that contain A_is.

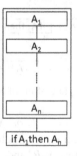

Fig. 3. Diagram of nested proof

Comments can be added to each proposition and one-step inference. Proofs written in natural language usually include additional information. Such information should be described in our diagram because the information helps learners interpret the proof. When comments are present, icons are displayed in the diagrams. The content of such comments appear when users hover the mouse cursor over the icons.

3   Creating Diagrams

In this section, we discuss our proposed methodology for creating diagrams, which includes constructing inference structures, inserting comments in proofs, and applying templates. Here, in the initial phase, an empty rectangle is set.

3.1   Constructing Structures of Proofs and Describing Comments

To create a new rectangle, users select an existing rectangle and choose to insert a rectangle as a premise or as a consequence. If the new rectangle is inserted as a *premise*, it is situated above the selected rectangle. However, if the new rectangle is inserted as a *consequence*, it is situated below the selected rectangle. Users can input an arbitrary sentence in natural language for each rectangle. Further, mathematical expressions are input using TeX notation. Proof structures are constructed by repeatedly inserting rectangles as described in this paragraph.

Comments are assigned to a single proposition or a one-step inference. When users select a single rectangle or a single vertical line and choose to insert a comment, an empty comment bubble is added. An arbitrary sentence with mathematical expressions can be written in the comments.

3.2   Templates

Templates that represent inferences used frequently in proofs are provided in order to create diagrams efficiently. To use these templates, users can select an empty rectangle and input the information required by each template. Fig. 4 shows an example of a template that represents proof by exhaustion.

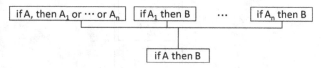

Fig. 4. Template of proof by exhaustion

The left "$\cdots$" symbol in Fig. 4 means A_i or A_{i+1} (*i is 1 to n-1*) and the right "$\cdots$" symbol represents a sequence of rectangles, including *if A_i then B*. This template requires a value for n and the content of A, B, and A_i. The templates are completed with information input by users. A nested structure can also be created using a template. The information required for a nested structure is the premise and the consequence.

Parts of sentences in rectangles that are related to a template are usually identical. For example, in Fig. 3, $n + 1$ rectangles have parts identical to B. Templates reduce the teachers' burden of writing identical sentences, and help prevent writing incorrect sentences.

4 Example of a Diagram

Fig. 5 illustrates an example of a proof diagram created by our proposed methodology. The diagram proves *if $a^2 + b^2 = c^2$, then at least one of a, b, and c is even.*

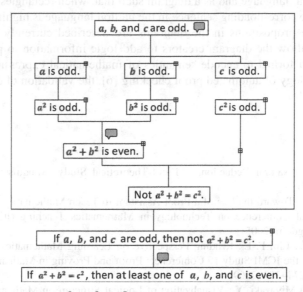

Fig. 5. Diagram of *if $a^2 + b^2 = c^2$, then at least one of a, b, and c is even.*

The comment bubbles that appear in the diagram indicate that comments have been assigned to certain propositions or inferences. In Fig. 5, the content of the uppermost comment is *a, b, and c are natural numbers*, the middle comment is *because the sum of two odds is even*, and the bottom comment is *by the law of contraposition*. Each proposition can be folded by clicking the icon on the upper-right corner of each rectangle. The icon ⊞ that appears on vertical lines indicates that there is a folded proposition at that location. The folded proposition in Fig. 5 is c^2 *is not even*. By clicking the icon ⊞, the proposition can be unfolded.

5 Concluding Remarks

In this paper, we discuss proof diagrams based on natural deduction and a method for creating these diagrams such that learners can understand proof structures intuitively. The diagrams comprise rectangles that represent propositions, and the propositions are connected with lines. The rectangles situated at the top of the diagram are premises, and they are connected to those situated at the bottom of the diagram, which are consequences. Comments can be annotated on the diagrams to show additional information to help the learners' understanding. The diagrams are created by repeatedly inserting a rectangle as a premise or as a consequence. Moreover, we provide templates that have typical proof structures in order to reduce the teachers' burden of creating diagrams.

In the future, the ability to read our diagrams would be linked to the skill of interpreting proofs written in natural language as the diagram. Because proofs are usually described in natural language, learners must grasp the structure of inferences from such proofs unassisted. We plan to develop a tool that displays a proof both as sentences in natural language and as a diagram such that, when rectangles in the diagram are clicked, the corresponding sentence in the natural language is highlighted.

Second, the propositions in the diagrams are described currently in natural language. If we allow the diagram creators to add logic information to propositions, to utilize the data format to encode semantics of mathematical expressions [5], and to use the technology of automated proof checking [6], the validation of diagrams might be possible.

References

1. Prawitz, D.: Natural Deduction: A Proof-Theoretical Study. Almquist&Wiksell, Stockholm (1965)
2. Narboux, J.: Toward the Use of a Proof Assistant to Teach Mathematics. In: The Seventh International Conference on Technology in Mathematics Teaching (ICTMT7), Bristol, United Kingdom (2005)
3. Yang, K.-L., Lin, F.-L.: Reading Perspective on Learning Mathematics Proofs. In: Proceedings of the ICMI Study 19 Conference: Proof and Proving in Mathematics Education, vol. 2, pp. 274–279 (2009)
4. Watabe, T., Miyazaki, Y.: Visualization of Logical Structure in Mathematical Proofs for Learners. In: Lee, R. (ed.) Computer and Information Science 2012. SCI, vol. 429, pp. 197–208. Springer, Heidelberg (2012)
5. MathML, http://www.w3.org/Math/
6. Rudnicki, P.: An Overview of the Mizar Project. In: Proceedings of the 1992 Workshop on Types for Proofs and Programs, pp. 311–330 (1992)

A Semantic Recommender System for Learning Based on Encyclopedia of Digital Publication

Mao Ye[1,2,3], Lifeng Jin[2], Zhi Tang[1,2], and Jianbo Xu[2]

[1] Peking University, Beijing, China
xjtuyemao@163.com
[2] State Key Laboratory of Digital Publishing Technology
(Peking University Founder Group Co. LTD.), Beijing, China
[3] Postdoctoral Workstation of the Zhongguancun Haidian Science Park, Beijing, China

Abstract. Digital publication is a useful and authoritative resource for knowledge and learning. How to use the knowledge in digital publication resources so as to enhance learning is an interesting and important task. Most of the recommender systems use users' preferences or history data for computation, which cannot solve the problems such as cold start, scarcity of history data or preferences data. A semantic recommender system is presented in this paper based on encyclopedic knowledge from digital publication resources, without considering history data or preferences data for learning the knowledge of a specific domain. Semantic relatedness is computed between concepts from the encyclopedia. The related concepts are recommended to users when one concept is reviewed. The method shows potential usability for domain-specific knowledge service.

Keywords: recommender system, digital publication, semantic relatedness.

1   Introduction

Digital publication has become one of the primary means for information circulation. It includes the digital publication of e-books, EPUBs, digital newspaper, digital magazines, digital encyclopedia, digital yearbook, and so on. The information in digital publication resource is normally useful and authoritative. It is an interesting and important task to associate different types of knowledge in digital publication resources in order to enhance learning. Since information retrieval (in terms of searching for relevant learning resources) is a pivotal activity in TEL (Technology Enhanced Learning), the deployment of recommender systems has attracted increased interest [1][2]. However, most of the recommender systems use users' preferences or history data for computation [3][4], which cannot solve the problems such as cold start, scarcity of history data or preferences data. Encyclopedia as digital publication is a kind of reference work containing a summary of information from either all domains of knowledge or a particular domain of knowledge in the format of articles or entries. It focuses on factual information to cover the concept for which the label stands. One purpose of an encyclopedia is to collect items around the globe and to organize the

C. Stephanidis (Ed.): HCII 2014 Posters, Part II, CCIS 435, pp. 189–194, 2014.

most important concepts into domains. A semantic recommender system is presented in this paper based on encyclopedia, without considering history data or preferences data for learning the knowledge of a specific domain.

2   Problem Domain

A typical encyclopedia mainly consists of concepts which usually describe and explain entities or knowledge points in its predestined domain. The knowledge contained in an encyclopedia may be denoted as $K = \{A, B\}$, where A is the set of labels and explanations in plain text of all concepts and B is other information than A in the encyclopedia, such as figures and pictures. The knowledge A may be represented as $O = \{o_1, o_2, \cdots, o_n\}$, where $o_i, i = 1, \cdots, n$ represents a concept. Each concept contains a label, which would be the name of the concept, and an explanation, which would be a short piece of text which describes the concept. Other concepts may be mentioned in the explanation of one concept. We suppose that the label of concepts in the encyclopedia is unique and encyclopedia contains the important concepts in one domain. Let $X = \{x_i, i = 1, \cdots, n\}$ be the label set in the encyclopedia where x_i is the label of the concept o_i. Let $Y = \{y_i, i = 1, \cdots, n\}$ be the explanation set where y_i is the explanation of the concept whose label is x_i. Therefore, it is known that $A = \{(x_i, y_i), i = 1, \cdots, n\}$ where x_i and y_i is the label and the explanation of the concept o_i respectively. When a concept o_i is reviewed by user, it is necessary to compute and recommend the related concept set $O_i^{'} = \{o_j \mid o_j \in O\}$ so that the user can learn or understand the concept o_i more effectively.

3   Semantic Recommender System

3.1   Semantic Relatedness Computing

Semantic relatedness is computed in this paper with concepts' labels $X = \{x_i, i = 1, \cdots, n\}$ and explanations $Y = \{y_i, i = 1, \cdots, n\}$ extracted from encyclopedia. Since one concept may be mentioned in other concepts' explanations and such concepts are often related with the original concept, we can extract the semantic relationship between the concepts by finding the relation among the text in explanations. The process to compute the relatedness can be summarized in the following steps.

Step 1: Extract concepts $O = \{o_1, o_2, \cdots, o_n\}$ from encyclopedia.

Step 2: For all concepts of O, extract concepts' labels $X = \{x_i, i = 1, \cdots, n\}$ and concepts' explanations $Y = \{y_i, i = 1, \cdots, n\}$.

Step 3: Compute the explicit relation from one concept O_i to another concept O_j by the equation $f_E(i, j) = \dfrac{\alpha(f_P(i, j) + f_N(i, j))}{1 + \alpha}$, where $\alpha \geq 1$ is a factor to control the relation strength. In the equation above, $f_P(i, j) = \dfrac{2}{1 + \exp(-\beta\mu)} - 1$ and $f_N(i, j) = \dfrac{f_P(j, i)}{\alpha}$, where $\beta > 0$ is a control factor and $\mu \geq 0$ is the number of occurrence of x_j in y_i.

Step 4: Build an explicit relation graph $G = (V, E)$ with the concepts O as vertexes and explicit relations between the concepts as edges. The edge's weight c_{ij} from the vertex O_i to O_j is set to $f_E(i, j)$.

Step 5: Build an auxiliary graph $G' = (V', E')$ according to explicit relation graph $G = (V, E)$, where $V = V'$. The weight of the edge from the vertex O_i to O_j in the graph G' is set to $c'_{ij} = -\ln c_{ij}$, where c_{ij} is the weight of the edge from the vertex O_i to O_j in the graph G.

Step 6: Compute the implicit relation from one concept O_i to another concept O_j by the equation $f_I(i, j) = \exp(-c(p^*_{ij}))$, where $c(p^*_{ij})$ is the cost of the shortest path p^*_{ij} from the vertex O_i to O_j in the graph G'. A classic algorithm to compute the shortest path is Dijkstra algorithm [5].

Step 7: Set the semantic relatedness from the concept O_i to the concept O_j with $f_E(i, j)$ if $f_E(i, j) \geq f_I(i, j)$; otherwise, set the semantic relatedness with $f_I(i, j)$.

3.2 Recommender System Based on Semantic Relatedness

The main process of the recommender system based on semantic relatedness is as Figure 1. Firstly, the concepts $O = \{o_1, o_2, \cdots, o_n\}$ of a specific domain are extracted from the encyclopedia selected for the domain. The concepts consist of labels and explanations. Ontology of the domain is then created with the concepts and the information extracted from other resources. Before the ontology can be built for a specific domain, domain experts are invited to create a schema for the domain firstly. Then the values of properties for the concepts as instances are extracted from the digital publication resources or the web resources for the ontology. The detailed process to create the ontology is well beyond the scope of the paper. Some methods or techniques can be found from the references [6][7][8]. After the ontology is built, the important concepts are saved as instances and the information or values are associated with the concepts. The semantic relatedness is then computed for the concepts $O = \{o_1, o_2, \cdots, o_n\}$ and will be saved as a matrix M in the system, where M_{ij} represent the semantic relatedness from o_i to o_j. When a concept o_i is reviewed by users, the row of o_i in M are extracted and the concepts o_j is sorted by the value of M_{ij} in descending order. Then $O_i' = \{o_j \mid o_j \in O\}$ is generated by selecting the top N concepts and are recommended to the users. The concepts in O_i' have better semantic relation with the concept o_i so that the user can learn or understand the concept o_i more effectively.

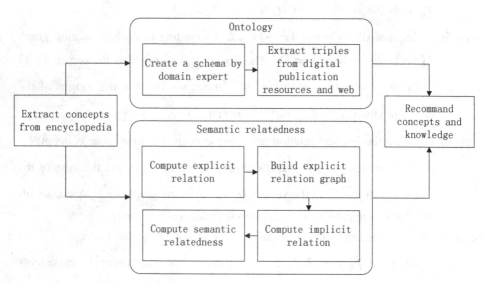

Fig. 1. The main process of the recommender system

4   A Case Study

A case of the concept Qinshihuang (秦始皇) is shown in this section to describe the early study results of the method. The concepts are extracted from three encyclopedias in the domain of history with the titles of the books "Encyclopedia of China, Chinese History I", "Encyclopedia of China, Chinese History II", and "Encyclopedia of China, Chinese History III" [9]. The number of concepts selected is 2392 for the experiment. Ontology is then built for the concepts selected. Semantic relatedness is computed between all the concepts by the method proposed with the parameters $\alpha = 2$ and $\beta = 1$. Because the semantic relatedness is computed by encyclopedias and there are normally encyclopedias of digital publish resources written in different languages, the method can be used in different linguistic environments. This is not the case for other semantic relatedness algorithms such as WordNet-based method [10], ESA[11] and WikiRelate![12]. The value of semantic relatedness is saved in the matrix M. Let o_i be the concept Qinshihuang, we get the row of o_i in M which represents the semantic relatedness from o_i to the other concepts. Top 50 concepts are selected within which 15 are shown in the table 1. The value in the field "Relation" is obtained from the matrix M. It is shown from the table that concepts related with Qinshihuang are found effectively. These concepts will be recommended to users when they review the concept Qinshihuang so that they can learn or understand it more effectively.

Table 1. Concepts recommended for the concept Qinshihuang

Concept	Relation	Concept	Relation	Concept	Relation
秦朝	0.936765502	吕不韦	0.661768490	赵高	0.462117157
李斯	0.932303602	陈胜、吴广起义	0.639763023	云梦秦律	0.462117157
蒙恬	0.836600870	黔首	0.629420632	匈奴	0.462117157
战国	0.796724106	秦郡	0.609794189	灵渠	0.462117157
秦国	0.757471222	秦二世胡亥	0.609794189	奴隶	0.398362041
…	…	…	…	…	…

5   Conclusions

Digital publication whose resources are useful and authoritative has become one of the primary means for information circulation. A semantic recommender system is proposed in this paper based on encyclopedia of digital publication for e-learning. Semantic relatedness is computed between concepts extracted from the encyclopedia for a domain. The concepts will be recommended to users for the original concept according to the semantic relatedness between them so that users can learn or understand the original concept more effectively. The recommender system works without considering users' history data or preferences data. This is the first stage investigation. The case shows its potential usability for domain-specific knowledge service. We will combine the knowledge in the constructed ontology to improve the effectiveness of the method in the future work.

Acknowledgment. The work was funded by China Postdoctoral Science Foundation and Beijing Postdoctoral Science Foundation of China.

References

1. Manouselis, N., Drachsler, H., Verbert, K., Duval, E.: Recommender Systems for Learning, pp. 1–20. Springer, Heidelberg (2013)
2. Verbert, K., Manouselis, N., Ochoa, X., Wolpers, M., Drachsler, H., Bosnic, I., Duval, E.: Context-aware Recommender Systems for Learning: A Survey and Future Challenges. IEEE Transactions on Learning Technologies 5(4), 318–335 (2012)
3. Bobadilla, J., Ortega, F., Hernando, A., Gutierrez, A.: Recommender Systems Survey. Knowledge-Based Systems 46, 109–132 (2013)
4. Carrer-Neto, W., Hernandez-Alcaraz, M.L., Valencia-Garcia, R., Garcia-Sanchez, F.: Social Knowledge-based Recommender System, Application to the Movies Domain. Expert Systems with Applications 39(12), 10990–11000 (2012)
5. Dijkstra, E.W.: A Note on Two Problems in Connexion with Graphs. Numerische Mathematik 1, 269–271 (1959)
6. Zouaq, A., Nkambou, R.: Evaluating the Generation of Domain Ontologies in the Knowledge Puzzle Project. IEEE Transactions on Knowledge and Data Engineering 21(11), 1559–1572 (2009)
7. Ameen, A., Khan, K.U.R., Rani, B.P.: Creation of Ontology in Education Domain. In: 4th International Conference on Technology for Education, pp. 237–238. IEEE Press, New York (2012)
8. Gaeta, M., Orciuoli, F., Paolozzi, S., Salerno, S.: Ontology Extraction for Knowledge Reuse: the e-Learning Perspective. IEEE Transactions on Systems, Man and Cybernetics, Part A: Systems and Humans 41(4), 798–809 (2011)
9. Encyclopedia of China, Chinese History I, II, III, http://shuyuan.apabi.com
10. Budanitsky, A., Hirst, G.: Semantic Distance in WordNet: An Experimental, Application-oriented Evaluation of Five Measures. In: Workshop on WordNet and Other Lexical Resources, Second Meeting of the North American Chapter of the Association for Computational Linguistics, Pittsburgh, USA (2001)
11. Gabrilovich, E., Markovitch, S.: Computing Semantic Relatedness Using Wikipedia-based Explicit Semantic Analysis. In: 20th International Joint Conference on Artificial Intelligence, pp. 1606–1611. Morgan Kaufmann Publishers Inc., San Francisco (2007)
12. Strube, M., Ponzetto, S.P.: WikiRelate! Computing Semantic Relatedness Using Wikipedia. In: 21st National Conference on Artificial Intelligence, vol. 2, pp. 1419–1424. AAAI Press (2006)

Design for All, Accessibility and Assistive Environments

User Interface Design for Disabled People Under the Influence of Time, Efficiency and Costs

Yashar Abbasalizadeh Rezaei, Gernot Heisenberg, and Wolfgang Heiden

Institute of Visual Computing
Bonn-Rhein-Sieg University of Applied Sciences, Germany
{yashar.abbasalizadeh,gernot.heisenberg,wolfgang.heiden}@h-brs.de
http://www.emotion-computing.org

Abstract. Applications being designed for disabled people so far are showing three main issues: *specific target user group*, *specialized user interface (UI)* and *interdependence problem*. In addition, three essential criteria do also affect the application's usability, namely *time*, *efficiency* and *costs*. In order to overcome these problems, we propose a different perspective of User-Centered Design (UCD) by dividing and analyzing the UI architecture design process over three interdependent spaces: User, Need and application. Finally we provide the reader with an algorithmic guideline towards minimizing the interdependence issue between interaction modalities.

Keywords: HCI, UI design, disabled people, User-Centered Approach.

1   Introduction

With the improvement in hardware and software technologies over the past few decades, interaction methods e.g. *touch-*, *vision-* and *speech-based* have become popular ways to interact with electronic devices. Besides all of these, an evolutionary approach called neuro-signal-based or the bio-signal-based has been tested successfully as laboratory prototype [1]. One important issue of most of the existing user interfaces on the market is that, due to low commercial profit, disabled people have been less attractive as target user group. In addition, the laboratory interface prototypes are generally specialized on a single goal (need) like writing and do not respond to other sub-goals such as reading, being mobile, communicating or being entertained. Another issue,called *interdependency problem* arises when two or more goals need to be performed at the same time with the same interaction modality. This relevant issue decreases the usability of the interface considerably. In this paper we propose a different perspective of *User-Centered Design*. For this purpose, three interdependent spaces are introduced:

1. **The User space** defines the type and the variety of the target user group. It can be categorized by different criteria like age, level of knowledge, gender, culture and health condition.
2. **The Need space**: Once the target user groups have been categorized, user needs should be identified by taking into account the objective behavior of

C. Stephanidis (Ed.): HCII 2014 Posters, Part II, CCIS 435, pp. 197–202, 2014.

the UI. This includes goals (needs) of the user that the software application has to fulfill by providing a certain functionality.

3. **The Application space** consist of software solutions provided by different domains such as *Computer Vision, Natural Language Processing, Signal Processing* etc. that can provide fast and reliable responses to interaction modalities.

In section three, an algorithmic approach is proposed for minimizing the interdependency problem. Finally, the result of our algorithmic approach is discussed by comparing it with appreciable multimodal HCIs that have been introduced to fulfill multiple needs and limitations of disabled people.

2   Related Work

To fulfill the needs of disabled people, various interfaces were devised by experts in the past, but these approaches were made to fulfill a particular need of a user group with a specific disability. For instance, [2] used a special face detection system for monitoring the physical activities of people who suffer from cerebral palsy. [3] devised a low cost eye tracking system for establishing a human-computer Interface for people who show limited movement of their bodies. In [4], gesture recognition is used as an interaction method for communication and provided a face tracking-based system for people who suffer from cerebral palsy to interact with a computer. In [5] speech and head tracking approaches are used to enable a hands free control of a computer and other devices, and [6] extended that approach by facial recognition. [1] introduced a similar approach, but instead of head tracking, face and hand gestures were used. [7] used touch-based and speech-based approaches in a mobile remote control unit to enable disabled people to control domestic appliances.

Problem Formulation: By studying and analyzing the above mentioned approaches and several more, the following problems have been identified: *Specific target user group* - In most of the cases, only one disability type is targeted by the application. This could cause problems as soon as the targeted user group is not able to make use of the application due to a secondary disability. For instance, an application provided for frail elderly suffering from vision impairment could probably not be used effectively because the usage of the application involves the users hands or the upper limbs. Even if it would not require the limbs but the auditory capability, this specific elder users could not make use of the application with the expected performance. *Specialized UI design* - The provided UIs target single specific tasks such as writing, speaking or mobility (controlling a wheel chair). However, this is not efficient for preparing people with multiple disabilities for higher education or professions because it would end up in providing separate applications for each single activity. *Interdependency problem* - It occurs when the target user groups are too general. For example, using a writing/reading system based on touch for people with visual impairment (braille) is extremely difficult to use if the user is also paraplegic and at the same time needs to control a wheelchair.

3   Approach for UI Design

One of the most important criteria for developing an effective User Interface (UI) is the *user scalability factor*. As discussed in the previous section, almost all of those UIs were trying to compensate physiological limitations by adding some special accessibility features. However, this approach drastically reduces the scalability of the interface. Hence, in the following we are introducing a novel *user-centered approach* for designing UI's for disabled people. The basic principle is to focus on the user and its needs by analyzing three interdependent spaces: *user, need* and *application space*.

User Space: WHO [8] says, there are more than one billion people with various disabilities all around the world, of whom approximately 150 million experience significant difficulties. Around 285 million are visually-impaired and 360 million are hearing-impaired. Different researchers provided distinct perspectives on the classification of disabilities, as follows [9]: *The Medical perspective* defines disabled people as people with a health problem, that is caused by disease, trauma, congenital or an accident. *The Socio-political perspective* focuses on an independent living philosophy rather than on a complex collection of conditions, no matter how people lost their functionality. *The Spectrum perspective* refers to the degree of functionality of certain senses such as the visual, the hearing or the tactile sense. *The Economic perspective* defines disabled people in terms of employability in the market. In the opinion of the World Health Organization (WHO) disabilities should neither be viewed as purely medical nor as purely social. A balanced approach is needed, providing appropriate weight to the different aspects of disability. Disability arises from the interaction of health conditions with contextual, environmental and personal factors. The International Classification of Functioning, Disability and health Association (ICF) adopts neutral language and does not distinguish between the type and cause of disability [9]. They describe disability in an easy and understandable way, with respect to human functioning and its limitations and structured the information in a meaningful way. We believe that no matter what the cause is or from what limitation disabled people suffer, they have to be seen as human individuals with the same needs as others. The only difference is the way of fulfilling their needs. In order to do so application and interaction designers need to study the corresponding need space.

Need Space: In this paper, we propose a new definition of "need" such as "the basic goals and activities associated to human interaction modalities". In other words, to identify basic goals and activities for vision impaired people, it is necessary to specify the data that the vision modality provides. They can be listed as follows: object detection, object identification, distance between the objects, distance to the objects. In order to complete the need analysis, it is essential to identify the role of each need in different life areas. For example, the object detection can be either detect words, sentences or a symbol for the purpose of reading. Or it could deliver the detection of tables, doors or a corridor for the purpose of moving. For the sake of completeness while identifying needs, a full range of activity and participation components was provided by the [9]. They used performance and capacity qualifiers to describe the individual's ability and performance during the execution of a task.

Application Space: The previous sections have shown that disabilities can be described as limitations of the degree of ability (DOA). In addition it showed how to analyze basic goals and needs corresponding to limitations resulted by the impairment in modalities. Now the question is, how to choose suitable substitutes in order to resolve or decrease the effects of such limitations.

Table 1. Substitution table shows alternative replacement for human body senses and actuators

		Sight	Hearing	Touch	Taste	Speech	Upper limb	Lower Limb	Skeletal muscles	Tactile graphic display	Tactile sensors	Text to Braille	Braille to Text	Eye gaze tracking	Head tracking	Facial gesture detection	Hand gesture detection	Text to Speech	Speech to Text	Sign language to Speech	ERP-based Control (EEG)	ERD/ERS-based Control (EEG)	Neuro-prosthetic /EMG-based	Manipulator arm	Non | Autonomous wheelchair	Environment mapping
Actuator	Skeletal muscles			*										*	*			*			*	*	*			
	Lower limb						*	*							*		*				*	*	*		*	
	Upper Limb			*		*	*							*	*		*				*	*	*	*		
	Speech	*	*		*	*										*	*	*	*	*						
Sense	Taste	*																								
	Touch	*									*															
	Hearing	*			*	*											*	*	*	*	*					
	Sight		*	*		*	*	*	*		*			*	*			*	*							*

Besides the phenomenon of natural substitution, the technological substitute also has important impact on the improvement of life conditions of disabled individuals. Table 1 summarized a number of senses, actuators and technologies that can be substituted by each other. On the other hand, there are situations that limit the technological substitute to specific conditions. For example, eye gaze tracking can be used as a mouse pointer unless the user is looking to a specific area, and speech to text performs reasonably good unless the user is in a noisy environment. In addition the mentioned disadvantages, the case has to be solved in which the individual is suffering from more than one disability at the same time since in such cases, apart from the adaptivity issue, the interdependency problem arises as well.

Reducing Interdependencies: For overcoming the above mentioned problem we propose a systematic approach in order to reduce interdependencies between tasks (see figure 1): In order to categorize users, cluster them into groups based on their limitation in DOA. It can be either binary (limited and not limited) or a multiple level classifier (min, average and high). The important is to cluster users into groups with the minimum amount of shared limitations. For the need identification, the information provided by the limited modality must be

```
Data: User information based on DOA
Result: Interdependencies between UI tasks
Input: Interaction modalities, ICF activity categorization, Substitution table
forall the Users do
    | Cluster users into groups based on Limitation of DOA;
end
forall the User groups do
    | Identify basic needs based on modality's behavior;
end
forall the Identified needs do
    | Specify tasks for need identification by considering ICF's activity categories;
end
forall the Tasks do
    | Choose appropriate technology from substitution table;
end
forall the Selected technologies do
    if Shared modality exists then
        | Interdependency
    else
        | No interdependency;
    end
end
```

Fig. 1. Systematic algorithm for the UI design approach

identified. For the task specification, it is highly recommended to follow the activity and participation guideline by [9] for analyzing appropriate tasks in all different life areas. From the substitution table select an appropriate technology corresponding to the identified tasks. Finally, for specifying the shared modality, compare all the selected technologies in order to identify their interdependency. This will result in a clear map of the applicability of tasks in sequential or parallel execution.

There are many factors that affect UI usability, but, the *time*, *costs* and *efficiency* criteria definitively show the highest impact. For example, an application for handicapped people that is controlled only by one event. In such application it is highly challenging and time consuming to change the focus and select a desired task such as typing a keyword to search in web browser. One solution for such a case is an UI which is extremely adaptable and intelligent that can increase the focus change and selection time by learning user preferences and adapt itself in an intelligent manner. Here, intelligence means that the UI should not represent the user preferences, but it considers the live events and also general preferred event and tasks as well.

4   Conclusions and Future Work

This paper is a modest contribution to the ongoing discussions about UI design for disabled people. Section two has shown that many applications that have been devised are lacking in several aspects: *Specific target user group, specialized design* and *interdependency*. The author's attention was focused on these three problems and as a result, section three proposed a comprehensive analytic UCD approach to overcome the identified problems. It should be noted that the interfaces of [10], [11] are the best examples of great designs and implementations so far, but in contrast to the proposed analytical UCD approach in this article, they also lacked in analyzing the *need space*. They mainly focus on combining a large number of interaction modalities for fulfilling specific need requirements, such as *communication* or *domestic life*. From the research being undertaken, it is possible to conclude that the depth analysis of user requirements and corresponding technologies has a special effect on scalability and usability of UIs. The proposed method can be used practically, not just for UI design for disabled people. It is an applicable mean for analyzing interdependencies for UI design for other user groups as well. On the basis of our research being presented in this paper, we have started to design and implement a user interface for people that can control only one facial muscle and hence can trigger one event at a time only. This work has been supported financially by the Institute of Visual Computing at Bonn-Rhein-Sieg University of Applied Sciences.

References

1. Millan, J.D.R., et al.: Combining brain-computer interfaces and assistive technologies: State-of-the-art and challenges. Frontiers in Neuroscience 4, 1–15 (2010)
2. Ong, C., Lu, M.V., Lau, B.: A face based real time communication for physically and speech disabled people. In: Assistive and Augmentive Communication for the Disabled, pp. 70–102 (2011)
3. Vazquez, L.J.G., Minor, M.A., Sossa, A.J.H.: Low cost human computer interface voluntary eye movement as communication system for disabled people with limited movements. In: 2011 Pan American Health Care Exchanges, pp. 165–170. IEEE (2011)
4. Murata, Y., Yoshida, K., Suzuki, K., Takahashi, D.: Proposal of an automobile driving interface using gesture operation for disabled people. In: 6th International Conf. on Advances in Computer-Human Interactions, ACHI 2013, pp. 472–478 (2013)
5. Karpov, A., Ronzhin, A.: Icando: Low cost multimodal interface for hand disabled people. Journal on Multimodal User Interfaces 1(2), 21–29 (2007)
6. Varona, J., Manresa-Yee, C., Perales, F.J.: Hands-free vision-based interface for computer accessibility. Journal of Network and Computer Applications 31(4), 357–374 (2008)
7. Valles, M., et al.: Multimodal environmental control system for elderly and disabled people. In: Proceedings of the 18th Annual International Conference of the IEEE Engineering in Medicine and Biology Society, vol. 2, pp. 516–517. IEEE (1996)
8. WHO: Draft action plan for the prevention of avoidable blindness and visual impairment 2014-2019. Sixty-Sixth World Health Assembly (2013)
9. ICF: International classification of functioning, disability and health / World Health Organization. World Health Organization, Geneva (2011)
10. Argyropoulos, S., Moustakas, K., Karpov, A.A., Aran, O., Tzovaras, D., Tsakiris, T., Varni, G., Kwon, B.: Multimodal user interface for the communication of the disabled. Journal on Multimodal User Interfaces 2(2), 105–116 (2008)
11. Pan, G., Wu, J., Zhang, D., Wu, Z., Yang, Y., Li, S.: Geeair: a universal multimodal remote control device for home appliances. Personal and Ubiquitous Computing 14(8), 723–735 (2010)

What Color? A Real-time Color Identification Mobile Application for Visually Impaired People

Sara A. Al-Doweesh[1], Felwah A. Al-Hamed[1], and Hend S. Al-Khalifa[2]

[1] Center of Excellence for Telecom Applications,
King Abdulaziz City for Science and Technology, Saudi Arabia
{saldoweesh, falhamed}@kacst.edu.sa
[2] Information Technology Department, College of Computer and Information Science,
King Saud University, Riyadh, Saudi Arabia
hendk@ksu.edu.sa

Abstract. In this paper we present an iPhone application that facilitates the operation of detecting colors for blind and visually impaired people in real-time. In order to detect colors, we take the input from the device camera then we process pixel values to produce the color using HSL color space, the detected color will be displayed as label on screen as well as uttering it. Moreover, the application can view a set of colors that match a specific color to help blind people choosing clothes before promenading. We tested the application on a set of blind and visually impaired people to evaluate the application accuracy and usability. Our evaluation showed that the application provides high detection accuracy of colors in different lighting conditions. Furthermore, the application satisfies its users' needs.

Keywords: Color Detection, Visually Impaired, Clothes Matching, Hue-Saturation-Luminance (HSL), Real-time Identification, Camera Phone.

1 Introduction

Latest global estimations indicate a dramatic increase in the magnitude of visual impairment in the world. Blind and visually impaired community has the right to live as normal people and we are responsible of facilitating their lives [1]. One of the challenging problems facing them is recognizing the color of things around.

Despite the existence of other techniques of color identification, such as electronic color detectors and tactile tags for marking clothes. Yet, these devices are stand-alone, which means the blind person has to carry them all the time and bear its weight. Furthermore, blind people who had no sense of color before have no way of knowing if a set of two or more color-combinations of clothes match or not [2].

According to problems mentioned previously, we decided to develop an iPhone application that detect the color of a chosen area and utter its name in Arabic. Moreover, it shows a set of suitable colors to help them in wearing appropriate clothes.

C. Stephanidis (Ed.): HCII 2014 Posters, Part II, CCIS 435, pp. 203–208, 2014.

2   Previous Work

Different applications were developed to help visually impaired and blind people identify objects' colors in real-life. This is done by utilizing the embedded camera and screen reader on smartphones [4]. Most of these applications apply image-processing algorithms either on captured images e.g. Kolorami and Color Helper or on a video stream to achieve real-time color identification e.g. Color Identifier.

Kolorami is an iPhone mobile application developed by Comparatel especially for color blind and visually impaired people. It allows the user to take a picture or import it from gallery and then analyze its colors and show the most three colors found in the picture with its approximate percentage [5].

Another application that analyses captured pictures is Color Helper 4 Men developed by Codete for Android users. It allows the user to take a picture and asks the user to determine a specific point to be analyzed and then identify the color and give suggestions for matching colors [6]. On the other hand, GreenGar, developed Color Identifier for iPhone users, works by moving the phone camera to the object center, then the application identifies the color by displaying and pronouncing its name [7].

From the previous discussion, we can see that existing applications either require the user to capture a picture in order to determine the object color, or provide real-time color identification in local language, besides, they show some sophisticated and rarely used colors. However in our application we will give Arabic speaking users the possibility to detect all colors in real time using their own language. Moreover, unknown detected colors will be approximated to nearest popular and known colors.

3   System Overview

Our application detects colors using HSL color space where Hue (H) refers to color name, Saturation (S) refers to color fullness and (L) is the Lightness of the color [9]. The system takes a pixel from the video stream of the device camera as an input, and then analyzes it to generate the color and output it in audio and text forms. Moreover, our application permits the user to view matching colors of the detected color in order to help visually impaired people in choosing clothes to wear. Our application consists of two main functions: Color Detection and Color Matching.

3.1   Color Detection

Color Detection is the process from when the user points the device camera on an item till the color name is viewed on the screen. There are two sets of colors to detect: the first is simple colors, which was made for blind people who never saw colors before. The second is complex colors, which contains more complex colors with different scales. Color is grabbed from the camera in Red-Green-Blue (RGB) model, since RGB channels interfere with each other and its chrominance and luminance are mixed, accordingly, a small variation in lightning will affect the rates for the red, green and blue components [8][12]. Thus, "As the three components (H, S, L) are independent in HSL color space, it is more suitable for color image analysis than

RGB color space" [9]. So, we convert the pixel value from RGB to HSL before determining the color. We did this by applying the equation used for RGB to HSL conversion as Kwanchai et al. mentioned in [3].

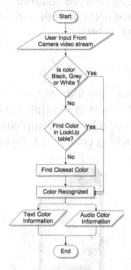

Fig. 1. Flowchart of Color Detection Process

Figure 1 illustrates the flow of our proposed system. After we have the H, S and L values for the pixel, we first check the values of saturation S and Luminance L to detect "*white*", "*black*", and "*gray*" colors. If the luminance L of a pixel is greater than 90, then the color is recognized as "*white*". On the contrary, if the luminance L of a pixel is less than 10 or (L <= 15 and S <=15) then the color is "*black*". The color is identified as "*gray*", when the saturation is less than 16 and luminance L matches one of these cases:

L <= 40→ Dark Grey, L <= 70→ Grey, L <= 80→ Silver and L <= 95→Light Grey

If the color is not White, Black nor gray, we search for it in the lookup table, if it is not found then: first we determine the category of the color in the pre-classified colors' categories that were classified depending on the hue value as in table 1.

Table 1. Color categories corresponding to hue values.

Hue Range	Color Category	Hue Range	Color Category
0 - 15, 346 - 360	Red	136 - 160	Spring Green
16 – 40	Orange	161 - 200	Cyan
41 – 45	Gold	201 - 255	Blue
46 – 60	Yellow	256 - 300	Purple
61 – 90	Yellow-Green	301 - 345	Pink
91 – 135	Green		

Next we calculate the difference between HSL value we obtained from the camera and the predefined HSL color values within the category. After finding the nearest value, the color name will appear on the screen and will be uttered also.

Figure 2 illustrates the color-detection interface in our system. The main window contains the video stream with point in the middle showing the exact location of the color that will be detected. Besides, there are three buttons at the bottom of the interface, button number 1 will switch between complex and simple colors, button number 2 will turn on Flash light to assist color detection in low light conditions, while button number 3 will be discussed next section.

3.2   Color Matching

Color matching function provides the user with some colors that matches a detected color in order to help the blind person in wearing suitable clothes. To accomplish this process, we used these three color schemes: complementary, split complementary and analogous to determine the matching colors [11]. Figure 3,4 illustrates an example.

  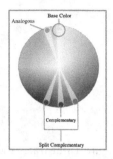

Fig. 2. Color Reader Main Interface, (1) indicates switching between complex and simple colors, (2) indicates turning on Flash light (3) indicates color matching

Fig. 3. Color Matching Interface. It shows the detected color and 4 matching colors that go with it

Fig. 4. Example of Color Schemes used to Match Color

4   Preliminary Evaluation

In order to demonstrate the effectiveness of our application, we discuss next the results of technical testing and user testing.

Technical testing was applied to measure the accuracy of color detection method. We tested our application under different lighting conditions (bright, natural and dark) to ensure our method can detect the correct color regardless of the light variation. We defined lighting conditions as follows: when all room lights are on, then it is bright lightening, dark lightening is defined when we depend on lampshade light only.

Table 2 illustrates the results of the technical testing. We obtained average success of 97.2% for color detection in bright lightening, 86.1% in natural lightening and 53.9% in dark lightening. However, results got worse on dark lightening where lighting conditions affects the value of the luminance (L) component of detected color.

Table 2. Color detection accuracy under different lighting conditions where 100% means the application always detects the color, 0% means the color is never detected

Color	Lighting Condition		
	Bright (%)	Natural (%)	Dark (%)
White	100	50	0
Gray	100	100	100
Black	100	100	100
Red	100	100	100
Dark Red	50	30	10
Pink	100	20	0
Fuchsia	100	100	80
Purple	100	80	70
Yellow	100	100	30
Orange	100	90	10
Brown	100	100	100
Beige	100	100	10
Green	100	100	100
Yellow-Green	100	100	70
Blue	100	100	10
Navy	100	100	30
Cyan	100	90	50
Sea Green	100	90	100
Average	97.2	86.1	53.9

Table 3. User testing results for 5 users

Tasks	Average Tasks Time (seconds)	Average Number of Errors
Identify cloth color	40	0
Turn on camera flash	36	0.4
Switch to complex color	20	0.2
Show suitable colors	33	0.2

Table 4. Average User feedback results where (1 is strongly agree and 5 is strongly disagree)

Statement	Average of user feedback results
Need for the application	1
Ease of use	1
Satisfaction	1

User Testing was applied to measure the usability of our application with end users. User testing was held at a local school for blind and visually impaired people. After introducing the application, five iPhone users (4 blind people, 1 visually impaired person) were asked to try our application and perform a set of tasks that are shown in Table 3 in order to gain an insight into how they are going to interact with the application. After that we asked them to give their feedback by rating the agreement and disagreement of some statements that is presented in Table 4 to see to what extent our application satisfies its users' needs. It is clear from the results that the application is easy to use, powerful and meets its users needs and expectations.

5   Conclusion and Future Work

In this paper we presented a real-time color identification iPhone application that helps blind and visually impaired people identify colors in real-life in an easy and effective way. Our algorithm for color detection is based on HSL color space and matching color algorithm is based on complementary, split complementary and analogous color schemes. Our evaluation showed that our application provides high detection accuracy of colors in different lighting conditions. Moreover, we found that the application is useful and satisfies its users' needs.

In order to make our application more valuable for cloth identification, we aim to improve the detection algorithm to detect cloth patterns besides colors.

References

1. Global trends in the magnitude of blindness and visual impairment,
   http://www.who.int/blindness/causes/trends/en/
2. Paisios, N., Subramanian, L., Rubinsteyn, A.: Choosing which Clothes to Wear Confidently: A Tool for Pattern Matching. In: Workshop on Frontiers in Accessibility for Pervasive Computing. ACM (2012)
3. Kwanchai, K., Prajin, P., Wichian, P.: Development of Object Detection Software for Mobile Robot using an AForce.Net Framework. In: Ninth International Conference on ICT and Knowledge Engineering, pp. 201–206. IEEE Thailand (2011)
4. Peng, E., Peursum, P., Li, L., Venkatesh, S.: A Smartphone-Based Obstacle Sensor for the Visually Impaired. In: Yu, Z., Liscano, R., Chen, G., Zhang, D., Zhou, X. (eds.) UIC 2010. LNCS, vol. 6406, pp. 590–604. Springer, Heidelberg (2010)
5. Kolorami,
   https://itunes.apple.com/us/app/kolorami/id394254215?mt=8
6. Color Helper, https://play.google.com/store/apps/
   details?id=co.codete.android.colorhelper
7. Color Identifier, http://itunes.apple.com/us/app/
   coloridentifier/id363346987?mt=8
8. Le, T.T., Tran, S.T., Mita, S., Nguyen, T.D.: Real Time Traffic Sign Detection Using Color and Shape-Based Features. In: Nguyen, N.T., Le, M.T., Świątek, J. (eds.) ACIIDS 2010. LNCS, vol. 5991, pp. 268–278. Springer, Heidelberg (2010)
9. Pan, R., Gao, W., Liu, J.: Color Clustering Analysis of Yarn-dyed Fabric in HSL Color Space. In: WRI World Congress on Software Engineering, WCSE 2009, vol. 2, pp. 273–278. IEEE, Xiamen (2009)
10. Tian, Y., Yuan, S.: Clothes Matching for Blind and Color Blind People. In: Miesenberger, K., Klaus, J., Zagler, W., Karshmer, A. (eds.) ICCHP 2010, Part II. LNCS, vol. 6180, pp. 324–331. Springer, Heidelberg (2010)
11. Rhyne, T.: Applying Artistic Color Theories to Visualization. In: Dill, J., et al. (eds.) Expanding the Frontiers of Visual Analytics and Visualization, pp. 263–283. Springer London (2012)
12. Toledo, F.J., Martínez, J.J., Garrigós, J., Ferrández, J.: Skin Color Detection For Real Time Mobile Applications (Spain In Field Programmable Logic and Applications). In: International Conference on FPL 2006. IEEE Spain (2006)

ACCESS: A Free and Open Source Arabic Assistive Technology Repository

Hend S. Al-Khalifa* and Muna Al-Razgan

Information Technology Department, College of Computer and Information Sciences,
King Saud University, Riyadh, Saudi Arabia
hendk@ksu.edu.sa, muna02@gmail.com

Abstract. In recent years the number of free/open source Arabic Assistive Technology (AT) software has increased, yet they are scattered and hard to find. In order to provide Arab users with easy access to Arabic AT software, AT repositories are created. In this paper we report our experience in creating ACCESS - an Open Source/Freeware AT software repository for Arabic speaking users.

Keywords: Open Source, Assistive technology, Accessibility, Arabic Language.

1   Introduction

Several free and open source Arabic Assistive Technology (AT) software are available online for people to download and use. Yet, the problem resides with the fact that these software are scattered in different locations, which makes these products hard to find, i.e. information for each product is available on its own website, with no easy way to overview all available software in one place.

Online AT repositories help users while searching for appropriate products. In order to provide users with easy access to AT software, hardware and peripherals, AT repositories are created. Some of the famous AT repositories are: EASTIN: European Assistive Technology Information Network [1], OATS: Open source Assistive Technology Software [2] and ATHENA a Free AT Software Inventory [3]. And recently the inception of Mada Portal (Qatar Assistive Technology Center) [4].

The number of such repositories available today is very few especially for Arabic speakers. Our developed repository intend to solve the problems associated with AT products in general and AT software in particular, by making the various free and open source Arabic AT software available to its users in one place and in an easily accessible form.

2   ACCESS Repository Overview

The repository as shown in Figure 1 has two main components:

1. **Product Page:** The product page is the most important component. It contains the list of all products. Products are classified based on type of disability and their ISO

---

* Corresponding author.

C. Stephanidis (Ed.): HCII 2014 Posters, Part II, CCIS 435, pp. 209–213, 2014.

Fig. 1. Screenshot of Access repository (access.edu.sa)

9999:2011 codes [5]. In ISO 9999 the products are categorized into classes, sub-classes, and divisions, where classes are the highest level and divisions are the lowest level of classification. For example, ISO 9999:2002 has 743 types of devices classified into 11 classes, 135 subclasses and each division contains a number of assistive devices. The different categorization would help the users to browse and search products based on their functionality and their ISO classification codes. Each product in the product page has metadata such as: software snapshot, its version, the disability covered, the system requirements for installation, type of platforms it supports, and most importantly, a downloadable link, through which the users can freely download the chosen product on their systems. The product page also allows the user to rate the product on a five-point scale and add comments.

2. **Search:** The repository provides two types of search, a simple search and advanced search. Simple search acts like a keyword search which will fetch all the related information from the database. Advanced search allows users to filter the results based on the different functionality (Category and ISO 9999 codes).

3   Methodology

The methodology we used to build ACCESS repository consists of several steps illustrated in the following sections.

3.1 Searching for AT Software Online

In order to search for useful Arabic AT software, we had searched: Google, Google-play, Apple store, browsers Add-ons, famous twitter accounts that disseminate new AT software besides AT repositories in other languages. A total of 114 software were found. We had excluded any software that does not work, or not intended for disabled people.

3.2 Installing and Testing AT Software

Once a software is found, we installed it on the appropriate platform such as PC, mobile phones, tablets or Mac computers. Once the installation is successful, we ran the software and check its intended use and functionality as described in the software website. While searching, we found two types of software: open source software and shareware software. For the open source software, the installation is straightforward. However, for the shareware software, we installed its trial version.

3.3 Documenting AT Software

After the successful installation and testing of each AT software, the ACCESS repository is populated with the software and documented in Arabic with the following metadata fields:

- **Software name**: the name of the AT software.
- **Software logo/image**: the software image or logo as it appears in the developer's website.
- **Disability category**: Each software is classified according to the available disability category; nonetheless, the category type can be increased if there is 3-5 software for specific disability not listed. For now the defined list contains the following disabilities: blindness or low vision, hearing, speech, moving, learning, and cognitive disability.
- **Description**: a description of the software functionality is provided along with its most important features.
- **Developer**: The company or the developer(s) name(s) is listed.
- **External download link**: a link is provided to the software website for download.
- **Version**: the version number of the software.
- **System requirements**: the compatible devices are listed, this includes: PC-Windows, Mac, iPad, iPhone, and iPod.
- **Language**: the language that is available for the software (Arabic or/and English).
- **Date of adding**: the date where the software was added to ACCESS repository.
- **ISO standard**: the class type of the ISO standard.
- **License**: the type of the license available e.g. open source or shareware.
- **Price**: either listed as free for open source software, or the price in local currency is displayed.
- **Share via twitter**: provide the availability to share the software via twitter.
- **Rate the software**: rate the software on a five-point scale for registered users.

- **Comments**: allow the registered users to add their comments about the software.
- **Related software**: this field provides images and links to other software available in the repository similar to the chosen software.

3.4   Repository Design

ACCESS repository was built using Drupal Content Management System (CMS). Drupal is a free content management software package that allows organizing, managing and publishing content easily, with an endless variety of customization. Drupal makes use of structures called "modules". Some modules, called core modules, are by default installed along with Drupal installation. Other modules can be installed when required during the design phase. In this project we have incorporated several modules such as simple search and advanced search, rating and share via Twitter. However, sometimes, we had to edit the code of the module especially with regards to accessibility features such as color, page layout, the ability to increase/decrees the font size of the repository, and the display of images.

Various search strategies were employed in ACCESS repository this includes: simple keywords search, search by disability category or search using ISO standard. In addition, the repository provides the ability to list all the available software in its database. The different search strategies are available in all pages of the repository.

Further information is also provided for each software page such as statistics showing the number of views a particular page gained.

3.5   Update and Maintenance

Updating and maintaining the repository is an important aspect to increase the number of available software to the Arab disabled personal. Routine checking for any updates in the available software added to the repository is done. There is also a suggestion form where registered users can suggest new software to add to the repository. Once any software is available ACCESS team search for the software, download and test it then add it to the repository.

4   Discussion

As explained in the previous section the information available for each software made ACCESS an easy to use repository. ACCESS repository (http://access.edu.sa) has been online for around eleven months with total of 114 Arabic AT software. To increase the repository exposure, it was disseminated via the university newspaper, twitter, and local conferences. So far the comments heard about the repository are positive and people are asking for more software to be added. The number of visitors during the past 11 months reached 340k.

5 Future Work

This paper presented our efforts in building the first Arabic AT software repository for Arab users. Software disseminated via ACCESS repository are tested and reviewed by computer experts in order to detect and point out reliability, installation, and compatibility issues.

Future plans include localizing existing AT software to Arabic by interested developers and volunteers. In addition, a mobile application will be developed for recommending newly added AT software to the repository for disabled people.

Acknowledgments. We would like to thank Hilah AlMazrou, Sunitha Robert and Akheela Khnaum for the involvement in the first stage of the project. We would also like to thank Manahel Al Twaim and Moneerah Al-Mohsin for carrying on the project, maintaining and populating the repository.

References

1. EASTIN - Your source of information on daily living equipment in Europe, http://www.eastin.eu/en-GB/whatIsEastin/index
2. OATS, http://www.oatsoft.org/
3. Free AT Software, http://access.uoa.gr/ATHENA/eng/pages/home
4. Mada Portal, http://madaportal.org
5. ISO 9999:2011, http://www.iso.org/iso/iso_catalogue/catalogue_tc/catalogue_detail.htm?csnumber=50982

Inclusive Design: An Interface for Users with Disabilities

Claudia Regina Batista[1], Vania Ribas Ulbricht[1], Marília Matos Gonçalves[1],
Tarcísio Vanzin[1], and Adhemar Maria do Valle Filho[2]

[1] Federal University of Santa Catarina, Department of Graphic Expression,
Trindade, 88040-900 Florianópolis – Santa Catarina, Brazil
claudia.batista@ufsc.br,
{vulbricht,marilinhamt,tvanzin}@gmail.com
[2] University of Vale do Itajaí, Computer Science, Itajaí – Santa Catarina, Brazil
adhe.valle@gmail.com

Abstract. This paper shows the interface development process for learning objects interface of the "Accessible WebGD" – a Virtual Environment of Education-Learning. This environment is destined for people without disabilities and deaf or blind people. Thus, in the interface it will have different technological resources, for example, LIBRAS interpreter for deaf people; media with high contrast for people with low vision; narration and didactic materials in braille for blind people; and others accessible and inclusive actions.

Keywords: Interface Design, Web accessibility, Digital Inclusion.

1 Introduction

"Accessible WebGD" is a Virtual Learning Environment (VLE) that was developed by researchers from Federal University of Santa Catarina, Brazil. The purpose of this environment is to teach spatial-graphic representation in an easy way, interactive and collaborative. Another relevant point, it refers to the proposal inclusive, i.e., should make possible the learning of this subject to a greater number of people, including those with disabilities, such as deaf people, blind people or with low vision. The "Accessible WebGD" is going to use the Moodle platform because of the following advantages: it is an intuitive tool and easy to use (usability), both for students and for teachers; it enables the creation of online courses; working groups and collaborative learning communities; it allows access through the Internet or local network; it is free software.

In this environment, the learning content will be presented through learning objects due to the following characteristics:

- Reusability is the possibility to use a single learning object in multiple contexts and different applications.
- Adaptability is the capability of adapt to different educational environments.
- Granularity is the possibility to encapsulate the content in parts.
- Accessibility allows access on different platforms.

C. Stephanidis (Ed.): HCII 2014 Posters, Part II, CCIS 435, pp. 214–219, 2014.

- Durability is the property that guarantees the material survival independently of changes and technology upgrades.
- Interoperability is the ability to work together (inter-operate) on different platforms.

Different technological resources are going to use in this environment, all with the same instructional objectives of the educational program and seeking to adequately serve needs of users learners.

In this context, the interface of learning objects is an important component to the success of this learning environment because through it is going to happen the understanding of the learning content and communication between the user-system. The interface is going to offer different medias destined for people with disabilities, such as LIBRAS1 interpreter for deaf people; media with high contrast for people with low vision; narration and didactic materials in braille for blind people; and others accessible and inclusive actions. This paper shows the interface development process of learning objects by "Accessible WebGD" and preliminary results of the research.

2   Interface Design

In a Virtual Learning Environment (VLE), the graphical user interface is the interlocutor scenario in Online Distance Education. This digital artifact should provide communication support during interaction between learners and, also, between them with the objects of study.

An interface poorly designed can present problems related to lack of usability, communication failures, compromised interaction, inappropriate layout, in the end it compromises the functionality and jeopardizes quality of web applications [2].

2.1   The Project Method

The project methods propitiate the realization of a structured, systematic and organized work, and help to identify specificities of the problem, because they provide a logic support for the development of projective activities [3].

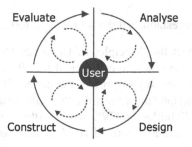

Fig. 1. Iterative Interface Design Process (Source: Mandel, 1997, p. 251)

---

[1] Brazilian sign language.

In this study, it was adopted the project method proposed by Mandel [5]: Iterative Interface Design Process; this method involves users, focuses prototyping and evaluation of the project, from the initial stages to the final product development. The figure 1 shows the process model:

Analysis Phase

In the analysis phase, the user information was collected and analyzed, such as: identification of the user profile, user tasks, and user requirements. The figure 2 shows the user model constructed on the basis of information from users.

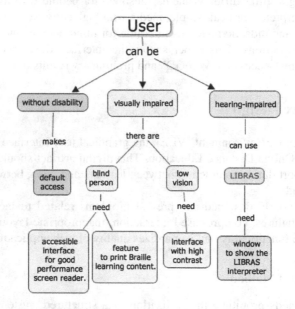

Fig. 2. Conceptual Map of User Profiles

Design Phase

In the design phase, it was established the following interface requirements:

— The interface must meet the Principles of Universal Design. In this way, all features are available in one interface is identical for all. Users can customize the interface manually according to your preference and needs.
— For deaf users: the interface must meet the "Brazilian standard about Accessibility in Communication – Subtitles on TV", specifically in item 7 that corresponds to the Guidelines for the window with LIBRAS interpreter (this window should occupy 1/4 of the screen).

— For low vision users: the interface should provide a function to adjust high contrast.

— For blind users: the interface must be implemented according to the W3C accessibility guidelines, enabling efficient use of the screen reader. Also, it should provide feature to print the content in Braille.

The Icons of the Interface

On the interface of "Accessible WebGD" (VLE), command buttons will be available to enable/disable functions necessary for user-system interaction. Icons will be used to communicate the functions of the buttons. The board 1 shows the icons proposed to represent the interface functions.

Board 1. The icons representing the functions of the interface

Function of Command Button	Icon
Next	▶
Return	◀
Exit	✕
Increase font size	AA
Reduce the font size	AA
Enable/Disable accessibility for deaf	
Enable/Disable the audible narration content (text and images)	
Enable/Disable high contrast (for low vision users)	
Help	?
Alert	!
Glossary	📖
Print content in Braille	Braille
Search	🔍

Interface Layouts.

The figures 3, 4 and 5 show interfaces developed for the "Accessible WebGD" (VLE).

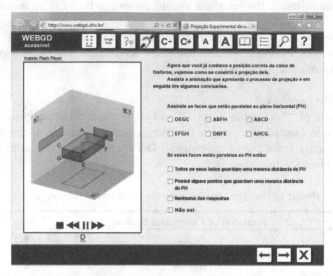

Fig. 3. Interface for users without disabilities and also blind user who will hear the information via screen reader. Static images, animations and videos contain audio description

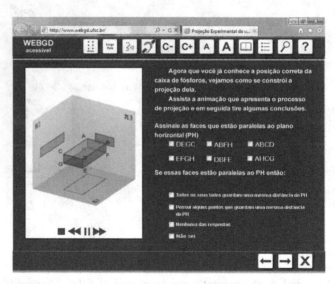

Fig. 4. Interface for users with low vision. Dark blue background and white or luminous yellow text are efficient contrast for reading and are considered enjoyable for users with low vision [4]

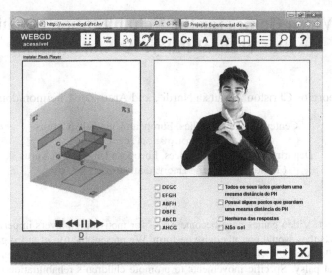

Fig. 5. Interface with window for LIBRAS interpreter destined for deaf users.

3   Final Considerations

The "Accessible WebGD" (VLE) the environment was not completed. Currently, the project is in the construction phase, where the content is being implemented. The ergonomics and usability evaluations of the interface will be made after implementation of the content.

It is emphasized that the socio-economic relevance of this research lies in the development of accessible digital material for learning (one of the bottlenecks to inclusive distance education).

References

1. Alvarenga, F.B.: Uma Abordagem Metodológica para o Projeto de Produtos Inclusivos. Tese (Doutorado) Universidade Estadual de Campinas, São Paulo (2006)
2. Batista, C.R.: Modelo e Diretrizes para o Processo de Design de Interface Web Adaptativa. Tese (Doutorado em Engenharia e Gestão do Conhecimento) – Programa de Pós-graduação em Engenharia e Gestão do Conhecimento, UFSC, Florianópolis (2008)
3. Bomfim, G.A.: Metodologia para Desenvolvimento de Projetos. Editora Universitária - UFPB, João Pessoa (1995)
4. Kulpa, C.C.: A Contribuição de um Modelo de Cores na Usabilidade das Interfaces Computacionais dos Usuários de Baixa Visão. Dissertação (Mestrado em Design) – Programa de Pós-Graduação em Design, UFRGS, Porto Alegre (2009)
5. Mandel, T.: The Elements of User Interface Design. John Wiley & Sons, Inc., New York (1997)

Using Video Games for the Rehabilitation of Children with Cerebral Palsy: A Pilot Study

Georgios Christou[1], Loutsia Nardi[2], and Areti-Zoe Cheimonidou[2]

[1] Center for Game Studies, European University Cyprus
christoug@acm.org
[2] Department of Health Sciences, European University Cyprus
{l.nardi,a.cheimonidou}@euc.ac.cy

Abstract. Video games have become a tool for motivating players in performing tasks they would not otherwise perform. We present the use of video games controlled through XBOX KINECT, to facilitate rehabilitation of children with cerebral palsy. Specific movements to promote children's rehabilitation of reduced balance and postural control were used with video games suitable for children between the ages of 5 – 12 years old. To evaluate the rehabilitation and motivation potential of the video games, a pilot study with 7 children between the ages of 9 – 12 years old was performed. The children played the aforementioned video games for 6 weeks, twice per week. Physiotherapists used the Paediatric Balance Scale to assess clinical their balance and postural control in 14 dynamic and static tasks before and after the experiment. The results are promising, both in terms of motivating children to attend their rehabilitation sessions, and in terms of rehabilitation potential.

Keywords: KINECT, video games, rehabilitation, cerebral palsy.

1 Introduction

Games are intimately tied to entertainment and pleasure. Video games in fact, are now a favorite pastime for both young and "young-at-heart". As a Nielsen study shows, online games are now more popular computer applications than email [1]. Because of this trend, and because games are thought of as fun, video games have been used in a host of other applications, to promote tasks that some may consider boring or uninteresting. Thus, serious games have been developed for education [2] and various types of training (such as medical and military) [3], and more recently gamification of various business processes has been proposed [4]. These applications leverage the fact that games motivate people to perform otherwise mundane tasks (for example people will kill insignificant monsters in World of Warcraft, solely to either complete game objectives or to level up their character – this is called grinding [5]). In this paper we discuss our attempt towards leveraging video games, played using the XBOX Kinect, that motivate children with movement difficulties to perform exercises that will help rehabilitate them. Specifically, we use the case of 7 children with cere-

C. Stephanidis (Ed.): HCII 2014 Posters, Part II, CCIS 435, pp. 220–225, 2014.

bral palsy on a a skiing video game, modified to incorporate rehabilitation movements to move the player's avatar.

Cerebral palsy is a term used to describe various posture and movement disorders seen in children who for various reasons developed a non-progressive lesion of the central nervous system [6]. The symptoms and disabilities of cerebral palsy vary greatly including motor and regularly cognitive disabilities with social implications later on when children have to go to school. Traditionally, intervention on such population targets the symptoms of motor impairments such as spasticity, decreased range of motion (due to muscular contractures), muscle weakness and decreased mobility, with a number of specialists being involved.

Currently, rehabilitation programs have begun to shift focus from minimizing deficits to enhancing functional participation/training, addressing in this way more aspects than solely motor dysfunction [7]. The implementation of exercises directly related to functions necessary for the child's everyday life, such as stair walking, has become a crucial aspect in clinical sessions, i.e. [8, 9]. In addition, experimental work in the field of motor learning and biomechanics [10] has led to models that pay attention to motor control, strength and aerobic capacity.

Treatment methods usually presuppose one to one contact between the physical therapist and the patient. Therapy can be a routine of practicing skills solely between the therapist and the patient, without much of parental involvement, in an enjoyable social activity indoors. Moreover, group therapy is not usually being conducted in this clinical population since the patients can be very diverse presenting attentional and cognitive deficits that resemble group work difficult. In either case the therapist at present can only provide individual treatment tailor made to the needs of each child at hand.

The current developments address the importance of child's participation in the therapy and function within a social environment via meaningful activities. The child's motivation and satisfaction is an issue gradually placed into focus, since motivation is an important factor for the success of the therapy [11]. Recent models identify the patient as an active participant in his/her own therapy, and the role of the physical therapist is to "coach" this process. The provision of children with some control over the therapeutic exercises, with variation in the sessions is desirable also for the fact that secondary improvements can be seen, such as a boost in problem-solving abilities and self-esteem [12]. Therefore, treatment methods should place the child as an active participant in his/her treatment and this presupposes high motivation and satisfaction levels.

Participation of the family in the treatment after a certain age when the child becomes part of the school environment is crucial. For the 5-12 years old children with normal cognitive level as well as for puberty, therapy will go on improving motor skills necessary for an adaptation to the school environment including ability to keep up with physical/social activities (participation in sports). It is at this point that exercise has to shift slowly from the physical therapy room to promote participation in the social environment via meaningful activities.

Thus, the motivation behind our research is to use activities that allow for social and physical interaction in a fun way that will motivate the child towards taking an active role in his/her treatment, all the while being entertained and motivated to do so. As video games have also been tied to other positive effects on children [13] we believe that in the long term video games for rehabilitation will enable a host of positive changes in the children that use them.

2   Video Game Design

The video game developed is a simple forward scrolling game, that requires the player to move a penguin left or right to go through pairs of flags and reach the end of the course without crashing. Time is limited, thus the children were required to finish the course before the time ran out. Figure 1 displays a screenshot from the game.

Fig. 1. A screenshot from the game used during the experiment

Our focus was on the way the player would interact with the game, because the interaction would provide the "hidden" rehabilitation abilities of the game. We considered three major platforms that are widely available to recognize player movement: Nintendo Wii, Playstation Move, and XBOX Kinect. We chose Kinect, because Kinect does not require the player to hold a controller. Rather, it recognizes the movements of the player through machine vision. A second reason that led us to choose Kinect over the other technologies was the ease with which we could find tools that support the modification of games so that they can work with the platform. The key to the video game was that it would be a normal game not designed for players with disabilities. As already mentioned, cerebral palsy was preselected as the syndrome that would be targeted by this pilot game. The video game interactions were thus designed by collaborating with physical therapists that specialize in neurological rehabilitation of children as well as adults, who selected specific movements that the players need to perform to interact with the game. For the pilot phase of the game, which included the completion of the first level, two movements were selected for player interaction. Figures 2 and 3 show the movements that move the avatar left and right in the game world.

(a)   (b)

Fig. 2. Movements for going left (a), and going right (b)

Here is another place where selecting Kinect was beneficial. Because the game will be used to rehabilitate as well as entertain, the movements needed to be performed as close as possible to an ideal standard. Because the Kinect SDK provides us with immediate access to a virtual skeleton of the player, we were able to fine tune motions so that the avatar of the player would not react, unless the movement performed was within an acceptable threshold of the expected motion. Hence, we expected that playing the game would provide real help towards rehabilitating its players.

3   Method and Results

The design was a pilot study with a pre – post test design. The participants were 7 children age 5 – 12 years old. The children were classified as GMFCS (5 of them) level I and (2 of them) level III. They were asked to play specific video games by first earning and then using the aforementioned movements. We used the game described in section 2. The children were standing (except the two children – level III sitting) and moving into flexion, extension, lateral bending, and flexion, extension for the 1st game and rotation instead of the side bending of the torso for the 2nd game with open arms. The children were trying to maintain balance and coordination to achieve the collection of the objectives in the game as fast as they could. The experiment ran for 6 weeks and for 2 times per week, and during a given week the children were asked to perform their normal rehabilitation program, and to also attend meetings during which they played the selected games. Physiotherapists used the Pediatric

Balance Scale to assess clinical their balance and postural control in 14 dynamic and static tasks before and after the experiment. We collected the average score (time and collection of objectives in the game) of their 12 sessions to see also the ability of coordination and balance. We interviewed parents and children for the participation in the game

According to the Pediatric Balance Scale (Maximum Score 56) we can see an improvement on balance and postural control after assessing the children at the end of the experiment in all the 7 participants. Also as we saw that the children from session to session were becoming better on their time finishing the game.

4   Future Work and Conclusions

In this article we have discussed our effort to build a rehabilitation game for children with cerebral palsy. We briefly explained how we designed the game, but more importantly we discussed how the interaction between the player and the avatar uses movements that aim towards rehabilitating the player.

Our very preliminary results are promising towards providing motivation to the player to perform those movements that allow for the player's rehabilitation, as was evident by the play session of one child, and the subsequent discussion with the child and its parent. We plan to continue pursuing this avenue, by testing the game with more children with cerebral palsy, and formally measuring their motivation through the Pediatric Volitional Questionnaire [15].

After the pilot testing, we plan a longitudinal study with a group of children with cerebral palsy using our game together with their physical therapy sessions, and a group of children that will not use our game. We expect that the group of children that uses our game will display more improvement after a period of months than the other group.

Acknowledgements. We thank our little volunteers and their parents for allowing us to work with him while building the game. We also thank Microsoft Cyprus for their kind donation of Microsoft XBOX 360 and Kinect.

References

1. Nielsen Wire What Americans Do Online: Social Media And Games Dominate Activity. City (2010)
2. Gros, B.: Digital games in education: The design of games-based learning environments. Journal of Research on Technology in Education 40(1), 23 (2007)
3. Chatham, R.E.: Games for training. Communications of the ACM 50(7), 36–43 (2007)
4. Deterding, S., Dixon, D., Khaled, R., Nacke, L.: From game design elements to gamefulness: defining gamification. ACM Press, City (2011)
5. Calleja, G.: Digital Game Involvement: A Conceptual Model. Games and Culture 2(3), 236–260 (2007)

6. Bax, M.: Terminology and classification of cerebral palsy. Developmental Medicine and Child Neurology 6, 295–297 (1964)
7. Steiner, W.A., Ryser, L., Huber, E., Uebelhart, D., Aeschlimann, A., Stucki, G.: Use of the ICF model as a clinical problem-solving tool in physical therapy and rehabilitation medicine. Physical Therapy 82, 1098–1107 (2002)
8. Schindl, M.R., Forstner, C., Kern, H., Hesse, S.: Treadmill training with partial body weight support in nonambulatory patients with cerebral palsy. Arch. Phys. Med. Rehabil. 81, 301–306 (2000)
9. Damiano, D.L., Vaughan, C.L., Abel, M.F.: Muscle response to heavy resistance exercise in children with spastic cerebral palsy. Dev. Med. Child Neurol. 37, 731–739 (1995)
10. Carr, J.H., Shepherd, R.B.: Movement science. Foundations for physical therapy in rehabilitation. Aspen Publishers, Gaithersburg (2000)
11. Kristen, H., Denise, R.: The influence of virtual reality play on children's motivation. The Canadian Journal of Occupational Therapy 72, 21–29 (2005)
12. Krichevets, A.N., Sirotkina, E.B., Yevsevicheva, I.V., Zeldin, L.M.: Computer games as a means of movement rehabilitation. Disability and Rehabilitation 17, 100–105 (1995)
13. Ferguson, C.J.: The Good, The Bad and the Ugly: A Meta-analytic Review of Positive and Negative Effects of Violent Video Games. Psychiatric Quarterly 78, 309–316 (2007)
14. Weber, J., Qvist, I.: Farseer Physics Engine. City (2006)
15. Harris, K., Reid, D.: The influence of virtual reality play on children's motivation. The Canadian Journal of Occupational Therapy 72(1), 21–29 (2005)

Persona Based Accessibility Testing

Towards User-Centered Accessibility Evaluation

Alexander Henka and Gottfried Zimmermann

Stuttgart Media University Nobelstraße 10 70569 Stuttgart, Germany
{henka,gzimmermann}@hdm-stuttgart.

Abstract. Web authors have a hard time understanding and applying accessibility guidelines. The guidelines are considered too technical, without providing sufficient support for problem solving. This results in bad usability of Web applications for people who rely on accessibility. In the field of designing Web applications and interfaces, the concept of personas, as a representation of the target audience, is well established. Personas are typically used to describe the user on a personal level, with their needs, preferences and habits. In this poster, we illustrate a new workflow approach for accessibility evaluations. We propose persona-based representations of accessibility guidelines for acceptance tests of Web applications, for web authors to gain understanding on the needs of people with disabilities and thus improve the accessibility of Web applications.

Keywords: human computer interaction, accessibility, personas, acceptance test, web accessibility guidelines, automatic testing, user-centered accessibility evaluation.

1   Introduction

For a large number of software developers, it is unclear how persons with disabilities interact with web applications. Several studies found that developers have issues to understand and classify accessibility guidelines [1][2].

Therefore, when checking the accessibility of a Web application, it is important to take the perspective of the end user, i.e. that reflects how an end user would interact with the system [3]. This involves testing the application as rendered in the browser, with dynamic code (e.g., JavaScript) being executed, and the user interacting with the application. This is essential for modern Rich Internet Applications (RIAs) in particular which render their user interface dynamically at runtime.

Many studies (see below) suggest that accessibility is strongly user-centered. Barriers occur when there is a mismatch between a user and a website in terms of interaction characteristics.

Brajnik [4] characterizes accessibility in a user-centered context: "*[Accessibility is when a] specific users with specific disabilities can use it [the software] to achieve specific goals with the same effectiveness, safety and security as non-disabled people.*" According to this understanding, a barrier is a condition, which prevents a

C. Stephanidis (Ed.): HCII 2014 Posters, Part II, CCIS 435, pp. 226–231, 2014.
© Springer International Publishing Switzerland 2014

specific user, who has specific traits and is using specific assistive technologies, from achieving his specific goals. A barrier is not just an defect on a web application, but an attribute of the interaction between the user and the system [4][5][6][7]. The occurrence of a barrier is user-dependent and defined by:

- The user and his specific traits
- The type of assistive technology being used
- The goal of the user
- The properties (defects) of the web application which prevent the accomplishment of the goals

Therefore, conformance tests cannot be used to fully clarify the accessibility of a web application, as discussed in [8] and [9]. The conformance to accessibility guidelines is a technical property of the website and doesn't take the specific traits of the user, his devices and assistive technologies into account.
Personas can be a way for a more user-centered accessibility evaluation. They are an established concept for focusing on the goals and needs of the users during the development of a product [10][11].

Personas use scenarios to describe the goals of the target audience. They are depicted as a description of a hypothetical user. This includes a name, a description of the daily routine and of devices and technologies that the hypothetical user uses to access a specific software product. Several studies showed the benefit of using the concept of personas for accessibility evaluations.
Schulz and *Skeide Fuglerud* [12] shared their experience of using personas, to convey the needs and preferences of people with disabilities. They claimed that using personas, including descriptions of their assistive technology and specific interaction patterns, helps web authors to focus on the user.

Baily and *Pearson* [13] introduced a tool for teaching web accessibility to undergraduate students. They used personas to describe information about assistive technology usage and specific interaction patterns by people with disabilities. Using personas for accessibility evaluation raises the awareness for the specific interaction between people with disabilities and web applications, which results in more accessible applications.

Vigo et. al [14] described the usage of context-aware guidelines. Those guidelines are based on the W3C Web Content Accessibility Guideines (WCAG) and filtered by a certain context, which is defined by the traits of a specific user and his assistive technology. Conformance evaluation focuses on the success criteria relevant for the context only.

Brajnik [5] presented the concept of a *barrier walkthrough*, which is derived from the usability inspection technique *cognitive walkthrough*. In a mental process, the evaluator imagines the usage of the software (or any product) through to eyes of a dedicated user, by answering questions like: "Is that information perceivable for the user?" or "Would the user know what to do at this point?". This enables developers to find more severe accessibility problems than with pure conformance tests.

In the scenario-based design the *cognitive walkthrough* technique is used as a way to evaluate software with personas [10].

Our proposed system addresses the needs of Web application authors. It can run automated acceptance tests, similar to unit tests. Rather than walking a list of technical problems that has been generated by a conformance-testing tool, the developer works with *personas* and *user scenarios*. We define a *user scenario* as an instance of a *use case*, but with concrete usage data. Each user scenario has an actor, represented by a persona. These personas and user scenarios provide the input for the acceptance tests.

Personas are used as illustration of the impact of accessibility guidelines and serve as actors in the scenario. They tell the test system how to test and which interaction patterns to use, e.g., "check only for specific success criteria (in WCAG 2.0) that are relevant for visually impaired people, and consider navigation by keyboard and via screenreader". These tests are executed in the Web browser of the client, in the same way as end users interact with them. A similar concept is introduced in [15].

The remainder of this paper is structured as follows: Section 2 introduces the general concept. Section 3 specifies the envisioned benefits of our proposed approach and section 4 provides an outlook on our next steps.

2   General Concepts of Our Approach

The underlying principle of our approach is to use personas as representation and illustration of accessibility guidelines (e.g., WCAG) for the developer. Each success criterion of the guideline is represented as a set of personas affected (possibly in varying degrees) by the success criterion. This requires an ontology, which maps accessibility guidelines to personas [16].

A persona also contains information about how they would interact with a Web application, together with a description of assistive technologies that the persona would possibly use. This information is essential for determining assertions for testing Web applications. It tells the test system which specific success criterion of a guideline to follow, and how to interact with the application, e.g., "use only tab navigation and test if the application is accessible with a screenreader". However, interaction between people with disabilities and software is usually more complex than in this brief example.

Using personas in this manner has several benefits:

A) Personas serve as representation of the accessible guidelines for the developer. From their origin, personas are designed to work as a representation of the target audience. According to [10], personas work because they tell stories, stories of real people and their traits, activities and problems. Rather than working with textual requirements, a persona consists of stories to illustrate the success criteria of accessible guidelines. Therefore, development teams can empathize with their target audience and use techniques like the barrier walkthrough to question features and functions. *Alan Cooper* expresses this concept as follows: *"We are designing for Rosemary, not for somebody!"* [11] ("Rosemary" is the name of a persona.).

B) Personas provide a machine-readable representation of the accessibility relations between success criteria, personas for whom the success criteria are relevant, and interaction patterns such as keyboard-only navigation, magnification, or the use of a screenreader. Along with the knowledge of the structure of the Web application to be tested, personas enable the test system to run extensive automated tests and thus support the development of accessible Web applications.

For each use case of a Web application, a user scenario with concrete usage data can be derived, by capturing the use case interaction with a real person (e.g., the developer). We call this a *user scenario blueprint*. This blueprint consists of real usage data and an interaction pattern. If combined with the information specified by a persona, it tells the test system what and how to test. The basic principle of the system is to follow the navigation pattern, according to the user scenario blueprint, but with the constraints given by the persona. Thus, the test system can automatically perform end-user acceptance tests, as introduced in a similar approach [17], by using techniques of Web crawler and JavaScript to execute interaction [3]. The user scenario and the persona (actor) can be modeled by using the interaction flow modeling language (IFML), the new standard for modeling the user interaction flow for software, based on UML [18].

If the system finds any problem, it can pinpoint to the affected persona, the corresponding success criterion, the location in the source code and highlight the relevant area in the browser. Besides a detailed explanation of the problems found, the test system should provide solid guidance for their solutions, warnings and errors [19]. The test can be repeated for all use cases and all personas. Figure 1 illustrates these concepts.

The term "responsive design" has been recently used to describe the adaption of Web applications on various target devices, platforms and browsers [20]. By expanding the test system to test across devices, acceptance tests can be executed, taking multiple target devices into account. The goal is to test each combination of scenario, persona and device (since *Rosemary* can either use her desktop computer or her smartphone).

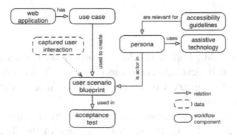

Fig. 1. Overview of the core concepts

3   Envisioned Benefits

In a nutshell, we envision the following benefits of this approach:

- Developers will gain a better understanding of accessibility, as compared to reading the plain guidelines.

- Testing the "real" accessibility of a RIA (based on its interaction flow) rather than its conformance to accessibility guidelines.
- Checking the accessibility of a RIA for a dedicated target audience, e.g., people with color blindness, by using as actors only personas linked to success criteria for that specific group.
- Cross-device tests can be conducted for Web applications that follow the "responsive design" approach.
- The accessibility of a web application can be sustained, following the continuous integration approach of modern software development. This implies running the acceptance tests again after changes to the application have been applied.

4   Current Status and Next Steps

This project is work in progress. So far, we have developed an HTML-based interactive high-fidelity prototype of an Integrated Development Environment (IDE), to simulate the later usage of our evaluation-workflow approach (as described in section 2). With the prototype we simulate the evaluation workflow for a single use-case of an application, create the scenario blueprint based on the selection of a persona, and conduct the accessibility evaluation.

As a next step, we will use this prototype to conduct user tests, with web authors and students from the field of computer science, to validate the workflow and the concept for its usability among web authors. A similar study showed the potential of such an integrated approach [21]. Besides the prototype, we are starting to implement a runnable version of our approach, to conduct further tests, so we can analyze the effectiveness of our approach in comparison with other accessibility evaluation methods.

References

1. Freire, A.P., Russo, C.M., Fortes, R.P.M.: A survey on the accessibility awareness of people involved in web development projects in Brazil. In: Proceedings of the 2008 International Cross-Disciplinary Conference on Web Accessibility (W4A), New York, NY, USA, pp. 87–96 (2008)
2. Greeff, M., Kotzé, P.: A lightweight methodology to improve web accessibility. In: Proceedings of the 2009 Annual Research Conference of the South African Institute of Computer Scientists and Information Technologists, New York, NY, USA, pp. 30–39 (2009)
3. Fernandes, N., Batista, A.S., Costa, D., Duarte, C., Carricco, L.: Three web accessibility evaluation perspectives for RIA. In: Proceedings of the 10th International Cross-Disciplinary Conference on Web Accessibility, p. 12 (2013)
4. Brajnik, G.: Beyond Conformance: The Role of Accessibility Evaluation Methods. Springer, Heidelberg (2008)
5. Cooper, M., Sloan, D., Kelly, B., Lewthwaite, S.: A challenge to web accessibility metrics and guidelines: putting people and processes first. In: Proceedings of the International

Cross-Disciplinary Conference on Web Accessibility, New York, NY, USA, pp. 20:1–20:4 (2012)

6. Petrie, H., Kheir, O.: The Relationship Between Accessibility and Usability of Websites. In: Proceedings of the SIGCHI Conference on Human Factors in Computing Systems, New York, NY, USA, pp. 397–406 (2007)

7. Kelly, B., Sloan, D., Brown, S., Seale, J., Petrie, H., Lauke, P., Ball, S.: Accessibility 2.0: People, Policies and Processes. In: Proceedings of the 2007 International Cross-disciplinary Conference on Web Accessibility (W4A), pp. 138–147. ACM, New York (2007), doi:10.1145/1243441.1243471

8. Brajnik, G.: Web Accessibility Testing When the Method Is the Culprit. Springer, Heidelberg (2006)

9. Kelly, B., Sloan, D., Phipps, L., Petrie, H., Hamilton, F.: Forcing Standardization or Accommodating Diversity?: A Framework for Applying the WCAG in the Real World. In: Proceedings of the 2005 International Cross-Disciplinary Workshop on Web Accessibility (W4A), New York, NY, USA, pp. 46–54 (2005)

10. Adlin, T., Pruitt, J.: The Persona Lifecycle. Morgan Kaufmann, MA (2006)

11. Cooper, A.: The Inmates are Running the Asylum. SAMS, Indiana (2004)

12. Schulz, T., Skeide Fuglerud, K.: Creating personas with disabilities. In: Miesenberger, K., Karshmer, A., Penaz, P., Zagler, W. (eds.) ICCHP 2012, Part II. LNCS, vol. 7383, pp. 145–152. Springer, Heidelberg (2012)

13. Bailey, C., Pearson, E.: Development and trial of an educational tool to support the accessibility evaluation process. In: Proceedings of the International Cross-Disciplinary Conference on Web Accessibility, New York, NY, USA, pp. 2:1–2:10 (2011)

14. Vigo, M., Kobsa, A., Arrue, M., Abascal, J.: User-tailored Web Accessibility Evaluations. In: Proceedings of the Eighteenth Conference on Hypertext and Hypermedia, New York, NY, USA, pp. 95–104 (2007)

15. Zimmermann, G., Vanderheiden, G.: Accessible design and testing in the application development process: considerations for an integrated approach. Universal Access in the Information Society 7(1-2), 117–128 (2007)

16. Lopes, R., Votis, K., Carriço, L., Tzovaras, D., Likothanassis, S.: Towards the universal semantic assessment of accessibility. In: Proceedings of the 2009 ACM Symposium on Applied Computing, pp. 147–151 (2009)

17. Watanabe, W.M., Fortes, R.P.M., Dias, A.L.: Using acceptance tests to validate accessibility requirements in RIA. In: Proceedings of the International Cross-Disciplinary Conference on Web Accessibility, New York, NY, USA, pp. 15:1–15:10 (2012)

18. Object Management Group, Inc. (OMG), Interaction Flow Modeling Language (IFML) (March 2013), http://www.omg.org/spec/IFML/1.0/Beta1/PDF/

19. Trewin, S., Cragun, B., Swart, C., Brezin, J., Richards, J.: Accessibility challenges and tool features: an IBM Web developer perspective. In: Proceedings of the 2010 International Cross Disciplinary Conference on Web Accessibility (W4A), New York, NY, USA, pp. 32:1–32:10 (2010)

20. Johansen, R.D., Britto, T.C.P., Cusin, C.A.: CSS browser selector plus: A JavaScript library to support cross-browser responsive design. In: Proceedings of the 22nd International Conference on World Wide Web Companion, Republic and Canton of Geneva, Switzerland, pp. 27–30 (2013)

21. Zitkus, E., Langdon, P., John Clarkson, P.: Inclusive Design Advisor: Understanding the Design Practice Before Developing Inclusivity Tools. Journal of Usability Studies (JUS), 127–143 (2013)

A GPS-Based Personalized Pedestrian Route Recording Smartphone Application for the Blind

Rabia Jafri[1] and Syed Abid Ali[2]

[1] Department of Information Technology, King Saud University, Riyadh, Saudi Arabia
rabia.ksu@gmail.com
[2] Araware LLC, Wilmington, Delaware, U.S.A.
syedabidali@gmail.com

Abstract. A GPS-based smartphone application for blind users is proposed which will allow them to record pedestrian routes to frequently visited destinations (e.g., supermarket, neighborhood mosque, etc.) and to retrieve them later for autonomous navigation. Unlike similar systems, which simply provide a route to a specified destination based on existing GPS maps which may not contain detailed information especially about pedestrian paths and alleys, our software is unique in that it will allow users to record a customized path to a particular destination based on personal considerations such as whether the area surrounding the route is well-lit and well-populated, the unevenness of the terrain and the absence of hazards (such as traffic intersections). A distress call option and auditory cues about user-specified obstacles will also be provided. The objective is to develop a low-cost, portable solution based on easily accessible technology to assist blind users in their daily outdoor mobility tasks.

Keywords: Visually impaired, blind, assistive technologies, navigation, mobile applications, GPS-based.

1 Introduction

Among the different senses which we utilize to determine our location and to navigate in our environment, the sense of sight is arguably the most pivotal one. Consequently, one of the major challenges faced by individuals suffering from vision loss is navigating from one location to another, especially outdoors. Even short trips on foot to familiar locations such as the supermarket or neighborhood mosque, may be hard to manage independently. Usual solutions to this problem include soliciting the help of a close friend or caregiver, acquiring a trained guide dog, or feeling the way with a white cane. However, a sighted human aide may not always be available (indeed, according to a recent report, 26% of blind adults in the United States live alone [1]), while both white canes and guide dogs can only be used to detect objects in close proximity to the user and are restricted in their capacity to detect obstacles in the path that are above his waistline (e.g., low-hanging tree branches). Also, they cannot provide the user information about his geographical location or his orientation in his current environment.

C. Stephanidis (Ed.): HCII 2014 Posters, Part II, CCIS 435, pp. 232–237, 2014.
© Springer International Publishing Switzerland 2014

The limitations of these traditional solutions have fueled research into developing more innovative means for aiding the blind in their daily mobility tasks, with numerous electronic aids being devised for this purpose in recent years [2, 3]. Several of these solutions make use of GPS, or global positioning satellite, a satellite-based navigation system, that provides exact location and time information in all weather conditions, anywhere on or near the Earth where there is an unobstructed line of sight to four or more GPS satellites. The system is maintained by the U.S. government and is accessible, free of charge, to anyone with a GPS receiver [4]. However, current GPS-based navigation aids for the blind suffer from the following drawbacks when utilized for pedestrian routes: Most of these devices simply make use of existing GPS maps which usually cover only major roads and locations and may not contain detailed information, especially about pedestrian paths and alleys. Many of them are standalone devices whose cost may be prohibitive for this user group (note that 90% of the visually impaired live in developing countries with limited financial resources [5]). Moreover, most of them sport complex interfaces with numerous choices and require extensive training before the user can use them effectively.

Most modern smartphones now come equipped with GPS receivers. Exploiting these as navigation tools offers the following advantages: Eliminates the need to carry around a separate device for navigation, provides access to the latest GPS maps via frequent, automatic updates and saves money by rendering it unnecessary to purchase a standalone navigation device. We, therefore, propose developing a smartphone-based application with a simple interface for blind users which will allow them to record pedestrian routes outdoors to frequently visited destinations by utilizing the phone's built-in GPS receiver. Our software will be unique in that it will allow the user (or his sighted caregiver) to record a customized path to a particular destination based on personal considerations such as whether the area surrounding the route is well-lit and well-populated, the unevenness of the terrain and the absence of hazards (such as traffic intersections). Our system will also provide some specialized functions taking the users' blindness into account, e.g., a "Find me" option which will allow the user to send a distress message with his GPS coordinates to his close friends in case he gets disoriented or hurt (bear in mind that 65% of the visually impaired are 50 years or older and suffer from several ailments related to old age [5]). Also, our application will allow the user to record the presence of obstacles on his path and will later provide auditory cues to alert the user that he is approaching a hazard and should exercise caution. The user interface to the system will be very simple to use and will afford interaction via tactile or auditory means. Our aim is to present blind users with a low-cost, portable application based on easily accessible technology to assist them in their daily outdoor mobility tasks.

The rest of this paper is organized as follows: Section 2 provides a brief overview of related work in this area. Section 3 describes our application and outlines its functionalities. Section 4 concludes the paper and identifies some directions for future work.

2   Related Work

Several standalone GPS-based navigation devices for the visually impaired have been proposed and developed in recent years: Yelamarthi et al. [6] have developed an RFID and GPS integrated system, Smart Robot (SR), which can guide a user to a new destination or create a new route on-the-fly for later use. The input unit, equipped with an RFID reader, GPS and analog compass, is mounted on a chassis which can roll alongside the user. Feedback to the user is provided via speech and vibrating motors on a glove. Though, similar to our application, this system provides the ability to record and retrieve new routes, however, as mentioned before, this is a standalone device which has to be separately purchased for assistance in navigation. Moreover, having a small robot unit rolling alongside one does not appear to be a practical option, especially when travelling over uneven terrain or in crowded areas..

Pathy et al. [7] have conducted a study in Kuala Lampur, Malaysia to test the usability of Trekker, a commercial tool that uses GPS and digital maps to help the blind to navigate in urban and rural areas. Even though, similar to our application, this device allows users to record personal points of interest (POIs) to create their own routes which they can retrieve later, however, they have to be online to create a POI. Furthermore, this is a standalone device with a complicated interface consisting of 33 multifunction buttons and requires comprehensive training for its usage. A newer version of this device [8] has fewer buttons and thus, appears more usable; however, its cost is prohibitive.

Prudhvi and Bagani [9] have proposed a system in which the user wears a glove equipped with various components including a GPS receiver for determining the user's position, a magnetometer and accelerometer to determine his orientation and SONAR for detecting obstacles. The device also provides other information such as time, date, object color, ambient light and temperature conditions. However, the system is yet to be implemented and tested.

Recently, some smartphone-based navigation applications to aid the visually impaired have also emerged: Koiner et al. [10] have developed a smartphone application which provides a user with audio instructions to guide him from a starting point to a destination by taking him from one predefined location (called a waypoint) to another along the way. The user can also choose a different waypoint while walking and the system will recompute the path from the new waypoint. However, the application does not appear to allow the user himself to create new trips or define waypoints – only the system administrator has this capability. Also, the system interface provides several extraneous functions (e.g., the ability to take a picture) and detailed GPS and sensor data information (coordinates, orientation angles, etc.). The system interface does not appear to be particularly tailored for blind users: It is mentioned that instructions will be verbally communicated every 5 seconds. However, there are a number of options on the interface - it is not clear whether the user will receive verbal or haptic feedback for these options or if he will need to receive training and have to memorize them. Another example of a GPS-based smartphone application is *iExplore* [11] which supports navigation in outdoor shopping complexes for visually impaired users through multi-modal data fusion. Exploratory studies for this system provide some invaluable insights into users' needs and expectations for a navigation aid. However, this product is targeted towards a specific kind of location (i.e., outdoor shopping complexes) and does not appear to provide the ability to record customized user-specified routes.

3   Application Description

We propose a smartphone-based application for blind users which will allow them to record pedestrian routes outdoors to frequently visited destinations (e.g., supermarket, neighborhood mosque, etc.) by utilizing the phone's built-in GPS receiver. This will enable the user to navigate to these locations autonomously later. Fig. 1 shows an example of a customized route that can be recorded using this application which will not be available on a standard GPS map.

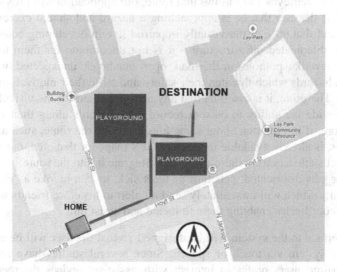

Fig. 1. Customized route recorded using the proposed application which would not be available on a standard GPS map

The main interface of the system will be very simple providing only two options: One for recording routes and the other for retrieving them. The details of these functions are described below:

1. **Record Route:** The system will ask the user for the route origin *A* and destination *B*. It will then create a route file with the name *AB* which will be stored in the system memory. To allow more flexibility, the application would permit multiple routes among the same endpoints to be recorded: If *n* routes with the same name already exist, the system will inform the user about this and will name the new route *AB_n+1*. From this point on, it will periodically keep recording the user's latitude and longitude coordinates via GPS and store them in a route array. When the user indicates that he has reached his destination, the route array will be stored in the file for this route.

2. **Retrieve Route:** The system will retrieve the array for the route requested by the user. The user's orientation would then be determined using the phone's built-in compass and the system will give him verbal directions about whether he needs to move straight, left or right until he reaches his destination. The directions would be intuitive and easy for the user to understand, e.g., "Turn right by 90°; walk straight for 15 meters, turn left by 45°, ..."

Our application will also provide some specialized functions taking the users' blindness into account:

- While recording a route, the system will allow the user to indicate if there is an obstacle along the way and the location of that obstacle will be saved as well. Later on, if the user retrieves and follows that route, our application will provide auditory cues to alert the user that he is approaching a hazard and should exercise caution. Bear in mind that 90% of the visually impaired live in developing countries [5] in areas with dilapidated infrastructure – it is not uncommon for them to encounter cracked sidewalks, potholes in the road, open manholes, unexpected bumps in the path, etc., hazards which threaten their safety and stifle their motivation to venture out alone. Therefore, it is essential that any navigation aid for the visually impaired should provide the ability to custom record such hazards along their daily paths. Furthermore, if information about some hurdles along the route, such as traffic intersections, is already available in existing GPS maps for that area, our system will also extract such data from these maps and integrate it into the route.
- If the user gets disoriented, gets hurt or feels sick, he can invoke a "Find me" option verbally which will immediately send an alert to his close friends with his current GPS coordinates enabling them to locate and assist him.

The user interface to the system will be designed so that the user will be able to interact with the system via touch or speech. Since several studies have reported that visually impaired users prefer to interact with assistive devices discreetly without drawing attention to their disability [12], we are planning to conduct some usability studies to determine which mode of interaction is preferred by most users as well as to identify any problems with the current system and to discover if there are any additional features which should be incorporated into this application.

4   Conclusion and Future Work

A GPS-based smartphone application with a user-friendly interface which allows blind users to custom record pedestrian routes and to retrieve them later for autonomous navigation has been described in this paper. The objective is to develop a low-cost, portable solution based on easily accessible technology which will assist blind users in their daily outdoor mobility tasks, boosting their self-confidence and making them more self-reliant.

The software will be extended in the future to integrate automated computer vision-based obstacle detection methods, which will significantly enhance the user's ability to interact with his environment in real-time. Since some studies have reported relatively low accuracy using the built-in GPS receiver [10], we will consider utilizing assisted and Bluetooth GPS as well to counter this problem. Furthermore (and this will be mainly based on the users' feedback during usability testing), the system will be enhanced to provide the user with other relevant information such as travel times, distance to destination, traffic and weather conditions, etc.

Acknowledgements. The authors extend their appreciation to the Deanship of Scientific Research at King Saud University for partially funding the work through the research group project number RGP-VPP-157.

References

1. Zuckerman, D.M.: Blind Adults in America: Their Lives and Challenges. National Center for Policy Research for Women & Families, Washington, DC (2004)
2. Dakopoulos, D., Bourbakis, N.G.: Wearable Obstacle Avoidance Electronic Travel Aids for Blind: A Survey. IEEE Transactions on Systems, Man, and Cybernetics—Part C: Applications and Reviews 40, 25–35 (2010)
3. Jafri, R., Ali, S.A., Arabnia, H.R., Fatima, S.: Computer Vision-based object recognition for the visually impaired in an indoors environment: a survey. The Visual Computer (2013), doi:10.1007/s00371-013-0886-1
4. Everyday Mysteries: Fun Science Facts from the Library of Congress, http://www.loc.gov/rr/scitech/mysteries/global.html
5. Visual impairment and blindness: Fact sheet number 282. Ed: WHO media center (2012), http://www.who.int/mediacentre/factsheets/fs282/en/
6. Yelamarthi, K., Haas, D., Nielsen, D., Mothersell, S.: RFID and GPS integrated navigation system for the visually impaired. In: 2010 53rd IEEE International Midwest Symposium on Circuits and Systems (MWSCAS), pp. 1149–1152 (2010)
7. Pathy, N.B., Noh, N.M., Moslin, S.I., Subari, M.D.B.: Space technology for the blind and visually impaired. In: 2011 IEEE International Conference on Space Science and Communication (IconSpace), pp. 206–210 (2011)
8. Trekker Breeze Handheld Talking GPS, http://www.humanware.com/en-usa/products/blindness/talking_gps/trekker_breeze/_details/id_101/trekker_breeze_handheld_talking_gps.html
9. Prudhvi, B.R., Bagani, R.: Silicon eyes: GPS-GSM based navigation assistant for visually impaired using capacitive touch braille keypad and smart SMS facility. In: 2013 World Congress on Computer and Information Technology (WCCIT), pp. 1–3 (2013)
10. Koiner, K., Elmiligi, H., Gebali, F.: GPS Waypoint Application. In: 2012 Seventh International Conference on Broadband, Wireless Computing, Communication and Applications (BWCCA), pp. 397–401 (2012)
11. Paladugu, A., Chandakkar, P.S., Peng, Z., Baoxin, L.: Supporting navigation of outdoor shopping complexes for visually impaired users through multi-modal data fusion. In: 2013 IEEE International Conference on Multimedia and Expo (ICME), pp. 1–7 (2013)
12. Golledge, R., Klatzky, R., Loomis, J., Marston, J.: Stated preferences for components of a personal guidance system for nonvisual navigation. Journal of Visual Impairment & Blindness 98, 135–147 (2004)

Inclusivity in the Digital Connected Home

Optimising the Accessibility of Digital Connected Home Technology for Disabled Users

Tim Pennick[1], Sue Hessey[1], and Yingyan Gu[2]

[1] BT Research and Innovation, BT Plc, Adastral Park, Ipswich, IP5 3RE
[2] Department of Mathematics, Imperial College London, London, SW7 2A7
{Tim.pennick,sue.hessey}@bt.com,
yingyan.gu11@imperial.ac.uk

Abstract. This paper introduces a Proof of Concept to demonstrate the feasibility and benefit of exploiting existing home management devices for disabled users. The model we present exploits an integrated platform exposing an API which can be utilized by a variety of User Interface approaches, including accessible Smartphones/tablets or more specialised hardware/software combinations. Future research will investigate the extent to which provision of suitable control technology can enhance feelings of wellbeing in disabled users, increase their independence, and enhance a sense of control over their living environment.

1 Introduction

In a report [1] commissioned by the UK government in 2008, the New Economics Forum (NEF) listed the following "5 Ways to Wellbeing":

- Connect
- Be Active
- Take Notice
- Keep Learning
- Give

For the purposes of this paper, we propose the addition of a 6th "way to wellbeing", namely Control, specifically control of the environment in which we live, or shared control where more than one person inhabits the same environment.

Control (or lack of) can be particularly experienced by elderly people [2] who may already be experiencing a sense of social isolation: Friends move away or die, financial constraints restrict travel and increasing habitual inertia adds further barriers to leaving the home. Self-confidence can be further eroded if, due to age-related disabilities any requirement for a change to room temperature, lighting etc has to be requested for action by another person. Enhanced independence can be expected where technology is employed to return control of these functions to the user, and to enable control of other aspects of the environment, such as security, power management, etc.

In terms of a business proposition, the fact that there is an ageing population globally makes the offer of "control" services for a Smart Home compelling – it is after all a growing market [3]. And for users the proposition is also compelling – it can enhance their quality of life, and can offer reassurance for their families.

2   Opportunities and Limitations of Technology for Disabled Users

A key component of recent developments in digital technology is the extent to which it is capable of being interconnected. Network technology in the home has supported the proliferation of devices for the management of features such as security, energy management, access to media devices, and communication. However, the proliferation of networked digital devices has the potential for negative as well as positive implications for disabled users. Analogue controls, for example, such as physical dials, buttons, switches, levers and valves were conventionally addressable by more than one of the 5 senses. In many cases they could be touched, seen, and heard. For instance, turning a dial might indicate progress by a visual and tactile arrow, and might emit clicks to indicate a change of state. The state of a real (as opposed to a metaphorical) radio button, could be felt, and seen, and a change in state of a group of these buttons could be heard.

Reducing the number of moving parts of this type both reduces the cost and increases the flexibility of the user interface, since extra functionality can be introduced without the requirement for additional physical controls. However, it also has the effect that interactions rely for the most part on a single sense, primarily visual output from the device. Where the relevant sense is impaired, backup strategies such as the ability to ascertain the state of a physical button by touch, are no longer available.

The more positive effect of this trend can be seen in the potential for customisation of digital technology. Although the graphical user interface is becoming increasingly ubiquitous in devices such as domestic kitchen equipment, energy and environmental control etc, the underlying technology can be designed to allow access options of many types to interact with the services they implement. Thus, in spite of possible disadvantages, it can be seen that this technology, while increasingly popular among the general population, has the potential to be truly life-enhancing for some groups of disabled users.

3   Smart Home Context

Technology to control appliances and environment in the home has been developing rapidly in the past years, encouraged by enhanced connectivity which has the effect of reducing the cost of control interfaces. Examples include Air Conditioning, Moisture detectors (for alarms triggered by leaking freezers or pipes), sensors to test whether doors and windows are open/closed, thermostats etc.

Currently, many of these have incompatible, proprietary interfacing strategies for operation via dedicated apps on smart phones and tablets. The potential benefits for disabled people of this new technology are obvious, but for many, the promise remains unfulfilled due to the incompatibility of the user interface, with assistive technology appropriate to a specific disability. The approach demonstrated by our Proof of Concept (outlined below) provides a user interface with flexibility to facilitate access by users with a variety of disabilities, primarily those with a visual impairment.

Fig. 1. Smartphone handset featuring Smart Home application used in the Proof of Concept

4   Proof of Concept

User Requirements

Our Proof of Concept (POC) user interface (see figure 1.) was based on the requirements of users with a severe visual impairment, though the model could be extended to incorporate the requirements of other disability groups, such as those with manual dexterity issues. The requirements of visually impaired users are of particular interest in this context since these users are currently excluded from the use of much of the current generation of Smart Home and media technology due to the almost total reliance placed on visual feedback employed by the associated user interfaces. Control of heating is an area with particular issues, since the user needs to be able to read the current temperature, the target temperature, the state of the heating system (on, off), the various programmes determining when the state will change, etc. This function was included in our Proof Of Concept (POC) together with sensors to indicate whether doors were open/closed. It also had the capability to control devices such as lamps.

Hardware and Software Approaches

The device chosen as the platform for the User Interface was a fifth generation Apple iPod Touch, as the VoiceOver screen reader which comes as standard with this device offers comprehensive Text To Speech conversion enabling voiced feedback. Encouraging results were also achieved using an iPhone 4, and a selection of Android devices.

An early decision in the development of our POC was the use of a web application, as this approach is particularly suited to portability across browsers and devices. The "web app" was built using HTML, CSS and JavaScript. It also makes use of the jQuery 1.X and jQuery Mobile libraries, which were chosen due to their cross-platform compatibility.

A core attribute of the design of the Web App was the W3C Access Initiative, Accessible Rich Internet Applications suite (WAI-ARIA) [4]. The ARIA suite was chosen as it assists the developer to ensure that information relating to the type and purpose of an object is correctly exposed to assistive Technologies so that it can be rendered to a disabled user in a meaningful way. By defining facilities that help Assistive Technologies to present rich content, WAI-ARIA provides a powerful set of tools that help developers make their web content truly accessible. Specifically, ARIA roles, states and properties are the semantic means by which information is conveyed to the User Agent and associated assistive technologies. Role attributes are assigned to elements to inform User Agents of the purpose, or role, of a particular element, its relationship to other elements, and subsequently how to handle each element.

Various browsers were used to validate the design of the "Web App" including Google Chrome, Internet Explorer 9 and Mozilla Firefox, the last of which was also used for its excellent debugging abilities via Firebug and its element inspector.

The ZWave protocol, designed to automate devices around the home, was used to enable the Wi-Fi element of the POC.

User Interface Options

Accessibility/Inclusivity is most likely to be achieved where the user interface can be optimised for the requirements of the user. These include, voice and gesture recognition and single-switch control for severely disabled users.

A secondary application was coded on top of the Z-Wave infrastructure to experiment with different kinds of interfaces – in this case the LEAP motion controller and aural interfaces, specifically clapping to extend the functionality for those experiencing difficulties with speech, for example.

Feedback can be provided via screens with configurable characteristics such as font size and contrast or using Speech Synthesis, and even Braille.

Prototype Testing

The POC web app was evaluated by a totally blind user, who in a mocked-up "home environment" tested the app via specific tasks such as detecting the state of doors and windows, setting and testing room temperature, and activating and de-activating devices plugged into the power switch using amended gestures and spoken feedback native to the iPod test platform.

For this POC, the user experience was continually developed and optimised via iterative requirements capture sessions conducted throughout the development period. Informal validation of this POC was considered sufficient ahead of a formal trial proposed for later in 2014, and the results gained from it will be used to inform the development of the trial version.

5   Conclusion

The initial evaluation demonstrated the validity of the concept sufficiently to conduct a trial with a small number of participants who will be able to use the basic functionality provided by the prototype in the participants' home environment. The trial's objective will be to evaluate the extent to which our accessibility model can help to increase the control of the home environment, and by extension to enhance the well-being of the user. By understanding in-home use, and by specifying specific functions (such as those covered in the initial prototype testing) we can, over a period of time, ascertain whether or not the application indeed offers enhanced control and less reliance on others, to enhance independence among the participant group.

In order to fulfil our research objectives of demonstrating the scope of technology to enhance independence and reduce social isolation, this Proof Of Concept should be considered to be a part of the overall Accessible Smart Home, which would include enhanced communications, and the option for remote monitoring by carers and health professionals. This holistic approach is intended to have multiple benefits for many user groups, going beyond the "user", including their entire community. Any future business case for development of such services will need to consider this holistic view.

References

1. Five Ways to Well-being: The Evidence, New Economics Forum. Report commissioned by UK Government Foresight project on Mental Capital and Wellbeing:
   http://www.neweconomics.org/publications/entry/
   five-ways-to-well-being-the-evidence
2. Older People, Technology and Community, Independent Age. Report, commissioned by the Calouste Gulbenkian Foundation (UK Branch),
   http://www.independentage.org/publications/research-reports/
3. http://www.inclusivedesigntoolkit.com/betterdesign2/why/why.h
   tml#./images/rsz_agevartop__260.gif
4. http://www.w3.org/WAI/intro/aria

A Wizard of Oz Study Exploring How Agreement/Disagreement Nonverbal Cues Enhance Social Interactions for Individuals Who Are Blind

Joshua Rader[1], Troy McDaniel[2], Artemio Ramirez Jr.[3],
Shantanu Bala[2], and Sethuraman Panchanathan[2]

[1] Hugh Downs School of Human Communication
Arizona State University, Tempe, AZ
[2] Center for Cognitive Ubiquitous Computing
School of Computing, Informatics and Decision Systems Engineering
Arizona State University, Tempe, AZ
[3] Department of Communication, University of South Florida, Tampa, FL
{jbrader,troy.mcdaniel,shantanu.bala,panch}@asu.edu,
aramirez@usf.edu

Abstract. Given their visual nature, nonverbal social cues, such as facial and head movements, are largely inaccessible to individuals who are blind, limiting the information gleaned during interactions. While social assistive aids have explored some nonverbal cues, such as detecting and communicating facial expressions, relatively few nonverbal cues have been explored. A thorough and systematic study has yet to investigate the importance and usefulness of many nonverbal social cues for individuals who are blind. This work takes this first step by beginning to explore the nonverbal cue of agreement/disagreement as indicated by head/body movements including head nod, head shake, leaning forward and leaning backward. To facilitate the investigation of the usefulness of nonverbal cues for individuals who are blind, we propose the use of a Wizard of Oz experiment to rapidly evaluate nonverbal communications using existing technologies rather than building new and complete systems. We first explore the usefulness of agreement/disagreement nonverbal cues using our existing Social Interaction Assistant platform in which most of the seemingly automated processes were manually performed by a wizard without the knowledge of participants. We conducted an experiment with 11 individuals who are blind or visually impaired involving one-on-one interactions with trained interviewers. Results show the potential of agreement/disagreement nonverbal cues within the social interactions of individuals who are blind.

Keywords: Social Interaction Assistant, social assistive aids, nonverbal communication, agreement, disagreement, haptic belt.

1 Introduction

Social interactions are an essential part of daily life that contribute to a person's general health and wellbeing. Social interactions are fundamental to friendships and other

C. Stephanidis (Ed.): HCII 2014 Posters, Part II, CCIS 435, pp. 243–248, 2014.
© Springer International Publishing Switzerland 2014

personal relationships; and have an indelible effect on who we are. However, there is limited access to the content conveyed during social interactions for those who are blind or visually impaired. Within a typical social interaction, 65% of the information exchanged is nonverbal, and 72% of nonverbal communication is visual [1]. Hence, individuals who are blind or visually impaired are severely limited in the amount of information they can glean from a social interaction. Furthermore, the inability to access facial expressions, body language, posture, and eye gaze can lead to potentially awkward and uncomfortable social situations for individuals who are blind. Overtime, situations such as these can lead to social avoidance and isolation.

While prior work [2-5] has developed, and to some extent, evaluated, social assistive aids for individuals who are blind, very few nonverbal cues have been investigated. Facial expressions are typically chosen for investigation, but nonverbal cues are extensive, rich and diverse, covering many other facets of nonverbal language. One possibility for the lack of a thorough and systematic study of the usefulness and importance of nonverbal cues for individuals who are blind might be the time and effort required to develop social assistive aids for various nonverbal cues. These technologies typically consist of sensing, processing and delivery components in which visual nonverbal cues are extracted using computer vision algorithms, and then relayed to the user through audio or haptic devices.

To avoid building new social assistive aids for each nonverbal cue to be communicated, we propose the use of a Wizard of Oz experiment to rapidly evaluate nonverbal cues for their usefulness and importance during social interactions involving individuals who are blind. A Wizard of Oz experiment [6] is an experimentation technique within the field of Human-Computer Interaction in which participants interact with a technology that is seemingly operating autonomously, but actually controlled completely or partially by the experimenter (wizard) without the knowledge of participants. Using this approach, we take the first step in exploring the usefulness of agreement/disagreement nonverbal cues for individuals who are blind. We use an existing Haptic Belt technology [5] in which head and body movements, specifically head nod, head shake, learning forward and learning backward, are manually recognized by the wizard, and subsequently sent to the haptic belt, delivering spatiotemporal vibrotactile patterns around the waist. We conducted an experiment with 11 individuals who are blind or visually impaired involving one-on-one interactions with trained interviewers. Results show the usefulness of a Wizard of Oz experimental approach, and the potential of agreement/disagreement nonverbal cues within the social interactions of individuals who are blind. The rest of the paper is structured as follows: Section 2 provides a review of social assistive aids. Section 3 introduces our proposed approach. Section 4 presents the results of a user study exploring the usability of the technology, and the relationship between nonverbal cues of agreement/disagreement and understanding. Section 5 concludes and provides possible directions for future research.

2   Related Work

Some prior work has explored social assistive aids that sense and deliver specific nonverbal cues to individuals who are blind including facial expressions [2, 3], interpersonal distance [4] and direction [5] of interaction partners. Rehman et al. [2]

proposed a vibrotactile chair to convey emotions to individuals who are blind by mapping the manifold of facial expressions to the back of a chair. Their proposed vibrotactile display consisted of three axes along which convey the intensity of one of three emotions being visually expressed by an interaction partner: happy, sad or surprised. Krishna et al. [3] mapped the six basic emotions (happy, sad, surprised, angry, fear and disgust) to the back of the hand using a vibrotactile glove to convey emotions through spatiotemporal patterns inspired by both emoticons and affective haptics. McDaniel et al. [4] mapped interpersonal distances to tactile rhythms presented through a haptic belt using the analogy of a heartbeat: an increased "heart rate" conveys that interaction partners are becoming closer, indicative of intimacy. McDaniel et al. [5] have also explored the use of haptic belts for conveying both direction and distance of interaction partners to enhance the situational awareness of individuals who are blind during dyadic, or larger, social interactions.

While some progress has been made, many nonverbal cues have yet to be explored in the context of social assistive aids. In this work, we explore four nonverbal cues of agreement/disagreement [7] (head nod, head shake, leaning forward, leaning backward) and their usefulness to individuals who are blind. Bousmalis et al. [7] reference Poggi's [8] work to establish the three ways in which a person can express agreement/disagreement: *Direct Speaker's Agreement/Disagreement, Indirect Speaker's Agreement/Disagreement,* and *Nonverbal Listener's Agreement/Disagreement.* In this work, we focus exclusively on Nonverbal Listener's Agreement/Disagreement. Bousmalis et al. outline a full list of Nonverbal Listener's cues of agreement/disagreement noting that head nod is the most prevalent cue of agreement; and head shake is the most prevalent form of disagreement. It is also important to note that these two nonverbal cues (head nod, head shake) are generally agreed upon as indicating agreement and disagreement respectively [7, 8]. Nonverbal cues of learning forward/backward are useful for discerning agreement/disagreement, respectively, as indicative of interest (learning forward toward your interaction partner) and disinterest (learning away from your interaction partner). Bousmalis et al. establish a much needed set of accepted cues of agreement disagreement, but much work remains to develop and evaluate social assistive aids that convey these, among other, nonverbal cues in useful ways such that they complement social interactions.

To the best of the authors' knowledge, this is the first study to investigate how agreement/disagreement nonverbal cues may add to or enhance dyadic (one-on-one) interactions for individuals who are blind. The current study implements these nonverbal cues using existing technology, particularly a haptic belt [5] designed and built at the Center for Cognitive Ubiquitous Computing, through which the proposed visual head/body movements were mapped to spatiotemporal vibrotactile patterns around the waist.

3   Proposed Approach

To quickly evaluate the usefulness of nonverbal cues during social interactions for individuals who are blind, we propose the use of a Wizard of Oz experiment [6] to simulate (1) nonverbal cue extraction from an interaction partner through manual observation and recognition by an experimenter (wizard); and (2) delivery of the aforementioned nonverbal cues to the user (individual who is blind or visually impaired) by which the wizard manually sends the cues (using software) to an existing technology such as an audio or haptic device. In a Wizard of Oz experiment, participants use a technology that is seemingly operating autonomously, yet is partially or completely controlled by an experimenter (wizard). While deceptive, Wizard of Oz experiments help gather usability feedback quickly to save time and effort by avoiding the building of complete systems. Participants not knowing that parts of the system are simulated is critical to obtaining realistic feedback. Therefore, wizards should perform *(1)* and *(2)* outside of the experiment room to discreetly observe the interaction taking place via live video streams. Dyadic (one-on-one) interactions are recommended over larger interactions involving three or more people given the ease at which cues may be extracted and conveyed. Interactions should involve one individual who is sighted (interviewer), who is informed about the Wizard of Oz study and briefed on the discussion topics well in advanced; and one individual who is blind or visually impaired (interviewee) who will not know this is a Wizard of Oz study. The interviewer should be someone who is trained in human communication, well-articulated and can carry a variety of discussion topics. The dyadic interaction may be semi-structured depending on the goals of the experiment. The mapping of nonverbal cues to the delivery technology will depend on the nonverbal cues being extracted, the technology being used, and the desired mapping between these modalities. In the next section, we describe our experiment exploring the usefulness of nonverbal cues related to agreement and disagreement conveyed through a haptic belt—an array of vibration motors placed around the waist.

4   Experiment

We conducted an Institutional Review Board (IRB)-approved experiment to examine the usefulness of nonverbal cues of agreement/disagreement in an interpersonal interaction for a person who is blind. In addition, the study explored the utility of the haptic belt as an effective means of relaying nonverbal communication. Utilizing previous research, we established four distinct vibrotactile cues to convey head and body movement that articulated nonverbal cues of agreement/disagreement: *Head Shake:* short vibrotactile pulses alternating at the left and ride sides of the waist (Left: 100 ms pulse, 150 ms gap, Right: 250 ms pulse, 200 ms gap, Left: 100 ms pulse); *Head Nod:* three short vibrotactile pulses at the midline (100 ms pulse, 150 ms gap, 250 ms pulse, 200 ms gap, 100 ms pulse); *Lean Forward:* three vibration motors centered at the midline vibrating simultaneously for 800 ms; *Lean Backward:* two vibration motors centered at the spine vibrating simultaneously for 800 ms. The experiment involved 11 participants (6 female, 5 male) recruited through the Disability Resource Center at Arizona State University. The age ranges of participants included 22 - 34 (4 participants); 35 - 44 (2); 45 - 54 (2); 55 - 64 (2); and 65 and over (1). Every participant was legally blind: 4 were totally blind, and 7 were visually impaired.

During the study, each participant engaged in a one-on-one interaction with a trained interviewer. These interactions consisted of thirty minute conversations covering diverse topics (Ex: What is your favorite type of music? Who would you like to see as the next President of the United States?), while an experimenter (wizard) trained in recognizing nonverbal cues, identified these cues from a live video stream, and delivered the cues to the haptic belt. During the interaction, only half of the discussed topics received cues (within-subject design) in an alternating pattern. The sequence of topics was randomized for each participant. Whether the interaction began with the haptic belt turned on or off was randomized. Through a post-experiment questionnaire, participants were asked a series of questions regarding the utility of the belt and the relationship between the nonverbal cues and understanding using a 5-point Likert scale from "Low" (1) to "High" (5). Once the study was completed, the Wizard of Oz experiment was revealed to participants.

Results regarding the utility of the belt were encouraging. Results indicate that the haptic belt was an effective channel of nonverbal communication. The following results are the average responses of all eleven participants as a group: "How easy was it to put on the belt?" M: 4.0, SD: 1.18; "How comfortable was the belt?" M: 4.45, SD: 0.69; "How easy was it to learn the vibration patterns?" M: 4.18, SD: 0.98; "How intuitive were the vibration patterns for the nonverbal cues they represented?" M: 4.0, SD: 1.00; "When experiencing vibrations with the belt, how easy was it to associate them with the nonverbal cues of the interviewer?" M: 4.09, SD: 0.94; and "How easy was it to combine the information received through the vibrations with that of the content of the conversation?" M: 4.00, SD: 1.0. These results indicate that the belt was easy to put on and comfortable to wear throughout the duration of the interaction. As well, they indicate that the chosen vibrotactile cues were easy to learn and intuitive for the nonverbal actions they represented.

Participants were also asked if the agreement/disagreement nonverbal cues (as conveyed through the belt) added to their overall conversation (across topics). They used a similar Likert scale as described before to convey how much this addition was: "Do you think that the information presented through the belt added to the conversation?" of which 8 of 11 participants answered yes with M: 3.38, SD: 1.5. This data shows that participants felt that agreement/disagreement nonverbal cues added to their interaction. Furthermore, the data is particularly compelling when participants are parsed into groups of totally blind vs. visually impaired. Three out of four totally blind participants responded that 'yes' the belt added to the conversation (M: 4.0, SD: 1.73); while five out of seven participants with some sight responded 'yes', but with M: 3.0, SD: 1.41. Participant understanding per topic was also collected, but more participants are needed to make more conclusive arguments regarding whether or not nonverbal cues of agreement and disagreement, as conveyed though a haptic belt in this study, enhance the perception of an interaction partner's agreement for specific conversation topics by an individual who is blind.

5   Conclusion and Future Work

We have explored the usefulness of nonverbal cues for agreement and disagreement during dyadic interactions involving individuals who are blind. A Wizard of Oz experiment was conducted to quickly assess the usefulness of these cues and the utility of the technology. Future work will involve the expansion of this study to include more participants and continued analysis. Using Wizard of Oz studies, we will explore other nonverbal cues including eye gaze and hand gestures.

Acknowledgements. We would like to thank the National Science Foundation (NSF) and Arizona State University (ASU) for their funding support. This material is partially supported by the NSF under Grant Nos. 1069125 and 1116360. We would also like to thank Vineeth N. Balasubramanian for his ideas and guidance during the planning of this study.

References

1. Knapp, M.L.: Nonverbal Communication in Human Interaction. Harcourt College Pub. (1996)
2. Rehman, S.U., Liu, L., Li, H.: Manifold of Facial Expressions for Tactile Perception. In: Proceedings of the IEEE 9th Workshop on Multimedia Signal Processing, pp. 239–242 (2007)
3. Krishna, S., Bala, S., McDaniel, T., McGuire, S., Panchanathan, S.: VibroGlove: An Assistive Technology Aid for Conveying Facial Expressions. In: Proceedings of the CHI 2010 Extended Abstracts on Human Factors in Computing Systems, pp. 3637–3642 (2010)
4. McDaniel, T., Villanueva, D., Krishna, S., Colbry, D., Panchanathan, S.: Heartbeats: A Methodology to Convey Interpersonal Distance through Touch. In: Proceedings of the 28th International Conference Extended Abstracts on Human Factors in Computing Systems, pp. 3985–3990 (2010)
5. McDaniel, T., Krishna, S., Balasubramanian, V., Colbry, D., Panchanathan, S.: Using a Haptic Belt to Convey Non-Verbal Communication Cues during Social Interactions to Individuals who are Blind. In: Proceedings of the IEEE International Workshop on Haptic Audio visual Environments and Games, pp. 13–18 (2008)
6. Martin, B., Hanington, B., Hanington, B.M.: Universal Methods of Design: 100 Ways to Research Complex Problems, Develop Innovative Ideas, and Design Effective Solutions. Rockport Publishers (2012)
7. Bousmalis, K., Mehu, M., Pantic, M.: Spotting Agreement and Disagreement: A Survey of Nonverbal Audiovisual Cues and Tools. In: International Conference on Affective Computing and Intelligent Interaction, vol. 2, pp. 1–9 (2009)
8. Poggi, I.: Mind, Hands, Face and Body: Goal and belief view of multimodal communication. Weidler (2007)

Open Web-Based Text-to-Speech Services for the Citizens

Spyros Raptis, Aimilios Chalamandaris, Pirros Tsiakoulis, and Sotiris Karabetsos

Institute for Language and Speech Processing – ATHENA Research Centre, Greece
{spy,achalam,ptsiak,sotoskar}@ilsp.gr

Abstract. A system is presented that offers a set of complementary services based on text-to-speech technology. The services and the underlying system that supports them are described. These services include: (a) a service for automatic document-to-speech conversion via e-mail, (b) an open library of audio books, and (c) a dynamic audio news service. The system seeks to maximize the availability and the social impact of text-to-speech technology, making its benefits widely available to the public through open services that address important daily needs of persons with visual impairments and reading difficulties.

Keywords: Speech synthesis, accessibility, open services, audio books, voice-enabled websites.

1 Introduction

Accessibility barriers to information and content, particularly to the ones that are in written form, place significant limitations to the independent living and social inclusion for people with disabilities. As text is well suited for massive and rapid communication, it has become the prevalent means for conveying information, not only in the personal and professional life but also in the relation of citizens to the public administration. As a result, citizens who are disadvantaged in decoding or efficiently handling textual information are in an extremely unfavorable position as they must rely on others to gain access to everyday information that concerns him.

Relevant studies in Greece and other countries have shown that there is a digital divide between the general population and people with disabilities. The limited access to ICT infrastructure, the relatively limited number of websites that meet the W3C accessibility standards and the lack of appropriate training and awareness are three key factors responsible for this digital divide [1]. Some of the measures often proposed for the digital integration of people with disabilities include the development of accessible websites and content relating to news, entertainment, education etc. as well as the participation of the State in providing specialized support software and access equipment.

The work presented here seeks to make a contribution in the above lines, focusing on persons with visual impairments or reading difficulties. They constitute a broad group of persons who are facing difficulties in handling text in written form. Speech is the main alternative to text, and is now considered to be an indispensable component of natural Human Computer Interaction. Its use is rapidly expanding from the

C. Stephanidis (Ed.): HCII 2014 Posters, Part II, CCIS 435, pp. 249–252, 2014.

desktop environment to the web and to online content [2-3]. Speech synthesis technology can automatically convert text into speech, thus making text content accessible to reading disabled persons.

The main focus of this work is on making openly available: (a) assistive technologies, based on text-to-speech technology, for serving everyday needs of people with reading disabilities; and (b) content of various types (informational content, newsfeeds, educational content etc.) and in various accessible forms.

The next section provides an overview of an online system that incorporates a set of digital services and digital content, and is tailored to the needs of visually impaired persons. This work is carried out under the project "Set of Open, Digital, Speech Services for the Citizens" (MIS: 303620), co-financed by Greece and the European Union.

2   System Overview

In this section, a set of complementary services based on text-to-speech technology and the underlying system that supports them are described.

2.1   The System Core

The core of the system is built on cutting edge *speech synthesis technology* that achieves high intelligibility and near-natural quality. It is based on the speech synthesis engine developed at ILSP/"Athena" and has been ranked at top positions in a recent specialized international contest [4]. The system currently supports Greek and English but due to its open architecture, it can be easily extended to accommodate for any other language. The synthesis engine is supported by extensive abbreviations and pronunciation lexica allowing it to efficiently handle out-of-vocabulary words and other special cases. The engine offers the ability to dynamically modify speaking rate and pitch level.

A *user management module* maintains information about users and their privileges, allowing for different access levels (anonymous, registered and accredited users as well as super users and administrators). Registered users are given personalization options as discussed below. Further to that, accredited users can upload content.

A *content management system* is employed for all the content handled by the system, especially for the digital documents managed by the Library service (Service 2 below).

The overall system architecture incorporates *load balancing* mechanisms targeted to the most computationally intensive part of the processing, namely speech synthesis, thus ensuring a more responsive overall performance.

2.2   The Digital Services

Service 1: Automatic conversion of documents to speech through email
Through this service, anyone will be able to send an email to predefined email addresses, attaching any document in txt, doc or pdf format. The service automatically

converts the attached document to high-quality synthetic speech and returns a reply message with a link to the corresponding audio file. The service offers a degree of personalization, allowing the user to configure and store his/her preferences regarding the characteristics of the synthetic voice to be used in the conversion.

Service 2: Online library of audio content
The Library will provide the basic infrastructure for the storage, management, retrieval and distribution of electronic documents in audio format. It uses a typical metadata scheme for the categorization and organization of content. The Library has built-in mechanisms for the automatic conversion of electronic books and documents in audio form. This way, e-books, magazines, manuals or any document uploaded will be automatically converted and be readily available in the form of an audio file or digital talking book that follows the DAISY standard (Digital Accessible Information SYstem - ANSI / NISO Z39.86). Adopting the DAISY open standard ensures interoperability with content produced or consumed by other technologies and devices.

The Library will offer an initial collection of audiobooks. This will include documents collected specifically for the purposes of the project and will be either free and open content or content for which specific permissions have been obtained. This will cover educational, literary, or other useful books, guides, monographs, conference proceedings, etc. Additionally, the Library will offer acoustic versions of selected public documents and documents from public organizations.

The Library will be open so as to accommodate for an increasing volume of content. Accredited users (public entities, educational institutions, associations of persons with disabilities, etc.) will be given the option to continuously upload new content. This way, the Library will bring significant added value to a range of public or charity institutions providing them with the means to render any document available in alternative, more accessible forms at practically no cost.

The service offers personalization options, through which a user will be able to set a profile of his/her preferences and interests. Based on this profile, users will receive notifications via email for all new content that matches their profile.

Service 3: Audio news alerts
On a daily basis, this service will retrieve news and informational content from different sources and news portals. The content will be presented in the portal in audio form through appropriate novel functionalities which will help users stay informed about current developments in the categories of their interest. Such functionalities include: the option to select and listen to specific news articles, the option to activate live audio news alerts through which the user will be able to listen to headings of news articles in real time as they are published on the portal etc. The news content will be obtained under permission from various sources including both high traffic private news portals as well as public informational websites.

2.3   The Overall Portal

The portal that will host the above services will fully comply with the W3C (WAI/WCAG) guidelines for accessibility at level AA. In addition, in order to further facilitate the accessibility of the target user groups, the portal will be voice-enabled offering functionalities for reading out the content of all webpages in a structured manner through synthetic speech as well as for providing support for voice-enabled navigation [5].

All of the above services will be openly available to all citizens. This way, citizens will gain access to reference content (audio books), dynamic content (news) and the ability to transform their own content into a format that meets their personal daily needs.

3   Progress and Timeplan

The system is currently at the final stage of development. A testing period will proceed, followed by an evaluation phase that will involve users from the targeted groups. The rollout of the final system is expected in autumn 2014. A preliminary limited version of the portal can be found at: www.openspeech.gr (in Greek).

Acknowledgements. The work presented here is carried out under the project "Set of Open, Digital, Speech Services for the Citizens" (MIS: 303620). The project is co-financed by Greece and the European Union, under the Operational Programme "Digital Convergence" and the Regional Operational Programmes.

References

1. Assessment of Digital Divide for Disabled Persons, Immigrants and the Third Age in Greece - Results, Conclusions & Recommendations. Observatory for the Information Society, http://www.observatory.gr/files/meletes/amea_ap_ac.pdf (in Greek)
2. Gilbert, M., Feng, J.: Speech and Language Processing over the Web: Changing the way people communicate and access information. IEEE Signal Processing Magazine 25(3), 18–28 (2008)
3. Deng, L., Wang, K., Chou, W.: Speech Technology and Systems in Human-Machine Communication. IEEE Signal Processing Magazine, Editors' Note 22(5), 12–14 (2005)
4. Chalamandaris, A., Tsiakoulis, P., Karabetsos, S., Raptis, S.: The ILSP Text-to-Speech System for the Blizzard Challenge 2013. In: Proc. Blizzard Challenge 2013 Workshop, Barcelona, Spain (2013)
5. Chalamandaris, A., Raptis, S., Tsiakoulis, P., Karabetsos, S.: Enhancing Accessibility of Web Content for the Print-Impaired and Blind People. In: Holzinger, A., Miesenberger, K. (eds.) USAB 2009. LNCS, vol. 5889, pp. 249–263. Springer, Heidelberg (2009)

Design, Implementation, and Evaluation of a Location-Based System for Investigating the Parameters of Place Meaning for Visually Impaired Users

Charalampos Rizopoulos[1,2], Lambros Lambrinos[1], and Angeliki Gazi[1]

[1] Department of Communication and Internet Studies,
Cyprus University of Technology, Limassol, Cyprus
{c.rizopoulos,lambros.lambrinos,angeliki.gazi}@cut.ac.cy
[2] Department of Communication and Media Studies,
National and Kapodistrian University of Athens, Greece
c_rizopoulos@media.uoa.gr

Abstract. This paper outlines the design, implementation, and evaluation methodology of a location-aware application intended as an aid to blind users who navigate urban spaces. The application is used in the context of a soundwalk whose purpose is to enable these users to indicate their level of emotional involvement with particular sounds emanating from specific areas of the city and provide a backdrop to the users' generation of place meaning based largely on auditory cues.

Keywords: Accessibility, place meaning, soundscape, affective interaction, location awareness.

1 Introduction

As demonstrated in previous work on the subject (e.g. [1, 2]), mobile communication devices such as smartphones facilitate the hybridization of urban space via the incorporation of digital, intangible information in the rigid spatial structure of the city. In addition to a wide variety of entertainment-oriented applications, this technology can be used to improve the accessibility of urban space to persons with disabilities, such as the visually impaired, who may experience considerable difficulties when it comes to autonomously navigating the city. Rendering the urban environment more accessible would allow such users to experience it in a more active and embodied fashion, which may in turn improve spatial learning and reinforce their emotional connection to space and its elements.

In addition to the safety and functional aspects of ordinary city life (i.e. effective guidance on how to get from point A to point B in the shortest possible time and at the least possible risk), the emotional aspects of normal everyday activity in the city are also important. Prolonged activity in a specific environment strengthens an individual's affective bond with that environment, which is the most important parameter of meaning attached to a unit of space. Essentially, space that is endowed with meaning

C. Stephanidis (Ed.): HCII 2014 Posters, Part II, CCIS 435, pp. 253–258, 2014.
© Springer International Publishing Switzerland 2014

becomes a place, and the absence of such meaning is often viewed negatively (e.g. "placelessness" / "non-place") [3]. In short, the meaning of an environment largely depends on its emotional connotations. The process of forming an emotional connection with a space ("place attachment") is inherently subjective and involves synthesizing multisensory information into a coherent whole and endowed with meaning[1]. In the case of blind persons, this information does not include the visual modality. Consequently, the relative importance of the other senses (primarily auditory information) is increased. Essentially, the blind individual's mental representation of the environment that may be significantly different from that of sighted persons on account of the former's incomplete spatial experience. As a result, environmental meaning can be expected to vary between blind and sighted individuals to a significant degree.

This paper describes a mobile application that was developed in light of the aforementioned considerations and aims to facilitate the blind users' interaction with the urban environment while also acting as a tool for ascertaining the ways in which environmental meaning differs between sighted and visually impaired individuals. The paper focuses on the latter topic and highlights the ways in which emotion-related data pertaining to the city can be acquired through this application.

2   Application Functionality

The application runs on Android 4.1 or higher and superimposes a layer of information on top of a map of the area (i.e. Google Maps or OpenStreetMap). On this layer, the users' trajectory and geo-located information is displayed (see below). Maps require an Internet connection. If no Internet connection is available, the map layer is not displayed; the users' trajectory and geo-located content are displayed whether or not an Internet connection is available. When in offline mode, the content generated during each session is uploaded to the server when an Internet connection becomes available. Thus, using the application does not necessarily incur any cost on the part of the user.

The initial prototyping for this application was conducted on a Samsung Gallaxy SIII and an LG P710 device.

2.1   Goals and Objectives

The primary idea behind the design of this application is accessibility by virtue of sensory substitution, i.e. the substitution of one sensory modality (in this case vision) with another (hearing) [4] – e.g. users are provided with audio or tactile (vibration) cues as to how close or far they are from a target location, but are also able to provide content using these sensory modalities. It encourages users to navigate and meaningfully interact with the city and its elements, and also allows them to indicate their

---

[1]   Although the term "attachment" implies a positive affective response, it is worth noting that the emotional connotations of a place need not be positive; negatively valenced environments (e.g. a concentration camp) are still endowed with place meaning and identity.

emotional disposition toward specific places either via an audio description (qualitative) or specific values corresponding to the two main dimensions of Russell's [5, 6] circumplex model of affect. In brief, the circumplex model, conceptualizes affective response to a stimulus as consisting of two distinct dimensions, arousal (the level of activation of the organism) and valence (the evaluation of the emotion-inducing stimulus as beneficial or harmful or, more broadly, as pleasant or unpleasant)[2].

2.2   Interaction Techniques

The application uses text-to-speech in order to make text-based information accessible to visually impaired users, but can also be used by sighted individuals. In the case of visually impaired users, auditory and tactile feedback is utilized. Users may at any time enter recording mode, during which they record an oral description of their current affective state or any additional information that may be relevant to their disposition toward a particular place. The recording is subsequently stored as geo-located content.

Regarding tactile input, users may double-tap on the screen, and slide to the appropriate direction. More specifically, sliding along the horizontal axis corresponds to setting the value of "valence", whereas sliding along the vertical axis corresponds to setting the value of "arousal". Both these quantities have five gradations (highly negative, slightly negative, neutral, slightly positive, and highly positive), represented on-screen by a 5×5 grid, the neutral point for both axes being the central part of that grid. Although five-point continua may potentially be more complicated to a visually impaired user, they provide a much more detailed snapshot of a person's emotional disposition when compared to the undoubtedly simpler three-point "scales" which offer no meaningful differentiation between degrees of "positive" or "negative".

An example of providing information on the affective state of a user using tactile input is the following: having started at a neutral position on both axes, users swipe the screen a number of times in the appropriate axis so as to select the desired emotional description in terms of arousal and valence. Each swiping gesture changes one of the two components of that description – e.g. one upward swipe results in selecting the value "slightly aroused". An additional upward swipe would set the value to "highly aroused". A subsequent leftward swipe would shift the valence component from the neutral value to that of "slightly negative". The two axes combined in this case describe an emotional disposition that is negative but not overly so, while at the same time being highly arousing – possibly corresponding to anger, tension, or fear.

Visually impaired users receive auditory feedback on the currently selected arousal and valence descriptions, both during the actual selection process (i.e. immediately after having made a swiping gesture) and prior to the final confirmation, which is signaled by a double tap on the screen. An additional double tap is required for finalizing the selected description.

---

[2]   There is some correspondence between Russell's dimensional conception of affect and categorical approaches (such as Ekman's [7] for example), as evident by the descriptors (such as "sad", "upset", "happy", "frightening", etc.) provided by Russell at specific points or at specific zones along the circumplex.

An indicative screenshot is shown in Fig. 1.

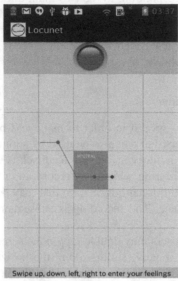

Fig. 1. An indicative screenshot of the application. The large button on the top is used to enter or exit voice recording mode. The dark-colored dot indicates the user's current location. Light-colored dots along the path are geo-annotations.

The application records the trajectory and activity of each individual user in the form of a line, and geo-located content generated by the user in that session ad a red-colored dot along that line; thus, a complete reconstruction of the users' movements through the city and geo-located content generation is possible.

3   Evaluation Scenario and Methodology

The application is to be deployed in a trial run through specific areas of the city of Limassol, Cyprus in the context of soundwalks. A soundwalk relies on active listening when navigating an environment. During a soundwalk, users are divided in groups and escorted through a predetermined series of locations. At every such location, users are exposed to certain auditory stimuli which are predicted to incite various emotional responses. The soundwalk method has been preferred over alternative methods that allow for unhindered movement throughout the city due to the advantages it offers for visually impaired users, who face issues of safety during their movement in the city. Given that this research will be undertaken in the city, which is an inherently uncontrollable environment, an additional advantage of the soundwalk method lies in its ability to ensure that all participants will be exposed to the same conditions, which will increase the validity of the conclusions that may be drawn.

The environment in which the soundwalk will take place encompasses various key locations of the city center of Limassol. The sites are sufficiently varied so as to provide a multitude of auditory stimuli from various parts of urban settings (see Fig. 2).

Fig. 2. The soundwalk route through the centre of Limassol

The application itself will be evaluated using a mixed methods approach. The application's usability will be ascertained my means of questionnaires, such as the System Usability Questionnaire [8], the simplicity of which compensates for the fact that it treats usability as a unidimensional construct. Additionally, short interviews will be conducted with the participants. In the case of visually impaired users, the questionnaire items will be integrated in these interviews. Data are to be analyzed both quantitatively and qualitatively in an attempt to capture a more holistic view of the application's functionality and the city's affective impact.

This application is expected to contribute to the documentation of the affective "image" of the city of Limassol: the map will be divided into a grid, and the affective response values provided by the participants will be aggregated for each cell of that grid and given an effective visualization aid, such as color. Thus, an "affective map" of Limassol that consists of zones colored according to the predominant affective response recorded by the users will result.

4   Future Work

A way of improving the application described in this paper is to extend its functionality and methods of communication with the surroundings so that it may be used in interior spaces, which pose a variety of additional problems for visually impaired users [9]. One potential way of achieving this is through the use of Near Field Communications (NFC) [9-11]. The use of NFC is expected to add to the perceived physicality of the interaction, since it forces the user to move very close to the intended area, practically at touching distance. Such a capability may be perceived as an alternate, digitally augmented form of distal perception on the part of visually impaired users. As a consequence, the detail of emotion mapping will potentially increase so as to encompass the interiors of public buildings in a city. Additionally, similar activities such as the one described herein may be repeated for other parts of Limassol or other cities in Cyprus. Furthermore, the unstructured use of this application by individual users can be expected to complement the data obtained through the soundwalk and highlight non-predetermined places of personal significance.

References

1. Diamantaki, K., Rizopoulos, C., Charitos, D., Tsianos, N., Gazi, A.: Theoretical and Methodological Implications of Designing and Implementing Multi-user Location-based Activities. Personal and Ubiquitous Computing 15, 37–49 (2011)
2. Diamantaki, K., Rizopoulos, C., Tsetsos, V., Theona, I., Charitos, D., Kaimakamis, N.: Integrating Game Elements for Increasing Engagement and Enhancing User Experience in a Smart City. In: Botía, J., Charitos, D. (eds.) Workshop Proceedings of the 9th International Conference on Intelligent Environments, Athens, Greece, July 16-17, pp. 160–171. IOS Press, Amsterdam (2013)
3. Low, S.M., Altman, I.: Place Attachment: A Conceptual Inquiry. In: Altman, I., Low, S.M. (eds.) Place Attachment, pp. 1–12. Plenum Press, New York (1991)
4. Visell, Y.: Tactile Sensory Substitution: Models for Enaction in HCI. Interacting with Computers 21, 38–53 (2009)
5. Russell, J.A.: Core Affect and the Psychological Construction of Emotion. Psychological Review 110, 145–172 (2003)
6. Russell, J.A., Pratt, G.: A Description of the Affective Quality Attributed to Environments. Journal of Personality and Social Psychology 38, 311–322 (1980)
7. Ekman, P.: Basic Emotions. In: Dalgleish, T., Power, M. (eds.) Handbook of Cognition and Emotion, pp. 45–60. John Wiley and Sons, Sussex (1999)
8. Brooke, J.: SUS: A Quick and Dirty Usability Scale. In: Jordan, P.W., Thomas, B., Weerdmeester, B.A., McClelland, I.L. (eds.) Usability Evaluation in Industry, pp. 189–194. Taylor & Francis, Abington (1996)
9. Upadhyaya, P.: Neef of NFC Technology for Helping Blind and Short Come People. International Journal of Engineering Research and Technology 2(6) (2013)
10. Ivanov, R.: Indoor Navigation System for Visually Impaired. In: Proceedings of the 11th International Conference on Computer Systems and Technologies (CompSysTech 2010), Sofia, Bulgaria, June 17-18, pp. 143–149 (2010)
11. Bae, K.Y., Jeong, Y.S., Shim, W.S., Kwak, S.J.: The Ubiquitous Library for the Blind and Physically Handicapped – A Case Study of the LG Sangnam Library, Korea. IFLA Journal 33, 210–219 (2007)

Development of a Touch Panel Interface that Provides Tactile Feedback Depending on the Surroundings

Hitoshi Tamura[1] and Yasushi Kambayashi[2]

[1] Department of Innovative Systems Engineering,
Nippon Institute of Technology, Japan
tamura@nit.ac.jp
[2] Department of Computer and Information Engineering,
Nippon Institute of Technology, Japan
yasushi@nit.ac.jp

Abstract. We have developed and evaluated a touch panel interface that provides tactile feedback depending on the surroundings. We attempt to provide map information for blind people and make the car navigation system replace the white cane for blind people. In the study, we emphasis on providing tactile feedback for blind users that reflects the surroundings. The design of the interface to tactile feedback is that the touch panel moves up and down with a touch position. Those movements provide the tactile feedback. In order to achieve the tactile feedback method, we have placed four servo motors at the four corners of the touch panel. The motors move up and down the panel. From the evaluation experiments, we have observed that it is possible for a blind user to recognize map information by touching the panel.

Keywords: Tactile feedback, Electric wheelchair, Multi touch panel, Assistive technology.

1 Introduction

Wheelchairs are the major moving apparatus for handicapped people. In the previous paper, we have reported our experiences about an interface that we have designed and implemented for electric wheelchairs that makes users recognize the surrounding circumference so that it prevents accidents. Even though we have implemented a viewer for the user that liberates the user from the constrained perspectives, we assumed that the user can see the display as well as the circumstances. We have not assumed the user of blind people. There are, however, a certain number of blind people who need to use wheelchairs.

Therefore, we have designed and implemented a touch panel interface that provides the wheelchair users tactile feedback over that circumstances. The motivation is an interface device for wheelchairs that provides similar functions of the white canes. The interface consists of a touch panel that moves up and down depending on the existence of any obstacles in front of the wheelchair. The surrounding information can be retrieved through the laser range finder (LRF). We employ usual surface capacitance for the touch panel, because our purpose is providing everyday apparatus and low cost is an important factor.

C. Stephanidis (Ed.): HCII 2014 Posters, Part II, CCIS 435, pp. 259–263, 2014.
© Springer International Publishing Switzerland 2014

2   System Configuration

The touch panel has four servo motors at the four corners that make the panel move up and down at three levels as well as incline the panel so that the user can feel the tactile sensation how far and which direction the obstacle is. The resolution of the touch panel is 512×666 pixels. The distance between the bottom and top position of the panel is 13mm, and it takes 0.085 second to move from bottom to top and vice versa.

By using this touch panel that moves up and down depending on the existence of any obstacle, the user can drives his or her wheelchair as if he or she walk with the white cane. Our first goal has been achieved. However, if we can provide some kind of navigation system for blind people, it should be useful. Our second goal is providing more accurate information than that of the LRF can provides.

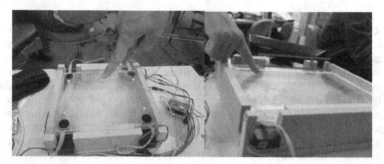

Fig. 1. A touch panel system equipped tactile feedback

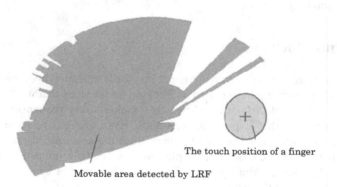

The touch position of a finger

Movable area detected by LRF

Fig. 2. A touch panel system equipped tactile feedback

Our assumption is that a blind user of the wheelchair would not drive unknown area alone. Therefore we do not need complete navigation system just as car navigation system. We only register the map information of the users' home or work place as well as immediate neighboring area.

The user is expected to touch the panel by using his or her finger, and the coordinates of the position of the fingertip are acquired by the connected microcomputer. The circumstances in front of the user are mapped into the panel so that panel functions as an invisible map of navigation system.

When the user touches a certain point of the surface, the position is calculated and mapped into the hidden map, and if the touched position is blocked by some obstacle, the touch screen rises to make the user sense the obstacle. Therefore, when the user drives his or her wheelchair, and go through a winding aisle, the user can sense the drivable route of the winding aisle on the touch panel. The user also can sense the corner of the aisle as the appearance of an open gap on the wall of the aisle.

3   Experiments for Performance Measurement

From the numerical experiments, we have observed that it is roughly possible for blind users to recognize map information by touching the panel. Even though the recognition accuracy by the tactile sense of this device is depending of the individual sensibility, the device achieved to provide base functionality.

For example, we have used a map in the experiments as shown in Fig. 3.

We acquired the following knowledge by the experiments using this simple map.

(1) It is generally possible the user can sense 16mm (on a panel) width as a route.

(2) It is enough to perceive width of a 12.5 mm up-and-down motion.

(3) For the feedback, the conditions that the high level indicates obstacles, the low level indicates road and the middle level indicates "start" or "goal" points are good enough for recognition.

We have observed that the participants tend to scan the whole panel with a finger first to perceive a route on the map. Thus the subjects have rightly recognized the topology of the graph of the route. Fig. 4 and Fig. 5 show how the subjects recognize the routes represented on the touch panels as the results of the experiments using this system. Fig.4 shows that many subjects have incorrectly recognized the routes. However, when a subject was advised that he should scan the panel beforehand, he could greatly improve the recognition rate (Fig.5).

Fig. 3. Simple maps for experiments

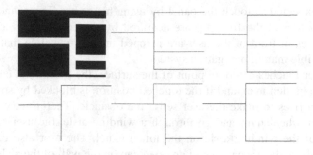

Fig. 4. Examples of result (tracing route)

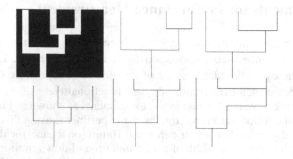

Fig. 5. Examples of result (scanning whole the panel before tracing)

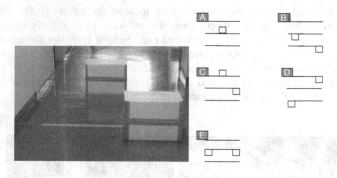

Fig. 6. Obstacles detection

Therefore we can conclude that blind users can drive his or her wheelchairs in well-acquainted places such as home or work place as well as immediate surrounding by using this touch panel navigation system.

In the emergency case, when the user must stop immediately, the panel inclines at maximum steep so that the user can sense the immediate obstacle in front of him or her (Fig. 6). We believe that the combination of the LRF and navigation map widen the activity area of blind people. We have observed, however, that it is hard for the LRF to detect moving obstacle as well as the LRF itself is moving.

We are well aware of the limitation of the touch panel interface. Even though it is very inexpensive, the accuracy is limited. We are planning to design and to implement a new touch panel that is able to provide unevenness so that the user can sense the route by his or her palm or multiple fingers instead of single finger.

In the current design, only a single point can respond by the technique of using the up-and-down motion of a panel. We are currently developing a new system; however, we extend the system that responds two points in the feedback system. The method is to lean the panel combining up-and-down motion of two points. Since leaning the panel as well as moving up and down makes a virtual three-dimensional structure, we have found that a user can easily understand the map by the expansion. Even though the experiments with touching two points and leaning the panel are still in preliminary stage, the new system improves the users' recognition ability, and the subjects give us favorable responses.

4   Conclusion and Discussion

We have proposed and developed a touch panel interface that provides tactile feedback depending on the surroundings. The design of interfaces for the tactile feedback is using a touch panel that moves up and down according to the touched position.

As tactile feedback method, we have placed four servo motors at the four corners of the touch panel. The motors move up and down the panel. The resolution of a touch panel is 512×666 pixels. A panel takes 0.085 second for moving up and down 13mm.

As the result of the experiments, we have found that it is possible for blind users to recognize map information by touching the panel. Feasibility study is now in progress using an electric wheelchair. Even though preliminary experiments suggest favorable results, there is some room for improvement. We are re-designing our interfaces while continuing to conduct the feasibility study to provide more flexibility to the users.

References

1. Dicianno, B.E., Spaeth, D.M., Cooper, R.A., Fitzgerald, S.G., Boninger, M.L.: Advancements in power wheelchair joystick technology: Effects of isometric joysticks and signal conditioning on driving performance. Am. J. Phys. Med. Rehabil. 85(10), 631–639 (2006)
2. Dicianno, B.E., Cooper, R.A., Coltellaro, J.: Joystick control for powered mobility: current state of technology and future directions. Phys. Med. Rehabil. Clin. N. Am. 21(1), 79–86 (2010)
3. Nakajima, Y., Yasuda, S., Yoshinari, S., Watanuki, Y., Tadano, S.: Development of a touchpad controller for an electric wheelchair. In: Dynamics and Design Conference, pp. 810–810 (2001) (in Japanese)
4. Maesako, T., Tamori, H., Shigemasu, K., Shimizu, Y., Sakamoto, T.: A Finger-Sensitive Multi-Functional Hemisphere Type Interface. J. Institute of Electronics, Information and Communication Engineers J70-A(3), 340–349 (1987) (in Japanese)
5. Asaoka, S., Murai, H., Tsuji, H., Tatsumi, H., Tokumasu, S.: The Concept of the Distance Field Model for Space Representation. In: Proc. 6th Int. Conf. on Intelligent Technologies, pp. 262–269 (2005)

Compilation of a Sign Language Database for Use in Medical Practice

Mina Terauchi[1], Keiko Watanabe[2], Yuji Nagashima[2], Naoto Kato[3],
Taro Miyazaki[3], Seiki Inoue[3], Shuichi Umeda[3],
Toshihiro Shimizu[3], and Nobuyuki Hiruma[3]

[1] Polytechnic University, 2-32-1 Ogawanishimachi, Kodaira-shi,
Tokyo 187-0035, Japan
[2] Kogakuin University, 2665-1 Nakano-machi, Hachioji-shi, Tokyo 192-0015, Japan
[3] NHK Science & Technology Research Laboratories 1-10-11 Kinuta, Setagaya-ku,
Tokyo, 157-8510, Japan

Abstract. This paper reports on a study into the establishment of a medical sign language database.

When visiting a medical institution, hearing-impaired patients are sometimes accompanied by a sign language interpreter. The interpreter's job is to correctly interpret the doctors' explanations. However, a problem arises in that medical sign language varies considerably in style from one region to another and has not been standardized.

We compiled a list of medical sign language with an emphasis on standardization of meanings and movements. For compiling the sign language terms, we consulted medical professionals, sign language interpreters and native signers. We tried to ensure that the resulting medical sign language include common expressions that can be easily understood by non-professionals. We also produced sign language instructions for medical terms that are hard to understand based on sign language alone, as well as other difficult terms.

1 Introduction

When visiting a medical institution, we receive an explanation on the medical condition and the treatment from a doctor or nurse. However, among medical terms there are many hard-to-understand words. A patient's inability to fully understand the doctor's explanation could be life-threatening, so it is essential for the patient and the attendant to correctly understand the doctor. If understanding is not enough, it is imperative to ask for a repeated explanation from the doctor or nurse. When visiting a medical institution, hearing-impaired patients are sometimes accompanied by a sign language interpreter. However, it is difficult to translate technical medical terms into sign language so the patient can understand. There are some books currently available in Japan that provide sign language words and example sentences for medical settings [1]– [3]. There are problems, however, in that some of the expressions included in such books are not widely accepted and sign language words have been created without any specific rules or consistency.

C. Stephanidis (Ed.): HCII 2014 Posters, Part II, CCIS 435, pp. 264–269, 2014.

Considering this situation, we have compiled and collected medical sign language words that are more easily understandable and are in wider usage. We have already defined 1,080 sign language words for 800 Japanese medical terms. Yet some terms can be confusing after being directly translated into a sign language word. For such terms, appropriate explanatory text has been provided. This report describes how to create medical sign language words and explanatory text, and introduces a part of the database that was experimentally developed.

2   Medical Sign Language Words

First, we briefly explain how we created medical sign language words. We created words mainly for commonly used words in a hospital setting, such as names of body parts, organs and bones, medical conditions and diseases, hospital departments, tests and equipment, and drugs. Table 1 shows word classification and examples.

Table 1. Medical word classification and example words

Classification	Example words
Body parts	Head, Face, Body, Skin, Eye
Organs and Bones	Stomach, Skull, Spine, intestine, lung
Medical Conditions and Diseases	Cold, High Blood Pressure, Stomatitis, Dizziness
Hospital Departments	Surgery, Gastroenterology, Internal Medicine
tests and equipment	echocardiography, MRI, endoscopic
drugs	mouthwash, antibiotics, powdered medicine, tablets
others	doctor, receptionist, medical history, recurrence

With the help of sign language interpreters, including health care workers, and native signers, we have already created 1,080 sign language words for 800 Japanese medical terms. The number of sign language words differs from that of Japanese words because ways of expressing vary from person to person, so there are sometimes multiple sign language words for one Japanese word.

For example, we have created two sign language words for the word gstomachh – an expression of tracing the stomach shape and an expression of using the manual alphabet, which are shown in Figure 1 (a) and (b), respectively. The animation images used in Figure 1 were created using TV program Making Language (TVML), which is currently being developed by NHK Science & Technical Research Laboratories.

With regard to phrases that include the word "stomach," such as "stomach ulcer" and "stomach camera," we created two types of sign language in order to standardize the way of expression. Therefore, the sign language words we actually created were increased in number. Most Japanese words have only one, two or three corresponding sign language words.

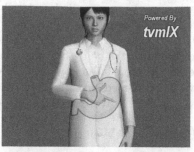

(a) Tracing the stomach shape

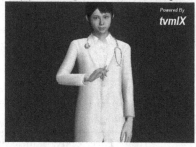

(b) Using the manual alphabet

Fig. 1. Sign language for the word "stomach"

3   Explanatory Text for Medical Sign Language

3.1   Problems of Medical Terms and Selection of Words

Medical terms are hard to understand when only looking at the name. There are many Japanese medical dictionaries available and the styles vary widely. Some include detailed descriptions and some provide example sentences for the purpose of translation, while others include generally used terms. However, the fact is that most of them are somewhat incomprehensible to non-professionals.

Take Kawasaki disease as an example. If it is directly translated from Japanese into sign language, the result is:

Kawasaki disease = $kawa$ (river) + $saki$ (small peninsula) + disease

It is almost impossible to understand the term since the sign language is created by transliterating each Japanese word.

Health care workers and non-professionals often interpret a certain disease name or symptom name differently. As seen in the example of "late childbearing," non-professionals tend to consider this phrase as meaning a woman who gives birth at a later age (35 or older). But in fact the Japan Society of Obstetrics and Gynecology defines the term as "first-time childbearing at a later age," i.e., a woman who gives birth for the first time at age 35 or older. Thus, it is necessary to add explanatory text to a case in which health care workers and non-professionals have different understandings, and misunderstanding can easily occur.

We have then included explanatory text that we created based on the medical sign language data already collected.

Conditions for selecting a word to be given explanatory text were determined as follows:

Condition 1

Some of the terms used in a medical setting are important and one's life can depend on them. We assumed a case in which a parent (a mother) with a hearing disorder brings his or her child to a hospital, because such a case is often time-critical.

Condition 2

We selected the names of diseases and symptoms that are common from the standpoint of nurses.

Condition 3

We preferentially selected terms that are hard to understand when transliterated to sign language.

We created example sentences for 69 medical terms. The procedure is described in the next section.

3.2   Procedures for Creating Explanatory Text

We created example sentences for selected words with the help of sign language interpreters, including health care workers, and native signers. The procedures are described by presenting the term "fundus examination" as an example.

Step 1

After a word is selected, a health care provider writes explanatory text in Japanese.

Writtenexplanatorytext

"Among all the blood vessels throughout the body, only those in the fundus can be seen by the naked eye. This examination is not only for detecting an eye disease but also for checking vascular conditions and presence or absence of bleeding. It can help in knowing the state of arteriosclerosis, diabetes, high blood pressure and others, so it can also be effective as a test for lifestyle-related diseases."

Step 2

A native signer and a sign language interpreter translate the Japanese sentence into sign language (a series of sign language words). It is preferable to use sign language words that are easier to understand for non-professionals and not to use technical terms. When a technical term must be used, it should be selected from the words already collected.

Translated sign language sentence
{ eye } { disease } { only } { not } { diabetes }
{ red } { vessel } { stiff } { disease }
{ hypertension } { exist } { not exist } { examine } { method }

Step 3

The sign language words that were translated in Step 2 are recorded as a video data.

Step 4

The video data recorded are Step 3 is verified with the cooperation of the health care worker, sign language interpreter and native signer. If there is a vague or confusing expression, the sign language sentence should be reviewed and recreated. When the recorded sign language sentence is transcribed into a written sentence, fundus examination is expressed as follows:

Transcribed sentence
"This is a method for not only detecting an eye disease but also checking the presence or absence of diabetes, arteriosclerosis and high blood pressure."

As described above, the translated sign language is simpler compared to the original sentence, but it is possible to convey the minimum necessary information. Another example is a case of bacterium and virus. Although each word is an individual term, we made only one explanatory text in order to clarify the difference between them.

Example: "Bacterium and Virus"

Written explanatory text
"Bacterium has cells and can grow on its own. Antibiotics can work effectively against it by destroying the cell walls. On the other hand, a virus is a pathogen smaller than bacterium. It can grow in other organisms but cannot grow on its own. A virus causes a disease. Antibiotics cannot work against it because it has no cells."

Translatedsignlanguagesentence
{Bacterium} {case} {bacterium} {inside} {cells} {exist}
{on its own} {grow} {can}
{virus} {case} {bacterium} {compared to} {very} {small}
{on its own} {grow} {difficult}
{For example} {human} {animal} {transmitted} {grow} {can}

4   Conclusion

This report reviewed how we created medical sign language words. We emphasized consistency of sign language and made the utmost effort to use sign language words that are easy for non-professionals to understand. We also created explanatory text for confusing medical terms. Corrections and further considerations for words that are required in a medical setting were conducted. Creating a database of medical sign language and explanatory text that is easy for non-professionals to understand is expected to help reduce the anxiety of the hearing impaired when they visit medical institutions.

We intend to continue collecting medical sign language words and creating explanatory text.

Acknowledgment. Part of this study was subsidized by a Grant-in-Aid for Scientific Research (A) 23240087, a scientific research grant by the Ministry of Education, Culture, Sports, Science and Technology.

References

1. Compiled by "Medical Sign Language" Editorial Board: Medical Sign Language, Medical Sign Language Series 1-3, separate volume, Publication Bureau of Japanese Federation of the Deaf (2009) (in Japanese)
2. Nakagawa, F. (ed.): Medical Sign Language Dictionary. Hiroshima Prefectural Sign Language Interpretation Research Association (2005) (in Japanese)
3. Costello, E.: Random House Webster's American Sign Language Medical Dictionary. Random House Reference (2000)

Study into Methods of Describing Japanese Sign Language

Keiko Watanabe[1], Yuji Nagashima[1], Mina Terauchi[2], Naoto Kato[3],
Taro Miyazaki[3], Seiki Inoue[3], Shuichi Umeda[3],
Toshihiro Shimizu[3], and Nobuyuki Hiruma[3]

[1] Kogakuin University, 2665-1 Nakano-machi, Hachioji-shi, Tokyo 192-0015, Japan
[2] Polytechnic University, 2-32-1, Ogawanishimachi, Tokyo, 187-0035, Japan
[3] NHK Science & Technology Research Laboratories 1-10-11 Kinuta, Tokyo,
157-8510, Japan

Abstract. This paper proposes a new NVSG element model with a focus on the linguistic structure of sign language. Morphemes in sign language consist of elements such as hand shape , movement and line of sight. An NVSG element description method is a method of describing morphological structure in an independent hierarchical structure.

Approximately 1,500 words have been described using the description method. After being described, the hierarchical structure of morphemes becomes easily comprehensible visually at a word level. Describing each element also allows us to search for a word from the word structure.

In the future, we intend to verify the possibility of sign language description in languages other than Japanese.

1 Introduction

Sign language is a visual language with no speech and is composed through manual markers (hand shape, hand movement, hand position, and palm direction) and non-manual markers (such as line of sight and nodding). Morphemes are composed of these multiple elements (articulatory organs).

Our goal is to construct a system that can automatically generate animation of translated sign language from spoken Japanese. To achieve this goal, it is necessary to have a method that can depict sign language and enable its analysis via computer. This paper proposes an NVSG element model, a hierarchical morphological description method that can describe the sign language structure. In this method, each element required to form a word is described independently for each morpheme in sign language.

We investigated means of describing manual markers objectively (including CL). We then described the sign language by using the NVSG describing method and compiled a dictionary that provides word structures.

2 How to Describe Sign Language

Different from spoken language, sign language has no widely used writing system. Known description methods include HamNoSys and SignWriting. However, these

C. Stephanidis (Ed.): HCII 2014 Posters, Part II, CCIS 435, pp. 270–275, 2014.

are iconic and aim to describe phonetic symbols. The NVSG element description method proposed here aims to describe morphological structures of words and generate animation by synthesizing them.

3   NVSG Element Model

In sign language, one word is represented by combining each element. Each element moves independently. To describe words in animation images, it is necessary to analyze how each element moves. Therefore, we decided to independently describe each element of the sign language.

Among elements, manual markers are described in an N element and V element, while non-manual markers are described in an S element and G element. Items related to hand shape, palm direction and hand position are described in the N element, while movement items are described in the V element. Among non-manual markers, line of sight is most important, so items regarding line of sight are described in the S element, while other non-manual markers are described in the G element.

3.1   N Element

In the N element, items related to hand shape, one of the components of manual markers, are described. Hand shape is represented by depicting how the finger shapes have changed. The state after the finger shape has changed is described according to Table 1. Numbers 1 to 4 were assigned to the fingers in order from index to pinky of both hands, with 5 assigned to the thumb.

Table 1. Codes for hand shapes

Hand shape		Code	
Relationship	Change in shape	Typical hand shape	Relaxed hand shape
Flexion of fingers	Extending	H	h
	Curving	B	b
	Folding	A	a
	Bending	F	f
	Standard shape	G	g
Relationship between fingers	Bonding	C	c
	Pinching	P	p
	Pushing the thumb	T	-
	Covering	V	-

The hand position (first position of the hand shape) is also described by using "@" in N element.

Example: {*tokui* (elation)} [1] = [Ns(H45 @nose) Vs(PR)]

---

[1] Sign language words are represented in {}. Japanese word are represented as italic.

3.2   V Element

In the V element, codes represent movements. Although movements in sign language look complicated, they can be classified as shown in Table 2, and each can be described by using a code. Writing out the movements with code can prevent differences in description from person to person and makes it possible to conduct computer analysis.

Example: {*hana* (flower)} = [NN(b0>h0) V(MV(transposed)))]RR(symmetric)
{*atama* (head)} = [N(H1) V(PT >> head)]

Table 2. Codes for movements

Movement		Code
Movement	Shift of position	MV (<u>M</u>o<u>v</u>e)
	Motion	MT (<u>M</u>o<u>t</u>ion)
Instruction	Pointing	PT (<u>P</u>oin<u>t</u>ing)
	Defining the area	PT:AREA
Presentation	Presentation	PR (<u>P</u>resentation)
Trace a Letter	Trace a Letter	TL (<u>T</u>race a <u>Le</u>tter)

4   Word Description in NVSG Element Model

This section covers how to describe specific sign language words by using the NVSG element model.

4.1   Describing Pattern of Manual Markers

The relationship between the V and N element of a manual marker is hard to understand because each element is independently described in NVSG element model. To solve this problem, the means of description were changed depending on the relationship between V and N elements, which makes the relationship between them more understandable. Based on the movement of both hands, the relationships between the V and N elements were classified into seven categories. Table 3 shows the classification and patterns.

The dominant hand, which often plays a significant role in sign language, is considered the strong hand, and the non-dominant hand the weak hand. They are represented by the letters "s" and "w", respectively. In other words, Ns means strong hand (dominant hand) in the N element and Vw means weak hand (non-dominant hand) in V element.

The structure of words can be clearly determined depending on which pattern is used.

Table 3. Description patterns of manual markers

	Description pattern	Definition
(1)	NsVs	Basic way of writing (when using only one hand)
(2)	[NsVs] [NwVw]	Basic way of writing (when using both hands)
(3)	Nw[NsVs]	When moving the strong hand while using the weak hand as a marker (e.g., when the weak hand is UM [unmarked])
(4)	NsNwV	When moving both hands in combination or symmetrically
(5)	NsVNw	When moving both hands in the same way (symmetrically) though the hand positions differ.
(6)	[NsVs] [&Nw]	When there is remaining shape in the weak hand
(7)	[&Ns] [NwVw]	When there is remaining shape in the strong hand

4.2 Word Description by Morphological Chain

When sign language animation is automatically generated, it is preferable that the movements are closer to those in actual sign language. Therefore, in the NVSG element model we added information that makes morphological chains more natural. Connections between sign language morphemes have specific features such as "remaining shape". Through animation reflects these features, it is expected that connection between morphemes will become more natural.

Remaining Shape. Remaining shape refers to a phenomenon that can occur when representing words with multiple morphemes: while a part of the previous morpheme remains, the next morpheme has already started. It is observed more frequently in the weak hand, which often plays a less important role than the strong hand.

Remaining shape is represented with the ampersand (&). For example, if it occurs in a weak hand, it is described as [&Nw].

Example: {*kazoku* (family)} = {*ie* (house)} + {*hitobito* (people)}
= [NN(C0) V(PR)]RN(touch),RR(symmetry) + [Ns(H45) Vs(MT(wave),MV(>out))] [&Nw]

5   CL (Classifier)

CL is an abbreviation for classifier, which means to make a classification. Considering that CL is required when creating a new word, we also reviewed the CL (classifier) of Japanese sign language. CL in sign language has a different definition depending on the researcher[1],[2]. In this report, CL is defined: What classifies the concept without any meaning; words in any word class can be CL. Studies have shown that CLs are found in manual markers (N and V element). We have made efforts to streamline the CL classification so that it does not include too many categories.

5.1   CL of Hand Shape

Since sign language is a visual language, external features of something, such as its size and shape, are represented as faithfully as possible. In this report, sign language for representing external features is conceptually classified focusing on hand shapes. Classification was carried out objectively, so it was possible to avoid ambiguity from one classifier to another.

CL of hand shape was classified into 10 categories in total. Table 4 shows the classification. Since this classification was implemented so that it does not include too many CL categories, one category has multiple hand shapes. The classification depended on what the hand shape means. For example, "man" and "woman" were put together as "CL:one". These two words seem to be considered as falling under a separate category of "man" and "woman" in terms of meaning, but categorization was based on the concept of hand shape without meaning. Thus, these two words have been classified in one category because they both are represented as "one being that stands straight" by the movement of holding up a finger.

Example: {*dansei* (man)} = [Ns(CL:one(H5)) Vs(PR)]
{*aruku* (walk)} = [Ns(CL: two(H12)it) Vs(MV(>$per2))]

Table 4. CL of hand shape

Category	Hand shape and body part	Meaning
one	H1	one straight line
	H5	man or human
	H4	woman
two	H12	two straight lines
	H45	two protrusions (tools)
many	h0	many things or unmarked
	H0	straight and stand, and many things
plate	C0	flat thing
circle	p1H234	round thing (2D)
	B15	circular and round thing
cylinder	p0	roll and round thing (3D)
	B(C1234)5	something whose diameter is longer that things represented by category "p"
square	F15	small square
ball	B0	spherical form
thickness	A15	thickness (thick)
	P1	thickness (thin)
stick	HN (head & neck)	head (G) & neck (arm)
	LF (leg & foot)	leg

5.2   CL of Movement

In CL of movement, semantic concepts like a gesture received from the sign language movement were classified. There are four resultant categories, as shown in Table 5. LVL means {*takai* (higher)} or {*ookii* (larger)} compared to a certain standard. ACT is a representation of mimicry, such as {*tenisu* (tennis)}. MAP is a representation of a movement or a state expressed by hand movements, such as {*aruku* (walk)} and {*yuki* (snow)}. GRP is a representation of a unity by a circular motion, such as {*zenbu* (all)} and {*tomodachi* (friends)}.

Example: {*ookii* (larger)} = [[NN(C1234H5)] V(CL:LVL(out))]
{*tenisu* (tennis)} = [Ns(G) Vs(CL:ACT(tennis))]

Table 5. CL of movement

Category	Meaning
LVL (Level)	change from a certain standard
ACT (Action)	mimicry, gesture
MAP (Mapping)	movement
	state
	shape trajectory
GRP (group)	unity

6   Conclusion and Future Issues

This paper is a study on how to write the language structure of sign language. A sign language morpheme dictionary was compiled by using our proposed NVSG description method. Approximately 1,500 words have been described. Three-dimensional motions for these 1,500 words were acquired through an optical motion capture system. The morpheme dictionary will be used for generating and synthesizing materials for linguistic analysis as well as sign language animation.

The NVSG element model is a method of describing the morphological structure of sign language in a hierarchical structure. Describing sign language makes computer analysis easier.

Codes are used in description. Doing so makes it possible to classify the sign language representations, and makes computer analysis easier. It was also shown that sign language movements that are seemingly complicated can be roughly categorized by using codes. CLs have also been defined and classified and can be utilized in generating new words.

In the future, we intend to investigate whether the NVSG description method can be used in sign language other than Japanese.

References

1. Mikos, K., Smith, C., Lentz, E.M.: Signing Naturally, Level 2. Dawn Sign Press, San Diego (1988)
2. Valli, C., Lucas, C., Mulrooney, K.J.: Linguistics of American Sign Language, An Introduction. Gallaudet University Press, Washington, DC (2002)

Design for Aging

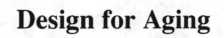

Technologies Developed for Older Adults:
Trends and Directions

Hend S. Al-Khalifa, Manahel Al-Twaim, Moneerah Al-Mohsin, and Muna Al-Razgan

Information Technology Department, College of Computer and Information Sciences,
King Saud University, Riyadh, Saudi Arabia
hendk@ksu.edu.sa

Abstract. Various studies stated that elderly community is the focus of many research discussing aging society or technology products developed for their assistance. Several technologies have been developed to cover different aspects in the elderly life. This study analyzes research papers published in the field of elderly technologies, covering the years 1992 through 2013. Our study involved analyzing 208 publications in terms of: research areas and technologies. Based on the previous overviewed research, this paper provides a brief insight about the different research and technologies developed for elderly people and explore their trends and future research directions.

Keywords: Elderly, Aging, Seniors, Disabilities, Internet, Assistive Technologies, Elder care, Robot, Games, Web Accessibility, Survey.

1   Introduction

Population ageing is increasing worldwide and it will continue growing for next decades. Many older adults suffer from chronic diseases, physical impairment and changes in their lifestyle due to aging. Through the past years, the need for technologies to aid elderly in their daily life attracted and raised awareness of many researchers. Also, it is notable that many technologies were developed and adapted in order to match with the elderly needs and to increase their quality of life.

This paper analyzes research papers published in the field of elderly technologies, covering the years 1992 through 2013. Our study involved analyzing 208 publications in terms of: research areas and technologies. Based on the previous analyzed research, this paper provides a brief insight about the different technologies developed for elderly people and explore their trends and future research directions.

2   Methodology

Papers collected in this study were gathered from ACM, IEEE, SpringerLink, and ProQuest databases. The selection started by searching for the following keywords: elderly technology, older adults, older people, seniors, and ageing. A refinement was

C. Stephanidis (Ed.): HCII 2014 Posters, Part II, CCIS 435, pp. 279–283, 2014.
© Springer International Publishing Switzerland 2014

then made by investigating the keywords and abstracts of each individual paper to include only those in elderly technologies field.

Then, papers were classified and grouped into clusters. This classification is based on hierarchical clustering method -bottom up- approach, where each observation is treated as singleton cluster at the outset and then successively merge (or agglomerate) pairs of clusters until all clusters have been merged into a single cluster moving up the hierarchy [1]. The classification clusters are driven from scanning the abstract of collected papers. The six clusters we reached are: Computer/Web Accessibility, Touchscreen Devices Interfaces Accessibility, Assistive Technologies, Robotics and Game for Elderly.

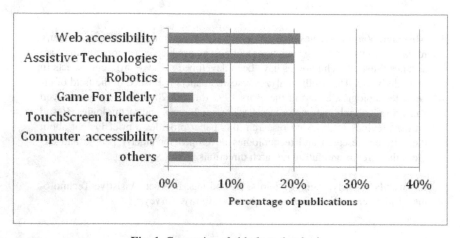

Fig. 1. Categories of elderly technologies

Figure 1 shows the categorization results. 21% of the papers have focused on web accessibility for elderly. This category is further divided into two subcategories: social networks and email. Furthermore, 34% of the papers discussed the accessibility of touchscreen devices. This category is further divided into smartphones and tablets. However, 20% of the papers talked about assistive technologies that enhance the capabilities of elderly to perform the necessary activities. The robotics category (10% of the papers) discussed technologies that are designed to aid elderly in their daily activities, while the computer accessibility category covered 8% of the papers. Additionally, the games that are designed for elderly have covered 4% of the papers. The remaining 4% of the papers (i.e. others category) have discussed different research topics e.g. ergonomics and effective computing.

3   Discussion

Over years there are variation of publications focusing on different elderly technologies, this section discusses the main topics and issues found in each category.

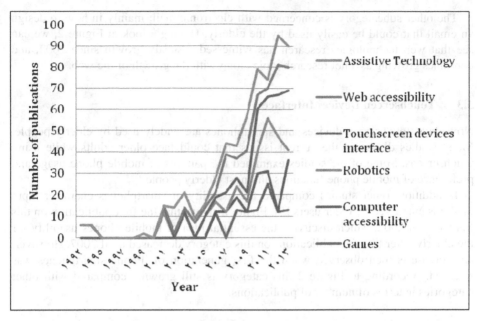

Fig. 2. Growth of publications of elderly technologies over years

3.1 Assistive Technology

The publications in this category have focused on producing technologies that assist older adults in overcoming aging barriers. This category covers a wide range of technologies from healthcare mentoring systems to home appliances.

Figure 2 presents the number of publications found under this category. We can see that there was a significant growth especially in the years 2009 to 2012 which indicates how important to have advanced assistive technologies for aiding elderly in this age. This category includes publications that are concerned with healthcare monitoring systems such as Sensing Systems for measuring Wellness of elderly, Medicine Dose Controllers and Disease Management. Another subcategory covered by this category is home appliances. This subcategory focuses mainly on technologies that help elderly to live independently such as wearable sensors, smart bed monitoring, and flow-sensors for water use in houses.

3.2 Web Accessibility

This category is concerned with aspects related to web accessibility such as: how to design a website that can be accessible by elderly, what are the principles and guidelines for designing a website targeting elderly, and the problems faced by elderly while surfing the web. This category is further divided into social networks and electronic mail subcategories. Social networks subcategory discusses topics such as making existing social networks more accessible by the elderly or designing social networks specifically for the elderly.

The other subcategory is concerned with electronic mail; mainly in how to design an email that could be easily used by the elderly. Having a look at Figure 2, we can see that web technologies research has witnessed a steady growth since 2002, and continues growing as a hot research topic along with the growth of the web.

3.3   Touchscreen Devices Interface

Nowadays, touchscreen devices and smartphones are widely used by elderly people. Many studies discussed the current issues that could face older adults while using touchscreens. Some of the studies examined the patterns of mobile phone usage and preference of mobile phone functions amongst elderly people.

In addition, other studies compared the usability of smartphones character input methods employed by older users [5]. Figure 2 shows that the first publication on this field was in 2002, which discussed the essential idea of mobile phones usability for the elderly, after that the publications on this category decreased until 2007. However, an increase is then observed when the first generation of iPhone smartphones was released. According to Figure 2 this category is still growing compared with other categories in terms of number of publications.

3.4   Robotics

The papers in this category discusses elderly needs, expectations and requirements for designing and developing robots that enhance their capabilities while performing the necessary daily activities. Figure 2 shows an increase in publications from 2009 to 2012 in this category. Many publications addressed the use of robots in elderly life and how the elderly prefer robot assistance for accomplishing their daily tasks. In Addition, some of these publications discuss the issue of the elderly acceptance to robots along with designing and evaluation of robots.

3.5   Computer Accessibility

The key concern of this category was interface design and evaluation of interfaces that meant to be used by the elderly. In addition, this category includes some guidelines and recommendations for designing and training elderly to use computers. Figure2 shows that this category is not steadily growing.

3.6   Game for Elderly

This category contains publications that discuss the designing of guidelines and evaluation of elderly games. The papers that fall in this category explore how games could increase elderly life quality, particularly games that employ gestures such as full-body motion control games [7]. Figure 2 shows that this category has got researchers attention starting from 2006, yet, the field is not well-researched compared to other categories.

3.7   Conclusion

From the previous overview of 208 publications in the field of elderly technologies, we can see that several research topics are gaining momentum and are possible for future research. Among the topics that worth researching include: the adoption of intelligent user interfaces and personalization [2, 3], developing multimodal interfaces [4], robotics and affective computing [6].

Acknowledgments. This project is supported by grant no. D-C-12-117 from King Abdulaziz City for Science and Technology.

References

1. Manning, C., Raghavan, P., Schütze, H.: Hierarchical clustering. In: Introduction to Information Retrieval. Cambridge University Press (2008)
2. Suryadevara, N., Quazi, M., Mukhopadhyay, S.: Intelligent Sensing Systems for measuring Wellness Indices of the Daily Activities for the Elderly (2012)
3. LeoraCulén, A., Bratteteig, T.: Touch-Screens and Elderly users: A Perfect Match? In: The Sixth International Conference on Advances in Computer-Human Interactions, ACHI 2013 (2013)
4. Rodrigues, É., Carreira, M., Gonçalves, D.: Developing a Multimodal Interface for the Elderly. Procedia Computer Science 27, 359–368 (2014)
5. Hamano, Y., Nishiuchi, N.: Usability Evaluation of Text Input Methods for Smartphone among the Elderly. In: 2013 International Conference on Biometrics and Kansei Engineering (2013)
6. Beer, J.M., et al.: The domesticated robot: Design guidelines for assisting older adults to age in place. In: 2012 7th ACM/IEEE International Conference on Human-Robot Interaction, HRI (2012)
7. Gerling, K., Livingston, I., Nacke, L., Mandryk, R.: Full-body motion-based game interaction for older adults. In: Proceedings of the SIGCHI Conference on Human Factors in Computing Systems (CHI 2012). ACM, New York (2012)

Understanding Elderly Needs for Designing a Digitally Extended Environment via Tablets

Patrizia Andronico[1], Salvatore Minutoli[1], and Ercan E. Kuruoglu[2]

[1] Istituto di Informatica e Telematica - CNR (IIT-CNR), Pisa, Italy
{patrizia.andronico,salvatore.minutoli}@iit.cnr.it
[2] Istituto di Scienza e Tecnologie dell'Informazione "A. Faedo" - CNR (ISTI-CNR), Pisa, Italy
ercan.kuruoglu@isti.cnr.it

Abstract. In this short communication we describe our methodological framework for developing an extended digital environment for the elderly. The core of our approach is based on probing elderly needs via storytelling to be interpreted in a wide sense. The probe consists of activities to be carried out by the experiment group, such as taking pictures, making a collage, writing a diary.

Keywords: participatory design, storytelling, elderly, user-centred design.

1   Introduction

The increasing of life expectation is a well-known phenomenon as are the related problems of maintaining an active ageing population. In Italy the aging index1 in 2013 is 151,4 elderly out of 100 youth, thus the population over 65 years old is now reaching 13 million [1]. In addition to the natural aging of the body and the possible diseases related to old age, many of them live alone. In recent years many governments have been investing in and many researchers are working to find solutions to improve the general quality of life of the elderly.

In recent years, we have seen at the same time an increase in mobile technology – smart phones or tablets - and the development of all types of applications, including social networks, for study, for entertainment, for the maintenance of relationships or connections among family members, and so on. The elderly also suffer the technological gap that keeps them distant from their own grandchildren, who were born to a digital world.

The aim of our research is developing digital means for an extended environment for elderly. For issues related to age and to the possible difficulty of movement or reduced social activities, in fact, the elderly are facing an increasingly reduced physical environment around them. One of our intentions is to recover part of the physical space via a virtual environment that can help them maintain a more active life.

A digital environment can provide a compensation for part of the reduced interaction of the elderly with the environment. Due to old age and the limitations that it

---

1   The ratio between people over 65 years old and youth up to 14 years old.

C. Stephanidis (Ed.): HCII 2014 Posters, Part II, CCIS 435, pp. 284–287, 2014.

brought, a manageable and usable environment should be one of the main things to take into consideration. The design of new technologies has changed and it is no more only a practical or usable design tool or application, but rather something that has inside some emotional aspect of the user experience. Designing an application framework for tablet to help elderly in their everyday activities and needs could let them feel still active in our society.

The choice of working with tablet technologies instead of smart phones is given by various practical aspects in relation to the difficulties that aging people could encounter. In fact the medium that is desired:

— Is light enough to carry everywhere the user moves to: elderly people may have problem in carrying heavy objects;
— Has a screen bigger than a mobile phone, even in a 7inch model: elderly with visual problems can interact with a tablet in a better way when compared to a smart phone;
— Has an easier interactability;
— Has no internet connection, but just wi-fi: reducing the other cost and taking advantage of the spreading of the wi-fi zone in all the cities;
— Has multiplicity of applications that are constantly being developed and downloaded for free;
— Has no sim card for call: again for reducing cost but also because we believe elderly who has their own mobile phone won't change the way they use it.

2   Storytelling as a Cultural Probe

Human beings have used the art of storytelling to tell stories, to teach, to communicate knowledge, or for entertainment. Storytelling in all its forms is the main way through which an individual imposes order to their experiences also to understand others and the differences of roles within the society. "At the family level, storytelling is used - often unwittingly - by parents to socialize their children, to teach what stories are appropriate and important, and aid their development in becoming competent tellers of the family's life stories. [2]"

Narrative approach is fundamental in Jerome Bruner vision of the creation of the self. According to Cultural Psychology in which Bruner and Vygotsky were two of the most important contributors, mind and culture cannot be separated. Life is a novel, according to Bruner and it is built by the stories we tell everyday to ourselves or to the others. "We organize our experience and our memory of human happenings mainly in the form of narrative – stories, excuses, myths, reasons for doing and not doing, and so on. .... Narrative, then, are a version of reality whose acceptability is governed by convention and 'narrative necessity' rather than by empirical verification and logical necessity, although ironically we have no compunction about calling stories true or false."[3] On the other way creativity for Vygotsky is in the society itself and help people in learning and internalizing things that help in generating new creative ideas [4].

3   Designing the Cultural Probe

To understand the inner thoughts of elderly that can help us in figuring out what should be the most useful app for people over 65 years old, we decided to implement a probe kit to work with and propose to our sample. The purpose is to capture some inner thoughts of the participants in a more relaxed way.

From the first developed in 1999 [5], the cultural probe was used in different research studies involving elderly population in different activities to explore in a creative way their domestic environments, their social network, health and assisted living [6]. A probe is a research methodology of user-centred design that can be useful for understanding human phenomena and exploring design opportunities [7].

A cultural probe is usually made of activities such as a diary, a list of photos to be taken, a map to draw, some pictures to comment. All of the material are intentionally open-ended. Due to the nature of the methodology, analysis is not easy and can bring some ambiguity, but it is for sure a creative way to talk about a group life in an informal way. Usually a probe kit is left to the experimental sample for a fixed period of time during which the group, individually, has to carry out the activities proposed. After that period all the materials is recollected and analyzed within the research team.

We designed a probe pack of activities in the form of a diary, visual and written, according to the theoretical framework illustrated in the previous chapter. Our kit consists of:

Table 1. activities of our cultural probe kit proposed to a sample of elderly

Activities	Action to be performed	Aim
Photos	A list of 20 items participants should explore taking pictures	Reflection on private life explored visually
Diary	A colored booklet to fill in with written thought or past stories	Reflection on the past and the current life in the form of a story, or a tale
Collage	A cardboard in which each participant has to create a collage following a given theme	Reflection in written and visual form of the given theme and finding of the materials they need to complete the task (picture, textile, written words, and so on).
Postcards	Postcards prepared with photos and an open comments area to be completed by participant	Reflections on pre-formed images and text

3.1   Experimental Set Up

Our cultural probe in form of diary was presented to a first group of elderly that usually attend classes at a special "university" for the elderly2. At the university there

---

2   UNI.DE.A. – Università degli Adulti, is a cultural association in Pisa established in 1983 providing educational courses and lectures in multidisciplinary topics for elderly.

are classes of practical artisanship, as well as classes on computing, history, cultural heritage, or scientific seminars. The group is particularly active in their daily lives and for this reason we decided to start from them. We believe that the experience gained from observing this group could inspire us in entering better the elderly population.

In the first meeting with one of the teachers of the university, we decided to arrange a meeting with all the elderly interested in our work. We explained the methodology and the tasks to be carried out to this group and we gave them two weeks to complete all the activities of the probe kit.

4 Towards the Design of the Extended Digital Environment

The data obtained via the probe provide us large amount of raw clues for the design of applications for tablet. We are in the phase of evaluating in the research group the results collected. Next step is to discuss the intuitions obtained from the evaluation phase with the experiment group to get their feedback which may require a second critical look into the data. This phase will be followed by the shortlisting of applications to be developed for tablets. The application prototypes will be tested by the same experiment group.

Acknowledgments. The authors would like to thank Angelo Pomicino, lecturer at UNI.DE.A. (University for Elderly in Pisa) for his liaison with the experiment group.

References

1. http://www.tuttitalia.it/statistiche/indici-demografici-struttura-popolazione/
2. Cassell, J., Ryokai, K.: Making Space for Voice: Technologies to Support Children's Fantasy and Storytelling. Proceeding of the Personal and Ubiquitous Computing (2001)
3. Bruner J.: The Narrative Construction of Reality. Critical Inquiry 18 (Autumn 1991)
4. Vygotsky, L.S.: Mind in society: The development of higher psychological processes. In: Cole, M., John-Steiner, V., Scribner, S., Souberman, E. (eds.) Harvard University Press, Cambridge (1978)
5. Gaver, W., Dunne, A.: PacentiE. Design: Cultural Probes. Interactions 6, 21–29 (1999)
6. Wherton, J., Sugarhood, P., Procter, R., Rouncefield, M., Dewsbury, G., Hinder, S., Greenhalgh, T.: Designing assisted living technologies 'in the wild': preliminary experiences with cultural probe methodology. BMC Medical Research Methodology (2012)
7. Mattelmaki, T.: Design Probes. University of Art and Design Helsinki (2006)

A New Smart Wearable Device Design Based on the Study of the Elderly's Mental Perception and Reading Usability

Yu-Min Fang, Yi-Jhen Huang, Bo-Cheng Chu, Chao-Wei Hsu,
Chien-Cheng Chang, and Meng-Hsien Hsun

Department of Industrial Design, National United University, Taiwan
{FanGeo,M0218003,U9918038,M0118003,
changcc,M0118005}@nuu.edu.tw

Abstract. The United Nations predicts the rate of population aging in the 21st century will exceed that of the previous century. For fulfill the need of the elderly, this research conducted a design project of the smart wearable system (SWS) to demonstrate three directions: integration and connection, in-depth interaction, and elderly-care awareness. Three commonly parts of the body wearing smart devices are investigated – wrist, upper arm, and the neck. The subjects were meant to wear the designed prototypes in a certain time and then fill in the questionnaire. The opinions and suggestions about the new and better add-on design guideline were collected; the data is integrated to conclude that the devices attached to the wrist are mostly accepted. A new proposal was created for a more reasonable and comprehensive interaction based on this study of the mental perception of the elderly and reading usability.

Keywords: Wearable Device, the Elderly, Usability.

1 Introduction

As the soaring population of the elderly in our society, the utility of personal computing devices is helpful for those aging seniors for health management [1]. With the assistance of the smart wearable devices and network systems for continuous monitoring of the elderly, the health condition can be well tracked by their families, and emergency situations can be reported to medical center immediately. Although the design concepts of SWS (Smart Wearable System) are highly helpful for the elderly, yet the integration between software and hardware is required for improvement to create the better user interaction with attentive and satisfactory personal emotion. To improve the interaction and connection anytime and anywhere, the real-time monitoring for physiological signals should be adopted. An add-on SWS is composed of an electric board equipped with additionally wireless transceiver and sensor components, as well as additionally battery module, supposedly attached to human body. However, applying add-on devices to users will result in mental awkwardness or discomfort while they wear these devices in the public area. Therefore, this research is designed

C. Stephanidis (Ed.): HCII 2014 Posters, Part II, CCIS 435, pp. 288–293, 2014.
© Springer International Publishing Switzerland 2014

with the prototypes of computer-aiding SWS plausibly attached to different body parts. The questionnaire surveys and interviews are conducted on the aging seniors to serve as the development reference for conceptual products. A new design proposal was created and dedicated to the aging seniors.

2   The Review of Scientific Literatures

2.1   The Aging Seniors and Wearable Device

The UN (United Nations) predicts the population of aging seniors in the 21st century will exceed that of the previous century [2], resulting in the rising demand for healthcare, assisted living, and promoting independence for the elderly. As applied in early stage, health technology is helpful to delay the aging process, and increase the quality of life and the independence of elderly. Also, it is helpful to reduce the cost of social care [3]. Some researches proves that health-monitoring technology is beneficial to decrease the hospitalization and death rate, improve mental life, and cultivate a healthier lifestyle for the elderly [4, 5]. To accomplish the previous achievements, the SWS is further integrated with wireless technology and information management required for physiology data and monitoring the health conditions of the elderly anytime and anywhere [6].

2.2   Case Study for Reference

In 2011, medicare imaging software company - OsiriX, announced the globally first smart sphygmomanometer availably linked to iPhone (Withings Smart Blood Pressure Monitor). The BodyMedia Company also promoted a product titled the SenseWear Systems available to monitor various physical conditions. Additionally, the Nike and GARMIN both step into the market of SWS for wrist products. The products are incorporated with wearable computers, wireless network, Bluetooth and Internet social activities. They can be worn on wrists to record the physical conditions of athletic activities anytime. Due to the emergence of these four products, a fact has been found the products of arm-wearable and wrist-wearable sensors for blood pressure, pulse and body temperatures have been widely commercialized in medicare realms.

Veari Company started to step into the realms of SWS to exhibit its Cloud Rings, tracking the health conditions of cervical vertebra and users' emotion by brainwave sensors attached to the neck. Additionally, the UK Bluetooth connector maker - CSR, cooperates with a jewelry company - Cellini, to promote a product - the Bluetooth Smart Jewellery. With the emergence of newly rising technologies of brainwave sensors, the Bluetooth Smart Jewellery can be used to analyze emotional feelings like attention, emotional arising, and relaxation through brainwaves. Inspired by these two reference cases, embedded detection module for emotion is possible and it can be designed to attach to human body- the neck.

2.3   The Bodily Parts Suitable for Wearable Computers

According to the research and analysis proposed by Chris Kasabach, the bodily parts suitable for wearable computers are featured with below points: (1) The symmetrical parts of human bodies must be featured with identical sizes; (2) When human beings are moving about, the bodily parts must be featured with less motion and flexibility; (3) The wearable bodily parts must be featured with very large continuous surface. The bodily parts conforming to aforesaid 3 points are separately necks, upper backs, upper arms, waists, wrists, thighs, calves and ankles [7].

3   Methods

3.1   Research Purposes and Steps

This research is aimed to explore the influence on the ease of use and acceptance among users when the SWS are worn on different bodily parts of users with the guidance and suggestion available for the design of upcoming products. The tested wearable bodily parts are summarized from relevant scientific literatures and market cases. The pretest questionnaires are previously designed and a pretest is also conducted to finalize the contents of formal questionnaires. Questionnaire surveys are conducted by using the Likert Scales to explore the acceptance for aging seniors to wear SWS.

3.2   Questionnaire Design

The first part in this questionnaire is meant to collect basic data of every individual case and mainly explore the personal trails and living habits of the aging seniors. The second part is divided into 3 parts, separately psychological feelings, physical feelings and information cognition. It is also conducted with the scoring assessment of Likert 7-point Scales to collect the data about the psychological feelings, physical feelings, and information cognition of those aging seniors use wearable computers.

3.3   Subjects

The subjects are 50 to 65 years old in Miaoli area, Taiwan, without the mental and physical illness. The basic information of the subjects show that 54.1% of them are older than 65 years, 29.1% of subjects are male, 70.9%, female, and 50% of subjects have the experience of using smart phone.

3.4   Stimulus

Through the analytical summarization about sensor items on markets, 3 bodily parts with potential development in the future are served as the subjects for questionnaire surveys. They are wrists, arms and necks, with the selection analysis of samples listed in Table 1. To avoid the influence only research results caused by interviewees' preference to product appearance, this research adopts the smart mobile devices with popularly ordinary sizes for design reference. The keypad size is followed by the reference of modal experimental design suggestion proposed by Lin [4] and Lee [8]. This experimental tool is applicable to the principles of remote home care products and it can be operable both indoors and outdoors available to monitor users' physical conditions anytime.

Table 1. The Analysis of Sample Selection

Factors			
Name	Neck Device	Arm Device	Watch Device
Embedded Module	Embedded Detection Module (No Data display)	Embedded Detection and Display Module (3.7-inch Touch Screen)	Embedded Detection and Display Module (3.7-inch Touch Screen)
Associated Device	Data display on the APP of personal smart phone	No	No
Usage Model	Users must wear the Neck Device with message display-ing function activated by smartphones.	Users must wear this device on arms and they can view the messages just lowering heads.	Users must wear this device on arms and they can view the messages just lowering heads.
Sensing Depth	Deepest detection	Only minor detection	Only minor detection
Sensing Item	Brain Wave for emotional Detection, Blood Pressure, Pulse	Blood Pressure, Pulse, Body temperature	Blood Pressure, Pulse, Body temperature
Size	415x40x3mm	115.2 x 58.6 x 9.3 mm	15.2 x 58.6 x 9.3 mm

4   Results and Discussions

This research emphasizes the influence on different bodily parts of users to use wear-able devices. Through the overall examination of ANOVA, as results indicate, differ-ent bodily parts show their significance on Q1.1.1 Demonstration Willing (F=3.702, significance p<0.05), Q1.1.4 Anxiety (F=6.997, significance p<0.05), Q1.3.1 Visibil-ity (F=3.228, significance p<0.05) and Q1.3.2 Legibility (F=3.974, significance p<0.05). It reveals the difference in the demonstration willing, anxiety, visibility and legibility of users worn on different bodily parts (Fig.1) and described in detail as below:

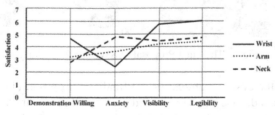

Fig. 1. The Averages of Wearing Bodily Parts

Demonstration Willing. As it can be found from descriptive statistical data, the average of wrist wearing is 4.63 rated above the average of the total sum, namely 3.58. It reveals the wrist wearing users of those aging seniors show strong willing to demonstrate the wearing bodily parts. However, the wearing part at necks has an average rated at 2.84. It is exactly the last bodily part for aging users for demonstration. However, on the whole, aging users always show weaker willing to demonstrate the wearable devices they wear.

Anxiety. The average of necks wearing reaches a high value at 4.74. However, the averages of wrist wearing and arm wearing are separately rated at 2.42 and 3.63. It reveals both wrist wearing and arm wearing cause less anxiety with the total average rated at 3.60. It can be seen aging seniors usually feel discomfort when using the wearable devices.

Visibility. The descriptive statistical data indicate a total average rated at 4.81 with every average of all items rated above 4. It reveals 3 different wearing bodily parts are all available for display viewing with the average of wrist wearing highly rated at 5.74. It can be seen wrist wearing provides the best viewing angle among different bodily parts.

Legibility: The descriptive statistical data indicate a total average rated at 5.04 with every average of all items rated above 4. Three different bodily parts wearing the devices of wearable computers can provide the best convenience for information reading. Among them, the average of wrist wearing is highly rated at 6.00. It can be seen a fact that wrist wearing provides the most convenient angle for information reading.

5   Conclusions and Suggestions

Based on the results as mentioned above, design principles are proposed. In accordance with these design principles, there are three proposals available for wrist wearing created. After the design evaluation and selection participated by invited experts, the finalized proposal is shown as below Fig. 2.

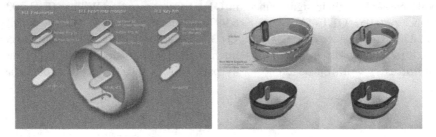

Fig. 2. The Final Proposal of SWS for the Elderly

Following are the design features for the finalized proposal: (1) The data of daily life and physical conditions can be recorded by a small sensor module; (2) It is available for computer analysis allowable for physicians to thoughtfully adjust the better lifestyles and medicare ways for those aging seniors; (3) Products are designed with a ring display providing aging seniors with the best convenience to review their physical conditions; (4) The appearance design of those athletic products like wrist rings and arm rings bring with a outlook quite different from the wearable monitoring devices for medicare; (5) Products are advantaged with the best privacy to reduce the reluctance for aging seniors to demonstrate the wears they have on; (6) Products are made of rubber to form a pleasant appearance and create comfortable wearing experience to reduce anxiety. In view of aforesaid features, these points initially conform to the researching structures and design guidelines for this research.

However, in view of technological feasibility, this proposal is required for further implementation. Additionally, further study is recommended to verify the aging users' willing to demonstrate their wearable devices in public. If the prototype and user testing can be improved, researcher can obtain more useful and in-depth knowledge and experience for further research in the future. Finally, the opinions collected from these surveys are valuable; and the final proposals are hoped to inspire other designers for further development.

Acknowledgement . The authors would like to thank the financial support by the National Science Council of Republic of China under grant number NSC 102-2410-H239-015 and NSC 102-2218-E-239-003.

References

1. Fang, Y.M., Hsu, C.W., Hsun, M.H., Chang, C.C.: The Exploratory Study for the Psychological Perception and User Attitude toward the Add-on Devices for the Elderly. In: 2013 IASDR Conference: Consilience and Innovation in Design, Tokyo (2013)
2. Department of Economic and Social Affairs, United Nations Population Division: World Population Aging 1950-2050 (2002)
3. Cluff, L.: The role of technology in long-term care. In: Binstock, R., Cluff, L., Meering, O.V. (eds.) The Future of Long Term Care, p. 103. Johns Hopkins University Press, Baltimore (1996)
4. Lin, C.Y.: A Study on Elder's User Acceptance to the Intelligent Home Care System. Master Thesis, Graduate Institute of Business and Management, Chang Gung University, Taiwan (2011)
5. Chou, C.C.: A study of technology acceptance and quality of life of elderly participants in the telecare service program. Master Thesis, School of Nursing, National Taipei College of Nursing, Taiwan (2009)
6. Chan, M., Estève, D., Fourniols, J.Y., Escriba, C., Campo, E.: Smart wearable systems: Current status and future challenges. Artificial Intelligence in Medicine 56, 137–156 (2012)
7. Gemperle, F., Kasabach, C., Stivoric, J., Bauer, M., Martin, R.: Design for Wearability. In: Second International Symposium on Wearable Computers, Pittsburgh, pp. 116–122 (1998)
8. Lee, C.F., Kuo, C.C.: A Study on the Operation of the Elderly for a Small Touch-screen. Journal of Design 9(4), 45–56 (2004)

Versatile Question-Answer Cards to Collect Personal Profiles from Seniors

Masatomo Kobayashi and Tatsuya Ishihara

IBM Research – Tokyo, 5-6-52 Toyosu,
Koto, Tokyo 135-8511, Japan
{mstm,tisihara}@jp.ibm.com

Abstract. Senior citizens often feel excluded from the digital world, leading to social isolation and preventing them from using personalized services to improve the quality of their lives. This can be caused by their limited skills with and passive attitudes towards the use of technologies. We tested a question-answer (Q&A) card interface to help senior citizens actively expose their personal experience, knowledge, and interests. A total of 50 senior participants answered 30,944 questions in six categories during the three months of our experiment, which indicated the Q&A interface effectively reduced the barriers for senior users to expose their profile information online. We also discuss some ways to analyze the collected data to investigate the profiles of senior citizens for the support of other new services.

Keywords: SNS, Analytics, Active Ageing, Digital Seniors, Gamification.

1   Introduction

Participation in the digital world (such as social networking services (SNS)) can prevent senior citizens from becoming socially isolated and improve the quality of their lives. However, even though the percentage of SNS users among the elderly population has increased [1], they tend to be passive users of information-communication technologies (ICT) and may hesitate in actively expressing their personal experience, knowledge, and interests [2][3]. Thus they cannot fully benefit from modern social analytics technologies, such as recommendation systems, though such mechanisms could help seniors with limited ICT skills derive greater benefits from online services.

We have developed a question-answer (Q&A) card interface to crowdsource micro-tasks to senior workers [4][5]. This interface can be useful not only for micro-tasking, but also for asking senior citizens about many types of information. To assess how well the interface encourages seniors to expose their information, we presented 3,489 questions in six categories to the members of a local SNS for senior residents. The Q&A card widget was embedded in the SNS. The tested categories included past work experiences, interests in jobs, interests in the local news, and everyday activities such as life-logging, as well as the micro-tasks.

C. Stephanidis (Ed.): HCII 2014 Posters, Part II, CCIS 435, pp. 294–298, 2014.

During the three months of the experiment, a total of 30,944 questions were answered by 50 senior participants, as summarized in Section 2. Their responses indicated that the Q&A card interface drastically reduced the perceived barriers for the senior citizens to input their information into the online system. The following sections cover the experimental design and results, and then show some ways the collected data can be analyzed, such as by clustering the participants based on their interests in various jobs and by linking their daily activities to a sense of fulfillment.

2   Experiment

2.1   Methods

Participants. A total of 50 senior citizens (members of an experimental local SNS for senior citizens) participated in the experiment. They ranged from 60 to 78 years old (*mean*=67.0, *SD*=4.4) (including two participants who did not report their ages).

Apparatus. The participants used their own desktop or laptop PC at home or in their workplaces. We used the Q&A card widget illustrated in [5], which was embedded in the portal of the SNS [6].

Question Categories. The participants were asked six different types of questions. Each (a) *past work experiences* question asked whether the participant had work experience in a specified job. (b) *Interests in jobs* asked whether the participant was interested in working on a specified job. (c) *Interests in local news* asked whether the participant was interested in a piece of local news. (d) *Everyday activities* asked what the participant did and how they felt that day. (e) *Words* asked about familiarity with a technical term, and (f) *proofreading* asked to proofread a sentence. All of the questions except some of the *proofreading* questions were multiple-choice. The details of (e) and (f) were reported in [4] and [5], respectively.

Procedure. Each participant saw up to 3,492 different questions in a random order. Each participant would see a specific question only one time, except for the "everyday activities" question, which reappeared each day. The participants could skip any question. The experiment ran for approximately three months, though some categories of questions appeared only during part of the three-month period.

2.2   Results

The statistics are summarized in Table 1. A total of 30,944 questions were answered by the participants. Each participant answered from 3 to 3,214 questions (*mean*=619, *SD*=734). Fig. 1 shows the daily numbers of the participants who accessed the SNS

Table 1. Overall statistics of the experiment

Participants		50
Questions		3,492
Total Answers		30,944
Answers/Person	Mean	619
	Max	3,214
	Min	3

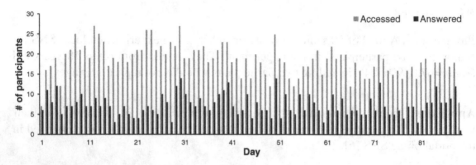

Fig. 1. The number of participants who accessed the SNS and who answered questions

(and thus might see questions) and the number of those who answered at least one question. On an averaged basis, about 20 participants accessed the SNS regularly, while about 10 participants answered one or more questions each day.

3   Collected Data Analyses

Here are some examples to illustrate the potential of the collected data to produce valuable information that can lead to better services for senior citizens.

Fig. 2 shows the clustering of the participants based on their interests in jobs. Using a dendrogram, they are roughly divided into three groups: those who have interests in a broad range of jobs, those who have interests mainly in professional and administrative jobs, and those who have little interest in working on jobs. This kind of analyses suggests the needs for different systems of offering jobs to each group.

Fig. 3 shows the correlation between participants' main daily activities and their sense of fulfillment for that day (collected using a 5-level scale). A heat map indicates that they felt a greater sense of fulfillment when they worked, enjoyed their hobbies, or left their homes. In contrast, housework produced lower levels of satisfaction.

Fig. 2. Clustering (dendrogram) based on the interests in jobs

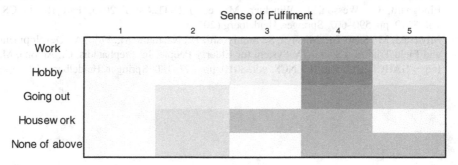

Fig. 3. Heat map of the sense of fulfillment for each type of daily activity

4   Conclusion

We showed our Q&A micro-tasking interface could be used for general purposes, such as asking about many types of information such as personal experience, knowledge, and interests. It helped senior citizens with limited skills and passive attitudes towards ICT actively expose their capabilities in the digital world, which is potentially useful for providing them with personalized services to improve the quality of their lives. The most promising advantage of the Q&A card interface seems to be its repetitive, interactive approach. This allows the system to ask senior citizens about large amounts of information only on an "as-needed" basis during their daily usage of ICT. This research tested some general questions and simple analyses, so additional studies are needed for better designs of the questions and for deeper analyses of various kinds of realistic applications.

Acknowledgements. We thank all of the participants in our experiment and Mr. Naomi Yatomi for his special efforts. This research was partially supported by the Japan Science and Technology Agency (JST) under the Strategic Promotion of Innovative Research and Development Program.

References

1. Pew Research Center, Social Media Update (2013), http://pewinternet.org/Reports/2013/Social-Media-Update.aspx
2. Kurniawan, S.: Older People and Mobile Phones: A Multi-Method Investigation. Int. J. Hum.-Comput. Stud. 66(12), 889–901 (2008)
3. Hiyama, A., Nagai, Y., Kobayashi, M., Takagi, H., Hirose, M.: Question First: Passive Interaction Model for Gathering Experience and Knowledge from the Elderly. In: Proc. PerCol 2013, pp. 151–156. IEEE (2013)
4. Ishihara, T., Kobayashi, M., Takagi, H., Asakawa, C.: How Unfamiliar Words in Smartphone Manuals Affect Senior Citizens. In: Stephanidis, C., Antona, M. (eds.) UAHCI 2013, Part III. LNCS, vol. 8011, pp. 636–642. Springer, Heidelberg (2013)
5. Kobayashi, M., Ishihara, T., Kosugi, A., Takagi, H., Asakawa, C.: Question-Answer Cards for an Inclusive Micro-Tasking Framework for the Elderly. In: Kotzé, P., Marsden, G., Lindgaard, G., Wesson, J., Winckler, M. (eds.) INTERACT 2013, Part III. LNCS, vol. 8119, pp. 590–607. Springer, Heidelberg (2013)
6. Miyazaki, M., Sano, M., Mitsuya, S., Sumiyoshi, H., Naemura, M., Fujii, A.: Development and Field Trial of a Social TV System for Elderly People. In: Stephanidis, C., Antona, M. (eds.) UAHCI 2013, Part II. LNCS, vol. 8010, pp. 171–180. Springer, Heidelberg (2013)

The Implementation of 3D Printing in Customized Interactive Design for Elderly Welfare Technology

Chor-Kheng Lim

Department of Art and Design, YuanZe University, Taiwan
kheng@saturn.yzu.edu.tw

Abstract. There are various technology products or IT services which can support elderly at home. However, most of them are designed without considering the individual preferences, needs and situations of elderly people. This study attempt to explore the concepts of elderly product design based on the theory of Emotional Design and aims at exploring solutions on how to meet the needs of the elderly through more humanistic aspects: "attractive" and "customized" technology products. Consequently, this study proposes the 3D printed "personalized" interactive flowerpot design for the elderly, called WATERS.

Keywords: Elderly welfare, 3D printing, interactive design, product design.

1 Introduction

Taiwan is becoming an aging society. Aging is not only an issue that advanced countries are facing today, but also a subject that future technology will address. In fact, each elderly person hopes to be cared, respected, and to enjoy convenience in life, and thus live happily and with dignity. These are basic needs of the elderly. Therefore, the welfare study of the elderly shall include humanistic concern. The current trend of the study involves cross-discipline study in both technological and humanistic fields. Humanistic concern is being addressed on the basis of technology.

Technology products are generally understood as the results of mass production per certain standard. Most of elderly welfare technology designs are designed without considering the individual preferences, needs and situations of elderly users (Malanowski et.al, 2008). However, design for the elderly have to achieve the needs of "personalization" because each elderly person has his/her distinct needs.

In addition to the requirement of "personalized", the elderly welfare technology design also emphasizes on the usability and explores how to enhance the technology acceptance and adoption, especially in the interactive design. Some attributes of interactive device evoke certain emotions and perceptions, which influence the user's behavior. Therefore, devices have to be not only useful but attractive, especially its appearance. Research on emotion and cognition has shown that attractive and beautiful things really do work better, as Donald Norman demonstrates in his book: Emotional Design (Norman, 2003). It is more probable for elderly to accept and adopt well designed interactive devices because these cover simultaneously their personalized functional, emotional and social needs.

C. Stephanidis (Ed.): HCII 2014 Posters, Part II, CCIS 435, pp. 299–303, 2014.
© Springer International Publishing Switzerland 2014

2   Research Objective

In order to meet the needs of "personalization" product designs, this study focuses on the new trend of design and manufacturing process. The 3D printing technology which enables *custom manufacturing* has created new ways to design. 3D printing enables small quantities of customized products to be produced at relatively low costs.

For recent years, the threshold for Rapid Prototyping technology has been lowered. 3D Printing is being widely used in various fields. Not only in advanced technology fields, such as aerospace, military, medicine, etc.3D Printing is also being popularized among general public. Low price 3D Printer sold to the consumers in the market include Makerbot, Cube 3D, and Solidoodle. Through a simple operation, "customized" product or things for daily use may be manufactured by 3D printing easily.

In the process of manufacturing interactive design product, 3D Printing plays an important role mainly because it can facilitate a customized and speedy production with high accuracy, thus meeting the requirement of designing parts for a highly interactive technology product. Moreover, through 3D Printing, many customized generative or parametric design shapes may be manufactured in a short time.

Therefore, this study aims at exploring solutions on how to meet the needs of the elderly through "customized" technology products, and proposing to produce "personalized" interactive products for the elderly through 3D Printing.

3   Design Concept

To enhance elderly users' willingness to adopt and use assistive technology at home, it should be perceived as compatible with their life-style, acceptable by their relatives and caregivers. Most elderly people prefer to stay in their own home and live an independent life as much and as long as possible. The research field of 'ageing at home' technology focuses on the needs of elders in their daily activities in their own homes (Dishman, 2004).Through interviews, this study has revealed that most of elderly people spend their time at home in *gardening* after they retire. It is thus expected to meet senior citizens' needs for being cared through creation of interactive products for their gardening activities.

The interactive device, **WATERS**, which is proposed in this study, has its name from a saying *"Water your family relationships as you water your flower-pots."* It is a customized interactive planter for the elderly, manufactured with 3D Printing technology, and also called "Customized Symbol Communication Planter."

The main design concept of WATERS is to use it as a platform, through the interaction between the elderly and planter, to nourish the relationship between the elderly and their children.

4   Design Prototype

WATERS Shapes Design
The shapes of these planters are inspired by Chinese symbols and Chinese zodiac. They were generated with generative design by using a parametric tool called Grasshopper. The elderly can pick a Chinese symbol of his/her preference (Figure 1).

The parametric tool then generates multiple planter shapes for the elderly to pick. The 3D Printer then "prints" the main container of the "customized" planter (Figure 2). The base of the planter employs the design of modulated manufacturing with Arduino as an interactive mechanism set at the base.

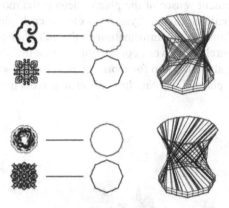

Fig. 1. Chinese symbols generative design

Fig. 2. 3D printed WATERS planters

WATERS Interactive System Architecture

The system architecture of WATERS is an open platform and it includes two parts: hardware (Body) and software (Brain). The hardware (Body) of this device is a customized 3D printed planter while the software (Brain) is installed in the planter base which operated by Arduino. It can be used in diverse interaction scenarios when installing different software or APP. For instance, it can present different interactive modes while changing the software (Brain).

WATERS Interactive Scenario

Every morning, the planter plays Chinese five-note music after it detects the humidity. Different music will be played for different humidity. The elderly will be guided to do various Chinese exercises with respect to the climate. While the music is played, the planter will also swing following the rhythm as if it exercises with the elderly. Once the human movement sensor of the planter detects the movement of the elderly, it will activate Automatic Sprinkler System to enable each planter to automatically watering. Later, the planter sends information to the cell phone or *desktop planter* of the children through wireless network connection, so that the children may know that their parents have already waken up for morning exercise and know what the weather is like at their parents' place. They can thus call their parents for greetings (Figure 3).

Fig. 3. Scenario of WATERS interactive planters

5   Conclusion

Consequently, this research proposes the "personalized" 3D printed interactive product called WATERS, the interactive planter for elderly and their children. In addition to meet the needs of the elderly through this "customized" interactive products, the main role of this interactive device is to nourish the relationship between the elderly and their children. This relationship connecting feature is based on emotional design concept, in order to make the elderly feel happy and warm while using the product. Furthermore, the usability of this daily use planter as an interactive device will more intuitive and humanistic. Technology of 3D printing is applied to the form manufacturing process of this product to meet the personal needs of the elderly. The customized components and parts are fabricated using 3D printer in a short time and low cost. This study finds that the implement of 3D printing in the elderly healthcare or welfare technology design is effectively.

References

1. Malanowski, N., Ozcivelek, R., Cabrera, M.: Active Ageing and Independent Living Services, The Role of Information and Communication Technology, European Communitiy (2008),
   http://www.umic.pt/images/stories/publicacoes2/JRC41496.pdf
2. Don, N.: Emotional Design: Why We Love (or Hate) Everyday Things. Basic Books (2003)
3. Dishman, E.: Inventing wellness systems for aging. Computer 37(5), 34–41 (2004)

Exploring the Potential of Gameful Interaction Design of ICT for the Elderly

Michael Minge, Juliane Bürglen, and Dietlind Helene Cymek

Berlin University of Technology Department of Cognitive Psychology and Cognitive
Ergonomics Marchstraße 23, Sekr. MAR 3-2 10587 Berlin, Germany
{michael.minge,juliane.buerglen,dietlind.h.cymek}@tu-berlin.de

Abstract. Due to increasing technologization and demographic changes, more
and more elderly people are facing the challenge of using information and
communication technology (ICT). ICT can be an essential facilitator for
positive aging by promoting the participation of elderly in society, as well as
activating their cognitive and motoric resources. However, elderly people often
struggle to use technical devices and therefore miss the benefits of digital age.
Feelings of helplessness and fear towards technology are often reinforced by
previous experiences that have been perceived as frustrating. We believe that
adding game elements to an ICT application can overcome some of the
motivational barriers which older adults face by providing pleasurable
experiences and hedonic value to the interaction with technology.

In the course of focus groups older adults appeared to be very open towards
gameful interaction design. Through an extensive interview study which we
conducted subsequently, we investigated the potential advantages and
requirements of this approach and whether it is to be used to assist the elderly.

Keywords: gamification, games, serious games, elderly people, motivation.

1 Introduction

Today, the majority of society uses ICT on a daily basis. People who do not or seldom
use these technologies, often senior citizens, may experience a growing gap between
them and the rest of society, since forms of communication and information retrieval
have changed fundamentally. Having social connections is an increasing contributor
to quality of life as people age. Thus, ICT should especially be designed for older
adults in order to facilitate their participation as active members in society.

Designing for elderly people first of all requires the consideration of ergonomic
and usability aspects. Eisma et al. (2004) for example found that "technology use in
general declines with age, but the use of more established and, possibly, easier-to-use
technology declines less rapidly". Renaud and Biljon (2008) investigated technology
acceptance in older users, which yielded the evidence that perceived usefulness and
ease of use determine the actual use and acceptance. A series of studies by Pohlmeyer
(2012) showed that non-instrumental product qualities such as aesthetics and
symbolic meanings are also relevant for the elderly, but that ergonomics were a more
important consideration for older users than for younger ones.

C. Stephanidis (Ed.): HCII 2014 Posters, Part II, CCIS 435, pp. 304–309, 2014.

Furthermore ICT design has to help overcome existing feelings of fear and helplessness associated with the interaction with new technologies. Such a hindering form of anticipated user experience (UX) often stems from negative experiences in the past, for example if previous systems have been perceived as being too difficult to learn and to use, or if older adults did not use any technology and therefore could not acquire relevant prior knowledge. We believe that creating more positive experiences with ICT for the elderly, with the help of game elements, could be a promising approach to motivate more elderly people to use ICT.

Creating positive emotions towards technology is highly associated with two concepts in the field of gameful interaction design. The first one is *gamification*, which is the "use of design elements characteristic for games in non-game contexts" (Deterding et al., 2011). Gamification is a very popular method to motivate users, especially in web and mobile applications. It is considered that gamification directly affects how users perceive and evaluate the interaction with a system. The second concept that promises higher motivation through game elements is *serious games*. In contrast to gamification, serious games describe fully fledged games with a "serious" intention. Such a "serious" intention is assumed for "any meaningful use of computerized game/ game industry resources whose chief mission is not entertainment" (Sawyer, 2007).

The core question with respect to the specific requirements and needs of our target group is: Which game elements can motivate elderly people? The number of senior citizens who engage in computer games is rising and therefore *silver gaming* hasbecome a trending topic during the last few years. First studies could already prove that playing digital games can activate cognitive, motoric and social resources (i.e. Gerling & Masuch, 2011). Nevertheless, there has not been much research until now, whether and how the larger group of older users could benefit from the concepts of gamification and serious games in non-gaming contexts, like ICT use. In particular, there is a lack of information about what actually motivates older people in their daily lives and especially how these motifs could be addressed by ICT.

One interesting approach to the motivating factors behind games is the framework of pleasurable experiences (PLEX) by Korhonen et al. (2009). The authors conducted interviews with young and middle aged computer gamers and asked them about their appeal to digital games. Responses were classified into a total of 22 motivational categories, such as discovery, completion, competition and thrill. As a result, a set of cards representing these categories was developed (http://www.funkydesign spaces.com). These PLEX cards are a helpful idea generation tool for designing gameful and pleasurable experiences, even for "serious" devices or applications. Up until now it is unknown which motivating factors are particularly relevant for older users, such that their consideration may help to make ICT easier and more accessible for the elderly.

In order to evaluate the general acceptance of the concepts gamification and serious games we first conducted two focus groups. Subsequently, an interview study was implemented aiming at discovering motivating factors of our target group.

2   Focus Groups

2.1   Method

In the first focus group we asked five senior citizens (60-80 years old) for their opinions on gamification and serious games in ICT applications. Both concepts were presented by showing existing application examples. In the case of serious games we introduced participants to a learning application for a specific software. The second concept, gamification, was presented by showing some typical game elements (points, levels, rewards, direct positive feedback) and giving examples where boring, annoying or monotonous activities could become more motivating through these elements. Afterwards participants discussed whether they would find these concepts helpful and motivating. Each participant rated the concept by pinning cards onto two pin boards.

In a second focus group (eight participants aged 60 to 80 years) conceptualized perceived advantages of gameful interaction design as well as possible reasons to reject the concept. Participants worked in groups of two and wrote their idea on cards which were attached to two pin boards again.

2.2   Results

Participants of the first focus group expressed that they found serious games very motivating or at least partially motivating. Serious games were rated as possibly helpful (less so than motivating). With respect to gamification there was no difference between "helpful" and "motivating", the concept was in general given positive ratings, but was less positive than serious games for learning overall. This was, according to the participants, due to a) gamification being less concrete and clear, b) gamification coming across as potentially superfluous due to points, ratings and leader boards, which the participants considered annoying and unnecessary performance pressure, and c) gamification lacking seriousness, which was mainly induced by "fun" feedback like flying balloons.

The potential lack of seriousness was also mentioned by the second focus group. Additionally, participants pointed out that users should have clear objectives and that they would reject the application if they get the impression to become isolated or an unnecessary waste of time. The positive effects reported by participants, were that they were able to discover the system independently, encounter new functionalities and to have more ambition to solve problems themselves.

In order to develop design options that take into account the perception of the elderly towards gameful interaction design and to identify patterns of motivation in older adults' lives, games, and ICT usage, we conducted a subsequent interview study.

3 Interview Study

3.1 Method

We conducted semi-structured interviews with 81 participants from age of 60 to 81 years. Interview guidelines covered questions concerning demographic data, lifestyle and free time activities, experiences and usage behavior of devices for information and communication, internet usage, dealing with technology in case of malfunctioning or usage problems, as well as (computer) game playing and the appeal of favorite games. Participants' answers were analyzed both qualitatively and quantitatively. Qualitative data was analyzed mainly following Mayring's (2010) Qualitative Content Analysis approach via categorizing inductively.

3.2 Results

Results reveal that hedonic aspects of an application are particularly important for a long-term use. In addition to the experience of fun, participants mentioned that achievement, stimulation and getting aroused by curiosity would be important aspects that increase their usage intention for a specific application.

With respect to gaming experiences, our results show that the elderly like playing games to a great extent. Nearly 80 % of the participants rated their affinity towards games at least at an intermediate level. The most favored games were card and board games, quizzes and crosswords. The motivational factors that underlie the appeal of games are shown in Table 1. Mental effort, social interaction and strategy have been found to be the most important categories.

Table 1. Appeal categories of games

Appeal categories of games	
Mental effort	Thought, concentration, attention
Social interaction	Community, society, exchange
Strategy	Combining, planning, flexibility
Competition	Performance comparison, winning
Pastime	Relaxation, no effort
Emotions	Fun, anger, surprise
Risk	Thrill, luck, excitement
Mastery	Collection, completion, successful conclusion
Tradition	Ritual, fashion, recollection, nostalgia

41 % of the sample reported to play computer games regularly. In contrast to offline and online applications, the experience of hedonic qualities like stimulation, aesthetics, distraction and fun, play by far the largest role in the appeal of computer games.

In order to find out which factors motivate the elderly in general in their daily lives, their individual hobbies were questioned, as well as the details as to why they were liked. Table 2 summarizes the identified motivation factors. Similar to the appeal of games it is again social interaction that strongly motivates the elderly as well as mastery and well-being.

Table 2. Appeal categories of hobbies

Appeal categories of hobbies	
Social interaction	Collaboration, teamwork, acknowledgement, helping others
Mastery	Creation, production, completion, creativity, originality
Emotion	Fun, freedom, pleasure, joy, enjoyment
Nature	Plants, animals, landscape, water, seasons
Exercise	Agility, mobility, sports
Relaxation	Pastimes, balance, peace, wellness
Initiative	Trying new things, openness, exploring curiosity
mental stimulation	Poetry, art, entertainment, fantasies
Knowledge	Background information, being up to date, learning

4   Conclusion

In our focus groups, the senior participants considered gamification and serious games to be promising approaches to overcome existing barriers to ICT usage. However, they emphasized that the success of the game approach depends on the specific implementation and design of the application, and that adding game elements should not necessarily lead to a general lack of seriousness or social isolation.

The results of our interview study indicate that what appeals to older adults in games is in some regards similar to the playful interaction categories as found by Korhonen et al. (2009). Even though our resulting appeal categories were derived inductively, many matched one or more PLEX categories. For instance the PLEX category challenge is obviously related to game category mental effort, fellowship (PLEX) corresponds with social interaction (games and hobbies) and completion (PLEX) relates to mastery (games and hobbies). Categories for relaxation and competition can also be found in the PLEX categories and in the categories of either games or hobbies. Competition was often mentioned as an appeal of games; however the focus group participants stressed that they did not enjoy aspects of quantification and comparison, when using software. Therefore implementing competition elements should be selected carefully. The many of similarities between category sets implicate that games, computer games and hobbies fulfill similar needs to some extent.

Nevertheless there are also categories in PLEX, which were not mentioned by older adults, with regard to game and hobby appeal, such as captivation, cruelty, eroticism, subversion and suffering. Also not all categories found for older adults had a counterpart in the PLEX categories, among these categories were nature, exercise, knowledge and tradition. These differences may be due to the different ages of the surveyed groups, but may also be the result of asking subjects for motivators in favored computer games in one group and for the appeal of favored games (all kinds of games) and hobbies in the other group.

In summary, seniors do like games and playful experiences. To design a more enjoyable ICT interaction for the elderly we therefore suggest to focus on the PLEX cards being similar to the categories we found for game and hobby appeal: challenge, fellowship, completion, relaxation and competition. Implementing these categories has already proven to be successful for technical devices. Integrating aspects of knowledge gaining, exercise, nostalgia and nature, which are not represented in the PLEX categories yet, may also contribute to more enjoyable interaction for older adults.

Acknowledgment. This research was supported by the German Federal Ministry of Education and Research as part of the "IKT 2020" initiative. We would like to thank Franziska Adler, Josephine Grauert and Sophie Neef for their superb work and Ingmar Wagner for many clarifying and helpful comments.

References

1. van Biljon, J., Renaud, K.: A Qualitative Study of the Applicability of Technology Acceptance Models to Senior Mobile Phone Users. In: Song, I.-Y., et al. (eds.) ER Workshops 2008. LNCS, vol. 5232, pp. 228–237. Springer, Heidelberg (2008)
2. Deterding, S., Khaled, R., Nacke, L.E., Dixon, D.: Gamification: Toward a Definition. In: CHI Workshop Gamification, May 7-12 (2011)
3. Eisma, R., Dickinson, A., Goodman, J., Syme, A., Tiwari, L., Newell, A.F.: Early user involvement in the development of information technology-related products for older people. Universal Access in the Information Society 3, 131–140 (2004)
4. Gerling, K.M., Masuch, M.: Exploring the Potential of Gamification Among Frail Elderly Persons. In: CHI Workshop Gamification, May 7-12 (2011)
5. Korhonen, H., Montola, M., Arrasvuori, J.: Understanding playful user experience through digital games. In: Proc. of DPPI 2009, October 13-16, pp. 274–285 (2009), https://research.nokia.com/files/p274%20-%20Korhonen.pdf
6. Mayring, P.: Qualitative Inhaltsanalyse. Grundlagen und Techniken, 11th edn. Deutscher Studien Verlag, Weinheim (2007)
7. Pohlmeyer, A.E.: Identifying Attribute Importance in Early Product Development. Exemplified by Interactive Technologies and Age. Berlin Institute of Technology (March 23, 2012), http://opus4.kobv.de/ opus4-tuberlin/frontdoor/index/index/docId/3274
8. Sawyer, B.: The "Serious Games" Landscape. Instructional and Research Technologies Symposium for the Arts, Humanities and Social Sciences (March 21, 2007), http://internet2.rutgers.edu/pres/speaker6-sawyer-final.ppt

Technology for Older People: A Critical Review

Helen Petrie[1], Bláithín Gallagher[1], and Jenny Darzentas[2]

[1] Human Computer Interaction Research Group, Department of Computer Science,
University of York, United Kingdom
{Blaithin.Gallagher,Helen.Petrie}@york.ac.uk
[2] University of the Aegean, Greece
jennyd@aegean.gr

Abstract. We will present the results of a critical review of research published in a range of peer-reviewed conferences in the period 2005 - 2012 on the use of technology to support older people. We explore what problems faced by older people are being addressed by the research; whether the research is motivated by user needs; the methodologies used; the levels of target user involvement in the research; and the outcomes achieved. Eight major topics of research have been identified: mobility and wayfinding; communication and social interaction; interaction with technology; using the web; access to and exploration of information; education; support for daily living; and games and play. In addition, we have categorized the research into four main types: research that proposes technologies for older people; research to understand the use of technology by older people and their attitudes to technology; research on guidelines, standards or other information to support developers and researchers; and research that on methodologies for working with older people in the development of new technological solutions. Important gaps and weaknesses in the current research portfolio are explored. The review will provide an overview of the state of the art of technologies for promoting independent living and wellbeing of older people, which should be useful for researchers, developers and practitioners in the field.

Keywords: Older people, Assistive technologies, User needs, Evaluation, Methodologies for working with older people.

1   Introduction

It is well known that many societies around that world are currently experiencing an aging of their population. The United Nations [7] estimates that in 2012, there were 841 million older people (they use a definition of people aged 60 years or older) worldwide and estimates that by 2050 the proportion of older people will increase to 21 per cent of total population or more than 2 billion people [6, 7]. If this prediction is born out, it will be the first time in history that the proportion of the population aged 60 years and over will be larger than the proportion of young people (aged under 15) [6]. The ratio of people of working age to older people, often known as the "aged

C. Stephanidis (Ed.): HCII 2014 Posters, Part II, CCIS 435, pp. 310–315, 2014.

dependency" ratio, is also very relevant. For example, in the European Union, for every person of 65 year or over, there are currently four people of working age (15 – 64 years); by the year 2060, it is estimated that there will be on two people of working age for each person of 65 for over [3].

These changes in the population have many implications, but of particular interest here is the consequences for the care of older people. In the coming years there will be far fewer younger people to help care for the older population. Technology has a vital role to play in filling this growing personnel gap. More technological support will be needed to enable more older people live independently in the community for older, and also to support their care in residential homes, hospitals and hospices.

For these reasons, we believe a critical review of current technology research and developments for older people is particularly timely. If technological support is likely to be used by older people, it needs to be useful and usable. To ensure this, it needs to be developed in a user-centred manner, taking into consideration the needs of users throughout the design process. Our review is investigating what problems faced by older people are being addressed by current research; whether the research is motivated by user needs; the methodologies used; the levels of target user involvement in the research; and the outcomes achieved.

2   Aims of the Current Review

The critical review covers relevant research published between 2005 to 2012. The review has been inspired by work carried out by Rogers Strong and Fisk [4] as they published a major survey of research on technology in relation to older people in 2005 which built on an earlier review by Czaja in 1990 [2]. They reported that very often the abilities and constraints of older users and were not taken into account in the development of technology.

3   Method

Research published in a selection of peer-reviewed conferences and journals was selected for inclusion in our review. The areas we focused on included "mainstream" outlets in human-computer interaction and human factors, as well as "specialist" outlets in gerontology, geronotechnology and rehabilitation technology. Journals and conferences were selected for inclusion based on their Impact Factor [5] and rankings by the Australian Research Council's ranking of journals and conferences [1]. From a list of possible conferences and journals, a random selection was made to reach a managable number. Table 1 lists the conferences and journals in the final selection.

Papers were included in the review if they included words relevant to older people and technology in the title, abstract or keywords. Terms included "older people", "older adults" and "elders" in mainstream conference or journal papers (which were by definition about technology) and in addition "computer/s", "assistive technology" and "online" in the specialist journals. A full set of the terms and how they were used is available at www.yorkhci.org/criticalreview/.

To ensure accuracy of selection of papers, either two researchers reviewed each conference proceedings or journal or the same researcher reviewed the proceedings or journal at least three months apart. Inter-coder reliability on the selection of papers was calculated on several sets and averaged over 90%.

Table 1. Conferences Proceedings and Journals included in the Review

Mainstream journals and conferences	
Journals	ACM Transactions on Computer Human Interaction Behaviour and Information Technology Human Computer Interaction Human Factors International Journal of Human-Computer Studies
Conferences	ACM Conference on Human Factors in Computing Systems (CHI) British Computer Society Interaction Specialist Group Conference (BCS HCI) IFIP TC 13 Conference on Human-Computer Interaction (INTERACT)
Specialist journals and conferences	
	ACM Transactions on Accessible Computing (ToACCESS) Educational Gerontology Gerontechnology Technology and Disability Universal Access to the Information Society
	ACM Conference on Computers and Accessibility (ASSETS) International Conference on Computers Helping People with Special Needs (ICCHP)

4   Results

A total of 5143 papers have been reviewed so far, 3823 in mainstream outlets and 1830 in specialist outlets. The number of papers relevant to technology for older people is 187, made up of 170 relevant solely to older people and 17 relevant to older people and people with disabilities. So far we have conducted detailed analysis of 131 of these papers.

We found that the papers divided into three types of research and development. These are:

Development of new technologies/systems: research and development that proposes emerging technologies or new uses of technologies for older people;

Understanding users: This is research that seeks to understand the use of technology by older people and their attitudes to technology;

Methods for working with older people: This research proposes methodologies for working with older people in the development of new technological solutions, or reflects on this area of research and development.

Table 2 shows the breakdown of the papers analysed so far into the three types of research. Just over three-quarters (75.6%) of the papers were about understanding older people, their use of technologies, experiences with technologies and attitudes to technology. The remaining papers were split evenly between proposals for new technologies and systems (11.5%) and methods for working with older people (12.9).

Table 2. Breakdown of papers by type of research and development

Research and development type	Mainstream outlets % (N)	Specialist outlets %(N)	Total % (N)
New Technologies/systems	15.4 (12)	5.7 (3)	11.5 (15)
Understanding older people	71.8 (56)	81.1 (43)	75.6 (99)
Methods for working with older people	12.8 (10)	13.2 (7)	12.9 (17)
Total	100.0 (78)	100.0 (53)	100.0 (131)

In addition, we found that the research could be categorized into 11 major topics, as listed in Table 3. So research on "mobility and wayfinding" might be proposing a new system to help older people with their mobility (so would fall in the "New technologies/systems" type of research) or it might be about understanding the issues that older people have with mobility (so would fall in the "Understanding older people" type of research). The "Methods for working with older people" we left as a topic in itself, as well as a type of paper.

Table 3. Breakdown of papers by topics addressed

Topic	Mainstream outlets % (N)	Specialist outlets % (N)	Total % (N)
Mobility and wayfinding (e.g. indoor, outdoor navigation)	6.4 (5)	1.9 (1)	4.6 (6)
Access to and use of information (e.g. search, health information)	3.8 (3)	9.4 (5)	6.1 (8)
Communication and social interaction (e.g. encouraging socializing, supporting communication, collaboration)	10.3 (8)	7.6 (4)	9.2 (12)

Table 3. (*continued*)

Interacting with/using technology (e.g. input/output, interaction techniques)	24.4 (19)	5.7 (3)	16.8 (22)
Attitudes to / experience with technology	7.7 (6)	24.5 (13)	14.5 (19)
Specific technology issues (e.g. security)	1.3 (1)	1.9 (1)	1.6 (2)
Education	0.0 (0)	20.8 (11)	8.4 (11)
The web (e.g. use, assessing accessibility, teaching developers about web accessibility)	2.6 (2)	3.8 (2)	3.1 (4)
Tasks of daily life (e.g. memory support, home monitoring, cooking, banking, exercise)	25.6 (20)	9.4 (5)	19.1 (25)
Games and gaming	5.1 (4)	1.9 (1)	3.8 (5)
Methods for working with disabled/older people	12.8 (10)	13.2 (7)	12.9 (17)
Total	100.0 (78)	100.0 (53)	100.0 (131)

Further analyses of the papers are underway and will be presented at the conference.

5   Discussion and Conclusions

The analysis of papers thus far has shown that there is a wide range of research on technology for older people. It is encouraging that so much of the research is about understanding older people's use and attitudes towards technology – this shows that researchers and developers are taking user-centred approaches, investigating older people issues around technology. The fact that this work is being published in such large numbers means there is a growing body of knowledge for researchers and developers entering the area to draw on.

The analysis of topics also shows that there is research on a wide range of different issues. Some of the common topics are to be expected: the most common area of research (19.1% of papers) is "Tasks of daily life", which is a very broad topic, but also reflects the interest in supporting older people in living independently but supporting them in a wide variety of tasks of daily life. However, at the other extreme, it is surprising that there is so little research on web accessibility for older people (only 3.1% of papers), as the web is such an important source of information, commerce and leisure. Researchers may not be aware that the Web Content Accessibility Guidelines (WCAG) [8] do not cover the needs of older web suers, and this is definitely an area that needs further research.

Further analyses are being undertaken to explore further gaps in the research, the actual level of involvement of older people and the outcomes achieved in the research. These will be reported at the conference and in subsequent publications.

Acknowledgements. The research is partly supported by funding from the European Union FP7 Marie Curie Programme under Grant Agreement No PIEF-GA-2011-303184.

References

1. Australian Research Council. Excellence in research for Australia (2010), http://www.arc.gov.au/era/era_2010/era_2010.htm
2. Czaja, S.: Human factors research needs for an aging population. National Academy Press (1990)
3. Giannakouris, K.: Population and social conditions. EuroStat Statistics in Focus 72/2008, Office for Official Publications of the European Communities (2008)
4. Rogers, W.A., Stronge, A.J., Fisk, A.D.: Technology and aging. Reviews of Human Factors and Ergonomics 1(1), 130–171 (2005)
5. Reuters, T.: The Thomson Reuters Impact Factor (2013), http://thomsonreuters.com/products_services/science/free/essays/impact_factor/
6. United Nations. World Population Ageing: 1950-2050 [11] (2002)
7. United Nations. World Population Prospects: The 2012 Revision, Highlights and Advance Tables [12] (2013)
8. World Wide Web Consortium. Web Content Accessibility Guidelines 2.0., http://www.w3.org/TR/WCAG20

A Barrier-Free Platform to Help Elderly People to Help Themselves

Sven Schmeier and Norbert Reithinger

DFKI - German Research Center for Artificial Intelligence,
Alt–Moabit 91c, 10559 Berlin, Germany,
{sven.schmeier,norbert.reithinger}@dfki.de

Abstract. The proportion of elderly people in German society has been increasing for decades. As a result Germany, and other industrial countries as well, are currently facing large demographic changes in terms of age structure and population size, changes that will only increase in the future. Furthermore, especially in bigger cities, the traditional family structures with more generations living together are disappearing.

Starting from these observations, the project *Barrierefreie Cloud für Senioren - WirlmKiez* (translated: A barrier-free Cloud for Seniors - We in our neighbourhood), funded by the German Ministry of Education and Research, aims to develop a platform where elderly people can get in touch with and help each other with everyday problems and issues. We plan to realise a virtual neighbourly help especially for elderly people who have no or very little social contact. Persons using the platform will be able to either provide support to others ("I can help to hang curtains", "I can help gardening", ...) or they can request for help ("I need to go to hospital for 4 days, who can take care of my cat"). The app will run on computers, smartphones, and tablets and will be very simple to use and appropriate for seniors. Its main features are creating a proposal or request by using natural language. Behind the scenes we will use shallow information extraction (IE) to extract the core information. After this we store the extracted information plus additional meta information like time and location on a central server (cloud). In the final step a generated request or proposal is offered to adequate users of the system, e.g. people who live nearby and are able to help or need help and connecting the persons in the end.

Keywords: Barrier-free, seniors, conversational interface.

1   Introduction

Seniors often need support in everyday situations especially for tasks that require a certain amount of physical fitness. Especially duties in the domestic home like cleaning windows, hanging curtains, cleaning wardrobes, lifting furniture, etc can be very dangerous or even impossible.

Furthermore the possibility of medical treatment from illness, falls, or other physical impairments is significantly increased with age. As a result older people

C. Stephanidis (Ed.): HCII 2014 Posters, Part II, CCIS 435, pp. 316–321, 2014.

are more vulnerable [Birgit Hibbeler , 2013], and therefore reluctant to take on regular responsibilities, e.g. keeping animals is often not possible without a larger support circle.

On the other hand, especially in western industrial cities, local social networks may not be very tight, friends may have moved away or died, and the traditional support structures found in so-called multi-generational families are becoming rare nowadays. As a result, the quality of life of elderly people suffers crucially. Among other things, hobbies and habits may have to be abandoned, and volunteer activities can no longer be carried out. Therefore, these impairments affect not only seniors, but also people who rely on them. Although people from the broader neighbourhood would often gladly help and respond quickly, in larger cities with higher anonymity, people are afraid to approach each other.

2   Our Goal

A still widespread misconception is that older people do not use modern information technology [Hartmut Wandke et al, 2012]. Statistics on Internet show a large growth for the *generation 60+*. In February 2011, 35.3% of that group used the internet actively, 17% already used the mobile internet[1]. Furthermore there are studies like [Meredith Skeels , 2006] which show that tablets are appropriate for users with less or no experiences with computers in general. Also the use of touch panels [Atsuo Murata et al, 2005] and spoken language [Daniel Sonntag et al, 2010] seems to be appropriate especially for seniors.

Our main goal is to develop a platform where elderly people can get in touch with and help each other with everyday problems and issues. In the long term we hope to realize a virtual neighbourhood to provide help for people who have no or very little social contact. The general functionality is very simple: people can make requests or offers for assistance to a bulletin board on the platform, which in turn can then be seen by other people and possibly answered. The main requirements of the platform are:

- User-friendliness and accessibility for people with little experience in dealing with computers or suffering of physical limitations (i.e., barrier-free usage). This point is especially important for the acceptance of the system by seniors.
- Protection of data privacy and security: Especially seen in the context of the latest news about the surveillance of online data, people are not willing to give away any personal data without sufficient protection and security.
- Location-based offers and requests: The users of the system should not be bothered by content that is not important to them.

We further hope that the system will also effect a connecting function in the neighborhood and hence cause an immediate increase in the quality of life of older people. They can perform again simple activities such as the cleaning of curtains and meet people from the immediate neighborhood at the same time. In that

---

[1] http://de.statista.com/statistik/kategorien/

way the social environment renews, the isolation that is getting stronger with age can be reduced. Also the social participation of older people is strengthened by providing and accepting help. Furthermore health hazards are avoided as dangerous activities are taken over by or done in cooperation with people of the neighbourhood.

3   The Approach

Our approach consists of a cloud-based system in which the technical components are embedded as shown in Fig.1

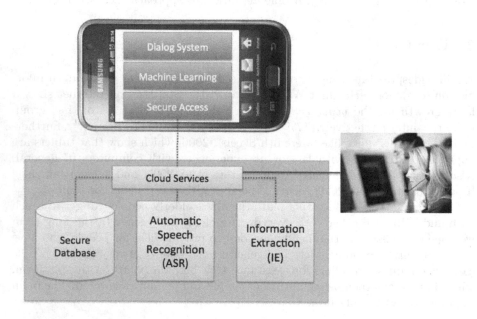

Fig. 1. The main concept of the system

We will realize the main goal, a barrier-free user experience, through a combination of three components:

- Automatic Speech Recognition (ASR) and Speech Synthesis [Marc Schröder et al, 2011] to transform speech into text and vice versa.
- Information Extraction (IE)[Jerry Hobbs et al., 2010] to extract the main information from the recognised text.
- Dialog System[Sven Schmeier, 2011] to ask the user for more information.

The process works as follows: A user talks to the system in the way he/she wants to: no commands need to be learned or recognized. The recorded speech is processed by the ASR component and the result is passed to the IE unit. The

Table 1. A partially filled action template from the sentence I need someone to help me take down my curtains at the last day in July. The person should come between 10 and 12 am.

Feature	Value
Type	Request
Subject	Take down curtains
Date	31st July 2014
Time-Frame	10:00 to 12:00 am
Time needed	n/a

IE unit extracts the information that is needed to fill an action template. Action templates consist of a type – in general this is the kind of request or offer – and typed slots that need to be filled (see Fig. 2)

If template slots cannot be filled, the Dialog System is activated and the user is asked (repeatedly) to complete the information. In our example the system would ask something like: *Do you have a rough estimate about how long the task will take?* The user's answer will then be processed and, if the template is filled completely, it will be stored in the system's Secure Database and pushed to possible helpers living around the location of the requesting user.

Additional components are:

– Machine Learning: The Machine Learning component tracks the users behaviour and tries to detect certain patterns in the requests. Examples for patterns are regular requests, automatic slot filling for similar tasks, alternating questions in the Dialog System to ensure a more natural process, etc.
– Secure access: For security we will use https connection and if possible we will make use of appropriate encryption methods [Roger Needham et al, 1994].

To secure the ecosystem in general, new users will be manually checked by customer agents.

4   Scientific and Social Impact

The use of the system, largely through natural language interaction adds substantial value for the target group of seniors compared to other existing (social) platforms in many respects. However, during the project, we will closely work together with the BAGSO (German Federation of Senior Citizens' Organisations) to ensure that it adds needed value. The whole development process will be carried out with the assistance of seniors, i.e. the targeted user group. Field tests to determine the parts in the system that need to be improved for everyday usage will conclude the project. At the end, our industrial partner will develop and release the final product based on our research.

In Fig.2 the different layers of the envisioned platform, services and goals are shown.

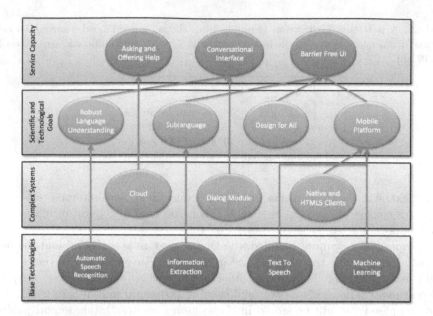

Fig. 2. The different layers, modules and services in detail

Acknowledgement. This research was conducted in the context of the project *Barrierefreie Cloud für Senioren - WirlmKiez* (funded by the German Federal Ministry of Education and Research, contract 16SV6323)

References

Birgit Hibbeler , 2013. Hibbeler, B.: Stationäre Behandlung: Der alte Patient wird zum Normalfall. Dtsch Arztebl 110(21), A-1036 / B-902 / C-898 (2013)

Jerry Hobbs et al., 2010. Hobbs, J.R., Riloff, E.: Information Extraction. In: Indurkhya, N., Damerau, F. (eds.) Handbook of Natural Language Processing, pp. 511–532. CRC Press, Boca Raton (2010)

Atsuo Murata et al, 2005. Murata, A., Iwase, H.: Usability of Touch-Panel Interfaces for Older Adults. Human Factors: The Journal of the Human Factors and Ergonomics Society Winter 47, 767–776 (2005)

Roger Needham et al, 1994. Needham, R., Wheeler, D.J.: TEA, a tiny encryption algorithm. In: Preneel, B. (ed.) FSE 1994. LNCS, vol. 1008, pp. 363–366. Springer, Heidelberg (1995)

Sven Schmeier, 2011. Schmeier, S.: Ein mobiles Übersetzungssystem für den Einsatz bei Notfällen im Kontext von AAL 5. In: Deutscher AAL-Kongress mit Ausstellung, January 24-25. VDE, Berlin (2012)

Marc Schröder et al, 2011. Schröder, M., Charfuelan, M., Pammi, S., Steiner, I.: Open source voice creation toolkit for the MARY TTS Platform. In: Proc. Interspeech, Florence, Italy

Meredith Skeels , 2006. Skeels, M.M., Kurth, A., Clausen, M., Severynen, A., Garcia-Smith, H.: CARE+ User Study: Usability and Attitudes Towards a Tablet PC Computer Counseling Tool for HIV+ Men and Women. In: AMIA Annu. Symp. Proc., pp. 729–733 (2006)

Daniel Sonntag et al, 2010. Sonntag, D., Engel, R., Herzog, G., Pfalzgraf, A., Pfleger, N., Romanelli, M., Reithinger, N.: SmartWeb Handheld — Multimodal Interaction with Ontological Knowledge Bases and Semantic Web Services. In: Huang, T.S., Nijholt, A., Pantic, M., Pentland, A. (eds.) ICMI/IJCAI Workshops 2007. LNCS (LNAI), vol. 4451, pp. 272–295. Springer, Heidelberg (2007)

Hartmut Wandke et al, 2012. Wandke, H., Sengpiel, M., Sönksen, M.: Myths About Older People's Use of Information and Communication Technology. Gerontology 58(6), 564–570 (2012)

Relative-Identity Management Based on Context

Allal Tiberkak[1,3], Tayeb Lemlouma[2], and Abdelkader Belkhir[1]

[1] Department of Electrical Engineering and Computer Science
Faculty of Science and Technology, University Dr. Yahia Fares Medea
Ain D'heb-Médéa - 26000 T, Algiers 16303, Algeria
allal.tiberkak@gmail.com,
tiberkak.allal@univ-medea.dz
[2] IRISA/ D2 (CNRS UMR 6074), BP 30219, Rue Edouard Branly 22302 LANNION Cedex
Tayeb.Lemlouma@irisa.fr
[3] Department of Computer Sciences
University of Sciences and Technology Houari Boumediene (USTHB)
BP 32, El Alia, Bab Ezzouar, Algiers 16111, Algeria
kaderbelkhir@hotmail.com, belkhir@lsi-usthb.dz

Abstract. Mobile devices nowadays are equipped with sensors and technologies that enable context evaluation. Those devices are not expensive in such a way that everyone can buy a smart phone easily. So, developing mobile context-awareness applications for helping dependent persons to deal with their everyday tasks is crucial. This paper aims to develop a new identities management system that runs on the dependent person's mobile device. This system will assist dependent persons by giving them information, advices, instructions and helps regarding their activities of daily living. The main idea is to use a simple communication way to identify objects and subjects in the surrounding context of the assisted person. In this paper, we propose efficient identification mechanisms that take benefits from our well understanding of the context. Our approach simplifies the use of the interaction between dependent persons and the system. Hence, unlike usual approaches, the identity of a given entity will not be universal by widely tailored it to the current person's context. In the case where the context is shared by many entities with the risk of identification ambiguity, our identification could use different means such as colors or locations towards others for identification of entities.

Keywords: identify, relative identity, context, context-awareness, profile.

1 Introduction

Holly Price is a five-year-old girl that has been saving her father's life when he fell into hypoglycemic coma by injecting him in the stomach with glucagon: a hormone that raises blood sugar [1]. This means that everyone can save life of other even he/she has limited capacities. The question is how can we inform a helper to do something for someone. Otherwise, how we can use profiles management and context awareness to communicate with a dependent person. A dependent person (e.g. deaf, blind and handicap.) is one who needs help and assistance to do common tasks.

C. Stephanidis (Ed.): HCII 2014 Posters, Part II, CCIS 435, pp. 322–327, 2014.

Identity is a set of information that permits to identify an entity in a unique way. This entity may be a person or an object [2]. Identity management is a set of operations that can be applied on identities, like definition, verification, creation, deletion, modification, etc. [3].

Data characterizing an entity represent the profile of such entity [4]. An entity can be an object or a person. Generally, objects are characterized by the physical information such as the size, weight, color, etc. However, peoples are characterized by demographic information such as age, race, etc. Modeling profiles is organizing the data to be understandable and processable by computers [5].

Information that describes situations of an entity represents the context of such entity [6]. In the other hand, context can be defined as the change of the profile values. In general, the context can be constructed by answering the following five questions: *who, what, when, where, why*. the *who* is the identification of the person, the *what* is the identification of the object, the *why* is the identification of the intention, the *when* is the time and the *where* is the location [7]. Context-awareness is the ability of an application or a system to discover and react to changes in the context [8].

Change in context can be easily captured by handheld devices such as smart phones, tablets, etc. Nowadays, handheld devices are equipped with various sensors (GPS, camera, microphone, accelerometer, etc.) that allow the sensitivity to changes in the context [9]. Also, they are equipped with communication technologies (GSM, UMTS, Wi-Fi, etc.) to be connected to networks (Internet, private networks, telephony, etc.) [10]. Moreover, the price of these devices as well as the subscription price for services is reduced by such a fate everyone can purchase smart devices and profit of offered services.

In [11] an architecture for context based Identity Management System using smart phones is proposed. This system permits the use of multiple sensors to evaluate the context and based on that evaluation it authenticates users with accuracy. It can check the identity of persons based on the context, but it cannot identify this person to others in simple way.

This paper aims to develop a relative identity management system. This system will assist dependent persons by giving them information, advices, instructions and helps regarding their activities of daily living. The main idea is to use a simple communication way to identify objects and subjects in the surrounding context of the assisted person. This work that will be presented in this paper is a major part of the following previous works.

In [12] we have proposed an architecture for home automation system. The main objective was to adapt indoor context to the preference of inhabitants. The architecture is composed of: sensors to evaluate the environment, actuators to act on environmental parameters (temperature, lighting, etc.) and database containing the profile of each inhabitant. In addition, a decision support system is proposed to calculate new environmental parameters values based on the current context and inhabitants profiles.

In [13] we have proposed a new middleware called *tinyUPnP* to enables interoperability between home devices. Proposed middleware works in same way the UPnP architecture, except that data control used by underlying protocols (SSDP, HTTP, SAOP and GENA) were reduced. So, our new protocols called *tinyHTTP*, *tinySOAP*, *tniySSDP* and *tinyGENA* were proposed. [20:36:51] T. L.: Consequently, by reducing messages size, the processing time and the amount of exchanged data were optimized.

2   Concept of "Relative Identity"

We define the new concept of *Relative Identity* to identify objects or subjects uniquely in a well-defined context. This implies that the identity may change with the change of the context and the change of the person for whom entities will be identified. Thus, identity will not be universally unique.

As illustrated in Figure 1, the red pen can be identified in several ways depending on its context and on to whom it will be identified. In case (a), it can be identified as "*the pen*"; in case (b) there are two pens, so the red one can be identified by "*the red pen*"; in case (c) it can be identified by "*the red pen*" or "*the thin pen*". For a person who cannot see red colors, the pen can be identified as the "*longest pen*" (case c). For a blind person, the system can use a voice message. In general, the relative identity system will be based on the person's profile: it can use textual messages for a person who can read text, voice messages if the person is not able to read or a picture for a deaf person who cannot read (e.g. with an arrow as shown in Fig. 1 (b)). The relative identification can consider other dimensions from the person's profile such as the speaking language, color blindness, etc.

(a)   (b)   (c)

Fig. 1. Red pen relative identification in different contexts: (a) the pen is alone, (b) two pens with the same form but one is red and the other is black, (c) tow pen with different forms

3   Architecture of Relative Identity Management System

The objective of our Relative Identity architecture is the development of a management system for identifying people and things in a simple way. As illustrates figure 2, the architecture is composed of the following elements:

- **Profiles Manager:** permits the user to update the profiles structure and consequently the way in which they will be processed by the *Context Manager*.
- **Profiles Data Base:** contains the current profile instances.
- **Context Provider:** it is the responsible for acquiring information from the environment and to deliver it to the *Context Manager*.
- **Context Manager:** it processes data received from the Context Provider. It calculates profiles values and updates Profiles Data Base. Also, it detects anomalies and notifies the *Identity Manager*.
- **Identity Manger:** its main role is to translate notifications coming from the Context Manager into an understandable and processable format.

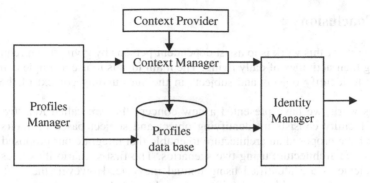

Fig. 2. Architecture of relative identity management system

4   Tests and Results

In order to test our solution we propose the following scenario. The system detects that the inhabitant (e.g. the father) is falling into a hypoglycemia coma and he needs a glucagon injection that is in the refrigerator. So, the system has to inform the nearest helper (e.g. the son/daughter) about the situation and what he/she has to do. It should send a message depending to the current context, such message could be *"your father needs a glucagon injection that is in the refrigerator, your father is in the bed room"*.

Note that the system message and choice of the nearest or more appropriate helper is the result of the context processing (i.e. the answers of the five questions discussed previously in the Introduction). In our scenario, the considered questions and answers are the following couples: ("who is the subject needing help?", "universal identity of that person into hypoglycemia coma"), ("who is the helper?", "universal identity of a person based on the profiles of the available helpers"), ("what happens", "a person is in hypoglycemia coma"), ("where is the person", "he is in the bad room"), ("what we have to do?", "glucagon injection"), ("where are the glucagon?", "it is in the refrigerator").

In case where the helper is the son, and he is blind and he understands only English, the system has to use voice provide required assistance. However, in the case where the helper is the daughter and she is deaf and cannot read text messages, the system has to use picture like illustrated in figure 3.

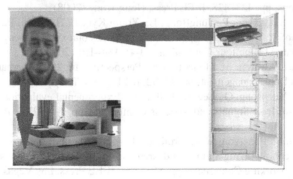

Fig. 3. The interpretation of the message "your father needs a glucagon injection that is in the refrigerator, your father is in the bed room" using a picture

5   Conclusion

The objective of this work is to assist dependent persons by giving them required help regarding their activities of daily living. The main idea is to use a simple communication way to identify objects and subjects in the surrounding context of the assisted person.

In this work, we have presented a new concept that we called *Relative Identity*. Relative Identity consists in identifying object and subject based on theirs context. Also, we have proposed an architecture to enable that integrate our proposed concept. We tested the architecture using two scenarios. The first scenario illustrates how the context elements are identified using textual message. However, the next scenario illustrates that it is possible to identify context elements by using pictures.

Relative Identify proposes an efficient way to identify situations, persons and actions and allows to take into consideration the context and its changes over the time.

References

1. http://www.dailymail.co.uk/health/article-2556831/Girl-5-saves-fathers-life-giving-injection-fell-diabetic-coma.html (acceded March 2014)
2. Coma, C., Cuppens-Boulahia, N., Cuppens, F., Cavalli, A.R.: Interoperability of Con-text Based System Policies Using O2O Contract. In: 4th International Conference on Signal Image Technology and Internet Based Systems, Bali, Indonesia, pp. 137–144 (2008)
3. Hidehito, G.: User-centric identity governance across domain boundaries. In: 5th ACM Workshop on Digital Identity Management, pp. 35–44. ACM, New York (2009)
4. Owusu, G., Voudouris, C., Dorne, R., Ladde, C., Anim-Ansah, G., Gasson, K., Connolly, G.: ARMS — application of AI and OR methods to resource management. BT Technology Journal 25(3-4), 249–253 (2007)
5. Skillen, K., Chen, L., Nugent, C.D., Donnelly, M.P., Solheim, I.: A user profile ontology based approach for assisting people with dementia in mobile environments. In: 34th Annual International Conference of the IEEE Engineering in Medicine and Biology Society, pp. 6390–6393. IEEE Press, San Diego (2012)
6. Heil, A., Gaedke, M.: Environment-Awareness: Quantitative Processing of Context Changes. In: Sixth Annual IEEE International Conference on Pervasive Computing and Communications, pp. 423–428. IEEE Press, Hong Kong (2008)
7. SungWoo, K., SangHyun, P., JungBong, L., YoungKyu, J., Hyun-mi, P., Amy, C., SeungEok, C., WooSik, C.: Sensible appliances: applying context-awareness to appliance design. Personal and Ubiquitous Computing 8(3-4), 184–191 (2004)
8. Hui, L.: Context Awareness: a Practitioner's Perspective. In: 2005 International Workshop on Ubiquitous Data Management, pp. 43–52. IEEE Press, Tokyo (2005)
9. Zhizhong, M., Yuansong, Q., Lee, B., Fallon, E.: Experimental evaluation of mobile phone sensors. In: 24th Irish Signals and Systems Conference, pp. 1–8. IEEE Press, Letterkenny (2013)
10. Baskett, P., Yi, S., Patterson, M.V., Trull, T.: Towards a system for body-area sensing and detection of alcohol craving and mood dysregulation. In: 10th IEEE Consumer Communications and Networking Conference, pp. 875–876. IEEE Press, Las Vegas (2013)

11. Paruchuri, V., Chellappan, S.: Context Aware Identity Management Using Smart Phones. In: 2013 Eighth International Conference on Broadband and Wireless Computing, Communication and Applications, pp. 184–190. IEEE Press, Compiegne (2013)
12. Tiberkak, A., Belkhir, A.: An Architecture for Policy-Based Home Automation System (PBHAS). In: 2010 IEEE Green Technologies Conference, pp. 1–5. IEEE Press, Dallas (2010)
13. Tiberkak, A., Belkhir, A.: tinyUPnP usage for home medical equipments control: case study diabetes management. In: World Congress on Computer and Information Systems 2014, International Conference on Cloud Computer Information Systems 2014, Hammamet, Tunisia (2014)

Games and Exergames

Research on Interactive Animation Design Based on Handheld Mobile Terminals

Dong Han*, Xue Han, and Yuan Wang

School of Computer Software, Tianjin University, Tianjin, China
379201586@qq.com, hx19891129@126.com,
play.wang1988@gmail.com

Abstract. Interactive animation has its own uniqueness, and apart from games, with artistic expression of traditional animation at the same time, reinforces the audience's participation, and opera interact. Based on handheld mobile devices, making interactive animated short film by created with a lot of new features. First consideration in the animated feature for the structures of branch development, after that interactive participative forms that appropriately and cleverly designed, thereby strengthening the expression of works .When you are using Unity3D tool to achieve specific interactive tasks, such as animated elements resource limitations and interface design are also factors that in the creation of to be considered.

Keywords: Mobile Entertainment, Storytelling and Location Based Gaming; Mobile Art, Interaction Design, Multi-branch Plot.

1 Introduction

1.1 Interactive Animation Development Survey

The interactive animation is known as the process of animation creation with the addition of interactive design. It is also a new type of animation that supports the event response and interactive functions when it is played. This interactive design has enabled the audience to participate in and even control the content of the animation being played.

As of now, there has not yet existed a systematic and comprehensive research system upon interactive animation or specialized organization both at home and abroad. The works in the earlier stage was featured by dull and unnatural content and also did not come off quite smoothly for the audience. The *SHOWGOOD* Company in China once presented a series called *Three Kingdoms* of *SHOWGOOD* by introducing a small game featured by controlling the movement of the thatched boat. Another work worth mentioning is the one called The *Fantastic Flying Books* of *Mr. Morris Lessmore* that was awarded as the best animation episode in the 84th session of Oscar in 2012. Besides the high-quality expression of arts, this work has also integrated the unique interaction into the plot, such as touching, rotating and sliding the screen to create a hurricane or pressing to activate a virtual piano (Fig. 1).

---

* Corresponding author.

C. Stephanidis (Ed.): HCII 2014 Posters, Part II, CCIS 435, pp. 331–337, 2014.
© Springer International Publishing Switzerland 2014

Fig. 1. In the *Fantastic Flying Books* of *Mr. Morris Lessmore* some users to participate in the print screen

1.2   Interactive Animation and Interactive Game Analysis and Comparison

The interactive animation is featured by the plot, participation and interaction. But it is also different from the video game. In order to work out more excellent interactive animations, further efforts should be made to understand the difference of them and also their properties. Therefore, a comparative analysis on the participation purpose, process and core value has been conducted, as seen in the table 1.

Table 1. Comparison of interactive games and interactive animation

Item Compared	Interactive Game	Interactive Animation
Target groups	Different types of game enthusiasts (typical)	Audience might be more widely
Participate for the purpose	Entertainment , Sports	Entertainment, education and publicity
Participate for the process	Involved with high frequency interaction process	Only in specific interactive participation
Main operating equipment	Screen contact tools, external sensors, professional	Equipment is given priority to with a finger
The development process	Completely development process	part preset a small plot trajectories
Value core	Competitive is the life of game	Stress and increase fusion to the plot and degree of

2   The Feature Study of the Interactive Animation Based on the Hand-Held Mobile Equipment

As the carrier of interactive animation, the hand-held mobile equipment has offered a variety of feasible and effective measures for animation creation. Therefore, a detailed analysis on the function feature will provide a basis for the interactive design in the animation.

1. The basic operation mode focusing on the input end of the multiple-point touch control, such as the control dragging and touch control.
2. The operation mode based on 3D gyro and acceleration sensor.
3. The interactive application of voice collection based on the in-built microphone.
4. The adjustment of the color and atmosphere in the whole setting(even the whole animation) based on the light   sensing and   geographical   coordinate   acquisition.

3   The Design Concept of the Interactive Animation *Resuscitation*

3.1   The Principle Analysis of Interactive Animation Script

Before the decision of working out an interactive animation   is made, it is quite important to take the feeling and response of the audience on the interactive part into consideration. As a matter of fact, the interactive content will also reduce the smoothness of the whole animation to a certain extent. It has become an issue of great concern to reduce the inconsistency brought by the addition of interactive tasks and also add in the interactive content in a proper manner.

What is more, the interactive part might bring about a change in the line of plot development. In the traditional animation, the plot is decided by the will of the creator alone. The biggest difference between the interactive animation and the traditional one is that the former has highlighted the interaction in which the audience can also exert a certain degree of influence upon the plot development.

Resuscitation is an animation devoted to an adventure. It is about a story of a robot dog as the leading role embarking upon a journey of difficulty and hardship so as to bring life to its master after a major catastrophe hitting the world. The adventure-themed animation can allow of more room for the interactive task in the turning point of the story, which has also blended the audience with the roles in it and also enable them to judge, choose or experience the adventure together in a interactive manner. During the course of finding joy in the animation, the audience will also fully appreciate the theme of the story.

3.2   The Correlation Analysis on the Multi-limbed Plot and Interactive Task in *Resuscitation*

The correlation between the multi-limbed plot and interactive task in *Resuscitation* has been illustrated in the figure2. In the left side, the plot development and the multi-limbed plot in the turning point has been well explained. In the right side, the feature of interactive animation in the last chapter has been fully utilized so as to elaborate on a series of operation modes used in the interactive task, such as screen touch, dragging, shaking and voice activation that correspond to the multi-limbed plot in four turning points in the left side.

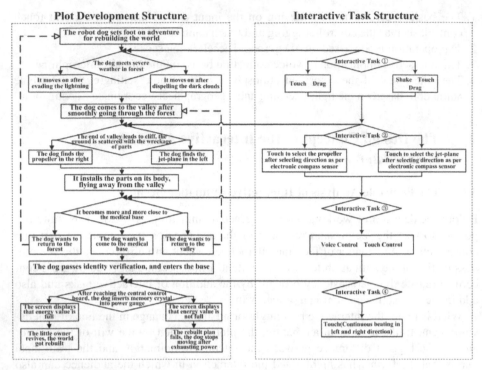

Fig. 2. In *Resuscitation* multi-branch plot and interactive task

3.3   The Realization of the Interactive Task in *Resuscitation*

First of all, the dog has to get through a forest in the middle of terrible weather.

As seen in the task 1, the audience is expected to drag the dog from the right side of the screen to left side, during which the lightning will take place without an alarm. Therefore, the audience should well manipulate the dog so as to avoid being hit by the lightning. If the audience would like to reduce the complexity of the task to move on to the next episode quickly, he can also shake the screen to lift the dark cloud and then drag the dog into the left side (Fig. 3).

Fig. 3. Forest interaction tasks

After passing the forest safely, the dog has to wander around in a desert for some days before reaching a valley leading to a cliff.

As seen in the task 2, the audience is expected to choose a flying tool for the dog. The in-built electronic compass sensor can be used to steer the flying tool by rotating the phone to the left or right. After choosing the direction, the audience should move ahead a little, accompanied by the picture in the screen moving accordingly. After the dog reaches the flying tool, the audience will need to click it(Fig. 4).

Fig. 4. Interaction tasks of choice props

After flying over the cliff and river, the dog will head toward the destination.

In the interactive task 3, the voice or touch control can be used to choose the location. The interactive interface herein is a map, marked with the medical base, valley and forest. The voice or touch control can be used to lead the dog to the destination, which will also make a change in the following plot(Fig. 5).

Fig. 5. Interaction tasks of select site

After reaching the medical based and passing the identity authentication, the dog will walk over to the central control platform and insert the memory crystal into the energy slot.

In the interactive task 4, the dog will place the memory crystal into the energy slot, followed by the energy slot coming out as a new interface. As the square map in the middle of the screen moves to the left or right at a constant speed, the audience should press the buttons at both sides alternately so as to fill in the energy to 100 percent(Fig. 6).

Fig. 6. Activation energy slot trough interaction tasks

The result of the task 4 will have a direct effect on how the story ends. Since the plot is open-ended, different choices in each interactive task will also lead to a difference in how the story develops and comes to an end.

4   The Test Upon the Interactive Task in the Unity3D Environment

The interactive tasks in *Resuscitation* are based on the Unity 3D which is known as a comprehensive game development tool, the programming language C# and JavaScript as well as Photoshop and MAYA. This interactive animation is also seen as an effort to explore the application on the Android platform. What is more, the finally release version is made on Android 2.3.6. , and has carried on the several of interactive task technology test.

5   Conclusion

The interactive animation can be seen as the combination of technology and art. As the technological innovation has brought about a transformation in the mode of operation and greatly enhanced the participation of the audience, which can be seen as the new feature of interactive animation.

In order to work out a multi-limbed plot, more efforts should be made to design the interactive task in the turning point of the plot where the audience can be involved in the task. It should be noted that the interactive task should not impair the integrity of the animation or simply attach it to the animation without due consideration. In addition, the feedback of the audience should be highly valued.

During the course of creation, the operation mode based on the instinct as well as the guidance effect of interactive task should be highlighted. What is more, the constraint upon the development task, operation environment and efficiency caused by the inability of the equipment should be addressed accordingly in real practice.

References

1. Preece, J., Rogers, Y., Sharp, H.: Interaction Design: Beyond Human - Computer Interaction. Wiley Press (2007)
2. Yan, L.: Study about interactive animation. Friends 11, 41–42 (2012)
3. Wang, K.: Study of the Art Form of On-line Interactive Animation. Art & Design 04, 50–51 (2007)
4. Wang, J.: The Design and Application of Interactive Animation in the Network Advertied. Xi'an University of Technology Press (2008)
5. Green. M., Alta, E., Sun, H.: Interactive animation: a language and system for procedural modeling and motion. Computer Graphics and Applications (2002)
6. Abe, Y., Popovic, J.: Interactive animation of dynamic manipulation. In: Proceedings of the 2006 ACM SIGGRAPH/Eurographics Symposium on Computer Animation, SCA 2006, pp. 195–204. Press (2006)

Visual Feedback of Fireworks Motivating Residents to Do Indoor Physical Activities

Yukio Ishihara[1], Makio Ishihara[2], Fuminori Hyodo[1],
Yuji Matsuzoe[3], and Keiji Yasukawa[1]

[1] Innovation Center for Medical Redox Navigation, Kyushu University, 3-1-1,
Maidashi, Higashi-ku, Fukuoka, 812-8582 Japan
{iyukio,hyodof,ykeiji}@redoxnavi.med.kyushu-u.ac.jp
[2] Faculty of Information Engineering, Fukuoka Institute of Technology, 3-30-1,
Wajiro-Higashi, Higashi-ku, Fukuoka, 811-0295 Japan
m-ishihara@fit.ac.jp
[3] Equipment Development Department, Manufacturing Center, Fuji Electric
Co.,Ltd., 1, Fuji-machi, Hino-shi, Tokyo, 191-8502 Japan
matsuzoe-yuji@fujielectric.co.jp

Abstract. In this study we propose a way to motivate healthy people
to do indoor physical activities more often. A lack of physical activity is
thought to be responsible for an increasing number of patients suffering
from lifestyle-related diseases. It is very important that people do physical activities regularly even though they are healthy. Thus we build a
prototype system where people see fireworks projected on the wall. These
fireworks will become more powerful, graceful and various as they keep
doing physical activities. Finally it is shown that progressive fireworks
are successfully displayed depending on the amount of time of physical
activities.

Keywords: fireworks, physical activity, gamification, health.

1 Introduction

There are an increasing number of people suffering from lifestyle-related diseases
such as hypertension, obesity and diabetes. According to WHO report in 2013,
obesity has nearly doubled since 1980 worldwide. 35% of adults (1.4 billion)
were overweight and 11% (500 million) were obese in 2008. At least 2.8 million
adults die each year as a result of being overweight or obese [1]. A lack of regular
physical activity and unhealthy diet are commonly believed to be major factors
for these diseases. Thus people are often advised to improve their lifestyles and
maintain their good health.

It would be no doubt that people encouragingly improve their lifestyles when
they have uncomfortable symptoms such as dizziness, nausea and fatigue or when
they have already been diagnosed as lifestyle-related diseases. When it comes to
healthy people, however, they are less likely to take any action until they have
symptoms even though their blood pressure and weight are close to the alert

C. Stephanidis (Ed.): HCII 2014 Posters, Part II, CCIS 435, pp. 338–342, 2014.
© Springer International Publishing Switzerland 2014

Fig. 1. Seven forms of fireworks

level. Therefore it is very important to motivate such healthy people to improve their lifestyles before they contract lifestyle-related diseases.

Recently it was found that daily health checks of blood pressure and weight affects people's attitudes on physical activity and healthy diet, leading to their better lifestyles. Although they don't need much effort to continue the checks, they become easily bored and end up going back to their previous unhealthy lifestyles unless they become actively engaged in maintaining their health.

Now there are several studies trying to improve people's lifestyles. In the work of Grimes et al. [2] and Orji et al. [3], educational games were developed to allow people to learn healthy meals through the play. As a result, it was shown that they had a positive attitude towards healthy diet after playing the games. Hamilton et al. [4] developed a mobile application that aims to motivate people to do a physical activity, specifically walking. For each of them, his/her step counts are visualized as buildings in a city on the mobile phone. The more steps he/she takes, the taller the buildings become. This city can be shared with his/her family members and friends. Therefore people gradually become motivated to walk longer in order to make their cities more attractive than those of the others. This application is one of the good examples incorporating gamification to entertain people as well as to motivate them to do physical activities. Gamification provides a way to apply game mechanisms into non-game contexts. It helps people get motivated to do their work in fun ways by introducing rankings, medals and social competition.

In this study, we take a similar approach to the study of Hamilton et al. [4] mentioned above. The difference is that we focus on indoor rather than outdoor physical activities. That is, the amount of time people do indoor physical activities is visualized as fireworks and the fireworks are presented to them. Furthermore, these visualized fireworks are not displayed on small screens such as mobile phones. To benefit from being in a house, instead, they are projected on the wall in more attractive and immersive ways.

Table 1. Three levels at each of which fireworks are visualized differently

Level	Color	Size and height of explosions
L1	B/W	small and low
L2	colorful	medium size and height
L3	colorful	big and high

The rest of this manuscript is organized as follows. In Section 2, it is explained the way how fireworks are visualized based on the amount of time of physical activities. Then our prototype system is demonstrated in Section 3. Finally we give concluding remarks in Section 4.

2   Visual Feedback of Fireworks

2.1   Visualizing Various Fireworks

In this study the amount of time people do indoor physical activities is visualized as fireworks. The longer they do physical activities, the more powerful, graceful and various the fireworks become. Fig. 1 shows seven forms of the fireworks. To vary each of these seven forms, three parameters are used: color, the size and height of explosions. These parameters are determined by each of three levels as shown in Table 1. L1 represents fireworks of the seven forms in small size and black-and-white, which explode at a low height. In contrast, L3 represents those in big size and full color. Fig. 2 shows fireworks of one of the forms, which are rendered at each of the three levels. Therefore fireworks of 21 kinds, combinations of the seven forms and the three levels, will be visualized. For simple reference, these 21 kinds are numbered one to seven for L1, eight to 14 for L2 and 15 to 21 for L3. Those at the same level are numbered in a predefined way.

It is said that daily walks of 8,000 steps are recommended for good health, which are equivalent to about a one hour walk each day at the speed of 120 steps per minute. Considering this, fireworks start with #1 and then #2 starts additionally after three minutes. Similarly #3 to #21 starts every three minutes as long as people keep doing physical activities. Furthermore the launching of fireworks is synchronized with their steps, so hopefully it would encourage them to make more steps in order to see more fireworks.

2.2   Detecting Vibration Caused by Physical Activities

A vibration sensor is used to detect vibration caused by residents' physical activities, or by them moving around in the house while they may be cleaning the room or going down to the kitchen for another cup of coffee. These activities could be any movements that cause vibration. Thus just watching TV and reading books are not supposed to be detected. It should be mentioned that vibration is caused by not only their physical activities but environmental factors such as traffic near the house. A simple filtering process is performed to extract the necessary vibration.

Fig. 2. Fireworks of three levels: L1, L2 and L3, which are shown in left to right

3   Experiment

Fig. 3(a) shows our prototype system. As shown in the figure, a vibration sensor, CPUKSNSS00 manufactured by Fuji Electric Co.,Ltd. Japan, is placed on the floor. And this sensor is connected to a PC that is equipped with a 2.5GHz Intel Core i5-2520M CPU, a 8GB RAM and Windows 7. Simulation software to display fireworks of the 21 kinds is coded on Microsoft Visual Studio 2010. This software is run on that PC and receives vibration data sent from the sensor, and then it visualizes the data as those fireworks. Finally images of the fireworks are projected from a projector.

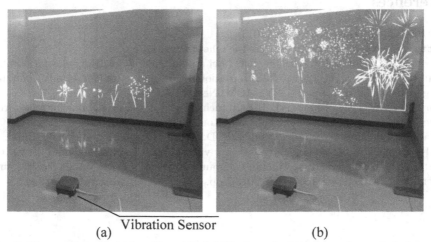

(a)   Vibration Sensor   (b)

Fig. 3. Fireworks projected on the wall. (a) Black-and-white fireworks explode low and (b) colorful and various ones explode bigger and higher in more attractive ways.

We conducted an experiment in a research laboratory to make sure our system works. A participant was asked to do a physical activity of walking. He didn't necessarily walk continuously, but he was allowed to take a break anytime. Fig. 3(a) shows fireworks that were seen when the accumulated amount of time of walking passed 15 minutes. After it passed 60 minutes, big and colorful fireworks were shown as in Fig. 3(b).

4   Conclusions

In this study we proposed a way to motivate healthy people to do indoor physical activities more often. The amount of time they do physical activities is visualized as fireworks. That is, the longer they do physical activities, the more powerful, graceful and various fireworks they see. Typically the amount of the time is visualized and displayed on mobile phones to inform them. In this study, taking an advantage of being in a house, the fireworks are projected on the wall in more attractive and immersive ways. An experiment was conducted to make sure our prototype system works. Through this experiment, it was shown that the progressive fireworks were successfully displayed depending on the amount of time of physical activities.

We are now planning to conduct a field study to find out the effectiveness in practical situations.

Acknowledgement. This study was supported by Creation of Innovation Centers for Advanced Interdisciplinary Research Areas Program, Ministry of Education, Culture, Sports, Science and Technology-Japan.

References

1. WHO. Obesity and overweight (2013),
   http://www.who.int/mediacentre/factsheets/fs311/en/
2. Grimes, A., Kantroo, V., Grinter, R.E.: Let's play!: mobile health games for adults. In: Proceedings of the 12th ACM International Conference on Ubiquitous Computing (Ubicomp 2010), pp. 241–250. ACM, New York (2010)
3. Orji, R., Vassileva, J., Mandryk, R.L.: LunchTime: a slow-casual game for long-term dietary behavior change. Personal Ubiquitous Comput. 17(6), 1211–1221 (2013)
4. Hamilton, I., Imperatore, G., Dunlop, M.D., Rowe, D., Hewitt, A.: Walk2Build: a GPS game for mobile exergaming with city visualization. In: Proceedings of the 14th International Conference on Human-Computer Interaction with Mobile Devices and Services Companion (MobileHCI 2012), pp. 17–22. ACM, New York (2012)

Music Synchronizer with Runner's Pace for Supporting Steady Pace Jogging

Tetsuro Kitahara, Shunsuke Hokari, and Tatsuya Nagayasu

College of Humanities and Sciences, Nihon University
3-25-40, Sakurajosui, Setagaya-ku, Tokyo 156-8550, Japan
{kitahara,hokari,nagayasu}@kthrlab.jp

Abstract. This paper describes a music player that automatically synchronizes the music playback speed with jogging pace. The importance of jogging is in running long distances at a steady pace, so it will be useful to alert when the pace varies. Focusing on the fact that a number of people jog while listening to music, we propose a method for telling the runner the pace variation by synchronizing the music playback speed with the runner's pace. Experimental results show that the proposed method facilitates to keep the runner's steady pace.

1 Introduction

Jogging is an effective way to increase physical fitness [1–4]. The importance of jogging is in running long distances at a steady pace, but this may not be easy for novices. Beginner runners sometimes run too fast and/or decrease their pace due to tiredness. If computing technologies can alert these runners of their pace variations to help them keep a steady pace, it would be useful in allowing them to enjoy jogging.

We focus on the fact that a number of people jog while listening to music with their portable music players (including smartphones). We then propose a method for telling the runner the pace variation by synchronizing the music playback speed with the runner's pace. After the runner's standard pace is measured, the playback speed automatically increases or decreases, according to the runner's pace as it increases or decreases. This method requires the runner to keep the standard pace in order to enjoy the music at its normal speed, therefore we expect that this method will spontaneously influence the runner to keep a steady pace.

There have been some attempts to support jogging using music. Rubisch et al.[5] developed a mobile-phone-based system that recommends musical pieces that have a close tempo to the target heart rate defined by the user-desired amount of oxygen consumption. Sakata et al.[6] proposed a concept called interactive jogging, in which the runner's pace is feedbacked as the change of music. These are similar concepts to ours, but their effects have not yet been confirmed through experiments. In this paper, we investigate the effects of our method by conducting experiments.

C. Stephanidis (Ed.): HCII 2014 Posters, Part II, CCIS 435, pp. 343–348, 2014.
© Springer International Publishing Switzerland 2014

2   Proposed System

The user wears an Android device on his/her hip using a belt and jogs while listening to music using the earphones or headphones connected to the Android device. After the music starts, it is then played back at the normal speed for 15 seconds, because the former five seconds are regarded as a setup time of running and the latter ten seconds are used for measuring the runner's standard pace. After measuring the standard pace, the system starts to synchronize the playback speed with the user's pace based on the method described below.

2.1   Preparation of Audio Signals

Audio signals of the target music with different playback speeds are generated on a PC in advance. In the current implementation, those with 0.5, 0.6, ..., and 2.0 times of the original speed are generated based on Phase Vocoder[7] using MARY Text To Speech Libary[8].

2.2   Measurement of Jogging Pace

The pace is measured with the acceleration sensor built in the Android device. The acceleration value $\alpha(t)$ defined by

$$\alpha(t) = |a_x(t) - a_x(t-1)| + |a_y(t) - a_y(t-1)| + |a_z(t) - a_z(t-1)|$$

is measured for every 80ms, where $a_x(t)$, $a_y(t)$, and $a_z(t)$ are the accelerations along the x-, y-, and z-axes, respectively. When $\alpha(t)$ is higher than an experimentally determined threshold α_θ, the step counter is incremented. The number of steps for the last four seconds is regarded as the jogging pace at that time.

2.3   Switching of Playback Speed

For every second, the system calculates the pace and accordingly switches the audio signal. As an example, when the pace at time t is 0.8 times the standard pace, the audio signal with 0.8 times of the normal speed is used.

3   Experiments

3.1   Experimental Condition

We conducted experiments on jogging using our system. There were ten participants, ages 22 to 23. Participant E exercises every month and Participant H exercises more than three times a week, while the remaining eight partcipants usually do not exercise. The procedure was as follows:

1. Try a two-minute jog three times, listening to music with the normal playback speed, at 30-s intervals.
2. Rest for enough time.
3. Try a two-minute jog three times again, listening to music with our system, at 30-s intervals.

To avoid order effects, we replaced Step 1 with Step 3 for half of the participants.

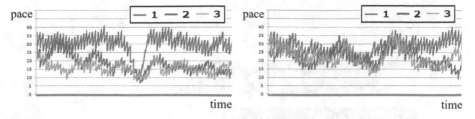

Fig. 1. Pace by Participant A with normal playback (left) and with our system (right)

We used a straight course and asked the participants to turn back around one minute after they started. We used "Tonight's the Night for Love" taken from RWC Music Database [8] and Acer ICONIA TAB A100 with Android 3.2.1.

3.2 Experimental Results

Table 1 lists the temporal average and standard deviation of the every-second jogging pace for each trial. Because the data for Participants I and J were lost due to device trouble, those were removed from the table. The results are summarized as follows:

1. Participant A's pace decreased at every trial with normal speed playback. Participant B's pace also varied between the trials. On the other hand, they jogged at consistent paces with our system.

Table 1. Temporal average and standard deviation of pace for each trial

(a) Our System

Participant	Trial 1		Trial 2		Trial 3	
A	28.0	2.0	21.0	2.0	21.0	3.0
B	21.5	4.0	23.8	3.9	22.4	3.0
C	22.8	4.0	22.4	3.6	21.4	3.4
D	27.5	3.4	30.0	3.7	29.6	3.4
E	30.2	5.1	27.7	3.9	28.8	5.0
F	11.1	2.0	12.0	2.3	11.2	1.8
G	27.0	4.1	22.8	3.5	19.4	3.3
H	24.7	3.8	29.5	5.1	30.1	4.6

(b) Normal Speed Playback

Participant	Trial 1		Trial 2		Trial 3	
A	29.5	0.5	22.5	10.5	15.5	3.5
B	10.4	2.8	20.9	5.3	24.2	3.6
C	26.4	4.3	23.2	4.3	23.3	4.2
D	26.2	3.5	26.3	3.7	25.7	3.5
E	27.2	5.1	26.1	4.1	27.4	4.2
F	10.8	1.6	12.5	3.7	12.7	2.3
G	19.3	3.9	19.4	4.1	18.6	3.1
H	8.2	2.1	21.8	4.0	24.6	4.9

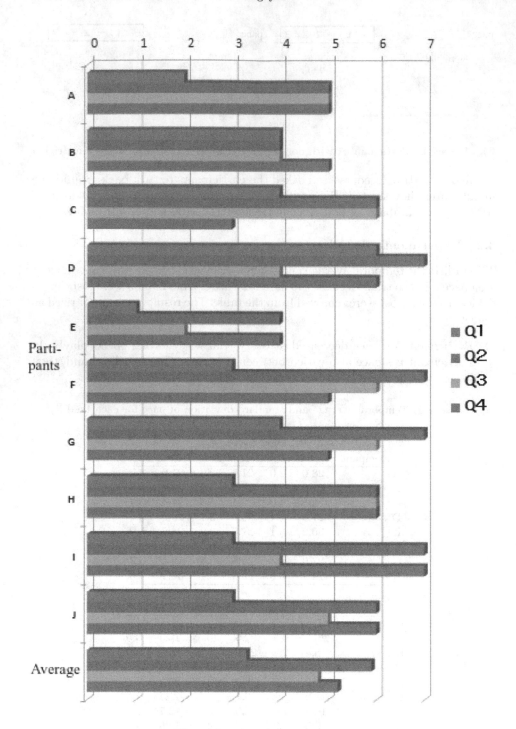

Fig. 2. Results of questionnarie

2. The standard deviations for the 2nd and 3rd trials were smaller with our system than with normal speed playback except for Participants E and H. This means that our system reduced pace variation caused by tiredness to some extent. The reason why this tendency was not shown in Participans E and H was that they frequently exercise unlike the other participants.

Details of every-second paces by Participant A are shown in Figure 1. The pace was made lower each trial with normal speed playback, while the pace with our system was not made lower. The pace largely decreased at turning back for normal speed playback, while the pace did not decrease with our system. This would be an effect of synchronizing music playback with the running pace.

3.3 Questionnaire

We asked the ten participants to answer a questionnaire consisiting of the following questions:

Q1 Did the music playback synchronized to your pace?
Q2 Did you consciously control the jogging pace according to the music?
Q3 Did you feel that jogging becames easy with our system?
Q4 Do you want to use this system in your daily life?

The questionnaire was conducted on a scale of one to seven.

The results are shown in Fig. 2. The result for Q1 was not high. Our system updates the playback speed at every second based on the avrage pace during last four seconds, so a little latency occured in the synchronization. This would be why the result of Q1 was not high. The result for Q2 was high. This means that synchronization of music playback speed with the jogging pace successfully raised the runner's consciousness of pace control. The results for Q3 and Q4 were also high on average. This means that our system is useful to support jogging by people without frequent exercise.

4 Conclusion

We proposed a method for presenting the variation of a jogging pace by synchronizing the music playback speed with the running pace and conducted experiments to confirm the effects of the method. The experimental results showed that this method effectively created steady pace jogging.

In the current implementation, audio signals with various playback speed are necessary to prepare in advance on a PC. Improving this will be one of the most important future issues. To do this, we plan to implement the Phase Vocoder[7] and achieve the music playback synchronization by generating the audio signal with the target speed in real time. In addition, we plan to distribute the software via Google Play and collect a lot of users' feedback for further improvement.

References

1. Makikawa, M., et al.: Portable Jogging Monitor Device and its Application for Health Management. In: Proc. APBME 2003 (2003)
2. Glaros, C., et al.: A Wearable Intelligent System for Monitoring Health Condition and Rehabilitation of Running Athletes. In: Proc. IEEE-ITAB 2003 (2003)
3. Mueller, F.F., et al.: Jogging over a Distance. In: Proc. CHI 2007 (2007)
4. Buttussi, F., et al.: MOPET: A Context-aware and User-adaptive Wearable System for Fitness Training. Artificial Intell. Med. 42, 153–163 (2008)
5. Rubisch, J., et al.: A Mobile Music Concept as Support for Achieving Target Heart Rate in Preventive and Recreational Endurance. In: Proc. Audio Mostly Conf. (2010)
6. Sakata, N., et al.: Situated Music: An Application to Interactive Jogging. In: Proc. ISWC 2006 (2006)
7. Flanagan, J.L., et al.: Phase Vocoder. Bell System Technical Journal 45, 1492–1509 (1966)
8. MARY Text To Speech, http://mary.dfki.de/
9. Goto, M., et al.: RWC Music Database: Music Genre Database and Musical Instrument Sound Database. In: Proc. ISMIR 2003 (2003)

An Intuitive Mobile Application for Notation of Group Dance Floor Plan*

Jeong-seob Lee

Graduate School of Culture Technology, Korea Advanced Institute of Science and Technology,
291 Daehak-ro, Yuseong-gu, Daejeon, Korea
Jslee85@kaist.ac.kr

Abstract. In this research, author suggests an interactive and intuitive mobile application to notate dynamic formation change in group dance which is the beauty of dance in conjunction with motion of a single human.Firstly, limitations of traditional notation systems and even less aids on floor plan were discussed. Those limitations results in inefficient and energy-consuming trial-and-error in creative work and inhibit artists' creativity.This research explores a new potential of digital media for notation of group dance formation. Essential information parameters to be a sound notation are investigated. Beneficial features of interactive digital media, such as synchronization with music which is crucial in dance notation, are discussed. Existing software products in various creating areas gave inspiration in design of interface.The mobile application is designed for users to intuitively draw and edit their own dynamic floor plan. User can record and review and share it highly effectively with other artists.This research is expected to help performing artist and expand their creativity.

Keywords: dance notation, group dance, floor plan, choreography, mobile application.

1 Introduction

Dance is an art of human body. Dance gets realized only through the body of dancers. Flourishing temporal and spatial pattern of body builds up artistic experience for audiences. As much as movement of a single dancer, the beauty and energy of dance comes out from dynamic and sophisticated locomotion and formation of multiple dancers.

To record, review, share and archive the choreography is one of the important and tricky parts in creation. While many notation systems have been researched in history, it is hard to say any of them became useful and popular enough to working choreographers. This situation also corresponds to floor plan of group dance. Many of them use improvised and arbitrary communication means like drawings and fingers which have difficulty and inefficiency.

---

* Supplement information including multimedia is provided at website.
http://jeongseoblee.wordpress.com/2014/03/21/groupdancenotation/

C. Stephanidis (Ed.): HCII 2014 Posters, Part II, CCIS 435, pp. 349–354, 2014.
© Springer International Publishing Switzerland 2014

In this paper, the author suggests a notation system for locomotion and formation of group dance that is based on interactive media. Google Android was used as its platform. Through literature review and field experience, typical pattern of how choreographers draw their floor plan was studied. Then, essential spatial and temporal data to be stored and intuitive user interface for dancers' cognitive pattern were discussed. Finally, those studies converged into an android application.

This application shows potential of interactive media on notation of group dance formation. It is expected to improve efficiency of choreography in various aspects and encourage more complicated and flourishing creation.

2   Background Research

2.1   History of Dance Notation

Notation of performing arts has been a long historical issue for the art area. Notation is essential for efficiently describing, sharing and archiving artistic works. Music notations have been established through centuries of dedication and modern staff notation works successfully in expressing music. On the other hand, notation of dance has been developed less successfully due to its characteristic of higher dimension of data and irregular expandability of vocabulary [1]. Historic work of Laban, or Labanotation, contributed to notate universal mechanism of motion Royal Ballet of England adopted "Choreology" by Rudolf Benesh later than the Labanotation. [1]

As a matter of fact, years of observations by the author on dancers and choreographers reveals that they have little interest in recording their movement on a sheet; many of them hardly believe it to be intuitive, effective or efficient way to communicate on their creation. Even the historical Merce Cunningham mentioned this problem. He thought dancers does not think and behave like symbols and logic in conventional notations when they are dancing [2].

Nowadays, some computational tools have been developed. Laban Writer[3] that digitalized labanotation, and Life Form and other several researches convert the labanotation into animation of a virtual dancer character [4–6].

2.2   Video and Dance Record

Appearance of video introduced enormous change in dance. Strict temporal and spatial limitation, which has been a characteristic of dance and other performing art, was drastically eased with video. Audience and other spectators do not necessarily need to share the same time and space with performers.

In aspect of dance recording, video became a well-functioning tool for creation. Many dancers and choreographers actively record dance through their working process. With the video, they review their work and improve it, communicate with dancers and other artists and archive it. Nowadays, by means of online video streaming services, every people in the world watch and learn dance choreography.

However, it doesn't mean video took place of all other communication tools. Cunningham [2] said video cannot clearly and precisely record dance solely without notation just like music cannot be recorded only with audio record without score. Every performance is re-interpretation of the original artwork; None of them can be same as the original [1]. Above all, video cannot exist before the realization of their imaginary creation. Hence, many dancers and choreographers develop their own habit of drawing or describing structure of their creation.

2.3   Notation of Locomotion and Formation

In Labanotation, notation of performer and its path on the stage basically looks like Figure 1. A pin and wedge indicate a dancer in starting position and finishing position respectively. Different shape of the pin indicates different gender. A path across the floor is indicated on the floor plan with an arrow from starting point to end point [1]. Many choreographers tend to draw their designed floor plan analogously to these.

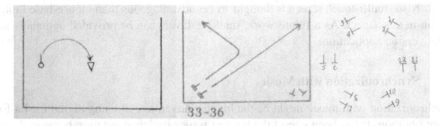

Fig. 1. Basic format of stage floor plan in Labanotation (source: [1], p.182,368, 377)

Problem is, when their choreography gets complicated, it requires drastically large numbers of drawings. One drawing expresses one queue on the stage. More formation queue requires more drawings. If each dancers start to move asynchronously, which they frequently do for richness of the work, drawing becomes very ineffective way of communication; It is not only hard for choreographer to draw on a paper but also confusing for dancers to understand it. Then some choreographers desperately bring their fingers to visualize paths of dancers.

3   Design Concept and Implementation

3.1   Goal of the Research

Goal of this research is to provide new notation tool of floor plan in choreography which is more efficient for expressing it and communicating with other artists. It requires information about time, position and rotation of dancers, which is quite multi-dimensional.

As aforementioned, choreographers often express their design of locomotion with drawing or their fingers, which is hardly an efficient communication. As we live in the age of digital media, we can think about new notation system with new media which has characteristic of higher dimension, multimodality and interactivity. Final form of the research is a mobile application that user can interactively draw, edit, simulate and share his/her floor plan with music.

3.2   Basic Structure

Basic structure of the application resembles to that of major 3D animation tools or video editing tools. Those computer software packages consist of a timeline with multiple parameters and key frames. The key frames designate values of parameters at certain time and parameter values are interpolated with them. Usually those parameters are displayed as stack of layers on timeline. By controlling the layers, user can delicately control parameters, but it occupies huge space on display and less intuitive.

As our goal of research is closer to draft sketch of an artist's idea rather than an accurate drawing, being intuitive take priority over precision. As size of the display is limited, multiple layers of the timeline are basically omitted and one single timeline is given. Also, multi-touch screen is thought to be advantageous than mouse-based interaction in this aspect. As a future work, multiple layers can be provided optionally for tablet version application.

3.3   Synchronization with Music

Synchronization with music might be the biggest advantage of using digital media for dance notation. It has been one of the biggest issues in dance notation because dance always needs to be considered with music together. Latest notation systems, Labanotation and Choreology, are designed to couple with musical notation to some extent and enable users to read music and dance side by side [1]. Especially, Choreology is drawn on staff to fulfill the condition. By means of digital media, we can provide a function that animates designed floor plan with synchronized music. Choreographers can see their floor plan design as an animation with music. It is effective for imagining, reviewing his/her work and communicating with other artists.

3.4   Data Structure

What kinds of information are needed to be handled as a notation of floor plan? Firstly, there should be dancers. Key frame-based structure is brought in and each dancer key frames. Each key frame stores parameters that include position, time and how long the dancer stays in the position. These parameters are very basic information to define locomotion of dancers. Also, dancer-key based structure can expect easy expansion of advanced parameters.

When an object (dancer) stays in one position for certain period, many animation tools model it with two key frames with same parameters but time. But that model is inappropriate in our case for two reasons; firstly, in that case, two key frames will perfectly overlapped on screen and it causes control error. Secondly, it is not intuitive for dancers. Dancers recognize time and space with where, when and until when. Therefore, storing dancer's staying time in the position is more appropriate.

3.5   User Interface

User interface of the application was implemented as Figure 2. It is designed to express key frame positions, paths, staying time and current position of dancers. Each linkage indicates a path of each dancer and each joint of the linkages indicates a key frame. Each triangle indicates position of dancers with respect to current time of music. Position of each key frame can be modified with touch & drag. Current time of virtual stage in the application is controlled with a slider at the bottom or by playing music with play button.

Other time-related functions are located at top-right side. Those include setting time and staying time of a key frame, adding and removing a key, adding and removing a dancer. Those were implemented as buttons to let users touch it listening to the music simultaneously, which is more efficient and intuitive than using other controller element for setting desired timing exactly.

Ability to load music file is provided so that user can design floor plan with music he/she want. Finally, user can save or load their floor plan design as 'project'.

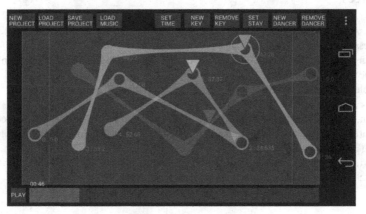

Fig. 1. Capture image of implemented notation application

4   Future Work

Our research provides a basic platform for notation of parameters. In addition to the implemented parameters, we can think about other advanced features to be stored. In addition to position and straight path information, rotational data can be added; heading direction of the dancer and circular path. Also, as dancers frequently move as a group, ability to control dancers as a group in the application might be desirable. Relationship between dancers, which is essential sometime to express choreographer's intention[1], is another promising idea.

Furthermore, another potential of this system is an aspect of simulation. It can evolve into a simulation tool to evaluate compatibility of plan such as collision between dancers or abnormal high speed locomotion.

To express all these information and functions, consideration of more effective user interface will be requested.

5   Conclusion

Notation of dance is ongoing obstacle for many choreographers and notation of floor plan takes big part of it. Focusing on the floor plan issue, we developed a mobile application-based notation system. Through the research, studies on principal data sets, proper data structure with expandability and intuitive user interface were discussed. This research will be improved to achieve more functionality and practicality in the future. It is believed that this research will help many choreographers and dancers design more sophisticated floor plan and, eventually, improve their artwork to the higher level.

References

1. Guest, A.H.: Labanotation: The System of Analyzing and Recording Movement. Sychology Press (2005)
2. Cunningham, M.: The dancer and the dance: Merce Cunningham in conversation with Jacqueline Lesschaeve (1998)
3. Venable, L., Sutherland, S., Ross, L., Tinsley, M.: Laban Writer 2.0,
   http://dance.osu.edu/labanwriter
4. Ryman, R., Fox, I., Ryman, R., Calvert, T.: Documenting dance for the 21st century: A translation interface between LabanWriter and Life Forms. In: Twenty-Second Bienn. Conf. (2001)
5. Calvert, T.: Animating dance. In: Proc. Graph Interface 2007 (2007)
6. Fox, I.: From Notation to Animation. In: Excerpt ICKL (1999)

Shake It Up: Exercise Intensity Recognizing System

Yang Kyu Lim[1] and Bo Kwang Shim[2]

[1] Graduate School of Culture Technology, KAIST, Korea
lim0386@kaist.ac.kr
[2] Anyteksys SDN BHD, Malaysia
jacob@anytek.com.my

Abstract. When we are doing exercise, we often listen to the music. We wanted to make a music player-based exercise intensive recognizing system. In this study, we focused on the motional aspect of hand and arm. The main concept is speed changing music player. A pedometer is the most common detecting tool for the exercise activities. Detecting swing of the body with smartphone –like a pedometer- to set as a downbeat for synchronizing music. We used smartphone gyroscope sensor to detect the downbeat gesture. Motion sensing with gyroscope is a common way in these days. We set the rotation rate of the pitch-axis at 2rad/s for filtering the unstable sensing of the gyroscope. After filtering, holding smartphone and staring movement can calculate the speed of the movement. Existing similar studies are using MIDI and PC to control *tempo* easily and do something more. In this study, we use only MP3 files, extract from CD. We make single application –*Shake It Up*- without any computer connection. We used time stretch to control the speed of MP3 files. After the application is ready, we had a user test to experience *Shake It Up*. Without a guide, all users were easily controlled BPM of the music. Some of them use this application as a music player on jogging with arm band. They said, they can hear the intensity of exercise with the speed of the music. We have to pay attention to the possibility of the future. After the test, we found a sequence of operation was very similar to orchestral conducting. It can be used to music practice tool for conductors. However, still *Shake It Up* cannot sync music file with the hand gesture speed point by point. We are finding out making extra tag files to synchronize and control each detailed point of music.

Keywords: smartphone, exercise, motion, music, BPM.

1   Introduction

Shake It Up is a handheld digital exercise intensity recognizing system that can be simply used by people in order to have an exercise [1].

Many people are listening to the music while exercising. The invention of MP3 made a light and simple music players better than Walkman and CD player. Most of the people who do aerobic exercise are listening a fast, strong, exciting, and progressive music. A slow and relaxing music is often played during the little movement exercise like yoga. When we exercise, we found that we are synchronized to the lis-

C. Stephanidis (Ed.): HCII 2014 Posters, Part II, CCIS 435, pp. 355–360, 2014.
© Springer International Publishing Switzerland 2014

tening music. The relation between music and exercise can be given a little more psychological energy and motivation to keep exercising. Music and exercise have a very close relationship.

We thought about that people can measure himself how strong, fast, and excite or light, slow, and relax when they exercise. We began to research and analyze the relationship between music speed and movement.

With the invention of the smartphone, MP3, telephone, and other devices are possible to carry in one hand together. Nowadays, there are already various sports-related applications in the market.

Shake It Up is using gyroscope in the smartphone to measure strength, pace, and intensity of self-exercise in real-time with the music.

2   Related Work

Our study is similar to pedometer which is a device that counts each step a person takes by detecting the motion of the person's body. Our goal is detecting the moment of the motion to change the BPM of the music.

Nowadays, there are lots of researches about Smartphones and devices related healthcare and sports activity. *Apple iPod* and *Nike Sports Kit* were the first start of this research. *Nike Sports Kit* has an extra sensor to measure the speed, distance, and calorie data. They can also upload the data to website with wifi connected *iPod* to compete against other people. *Nike* uploaded the *Nike plus* application series to the app store to use without sports kit anymore [2, 3, 4].

There are also motion detective wristband type devices -*Nike Pure Band*, *Misfit*, and *Fitbit* series- in the market [5, 6]. Some of are activated as a single device, but most of devices have to connect with smartphone. After finishing the exercise, saved data can be checked by the smartphone and PC. Most of these devices only focused on the distance and speed of the exercise with GPS sensor. It is hard to detect the real-time exercise intensity by these devices in these moments.

Galaxy Gear is an android based smart watch made by Samsung Electronics [7]. Pre-installed pedometer application is using built-in accelerometer to get a motion detection. And user can install the healthcare applications to synchronize with smartphone applications. User can check the real-time status of the data from little screen. However, developing galaxy gear application does not allow for personal development and any other devices except galaxy series.

Noom series are food and exercise logging application [8]. User can simply put the name of the food to automatically calculate the calorie. Using GPS to detect the speed and location of the people who is doing exercise. When exercise begins, *Noom* automatically activate the music player. Playing music with exercise is similar to our study. However, the current exercise intensity is hard to measure in real-time in single *Noom* application. Using sub-brand *Cardio trainer* application and *Polar Heartbeat Detector* together can make up for detecting the current intensity of the exercise. But it is difficult for common people to use and buy specialized equipment (Fig. 1.)

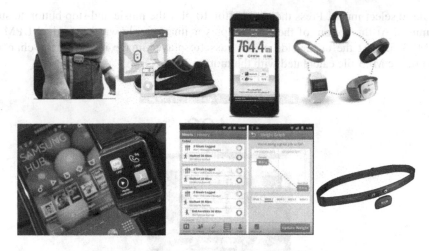

Fig. 1. Pedometer, Nike Spots Kit, Nike Plus, wristband type devices, Galaxy Gear, Noom, and Polar Heartbeat Detector

3 Design and Implementation

Some details of *Shake It Up* are as follows. Each of MP3 file has own information tag, *ID3* [9]. BPM information is one of them. First, the user inputs a BPM information matched with original music on PC (Fig. 2.). Save the BPM information attached MP3 file to the smartphone. Start application and hold a smartphone with the hand or wear with the armband. When you start to exercise, music will slower and faster depending on the strength of the arm.

Fig. 2. Input BPM information on *ID3* tag program

3.1 Design

Shake It Up is designed to simply and easily. The basic design of the form is a cassette tape player that everyone knows already. Pressing a cassette tape image on the middle to select music. Press the play button to play the music and stop button to stop the music. At the bottom of the cassette player image is shown the original BPM of the MP3 file. At the upper side of the cassette player image is shown the changed BPM of the MP3 file calculated with the motion (Fig. 3.).

Fig. 3. Shake *It Up* screen capture

3.2   Interface

The *Shake It Up* is an iOS7-based application that can be used on the iPhone. We used smartphone gyroscope sensor to detect the swing of the arm. Motion sensing with gyroscope is a common way in these days. We used *Apple CMAttitude* to access the data, which includes the rotation degrees for each of the three axes [10]. The body movement can be calculated via the pitch-axis of the gyroscope. For the noise filtering in the gyroscope a speed limitation of the rotation rate is used. We set the rotation rate of the pitch-axis at 2rad/s for filtering the unstable sensing of the gyroscope. After filtering, exercising data can be stable (Fig. 4.).

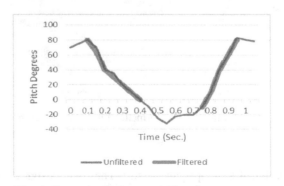

Fig. 4. Comparison of raw and filtered gyroscope

The music BPM can be controlled by calculating the movement time between each beat. The movement between each beat is calculated according to the formula shown below.

$$BPM = 60 \ sec \ / \ (time2 - time1)$$

Combination of the formula and the hand movements, the music BPM will increase or decrease. To control BPM of the music, we need to have time stretch technic. Our time stretch technic is based on Dirac3 demo code from the DSPdimension [11].

Existing similar studies are using MIDI and PC to control BPM easily and do something more. In this study, we use only MP3 files, extract from CD. We make single application –*Shake It Up*- without any computer connection.

4   Evaluation

We simply tested ten random people in a day. We wanted to know usability and the effects of the application. Two types of smartphone grips -holding hand and wearing armband- were tested.   Before the test, ten people were given a short duration to understand the application. Without a guide, all participants were easily controlled BPM of the music. Then, they tried *Shake It Up* on a treadmill. During the exercise, we let each user have own time to feel free.

After exercise, the participants were surveyed about *Shake It Up*. The survey inquired about their interest, concentration, and sense of accomplishment during the exercise. There was very positive (5), positive (4), normal (3), negative (2), and very negative (1) scores to answer. Each category got 3.7, 3.1, and 3.6 point over 'Normal'. On average, it was not great but it was not bad (Table 1.).

Table 1. Survey rating by category

	Interest	Concentration	Sense of accomplishment
Very Positive (5)	2	1	3
Positive (4)	4	3	3
Normal (3)	3	4	2
Negative (2)	1	1	1
Very Negative (1)	0	1	1

5   Conclusion

Shake It Up is a system through which a person can simply and easily recognize the intensity of the exercise without extra device. Buying an extra device for general people's exercise is uncomfortable. Simple exercise can keep people's health. Keep measuring the condition of exercise can be more effective. In this point of view,

Shake It Up is trying with music speed controlling system to overcome a lonely solo exercise.

We have to pay attention to the possibility of the future. The first is many types of exercise should be able to use. In this study, we tested only little range of exercise, a treadmill. In the future, we will expand our application to many kinds of exercises.

The second, we need online data sharing system like other applications. We can save our data and share with our friends to have much more competitive. Motive for participating in exercise can be made by competitors.

After the test, we found a sequence of operation was very similar to orchestral conducting. It can be used to music practice tool for conductors. However, still *Shake It Up* cannot sync music file with the hand gesture speed point by point. We are finding out making extra tag files to synchronize and control each detailed point of music.

References

1. 4tunes (Yang Kyu Lim), App Store 'Shake It Up',
   https://itunes.apple.com/app/id654879979
2. Nike Inc., Nike Plus, https://secure-nikeplus.nike.com/plus/
3. Apple Inc., Nike Sports Kit,
   http://www.apple.com/kr/ipod/nike/sync.html
4. Nike Inc., App Store, 'Nike+ Running',
   https://itunes.apple.com/ko/app/nike+-running/id387771637
5. ©misfit wearables, Misfit series, http://www.misfitwearables.com/
6. Fitbit Inc., Fitbit series, http://www.fitbit.com/
7. ©Samsung, Galaxy Gear, http://www.samsung.com/sec/galaxynote3/
8. Noom Inc., Noom, http://www.noom.com/
9. Wikipedia, ID3, http://en.wikipedia.org/wiki/ID3
10. Apple Inc., Apple CMAttitude, https://developer.apple.com
11. DSPdimension, Dirac3, http://www.dspdimension.com/

Touch Screen Rehabilitation System Prototype Based on Cognitive Exercise Therapy

Fuyuki Matsushima[1], Roberto Gorriz Vilar[2], Keita Mitani[1], and Yukinobu Hoshino[1]

[1] Kochi University of Technology
Tosayamada, Kochi, Japan
[2] Polytechnich University of Valencia
Valencia, Spain
140159w@ugs.kochi-tech.ac.jp,
{rogorvi,keita.mitani.kut}@gmail.com,
hoshino.yukinobu@kochi-tech.ac.jp

Abstract. In recent years the number of rehabilitation patients all over the world is rapidly increasing as society ages and stroke and dementia spread. Continuous rehabilitation helps physical and mental maintenance and recovery. However, the recovery process involves hard and dull work which can result in the patient abandoning the treatment. This problem requires a solution both effective and agreeable. Nowadays, cognitive exercise therapies are widely used to combine mental and physical function recovery. We introduce touch panel ad-hoc developed games into this therapy, motivating the user to actively participate in the rehabilitation and making the whole process reliable and days touch screens are commonly used in daily life, re-moving the need for an initial learning stage. This makes touch screens a perfect inter-face for people all ages, even if their mobility is reduced. In this paper, a prototype touch screen rehabilitation system based on cognitive exercise therapy is developed. Two applications are used to ensure rehabilitation reliability: Whack-a-Mole and Simon games. A usability evaluation test is employed to assess system's effectiveness. Additionally, two different touch screens were used, tested and evaluated.

Keywords: Rehabilitation, Touch screen, Cognitive exercise therapy, Usability evaluation.

1   Introduction

In recent years the number of rehabilitation patients all over the world is rapidly increasing as society ages and stroke and dementia spread. Continuous rehabilitation helps physical and mental maintenance and recovery. However, the recovery process involves hard and dull work, which can result in the patient abandoning the treatment. This problem requires a solution both effective and agreeable. Today, cognitive exercise therapies are widely used to combine mental and physical function recovery. We introduce touch panel ad-hoc developed games into this therapy, motivating the user to actively participate in the rehabilitation and making the whole process reliable and

C. Stephanidis (Ed.): HCII 2014 Posters, Part II, CCIS 435, pp. 361–365, 2014.

days touch screens are commonly used in daily life, removing the need for an initial learning stage. This makes touch screens a perfect inter-face for people all ages, even if their mobility is reduced. In this paper, a prototype touch screen rehabilitation system based on cognitive exercise therapy is developed. Two applications are used to ensure rehabilitation reliability: Whack a Mole and Simon games. A usability evaluation test is employed to assess system's effectiveness. Additionally, two different touch screens were used, tested and evaluated.

2   Application for Experiments

Cognitive exercise therapy is a rehabilitation method, which have the cognitive cycle, "See" → "Confirm" → "Think". This therapy should make patients self-conscious about this cycle in continuous rehabilitation naturally. Experiments test this cycle on visual game using hand stroking. Two kinds of applications were created for experiments. The first application is a mole game. The effectiveness of the rehabilitation is reported about this game. (See Fig.1) [1][2].

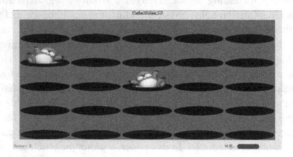

Fig. 1. Mole game

Second application is a Simon game. Rehabilitation patient is likely to be aware of the cognitive cycle this game. (See Fig.2)

The game process is a memory task game and a game screen has a narrow visual area. Hand stroke is short and the Recognition factor is greater than the exercise factor. Players can concentrate to the game task. Therefore participants work that cycle naturally.

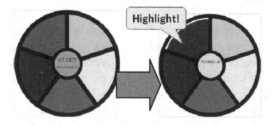

Fig. 2. Simon game

3   Evaluation of Experiment

Second application is a Simon game. Rehabilitation patient is likely to be aware of the cognitive cycle this game. (See Fig.2) Usability evaluation method is used in the evaluation of experiment. In addition, subjects are 9 male and female healthy. All subject's extremities are no problem healthy. Mean age is 20.6 and standard deviation is ± 1.26. NEC touch panel and touch panel acrylic was prepared for comparison. Capacitive sensor is used in acrylic touch panel.   Optical sensor is used in NEC touch panel.

3.1   Experimental Task

Table 1 shows the subject tasks in the experiment of Mole game. The subjects wore a weight band in Task2 and Task4. This band weight is 500g. Subjects wore the dominant hand. Those tasks are test of the simulated rehabilitation. This weight is to simulate the handicap of the arms.

Table 1. Task of Mol game

Task	Matrix	Mole	Speed [ms]	Total Mole [time]	Weight
Task 1	3*2	One	800	20	No
Task 2	3*2	Two	1600	20(40)	Add
Task 3	5*5	Two	1450	20(40)	No
Task 4	5*5	Two	1750	20(40)	Add

Player pushes the button color to order. The order of pushed button was reproduced. After that, player must reproduce that order by pushing the buttons. As the game progresses, the number of buttons to be pressed increases. Screen of Simon game experiment is fig.3. This is the start screen, which arranges 5 color buttons round. One push is one point. Game clear Score is at 10 points then Task is over. If a player made a mistake in the middle, Score is reset to 0. In this case, player must restart a game from start screen.

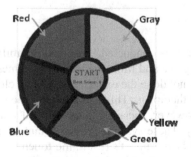

Fig. 3. Simon game detail

3.2   Experimental Results of Mole Game

We asked players 5 factors question. There are 'Favorite', 'Operatively', 'Continuity', 'Response' and 'Visibility'. Impression result is shown fig.4.

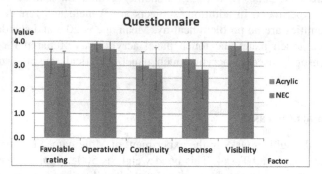

Fig. 4. Impression result of Mole game

3.3   Experimental Results of Simon Game

We asked players 5 factors question. There are 'Favorite', 'Operatively', 'Continuity', 'Response' and 'Visibility'. Impression result is shown fig.5.

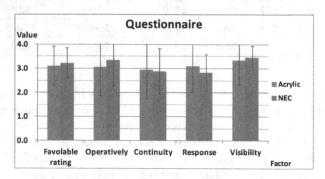

Fig. 5. Impression result of Mole game

4   Conclusion

An evaluation experiment was conducted. Proposal rehabilitation systems was compared, are using a Simon game and Mole game. These games are effective in rehabilitation. However, we have not done the experiment for the elderly. This research has to interview to occupational therapists. This is next step. The touch panel using the optical sensor was better. However, these systems are still inadequate according to the cognitive exercise therapy. These systems are important "feeling touch" with the cognitive exercise therapy. By experiment's result, the touch panel ideal is a tactile sensor type for rehabilitation system. For the future, we will experiment with a variety of touch panel interface.

References

1. Naoki, Y., Syougo, N., Takashi, I.: A computer-controlled multi-purpose rehabilitation system for evaluation and exercise using special input-output modules. In: Proceedings of The 15th Japanese Conference on the Advancement of Assistive and Rehabilitation Technology, pp. 21–24 (2000)
2. Burke, J.W., Morrow, P.J., McNeill, M., McDonough, S., Charles, D.: Vision Based Games for Upper-Limb Stroke Rehabilitation. In: IMVIP 2008: Proceedings of the 2008 International Machine Vision and Image Processing Conference, pp. 159–164 (2008)

Mobile Phone Casual Games Design
with Appeal to Children

Vasiliki Aggelopoulou and Irene Mavrommati

Hellenic Open University School of Applied Arts Athens, Greece
v.aggelopoulou@gmail.com, mavrommati@eap.gr

Abstract. In this paper, we will present the design decisions, evaluation and conclusions stemming from the process of making a set of three casual games, characterized by a common design style and simple scenario..

Keywords: casual games, mobile games, memory game, character, scenario.

1 Introduction

The game is an integral part of the human life starting from early childhood. Children are becoming very familiar with the use of computer technology, from a young age, and especially with the use of mobile phones. Young kids, i.e. between the age of 4 and 9, can prove to be very capable and competent operators of these appliances. Although are not usually the owners of mobile phones, they often use the phones of their parents in order to play casual games in a variety of settings. They often use the phones to play games that their parents usually selected and bought, when in waiting or travel time, when relaxing at home, or for keeping entertained and quiet in a social visit or restaurant.

The casual games are a well known class of computer games, appealing to a wide audience. They form a very wide variety and are characterized by simple rules, fast learning curve, and no commitment (in contrast with other more complex games). Because of these characteristics casual games are considered to be ideal to engage and motivate young children.

2 Design of a Set of Casual Games Aimed for Kids

A set of three games were designed and developed in the course of a Master thesis, in the Graphic Arts and Multimedia postgraduate course of the Hellenic Open University. The game types selected were widely established, similar to many games that can be easily found in the internet, but are also widely known in their standard paper form. What distinguished these games from the plethora of similar games available was that they specifically targeted in having a very recognizable aesthetics identity, characters and script. Thus they were able to differentiate from the competition, in order to aim for targeting the preference of children.

C. Stephanidis (Ed.): HCII 2014 Posters, Part II, CCIS 435, pp. 366–370, 2014.

Fig. 1. Start up screens from the Amnesia of Who memory game, introducing the characters

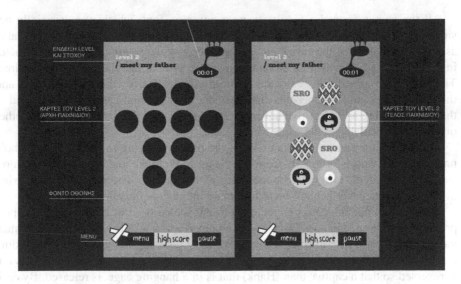

Fig. 2. Gameplay screens of the memory game: Amnesia of Who

The types of casual games that were developed are:

- A memory game titled "amnesia of Who" (Fig 1., Fig.2)
- A hangman game titled "unhang Hank" (Fig.3)
- A maze game, titled "love is in the air" (Fig. 4)

Fig. 3. Screens from the "Hangman" casual game: Unhang Hank

All the games formed a family, using a common font, which was especially designed for these games, and graphic design of characters and general style identifiable as a set. The design of the casual games focused on the creation of a central character in each game and a small story around them, in order to attract the interest of children. The evaluation aimed to asses if the children could identify with the characters and their adventures, and weather this characteristic of the casual games would appeal to them, thus giving a competitive advantage to these casual games as opposed to other ones that are available in the game marketplace.

In the memory game Amnesia of Who, the player is trying to help the hero who's name is Who, who is originally from the planet MakeMake and has amnesia as a result of an accident, to remember members of his family. The game has increasing difficulty as the player helps Who to find more members of his family.

Certain gaming elements were adapted to the scenario, in order to be more appropriate for children. Unhang Hank for example (Fig.3) which is a typical hangman game (the player trying to find the secret word by guessing letters), instead of adding body parts and ultimately 'hanging a man" (which is the game's usual game play), it is reversed so that a captive man (Hank) that is in a hanging cage, is released. By each correct guess, the player is gradually breaking a bit off the cage so that eventually the man in the cage can escape.

In *Love is in the Air* the player helps with his/her finger the alien hero, Noa, to reach his loving match Noi, through an animated maze (Fig.4). There is no single correct route, as the maze elements move and change the correct route on the fly. It differs to the other two games in that it has a gameplay consists of several very different mazes with animated elements (i.e. UFOs, Pools with fish, aliens, etc). It is characterized by increased difficulty, large variety, surprise (in what will follow), and funny animated elements.

Fig. 4. Love is in the Air: an animated maze game with variety and increasing complexity

3   Evaluation

The memory game titled as "amnesia of Who" was designed, programmed (along with its original music score and sound design) and was presented to a number of 5 children, aged between 4-9 years old, for an initial evaluation in order to get a valid feedback [5]. The evaluation used a 12-questions likert scale questionnaire, with criteria based on Game Usability Heuristics [2], while the criteria mentioned in [3],[4] were also considered.

All three games have a common underlying graphical style so that they form a very recognizable set. Each game has an underlying simple scenario, a trait that is not common practice for casual games in general. As was pointed out from the games evaluation, the existence of a simple scenario line as well as the choice of bold graphics and colors were specific characteristics that attracted the interest of children's and made the games much more enjoyable in the age group between 4 and 9.

Especially regarding the enjoyment factor to the games, the subjects responded very positively. The emotional involvement of the children, -achieved via the game scenario whereby the kids tried to help the hero in each case-, was a crucial defining factor towards their overall enjoyment.

The evaluation also pointed out at other possible adjustments for further improving this type of game typology. Further details on the design concepts and evaluation can be found in [1].

Acknowledgements. We would like to thank Vaso Dimitriou, composer and musician, who has composed the music and created the sound design in the game "Amnesia of Who"; and George Birbilis, computer and informatics engineer, who consulted on game requirements and programmed the game for windows mobile phones. Without them, the games described here would not have come into 'life'.

References

1. Vasiliki, A.: Master Degree thesis in Graphic Arts-Multimedia. School of Applied Arts, Hellenic Open University
2. Desurvire, H., Wiberg, C.: Game usability heuristics (play) for evaluating and designing better games: The next iteration (2009), http://www.behavioristics.com/downloads/DesurvireFinalHCI09PLAY.pdf
3. Falstein, N., Barwood, H.: The 400 Project (2006), http://theinspiracy.com/400_project.htm
4. Koivisto, E., Korhonen, H.: Mobile game playability heuristics (2006), http://www.forum.nokia.com/
5. Nielsen, J. (2006), http://www.nngroup.com/articles/quantitative-studies-how-many-users/

"Logical Blocks" Multimedia Game Development for Students with Intellectual Disabilities

Cecilia Sik Lanyi, József Klung, and Veronika Szücs

University of Pannonia, Veszprem, Hungary
lanyi@almos.uni-pannon.hu, kungl_jozsef@freemail.hu,
szucs@virt.uni-pannon.hu

Abstract. This paper presents the design process of an interactive game that can help to improve the recognition-skills of the children with intellectual disability, so later they can make their way in life easier. This article presents the interactive game, which is based on the traditional logical blocks tutorial. The game has been tested by special education teachers and students with moderate intellectual disabilities. According to teachers' view the game is useful for teaching students with moderate intellectual disabilities.

Keywords: intellectual disability, multimedia game, user needs.

1 Introduction

The purpose of the research showed in this article, was to create an interactive game for students with intellectual disability. In Hungarian education system the traditional logical blocks games set (Figure 1), which is made of plastic, is used for teaching mathematics for first-grade elementary school children aged 6-7. This article presents the development process of the interactive game "Logical blocks" based on the plastic game set; the functional and non-functional requirements; and the testing of the prepared game by special education teachers and students with moderate intellectual disabilities in a special education school. The hypothesis is verified by this: the "Logical blocks" interactive game, which was designed for young students – based on the already proven, traditional teaching material for math education, – is a useable teaching material for students with moderate intellectual disabilities.

1.1 Games in the Education

Instructional computing is widely used for classroom multimedia digital media presentations and interactive exercises for interactive computer-based training. There may be real benefits in using games for learning: "…research has shown that learning is much more effective when the student has fun" [1]. This is one of the main reasons for using games to educate, as much more is learned when the student is enjoying the education. Another reason is that "…computer games provide a good environment for learning because they are able to give instant feedback to the player, which is highly beneficial for learning" [2], [3].

C. Stephanidis (Ed.): HCII 2014 Posters, Part II, CCIS 435, pp. 371–375, 2014.

2   Developing Method

The software is being made using Adobe Flash CS4 and with ActionScript programming language. The user interface is very simple and very clearly organised. It is important for the target group, because in this way they are able to concentrate on the new information being presented rather than any additional burden created by non-intuitive navigation [4].

2.1   Specification of Requirements

The most important aspects of the design were the requirements of the special needs school. One of the requests was to allow access from all sub-menus with one click back to the main menu, so that the children cannot get lost in the "maze" of the program. Another important request was to incorporate clear markings, buttons and icons, so that it would be always possible to know exactly what will happen after the use of a given element. A further request was that everything that appears in a written form should also be read out aloud, so that younger children, or children, who cannot read could also understand the tasks to be done. An additional request was to create a demonstration site for every task. Here, information about the use and operation of the game can be found. The program should read out the tutorial of the task and at the same time should present the tasks step by step. After the task is clear, the users can push the 'next' button they can proceed and begin using the application.

Furthermore, a general guideline was that at different games, the same or similar elements should be guided by the same buttons (e.g. the exit button is the same everywhere). In the case of the use of colours we should also be consistent, this is the reason why there are no disturbing backgrounds or images while using the application.

2.2   The "Logical Blocks" Game

The "Logical-blocks" game idea is based on the traditionally used physical game "logical bricks" (Figure 1).

Fig. 1. Traditionally used "Logical bricks" in the early elementary education

Using the "Logical-blocks" game the task is going to be to recognize forms and colours with the long-known logic bricks lab, so that their skills can improve. On the basis of colours they can differentiate rings, squares and triangles, small and big, hollow and full slabs. It can make the learning and the improvement more enjoyable for them. This method has been applied everywhere, in the kindergarten as well as in schools. Having an idea from this, a well-known game into the computer was brought, so that the modern digital technic can take a part in teaching.

Some tasks will be achieved on different difficulty levels, which can help to improve the children's skills step by step. After they have easily recognised the shapes, they can also play with games, from which some easier tasks will also be achieved in which they can use their newfound skills.

Every task was presented appropriately for the children. Thinking about the possibility that they cannot write yet as an effect of their disability or simply because of their age, every description or the texts printed out in the tasks are going to be read out, since the program is first of all for smaller children. The submenus, of the "Logic-blocks" game are (Figure 2): Simple sorting, Sorting into sets, Pattern production, Quantities large and small signals relational practice, as a reward building formations, figures from the blocks.

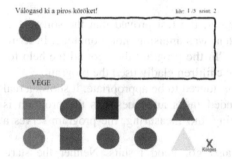

Fig. 2. Sort out the red circles!

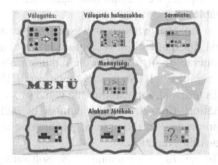

Fig. 3. The main menu of the game

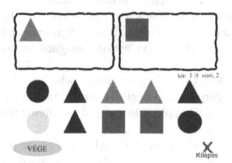

Fig. 4. Sorting into two sets

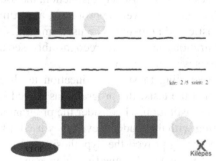

Fig. 5. Pattern production task

An example for sorting into sets can be seen on Figure 3., where the task for the student is to sort out, from the pictures in two rows at the bottom of the screen, the required images to the black frame at the upper right corner of the screen; e.g. sort out the red circles, for which the instruction is written in the upper left corner of the screen.

Figure 4 shows the sorting into two sets, here the task is to sort the green triangles to the left set, and the red squares to right set. Figure 5 presents an example for the pattern production task. In the upper line the student can see the pattern that he/she has to create, e.g. after blue and red squares a yellow circle should follow. This pattern should be continued with picking out the correct item from the two lines of objects at the bottom of the screen.

3   Test and Results

The game has been tested in a school, where students with moderate intellectual disabilities are studying. In the testing 15 children between the ages of 10-16 have participated. The testing was performed by a special education teacher. During the test four aspects were examined: applicability, operability, graphics, and whether it's enjoyable.

In the case whether it was enjoyable or not, the test proved that the software is good. Its application was not tiring; its content was amusing, not monotone. In terms of operability it fully met the requirements. "In the program they got all the help for the handling". It can be said that, overall, the children gladly used the program.

In terms of applicability the game was considered to be appropriate. It shows a real situation. Considering the number of included tasks and questions the program is appropriate. "In the case of teaching counting and measuring, the program serves a gap-filling function."

In regard to operability, the software also got good results. Neither the starting/quitting nor the usage of the program meant any problem, because of the helping signs for orientation. The contents were duly separated from each other. The sounds and images did not cause any distraction; the used speaking voice was understandable.

The graphics were appropriate, according to the feedback users considered it to be realistic and amusing. The used images, shapes were adequate. The backgrounds and illustrations used were recognizably separated. The action options assigned to the shapes were followable.

According to special education teacher, Mrs.Lilla Vági's opinion, who has performed the tests, the program has served its purpose and is gladly used at the educational institution. "I consider the program as a well-applicable material and during the testing with the students even they used it kindly."

The testing proved the hypothesis, according to which the "Logical blocks" is an interactive game, designed for elementary school students' math education – based on the already used traditional educational material – and is useful for the development of students with moderate intellectual disabilities.

4   Conclusion

In this paper the design and evaluation of the "Logical Blocks" game and its user interface have discussed. This game was developed for students with learning difficulties to help them learn the logical thinking and activities of daily living and at the same time to teach them how to use the computer and how to navigate on the Internet. Because learning the „and" and „or" logical function is very important. Without this knowledge searching a phrase on the internet is impossible. Teaching counting measurements and logical thinking, this game is a niche modern education tool.

As a final result, a successful game was created to help them getting over disabilities and getting integrated smoothly into the society. The „Logical Blocks" game's usability and pedagogical test was made in the Kozmutza Flora Special School in Veszprem.

References

1. Koops, M.C.: Digital adventure game-based learning (2008),
   http://www.drkoops.nl
2. Prensky, M.: Digital natives, digital immigrants. On the Horizon, NCB University Press 9(5) (2001)
3. Brown, D.J., Shopland, N., Battersby, S., Tully, A., Richardson, S.: Game On: accessible serious games for offenders and those at risk of offending. Journal of Assistive Technologies 3(2), 13–25 (2009)
4. Sik Lanyi, C., Brown, D., Penny Standen, P., Lewis, J., Butkute, V.: Results of user interface evaluation of serious games for students with intellectual disability. Acta Polytechnica Hungarica 9(1), 225–245 (2012)

Lower Member Game for Exercising Using Affordable 3DUIs

Alvaro Uribe-Quevedo[1], Sergio Valdivia-Trujillo[1],
Eliana Prada-Dominguez[1], and Byron Perez-Gutierrrez[2]

[1] Industrial Engineering, Mil. Nueva Granada University, Bogota, Colombia
alvaro.j.uribe@ieee.org, {sergiodragoon,elugreen}@gmail.com
[2] Mechatronics Engineering, Mil. Nueva Granada University, Bogota, Colombia
byron.perez@ieee.org

Abstract. Exercising requires the execution of repetitive activities with commitment and motivation that may not be present in all cases. Currently, the advances in mechanical, electronics and computer sciences have resulted in the development of several affordable 3DUIs used in entertainment such as the Wiimote, the Play Station Move, the Kinect and the newer trends like the MYO and the Epoc Emotive. 3DUIs have opened several possibilities of application in the wellbeing area outside physical rehabilitation; applications in entertainment, in exercising and even occupational healthcare are being developed. This project explores the development of game application for encouraging lower member exercises with game mechanics and affordable 3DUIs for impacting most users, whereas they are owners or newcomers to these technological trends. The proposed system integrates a gaming 3DUI with a smartphone for offering a portable and flexible solution that allows monitoring and motivating the user for performing preventive or corrective exercises.

Keywords: 3DUI, Exercise, Game, Therapy.

1 Introduction

Virtual Reality (VR) have been used as physical therapy tools given their immersive and interactive features for encouraging and improving rehabilitation processes while monitoring, quantifying and enhancing the quality of life of the user [1]. Current developments in the field have been focused providing interactive and immersive environments for patients recovering from stroke [2], focusing on motivation and distraction for succeeding on the rehabilitation process.

Although these developments are focused on patients, VR and game mechanics may be translated to other health-related scenarios for preventing musculoskeletal disorders. The World Health Organization (WHO) establishes that 20% of the world's population suffers some type of musculoskeletal disorder, and these are among the most common cause of work absence [3]. Most available solutions are offering entertainment and gamified fitness approaches based on motion capture based on 3DUI and games [4] and monitoring systems estimating burned calories, taken steps [5], thus, presenting a suitable scenario for developing an application for preventive exercising.

C. Stephanidis (Ed.): HCII 2014 Posters, Part II, CCIS 435, pp. 376–380, 2014.
© Springer International Publishing Switzerland 2014

This work presents the development of a lower member-exercising application using affordable 3DUIs as a complimentary tool for lower member exercising using game mechanics. The development is focused on a PC and Android version providing motion tracking for further assessment and game elements for increasing interest.

2   Methods

The first step in the development process is to identify the system's architecture for defining the corresponding inputs and outputs accordingly to the user and chosen feedback. The system receives inputs from the end user, the health-care administrator and the developer, as presented Fig.1.

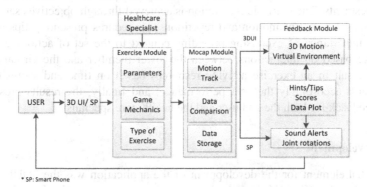

Fig. 1. System Architecture

The end user selects the exercise through arm and hand motions; once the exercise is chosen, the system tracks, compares and reports the motion data. The goals and mechanics of the exercise is determine by the health-care considering ranges of motion, repetitions and suitable movements. These are the fundamental aspects of the VR mechanics in the application. The feedback provided by the system allows the end user to monitor and keep track of his progression, for further medical assessments that may allow detecting or adjusting the exercises accordingly to the needs. An additional feature is the mobile subsystem that allows performing exercises with an Android smartphone; it presents the user with options for performing lower member exercises with motion tracking performed by the device's accelerometer.

2.1   Lower Member and Exercise Characterization

Lower member musculoskeletal disorders may affect human locomotion causing work absence and difficulties for performing daily activities [6]. Locomotion is possible thanks to the bones, muscles and ligaments that provide support and motion through extension/flexion and adduction/abduction provided in the joints. Major muscle activity during gait is found on the iliopsoas, gluteus maximus, gluteus medius, hamstrings, quadriceps, pretibial muscles and calf muscles [7], thus, weakened muscles may alter equilibrium and locomotor skills [8]. Basic exercises flexion/extension and abduction/adduction whose goal is to correct or prevent alterations; improve or reestablish motion; prevent or reduced health risks; and finally, optimize the overall health condition [9]. The chosen exercise is presented in Figure

2.2 Game Mechanics

The objective of the game mechanics is to provide an additional goal to the exercising process focusing on the formal game elements such as the players, objectives, procedures, rules, resources, conflicts and results [10]. The player has to accept the rules and objectives of the application for start using it; the approach taken takes advantage of the intrinsic motivation within every person for having an optimal physical health without mobility restraints. The extrinsic motivation is achieved through objectives set to obtain scores based on range of motion and repetitions; procedures presenting tips and hints about the importance of exercising providing context to the set of actions during the game; rules based on interactions between the lower member and the virtual environment that result in an exercise activity; resources based on time and scores obtained from rewards accordingly the user performance; and finally, the results presented to provide feedback for both the end user and the health-care specialist.

2.3 Development

A primordial element for the development of the application was the 3DUI, a survey presented that the Kinect [11] was the most common among the interviews users, because of the development possibilities with Microsoft's SDK for non-gaming applications [12], over others like Sony's PSMove [13]. The application is modularly developed in two main modules, one for PC and other for Android smartphones. The prototype for PC was developed using Unity3D free [14] and Zifu Kinect ZDK demo [15], the goal of using such technologies was to validate their suitability for fast developing an exercising gaming app. The development is composed of scripts running interaction between the tracked body, its 3D virtual avatar model and the environment accordingly to the goal of the exercise, considering its physics, rewards and important information about the activity. The mobile prototype allows exercising, scoring points and tracking user motion by placing the smartphone on the thigh or shank accordingly to the lower member part of interest. Both application measures flexion/extension motion and emit alerts on how well the exercise is executed. The dada can be synchronized with the PC application so both modules can keep track of user performance.

3   Results

A game application for lower member exercising was developed; it is composed of a PC and a mobile module using motion tracking. The PC module presents a virtual environment where the user kicks a ball in order to hit targets by performing flexion/extension as presented in Fig.2. During the activity, the user score points, while tracking and storing lower member motion for later assessment. The data contains information about position and orientation, providing measures and quantification.

The mobile module tracks the motion accordingly to the chosen exercise, without a 3D virtual environment. The feedback relies on scores depending on how well the execution was. Portability was achieved in both systems as the motion data can be imported and exported for keeping track of the activities. The application is design to be run on a smartphone attached to the lower member, thigh or shank as necessary, a test of the application is presented in Fig.3.

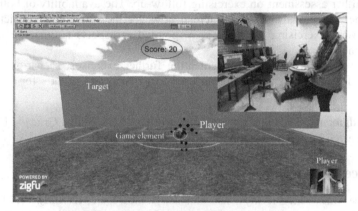

Fig. 2. Developed application GUI

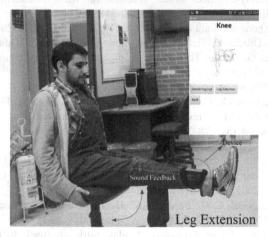

Fig. 3. Mobile app test with leg extension

For validating the developments, a survey was applied on potential users obtaining the following results: 80% do some form of exercise; 50% do it weekly, 25% daily and 25% monthly; 40% do it for fun, 20% for health and 20% for entertainment; 60% prefer exercising in open spaces, 20% at the gym and 20% at home; 60% own a Kinect, 20% a PSMove and 20% a Wiimote; 60% consider the application to be very useful and 40% useful; and finally, 100% would be interest in using the application.

4   Conclusions

The developed application allowed users to interact with an object going forward them and kick it away with flexion/extension lower member movements. From the survey it is possible to conclude that users are interested in complimentary tools for exercising that takes advantage of affordable 3DUIs such as the Kinect. Although the application only allows flexion/extension motion, users entertained while exercising, and also manifested curiosity in knowing and having access to the motion captured data for further assessment on exercising follow-up. The availability of both PC and Smartphone modules also caused interest, however the movement restrictions and lack of several exercising scenarios were pointed as aspects to improve in further developments.

Future works will focus on implementing further exercises, scenarios and game mechanics for interaction, focusing on user experience and reports for medical assessment.

Acknowledgments. The authors would like to thank Mil. Nueva Granada University and its Research Division for supporting Project ING1545.

References

1. Andreae, M.H.: Virtual reality in rehabilitation. B. Med. Jour. 312(7022), 4 (1996)
2. Jack, D., Boian, R., Merians, A.S., Tremaine, M., Burdea, G.C., Adamovich, S.V., Poizner, H.: Virtual reality-enhanced stroke rehabilitation. IEEE Transactions on Neural Systems and Rehabilitation Engineering 9(3), 308–318 (2001)
3. Lidgren, L.: The bone and joint decade 2000-2010. B. WHO 81(9), 629–629 (2003)
4. Nap, H.H., Diaz-Orueta, U.: Rehabilitation gaming. In: Arnab, S., Dunwell, I., Debattista, K. (eds.) Serious Games for Healthcare: Applications and Implications, pp. 50–75. IGI Global, Hershey (2012)
5. FitBit Personal Fitness, http://www.fitbit.com/us
6. Lawrence, R.C., Helmick, C.G., Arnett, F.C., Deyo, R.A., Felson, D.T., Giannini, E.H., Wolfe, F.: Estimates of the prevalence of arthritis and selected musculoskeletal disorders in the United States 41(5), 778–799 (1998)
7. Cuccurullo, S., Uustal, H., Baerga, E.: Gait analysis (2004)
8. Lewek, M., Rudolph, K., Axe, M., Snyder-Mackler, L.: The effect of insufficient quadriceps strength on gait after anterior cruciate ligament reconstruction. Clinical Biomechanics 17(1), 56–63 (2002)
9. Warburton, D.E., Nicol, C.W., Bredin, S.S.: Health benefits of physical activity: the evidence. CMAJ 174(6), 801–809 (2006)
10. Fullerton, T.: Game design workshop: A playcentric approach to creating innovative games. CRC Press (2008)
11. Microsoft Kinect, http://www.xbox.com/en-US/Kinect
12. The Kinect Effect, http://www.xbox.com/en-GB/Kinect/Kinect-Effect
13. Sony Play Station Move, http://us.playstation.com/ps3/playstation-move/
14. Unity 3D, https://unity3d.com/unity
15. Zigfu Kinect ZDK, http://zigfu.com/en/downloads/browserplugin/

Health and Well-Being

AraMedReader: An Arabic Medicine Identifier Using Barcodes

Norah I. Al-Quwayfili[1] and Hend S. Al-Khalifa[2]

[1] Center of Excellence for Telecom Applications, King Abdulaziz City for Science and Technology, Riyadh, Saudi Arabia
nalquwayfili@kacst.edu.sa
[2] Information Technology Department, College of Computer and Information Sciences, King Saud University, Riyadh, Saudi Arabia
hendk@ksu.edu.sa

Abstract. AraMedScanner is a prototype application that mainly helps the visually impaired to identify medicines by scanning their barcode and retrieving their information from a medical database. This paper presents an overview of AraMedScanner's features and shows preliminary evaluations conducted with blind people. The results of the evaluations revealed the application limitations and leaded to new future improvements.

Keywords: Medicine Identification, Barcode, Mobile computing, Assistive Technology, Visually Impaired.

1   Introduction

Nearly one million people in Saudi Arabia have visual impairment [1]. Visually impaired people confront a lot of difficulties in their daily life including the challenge in identifying medicines and reading their facts. As the process of medicines use is often considered a daily task, blind people always find it difficult to continually ask for sighted people help [2].

Various technologies (such as smartphone, phone line system, RFID and barcode scanners) have been utilized in order to help blind people and to get deeper understanding of their needs. All the developed systems aimed to assist blind people in different aspects of their life like: shopping, object recognition, face recognition, etc.

Still, there exist systems with new technologies that have not reached the level of delivering all their needs, either due to the requirement of special hardware and external devices or as a result of their high costs, e.g. barcode scanner devices.

Nowadays, with the growing trend of ubiquitous technologies; mobile devices are being considered a useful tool to support daily life needs. Many applications have been developed to facilitate daily life activities. But still the wide spread of these applications is not enough; since it rarely target blind people as the main users.

Our suggested solution is a smartphone application that aims to assist Arabic speaking blind and visually impaired people to identify medicines by scanning their barcode, get the medicines' information and manage their schedule.

C. Stephanidis (Ed.): HCII 2014 Posters, Part II, CCIS 435, pp. 383–388, 2014.

In this paper, we present a prototype application that mainly gives blind people the ability to scan medicines' barcode and retrieve their information from a medical database. As well, the paper shows the results of two preliminary evaluations carried out on blind people and the concluded suggestions and improvements to our application.

2   Related Work

Many systems and applications have been developed in order to get better understanding of visually impaired people needs. Technologies used in these systems vary from one to another and the systems differ in their use and purpose.

Many of the systems were concerned about shopping accessibility. Trinetra is an example of using an external device (barcode scanner) to help blind people in identifying products [3]. BlindShopping is another example of an application that is dedicated to help blind people navigate and identify products independently using RFID for navigation and QR code or Barcode through the smartphone camera for identifying products [4]. A similar smartphone application is an application that enables visually impaired users to find and read products barcode in real-time. The find and read process of the application passes two levels, the determination of barcode position and identification of the barcode and the retrieving of the corresponding product information from the database [5].

Another technology used in shopping accessibility is ShelfScanner, a real-time detection system of products in shelf store. This application depends on GroZi-120 dataset as products reference. The dataset is an available set of 120 grocery products that have been captured in different conditions [6].

For object identification, an application developed, based on Speeded Up Robust Features (SURF), which is a detector and descriptor algorithm that accelerates the interest point localization process, which maintains images' properties. The application helps blind people to find missing personal items through wearable camera connected to a computer [7].

In the medical field, an existing system in Hungary has been built and called Medicine Line system, which helps visually impaired people to reach medicines information easily through their mobile phones. The system consists of a speech recognizer for medicines' names, database and Speech Synthesizer [8]. Another system in the medical field, which is closest to our proposed system, is a system to help visually impaired people identify medicines based on their box visual features such as shape, color, etc. The experiment of this system was done on Windows OS using static webcam. Detection process passed the SURF features and in order to reduce processing time the Oveated model proposed by Gomes has been used [9].

As shown previously, the existing systems aimed to assist blind people in different ways and in different aspects of life. Yet, no portable system is found that is dedicated for identifying medicines in real-time and present their facts in an accurate way. And most importantly, no system was found that supports Arabic language. Our solution, unlike existing systems, is a portable smartphone application mainly targeting Arabic Speaking blind and visually impaired people. Developed to assist blind people to know exactly which medicine box they are holding, what its facts and give them the ability to add furthermore information as needed. In addition, blind users will have the ability to manage the medicine they currently take and set reminders.

3   Proposed System

The proposed system is a prototype Android application developed to help blind people identify medicines through barcode tags that are placed on medicines' boxes.

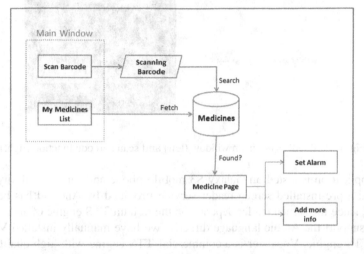

Fig. 1. Application Architecture

All the application's controls are accessible through Android screen reader, thus whenever the blind user presses on a control in the application it will be read by the screen reader. In some cases, like the instructions, the application fires an accessibility event that makes the TTS (Text-To-Speech) feature reads a specific sentence.

As shown in figure 1, the application starts with two options in the main window. First is the scanning of medicines' barcode option, which access device's camera to give the blind user the ability to scan the medicines barcode in real-time. The function starts with two instructions to the user: (1) "Try to point the camera correctly to the barcode tag" and (2) "Put a distance between the camera and the medicine box". When the barcode is detected, the medicine's information will be obtained, only if it exists in the application's medicine database. The database of medicines is obtained from the Saudi Food and Drugs Authority website, which includes all registered medicines' list in Saudi Arabia market [11]. The scanner feature in the application is built from Scandit [10], a barcode scanner API that accesses device's camera and starts real-time barcode detection.

The second option in the application is to display a list of medicines that the user currently takes. Moreover, if the medicine is on the user's list; the user will have the ability to set an alarm for the medicine and add further information about it.

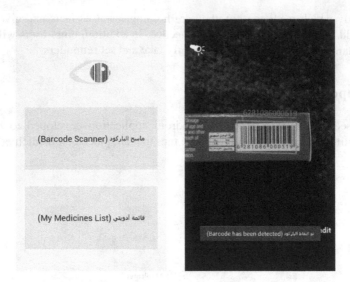

Fig. 1. AraMedReader main window (left) and scan barcode function (right)

The application is tested on Galaxy S3 mobile phone and for accessibility feature, TalkBack; a pre-installed screen reader service provided by Android has been used. However, since the screen reader depends on the default TTS engine of android which does not support the Arabic language directly; we have manually installed Vocalizer, another TTS engine. Vocalizer is a commercial TTS engine with high quality speech synthesizer that supports Arabic language, the Arabic voices packages have been downloaded from Vocalizer website [12].

4   Preliminary Evaluation

A visit to a blind organization has been conducted, and two blind people were chosen to perform the first evaluation of this application. They were asked to perform the following tasks: Scan Medicine's barcode, Add medicines to 'My Medicines List' and Set an alarm for the added medicines.

Both blind users have struggled in the first task, faced difficulties in pointing the camera correctly in order to detect the barcode. We found out that while the user is trying to point the camera she cannot determine whether the barcode has been detected or not yet, as there is no cues to indicate barcode's position. As a solution for the problem, we suggest to include an audio sound that starts playing once the user starts scanning the barcode, and stops once the barcode is detected.

After adding the suggested modifications to the application, another evaluation session has been carried out with a third blind user. A group of medicines boxes have been picked randomly from the user's medicines, three out of ten boxes only found containing barcode tags; this means not all medicines in the Saudi market contain barcode tags.

As a starter task, the blind user was asked to scan the barcode of the three boxes. In this evaluation session we tried to provide some verbal hints to the blind user regarding the preferable distance that should be between the camera and the box and where the barcode is likely found.

The results were as the follows: the first box took two minutes from the blind user to scan the barcode, the second box took five minutes and the third one took eight minutes. The difficulty in pointing the camera depends on barcode's position in the box, as it has no standard position for it.

The blind also was asked to perform other tasks such as opening the medicines list and setting the alarm, but she was confused and was not sure how to perform them.

From the previous evaluation and based on our observations we can find some limitation of our system. First, as was previously mentioned, not all the medicines boxes found in the market have a barcode tag; which means as long as the blind user cannot know if the box has barcode or not the application will be useless. Second, the problem of pointing the camera correctly to the barcode, which is considered one of the most known obstacles that blind people face in order to use the camera [13]. This issue was studied as part of a qualitative study to support blind people take pictures using mobile applications. The survey indicated that the most common problems with general photography-related activities are the problems of aiming, focusing and positioning and framing while taking a photo [13].

Therefore, the limitations of our application are not new and considered one of the common problems in blind people technologies. However, the application still in progress and there will be a next version that holds modifications to simplify the application to blind people and make it more accessible. The suggested solution that solves the problem of finding the barcode tag and solve the fact that not all Saudi medicines boxes contain barcode tag, is to use another technology beside barcode scanning like augmented reality and object recognition.

5 Conclusion and Future Work

This paper is an attempt to develop a smartphone application that helps the Arabic Speaking blind people identify medicines through their barcode tags. The barcode detection feature is built based on Scandit, a real-time barcode detection APIs. The prototype application offered a medicine's barcode scanner; a display of the list of medicines that the blind currently takes and a medicine's reminder function. In order to evaluate the prototype and determine the application's accessibility and the usefulness of its features, two preliminary evaluations have been conducted. The first evaluation obtained results that leaded to the suggestion of new improvement of the application. The second evaluation revealed the application major limitations. Firstly, as the result showed, not all medicine boxes in Saudi Arabia contain barcode tags. Secondly, as there is no standardized position for the barcode tag in the boxes; the blind takes a long time before reaching the barcode position correctly. Thirdly, blind people were confused during navigating the application.

However, the application still in progress; thus, as a future work there will be a next version of the application that holds new improvements that simplify the application for blind people. And as a solution for the boxes that misses barcode tags, augmented reality and object recognition will be used alongside with barcode detection. Finally, the beta version of the application is available for download from [14].

References

1. Al-Hamid, N.: Nearly 1 million in KSA are visually impaired" Arab News, http://www.arabnews.com/news/463054 (accessed: September 30, 2013)
2. Erin, B., Meredith, R.M., Yu, Z., Samuel, W., Jeffrey, P.B.: Visual challenges in the everyday lives of blind people. In: CHI 2013 Proceedings of the SIGCHI Conference on Human Factors in Computing Systems, pp. 2117–2126 (2013)
3. Lanigan, P.E., Paulos, A.M., Williams, A.W., Rossi, D., Narasimhan, P.: Trinetra: Assistive Technologies for Grocery Shopping for the Blind. In: 2006 10th IEEE International Symposium on Wearable Computers, Montreux, pp. 147–148 (2006)
4. López-de-Ipiña, D., Lorido, T., López, U.: BlindShopping: Enabling Accessible Shopping forVisually Impaired People through Mobile Technologies. In: The 9th International Conference on Smart Homes and Health Telematics, Montreal, Canada, pp. 266–270 (2011)
5. Tekin, E., Coughlan, J.M.: A Mobile Phone Application Enabling Visually Impaired Users to Find and Read Product Barcodes. In: Miesenberger, K., Klaus, J., Zagler, W., Karshmer, A. (eds.) ICCHP 2010, Part II. LNCS, vol. 6180, pp. 290–295. Springer, Heidelberg (2010)
6. Winlock, T., Christiansen, E., Belongie, S.: Toward real-time grocery detection for the visually impaired. In: The Computer Vision Applications for the Visually Impaired Workshop (CVAVI), San Francisco (2010)
7. Chincha, R., Tian, Y.: Finding objects for blind people based on SURF features. In: BIBM Workshops: IEEE, pp. 526–527 (2011)
8. Németh, G., Olaszy, G., Bartalis, M., Kiss, G., Zainkó, C., Mihajlik, P., Haraszti, C.: Automated Drug Information System for Aged and Visually Impaired Persons. In: Miesenberger, K., Klaus, J., Zagler, W.L., Karshmer, A.I. (eds.) ICCHP 2008. LNCS, vol. 5105, pp. 238–241. Springer, Heidelberg (2008)
9. Benjamim, X.C., Gomes, R.B., Burlamaqui, A.M.F., Gonçalves, L.M.G.: Visual identification of medicine boxes using features matching. Paper presented at the meeting of the VECIMS (2012)
10. Barcode Scanner Scandit SDK, https://ssl.scandit.com/account/sdk (accessed: September 29, 2013)
11. Saudi Food and Drug Authority, http://www.sfda.gov.sa/ar/Pages/default.aspx (accessed: October 10, 2013)
12. Vocalizer for NVDA, https://vocalizer-nvda.com/ (accessed: January 24, 2014)
13. Dustin, A., Lourdes, M., Sri, K.: A Qualitative Study to Support a Blind Photography Mobile Application. In: Proceedings of the 6th International Conference on PErvasive Technologies Related to Assistive Environments, PETRA 2013, Rhodes Island, Greece (2013)
14. AraMdScanner, https://play.google.com/store/apps/details?id=com.med.reader

"Two Faces and a Hand Scan"- Pre- and Postoperative Insights of Patients Undergoing an Orthognathic Surgery

Luisa Bremen[1], Johanna Kluge[1], Martina Ziefle[1],
Ali Modabber[2], Evgeny Goloborodko[2], and Frank Hölzle[2]

[1] Chair of Communication Science, Human Computer Interaction Center
RWTH University, Aachen, Germany
[2] Department of Oral and Maxilofacial Surgery, Universitätsklinikum Aachen,
RWTH Aachen, Germany
{Bremen,Kluge,Ziefle}@comm.rwth-aachen.de,
{AModabber,EGoloborodko,FHoelzle}@ukaachen.de

Abstract. The current study deals with an empirical approach to an improvement of the patient and doctor relationship of patients undergoing an orthognathic surgery. The aim is the development of an information and communication concept for a smooth and positive treatment for medicine and patient. Such an intervention is a decisive experience and needs to be treated very sensitive. Patients with jaw modulation often suffer from medical-functional as well as psychological problems. Also after surgery, the change of appearance might lead to adjustment disorder. Therefore, a well-elaborated treatment is needed and essential. Retrospective already operated patients were interviewed regarding their expectations, fear, hopes and wishes as well as their individual experience with the surgery. The addition of technical support in form of a 3D scan was also assessed. First results portray a big need of an improved medical education concept as well as an overall positive assessment of the 3D scan.

Keywords: Orthognathic surgery, medical treatment, information and communication concept, 3D Scan.

1 Introduction

Inherent or development related dentofacial abnormalities have a serious impact on medical-functional as well as on psychological well being of patients. Patients with jaw modulation often suffer from functional problems such as problems chewing, swallowing or even speaking properly. Moreover, also psychological problems e.g. emotional instability or low self-esteem because of "abnormal" appearance are just a few from many associated psychological difficulties [1-2]. An orthognathic treatment solves the functional problems of patients, but also may change their facial features. The face, as being one of the most complex parts of the body, reflects the individuality and social identity [3]. Changing ones´ face means changing ones´ identity. The face is a highly sensitive part of the identity of a person: it distinguishes persons, expresses emotions it stands for the appearance of a person [4]. Changing this

C. Stephanidis (Ed.): HCII 2014 Posters, Part II, CCIS 435, pp. 389–394, 2014.
© Springer International Publishing Switzerland 2014

meaningful part of the body results in often-dramatic modification. Objectively speaking, a surgery improves all the issues and problems a person is dealing with and enhances quality of life [5]. However, subjectively speaking, such a surgery requires a rapid integration of ones´ new facial appearance into the self-concept. Additionally, the process of an orthognathic intervention is very painful, long and risky that is why it causes a lot of fear. Last but not least, postoperative disgruntlement because of changed appearance might lead to adjustment disorder   [6]. This intervention therefore has to be handled with sensitivity and with a good psychological support. In order to support patients in an optimal way, a well-elaborated treatment needs to be designed. Our main research question is in how far the psychological strain, the consequences for the individual appearance and identity changes can be supported with the help of a sensitive information- and communication strategy.

In order to develop such a concept our study is arranged into two parts. The first part depicts results on a retrospective interview and questionnaire with patients who have already undergone surgery. An overview of these results will be presented in this paper. In a second step, a prospective study is conducted with patients who are still in treatment. Participants assess a questionnaire at five different moments during a time period of 6 months with different medical education type. One is conventional with plaster models. The second is a 3D simulation   [7], which already portrays the supposable facial appearance of the patients after surgery. In the end, results of the retrospective and prospective study will be evaluated, triangulated and are introduced into an information- and communication-concept.

2   Method and Results

In order to investigate patients´ satisfaction and needs before, during and after a surgery, we decided on a longitudinal study with standardized and self-administered interviews and questionnaires. The first part (retro perspective) of the study was explorative to get insights into the real needs and feelings of patients with an orthognathic operation. In order to understand the individual experiences in detail and to sense the way of coping of patients that already finished their treatment, a face-to-face interview was chosen. Additionally, patients were scanned with a 3D hand scan for two purposes: firstly, for the assessment of quality and usability by patients and secondly for technical data collection.

Interview and Questionnaire. An interview and questionnaire guideline was created, based on theoretical research and the status quo of findings in the relevant research field. Interviews were conducted face-to-face; with questionnaires, we reached participants via Internet. The survey instruments consisted of questions concerning: demographic data, personality traits, information type, positive and negative expectations before surgery and in how far they came true afterwards, social reaction, acceptance and support before and after surgery, assessment of education and treatment of doctors as well as acceptance of 3D scan and outlook for future patients.

Sample. 22 Participants with jaw surgery experience took part in the study with an age range from 20 to 62 years (M=33;SD=12). 14 participants were female and 8 were male. Participants were former patients of the university hospital Aachen and were contacted by their agreement to **take** part into research. Surgery was undergone between 3 and the latest 8 years ago from time of interview. The profession of patients compasses a wide range of activities (student, employees, free-lancer, baker, cosmetician, etc.).

Results. Results were analyzed by **frequencies** and qualitative data analysis by Mayring [8]. Open answers were collected and categorized and will be reported in the following part.

- *Reasons for surgery.* As people are individual, also reasons for undergoing surgery differs from patient to patient. The most mentioned reason was the functional one (45,5%, problems chewing), followed by aesthetic reasons (36%) such as facial appearance. Beside, social (5%), comorbid disorders (5%) and no medical reasons (8%) were named.
- *Information search.* Asked about where patients searched for information about the surgery and healing process, 55% received their information in the medical education by the medicine. Specifically asked, in which kind of media they informed themselves, Internet (60%), other experts (30%), secondary literature (30%) and contact with experienced patients were mentioned (18%). It turns out, that the medical education seems to be the most important information resource.

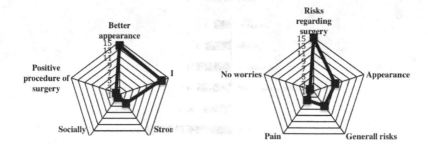

Fig. 1. Left: Categories of named expectations. Right: Categories of named worries. Multiple replies possible (N=22).

- *Expectations and hopes.* Participants were asked to remember their expectations they had before undergoing surgery. Figure 1 portrays the number of namings, participants reported. Multiple replies were possible. The outer black line in figure 1 left depicts the most mentioned expectations before surgery. Better appearance (14 namings) as well as the improvement of the jaw function (13 namings) was of great importance. Expectations and hopes, affecting the surgery, were often attached to the social life of the patients and their optic appearance. One expectation, which stands for the improvement of appearance, was "I was looking forward to have an open, unforced laugh" (female, 42 years). Functional reasons for the treatment were on the one hand directly linked to problems with chewing, swallowing, etc. On the other hand patients reported about physical complaints that derive from the malposition of the jaw, such as headache and tinnitus. Participants told us about suffering from physical complains and the decreasing quality of life resulting from this. One participant described e.g.: "Ringing in my ears and headache accompanied me daily. I had a hard time going to work, I was so restless due to the ringing and lack of sleep" (male patient, 40 years). His expectation on the surgery was evident (functional improvement). All in all, the responses correspond to the big influence a jaw modulation has both on the psychological well being and the functional problem as well the hope to solve or at least improve these problems. Finally, 10 patients stated that 100% of their expectation came true; the rest stated that at least 50% to 80% of their hopes arrived.

- *Fears and worries*. With such a hard and long treatment also fears and worries come along with hopes. Again multiple responses were possible. Participants were mainly afraid of emerging risks (15 naming) due to the surgery such as fear of complications, dying nerves as well as bad consequences among others. Fear of not receiving the expected appearance followed (7 naming), next to fear of pain (4 naming) (see figure 1 right). Half of the patient reported that at least one worry came true (nerves dying, strong pain, etc.).

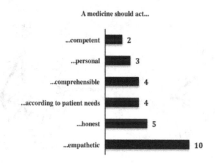

Fig. 2. Reported advice; Multiple responses possible ($\sum$=28 responses; N=22)

- *Advice to medicines*. Since the aim of the retrospective investigation was to get deeper insights into patient's needs who undergo surgery, the most important question was regarding the patients advice for medicines. It was an open question; multiple responses were possible. As being most important, participants mentioned the relationship between medicine and patient (25 naming), followed by communication and interaction (16 naming), good preparation of time and process after surgery (11 naming), medical expertise (10 naming), honesty (8 naming) and medical interaction (5 naming). Moreover a scenario was defined and had to be answered: *"Imagine, a medicine would ask you as an expert to give him advice on what he has to focus on particularly in order to be a good medicine?"*. Results can be seen in figure 2.

- *3D scan.* The willingness to include technical support in form of a 3D scan was assessed. Patients were introduced into a 3D program   [7], a picture of their face was taken and it was illustrated how the face could be turned and changed with the help of program features. This method allows, to give patients a possible picture of their face before surgery, portraying how they will look afterwards. 100% of the participants assessed it as a very positive method.

3   Discussion

This study represents a first empirical approach to an improvement of the patient and doctor relationship of patients who undergo orthognathic surgery. The aim was to identify first aspects among the medical treatment, which are essential for the development of an information and communication strategy including innovative technical support in form of a 3D scan. In the study former patients who have already experienced their treatment were interviewed and data was collected qualitatively. The data portray that patients with jaw malposition suffer from psychological and physical difficulties. The decision for a correction was described as a very decisive experience, which carries many worries but also expectations. Information about the treatment was mainly collected in the medical education the medicine has to hold before surgery. Therefore, the medical education is among the whole treatment the essential source for patients questions and needs special focus regarding a treatment improvement. As participants reported, the information has to be communicated sensitively and patients discomfort has to be taken seriously. Additionally, data showed that a visualization of the expected treatment result of the face would be very appreciated by patients and might lead to a higher overall satisfaction of the long and hard process.

The current data presented qualitative data in a retro perspective. Based on these findings, a second study is already running, focusing on the prospective time. Patients who are going to receive surgery participate and assess on five different periods of time the treatment (before surgery, 10 days after, 1 months after, 3 and 6 months after surgery). In order to evaluate the medical education including a 3D scan, patients are randomly divided into two groups. One groups receives the conventional medical education, the second group is educated with the help of the 3D scan of their current face before surgery converted into the expected face after surgery. In the end, results of the retro perspective study and the prospective study will be triangulated and introduced into an information and communication strategy.

Limitations of study and research duties. So far the study only includes German participants. The influence and experience of participants being from different cultures has to be included. A further aspect is the size of our sample. In order to report representative data, the sample has to be enlarged. On a long term, the question appears in how far an information and communication strategy in the field of jaw malposition under regard of technical devices for patient information is transferable to other medical fields.

4   Conclusion

In this paper, we presented an empirical approach to the improvement of the patient and doctor relationship especially in the orthognathic treatment. Interviews were conducted with patients who have already undergone a surgery. Results show, that there is a big need of the improvement of the medical education including innovative technical support (3D scan). The evaluation of such a treatment method is currently running in the prospective part of the study. The results will finally serve for the development of an information and communication concept for the medical treatment with the addition of 3d scan.

Acknowledgements. Authors would like to thank Florian Peters, Laura Burbach and Sarah Völkel for their research support. A special thank goes to all the participants who took part. The Excellence Initiative of the German Research Foundation DFG funded this work.

References

1. Philipps, C., Asuman Kiyak, H., Bloomquist, D., Turvey, T.: Perceptions of Recorvery and Satisfaction in the short term after Orthognathic Surgery. Journal of Oral and Maxillofacial Surgery 62(5), 535–544 (2004)
2. Modig, M., Andersson, L., Wårdh, I.: Patients' Perception of Improvement after orthognathic surgery: Pilot study. British Journal of Oral and Maxillofacial Surgery 44(1), 24–27 (2006)
3. Ekman, P., Friesen, W.V.: Constants across Cultures in the Face and Emotion. Journal of Personality and Social Psychology 17(2), 124–129 (1971)
4. Rivera, S., Hatch, J., Rugh, J.: Patients' own reasons and patient-perceived recommendations for orthognathic Surgery. Seminars in Orthodontics 6(4), 259–269 (2000)
5. Rustemayer, J., Gregersen, J.: Quality of Life in orthognathic surgery patients: Post-surgical improvements in aesthetics and self-confidence. Journal of Cranio-Maxillofacial Surgery 40(5), 400–404 (2012)
6. Cunningham, S.J., Crean, S.J., Hunt, N.P., Harris, M.: Preparation, perceptions, and problems: a long-term follow-up study of orthognathic surgery. The International Journal of Adult Orthodontics and Orthognathic Surgery 11(1), 41–47 (1996)
7. 3D Sahpe Gmbh, http://www.3d-shape.com/produkte/face_d.php
8. Mayring, P.: Einführung in die qualitative Sozialforschung. Eine Anleitung zu qualitativem Denken. Psychologie Verlags Union, Weinheim (1996)

Exploring the Relationship between Location and Behaviour in Out of Hours Hospital Care

Michael Brown, James Pinchin, Jesse Blum, Sarah Sharples, Dominic Shaw,
Gemma Housley, Sam Howard, Susan Jackson, Martin Flintham,
Kelly Benning, and John Blakey

Horizon Digital Economy Research
University of Nottingham, Nottingham, NG7 2TU, UK
michael.brown@nottingham.ac.uk

Abstract. 'Out of Hours' (OoH) hospital care involves a small number of doctors covering a very large number of patients. These doctors are working in stressful environments, performing complex tasks and making difficult task prioritisation decisions, yet little data exists to aid in improving the working practices or to ensure junior doctors are adequately prepared for OoH working. Historically, this has been owing to complex and expensive processes to capture this data; however recent advances in indoor positioning technologies has the potential to automate and improve the capture and availability of data that may help alleviate the burden of OoH care on at a personal and hospital level. This paper describes our work to combine cutting edge indoor positioning technologies from OoH working with and a newly deployed in-ward electronic tasking system. Here we describe data collection via traditional methods, clinical tasking systems, and indoor positioning solutions. We further describe our understanding from such data of the effect of physical layout and current working practices on task completion and time spent in transit, which ultimately may inform improvements to working practice within OoH care. Finally we discuss potential relevance to other work domains.

Keywords: Human Factors, Indoor Positioning, Out of Hours, Task Prioritisation, Clinical.

1   Introduction

Hospitals operate in an 'Out of Hours' (OoH) mode outside the traditional working day (which in the UK is 9-5, Monday to Friday, non-Holidays). OoH care tends to involve a small number of doctors treating a very large number of patients. For example in a large hospital, Nottingham City University Hospital it is typically 5-7 doctors to cover 700 patients over 24 wards. During these OoH shifts doctors work in stressful environments, perform complex tasks, and constantly make difficult task prioritisation decisions. They must simultaneously navigate large and often unfamiliar sites to locate wards, patients, other staff, and equipment.

Reducing stress and fatigue for these doctors is crucial to reducing error rates, and is a significant step towards minimising the preventable mistakes in hospitals which are estimated to cause hundreds of thousands deaths every year [12].

C. Stephanidis (Ed.): HCII 2014 Posters, Part II, CCIS 435, pp. 395–400, 2014.
© Springer International Publishing Switzerland 2014

The first hurdle in improving OoH care is to understand current practice/staff behaviour in order to identify both best practice and areas for improvement. Yet very little data exists regarding how these doctors move around hospitals and complete tasks over the course of their shifts [6]. Obtaining detailed data about OoH working practice may pave the way to optimise hospital layout and the effective incorporation of location into the staff tasking process In addition, such data can potentially feed into medical training to ensure junior doctors are adequately prepared for OoH working.

Historically, studying the behaviour of hospital staff has been a complex and expensive process involving a staff member physically 'shadowing' doctors at work. Recent advances in indoor positioning technologies enable the automated collection of high accuracy indoor location data [12]. The following describes methods that may be used to understand the effect of physical layout and current working practices on task completion and time spent in transit in OoH environments.

2   Review of Methods for Studying Out of Hours Care

Here we present various ways in which the behaviour of OoH Doctors can be studied, either directly or via location analysis. The methods are categorized within: traditional methods, tasking data, and location analysis.

2.1   Traditional Methods

Self-Report. Perhaps the most obvious ways of studying behavior is through self-report, or simply asking those who experience the phenomena about how they behave. Self-report methods include, but are not limited to: interviews, focus groups, diary studies and questionnaires. For example, a study developing a simulator to help junior doctors deal with night shifts [6] involved a series of focus groups and interviews exploring the expectations and experiences of medical students/junior doctors in relation to OoH working.

Self-report measures have the advantages of being non-invasive, may produce rich qualitative data, and are relatively easy to employ, however they are also difficult to scale, highly subjective, and vulnerable to a range of potential reporting biases [1].

Direct Observation. A second method commonly employed to studying behavior in workplaces is that of direct observation; involving researchers watching what workers are doing. A range of methods and methodological frameworks can be applied to guide how this is performed, data is recorded and analysis completed, such as ethnography, ethnomethodology, time-and-motion studies, and structured observation.

Richness of data is again an advantage of these methods, and compared to self-reporting, direct observation removes the potential for reporting bias from participants. However, observer effects may still influence the subjectivity of findings. Some techniques embrace this subjectivity as a core value of the method (e.g. [7]) where others use highly structured data collection and reporting in order to minimize its influence (e.g. [8]). Other than subjectivity, the main disadvantage of direct observation methods is the prohibitive cost of running observations at scale and subsequently the lack of generalizability of findings.

While both of these types of method are useful tools for collecting rich qualitative data about OoH working, their costs and subjectivity limit the generalisability of findings which is critical if these findings are to inform safety critical decision making.

2.2   Tasking Data

Recent advances in technologies to support OoH working such as the wireless working system described by Blakey et al [3] mean that increasing numbers of hospitals have potential to automatically capture task allocation and completion information from which behavior can be inferred. For example Blakey, Fern and Shaw [2] use such a system to explore the 'August Effect', i.e. the impact of newly qualified doctors joining teaching hospitals en mass has on quality of care, focusing on OoH working. These data present a valuable source of behavior information which is easily scalable and cheap to capture if appropriate infrastructure is already in place.

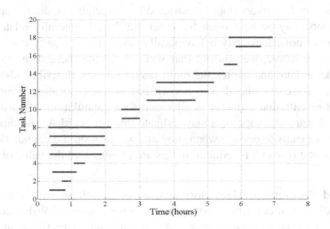

Fig. 1. A Gantt chart depicting accept/complete times for tasks from an OoH shift

Unfortunately, in isolation this type of data only allows high level analysis of task frequency as co-occurrence of tasks on the system, and system appropriation behaviour such as marking tasks as completed in batches. This reduces the value of individual task behavior timings. Consider, for example figure 1, which shows a sample of tasking data collected for a single doctor over one shift at Nottingham University City Hospital. This data shows the range of times doctors are assigned to multiple tasks, but does not present information with which to determine any particular task being performed at a given time In addition, such task data do not provide any insight into sub-task behaviour (such as finding a cannula, finding a patient, and placing items in the 'sharps bin').

2.3   Location Data

We propose that positioning data has the potential to provide insights into staff behavior in situations such as OoH care when tasks are geospatially distributed and the nature of tasks undertaken is related to current location [10].A range of potential technical solutions exist for establishing position in indoor environments, as described in detail by Brown, Pinchin and Hide [5]. For the purposes of this work we focus on three such methods based on the practicalities of working in hospital environments.

Security Swipe Card Logging. Hospitals contain many areas for which access is restricted, often though the use of swipe points linked to ID cards which open doors. Modern swipe card systems tend to log who has used them and when, giving a potential high accuracy by low frequency positioning solution, i.e. when someone swipes their card to access a location we can be reasonable certain they are located a short distance from the swipe point itself and about to enter the restricted area associated with it.

This data source is of limited use in isolation, as it tends to be spatially sparse & contain omissions (not every door is restricted by swipe access, doors may be propped open and doors may be held open for other staff) and generally relates to specific areas which are not necessarily behaviourally interesting (usually outside a ward or storage unit). However, we contend that when available these data may be used to enhance tasking data, and unpick the multi-tasking issues, described above, when the individual tasks are associated with known but different locations. For example, if tasking data reveals that a doctor is allocated to a cannulation in ward A and drug prescribing in ward B, swipe data may indicate entry to ward A, and thus would provide us with a means to deduce when they are working on the cannulation task. Further experimental research is required in this area to measure the value of swipe data.

WiFi Based Positioning. Many hospitals, especially those with wireless working systems (such as that described above), have high densities of WiFi access points in order to provide robust network connections throughout a site. Consequently, the use of WiFi signal strength captured by a wireless device (such as a mobile phone) has the potential to produce a positioning solution which is accurate to room level. Pinchin et al [9] for example, introduce a system for collecting and fusing WiFi data with tasking data, in order to explore task management behavior. This work shows algorithms that may be used to discriminate place (and therefore task) in some cases, although further research is required in this area towards a more universal solution.

WiFi data may provide more robust datasets than swipe cards (for instance fewer missing data points from behaviours such as people holding doors open for each other), as well as a more precise data set in that WiFi coverage may be widespread across all the rooms of a ward, whereas swipe cards tend to only be used at the entrance to a ward, or for special rooms. Both WiFi and swipe cards require alternative infrastructures and therefore, may be more or less appropriate for use depending on the context, and also may be used to supplement each other's positioning data.

Foot Mounted Inertial Navigation. A third positioning solution is dead reckoning based on foot mounted inertial measurement unit. This dead reckoning form of navigation measures the acceleration and rotation of the foot from a fixed starting point in order to determine current position/movement over time. Numerous previous publications [4,11] describe systems which uses this technology to produce positioning accurate to under 1 meter.

Figure 2 shows an example of the type of output this method produces with a trace showing movement though a ward and stop positions. These data are sufficiently accurate to determine movement between, and stops at, specific sub-room activity areas (such as patient beds, nurses' stations, drug stores and notes trolleys). Thus, this method has the potential to identify sub-task behaviours (such as looking at notes or searching for equipment). However, the technology involved is more invasive than the other two location methods, both physically (staff must wear a foot mounted sensor) and in terms of staff privacy/security (due to the highly accurate data collected).

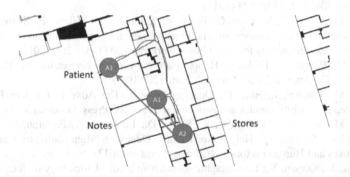

Fig. 2. Example output from Inertial Based Positioning with stop positions

3   Discussion

This paper has described methods for understanding staff behaviour during OoH hospital shifts. Traditional methods suffer from considerable limitations to their scalability and accuracy. Current forms of tasking data begin to provide course grained views of clinician activity, but as yet cannot be used to gain sufficient understanding of the clinical situations in order to make substantial alterations to working practice. Positioning data, especially when combined with the tasking data, however, has considerable potential to capture empirical evidence of existing behaviours in a scalable manner and reveal opportunities for improvements to hospital infrastructure and procedures in order to minimise clinician burden.

The concept of position based behaviour observation also has the potential to be applied in other work domains where tasks are spatially distributed and the nature of behaviour is dependent on current location (such as the construction industry).

Further work is needed to refine location based solutions, to understand how best these methods can be used together, and to confirm their practical values within OoH hospital situations and other work domains.

Acknowledgements. This work was funded by the RCUK Horizon Digital Economy Research Hub grant, EP/G065802/1.

References

1. Adams, A.S., Soumerai, S.B., Lomas, J., Ross-Degnan, D.: Evidence of self-report bias in assessing adherence to guidelines. International Journal for Quality in Health Care 11(3), 187–192 (1999)
2. Blakey, J.D., Fearn, A., Shaw, D.E.: What drives the 'August effect'? A observational study of the effect of junior doctor changeover on out of hours work. JRSM Short Reports 4(8), 2042533313489823 (2013)
3. Blakey, J.D., Guy, D., Simpson, C., Fearn, A., Cannaby, S., Wilson, P., Shaw, D.: Multi-modal observational assessment of quality and productivity benefits from the implementation of wireless technology for out of hours working. BMJ Open 2(2) (2012)
4. Brown, M., Pinchin, J.: Exploring Human Factors in Indoor Navigation. In: The European Navigation Conference 2013, Vienna, Austria (2013)
5. Brown, M., Pinchin, J., Hide, C.: Opening Indoors: The Advent of Indoor Positioning. In: Contemporary Ergonomics and Human Factors. CRC Press, London (2013)
6. Brown, M., Syrysko, P., Sharples, S., Shaw, D., Le Jeune, I., Fioratou, E., Blakey, J.: Developing a Simulator to Help Junior Doctors Deal with Night Shifts. In: Contemporary Ergonomics and Human Factors. CRC Press, London (2013)
7. Charmaz, K., Olesen, V.: Ethnographic research in medical sociology its foci and distinctive contributions. Sociological Methods & Research 25(4), 452–494 (1997)
8. Mintzberg, H.: Structured observation as a method to study managerial work. Journal of Management Studies 7(1), 87–104 (1970)
9. Pinchin, J., Brown, M., Blum, J., Shaw, D., Blakey, J.: 2014 IEEE/ION Position, Location and Navigation Symposium (2014)
10. Pinchin, J., Brown, M., Flintham, M., Sharples, S., Shaw, D., Housley, G., Blakey, J.: Location Analysis for Hospital Doctors Working Out of Hours. In: Proceeding of the 2013 Digital Economy Conference, Salford, UK (2013)
11. Pinchin, J., Hide, C., Moore, T.: A particle filter approach to indoor navigation using a foot mounted inertial navigation system and heuristic heading information. In: International Conference on Indoor Positioning and Indoor Navigation, IPIN (2012)
12. The Royal College of Physicians. Hospitals on the edge? The time for Action. The Royal College of Physicians, London (2012)

The Assistive Device Design for Macular Hole Surgery Postoperative Face-Down Positioning

Yi-Yang Gao, Cheng-I Tsai, Ssu-Erh Hsu, and Ming-Hsu Wang

Department of Industrial Design, Chang Gung University,
Taoyuan,-Taiwan R.O.C.
citsai@mail.cgu.edu.tw

Abstract. Doctors more often choose to apply pneumatic retinopexy therapy to retinal detachment patients. Successful rate of pneumatic retinopexy depends on can comply with requirement of supine posture. This study is focusing on design and application of how the successful rate of surgery of pneumatic retinopexy can be improved and on the user' s experience of this aid design. This study did confirm that a recovery table helped reduce burden of necks and shoulders.

Keywords: pneumatic retinopexy, universal design, rehabilitation tables.

1 Introduction

As the technology advances, people's lifestyles are changing gradually, for example many people are staring at the screens for hours each day without having any rest. It has shown that those who are in severe myopia are 131 times more likely to be prone to retinal detachment. Doctors more often choose to apply pneumatic retinopexy therapy to retinal detachment patients. By injecting a certain gas which is able to expand in eye balls to the vitreous bodies, pneumatic retinopexy is applied to seal the tears by buoyancy and surface tension of the gas. However, patients need to follow doctor's instruction to remain in a specific supine posture in a fairly long time in order to keep the retinal in properly pressurized position.

Such surgery can reach around 80% successful rate for patients who are in preliminary stage. While correct post-surgery posturing is a key factor leading to success of the surgery, if patients can strictly follow the instruction of maintaining supine posture for more than 16 hours per day, post-surgery repair rate can reach up to 95%. According to the survey of Linkou Chang Gung Hospital over the re-entered patients within 14 days, because of lack of appropriate aids, it has been found that those who need to receive surgery repetitively due to being unable to comply with supine position requirement. Thus, when those patients try to maintain supine position, considerable burdens are resulted to the necks, shoulders, and other parts of the body, and leads to problems such as post-surgery inappropriate supine posture or insufficient supine posture time, or further reduce the post-surgery repair rate.

C. Stephanidis (Ed.): HCII 2014 Posters, Part II, CCIS 435, pp. 401–406, 2014.
© Springer International Publishing Switzerland 2014

2   Literatures

2.1   Discussion on the Retinal Detachment

Current Status of Diseases of Retinal Detachment. Since Taiwan is currently step-ping into an aged society, people are more tended to suffer from retinal disorders, age-related macular degeneration, retinal detachment, and other retinal related diseas-es resulting from diabetes, hypertention, and severe myopia. If people do not increase with their own level of cautiousness, it is foreseeable in 2020 the population of patients can double or triple and the resulted medical costs would also increase in multiple folds (Cheng, Chiou, Lo, & Lu, 2006). According to analysis of eye-related disease from the National Health Insurance Research Database from 1999 to 2003, it has been shown that the population of retinal-related diseases in the 5 years reaches 188,370. The averaged prevalence rate of diabetic retinal disorders and that of aged-related macular degeneration are 2.81% and 8.54%, respectively.

Relevant Researches on Pneumatic Retinopexy. Since 1985, due to the features of causing less injury to eye tissues, no severe complications, and less medical costs, pneumatic retinopexy is currently a trend for retinal surgery (Brinton & Hilton, 2001). According to evaluations, at least 40% of patients of rhegmatogenous retinal detach-ment chose this therapy and reached a certain level of therapeutic effect. From 2003 to 2005, Taiwanese eye doctors have conducted researches of half-year tracing re-searches over 60 patients of retinal detachment, and it has been showing that the suc-cessful repair rate after operation of pneumatic retinopexy only is 60%, whereas when the operation is applied together with other surgeries the repair rate reaches 100% (Tsai, Chang, Chou & Liou, 2007).Successful rate of pneumatic retinopexy depends on 3 key factors (Chan, Lin, Nuthi, & Salib, 2008): (i) Whether applied together with cryopexy or laser coagulation. (ii) Gas injected to eye balls. (iii)Whether the patient can comply with requirement of supine posture for 5-7 days, or even 7-14 days, until the retinal re-attached or the tears sealed.

2.2   Gist of User-Oriented Designs

Current Status of Supine Postures of Patients Received   Pneumatic Retinopexy.
For repairing the retinal to re-attach, patients of retinal detachment have to adopt su-pine postures for several weeks after surgery. However, patients are often not able to continuously remain as supine posture which is an unnatural one as shown in figures below.

Table 1. supine posture

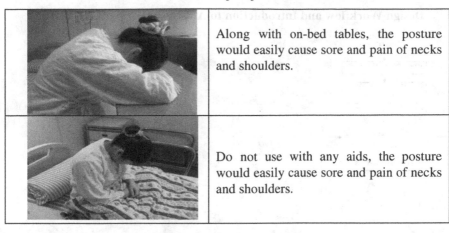

	Along with on-bed tables, the posture would easily cause sore and pain of necks and shoulders.
	Do not use with any aids, the posture would easily cause sore and pain of necks and shoulders.

Discussion on Design-Orientation. Researchers have been showing that constantly repetitive movements, excessive forcing, or adopting inappropriate postures would cause accumulative professional injuries. Such injuries resulting from repetitive wear-outs and strains of tendons, tendon sheaths, ligaments, nerves and muscles account for majority of causes of labors' musculoskeletal discomforts (Kasdan & Kasdan, 1991). Therefore, the user-oriented designs and ideas prioritize on how the level of fatigue can be effectively decreased. Also, the scope of users' arms and legs stretching room when in supine postures is also influential to comfortableness.

2.3   Comprehensive Designs

The Future Trends in Comprehensive Designs. In a seminar in visiting Taiwan Creativity Design Center in March 2004, German Executive Director of iF Design Awards Ralph Wiegmann clearly pointed out that the Awards praise a Universal Design of global prevalence instead of a fashion merchandise of merely refined material or cultural styles. He also emphasize that "from the perspective of industrial design, a design of merit is one that creates a product which can be used by anyone".

Concept of Universal Design. Universal Design is one of the most important trends in history of aid development. The concept of Universal Design should be construed in a sense that an aid can provide convenience to the handicaps, as well as being used by anyone. Thus, it is hoped that the subject population of aid usage can be expanded from the basis of the design so that the designed and produced aids can be available for everyone in a largest scope (Hsu, 2008).

3   Introduction to Design and the Surveys on Users

3.1   Design Workflow and Introduction to Aid Design

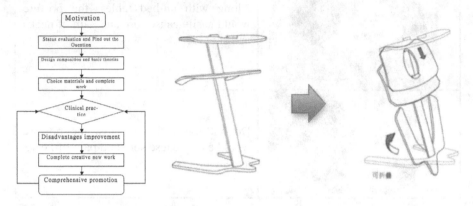

Fig. 1. Design Workflow   **Fig. 2.** By folding it can be placed underneath the bed or any other spaces

this design is user-oriented and emphasize on : I. Comfortableness, II. Safety, III. Convenience of Shelving, and IV. Esthetics

Based on user-oriented designs, comfortableness, esthetics, convenience of shelving are all factors to design. Users can use the aids together with any kinds of chairs, for example, when the head is placed easily on the table surface of the aid both arms would be able to reach out spaciously and legs stretch out freely. When the design is simple and direct the aid is more of esthetics.

3.2   Surveys on Users' Preference

User's experience and preference is a critical factor to the orientation of designs. We created an environment that is similar to hospital for users to experience. Users are requested to fill in satisfaction questionnaires so that the surveyors are able to understand the subjective mindset and feelings. A questionnaires survey on 20 patients using recovery tables after surgery by random sampling was done. The individual acceptance of such device is reviewed under simple scoring in terms of 4 concepts: comfort, safety, handy storage and good looking. The figures of satisfaction in comfort, safety, handy storage and good looking are 69.4%, 69.2%, 72.6% and 66.0%, respectively. The satisfaction pursuant to individual body sizes by 51% pinpoints that such design is unfriendly to diverse users. On the other side, the satisfaction in comfort by 74.0% proves that such device did help advance compliance of lying gesture by reduced labor load.

The questionnaires survey identified some findings as follow. Such device helped users lessen burden of necks and shoulders, but comfort of shoulders and clearance of hands were unsecured since the top and middle levels are not well designed. In fact, most users accustomed to reading or using handheld devices are in need of adequate room. The findings indicate that such assistive device helped advance personal willingness as well as compliance of lying gesture in a long run for pneumatic retinopexy due to reduced burden of necks and shoulders and less fatigue. The positive feedbacks and precious advices were noted as well. Such outcome identifies high acceptance of a recovery table after surgery as well as the references to its future direction and ideas of promotion.

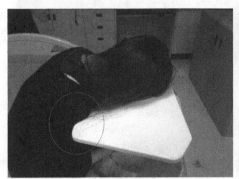 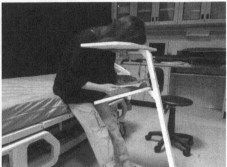

Fig. 3. Shoulder interference   **Fig. 4.** Hand space

4   Conclusions

This study did confirm that a recovery table helped reduce burden of necks and shoulders. The data acquired and assayed identify less fatigue, but satisfaction fails to be high due to issues in appearance, good looking, prices and how to use. Thus, design shall include the mental factors such as good looking, how to use and price besides physical concerns.

This study fails to employ comparative research owing to the insufficient literature relating to recovery tables. According to the preceding data assayed and remarks concluded, it is suggested to do more studies on design with flexile heights and adequate rooms for heads and hands as well as simple operation free of impact on good looking for advanced satisfaction. Also, the author is expecting to initiate profound research and review on related issues by promoting such assistive device.

Acknowledgement. The research presented in this article was funded by a grant from Chang Gung University Research Program (CGURP UARPD3C0011) support this study.

References

1. Brinton, D., Hilton, G.: Pneumatic retinopexy and alternative retinal detachment techniques. Retina 3, 2047–2062 (2001)
2. Chan, C.K., Lin, S.G., Nuthi, A.S., Salib, D.M.: Pneumatic retinopexy for the repair of retinal detachments: a comprehensive review (1986–2007). Survey of Ophthalmology 53(5), 443–478 (2008)

3. Cheng, R.-H., Chiou, H.-Y., Lo, H.-C., Lu, D.-W.: Taiwan Retinal Disease Study: Prevalence And Risk Factors. Taiwan J. Ophthalmol. 45(3), 171–177 (2006)
4. Hsu, Y.-L.: Elderly Welfare technology and tele-home care technology. Tsang Hai (2008)
5. Kasdan, M.L.: Kasdan: Occupational hand & upper extremity injuries & diseases. Hanley & Belfus, Philadelphia (1991)
6. Tsai, C.-Y., Chang, T.-J., Chou, P., Liou, S.-W.: Pneumatic Retinopexy for Rhegmatogenous Retinal Detachment. Taiwan J. Ophthalmol. 46(1), 8–12 (2007)

eNurse. A Mobile System for Improving the Quality of Treatment for Cancer Survivors

Adrian Iacomi and Thomas Pederson

IT University of Copenhagen, DK-2300 Copenhagen, Denmark
contact@adrianiacomi.com, tped@itu.dk

Abstract. In this paper we make a short analysis of the existing cancer care system, and we identify the elements that can improve the quality of treatment for cancer survivors. Through literature reviews and patient interviews we have identified two of the most important: doctor efficiency and patient active involvement. Our findings have shown that to improve both of them, a better communication system between patients and caregivers is required. Our project was made with three design iterations, each including testing sessions with real patients and healthcare personnel. We have used two main heath care theories: patient empowerment and post-traumatic growth. The resulting system has two separate web apps, one for the doctors and one for the patients.

Keywords: eCare, Cancer survivors, Mobile apps, Patient Empowerment, Post-traumatic Growth, Cancer care.

1 Introduction

In 2008, the number of given cancer diagnostics was of 12.7 million just in the United States [1], and since then this number has increased slowly. This is a disease that affects males and females, disregarding the age or the social status. Alongside the patients there are other categories affected by the disease: family, friends, co-workers and medical personnel. Doctors at their turn are overcrowded with patients and have a very limited amount of time to dedicate to each of them, not to consider the stress level they endure. Right now there is no dedicated eCare system for cancer survivors, even if the same problems are encountered in Denmark, Romania, UK and US (countries on which we have focused our research).

The present paper is based on the master thesis with the same name [1], with a focus on the research made and the resulting system.

2 Methodology

The research was based on classical User Experience (UX) principles as described by Unger [2] and has followed through the entire design process an iterative cycle with three phases, each of them including design, implementation and evaluations periods. The initial research was based on various interviews [1], [3] with cancer survivors and

C. Stephanidis (Ed.): HCII 2014 Posters, Part II, CCIS 435, pp. 407–412, 2014.
© Springer International Publishing Switzerland 2014

on articles on cancer care [4] published in oncology oriented mediums. An important element was the creation of the Cancer survivor environment (Fig 1) which helped us a lot during the creation of the personas and scenarios necessary during the design cycles.

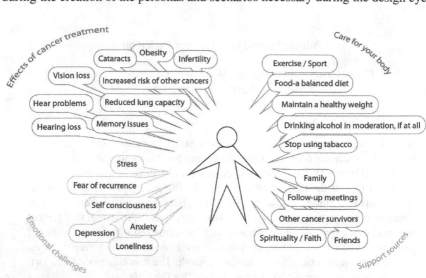

Fig. 1. Cancer survivor environment

Design Process. To create the final system, we have gone through an iterative design process described in detail in Fig 2.

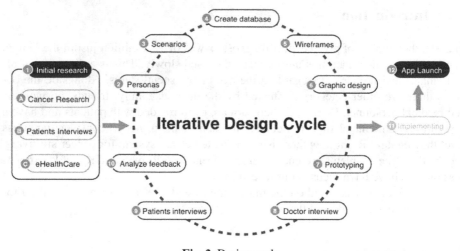

Fig. 2. Design cycle

During our research we have conducted several interviews [1] with cancer patients from Romania, cancer care medical personnel from Denmark and we have concluded several interviews with one of the best oncology experts in Romania. The existing cultural differences between these systems where not controlled for. The patients selected for interviews were coming from various social backgrounds and were in different stages of treatment. Based on them we have created personas and scenarios to test the apps.

After each implementation phase we have conducted user tests with the latest version of the application with both patients and the oncology expert who has supported us during the tests.

3   System Design

In the creation of the system we have taken into consideration two new theories in medical care: patient empowerment [6] and post-traumatic growth [5]. Both theories are focused on the patient and the responsibly that is given to him during the treatment process.

During our initial research we have found out that a considerable amount of information is lost in-between visits and also that the doctors are using the small amount of time of the meeting to focus on the existing symptoms and empowering the patients (ex: encouraging them to be able to continue treatment) instead on focusing solely on finding solutions.

Some of the information lost in the existing system are related to:

- The real mental status of the cancer survivor (between the presented feelings/symptoms of the patient and his/her real ones can be huge differences);
- The exact symptoms (severity, duration, etc.) that occur in-between medical visits
- Other mental and physical challenges that the patients are facing;
- The time dedicated to his/her treatment;
- The current health status (resulted by summing up the achievement level of the goals and the values of the health parameters – which have to be in the accepted values);

System Requirements. To reach a wider range of patients and medical systems (inside EU and outside) the proposed system needed to comply to certain necessities: platform coherence (disregarding the operating system: Android, iPhone, etc.), scalability (any device size), synchronization (between doctor and patient's app in real time), clarity of the data (visualization tools for patients and doctors), high usability (as we have a wide range of patients), more visual oriented, to perceive the information faster and clearer and affordable (to reach more patients and doctors).

4   eNurse System

The resulting system has switched focus several times by trying to find the most pressing issues of the oncology care system. We have started from one app dedicated only for the patients and in the present we have two different applications for the patients and the doctors.

Doctor's App. This application contains the medical files (Fig 3) of all their patients and as well a connection with medical networks. It is a strongly visual app with focus on current health status of the patient.

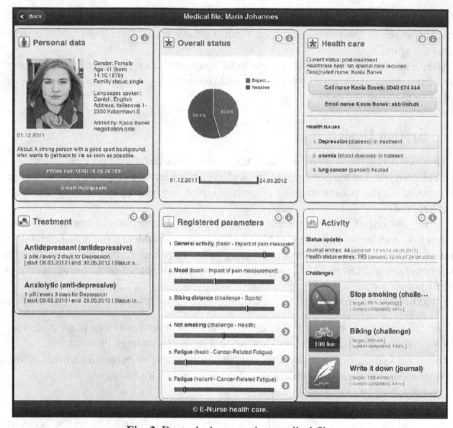

Fig. 3. Doctor's App – patient medical file

Doctor's App main features:

- Patient list with real-time updated health status and complete medical file;
- Health parameter toolbox – which allows the creation of a daily health status form to be completed by the patient. The parameters are customized for each patient and are offering a precise image of the patient status.
- Medical appointment system with a connected calendar;
- Graphical representation of the health status and the parameters of the patients;
- Motivational tools for patients – creation of small challenges (ex: walking a short distance every day, which can still be a challenge for a cancer survivor).

Patient's App. The mobile app is created in HTML5 so can be used on all major mobile platforms (tablets included). The main features are:

- Patients can record their current health status (by using a very simple form with checkboxes, sliders, etc.);
- Updates received by RSS feed with selected oncology news;

- Appointments / Calendar system to track their medical meetings (note: cancer survivors are going to several doctors and several medical facilities during their treatment);
- Challenges system – that empowers them by following small challenges that can be achieved (created by the doctor). An example of a challenge is walking every two days 1km, which for a healthy person is not a challenge but for a cancer survivor it can be a serious one;
- Medication list;
- 24/7 connection with medical staff aware of their current condition;
- A "humanized" medical system in which the patient can always see the image of the doctor he is going to meet and the main contact person (which is a head nurse usually).

5   Conclusion

The quality of treatment remains a very complex domain of which we have just scratched the surface and managed to address just few of the issues, and due to the short period of time is hard to truly assess the impact of such a system on the quality of treatment.

Nevertheless, during our tests with real patients and working together with the medical stuff we have filled the gap in which a great quantity of data was being lost. Also we have pointed out few of the major fails of the existing system and we have offered a modern solution to them.

After the research we have pointed out the most important findings:

- A standalone app is useless without the support of an entire system that involves oncology experts.
- The existing medical system can support such a sub-system, but it will require severe modifications.
- By using eNurse, even for a short amount of time, a doctor can decrease the time spent on assessing the patient health status, and dedicate more time for searching solutions for the patients.
- Patient empowerment can be applied to cancer survivors - from the interviews we have conducted we can conclude that using challenges can give them a higher empowerment. Still, to truly asses this feature we have to test further and for a longer period of time.

6   Future Work

The existing system is just a working prototype with limited functionality. So to improve eNurse we need to have a fully working prototype to be tested with a higher number of patients (fifty at least) on a much longer period of time, which in this case should be of at least one year, to actually observe improvements in the behavior of the patients and also to analyze the communication flow between survivors and the medical system. Also a very important part would be an extensive collaboration with a medical center and oncology experts.

References

1. Iacomi, A.: eNurse. A mobile system for improving the quality of treatment for cancer survivors. IT University of Copenhagen MSc. Thesis (2012)
2. Unger, R., Chandler, C.: A project guide to UX Design. New Riders (2009)
3. Survivors Interviews. LivesStrong Foundation website (2012),
   http://www.LiveStrong.org/Get-Help/
   Learn-About-Cancer/Survivor-Interviews
4. Devane, C.: Cancer Survivorship. Nursing Times (2009)
5. Tedeschi, R.G., Calhoun, L.G.: Posttraumatic Growth: Conceptual Foundations and Empirical Evidence. Psychological Inquiry 15(1) (2004)
6. Lau, D.H.: Patient empowerment - a patient-centered approach to improve care. Hong Kong Med. 8(5) (2002)

The Investigation of Acoustical Environments in Elderly Mental Hospital

Wei Lin[1,*] and Hsuan Lin[2]

[1] Department of Interior Design, Hwa Hsia Institute of Technology, Taipei, Taiwan
weilin@cc.hwh.edu.tw
[2] Department of Product Design, Tainan University of Technology, Tainan, Taiwan
te0038@mail.tut.edu.tw

Abstract. Acoustic conditions in hospitals have been shown to influence a patient's physical and psychological health. Noise levels in Beitou Armed Forces Hospital were measured among various times. Sound pressure levels were logged every 30-seconds over a period in different locations: at the nurses' station, in the hallway, and in a patient's room. Results show that current noise level guidelines were exceeded regularly; despite this the surveys showed most patients were not very annoyed with the noise. Additionally, no relationships were found between a patient's gender or age to various noise responses. Overall this study did not find very large changes in sound levels in various time periods and overall patient noise perception will be discussed in the further work.

Keywords: Elderly mental hospital, Acoustical environments, Subjective evaluation.

1 Introduction

The current aging society in Taiwan for the elderly health care environment is becoming attention, noise control has also become the primary research. For all the countries of the world, it have been built for hospitals interior noise value and sound quality criteria of the proposed classification system which develop autonomy ways to improve hospital noise. Department of Health Science and Technology Research of Taiwan proposed the related research project which is noise hazards in hospital environments cause in the level of anxiety [1]. Physiological and psychological effects of noise for patients has been a considerable number of researches for the reference. Researches of noise effects for medical space are from the beginning of the 1960s. With the constantly increasing medical equipment unit, high-decibel noise levels is main factor for resulting in high-impact physical and mental health of the patient [2].

In the U.S. study survey found that the average noise hospital space is about 55 dB (A) [3] [4]. 150 patients after surgery for investigation, averaged result is up to 95% correlation between the amount of noise and the patient's anxiety [5]. In addition, many studies found that noise is the main factor which cause patient "psychological pressure" [6]-[11]. The prolonged exposure to high noise environment led into the

---

* Corresponding author.

C. Stephanidis (Ed.): HCII 2014 Posters, Part II, CCIS 435, pp. 413–418, 2014.

patient's psychological stress and physical pain with a direct impact on wound healing and lead to slow growth in time to stay in the hospital treatment [12], serious noise environments cause physical and psychological concurrency problems [13]. In this study, elderly who stay in mental hospital and have medical treatment for insomnia, anxiety, emotional disorders and other mental disorders are the object, sound measurements in Beitou Armed Forces Hospital is be taken. In order to understand the correlation between objective sound distribution of the ward unit noise and subjective test, patient questionnaires are also made to comprehend subjective feelings of the psychological impact by noise sound. The purpose of this study is as follows:

(1). Understand the current environmental conditions of care for Geriatric Psychiatry.
(2). For elderly patients to provide the relationship between the noise impact and subjective psychology.
(3). Enhance care unit nurses noise control attention, improve noise control standards.
(4) Finally, expect to improve the noise environment in the development of psychiatric care space and to create a truly high-quality quiet environment of treatment.

2   Methods

To understand the correlation between with the noise frequency characteristics of the ward nursing unit and subjective with a tolerance of feeling, acoustical measurements of Geriatric Psychiatry Medical Center of Beitou Armed Forces Hospital as a foundation may be taken, questionnaires assessment may also conduct to realize the patients' psychological impact of noise. The main structure and content of the steps of this study described below:

2.1   Objective Evaluation

Measurement location is at Geriatric Psychiatry Medical Center of Beitou Armed Forces Hospital for monitoring the status of field sound environmental conditions. Elderly psychiatric hospital offer a treatment for elderly who are suffering from insomnia, anxiety, mood disorders and other mental disorders, and the recuperation space and related service space are the target spaces for monitoring indoor noise distribution prone shown in Fig. 1.

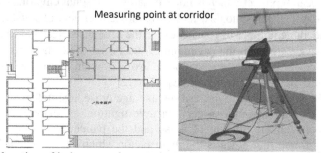

Fig. 1. Plane for location of indoor sound measuring points with sound meter de vice in Beitou Armed Forces Hospital

The main noise sources including hospital space monitoring mobile source - wheelchairs, hospital beds, medical carts, voice chat and other health care workers communication etc. Stationary noise including, pantry and indoor air-conditioning (machine) between devices, such as background noise in the ward. Measuring equipment for the requirements of IEC TYPE 1 decibel meter as a measuring instrument (Shown in Figure 2) is used, mobile noise assessment parameters is based on LAeq (10min), stationary noise is on NC value.

2.2   Indoor Sound Environment Measurement

Measuring height from the floor is 1.2 ~ 1.5-m and is away from windows 1.5-m. Every three minutes the is recorded by equivalent sound level (LAeq). Referring to the CNS 7183 noise level measurement method, 30 seconds integration of sound pressure level in 1/3 octave band for 20 Hz to 20000Hz is calculated by real time analyzer (Comply with requirement of Type 1, IEC standard).

$$\overline{Lp} = 10\log_{10}\frac{1}{N}\left(\sum_{i=1}^{N}10^{Li/10}\right)\qquad(1)$$

2.3   Measurement Configuration and Space Description

Measuring targets are physical and mental wards space in Beitou Armed Forces Hospital Medical Center, spatial arrangement at physical and mental center, such as the entrance, physical and mental wards, nursing stations, group therapy rooms and pantries etc are selected. Spatial distribution of the measuring point sources for mobile noise set are walkways, public telephone areas, pantries and other indoor spaces and for stationary noise set are the ward, consulting space, equipment and service space.

2.4   Subjective Evaluation

Based on data quantities of measurements, subjective questionnaire will be applied for patients to understand the actual subjective feelings in order to assess consistency for the psychological impact of noise and objective discussion of the space condition. Finally, to provide space planning optimization of the design proposals.

2.5   Measurement Results of Mobile Noise

The assessment of the noise sources are stationary and mobile noise, Mobile Indoor noise, compared with mechanical carts, noisy sound and the sound of conversation are set in the open aisle space and administrative space. Measuring height from the floor is 1.2 ~ 1.5-m and is away from windows 1.5-m. Every three minutes the is recorded by equivalent sound level (Leq). The results is shown in Table 1.

Table 1. Measurement results of mobile noise

Measurement location	Leq dB(A)	L$_{max}$ dB(A)	L$_{99}$ dB(A)	Leq $_{20\sim200Hz}$ dB(A)
Ward corridor A (with activity)	58.7	62.4	56.3	50.6
Ward corridor B (with activity)	54.1	60.3	53.4	46.4
Subject within group	49.8	58.8	47.4	40.1

2.6   Measurement Results of Stationery Noise

The 30 seconds integration of sound pressure level in 1/3 octave band for 20 Hz to 20000Hz is calculated by real time analyzer. Referring to the CNS 7183 noise level measurement method, 30 seconds integration of sound pressure level in 1/3 octave band for 20 Hz to 20000Hz is calculated by real time analyzer. The results is shown in Table 2.

Table 2. SPL values of 1/3 octave band in 63 Hz to 4000Hz and NC value

Frequency Location	63 Hz	125 Hz	250 Hz	500 Hz	1K Hz	2K Hz	4K Hz	NC
Group therapy room	47.4	42.8	44.8	28.1	22.9	24.7	19.9	35
Meeting room	30.7	32.0	31.8	28.6	21.2	18.9	16.2	25
Psychology Assess- ment Room	36.1	39.3	39.2	36.0	28.6	25.7	23.4	35
Head nurse office	30.6	43.9	38.8	36.9	28.7	28.1	25.7	35
Ward (old air- conditioning)	52.1	53.3	47.4	41.7	34.2	27.9	24.1	40
Ward (renwe air- conditioning)	45.4	47.8	44.8	41.0	33.6	27.4	22.6	35

2.7   Subjective Evaluation

Thirty patients who made evaluations at the hospital. They were all have healthy hearing and asked about the air conditioner, hospital beds, medical carts, voice chat and other health care workers communication for mobile noise, and indoor air-conditioning (machine) between devices, such as background noise in the ward is for stationary source. A questionnaire was used that consisted of 5-point semantic scales with verbal descriptors defining the extremes at each end. The 3 point in each scale implied the unpleasant of perception. The results is shown in Fig. 2.

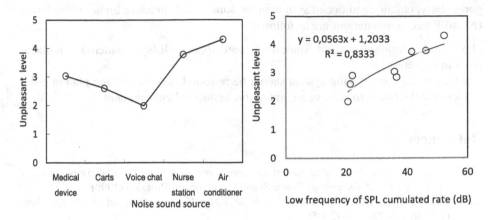

Fig. 2. Unpleasant level as a function of noise sound source **Fig. 3.** Unpleasant level as a function of low frequency of SPL cumulated rate (dB)

Subjective questionnaire applied for patients to understand the actual subjective feelings in order to assess consistency for the psychological impact of noise and objective discussion of the space condition. The results show the highly positive correlation between Unpleasant level and Low frequency of SPL cumulated rate (r= 0.90, R^2= 0.83) (shown in Fig. 3).

3   Discussion

From results of Indoor mobile noise measurement, a semi-open space such as walkways, public telephone areas and other public spaces was a targets of investigation. The averaged 50dB (A) Leq dB (A) is calculated, far exceeding the Noise Control Act standard 40dB (A) (the hospital is the first level of standard), in particular during certain hours of the aisle of the sound level can reach 58.7dB (A). Hospital need a quiet place for spiritual space should raise standards and precisely control. Recommendations are as follows:

(1). Installation of sound-absorbing material of the ceiling and walls to reduce the noise of the distribution and diffusion in the public space.
(2). For ease of management and assistance needs of patients, the nursing station staff voice conversations are self-control and easily generated noise of space, such as group activity room of zoning to reduce noise interference to each other sounds.

Measurement results of the stationary sources (background noise) was found, such as ward space due to the adoption centralized air conditioning system, air-conditioning machinery and equipment for self-generated noise averaged NC35, in particularly, old air conditioned system in the some wards produce higher noise levels (NC40). Recommendations are as follows:

(1.) Sound isolation doors and windows in ward space will be considered to replacement in the future.
(2.) Central air conditioning system should be re-round reviewed of the plan in order to facilitate the future to achieve a comfortable acoustical environment.

References

1. Tsai, S.F.: The study of noise hazard and annoyance in a large hospital. Department of Health Science and Technology Research and Development Program (1998)
2. Busch-Vishniac, I.J., et al.: Noise Levels in Johns Hopkins Hospital. J. Acoust. Soc. Am. 118(6), 3629–3645 (2005)
3. Falk, S.A., Nancy, F.W.: Hospital Noise-Levels and Potential Health Hazards. The New England Journal of Medicine 289(15), 774–781 (1973)
4. Falk, S.A., Woods, N.: Noise Stimuli in Acute Care Area. Nursing Research 23, 144–150 (1974)
5. Topf, M.A.: Physiological and Psychological Effects of Hospital Noise Upon Postoperative Patients. Dissertation Abstracts International 43, 4202 (1983)
6. Wysocki, A.B.: The Effect of Intermittent Noise Exposure on Wound Healing. Advances in Wound Care 9(1), 35–39 (1996)
7. Ragneskog, H., Gerdner, L.A., Josefsson, K., Kihlgren, M.: Probable Reasons for Expressed Agitation in Persons with Dementia. Clinical Nursing Research 7, 189–206 (1998)
8. Dyson, M.: Intensive Care Unit Psychosis, the Therapeutic Nurse–Patient Relationshipand the Influence of the Intensive Care Setting. Analyses of Interrelating Factors. Journal of Clinical Nursing 8, 284 (1999)
9. Holmberg, S.K., Coon, S.: Ambient Sound Levels in a State Psychiatric Hospital. Archives in Psychiatric Nursing 13(3), 117–126 (1999)
10. Maschke, C., Tanja, R., Karl, H.: The Influence of Stressors on Biochemical Reactions-a Review of Present Scientific Findings with Noise. Int. J. Hyg. Environ. Health 203, 45–53 (2000)
11. Christensen, M.: Noise Levels in a General Intensive Care Unit: A Descriptive Study. Nursing in Critical Care 12(4), 188–197 (2007)
12. Minckley, B.B.: A Study of Noise and its Relationship to Patient Discomfort in the Recovery Room. Nurs. Res. 17, 247–250 (1968)
13. Hagerman, I., et al.: Influence of Intensive Coronary Care Acoustics on the Quality of Care and Physiological State of Patients. International Journal of Cardiology 98(2), 267–270 (2005)

The Design and Evaluation of Mobile HCI in Dietary Intake Estimation

Ying-Chieh Liu[1,*], Chien-Wei Lee[1], Chien-Hung Chen[2], and Zhao-Yang Yang[3]

[1] Industrial Design Department, Chang Gung University, Tao-Yuan, Taiwan
ycl30@mail.cgu.edu.tw, s923446@gmail.com
[2] Institute for Information Industry, Taipei, Taiwan
marken@iii.org.tw
[3] Industrial Design Department, Tatung University, Taipei, Taiwan
cyyan@ttu.edu.tw

Abstract. This research designs and evaluates app interfaces designed to estimate and record dietary intake. Effect and user's preference are taken for consideration. Three potential interfaces are proposed, i.e., a) interactive photo interface; (b) a sketching interface, and c) a resizable shape interface. Trials with 38 university students indicate that a) and b) both provide some useful features, but there is a preference for the interactive photo interface. Future research will focus on design enhancements to improve user experiences in different target groups.

Keywords: Mobile HCI, portion size estimation, dietary intake, subjective evaluation.

1 Introduction

An increasing number of mobile apps focus on issues related to health care and public health, but few studies have examined the appropriateness and utility of such apps including from a Human-Computer Interaction (HCI) standpoint (Chesanow & Fogg, 2013). Dietary management is an essential component of weight management and the prevention of clinical diseases (Kuczmarski et al., 1994; Byrd-Bredbenner et al., 2004). A critical issue in effective dietary management is the process of estimating portion sizes. This process typically entails three individual abilities, namely perception, conceptualization and memory, through which the user relates the size or amount of food, consumed to pre-set portion sizes, develops a mental picture of the amount, and recalls the amount of food consumed. This process in frequently subject to errors (Cypel et al., 1997; Slawson & Eck, 1997; Hunter et al., 1998; Ervin & Smiciklas-Wright, 2001; McGuire et al., 2001) which can negate the impact of dietary control or even jeopardize personal health (Arroyo et al., 2007).

Special purpose apps can be designed to provide users with effective and real-time estimates of portion sizes and amounts of unfinished food. Such features could present a significant improvement over current practices which are time-consuming,

C. Stephanidis (Ed.): HCII 2014 Posters, Part II, CCIS 435, pp. 419–423, 2014.

inconvenient and error-prone. This study investigates the design of such innovative aids with subjective user evaluations. Users were asked to use design alternatives with different user interface concepts aiming to determine interface design factors which are conducive to effective use.

2   Design

This research adopts an iterative user-centered design process from Bandura's social cognitive theory (1977) to investigate potential design interfaces in the portion esti-mation process under specific environmental conditions. The design approach entails proposing, evaluating, and selecting design alternatives so as to eventually obtain an effective and user-friendly design. All designs 1) present a selection of pre-determined images of foods and associated portions for user consideration, or 2) use handy comparators so users don't need supplemental pocket guides or memory aids to determine an equivalent serving size. One interface design alternative is proposed from the concept of pre-determined images, namely interactive photo interface. Two design alternatives are proposed for the comparators: 1) a sketching-based interface and 2) a shape-resizing interface. Fig. 1 illustrates the sketching-based interface oper-ation. In Fig. 1(a), the user selects a specific food, followed by a comparator (e.g., credit card) in Fig. 1(b). The user then describes the portion size by shading in the appropriate area by scribbling as shown in Fig. 1(c). The user then completes the activity and submits the data for calculation and storage as shown in Fig. 1(e).

In resizing tasks, users select a given initial shape (e.g., circle, ellipse, square) and then baseline the shape against the comparator based on their own experience. The area of the initial shape is enlarged or reduced by dragging its side. The shape resizing task proceeds as follows: Selecting a food item (see Fig. 2(a) and a comparator (Fig. 2(b). In Fig. 2(c), a predefined shape (in this case, a semi-transparent blue square) is superimposed above the comparator. The user drags the shape to indicate the portion size in relation to the comparator and confirms the completed size (Fig. 2(d)). The difference between these two interfaces is that the sketching interface involves a men-tal picture based on a scribble, while, the shape-based interface allows the user to resize a pre-defined shape by dragging its boundary to modify its shape and size.

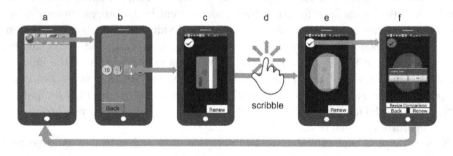

Fig. 1. Sketching interface operation

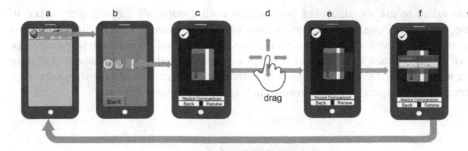

Fig. 2. Shape resizing interface operation

As for the interactive photo, the user selects a picture of the actual food item from a menu (Fig. 3(a)), which is then superimposed on a place setting including a plate, chopsticks and spoon for size reference (Fig. 3(b)). The user then flicks left or right to increase or decrease the size of the food object relative to the size of the place setting objects (Fig. 3(c)).the user first takes a picture of the size of the real food portion next to certain objects. Once the user has found an appropriate size relation, he/she confirms the selection (Fig. 3(d)) and completes the action (Fig. 3(e)).

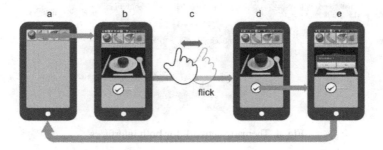

Fig. 3. Interactive photo interface operation

3   Initial Subjective Evaluation

An initial subjective evaluation using open-ended questions was conducted to assess interface preference. We recruited 38 students at Chang Gung University in Taiwan, 26 males and 12 females between the ages of 18 and 27 years old. The test group was split into two subgroups to test the different interfaces, with group A (12 females 6 males) testing the interactive photo interface, and group B (14 females, 6 males) testing the sketching interface. Due to time constraints, the resizable interface was not included in this evaluation. A range of 18 food items was selected to ensure consistency and variety (apple, orange, banana, corn, cake, pizza, pork slice, fish, corn flakes, seeds, soya, vegetable, milk, black tea, honey, jam, rice, and tofu). In group A, each subject was asked to visualize a specific food portion using the interactive photo function on a mobile device with a 4.3 inches touch panel. In group B, each subject was asked to use the sketching interface. In both groups, all subjects were asked to use their respective interfaces to process all 18 food items a single time. The two groups then switched to the other interface and repeated the evaluation process for five minutes which only allowed subjects to experience the design without repeating the testing of all 18 items.   Subjects were then asked to complete a questionnaire with three open-end questions to determine their interface preferences.

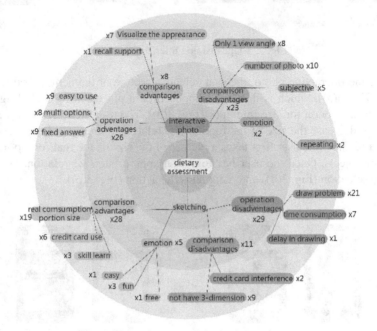

Fig. 4. Thematic network for both interfaces

4   Results

The thematic network method (Martin & Hanington, 2013; Lee & Fielding, 1996) was used to summarize subject response to both interfaces (Fig. 4). Responses dealt with two specific tasks: conducting food portion comparisons and operating the interface. Advantages cited for the interactive photo included ease of use (9 respondents), a predefined selection of images to represent specific portion sizes (9), and fixed answers (9 subjects). Subjects also indicated concerns regarding the limited selection of food images (10 subjects) and that food images were only portrayed from a single angle (8). As for the sketching interface, most subjects liked that the interface allowed them to draw shapes and sizes that could accurately reflect the food portions (19 respondents) using a handy comparator (6). However, subjects experienced difficulties drawing specific sizes and shapes (21 respondents) and felt the process was time consuming (7). Also, a cost-effective means must be found to expand the variety of food images used in the interactive photo interface. For the sketching interface, operations need to be streamlined to reduce the time and effort needed to draw a specific shape. Further testing is also required to objectively evaluate estimation errors and operating time requirements.

References

1. Arroyo, M., De la Pera, C.M., Ansotegui, L., Rocandio, A.M.: A short training program improves the accuracy of portion-size estimates in future dieti-tians. Arch. Latinoam. Nutr. 57(2), 163–167 (2007)
2. Byrd-Bredbenner, C., Schwartz, J.: The effect of practical portion size measurement aids on the accuracy of portion size estimates made by young adults. Journal of Human Nutrition & Dietetics 17(4), 351–357 (2004)
3. Chesanow, N., Fogg, B.: Can Health Apps Help Patients Change Their Behavior? (June 2013), http://www.medscape.com/viewarticle/806734 (retrieved)
4. Cypel, J., Guenther, P., Petot, G.: Validity of portion- size measurement aids: A review. J. Am. Diet. Assoc. 97, 289–292 (1997)
5. Ervin, R., Smiciklas-Wright, H.: Accuracy in estimating and recalling portion sizes of foods among elderly adults. Nutr. Res., 703–713 (2001)
6. Hunter, D., Sampson, L., Stampfer, M., Colditz, G., Rosner, B., Willett, W.: Variability in portion sizes of commonly consumed foods among a population of women in the United States. Am. J. Epidemiology 127, 1240–1249 (1998)
7. Kuczmarski, M.F., Moshfegh, A., Briefel, R.: Update on nutrition monitoring activities in the United States. Journal of the American Dietetic Association 94(7), 753–760 (1994)
8. Lee, R.M., Fielding, N.: Qualitative Data Analysis: Representations of a Technology: A Comment on Coffey, Holbrook and Atkinson'. Sociological Research Online 1(4), 55 (1996)
9. Martin, B., Hanington, B.: Universal Methods of Design, 1st edn. Rockport, United States of America (2012)
10. McGuire, B., Chambers IV, E., Godwin, S., Brenner, S.: Size categories most effective for estimating portion sizes of muffins. J. Am. Diet. Assoc. 101, 472–474 (2001)
11. Slawson, D.L., Eck, L.H.: Intense practice enhances accuracy of portion size estimation of amorphous foods. J. Am. Diet. Assoc. 97, 295–297 (1997)

Usability Evaluation of Home-Use Glucose Meters for Senior Users

Hsin-Chang Lo[1,*], Cheng-Lun Tsai[2], Kang-Ping Lin[3],
Ching-Chang Chuang[1], and Wen-Te Chang[1]

[1] Department of Product Design, Ming Chuan University
{lohc,ccchuang,mimi}@mail.mcu.edu.tw
[2] Department of Biomedical Engineering, Chung Yuan Christian University
clt@cycu.edu.tw
[3] Department of Electrical Engineering, Chung Yuan Christian University
kplin@cycu.edu.tw

Abstract. Self-monitoring of blood glucose technique provides diabetic mellitus patients a simple and real-time method to monitor their blood sugar at home. In order to understand the interface design problems in home-use glucose meters, the aim of this study was to realize if senior users were able to easily and effectively operate glucose meters via usability evaluation. Five senior users of above 65 years old who never use home-use glucose meters before were recruited to operate typical tasks: a. changing lancet, b. inserting a strip to turn on the meter, c. lancing, d. waiting for the result and e. discarding lancet. The experiment process was recorded for further interview. The results demonstrated that the key factors that caused operation errors were found on lancing device and test strip instead of the glucose meter. Especially for seniors that had memory degradations, they needed side by side assistance to finish the tasks.

Keywords: Senior user, Glucose meter, Usability evaluation.

1   Introduction

According to International Diabetes Federation (IDF), diabetic population in the world has reached 382 million in the end of 2013. It also reported that 10% of the global population will have diabetes by 2035[1]. Self-monitoring of blood glucose techniques provides diabetic mellitus patients a simple and real-time method to monitor their blood sugar at home which helps avoids tiring transportations between home and medical facilities. For seniors with high risk in diabetes mellitus, home-use glucose meters still presence many interface design defects which can easily cause operation errors. In 2005, the United States Food and Drug Administration (FDA) issued a Medical Device Report of Abbott glucose meters to warn users that the Abbott glucose meters provided mg/dL and mmol/L, two different measuring units. When users were setting time and date of the meters, accidentally switching to another measurement could happen. Unknowingly reading the wrong glucose values could subsequently cause wrong dosage of insulin injection or losing control of diet. It resulted in

C. Stephanidis (Ed.): HCII 2014 Posters, Part II, CCIS 435, pp. 424–429, 2014.

multiple incidents of serious high blood sugar or hyperglycemia that endangered lives in the U.S. [2]. Although many seniors are willing to use new technology-applied products, the aging process degenerate the physiological functions. For instance, visual degenerations that common to seniors cause difficulties in seeing the operating interface of the products clearly; decreasing muscle strength and finger sensitivity resulting from motion function degeneration cause difficulty for seniors to operate small buttons [3]. Psychologically, cognitions, comprehensions as well as learning abilities also show signs of degradations through aging. Therefore when senior users are in contact with new products, they may face obstacles in learning that they cannot correctly use them.

In order to compensate the condition of inexperienced seniors using products, related studies shown that usability evaluations are effective methods that can improve the interactions between seniors and medical devices [4,5]. Usability evaluation has been widely implemented in the process of product evaluation and system development [6,7]. Despite that the evaluation methods are not originally developed for medical system, applications on medical devices to evaluate interfaces continue to grow. Users are invited to do typical tasks for researchers to identify the operation flow which errors happen on and users having difficulties with in order to discover design defects [8,9]. The most important issue of medical device usability evaluation is to understand the interactions between users and products. In addition to improve the health of people, it is meant to reduce the probabilities of medical malpractice and ensure the safety of the people as well [10]. Beuscart-Zéphir [11] indicated that many actual cases shown that medical equipment, such as infusion pumps, hand-held electronic prescribing devices and computerized order entry, are in fact prone to human errors. Therefore, the aim of this study is to realize the usability of commercial home-use glucose meters for senior users. And the study results are expected to provide interface design recommendations for new home-use medical devices.

2   Method

2.1   Subjects

Five seniors, 3 females and 2 males, above age of 65 (average 70.9) years old were recruited for this study. All of the test subjects had no upper limb disability, no cognitive impairment, and had no previous experience in using home-use glucose meter independently.

2.2   Instrumentation

Two commercial home-use glucose meters were chosen for the experiments: One-Touch UltraEasy, johnson & Johnson and FreeStyle Freedom Lite, Abbott (Fig.1).

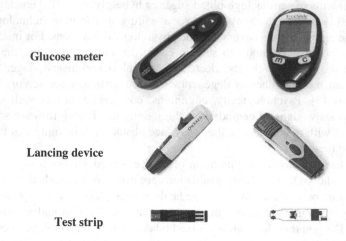

Glucose meter

Lancing device

Test strip

Fig. 1. Two commercial home-use glucose meters, (L)OneTouch; (R)FreeStyle.

2.3   Experiment Protocols

The experiment protocols were described as followed:

1. First, the researchers would explain the glucose meter operation instructions to the subjects, and allowed them to have 10 minutes to practice using the two meters.
2. The researchers would then explain the test procedures, operation tasks and things to be aware of during experiments.
3. Next, subjects operated five operation tasks in orders, which started from task a to task e, and they should achieve the default target of all the tasks with no time limit.

a. changing lancet

    a.1 open the lancing device cap.

    a.2 insert the lancet.

    a.3 replace the lancing device cap.

    a.4 adjust the lancing depth.

    a.5 cock the lancing device.

b. inserting a strip to turn on the meter

    b.1 open the test strip vial lid.

    b.2 remove a test strip.

    b.3 close the test strip vial lid.

    b.4 insert a test strip into the meter.

c. lancing

    c.1 wipe the lancing area with an alcohol pad.

    c.2 hold the lancing device against the finger and press the release button.

    c.3 apply the correct solution to the test strip.

d. waiting for the result

    d.1 read the result from the meter screen.

    d.2 dispose the test strip.

e. discarding lancet

    e.1 open the lancing device cap.

    e.2 remove the lancet.

    e.3 replace the lancing device cap.

4. The experiment process were recorded using a digital camera to record the actions of subjects using the glucose meters for further analysis and reference of video/audio retrospection.

In order to avoid learning effects, glucose meters were chosen randomly by subjects. A five-minute break was taken between each experiment.

Fig. 2. One of the subjects was operating OneTouch glucose meter.

3   Results and Discussion

From our observation and interview, we found that users spent more operation time in task a and task b, than other three tasks. The lacing device and test strip were the major parts involved in the above two tasks, the discussion of this study focuses on those two items.

3.1   Lacing Device

The sub-task of task was a.1 open the lancing device cap. Both lacing devices both had different shapes and colors to distinguish the devices and its cap which provided information that the lancing device and the cap were detachable. However, the information of how to detach the cap was not clear. Users would try to unscrew or pull the cap. Use error occurred when the users were unable to realize that the lancing cap should be snapped open. Additionally, for those subjects who had weakened hand muscle strength it was difficult to pull open. It required greater effort and repeat attempts to achieve.

Sub-task "a.5 adjusts the lancing depth" was the bottleneck for the novice user. If those users adjusted lancing depth too deep might increase the pain they felt during lancing. On the contrary, if the lancing depth was not enough, it might cause test failure because of insufficient in blood sample. OneTouch lancing device was designed to adjust lancing depth by twisting the device, which could cause confusion with pulling open the cap. Subjects tended to mistakenly adjust lancing depth by trying to unscrew the device cap.

3.2   Test Strips

Test strips used usually differentiate the side of inserting into the meters and the sampling side by graphics. This study discovered that most of the subjects did not carefully observe the differences of the graphics before use. They inserted the strip without confirming the correct insertion side and thus leaded to use error. The possible explanation could be that the graphic on the test strip was not specific and also due to impaired vision that happed to most seniors participants. For instance, errors usually happened when most of the users did not notice the arrow instruction or failed to understand the meaning of the arrow.

Most of the commercial glucose meters can automatically turned on by inserting the test strip. Although it supposed to be a considering and convenient design, this study shown that OneTouch could still turn on even the test strip was not properly placed in (wrong insertion direction or not fully inserted). The meter could be turned on just because the test port was disturbed. When the subjects realized they made mistakes and tried to give second attempt, it required to reboot the device or the test strip was contaminated by blood even further caused lancing failure. Therefore, the test strip should design with a clear graphic to let users realize that it is set up correctly.

3.3   Glucose Meter Operation Procedures

Most of the subjects could not remember all the operation procedures after the researchers explained the process. They usually required researchers gave step-by-step reminders to finish all the tasks. It proved that the operation procedures of commercial glucoses meters were burdensome for novice senior. Most subjects failed to remember correct procedures because the tasks were too complicated to memorize. This study found that even the subject had performed the same task more than twice they still forgot, hesitated, paused or made mistakes. Aging accompanies with short-term memory degeneration. It is hard for seniors to remember the instructions they read orderly [12]. Most of the home-care medical products use new technologies and consist of multiple functions. However, senior users usually lack for experience in using technological products for which it is hard for them to understand various functions and complicated operating interface [13]. We found that when senior subjects operating complicated devices, such as glucose meter, the concerns of being unfamiliar with the products may result in operation errors.

4   Conclusion

This study recruited seniors to operate two types of home-use glucose meters to evaluation usability. Results revealed many operation problems in practical use. The crucial factors that caused use errors involved lancing devices and test strips rather than glucose meters. If the above two parts can be further designed more thoroughly, the usability of seniors using home-use glucose meters can be effectively improved.

Acknowledgement. The authors appreciate the participation of senior users. This work was sponsored under grant NSC 102-2410-H-130 -068 - by the National Science Council and DOH102-FDA-51002 by Ministry of Health and Welfare, Taiwan.

References

1. International Diabetes Federation (IDF), http://www.idf.org/
2. U S Food and Drug Administration News (2011), http://www.fda.gov/bbs/topics/NEWS/2005/NEW01250.html
3. Dall, P.M., Kerr, A.: Frequency of the sit to stand task: An observational study of free-living adults. Appl. Ergon. 41, 58–61 (2010)
4. Demiris, G., Rantz, M., Aud, M., Marek, K., Tyrer, H., Skubic, M., Hussam, A.: Older adults' attitudes towards and perceptions of "smart home" technologies: a pilot study. Med. Inform. Internet Med. 29, 87–94 (2004)
5. Ehmen, H., Haesner, M., Steinke, I., Dorn, M., Növercin, M., Steinhagen-Thiessen, E.: Comparison of four different mobile devices for measuring heart rate and ECG with respect to aspects of usability and acceptance by older people. Appl. Ergon. 43, 582–587 (2012)
6. Nevala, N., Tamminen-Peter, L.: Ergonomics and usability of an electrically adjustable shower trolley. Int. J. Ind. Ergonom. 34, 131–138 (2004)
7. Lintula, M., Nevala, N.: Ergonomics and the usability of mechanical single-channel liquid dosage pipettes. Int. J. Ind. Ergonom. 36, 257–263 (2006)
8. Rosenbaum, S., Rohn, J.A., Humburg, J.: A toolkit for strategic usability: results from workshops, panels, and surveys. In: Proceedings of the ACM CHI 2000 Conference on Human Factors in Computing Systems, pp. 337–344. ACM Press, New York (2000)
9. Bastien, J.M.: Usability testing: a review of some methodological and technical aspects of the method. Int. J. Med. Inform. 79, e18–e23 (2010)
10. Sainfort, F., Jacko, J.A., Booske, B.C.: Human–computer interaction in health care. The human–computer interaction handbook. Lawrence Earlbaum Associates, London (2003)
11. Beuscart-Zéphir, M.C., Elkin, P., Pelayo, S., Beuscart, R.: The human factors engineering approach to biomedical informatics projects: state of the art, results, benefits and challenges. Yearb. Med. Inform. 109–127 (2007)
12. Hickman, J.M., Rogers, W.A., Fisk, A.D.: Training older adults to use new technology. J. Gerontol. Ser. B-Psychol. Sci. Soc. Sci. 62, 77–84 (2007)
13. Lee, C.F., Kuo, C.C.: A pilot study of ergonomic design for elderly Taiwanese people. In: Proceedings of the 5th Asian Design Conference-International Symposium on Design Science, Seoul, Korea (2001)

Usability Evaluation of Hospital Websites in Nigeria: What Affects End Users' Preferences?

Shakirat O. Raji[1], Murni Mahmud[1], Abu Osman Tap[1], and Adamu Abubakar[2]

[1] Human Centered Design Group (HCDG), Department of Information Systems,
Kulliyah of Information and Communication Technology International Islamic University Malaysia
peacefultosin@hotmail.com, {murni,abuosman}@iium.edu.my
[2] Intelligent Environment Research Group (INTEG),
Department of Information Systems, Kulliyah of Information and Communication Technology
International Islamic University Malaysia
adamu@kict.iium.edu.my

Abstract. Hospital providers need to deliver satisfactory services in a specialized field which involves a great number of stakeholders with different concerns, needs and requirements. Some hospitals' policies have been focused on providing health and medical services to the public. Less attention has been given to the responsibility to provide useful, accurate health information of high quality to their key publics mainly by facilitating interactive communication with patients, citizens and physicians and community services. To date, hospitals are turning increasingly towards the Internet and have developed their own web presence in order to enhance interactive communication practices. The research evaluated the usability of hospital websites in Nigeria, focusing on two websites in south- west of the country. Evaluation criteria for assessment were developed. The results provided empirical evidence that websites should be easy to use as well as aesthetically pleasing but must be rich in information content.

Keywords: Usability, Aesthetic Design, Hospital Websites, Evaluation.

1 Introduction

Many patients access the internet for comprehensive hospital information and hospital selection. Medical expertise is not the only selection criterion for those seeking medical help; additional service and trust also play a role [1]. In the competition among hospitals, the question of how a clinic should present itself on the web has set up competition among hospitals. Therefore, hospital websites are becoming an industry standard as patients (consumers) and health professionals use web resources for information, research and communication. Nowadays, citizens are aware of this historic change that is taking place and they are the drivers of a growing demand for a wide-scale adoption of web channels, within contexts such as healthcare services [2] where exchange of information between patient and care provider is formal. However, patients face difficulties when searching the Internet for health- related information, because of information overload or the complexity of the information [3]

C. Stephanidis (Ed.): HCII 2014 Posters, Part II, CCIS 435, pp. 430–434, 2014.
© Springer International Publishing Switzerland 2014

Usability, which is a well-defined concept in user interfaces and websites, connotes the ease with which people can employ a particular tool or other human-made object in order to achieve a particular goal [4]. Nielsen [5] explains Usability as a quality attribute that assesses how easy interfaces is to use. When evaluating the user interfaces for usability, it can be defined as "the perception of a target user of the effectiveness (fit for purpose) and efficiency (work or time required to use) of the interface". Usability improves the design of user interfaces by evaluating the organization, presentation, and interactivity of the interface [6]. Usability is a key measurement for evaluating the success of an organization's web presence [7]. The concept of usability is a key theme in Human-Computer- Interaction (HCI). Research in HCI has shown that the study of human factors is important to the successful design and implementation of technological devices [8].

Norman [9] claims that aesthetic design can be more influential in affecting user preferences than traditional operational usability. Not only is beauty an important quality of a product but it also influences users' judgments [10].   Studies have shown the relationship between the perceived aesthetic quality of a system's user interface and overall user satisfaction [11], [12], claiming that aesthetic design can be a more important influence on users' preferences than traditional usability [9]

In this study, we evaluated two hospital websites in Nigeria, investigating the relationships between content, presentation, usability and memory and their importance to users' preferences.

2   Methodology

Two hospital websites were selected; one public hospital website and one private hospital website, namely: Lagos University Teaching Hospital and St. Nicholas Hospital. The two websites were picked for their variation in usability, content and aesthetic design. The two websites represent the most popular hospitals in the south-west of Nigeria.

2.1   Participants

47 participants, ranging from health professionals as to prospective patients, participated in the evaluation exercise. All participants were expert web users but none had prior knowledge of the two hospital websites. All participants volunteered and no incentive was provided for their participation. All participants gave written consent.

2.2   Procedure

Each participant worked individually for almost an hour in evaluating the hospital websites. The websites were evaluated for usability, content, aesthetic design and information quality. Each participant examined the websites one after the other. The criteria consisted of four categories with subcategories / dimensions (Table 1). The subjects rated each site on a 1-5 scale which can be viewed in Table 3.

Table 1. Assessment Criteria

Evaluation Criteria	Dimensions
Usability	Visibility, navigation, flexibility, efficiency, ease of use
Accessibility	Ease of retrieval
Aesthetic Design	Visual attractiveness, appropriate choice of colours Images, fonts, consistency
Information Quality	Accurate, relevant, reliable, concise, timely

3   Results and Discussion

Table 2 below shows demographics of the participants based on selected variables (age, gender, education, computer experience and Internet experience).

Table 2. Demographics of Participants

Variable	Frequency	Percentage
Age		
20-25	10	21.3
26-30	10	21.3
31-35	12	25.5
36-40	10	21.3
41-45	5	10.6
Gender		
Female	21	44.7
Male	26	55.3
Education		
Bachelor	30	63.8
Masters	13	27.7
PhD	4	8.5
Computer Experience		
20-25	16	34.0
26-30	10	21.3
31-35	10	21.3
36-40	6	12.8
41-45	5	10.6
Internet Experience		
20-25	18	38.3
26-30	10	21.3
31-35	8	17.0
36-40	7	14.9
41-45	4	8.5

4   Discussion

As illustrated in Table 3, 47 participants rated each website according to the criteria based on a Likert scale of 1 to 5 (1 equals strongly disagree and 5 equals strongly agree).

Table 3. Participants Rating the Hospital Websites

Hospital Website	Evaluation criteria	Strongly Disagree	Disagree	Neutral	Agree	Strongly Agree
St. Nicholas Hospital	Usability	0	4	3	8	7
	Accessibility	0	4	3	8	7
	Aesthetic	0	3	9	9	7
	Design Information Quality	0	3	4	9	7
Lagos University Teaching Hospital (LUTH)	Usability	0	15	4	6	0
	Accessibility	0	18	2	0	0
	Aesthetic	0	16	3	0	0
	Design Information Quality	5	16	3	0	0

The usability scores of the two hospital websites with regards to performance in terms of the four categories are summarized as follows:

1. Usability: St. Nicholas was rated high in all dimensions by 15 participants; for Lagos University Teaching Hospital (LUTH), only six participants agreed to all the dimensions under usability.
2. Accessibility: 18 participants disagreed that LUTH was accessible, as compared to the 15 participants rating St. Nicholas has highly accessible.
3. Aesthetic Design: LUTH still recorded a low score.
4. Information Quality: participants rated St. Nicholas as rich in terms of information quality, as compared to LUTH.

The overall scores showed that the St. Nicholas hospital website was preferred by users.

5   Conclusion

The developed usability criteria which are specific to hospital website evaluation would provide guidance for designers of such websites regarding website features that should be taken into consideration. This study also revealed that when it comes to hospital websites, the information quality, which has to be the health information, is as much important as aesthetic design and usability.

References

1. Wendland, K., Planz, C., Oldorf, P.: Optimal Solutions for Hospital Websites. In: 14th IEEE International Requirements Engineering Conference, RE 2006 (2006)
2. Kreps, G.L., Neuhauser, L.: New Directions in EHealth Communication: Opportunities and Challenges. Patient Education and Counseling 78(3), 329–336 (2010)
3. Sommerhalder, K., Abraham, A., Zufferey, M.C., Barth, J., Abel, T.: Internet Information and Medical Consultations: Experiences from Patients' and Physicians' Perspectives. Patient Education and Counselling 77, 6 (2009)
4. Mchome, S., Sachdeva, S., Bhalla, S.: A brief Survey: Usability in Healthcare. In: International Conference on Electronics and Information Engineering (ICEIE 2010), Kyoto, vol. 1, pp. 464–467 (2010)
5. Nielsen, J.: 25 years in Usability. Jakob Nielsen's Alertbox (April 21, 2008)
6. Schneiderman, B., Plaisant, C., Cohen, M., Jacobs, S.: Designing the user interface. Strategies for Effective Human-Computer-Interaction, 5th edn. Addison-Wesley, Boston (2009)
7. Agarwal, R., Venkatesh, V.: Assessing a firm's web presence: A heuristic evaluation procedure for the measurement of usability. Information Systems Research 13(2), 168–186 (2002)
8. Wang, J., Senacal, S.: Measuring Perceived Website Usability. Journal of Internet Commerce 6(4), 97–112 (2007)
9. Norman, D.: Emotional Design: Why we Love (Or Hate) Everyday Things. Basic Books, New York (2004)
10. De Angeli, A., Sutcliffe, A.G., Hartmann, J.: Interaction, usability, aesthetics: What influences users' preferences? In: Proceedings of DIS 2006, Designing Interactive Systems. ACM Press, New York (2006)
11. Lindgaard, G., Dudek, C.: what is this evasive beast we call user satisfaction? Interacting with Computers 15, 149–188 (2003)
12. Tractinsky, N., Shoval-Katz, A., Ikar, D.: What is beautiful is usable. Interacting with Computers 13(2), 127–145 (2000)

Professional Natural Interfaces for Medicine Applications

Illya Starodubtsev[1], Vladimir Averbukh[1],
Nataly Averbukh[2], and Dmitriy Tobolin[3]

[1] Krasovskii Institute of Mathematics and Mechanics, Ural Branch Russian Academy
of Sciences, Yekaterinburg, Russia
[2] Urals Federal University, Yekaterinburg, Russia
[3] AngioSystems Ltd., Russia

Abstract. This article focuses on the problems of development of control systems and medical equipment medical professional interfaces. In our paper we propose a solution to the problem, using gesture language and contact-less motion capture.

Keywords: NUI, natural interfaces, professional interfaces, gesture, depth map, medical equipment, control.

1 Introduction

Our interest lies in the field of development of interfaces for professional work. Including work with the medical equipment. It means control of the medical robot, control during diagnostics and the operation, remote control (teleoperation).

1.1 Problem

During deal with the equipment it is necessary to consider the following things.

1. **Sterility**. During the surgery, the doctor is obliged to keep sterility mode. It leads to restriction of use of hardware tools (button, stick, arm, etc.). As well as a passive / active motion capture markers on the body of a surgeon.
2. **Specialized activity**. These interfaces are not oriented to mass users, so it should use a specialized activity.
3. **Quality assessment**. There is a problem of an assessment of quality of such natural interfaces. In our opinion the usual quality assessment methods are not applicable here. In the case of professional interfaces should be considered, in addition estimates of the rate and accuracy of action, a stress level during user activity. To assess stress is possible through surveys and interviews, and by objective measurements.

C. Stephanidis (Ed.): HCII 2014 Posters, Part II, CCIS 435, pp. 435–439, 2014.

1.2 Overview

Research in this field is making steady headway. There are very interesting published over the past two decades. The close problem statements are contained in [1,2,3,4,5]. In these papers a way to assess the quality of the medicine sterile interfaces is given. However, a number of parameters are controversial (for example measuring objectivity and representativeness). On our opinion these approaches are needed to be determined more precisely.

Most of works has a number of drawbacks

1. **Pose vs trajectory.** In the great majority of papers the final control gesture is based on the (carpal) pose without hand trajectory in space. Or based only on the trajectory, without regard (carpal) pose.
2. **Binding to the hardware.** Algorithms and methods is rigidly bound to a specific technology.
3. **Non-flexibility.** In most cases, there are no opportunities to customize and make changes when conditions change or tuning to a specific operator/problem.

1.3 Problem

It is necessary to develop a system of gesture control for medical equipment. It is necessary to

1. Consider observations above described.
2. To design a flexible and convenient system.
3. To design a reliable system.
4. Consider the specifics of the doctor-operators work.

To consider the work specifics were analyzed real activity of the doctor during surgery and diagnostics [6]. Based on the analysis conclusions are drawn:

1. Control gestures should contain information about the pose and spatial information. Information about a pose a lesser extent, about the spatial trajectory more.
2. Gesture language should contain the native fuses which protect against "random" movements. They are of different nature for different types of manipulation.
3. Using virtual instruments such as real analogues, reduces the barrier to entry and increase the stability of the operator work.
4. To control the obsolete equipment designed for "classical" input devices (mouse and keyboard) is working well the idea of *touch-less-screen* + simple gesture language based on analysis of the *point-of-touch*.

2 Techniques Used

In the operating room conditions to use active markers for motion capture or passive markers on the body of doctor is not allowed. Also, the use of color information leads to complication of algorithms (compensation lighting conditions, suppression of active shadow). This leads to a drop in reliability.

To resolve this we will use information about the depth of the scene.

Definition 1. *Will be called* **depth map scene** *point cloud. Such that each point contains the distance from the origin point of the ray intersects with an object in the scene of a spherical coordinate system or infinity if there is no possibility to calculate the distance.*

$$DepthMap_{Spherical} = \{(\theta, \phi, \rho) : \theta, \phi \in [0, 2\pi], \rho \in \mathbb{R} \cup \infty, \rho = dist(O, P)\}, \quad (1)$$

where O is the origin point and P is an object point.

Obviously, that can be easily represented as a cloud of points in the Cartesian coordinate system:

$$DepthMap_{Cartesian} = \{(x, y, z) : x, y, z \in \mathbb{R}^3 \cup \infty\}. \quad (2)$$

2.1 Pose and Trajectory

Using both methods of processing (carpal) pose and trajectory (position) hand in space produces a favorable result. To use this the system modifiers was developed.

Definition 2. *We will call the* **modifier** *function having at the input state of the system and enabling the output to logical true if the state of the system satisfies certain conditions, and false otherwise.*

$$Mod : S \longmapsto \{TRUE, FALSE\}, \quad (3)$$

where S is system state.

Notes and Comments. There may be different types of modifiers. From simple button type or manipulation area (the trajectory of interest is treated as a point in the area and is ignored otherwise). To the complex, such as having recognized carpal complex poses or initiating/final gestures. Modifiers affect the interpretation of the results of the analysis of the trajectory.

Using a system of modifiers can be easily (naturally) used path analysis and carpal pose together. And not only.

Through this, it can be easily to build complex gesture languages suitable, comfortable and applicable for a specific task or for a specific person.

2.2 Full-Body and Point Based Interaction

There are two basic approaches to capture the movement to create a gesture language. It is:

1. **Full-Body Based Interaction.** In this case there is recognition full poses a human operator. This provides advantages like:

- It is allow to use information about the position of the set of points, such as hands, feet, elbows, torso, head, etc.
  For example, it is easy to make a pointing gesture as a ray from the elbow in the direction of the carpal.
- With contextual information about the position of other parts of the body in space, easily identifiable point of interest, if more than one. Even with partial (or full) overlap.
  For example, it is always possible to distinguish the right from the left hand.
- Using the information on the form (length, cross-sectional radius) body parts is not difficult to recover the trajectory of point of interest in the partially overlapping the visible part of the limb.

However, this method requires more complex algorithms and more computing resources. Also, it is not efficient when it want to recognize a non-regular (non-standard) or non-humanoid object.

2. **Point Based Interaction.** In this case there is capturing and tracking of the point of interest without reference to the context. This provides advantages like:
   - It is allow to tracking an irregular skeleton. For example, the operator has a big instrument in the hands.
   - It is allow to tracking an arbitrary object. For example, it may be the end of instrument or pointers.
   - Low computational cost.

However, to identify points need to use the additional information. For example, the proximity of the position given the history. This can be problematic when point is overlapped, or the distance between two points is low.

As can be seen, both approaches have their advantages and are useful in certain situations. To avoid selecting implemented both approaches.

"Full-Body" Approach. To track a cloud of points in the space corresponding to the operator projected on the plane of observation. Projection is multi-surface flat figure with self-intersections. For the projection procedure is applied skeletization. Next, create a master skeleton. And for the obtained (test) and master skeleton solved the problem of minimizing the energy of the residual by using a hierarchical representation. More in [7]. This approach allows to calibrate by one pose and be adjusted to suit various user settings.

"Point" Approach. To track is used analysis of the amount of motion in the frame. This is done using the cumulative difference buffers. More in [8]. This approach has complexity $O(n)$ on the number of operations and required memory and allows to track an arbitrary object. Point of interest initiated by special gesture.

2.3 Binding to the Hardware

In the case of tight binding to a specific hardware reduces overall system reliability. This makes difficult the timely updating of equipment or quick replacement in case of its failure. Especially when the equipment becomes obsolete.

In the case of the possibility to use different algorithms is increasing a flexibility and applicability. This allows to configure to specific user and a specific task. Which increases the efficiency and reliability.

To provide flexibility modular architecture introduced. Hardware module carried out of the kernel. This allows you to maintain different types of depth sensors by writing a plugin - reader/converter (like a driver). Now, there are plugins for some types of lidar, RGBD cameras, stereo cameras, TOF and rangefinders.

As well as algorithms. Analysis module can be replaced with a more appropriate without changing the kernel. In combination with the modifier system it is give excellent result for flexibility to the system.

3   Prospects

As near term prototypes of interfaces for real medical devices are considered. In particular prototype design gesture interface for control of Angiographic Systems conducted.

Another direction of our research and development is related to the use of gesture and motion capture interface to monitor and create an accurate log for modern cardio surgeries.

References

1. Wachs, J.P., Stern, H.I., Edan, Y.: Parameter search for an image processing fuzzy C-means hand gesture recognition system. In: Proc. of IEEE Intl Conference on Image Processing, ICIP, Spain, vol. 3, pp. 341–344 (2003)
2. Stern, H.I., Wachs, J.P., Edan, Y.: Human Factors for Design of Hand Gesture Human-Machine Interaction. In: IEEE International Conference on Systems, Man and Cybernetics, SMC 2006, vol. 5, pp. 4052–4056 (2010)
3. Wachs, J.P.: Gaze: Posture and Gesture Recognition to Minimize Focus Shifts for Intelligent Operating Rooms in a Collaborative Support System. International Journal of Computers Communications & Control 5(1), 106–124 (2010)
4. Kristensson, P.O., Nicholson, T.F.W., Quigley, A.: Continuous Recognition of One-Handed and Two-Handed Gestures using 3D Full-Body Motion Tracking Sensors. In: Proceedings of the ACM International Conference on Intelligent User Interfaces, pp. 89–92 (2012)
5. Jacob, M., Wachs, J.P.: Context-based Hand Gesture Recognition for the Operating Room Pattern Recognition Letters (2013) (article in press)
6. Averbukh, V., Starodubtsev, I., Tobolin, D.: The Gesture Interface for Control of Angiographic Systems. Modern computer technology. In: Proceeding of International Russian-Korean Conference, pp. 97–107. UrFU, Ekaterinburg (2012)
7. Starodubtsev, I.: Motion captire based on flexible skeleton hierarchy. Scientific and Technical Bulletin of the Volga Region 1, 159–162 (2014)
8. Starodubtsev, I.: Depth map based initialized motion capture and tracing for gesture interface. Scientific and Technical Bulletin of the Volga Region 3, 264–268 (2013)

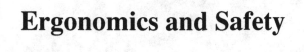

Ergonomics and Safety

The Slip-Resistance Effect of Tread Grooves and Floor Roughness on Different Liquid Thickness

Ching-Chung Chen[1], Hui-Chun Chen[2], Liwen Liu[3],
Fang-Ling Lin[4], and Chih-Lin Chang[4]

[1] Information Management, Hsing Wu University of Science and Technology,
New Taipei City, Taiwan
095165@mail.hwu.edu.tw
[2] Business Administration, Hsing Wu University of Science and Technology,
New Taipei City, Taiwan
078011@mail.hwu.edu.tw
[3] Institute of Occupational Safety and Health, New Taipei, Taiwan
liwen@mail.iosh.gov.tw
[4] School of General Education, Hsiuping University of Science and Technology,
Taichung City, Taiwan
{fingling,salamen}@mail.hust.edu.tw

Abstract. The coefficient of friction between shoe sole and floor is the most critical environment factor influencing slipping risks. When the shoes tread on the surface covered by liquid, the slip resistant of floors are reduced by the squeeze-film effect and the risks of falling are increased. The prior researches discussed mostly the relationship between floor roughness and COF, the discussions of the impact of liquid thickness on COF are relatively rare. This study measured the slip resistance effect of tread groove and floor roughness under different liquid thickness by adopting Brungraber Mark II slipmeter. The results showed that the tread groove, floor roughness and liquid thickness are all factors influencing the COF. The COF of non-tread groove footwear decreases significantly while the liquid thickness larger than 1mm or the floor roughness Ra less than 2μm.

Keywords: slip-resistance, coefficient of friction, liquid thickness.

1   Introduction

Slip and fall happen to many people and cause serious injuries which might be fatal. The Labor Inspection Annual Report [1-5], publish by the Council for Labor Affairs annually, indicates that fall incidences were the most common occupational injuries in Taiwan. This accounted for 15.97% of all occupational incidences from 2008 to 2012. Leamon & Murphy [6] pointed out that the fall incidences take 17% of all occupational incidences in USA and 20% of all occupational incidences in UK annually, and all those slipping and falling incidences lead huge losses at the workplaces. Liberty Mutual [7] reported the occupational injuries had caused 50.01 billion dollars

C. Stephanidis (Ed.): HCII 2014 Posters, Part II, CCIS 435, pp. 443–448, 2014.

losses during 2009. At year 2009, falling had placed at the second position among all incidents (15.8%) and had caused 7.94 billion dollars losses in USA. Federal Institute for Occupational Safety and Health (BauA) [8] indicated that more than 20% of occupational incidents were caused by falling which produced 300 million euro dollars insurance benefits and 8 billion euro dollars losses. Therefore, falling could produce dramatic damages.

Falling mainly happens while the friction between shoe sole and floor is not enough. The friction between shoe sole and floor can be measured by the Coefficient of Friction (COF) which is the most critical environment factor influencing slipping risks. Leamon & Murphy [6] also indicated 2/3 of falling and slipping are caused by slippery. Chang et al. [9] pointed out that COF is the main item to measure the degree of slippery between shoe sole and floor. The higher the COF is, the higher the degree of anti-slippery will be. Many researches have shown that the material of floor, the roughness of floor surface, the floor contaminations, the footwear material, and the tread grooves are all the factors influence the friction measurements [10-12]. Chang [13] further indicated that the liquid thickness has stronger influences than the floor roughness.

In public area and workplaces, the floors covered by liquid are happen all the time. When the floor covered by water, detergent, oil, or other liquid, those liquid will increases the time to contact the tread with the floor. Before the liquid is discharged from the surface between tread and floor, the friction could not be produced. Therefore, the slip-resistance effect will decrease significantly and the falling and slipping will happen dramatically. When the shoes tread on the surface covered by liquid, the influences can be described by squeeze-film effect.

Moore [14] introduced the squeeze-film effect and its function is as followed:

$$t = \frac{K\mu A^2}{F_N}\left(\frac{1}{h^2} - \frac{1}{h_0^2}\right)$$

Where t is the time needed to reduce the liquid thickness from initial h0 to h, F_N is the normal forces, K a shape constant, μ the viscosity of liquid, and A the contact area between the surface. From the squeeze film equation, it is easily to find that the time of falling has positive relationship with the thickness of liquid. The higher the viscosity of an object is, the longer the falling time will be. Therefore, when a person treads on the floor covered by liquid, t is longer or $\frac{dh}{dt}$ is smaller, the contacts between shoe sole and floor will be delayed and the opportunity to fall will be increased.

According to the equation of squeeze film by Moor [14], the thicker the liquid thickness is, the longer the time to contact the tread with the floor and the higher the risk of slipping will be. Burnfield and Power [15], Kulakoski [16] also point out the liquid thickness will affect the measurement of the friction. However, they didn't discuss how the influence of liquid film thickness on the coefficient of friction. William English [17] and Chang [13], Li et al. [18] described that at the surface contaminated by liquid or oil, rough surface of floor will be helpful on improving the squeeze film effect caused by liquid. Leclercq et al. [19], Kim and Smith [20], and Grönqvist [21] indicated that the tread groove design could discharge liquid contaminations (such as water and oil) quickly while the footwear touches the floor, decrease the time while footwear contact the floor, and reduce the risk of slipping and falling.

Concluded the researches mentioned above, the effect of slip resistance can significantly increase by improving the tread groove design and floor roughness. Therefore, this study discussed the slip-resistance effect of tread grooves and floor roughness under different liquid thickness.

2   The Methodology

The study performed a 3 factors experiment by adopting tread and non-tread Neolite shoe materials and three floors with same material, same thickness but different roughness to measure the coefficient of friction.   Each treatment measures 6 times of friction coefficient and 180 (2*3*5*6) measurement values in total.   The differences between tread and non-tread Neolite shoe materials are the tread shoe material was craved with 1mm width and 3mm deep grooves separated every 3mm on the sole.

The roughness of three different tiles was measured by Mitutoyo® SJ-301 surface roughness tester.   The measurement principle followed the suggestions of Chang [13].   The tiles was cut into 2.5mm and 12.5mm separately and adopting the value of Ra and Rtm as the measurement parameters where Ra is the average height of central lines on vertical section and Rtm is the average height between the higher and lower point of the surface.   The Ra of three tiles are 7.05µm, 4.03µm, 1.94µm and Rtm are 55.73µm, 26.89µm and 14.21µm separately.

Furthermore, the experiments conduct with the wet floors which sink in water for 24 hours without water mark.   There are 0.5mm, 1mm, 1.5mm, and 2mm notch separately designed on the experiment platforms to control the thickness of water.   After each hit with Brungraber Mark Ⅱ, the liquid inside the notches will be drained by a small water pump and cleaned by an air compressor, then, same amount of water will be added to perform the next experiment to insure the thickness of water is constant.

The BM II slipmeter was used in the friction measurements. This slipmeter is commonly used in the USA for field study involved slipping & falling incidences. The standard test method of using the BM II is published by the American Society for Testing and Materials (ASTM) [22].

Finally, the study applied descriptive statistics and ANOVA to discuss the influences of shoe material, floor roughness and liquid thickness on COF.   While the factor reaches the level of significant at $\alpha=0.05$, the Duncan Multiple Range then further conducted to analyze the multiple comparisons.

3   The Results

The COF and the losses of friction tested under various shoe materials, floor roughness and liquid thickness are shown as Table 1. As shown in Table 1, the COF of tread grooves is higher than the one of non-tread grooves.   Except the combination of non-tread grooves and 0mm liquid thickness, the COFs are negatively related to the liquid thickness.

The results of ANOVA analysis demonstrate that the influences of shoe material, floor roughness and liquid thickness on COF are all significant ($p<0.001$) and the two-way and three-way interaction effects are also significant ($p<0.001$). The results of Duncan's multiple range test shown in Table 2, the average COF of tread groove is higher than those of non-tread groove and the sequences of the average COF for three different tiles are tile A(Ra=7.05μm), tile B(Ra=4.03μm) and tile C(Ra=1.94μm). The average COF of liquid thickness is reduced while the thickness getting thicker. The value of COF is the largest one with the liquid thickness equals zero, and the value of COF is the smallest one with the liquid thickness equals 5mm.

Table 1. The mean and standard deviation of COF under conditions

Shoe material	Tiles	Liquid thickness				
		0mm	0.5mm	1mm	1.5mm	2mm
tread	Tile A	0.430	0.387	0.383	0.363	0.360
	(Ra=7.05μm)	(0.015)	(0.012)	(0.012)	(0.005)	(0.000)
	Tile B	0.425	0.398	0.373	0.363	0.355
	(Ra=4.03μm)	(0.014)	(0.012)	(0.015)	(0.012)	(0.008)
	Tile C	0.362	0.332	0.333	0.308	0.305
	(Ra=1.94μm)	(0.015)	(0.010)	(0.014)	(0.012)	(0.010)
Non-tread	Tile A	0.425	0.352	0.292	0.250	0.245
	(Ra=7.05μm)	(0.010)	(0.008)	(0.010)	(0.000)	(0.005)
	Tile B	0.393	0.287	0.250	0.240	0.215
	(Ra=4.03μm)	(0.008)	(0.012)	(0.000)	(0.006)	(0.010)
	Tile C	0.410	0.043	0.042	0.037	0.035
	(Ra=1.94μm)	(0.009)	(0.008)	(0.008)	(0.005)	(0.005)

Table 2. Duncan's multiple range test results

Factors	Level	Average COF	Group*
Shoe materials	tread	0.365	A
	Non-tread	0.234	B
Floors	Tile A (Ra=7.05μm)	0.349	A
	Tile B (Ra=4.03μm)	0.330	B
	Tile C (Ra=1.94μm)	0.221	C
Liquid thickness	0mm	0.408	A
	0.5mm	0.300	B
	1mm	0.279	C
	1.5mm	0.260	D
	2mm	0.253	E

*Different letters in group indicate they were significantly different under α=0.05.

Figure 1 reveals the interaction effects of material, floor and liquid thickness. On all floors, the thicker the liquid is the lower the COF will be no matter the shoe material is tread or non-tread. For tile A and tile B, the COF of tread groove is higher than the one of non-tread groove, and the COF of non-tread groove is significantly drop down while the liquid getting thicker especially the thickness is over 1mm. For tile C, the COF of non-tread groove is reaching zero while the floor covering with liquid. Therefore, the design of tread groove and floor roughness will be useful to improve the impact of liquid thickness on COF reducing and promote the effect of slip resistant. The effect is most significant while the tread groove Ra is less than 2μm and tested on tile C.

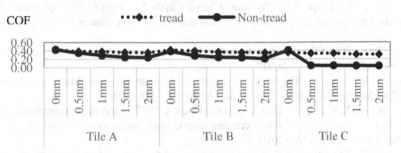

Fig. 1. The interaction effect of shoe material, floor and liquid thickness

4   Conclusion

Many researches have pointed out the floor, the roughness of floor, contaminations, shoe materials and tread grooves are all factors influencing COF. The results of this study demonstrated that the tread groove is the main factor affecting COF followed by floor roughness and liquid thickness. The results about the liquid thickness are quite opposite from the results of Chang [13] who believed the liquid thickness has stronger impacts on COF than floor roughness does. Same as the prior researches, the coefficient of friction can be proved by using the tread grooved footwear and rough floors. On the other hand, the slip resistance effect can also be improved by reducing the influence of liquid thickness on COF [13], [17-21]. In total, the rougher the floors is, the higher the COF will be. And, the thicker the liquid thickness is, the lower the COF will be. Therefore, the tread groove footwear will be the key solution to avoid the falling and slipping on the floor covered by liquid.

Acknowledgments. This research was financially supported by the National Science Council of the Republic of China under the grant NSC 101-2221-E-266-001.

References

1. Labor Inspection Annual Report, Council of Labor Affairs of ROC, Taipei (2008) (in Chinese)
2. Labor Inspection Annual Report, Council of Labor Affairs of ROC, Taipei (2009) (in Chinese)

3. Labor Inspection Annual Report, Council of Labor Affairs of ROC, Taipei (2010) (in Chinese)
4. Labor Inspection Annual Report, Council of Labor Affairs of ROC, Taipei (2011) (in Chinese)
5. Labor Inspection Annual Report, Council of Labor Affairs of ROC, Taipei (2012) (in Chinese)
6. Leamon, T.B., Murphy, P.L.: Occupational slips and falls: more than a trivial problem. Ergonomics 38(3), 487–498 (1995)
7. Liberty Mutual Research Institute for Safety. Annual Report of Scientific Activity. USA: Hopkinton, M.A. (2011), http://www.baua.de
8. Chang, W.R., Grönqvist, R., Leclercq, S., Myung, Makkonen, L., Strandberg, Brungraber, R.J., Mattke, U., Thorpe, S.C.: The role of friction in the Measurement of slipperiness, part 1; Friction mechaniness and definition of test conditions. Ergonomics 44(13), 1217–1232 (2001)
9. Chang, W.R.: The Effect of Slip Criterion and Time on Friction Measurement. Safety Science 40(7-8), 593–611 (2002)
10. Chang, W.R., Matz, S.: The Slip Resistance of Common Footwear Materials Measured with Two Slipmeters. Applied Ergonomics 32(6), 549–558 (2001)
11. Liu, L.W., Li, K.W., Lee, Y.H., Chen, C.C., Chen, C.Y.: Friction measurements on "anti-slip" floors under shoe sole, contamination, and inclination conditions. Safety Science 48(10), 1321–1326 (2010)
12. Chang, W.R.: The Effect of Surface Roughness and Contaminants on the Dynamic Friction between Porcelain Tile. Applied Ergonomics 32, 173–184 (2001)
13. Moore, D.F.: The friction and lubrication of elastomers. International Series of Monographs on Material Science and Technology. Pergamon Press, Oxford (1972)
14. Burnfield, J.M., Powers, C.M.: Prediction of slips: an evaluation of utilized coefficient of friction and available slip resistance. Ergonomics 49(10), 982–995 (2006)
15. Kulakowski, B.T., Buczek, F.L., Cavanagh, P.R.: Evaluation of performance of three slip resistance testers. Journal of testing and Evaluation 17, 234–240 (1989)
16. William English, Pedestrian Slip Resistance, 2nd edn. Rose Printing Company Inc., New York (2003)
17. Li, K.W., Chang, W.R., Leamon, T.B., Chen, C.C.: Floor slipperiness measurement: friction coefficient, roughness of floors, and subjective perceptive under spillage conditions. Safety Science 42, 547–565 (2004)
18. Leclercq, S., Tisserand, M., Saulnier, H.: Tribological concepts involved in slipping accidents analysis. Ergonomics 38(2), 197–208 (1995)
19. Kim, I.J., Smith, R.: Observation of the Floor Surface Topography Changes in Pedestrian Slip Resistance Measurements. International Journal of Industrial Ergonomics 26(6), 581–601 (2000)
20. Grönqvist, R.: Mechanisms of Friction and Assessment of Slip Resistance of New and Used Footwear Soles on Contaminated Floors. Ergonomics 38(2), 224–241 (1995)
21. American Society for Testing and Materials, F-1677-05. Standard method of test for using a portable inclinable articulated strut slip tester (PIAST), American Society for Testing and Materials (2005)

Human Factor and Ergonomics in Essential Requirements for the Operation of Technical Equipment

Adam Górny

Poznań University of Technology, Faculty of Management Engineering
ul. Strzelecka 11, 60-965 Poznań, Poland
adam.gorny@put.poznan.pl

Abstract. The goal of ensuring the safety of technical equipment users lies at the heart of all design requirements classified as essential [3]. To achieve proper compliance with such requirements, it is essential to adopt solutions which meet the needs and expectations of the concerned parties. The choice of solutions must reflect the profiles of users, who are described as the so called human factor, as well as any criteria helpful in achieving the best possible matches for particular worker profiles. Described in terms of ergonomic criteria, the solutions should be seen as an integral part of the design process. By accounting for ergonomic criteria in such a process, it is possible to ensure that the conditions in which technical equipment is operated live up to the desired level of human-friendliness.

Keywords: Ergonomics principles, technical equipment, essential requirements.

1   Introduction

The requirements of the European safety system are designed to ensure that equipment is operated without endangering any involved persons.

Compliance with such requirements is, in fact, the prime responsibility of machine and equipment designers. The required safety level is achieved by applying solutions which comply with guidelines set out to serve as fundamental requirements. Compliance with such requirements, which incorporate technical safety principles, is achieved in a three-stage design process [2], [3], [7], [12]. Practicable solutions have been described in the new approach directives and further elaborated in harmonized standards containing sample measures to be taken to ensure conformity with the essential requirements.

To achieve protection against hazards, it is crucial to identify operational requirements and provide all those involved in the work process with proper guidance on working principles [4], [9].

Requirements as well as the ways to satisfy them must account for the specific profiles of users (the so called human factor) [1], [5], [11], so as to ensure the achievement of the required safety levels, protection against hazards and compliance with

C. Stephanidis (Ed.): HCII 2014 Posters, Part II, CCIS 435, pp. 449–454, 2014.
© Springer International Publishing Switzerland 2014

ergonomic design criteria. The ergonomic criteria, which are pivotal for ensuring that machines meet human needs and expectations, should be seen as an integral part of the design process. Leaving them ignored will bar the way to achieving conformity with the fundamental requirements.

2   Identifying the Design Requirements

2.1   Technical Safety Criteria

The purpose behind seeking compliance with technical safety requirements is to ensure safety in the operation of technical equipment. Safety requirements must allow workers to operate technical equipment without creating hazards or making the work strenuous for persons performing their assigned duties. This applies to operation in the face of anticipated hazards and to the option for defining the parameters of such hazards as well as to circumstances which cannot be foreseen [9]. In selecting adequate safety precautions, one should account for all individuals known to be involved in the operation. Particular focus should be placed on operators as well as maintenance and support services.

At each stage of operation, a major role is played by ergonomic criteria which describe the adjustment of technical equipment to user needs and expectations [5], [6], [8], [11]. In applying ergonomic criteria in the design process and in planning the conditions for the performance of operator tasks, emphasis should be placed on minimizing loads and strains. This can be achieved by [3]:

— accounting for the diversity of physical characteristics among operators,
— ensuring sufficient room for the safe performance of motions involved in the work of operators,
— ensuring that operators may utilize the machine's entire range of movements,
— ensuring the equipment can be overseen without the need for maintaining concentration for overly prolonged periods,
— ensuring the operator and the machine in their charge have ways available to effectively exchange messages.

The solutions must be instrumental to reducing hazards and strenuousness by relying on ergonomic criteria in technical equipment design. The top priority consideration in the process is human safety [1], [10].

Relevant requirements apply to all areas of potential hazard during equipment operation in keeping with operating manuals as well as during maintenance and repair work. In particular, this applies to controls and control systems, rules for normal and emergency activation and shutdowns, protection against hazards resulting from the ejection of objects and the emissions of gas and fumes, protection from moving parts and other items as well as protection against frost bites, burns, fire, explosions and electric shocks [2], [3].

The fundamental requirements designed to protect humans are associated with ergonomic criteria and determine the use of ergonomic principles in the design of technical machinery and equipment. These requirements ensure the proper:

— interaction between man and machine,
— collaboration among all individuals involved in equipment operation,
— compliance with psychological and social requirements pertaining to the operation of technical equipment,
— enhancement of human abilities to perform hazard reducing tasks.

Such ergonomic requirements and solutions help achieve the desired safety levels by employing design determinants which ensure the achievement of safe operating conditions. Furthermore, such requirements and solutions ensure safe operation by unambiguously defining how equipment operation is to proceed [7], [12].

2.2   Compliance with Design Requirements and Solution Development

The key requirements designed to ensure technical equipment operating safety are enshrined in the relevant legislation based on the principles embodied in the New Approach. The central legislative instrument for this purpose is Directive 2006/42/EC [2] which calls for the use of design solutions for the achievement of the desired technical compliance and to eliminate hazards.

In order to ensure compliance with the fundamental requirements during technical equipment design, it is necessary to verify the needs of all concerned parties while accounting for market demands. When assessing the option of applying specific solutions, proper account also needs to be taken of hazard assessments and the impact of hazards on any persons involved in the work. The design assessment methodology relies on the guidelines of the EN ISO 12100 [3] standard under which one is required to:

— identify any risks and limitations associated with the operation of technical equipment,
— verify requirements laid down in harmonized standards B and C,
— assess risks associated with operating technical equipment,
— apply prescriptive solutions to allow for the mitigation of impacts of the risk factors,
— ensure oversight over risk mitigation and define measures necessary to ensure that the required safety level is maintained continuously throughout the operation of technical equipment.

The procedure followed to achieve the expected level of compliance with the fundamental requirements is shown in Figure 1. The measures to be taken to that end should be seen as a strategy to minimize any risks taken with respect to technical equipment.

To ensure the work process proceeds effectively, the designer needs to recognize the ergonomic criteria essential for producing human-friendly solutions. The critical elements of such solutions are presented in Table 1.

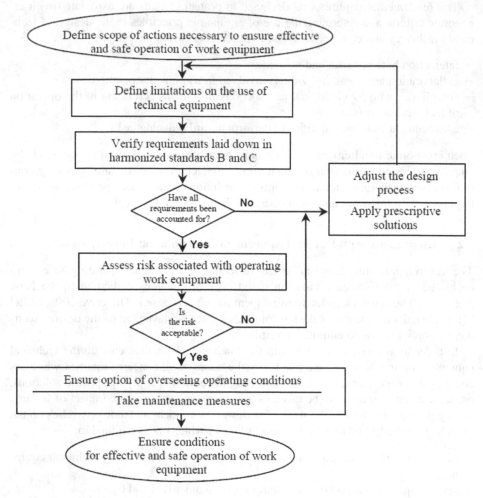

Fig. 1. Algorithm designed to ensure compliance with fundamental requirements.

In the measures taken, particular attention needs to be paid to the human factor, which is critical for [4]:

— applying ergonomic principles in the design process and producing work factors and workstations,
— any natural working skills and working skills acquired by workers,
— the awareness of hazards among any exposed individuals,
— the conviction that the tasks can be performed with unintended departures from the desired course of work,
— workers' propensity to deviate from adopted safe working procedures.

To gain the certainty that the actions taken to minimize hazards are indeed effective, designers need to account for attempts to block certain measures and by-pass any existing safety precautions and systems. When dealing with the human factor, it is essential to learn why attempts to block measures and circumvent safety systems might be made.

Table 1. Role of ergonomic criteria and requirements accounted for in the design process

Design stage	Role of ergonomic criteria and requirements (associated with the human factor)
Identification of hazards and limitations	- define factors which reduce work effectiveness, - help identify factors which contribute to strenuousness, - help assess the significance of individual factors associated with persons entering workplace and their work engagements.
Verification of prescriptive requirements	- indicate standards containing ergonomic criteria of significance for the design process, - identify standards which help raise the effectiveness of operating technical equipment.
Risk assessment	- help apply ergonomic criteria in risk assessment, - bring particular attention to hazards affecting people in the equipment work zone.
Mitigation of risk factor impact	- indicate ergonomic solutions which mitigate the impact of risk factors, - help incorporate ergonomic criteria into risk impact mitigation process.
Oversight over risk mitigation	- help oversee the application of ergonomic criteria in risk mitigation.
Continuous maintenance of required safety level (compliance with requirements)	- treat ergonomic requirements as an integral part of design process.

3   Conclusions

While the responsibility for worker safety associated with the operation of technical equipment rests with the employer, the party liable for ensuring the proper conditions to achieve safety lies with the manufacturer which is subject to the fundamental requirements. Technical equipment should satisfy safety specifications and ergonomic requirements throughout its usable life. One needs to bear in mind that the majority of accidents and incidents result from failures to provide employees with proper procedures. Particularly high rates of errors leading to accidents can be found in maintenance operations. The reason for this is that maintenance work is highly complex and that maintenance personnel frequently work under time pressure, under insufficient supervision, without the required knowledge and under adverse external circumstances. Furthermore, errors made in the course of maintenance work often result in delayed accidents occurring during the regular operation of technical equipment [4]. As a consequence, since maintenance work is likely to contribute to accidents, it requires technical and organizational solutions which maximally reduce the likelihood of untoward events.

The ergonomic requirements applied in the design process should be perceived as an integral part of the body of requirements intended to ensure the safest possible operation of technical equipment. Ergonomic criteria highlight the necessity to adjust technical equipment to the needs of users (operators, technical service providers) so as to avert any identified hazards.

The design safety requirements defined as fundamental should also be seen as guidelines for the development of conditions which ensure effective performance of work [11]. Such requirements must account for ergonomic criteria which need to be seen as mandatory.

References

1. Butlewski, M., Tytyk, E.: The assessment criteria of the ergonomic quality of anthropotechnical mega-systems. In: Vink, P. (ed.) Advances in Social and Organizational Factors, pp. 298–306. CRC Press, Taylor and Francis Group, Boca Raton (2012)
2. Directive 2006/42/EC of the European Parliament and of the Council of 17 May 2006 on machinery, and amending Directive 95/16/EC (recast) Official Journal L 157, p. 24, as amended (June 9, 2006)
3. EN ISO 12100, Safety of machinery. General principles of design. Risk assessment and risk reduction, European Committee for Standardization, Brussels (2010)
4. Górny, A.: Assessment of compliance with minimum safety requirements in machine operations: A case of assessing the control devices of a press. In: Arezes, P., et al. (eds.) Occupational Safety and Hygiene, pp. 497–501. CRC Press, Taylor & Francis, London (2013)
5. Górny, A.: Ergonomics in the formation of work condition quality. Work: A Journal of Prevention, Assessment and Rehabilitation 1(suppl. 1), 1708–1711 (2012)
6. Górny, A.: Ergonomics in occupational safety formation – ergonomic requirements in system managements of industrial safety. Foundations of Control and Management Sciences 11, 127–137 (2008)
7. Górny, A.: Essential requirements in ergonomics standards harmonized with the European Parliament and the Council Directive 2006/42/EC. In: Pacholski, L.M., Marcinkowski, J.S., Horst, W.M. (eds.) Proceedings of the XXIInd International Seminar of Ergonomics Teachers, pp. 37–47. Poznan University of Technology, Institute of Management Engineering, Poznań (2006)
8. Gołaś, H., Mazur, A.: Macroergonomic aspects of a quality management system. In: Jasiak, A. (ed.) Macroergonomic Paradigms of Management, pp. 161–170. Poznan University of Technology, Poznan (2008)
9. Jasiulewicz-Kaczmarek, M.: The role of ergonomics in implementation of the social aspect of sustainability, illustrated with the example of maintenance. In: Arezes, P., et al. (eds.) Occupational Safety and Hygiene, pp. 47–52. CRC Press, Taylor & Francis, London (2013)
10. Mazur, A.: Shaping quality of work conditions. In: Dahlke, G., Górny, A. (eds.) Health Protection and Ergonomics for Human Live Quality Formation, pp. 31–44. Publishing House of Poznan University of Technology, Poznan (2009)
11. Mrugalska, B.: Environmental disturbances in robust machinery design. In: Arezes, P., et al. (eds.) Occupational Safety and Hygiene, pp. 229–236. CRC Press, Taylor & Francis, London (2013)
12. Mrugalska, B., Kawecka-Endler, A.: Machinery Design for Construction Safety in Practice. In: Stephanidis, C. (ed.) Universal Access in HCI, Part III, HCII 2011. LNCS, vol. 6767, pp. 388–397. Springer, Heidelberg (2011)

Changes in Biological Data during Prolonged Use of a Learning Support System and the Effects of a Rest Break

Kaoru Honda[1] and Fukuyo Honda[2]

[1] Faculty of Literature and Social Sciences, Yamagata University, Japan
honda@human.kj.yamagata-u.ac.jp
[2] Faculty of Medical Science and Welfare, Tohoku Bunka Gakuen University, Japan
fhonda@rehab.tbgu.ac.jp

Abstract. The use of a learning support system can give rise to complaints of pains in the shoulder and arm and of asthenopia in many people. The increased feeling of fatigue is considered to be due to prolonged personal computer use, making this type of learning a heavy burden for learners. However, few studies have focused on how to measure the effect of prolonged use of a learning support system on the learner's physical condition. Evaluation of this type of learning has been attempted using biological data, but optimal measuring methods and data processing have not been established to evaluate the physical effects of this type of learning. The aims of the present study were to measure biological data (brain waves and heart rate) when learners were subjected to a continuous problem solving session that involved calculation, reading, and collation (problem-solving tasks), to analyze the temporal changes that occurred in the measured biological data, to examine the validity of the measurements of mental activities and burden, and to evaluate the effects of taking a break during the session.

Keywords: learning support system, prolonged use, fatigue, biological data, brain wave, heart rate.

1 Introduction

The use of a learning support system can give rise to complaints of pains in the shoulder and arm and of asthenopia in many people. The increased feeling of fatigue is considered to be due to prolonged personal computer use, making this type of learning a heavy burden for learners. However, few studies have focused on how to measure the effect of prolonged use of a learning support system on the learner's physical condition. Evaluation of this type of learning has been attempted using biological data, but optimal measuring methods and data processing have not been established to evaluate the physical effects of this type of learning. The aims of the present study were to measure biological data (brain waves and heart rate) when learners were subjected to a continuous problem solving session that involved calculation, reading, and collation (problem-solving tasks), to analyze the temporal changes that occurred in the measured biological data, to examine the validity of the measurements of mental activities and burden, and to evaluate the effects of taking a break during the session.

C. Stephanidis (Ed.): HCII 2014 Posters, Part II, CCIS 435, pp. 455–460, 2014.

2   Methods

2.1   Experiments

(1) Experiment 1. In experiment 1, the subjects were asked to solve calculation, reading, and collation problems as modeled learning problems. In the calculation problem, the subjects were asked to use the computer mouse to click on (select) one numeral from a set of numerals from 0–9 enclosed by a box so that the selected numeral agreed with the first numeral of the answer to a one-digit addition problem displayed at the center of the screen. The numerals 0–9 were displayed near the one-digit addition. In the reading problem, the subjects were asked to click (select) on one of 10 colored squares so that the selected square agreed with the Chinese character indicating the color of the square displayed at the center of the screen. The 10 squares were displayed near the Chinese character. In the collation problem, the subjects were asked to click (select) on one of 10 symbols enclosed by the box so that the selected symbol agreed with the symbol displayed at the center of the screen. The 10 symbols were displayed near the symbol displayed at the center of the screen. The subjects were asked to sit on a chair in a comfortable position. The subjects were then asked to face the screen, and the mouse position was adjusted. At the start of the experiment, the subjects were instructed to "please solve the problems without stopping." The subjects were four male university students aged 19–20 years.

After explaining the content of the experiment, a preliminary training task was performed for 2 minutes. The subjects then took a 5-minute break while sitting on a chair in a comfortable position. After confirming that the subjects were calm, the experiment was launched. The subjects were asked to solve the calculation, reading, and collation tasks for 60 minutes (20 minutes each) without stopping. The subjects could select the order of the problems at random.

(2) Experiment 2. In experiment 2, the subjects were asked to solve the calculation problem described in experiment 1. The subjects were six male university students aged 21–24 years.

After explaining the content of the experiment, a preliminary training task was performed for 2 minutes. The subjects then took a 10 minute break while sitting on a chair in a comfortable position. After confirming that the subjects were calm, the experiment was launched. The subjects were asked to solve calculation problems for 30 minutes, to take a 10 minute break, to continue solving calculation problems for a further 30 minutes , and then to take another 10 minute break (a total of 80 minutes).

2.2   Processing of Biological Data

Measurement of brain waves: Electrodes were placed on three points (Fp1, Fp2, and A1) in accordance with the international 10–20 system. For data processing, brain waves were classified into three bands: θ waves (4–6 Hz), α waves (7–13 Hz), and β

waves (14–30 Hz). During various mental activities such as stimuli and mental arithmetic, β waves are said to be dominant [1][2]. Therefore, we focused on the appearance of β waves and evaluated changes in mental activities.

Measurement of heart rates: Electrodes were placed on three points of the chest in
accordance with the bipolar lead CM_5. Heart rate data were processed by power spectrum analysis of RR-interval data using wavelet transform, in which the total power of
0.05–0.15 Hz was defined as the LF component and 0.15–0.475 Hz was defined as
the HF component. The balance between sympathetic and parasympathetic nerve
activities is generally analyzed based on the ratio of the LF component to the HF
component [3]. Therefore, we calculated the LF/HF ratio and observed sympathetic
nerve activities (indicative of a burden on the living body).

3   Results and Discussion

(1) Experiment 1. Figure 1 shows the changes in β waves during the 60 minutes of
the problem-solving tasks (the average of the four subjects). The β waves increased
after the initiation of each of the three problems and a peak was observed in each of
three time zones (the elapsed time of 20, 40, and 60 minutes), corresponding to the
three problems. In other words, when the type of problem changed, mental activities
first decreased and then gradually increased.

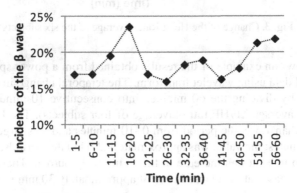

Fig. 1. Change of the brain waves (β wave)

Figure 2 shows the variations in R-R intervals during the performance of problem-
solving tasks. R-R intervals shorten when each subject starts the tasks. R-R intervals
for three subjects A, B and D transition at a constant value. Figure 3 shows the average of the subjects' R-R intervals to observe time-dependent variations of R-R intervals. R-R intervals shortens as soon as the subjects begin a task, and is the shortest in
around 30 minutes.

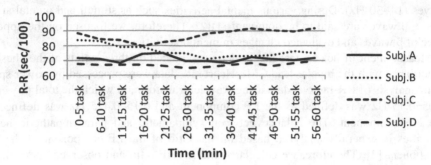

Fig. 2. Change of the Heart Rate

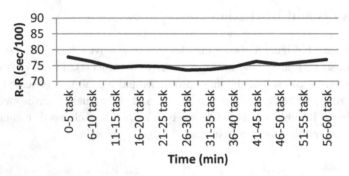

Fig. 3. Change of the Heart Rate (average of the six subjects)

Figure 4 shows an example of the results obtained from a power spectrum analysis for RR-interval data using wavelet transform. The temporal change in the LF/HF ratio was examined by dividing the 60 minutes into consecutive 10 minutes periods and calculating the average LF/HF ratio (average of four subjects). The LF/HF ratio was slightly larger than 1.5 in the period from 0–10 minutes and was largest in the period from 30–40 minutes; the value was approximately 2.0 in later periods. The increase in the LF/HF ratio indicates an increase in the living body burden. Therefore, the living body burden increased at the elapsed time of approximately 30 minutes.

(2) Experiment 2. Figure 5 shows the variations in R-R intervals during the performance of the task (calculation problem). When each subject begin the task, R-R intervals tend to shorten. And, after a rest (40 minutes later), the decrease in R-R intervals is small. Figure 6 shows the average of the subjects to observe time-dependent variations of R-R intervals. R-R intervals shorten rapidly when calculation tasks started, and R-R intervals become the shortest after around 25 minutes. And, after a rest (10 minutes), the width of R-R intervals increases. And, after a rest (40 minutes later), these variations of R-R intervals are small.

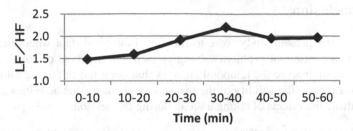

Fig. 4. Change of the power spectrum (LF/HF)

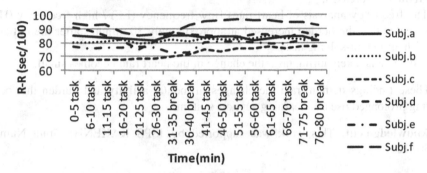

Fig. 5. Change of the Heart Rate

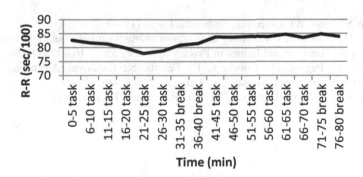

Fig. 6. Change of the Heart Rate (average of the six subjects)

To see the effect of the rest, Figure 3 and Figure 6 are compared. When the subjects go on each tasks without a rest break consecutively for 60 minutes, the short states of R-R intervals continues until end. But, if the rest is taken for ten minutes during the tasks of 30 minutes, the change in the R-R intervals after the rest becomes small. It is that a living body burden is high that there are many heart rates [4]. In other words, taking a 10 minute break during the session inhibited the increase in the living body burden.

4   Conclusion

The aims of the present study were to measure biological data when learners were subjected to a continuous problem solving session that involved calculation, reading, and collation, to analyze the temporal changes that occurred in the measured biological data, to examine the validity of the measurements of mental activities and burden, and to evaluate the effects of taking a break during the session.

1. The β brain waves at each time zone during a 60 minute problem solving session were attenuated when the type of problem was changed and these waves then gradually increased.
2. The frequency analysis of heart rates [low frequency (LF) / high frequency (HF)] revealed that the burden increased at approximately 30 minutes after the initiation of the problem-solving tasks.
3. If the rest is taken during task, the change in the heart rate becomes small.

These findings demonstrate the changes in mental activity and burden that occur during prolonged use of a learning support system.

Acknowledgment. This work was supported by JSPS KAKENHI Grant Number 24501123.

References

1. Miyake, S.: Comfort Engineering. Senbundo, Tokyo (1994)
2. Wilson, G.F., Swainb, C.R., et al.: EEG power changes during a multiple level memory retention task. International Journal of Psychophysiology 32(2), 107–118 (1999)
3. Malliani, A., Pagani, M., Lombardi, F., Cerutti, S.: Cardiovascular neural regulation explored in the frequency domain. Circulation 84(2), 482–492 (1991)
4. Yamaji, K.: Science of Heart Rate. Taisukan Publishing, Tokyo (1981)

A Study of Movement Characteristics in Fine Operations Using TV Monitor

Hiroshi Ichikawa[1], Hiroo Hirose[2], Yoshito Yamamoto[3], and Takeshi Ozaki[2]

[1] Faculty of Home Economics, Otsuma Women's University, Tokyo, Japan
ichikawa.h@otsuma.ac.jp
[2] Faculty of Management of Administration and Information,
Tokyo University of Science, Suwa, Japan
hirose@rs.tus.ac.jp, ozaki@rs.tus.ac.jp
[3] Faculty of Science, Tokyo University of Science, Tokyo, Japan
yama@rs.tus.ac.jp

Abstract. In the manufacturing industry, fine processing tasks advance as the products become smaller. These tasks are usually carried out by industrial robots and automation systems to improve the quality and reliability of products. However, there are a lot of tasks such as products finishing and adjusting/inspecting the finished products that workers have to do at their work sites. Therefore, an analysis of the learning process of work with micromotion, performance assessment and workload assessment are important subjects. This study examines the effect of monitor magnification on worker's motion and workload for positioning as an example of micro-manipulation tasks. We describe motion time and heat rate (HR) to measure workload in the positioning process.

Keywords: Fine operation, TV monitor, Movement characteristics, Workload.

1 Introduction

In the manufacturing industry, fine processing tasks advance as the products become smaller. These tasks are usually carried out by industrial robots and automation systems to improve the quality and reliability of products. However, there are a lot of tasks such as products finishing and adjusting/inspecting the finished products that workers have to do at their work sites. Especially, setting and adjusting the tool in infrequent operations including a setup change depends on skilled workers and needs their flexibility. Because a product design is often changed in trial production, it is difficult to automate this process and the manufacturer must rely on the workers' skills to cope with such a design change. Likewise, automatization of the fine pattern inspection, including pattern recognition, has been researched and implemented, but there are still many cases in which the workers should perform visual inspection of products by a microscope in the initial mass production or small-lot production.

For example, when micro fabricating a printed wiring board, the workers always conduct visual inspection to carry out work with fine adjustment and detect failures,

C. Stephanidis (Ed.): HCII 2014 Posters, Part II, CCIS 435, pp. 461–466, 2014.

such as a broken wire and short circuit, while looking through the microscope or watching an enlarged image on a TV monitor.   Since the eyes and hands of the workers that are different from the actual motion must cooperate with each other when their enlarged images are displayed on such a monitor, it seems to be difficult to apply the conventional motion study and workload knowledge to this work.   Therefore, an analysis of the learning process of work with micromotion, performance assessment and workload assessment are important subjects.

With advances in information technology, work with micromotion using pointing devices such as a computer mouse is increasing in an interface environment consisting mainly of graphical user interfaces (GUI) in not only the manufacturing department but also the general affairs department and the design department using computer aided design (CAD).   In these tasks, the movement of mouse pointer displayed on the monitor does not accord with the movement of worker's hand to use a computer mouse or tablet, so that the worker's visual sense is considered hard to collaborate with his/her motion[1][2][3]. As for fine movements, there is report about the degree of difficulty of coordinating the eyes and the hands[4][5]. However, the relation between fine operation and workload is seldom considered.

Hereafter, this study examines the effect of monitor magnification on worker's motion and workload for positioning as an example of micro-manipulation tasks.   We describe motion time and heat rate (HR) to measure workload in the positioning process.

2   Experimental Method

Subjects **for experiment:**.

The subjects were 6 male university students with normal visual sense and cardiopulmonary function between 20 and 24 years of age.

Task content:.

To examine the effect of TV monitor magnification on worker's motion and workload, an experiment was conducted under the following conditions.   The subjects performed the positioning task while watching an enlarged image on the TV monitor. At this time, the subjects used a pencil and positioned two targets (squares).   This experiment set a single trial motion to 10 reciprocating motions and made the subjects execute 10 trial motions.   We determined the monitor magnification to two levels of 10 times and 20 times, the side length of individual squares (two targets) to two levels of 0.5mm and 1mm and the distance between two targets to two levels of 1mm and 2mm and measured the heart rate (R-R interval) and motion time in the subjects in four types of task conditions.   Here, the code "w.5d2" presents the task conditions that the side length of individual squares (two targets) is 0.5mm and the distance between two targets is 2mm (Fig. 1).

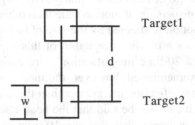

Fig. 1. Experimental work

We attached a heart rate monitor to the subjects and instructed them to sit on a chair and keep their minds at rest in a comfortable position. We measured the heart rate (R-R interval) in the subjects at rest for 5 minutes before staring the task. The task procedures were provided at random and the subjects took a 5-minute break between the tasks.

3   Experimental Results and Discussion

Fig. 2 shows the mean value of motion time in the task conditions. Although there is dispersion of motion time between the subjects and between the task conditions, motion time at a 20-time magnification is longer than that at a 10-time magnification in the task conditions. When the t-test was performed for the mean value of motion time at the 10-time and 20-time magnifications, there was a significant difference between them at the 1% significance level (t=4.06, df=23, p<0.01).

Fig. 3 shows the coefficient of variation (CV = Standard deviation/Mean value). Dispersion of motion time at a 20-time magnification is greater than that at a 10-time magnification in the task conditions. When the t-test was performed for the mean value of the coefficient of variation at the 10-time and 20-time magnifications, there was a significant difference between them at the 1% significance level (t=6.06, df=23, p<0.01).

Fig. 4 shows the heart rate fluctuation (Working heart rate/Resting heart rate x 100) in the task conditions. The working heart rate is higher than the resting heart rate and the increase in heart rate fluctuation in the tasks at a 20-time magnification is greater than that at a 10-time magnification. When the t-test was performed for the mean value of the heart rate fluctuation at the 10-time and 20-time magnifications, there was a significant difference between them at the 5% significance level (t=2.61, df=23, p<0.05).

As a result, it is proven that the tasks at higher magnification produce the greater mean value and dispersion of motion time and the difficulty of these tasks is high.   It also seems that the tasks at higher magnification cause the heavier workload from the result of the calculated heart rate fluctuation.

Fig. 5 shows the mean value and standard deviation of motion time in the task conditions in all subjects. Out of the said task conditions, the codes "w.5d1" and "w.5d2" meaning that the side length of individual squares (two targets) is 0.5mm produce the greater mean value and dispersion of motion time than other codes. This indicates that the difficulty of micromotion is affected by the size of targets.

In the subjective survey after the completion of this experiment, the subjects answered that the tasks at a 20-time magnification were easier than those at a 10-time magnification. As abovementioned, however, the mean value and dispersion of motion time at a 20-time magnification are greater than those at a 10-time magnification in the task conditions. It can also be said that the heart rate fluctuation in the tasks at a 20-time magnification is greater than that at a 10-time magnification, leading to the heavier workload. It is believed that as the monitor magnification becomes higher regardless of subjects' burden, the difference between visual information and actual motion increases more, the recognition process before starting motion becomes complicated and then the subjects' workload increases.

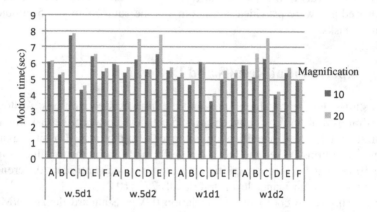

Fig. 2. Motion time in subjects

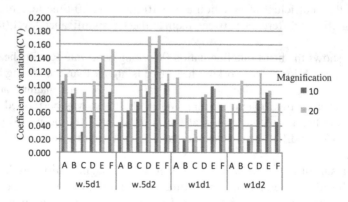

Fig. 3. Coefficient of variation of motion time

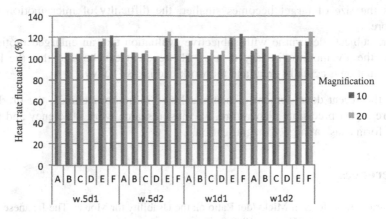

Fig. 4. Heart rate fluctuation

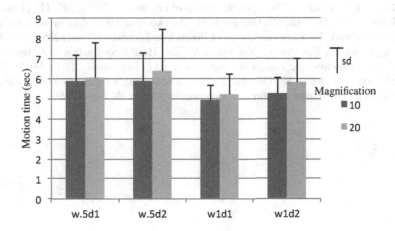

Fig. 5. Mean value and standard deviation of motion time in all subjects

4   Conclusion

We have studied the effect of monitor magnification on worker's motion and work-load for positioning as an example of micro-manipulation tasks. In this experiment, we found the following results:

1. When the subjects make the proper motion while watching an enlarged image on the TV monitor, it takes a longer time in motion as the monitor magnification becomes higher.   The motion-time dispersion also increases.
2. When the subjects make the proper motion while watching an enlarged image on the TV monitor, the heart rate fluctuation increases more to bring the heavier work-load as the monitor magnification becomes higher.

3. As the size of target becomes smaller, the difficulty of micromotion increases more.
4. The subjects determine with subjective evaluation that an enlarged motion image on the TV monitor is easy to use. However, it can be said that the heart rate fluctuation is actually great and the workload is also heavy.

With the recent development of nanomachines in micromachines, the products will require higher precision. Therefore, we must research work efficiency and workload to perform a task at higher magnification.

References

1. Murata, A.: Effects of Micky/dot Ratio on the Usability for Mouse. The Japanese Journal of Ergonomics 28(5), 259–264 (1992)
2. Murata, A.: Experimental Evaluation on Usability for Pointing Devices in Human-Computer Interaction. The Japanese Journal of Ergonomics 28(3), 107–117 (1992)
3. Ichikawa, H., Homma, M., Umemura, M.: An experimental evaluation of input devices for pointing work. International Journal of Production Economics 60-61, 235–240 (1999)
4. Miyashiro, N., Koshiba, T., Yokomizo, Y.: Eye-Hand Coordination and Motion Characteristics on Microscopic Task. The Japanese Journal of Ergonomics 28(1), 33–39 (1989)
5. Shibazaki, H., Noda, K., Enkawa, T.: Effects of Feedback's Discreteness on Fine Positioning Tasks. The Japanese Journal of Ergonomics 32(3), 139–148 (1996)

Integrating Safety, Health and Environment (SHE) into the Autonomous Maintenance Activities

Małgorzata Jasiulewicz-Kaczmarek

Poznan University of Technology, Poznan, Poland
malgorzata.jasiulewicz-kaczmarek@put.poznan.pl

Abstract. In the manufacturing industry, Total Productive Maintenance (TPM) is a very effective tool for improving product quality, productivity as well as safety of employees. In the paper a part of research on implementation of TPM in medium-sized industrial company is introduced. The goal of the paper was analysis of efficiency of promotion of safety and hygiene issues during Autonomous Maintenance pillar implementation.

Keywords: TPM, Autonomous maintenance, SHE.

1 Introduction

Achieving competitive advantage requires building and developing strategies and procedures taking into consideration needs and expectations of stakeholders of a company. Typical postulates of stakeholders include financial aspects (f.ex. returns on capital invested), as well as environmental (f.ex. decrease in emissions and wastes) and social issues (f.ex. safety and hygiene of work). To respond to these challenges companies undertake numerous actions. They implement quality management systems, safety and hygiene of work management systems, environmental management systems [1], [2], introducing elements of CSR [3], [4] to their strategies and promoting safe behavior with BBS approach implementation [5], [6].

Maintenance, as a key process within corporate internal value chain is an active participant of realization requirements of company's stakeholders

Maintenance is defined as activities intended to preserve or promptly restore the safety, performance, reliability, and availability of plant structures, systems, and components to ensure superior performance of their intended function when required. In literature maintenance function is usually analyzed in the context of its role in achieving economic and ecologic efficiency, which refers to efficient use of f.ex. electric energy, high level of products manufactured or competitiveness of a company. Simultaneously, it also contributes significantly to occupational safety and health. Maintenance influences the safety and health of workers in two ways. First, regular maintenance that is correctly planned and carried out is essential to keep both machines and work environment safe and reliable. Second, maintenance itself has to be performed in a safe way, with appropriate protection of maintenance workers and others present in the workplace [7].

C. Stephanidis (Ed.): HCII 2014 Posters, Part II, CCIS 435, pp. 467–472, 2014.

2   Total Productive Maintenance

Total Productive Maintenance is a unique Japanese philosophy. TPM provides a comprehensive, life-cycle approach to equipment management that minimizes equipment failures, production defects, and accidents. It involves everyone in the organization, from top-level management to production mechanics, and production support groups to outside suppliers. TPM is based on teamwork and provides a method for the achievement of world-class levels of overall equipment effectiveness through people and not through technology or systems alone [8], [9].

TPM initiatives as suggested by Japan Institute of Plant Maintenance (JIPM) involve eight pillars: autonomous maintenance; focused improvement; planned maintenance; quality maintenance; education and training; safety, health and environment; office TPM; and development management [10]. The basic goal of achieving "zero" culture, defined as „zero defects", „zero complaints", „zero accidents", „zero waste", „zero lacks in quality".

3   Autonomous Maintenance

The autonomous work group was the first of the formal group concepts advanced for the conscious design of group work systems. Based upon socio-technical work design theory, the concept of the autonomous work group emphasized the organizational independence of the work unit. Work units were decoupled from organizational systems of monitoring and control (supervision) in order to internally self-regulate work tasks. At the core of world-class   maintenance performance is something called autonomous maintenance. In this context, the term autonomous doesn't mean performing maintenance in a vacuum or solely by the traditional maintenance department. The purpose of Autonomous Maintenance is to minimize maintenance costs and downtime costs at a given quality of production whilst at the same time fulfilling the requirements of safety [11].
Operators learn the maintenance skills they need to know through a seven-step maintenance program: initial cleaning, countermeasures to sources of contamination, cleaning and lubrication standards, overall inspection, autonomous maintenance standards,   organize and manage the workplace, carry out ongoing autonomous maintenance and advanced improvement activities.

Implementation of the AM program requires preparing operators for active partnership with maintenance department staff not only in technology area (f.ex. inspection scheme), but also in safety and ergonomics area. All the actions taken within each of the seven steps should be performed in a safe way.

4   Research

The company the research was conducted in is well settled in the market, as it has been operating for over twenty years. Decision on TPM implementation was taken four years ago. The first two years of project implementation required building proper organizational structure, identifying and appointing people responsible for predefined actions and organizing   trainings for employees striving for building awareness, team work and 5S practices implementation.

The next step of project realization, conducted parallel to 5S practices development, was   preparing operators to take over part of responsibilities of maintenance staff which means introduction of autonomous maintenance. The program of trainings was developed in the organization to build operators knowledge and skills for safe performance of simple service actions create pro-active attitude towards problems identified. Parallel to trainings, there are operational activities performed at predefined machines. Every training, apart from content focused on technical aspects, includes also content referring to work safety.

The goal of the research conducted in the company was determination whether trainings organized, procedures and instructions developed and managers commitment promote safety and hygiene of work principles efficiently. The research was conducted for 46 operators (21 women and 25 men). All the operators participating in the research were part of the project from the very beginning. The research was done with a questionnaire. The questionnaire included 16 questions (statements):

1. It is important that everybody knows consequences of failures
2. Unexpected things happen all the time
3. Knowledge on safe principles of work helps me to identify threats
4. I understand necessity of application of individual protection means
5. There is still lot to do in safety and hygiene of work area
6. AM trainings improved my knowledge on safety of work issues
7. In situations requiring fast reaction, obeying rules is just enough
8. Developed procedures enable safe work performance
9. I believe that deviation from procedures/ instructions is acceptable if there are no consequences or just a small risk
10. Following detailed instructions   makes work difficult
11. Maintaining cleanness standards influences safety of work
12. My colleagues obey procedures and instructions
13. My work environment allows me to be effective and efficient
14. I keep my supervisors informed on incorrectness in machines work
15. In my company, employees initiatives striving for safety and hygiene of work are supported
16. My supervisors discipline and correct me when I work against procedures/ instructions

The level of meeting predefined requirements was assessed by operators within 1 to 5 scale, where 1 means "I totally disagree' while 5 is "I totally agree". The results of the research are presented in the figure below (figure 1).

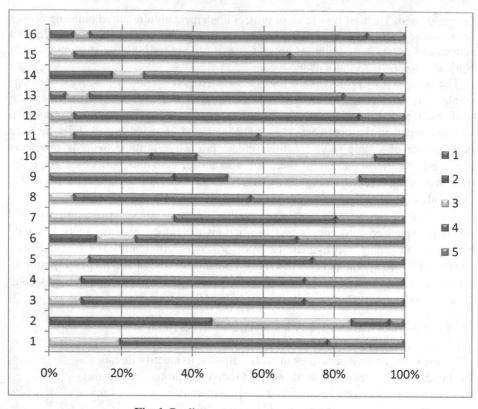

Fig. 1. Replies operators - cumulated values

The way operators perceive their actions performed within AM pillar is reflected in their supervisor assessment. The assessment is conducted once a month and includes 5 criteria. Because of the research range two criteria are going to be presented: commitment to AM actions and obedience of safety and hygiene of work principles and promoting safe work environment. Results of the supervisor's assessment are referred to the same place the research among operators was conducted in.

Employees commitment to Autonomous Maintenance actions is assessed by their supervisors in five-level scale:

1. Participates in trainings but does not apply knowledge gained there in practice. Demonstrates aversion to taking up additional activities.
2. Participates in trainings but does not apply knowledge gained there in practice. Correctly, however not systematically follows AM schedules.
3. Participates in trainings and applies knowledge gained there in practice in standard situations.
4. Participates in trainings and applies knowledge gained there in practice willingly.
5. Participates in trainings. Deals with non-typical situation without any help.

The supervisor applies the same scheme for assessment of operators obedience to safety and hygiene of work principles and promoting safe work environment.

1. Despite commands does not care for own or others safety, often does not follow safety and hygiene of work procedures
2. There have been cases of encroaching upon safety and hygiene of work regulations or procedures; personal protection means are not used; increased supervision is required.
3. Obeys safety and hygiene of work regulations and procedures, uses personal protection means
4. Obeys safety and hygiene of work regulations and procedures, uses personal protection means; actively supports safety and hygiene of work regulations obedience
5. Fully obeys safety and hygiene of work regulations and procedures; actively supports safety and hygiene of work regulations obedience and safety of work improvement

The results of operators assessments by their supervisor in a month in which survey among   operators was conducted is introduced in the figure below (figure 2).

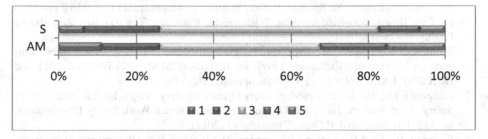

Fig. 2. Employees assessment by their supervisor

The research conducted leads to the conclusion that actions undertaken in a company and striving for promotion of safety and hygiene of work principles are efficient. Most employees are aware of necessity to perform according to rules predefined in procedures and instructions and see the necessity to implement further improving actions. The attitude of managers is also worth mentioning as according to most employees managers support and promote principles of safe work performance and discipline obedience of these principles. It is especially important as managers' attitude supports and determines success in changes implementation.

5   Summary

The goal of autonomous maintenance in TPM is, among others, preparing operators to active partnership with maintenance staff, striving for general safety improvement, equipment reliability and work safety.

Operators can make or break maintenance effectiveness. Without interrupting their production work, operators can easily prevent breakdowns, predict failures and prolong equipment life if they become more intimately familiar with the machinery they run every day. But to do this, they must become highly equipment conscious, and that can require some intense training

References

1. Gołaś, H., Mazur, A.: Zarządzanie jakością. Wydawnictwo Politechniki Poznańskiej, Poznań (2011)
2. Górny, A.: Ergonomics aspects of CSR in system shaping the quality of work environment. In: Vink, P. (ed.) Advances in Social and Organizational Factors, pp. 541–550. CRC Press, Boca Raton (2012)
3. Misztal, A.: Przegląd standardów uzupełniających systemy zarządzania jakością w wybranych branİn: Problemy Jakości, pp. 30–33. Wydawnictwo SIGMA-NOT, Warszawa (2009)
4. Saniuk, A., Saniuk, S.: Monitoring and control of strategy realization in make-to-order manufacturing. In: Carpathian Logistics Congress CLC 2013, Cracow, Poland, Tanger (2013)
5. Sadłowska-Wrzesińska, J.: Bezpieczeństwo behawioralne (BBS), społeczna odpowiedzialność biznesu (CSR) i dialog społeczny – współczesne wyzwania bezpieczeństwa pracy. In: Knosala, R. (ed.) Innowacje w zarządzaniu i inżynierii produkcji. Tom II, pp. 606–616. Oficyna Wydawnicza Polskiego Towarzystwa Zarządzania Produkcją, Opole (2014)
6. Jasiulewicz-Kaczmarek, M., Drozyner, P.: Preventive and Pro-active Ergonomics Influence on Maintenance Excellence Level. In: Robertson, M.M. (ed.) EHAWC 2011 and HCII 2011. LNCS, vol. 6779, pp. 49–58. Springer, Heidelberg (2011)
7. Butlewski, M.: The issue of product safety in contemporary design. In: Salamon, S. (ed.) Safety of the System, Technical, Organizational and Human Work Safety Determinants, pp. 112–120. Red. Wyd. P Częst, Częstochowa (2012)
8. Willmott, P.: Total Productive Maintenance: The Western Way. Butterworth-Heinemann, Oxford (1994)
9. Yamashima, H.: Challenge to world-class-manufacturing. International Journal of Quality & Reliability Management 17(2), 132–143 (2000)
10. Rodrigues, M., Hatakeyama, K.: Analysis of the fall of TPM in companies. Journal of Materials Processing Technology 179(1-3), 276–279 (2006)
11. Mugwindiri, K., Mbohwa, C.: Availability Performance Improvement by Using Autonomous Maintenance – The Case of a Developing Country, Zimbabwe. In: Proceedings of the World Congress on Engineering 2013, London, U.K., vol. I (2013), http://www.iaeng.org/publication/WCE2013/WCE2013_pp715-720.pdf

Relationship between Comfortable Feelings and Distribution of Seat Pressure in Sustaining a Sitting Posture for a Long Time

Yasuyuki Matsushita, Noriaki Kuwahara, and Kazunari Morimoto

Graduate School of Science and Technology Kyoto Institute of Technology Matsugasaki,
Sakyo, Kyoto 606-85858, Japan
{yasuoyasuoyasu,noriaki.kuwahara,morix119}@gmail.com

Abstract. It is necessary to clarify the method for measuring a comprehensive evaluation from plurality criteria of the physical load when they sitting on a chair, because they cannot access their sitting posture during a continuous working. Further, in order to provide a chair that fits the user, it is important to find simple evaluation method of comfort when sitting on a chair. Further, in order to develop a good chair that fits to the users, it is important to find simple evaluation method on comfortable sitting conditions when sitting on a chair. The aim of this paper is to show some rating factors on comfort or discomfort when sitting on a chair for a long time. The experiment was carried out using an office chair. Body pressure distribution of the buttocks was measured by electrical seat sensor for an hour of one session. In addition, they were interviewed on five items of subjective evaluation every five minutes during an hour sitting situation. According to the experiments, we found that elapsed time and two feature values of the total load area of the body pressure distribution and the ratio of the particularly highly pressure area are effective to predict discomfort. And we derived a regression equation to predict the increase of discomfort using the average pressure distribution when they are sitting.

Keywords: chair, comfort, pressure, posture.

1 Introduction

Workers, some occupations of clerical staff and programmers etc., spend a lot of time to sit on office chair during all day long. They do not become something of the physical problem directly in compared to the senior persons because they can change the sitting posture by themselves and do not obstruct their bloodstream for maintain their posture. However, they get tired of keeping the same posture for a long time during all day, and it generates huge fatigue and pain to them. These situations will derive a low motivation and low efficiency of their works.

We have to clarify the reason of their fatigue, pain and relations of decrease of the comfort, to occur by continuing sitting down of the chair for a long time because we

C. Stephanidis (Ed.): HCII 2014 Posters, Part II, CCIS 435, pp. 473–478, 2014.
© Springer International Publishing Switzerland 2014

want to discover some condition of the chair to be able to sit down on comfortably for
a long time.

2   Method

2.1   Participants

Thirteen adult volunteers (7 male, 6 female) with no history of low back pain were
recruited from our university community. Anthropometric data including, height,
weight, leg length and torso length were collected. These data were used to calculate
body mass index (BMI), and leg–torso ratio (LTR).

2.2   Experimental Apparatus

We used the wheelchair and the office chair to evaluate comfortableness in sitting
conditions using an office chair with elbow rest and five legs with casters. The height
of seat when sitting and inclination angle of the backrest are adjustable. The seat and
backrest are covered with a cushion. The office chair of the size that resembled a
used wheelchair was used to facilitate comparison (Fig. 1).

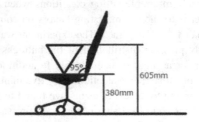

Fig. 1. Size of office chair

2.3   Protocol

We measured some pressures of body-touched on sitting areas and degree of comfortableness feelings for an hour of each session using the office chair with armrest, backrest, and foot support. They watched a movie of the monitor in front of them during
sitting on chair. They were interviewed in every five minutes using subjective rating.
Questionnaire survey is carried out to evaluate feelings of 13 subjects. (1) fatigue of
cervix, waist, foot and whole body, (2) feelings cramped of a part touching it with the
chair, stability, pain of the buttocks, and comfort.

We measured the body pressure distribution of the buttocks and the back by using
pressure sensor sheet (Xsensor Pressure Mapping System X3). Moreover the movements of the neck, shoulder, elbow, wrist, waist, knee, and ankle in left side were
captured by 3D measuring system.

3   Results

3.1   Method of Predicting the Discomfort by the Subjective Evaluation

We propose the discomfort or comfort situation conditions in sitting on chair from analyzing getting the data of the subjective evaluation. Then we conduct the correlation analysis in order to evaluate the relation among question items. Table 1 shows the correlation coefficients between subjective rating items. We can see the strong or medium positive correlation among all items in 0.1% level.

Table 1. Correlation coefficients between rating values of fatigue

	Shoulder stiffness	Cramped of the back	Pain of the buttooks	Fatigue of the waist	Cramped of the thighs	Fatigue of the thighs	Fatigue of the calf	Unstableness of upperbody	Unstableness of waist	Slipperine -ss	Fatigue of whle body	Discomfort
Fatigue of the neck	.871	.792	.696	.620	.633	.694	.729	.694	.568	.560	.659	.641
Shoulder stiffness	—	.665	.710	.656	.515	.675	.753	.747	.511	.549	.701	.675
Cramped of the baok		—	.696	.593	.672	.656	.641	.606	.568	.517	.625	.630
Pain of the buttooks			—	.775	.488	.548	.582	.726	.663	.651	.826	.870
Fatigue of the waist				—	.490	.547	.565	.751	.702	.638	.796	.847
Cramped of the thighs					—	.779	.664	.545	.583	.524	.486	.424
Fatigue of the thighs						—	.869	.578	.359	.379	.561	.515
Fatigue of the oalf							—	.682	.342	.456	.629	.592
Unstableness of upperbody								—	.746	.761	.797	.767
Unstableness of waist									—	.842	.701	.676
Slipperine -ss										—	.683	.658
Fatigue of whle body											—	.922

To expresses the degree of discomfort feeling during office work, we can propose the regression equation by multiple regression analysis with forced entry as an explanatory variable 10 items other than comfort, pain of the buttocks and fatigue whole body. We used absolute values of the explanatory variables which standardized coefficient β are two or more. Then we derived regression eq. (1) by using multiple regression analysis

(Degree of discomfort) = -0.244 + 0.596×(fatigue of the whole body) + 0.251×(pain of the buttocks) + 0.247×(fatigue of the waist)   (1)

$$R^2 = 0.903, F(3,152) = 474.280, p < 0.001$$

Moreover the fatigue of whole body could be calculated by the regression eq. (2).

(Fatigue of the whole body) = 0.662 + 0.502×(stability of the buttocks)+ 0.362×(fatigue of the waist) + 0.531×(fatigue of foot)- 0.343×(feeling cramped of a part touching it with the chair)   (2)

$$R^2=0.751, F(4,151)=113.905, p<0.001$$

3.2   Method of Predicting the Discomfort by the Body Pressure Distribution

To predict the degree of discomfort feeling body pressure distribution was divided into the four ranges (0.3-1.1N/cm is the low pressure area, 1.1-1.5N/cm is the medium pressure area, 1.5- 2.2N/cm is the high pressure area, 1.8-2.2N/cm, 2.2N/cm or more is the over pressure area.)   Fig. 2 shows the average pressure distribution of all the trials of each participant. Numerical value of the right side of bar shows the rating value on discomfort feeling.

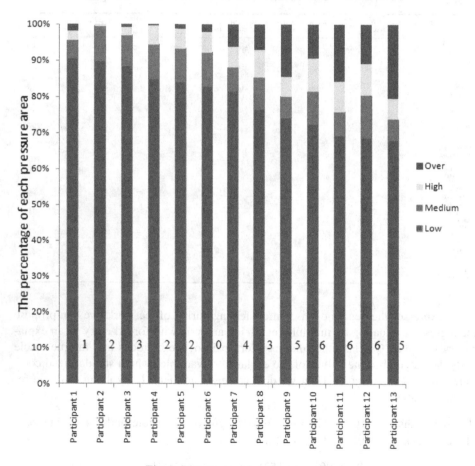

Fig. 2. Percentages of each pressure area

We tried to make new formulae for predict the degree of discomfort by using feature amount of body pressure distribution of each time in a short time when they sit down continuously for an hour. Regression eq. (3) was derived by using the average of the explanatory variable coefficients and constant of the regression equation in $t \geq 15$.

(Degree of discomfort) = 4.670 + 28.958×(area of over pressure)- 0.0056×(area of all pressure)   (3)

$$R^2 = 0.765$$

The coefficient of determination was especially high during the point of $25 \leq t \leq 40$. The average of correlation coefficients between the predicted values and the rating values of discomfort was 0.872.   To evaluate the effectiveness of this approach the leave-one-out cross-validation method was done. Fig. 3 shows the time variation of the difference between the predicted values and the rating values.

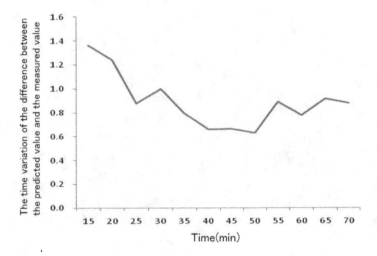

Fig. 3. Change of difference between the predicted values and the rating values

4   Results

The subjective evaluation of the pain of the buttocks, fatigue of the waist and whole body were relevant to the increase of discomfort. And the fatigue of the whole body was largely influenced by stability of the waist and fatigue of the calf. On the other hand, the increase of the feeling cramped of the thighs suppressed the increase of the fatigue of the whole body. Therefore, for designing the chair, it is important to pay attention to particular the decrease of the pain and fatigue of the waist. And it is necessary to consider the reduction of the fatigue of the calf and improve the stability of the waist by cramping. From the body pressure distribution, it is possible to obtain a highly accurate prediction by using the feature value of the body pressure distribution data from 35 minutes to 50 minutes after the start of sitting. Seated posture gradually became unstable in the passage of sitting time. Therefore, it was assumed that the change of the body stability was affected by the accuracy of prediction derived from body pressure distribution.

References

1. Steven, M.C., Peter, J.K.: Effects of backrest design on biomechanics and comfort during seated work. Applied Ergonomics 38, 755–764 (2007)
2. Giuseppe, A., Giorgio, C.S., Marco, R.: Method for the analysis of posture and interface pressure of car drivers. Applied Ergonomics 33, 511–522 (2002)
3. Gordon, A., Jerome, V., Steven, J.C.J., Postural, M.: versus chair design impacts upon interface pressure. Applied Ergonomics 37, 619–628 (2006)

Self-assessment of Maturity of Organization in Terms of Occupational Health and Safety with the Recommendations of ISO 9004:2010

Anna Mazur

Poznan University of Technology, Department of Management Engineering,
ul. Strzelecka 11, 60-965 Poznań, Poland
anna.mazur@put.poznan.pl

Abstract. Companies focused on achieving long-term success analyze their performance in many areas, among which issues of health and safety cannot be overlooked. In the following paper an example of implementation of self-assessment methodology recommended by ISO 9001:2004 for corporate's safety and hygiene of work area is introduced. Self-assessment of maturity of organization in this area is conducted with reference to strategy and management system, resources, processes of organization and outcomes monitoring, as well as to improvement and self-learning.

Keywords: maturity, maturity of organization, occupational health and safety, ISO 9004:2010 standard.

1   Introduction

International standard ISO 9004:2010 promotes self-assessment as an important tool for the review of the maturity level of the organization. A mature organization performs effectively and efficiently and can achieve sustained success by [5]:

— Understanding needs of parties involved,
— Understanding and still monitoring changes in the organization's environment,
— Effectively identifying possible areas for improvement,
— Defining strategies and policies and consistent realization its,
— Setting relevant goals,
— Managing its processes and resources,
— Demonstrating confidence in its employees leading to increased motivation,
— Establishing mutually beneficial terms of cooperation with suppliers and other partners.

This international standard provides guidance to support the achievement of sustained success for any organization using a quality management approach. Assumptions of quality management system include in its structure elements of work environment [2], on the other hand z safety and hygiene of work management systems

C. Stephanidis (Ed.): HCII 2014 Posters, Part II, CCIS 435, pp. 479–484, 2014.
© Springer International Publishing Switzerland 2014

(f.ex. OHSAS 18001, PN-N 18001) can be integrated with quality management systems thanks to numerous common parts. It is possible to adapt these recommendations to self-assessment in occupational health and safety area, allowing organizations to assess the maturity in this area. It is particularly important to build self-assessment modes as in large corporations improvement actions were always launched in one domain only and then spread on the entire organization, which can be an important and valuable benchmark. Excellence of the company in health and safety of employees will improve other areas of company action [8].

2   Maturity of Organization

Mature organization is the one oriented to achieving sustained success which means striving for the ability to achieve and maintain objectives in the long term [4]. Functioning of organization depends on influence of its environment, with special reference to macro-environment including legal regulations, as well as social and demographic aspects [9]. Such approach is especially important in the aspect of safety and hygiene of work issues. Legal requirements and standards, as well as environmental issues determine safety level in organizations. The aspect as important is competitive environment and the role of internal and external stakeholders. Stakeholders is person or group having an interest in the performance or success of an organization, for example: customer, owners, people in an organization, suppliers, bankers, unions, partner or society [4]. In mature organizations the term stakeholders should be used in place of the term customers (internal and external). It is necessary to identify stakeholders interested in management system, as well as relations between them since they are supposed to enable appointing a common, general goal and motivate to active cooperation, participation and striving for the goals appointed achievement [6] also in the area of occupational health and safety. In organizational maturity assessment from safety and hygiene of work point of view the aspect of work conditions level assessment [10] and shaping ergonomic aspects of quality of work conditions [3] are also essential. All the areas of mature organizations functioning (including safety of work area) and mutual relations between them should be manager, maintained and improved. Human factor should not be neglected as all the decision and operations processes involving human factor include personal risk which results from employees competences, tasks division and ability to mutual communication [1]. An important element of formation and exploitation of a management system is its improvement on the basis of experience from improvement of the system as well as partner relationships, cooperation with beneficial suppliers, customers, and other stakeholders. Defining and deploying strategies, policies and relevant objectives will also related with shaping of safety culture. Process management and resource management is another area of organization management system, which also should be assessed with the point of view of organizational maturity in regard to health and safety aspects. In cases where the organization operates and makes progress, available resources determine the result of processes of the organization. In such circumstances, the resources possessed (type, quantity, quality) and execute the processes will have an impact on the functioning of the organization. Corporate management system focused at continuous increase in benefits of organization and its stakeholders should include strategies of agility, efficiency and sustainability. Sustainability is becoming a significant component of operational and competitive strategies in an increasing number of companies. The idea combines economic, environmental, and social aspects of a activity of an organization. Social sustainability is implemented in concepts such as preventive occupational health and safety, human-centred design of work, empowerment, individual and collective learning, employee participation, and work -life balance [7].

3   Self-assessment of the Organization Maturity in Terms of Occupational Health and Safety

Methodology of self-assessment recommended by ISO 9004:2010 identifies five levels of maturity for elements assessed, starting with the first base level, and finishing with the best practice. Self-assessment is conducted both at the strategic level referring to key elements of organization, and at the tactic and operational level (f.ex. it is performed by managers, line managers and process owners) referring to elements of organization, its processes, resources and outcomes. Self-assessment of organizational maturity in the area of safety and hygiene of work (according to recommendation of ISO 9004:2010 standard) includes:

— Strategy and policy,
— Resources management,
— Proces management,
— Monitoring, measurement, analysis and review,
— Improvement, innovation and learning.

Self-assessment realization at every level of maturity requires application of numerous methodologies and tools supporting its performance. For example, to assess the area of strategy and policy, there are five levels of maturity identified, and they are presented in the table 1:

Table 1. Organizational maturity levels in the area of strategy and policy

Level 1	Level 2	Level 3	Level 4	Level 5
Short term goals of safety are deployed into everyday operational activities.	Safety strategy and politics are translated into goals at various levels of organization.	Measures for progress in achieving strategic goals in terms of safety are applied. Positive and negative discrepancies with plans are analyzed and actions are undertaken.	Measurable safety goals are defined for every process and level of organization and they are consistent with strategy.	Strategy, policy and safety goals are reviewed and updated with use of data from monitoring and analysis of organization's environment.

Organizations can be at any level of maturity. The important rule is the fact that it is impossible to upgrade maturity level without meeting all the requirements of the previous level. Hence, it is crucial to measure results of one level before the decision on upgrading is taken. The measurement at every level requires development of independent plans guaranteeing meeting the assumption of previous level to enter the next one. The tool which can be used for that purpose is Force Field Analysis methodology. The methodology can be applied for assessing ability to implement changes. It enables identification of contradictive factors of a predefined change: driving forces and factors having positive influence on implementation of planned changes and inhibitory forces and factors representing negative influence on the changes mentioned. Force Field Analysis methodology is applied to planning and assessment of actions at the second level of strategy and policy area: Safety strategy and politics are translated into goals at various levels of organization. Application of the methodology is presented in the figure 1.

Fig. 1. Example of use Force Field Analysis to assess the level 2 for strategy and policy aspect

Application of Force Field Analysis allows to analyze situation of organization at any level of maturity currently. Focusing at stressing positive factors and minimization of risk of occurring negative factors will contribute to efficient meeting of requirements of a given maturity level. Identification of negative factors is crucial as their consciousness provides faster reaction to a negative factor appearing. For example, analysis and elimination of negative factors connected with understanding safety politics can be performed with ACORN test. The superior goal defined in safety politics is striving for continuous improvement and providing safe and hygiene work conditions. The example of application of ACORN test to analysis of previously presented safety politics is introduced in the table 2.

Table 2. Example of use ACORN test for analysis of the understanding of security policy

Accomplishment	Organization did not finish tasks connected with guaranteeing safe work conditions as they are performed in continuous cycle
Control	Predefined areas of safety policy were communicated to employees at various organizational levels in form of goals and are controlled with respect to their correct performance
Only objectives	Primary assumption is realization of safety policy which results in identification of goals strictly connected with improvement and ensuring safe and hygienic work conditions.
Reconcilation	Goals are defined in the way enabling realization of quality policy and goals independence (so that they were not contradictive)
Numbers	Results of realization of tasks are currently available. They can be translated to methodologies for achieving goals measurability

Application of methods and tools supporting assessment of predefined levels of organizational maturity is necessary and essential for accurate diagnostics of corporate's situation.

4   Conclusions

Self-assessment provides global review of achievements of organizations at the first levels of management system maturity, as safety and hygiene of work area should be its integral part. Regular self-assessment of level of maturity of organization is also the first step in striving for predefined level of excellence.

The information gained from the self-assessment could also be used to:

- Simulate comparisons and share learning throughout the organization,
- Benchmarking with other organizations,
- Monitor progress of the organization over time, by conducting periodic self-assessment,
- Identify and prioritize areas for improvement.

Safety and hygiene of work area is very important because of its influence on long-lasting success of each organization. Self-assessment with respect only to work environment and human factor and its competences does not provide a full picture of maturity of organization in terms of safety and hygiene of work. Translating requirements of ISO 9004:2010 towards the area of organization's functioning in which elements of organization, its resources and outcomes are assessed, provides results actually reflecting level of maturity of organization in terms of safety and hygiene of work.

References

1. Golas, H, .: Personal risk management. In: Stephanidis, C., Antona, M. (eds.) UAHCI 2013, Part I. LNCS, vol. 8009, pp. 175–184. Springer, Heidelberg (2013)
2. Górny, A.: The Elements of Work Environment in the Improvement Process of Quality Management System Structure. In: Karwowski, W., Salvendy, W.G. (eds.) Advances in Human Factors, Ergonomics, and Safety in Manufacturing and Service Industries. CRC Press, Taylor & Francis Group, Boca Raton (2011)
3. Górny, A.: Ergonomics in the formation of work condition quality. Work: A Journal of Prevention, Assessment and Rehabilitation 1(suppl. 1), 1708–1711 (2012)
4. ISO 9000:2005 Quality management system- Fundamentals and vocabulary (2005)
5. ISO 9004:2009 Managing for the sustained of an organization – A quality management approach (2009)
6. Jasiulewicz-Kaczmarek, M.: Participatory Ergonomics as a Method of Quality Improvement in Maintenance. In: Karsh, B.-T. (ed.) EHAWC 2009. LNCS, vol. 5624, pp. 153–161. Springer, Heidelberg (2009)
7. Jasiulewicz-Kaczmarek, M.: The role of ergonomics in implementation of the social aspect of sustainability, illustrated with the example of maintenance. In: Arezes, P., Baptista, J.S., Barroso, M., Carneiro, P., Lamb, P., Costa, N., Melo, R., Miguel, A.S., Perestrelo, G. (eds.) Occupational Safety and Hygiene, pp. 47–52. CRC Press, Taylor & Francis, London (2013)
8. Jasiulewicz-Kaczmarek, M., Misztal, A., Butlewski, M.: The holons model of quality improvement and measurement in SMEs. In: Book of Proceedings of Global Innovation and Knowledge Academy (GIKA) Conference, University of Valencia, Spain (2013)
9. Kałkowska, J., Pawłowski, E., Włodarkiewicz-Klimek, H.: Zarządzanie organizacjami w gospodarce opartej na wiedzy. Wydawnictwo Politechniki Poznańskiej, Poznań (2013)
10. Mazur, A.: Application of fuzzy index to qualitative and quantitative evaluation of the quality level of working conditions. In: Stephanidis, C. (ed.) HCII 2013, Part II. CCIS, vol. 374, pp. 514–518. Springer, Heidelberg (2013)

Designing Smart Home Technology for Fall Prevention in Older People

Ather Nawaz[1], Jorunn L. Helbostad[1], Nina Skjæret[1], Beatrix Vereijken[1],
Alan Bourke[2], Yngve Dahl[3], and Sabato Mellone[4]

[1] Department of Neuroscience, Norwegian University of Science and Technology, Norway
[2] Laboratory of Movement Analysis and Measurement, EPFL, Switzerland
[3] SINTEF ICT, Norway
[4] Department of Electronics, Computer Science and Systems,
University of Bologna, Italy
{ather.nawaz,Jorun.Helbostad,Nina.Skjaret,
Beatrix.Vereijken}@ntnu.no
alan.bourke@epfl.ch, yngve.dahl@sintef.no,
sabato.mellone@unibo.it

Abstract. Falls in older people constitute one of the major challenges in health-care. It is important to design technologies that can help prevent falls and improve falls management. Smart home technology could be of importance in this context, but the technology has to be user-centred or adapted to be useful in this particular context. This study assessed usability of paper and interactive proto-types of a smart home touch screen panel. The study implemented five scena-rios related to fall risk, fall assessment and exercise guidance, designing a smart home interface for independent living in general and fall management in partic-ular. A usability evaluation showed that older people had positive experiences when using the touch screen interface. The study demonstrated the need for us-er-centred interfaces for older people in the context of falls prevention.

Keywords: Falls, Seniors, Scenarios, Usability, Evaluation, Smart home, Interface design.

1 Introduction

Falls in older people constitute one of the major challenges in healthcare. Falls are an important public health issue. Each year, 35% of people over the age of 65 experience one or more falls. Between 10 and 25% of fallers sustain a serious injury [1]. This has implications regarding independence, reduced quality of life, and health care costs [1]. Therefore it is important to design technologies that can help prevent falls and improve falls management. Smart home technology could be of importance in this context, but the technology has to be purpose-designed or adapted to be useful in the context of fall prevention and fall management service.

Smart home technology often is envisioned to contribute to increased safety, secu-rity and well-being of people with special care needs. However, user acceptance of

C. Stephanidis (Ed.): HCII 2014 Posters, Part II, CCIS 435, pp. 485–490, 2014.
© Springer International Publishing Switzerland 2014

smart home technology that aims to serve assistive purposes is generally low among elderly people. Therefore the technology needs to be developed through an iterative, user-centered design (UCD) approach [2]. The system and technology constantly take into account input from different stakeholders of the system to improve usability of the system. In the context of fall management, stakeholders include senior citizens, doctors, health professionals and physiotherapists.

This study aimed to assess the usability of paper and interactive prototypes of a smart home touch screen panel. A user-centered design approach was employed to collect the requirements of a smart home system for fall management. On the basis of such requirements, the interface of a smart home system was developed. Subsequently, usability evaluation of the smart home system was conducted with older people.

2   Scenarios for Requirement Analysis

Different approaches exist to assess the user-centered design aspect of technologies. Scenarios can be used as a way to explain conditions in which a system can be used. A scenario is an idealized but detailed description of a specific instance [3]. The goal of scenarios is to identify situations in which the system can be used. In this sense, a scenario presents and situates solutions [4].

The system requirements for smart home systems for fall management were defined through development of scenarios. The scenarios represented everyday tasks of relevance for older home-dwelling persons that can contribute to prevent and manage falls. These scenarios were developed based on input from 17 human movement scientists, physiotherapists, health professionals and human-computer interaction researchers. Through internal consensus, the decision was made to focus on a set of five core scenarios in which smart home systems can be used by seniors. These scenarios include: Exercise, Exergame, Walking, Fall detection, and Self-test. The core scenarios descriptions were used to select the required technology and develop the appropriate user interaction and user interface.

2.1   Scenarios Description

The following section describes the scenarios, their underlying concepts, and the deployment solutions.

Exercise. Kari's physiotherapist has recommended she try to incorporate some exercises into her daily routine to improve her muscle strength and balance, while requiring no extra time.

Concept: She is taught how to use the furniture and items in her home to do some muscle strengthening exercises. She is reminded about the exercises and given a demonstration of them via the interface (video clip, animated gif). She can schedule these exercise reminders or else, if she chooses, she can also select to do the exercises at any time.

Deployed Solution: By using the touch screen interface, the user can select to view video exercises for strength and balance tailored to older adult users. These videos are also scheduled to appear as a reminder to the user to perform the exercises at an appropriate interval, selected upon installation. Motivational messages are delivered to the user upon completion of a short questionnaire regarding the exercises.

Exergames. Ingrid heard about an exergame from a friend who said the game was entertaining, challenging and would help her to improve her balance and stepping ability.

Concept: Ingrid interacts with the smart home panel to select the appropriate time for here exergame use. The smart home system reminds Ingrid when it is time for her exergame via persuasive messages. Her score is saved and a record of improvement is available to her.

Deployed Solution: The user is prompted to use the exergame via a touch screen interface or they can select to use the exergame independently. Instructions are given to the user on how to use the exergame. Once finished the user's performance indicators are saved by the system and used to select the appropriate level for subsequent use. Persuasive and motivational messages are given to the user at the start of the game and upon finishing to provide encouragement.

Walking. Albin has become less active after his wife died 3 months ago. His physician encourages him to do more outdoor activity.

Concept: Based on feedback regarding weather conditions, the smart home system encourages the user to participate in outdoor walking. The user receives feedback on the distance walked and the length of time of walking based on smartphone monitoring and the smart home user interface, respectively.

Deployed solution: The user can assess the weather forecast via the touch screen interface to see whether the weather forecast is suitable for an outdoor walk. The user then selects the outdoor walk button on the 10-inch touch screen and commences the outdoor walk with the smartphone attached; they select to finish the outdoor walk upon return. If the user has improved walking time a motivational message is delivered. The user can also be prompted to go for an outdoor walk. Alternatively, the user can postpone the reminder for a certain amount of time.

Fall Detection. Kirstin fell in her living room some time ago. She injured her wrist, but was able to recover back to a standing position and contact help. She has since become concerned about not being able to get up and get help if she falls at later time.

Concept: Kirstin wears the Smartphone which works as a fall-detection sensor. If the user experiences a fall, the smartphone communicates with the smart home system and prompts the user to indicate whether they have fallen or not. If the user does not respond, cameras located in the home can be switched on to assess the situation. Thus, falls can be detected in different ways.

Deployed solution: If a specific movement signature is measured by the embedded inertial sensors in the phone attached to the user that resembles a fall signature, a message is sent to the smarthome system to raise a fall alarm. The touch screen interface then prompts the user to indicate whether they have fallen or not. If no response is given, it is assumed that an actual fall has occurred and the alarm will be sent to an alarm central.

Self-test. Clemmensen is approaching 89. Clemmensen´s physiotherapist suggests to him to test his physical performance by regular measurement of his gait speed.

Concept: Clemmensen's gait speed is measured through a combination of the sensors and interfaces that are located around the home.

Deployed Solution: The user's gait speed is measured through a combination of pressing buttons on the 10-inch wall mounted touch screens and buttons located around the residence. The time taken to activate the combination of buttons in combination with the distances between them is used to estimate gait speed.

3   User Interface Design

A number of key elements were taken into account when designing the user interface for elderly users. For example, icons must be large enough to allow coarse pointing and seniors should be able to easily distinguish between the foreground and background colours.

The interface was evaluated using the system usability scale (SUS) [5]. SUS is a ten-item scale which provides a subjective assessment of the usability of a system.

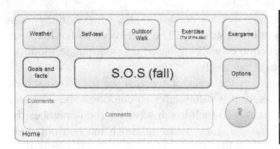 

Fig. 1. The mock-up (*left*) and interactive prototype (*right*) of the user interface on a 10-inch smart home screen

As listed previously, the user interface for the Smart home system interface was designed with 5 main scenarios. The interface of the smart home technology was developed on the basis of these scenarios and allowed the older people to select any of the main actions. As shown in figure 1 (left), a mock-up was developed to visualize the interface of the system. The functional touch screen user interface was deployed on a 10" 16:19 LCD developed by Bticino[1]. Figure 1 (right) shows the deployment inside Bticino's smart home interface.

---

[1] http://www.bticino.it/cons/content/dettaglio/prodotti/bt_28/
MultimediaTouchScreen/bt_8

4   Usability Evaluation of Smart Home User Interface

The usability evaluation of the smart home touch screen interface was conducted with five senior citizens with an average age of 77±6 years (range from 72-87 years). To show the full functions of the system, high-fidelity paper prototypes were used in addition to a functional touch screen interface. The participants were asked to think aloud when exploring and performing different activities using the interface.

Fig. 2. An example of interactive prototype (left) and paper prototype (right) used in the usability experiment

First, the participant started to explore different options on the interface of the touch screen. The interface was in English. A high fidelity paper prototype in Norwegian was initially provided along the touch screen interface (figure 2, left). Later participants were offered the possibility to explore these options of the interface on the paper prototype in Norwegian which was placed in a rectangular box (figure 2, right).

Table 1. System usability of smart home touch interface

System usability scale questions	Mean	SD
This system will help me stay in shape	3,8	0,84
The system is simple to use at home	4,0	0,00
System is motivating and fun	4,0	0,71
I will tell family and friends that I use this system	4,2	0,84
I will setup this system at home	4,5	0,58
I will prioritize to buy this system even if it costs much	3,2	1,48
I will be able to use the system on my own	4,4	0,55
*It does not seem difficult to use the system	3,4	0,89
I will use it in the near future (soon)	3,8	0,84
The system fits with other seniors as well	3,8	1,10

* Inversed the question

Rating: 1= strongly disagree, 2= disagree, 3 = neutral, 4 = agree, 5= strongly agree

The results of SUS showed that older people liked the interface and a positive reaction was received for usefulness and usability of system, see table 1. Usability issues that came up were: confusion between the interface of the manufacturer and the space dedicated to the interface for physical activity and fall management, readability difficulty, and inactive screen. The participants wanted to be reminded about activities to be performed. These recommendations will be used by Bticino to further refine and update the final user interface.

5   Discussion and Conclusion

The study implemented five scenarios related to fall risk, fall assessment and exercise guidance to be used to prevent and manage falls by use of smart home technology. To show the full functions of the system, the study used high-fidelity paper prototypes and a functional interactive prototype for system evaluation.

The usability evaluation showed that participants had positive experiences when using the touch screen interface. The positive experience of the seniors suggests that technologies should be designed to fulfill the particular needs of seniors. Usability issues that came up were: confusion between the interface of the manufacturer and the space dedicated to the interface for physical activity and fall management, readability difficulty, and inactive screen. The participants suggested to be reminded about activities to be performed. The study demonstrated the need for developing interfaces particularly for older people in the context of falls prevention.

This study underlines the importance and need to design smart home technologies for independent living in general, and for preventing and improving management of falls and fall-related activities for older people.

Acknowledgement. The research leading to these results has received funding from the European Union Seventh Framework Programme (FP7/2007-2013) under grant agreement FARSEEING n° 288940. FARSEEING aims to promote better prediction, identification and prevention of falls with focus on ICT devices.

References

1. Department of Health, Falls and Fractures: Effective Interventions in Health and Social Care. DH (2009)
2. ISO 9241, Ergonomics of Human–System Interaction—Part 210: Human-Centred Design for Interactive Systems, International Organization for Standardization (ISO), Geneva, Switzerland (2010)
3. Young, R.M., Barnard, P.: The use of scenarios in human-computer interaction research: Turbocharging the tortoise of cumulative science, vol. 17. ACM (1986)
4. Bødker, S.: Scenarios in user-centred design—setting the stage for reflection and action. Interacting with Computers 13(1), 61–75 (2000)
5. Brooke, J.: SUS-A quick and dirty usability scale. In: Usability Evaluation in Industry, pp. 189–194 (1996)

3D Hand Anthropometry of Korean Teenager's and Comparison with Manual Method

Se Jin Park[1], Seung Nam Min[2], Heeran Lee[1],
Murali Subramaniyam[2], and Sang Jae Ahn[3]

[1] Division of Convergence Technology,
Korea Research Institute of Standards and Science, Daejeon 305-340, Korea
{Sjpark,heeranlee}@kriss.re.kr
[2] Center for Medical Metrology, Division of Convergence Technology,
Korea Research Institute of Standards and Science, Daejeon 305-340, Korea
msnijn12@kriss.re.kr, murali.subramaniyam@gmail.com
[3] Department of Electrical and Computer Engineering, Korea Aerospace University,
Goyang 412-791, Korea
sangjae2006@naver.com

Abstract. The requirements of wearing products fitting comfort was continuously increasing and considerable attentions had been paid for a long time. The assessment of the physical dimensions of the human hand provided a metric description to establish human-machine compatibility. Higher accuracy in hand anthropometric measurements could be achieved with the aids of an image analysis system. Scanning of hand surfaces either 2D or 3D was an alternative method for manual measurements. Three-dimensional anthropometry may lead to significant improvement in fitting comfort of wearing products. The purpose of this study was to measure 3D hand anthropometry and compared it with manual methods. For that purpose, 10 hand measurements of the right hand (lengths, breadths, and circumference of hand and fingers) were taken from 1,700 middle and high school students by age ranged from 13 to 19 years old. The hand was measured by manual (using anthropometric sliding, spreading calipers and measuring tape) and using a high-resolution 3D hand scanner (NEXHAND H-100, Knitech, South Korea) with the scanning accuracy ± 0.5 mm. From the scanned data, the hand measurements were extracted using scanning software (Enhand, Knitech, South Korea). Mean and standard deviation for each hand measurements were calculated. T-test statistical test on the data revealed that there was no significant difference between the manual and 3D hand measurements (p > 0.05). Therefore, 3D anthropometry can be replaced with manual methods. The data gathered may be used for ergo-design applications of hand tools and devices. And also it can provide a great help to develop a hand anthropometry database for hand wearing products.

1 Introduction

Anthropometric data are one of significant factors in designing machines and devices. Incorporating anthropometric data would yield more effective designs, ones that are

C. Stephanidis (Ed.): HCII 2014 Posters, Part II, CCIS 435, pp. 491–495, 2014.

more user friendly, safer, and enable higher performance and productivity. The assessment of the human hand physical dimensions provides a metric description to establish human-machine compatibility [1, 2, 3]. To protect hands from the hazardous work environments workers are commonly used the gloves [4]. The experts in the certain sports used the custom-made gloves to their personal specification requirements. Pressure therapy gloves were mainly found in the area of pressure therapy, those gloves are designed to apply acceptable pressure to hand and fingers with the purpose to increase the rate of scar maturation, prevent contracture formation, and enhance cosmetic appearance without impairing circulation [5, 6, 7, 8]. There are many types of gloves available in the market to protect against a wide variety of hazards. An accurate and effective measurement of hand anthropometric dimensions is crucial to optimize the effectiveness and practical use of the gloves [4]. There are two hand measurement methods namely direct and indirect. Direct measurement method used the tools such as flexible measuring tape, calipers, martin anthropometry device, measuring boards and rulers are traditionally used to obtain hand dimensions [9]. The indirect methods such as three-dimensional (3D) image analyses have been widely adopted for taking body dimensions in the design of various products including medical, garments, safety instruments, etc., [10, 11, 12, 13, 14]. Along with the 3D image analysis, multi-camera photogrammetric systems based on two-dimensional (2D) images for body measuring have been developed in various studies [15, 16].

The objective of the present study was Korean teenagers' hand anthropometric measurements by using indirect method using 3D scanner and compare against the direct measurement method. This research work aims to provide a useful reference for the development of hand anthropometry database.

2   Method

2.1   Participants

Ten measurements (lengths, breadths, and circumference of hand and fingers) of the right hand from 1,700 middle and high school students were measured and their age ranged from 13 to 19 years old. Table 1 showed participants demographic information.

Table 1. Demographic information for participants

	Height (mm)	Weight (kg)	BMI
N = 1,700	1593.37±52.26	52.72±8.26	20.73±2.88

2.2   Methodology of Measurement

The instruments used for the manual measurements were the anthropometric sliding and spreading calipers, and measuring tape (martin anthropometer). The instrument used for the indirect measurements was a high-resolution 3D hand scanner (NEXHAND H-100, Knitech, South Korea) with the scanning accuracy ± 0.5 mm. The 3D scanner generates a 3D digital hand, and then computer software (Enhand,

Knitech, South Korea) measures 3D hand dimensions from the digital hand (Fig. 1). The generated 3D digital hand with its several dimensions can be directly applied to design of product shape. Mean and standard deviation for each hand measurement were calculated and compared.

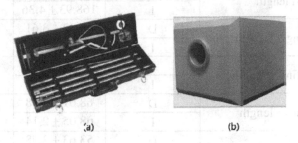

(a)   (b)

Fig. 1. Measurement tools used (a: Martin anthropometer, b: NEXHAND H-100 hand 3D scanner)

The selected hand dimensions measured from the direct and indirect methods were showed in Fig. 2

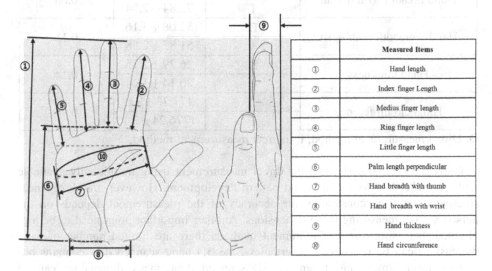

	Measured Items
①	Hand length
②	Index finger Length
③	Medius finger length
④	Ring finger length
⑤	Little finger length
⑥	Palm length perpendicular
⑦	Hand breadth with thumb
⑧	Hand breadth with wrist
⑨	Hand thickness
⑩	Hand circumference

Fig. 2. Hand items measured from the direct and indirect methods

3   Results and Discussion

The t-test was performed to compare the significance between the direct and indirect measurement methods (Table 2) for the measured items.   The t-test results showed that there were no significant differences between two measurement methods for whole items measured.

Table 2. Right Hand Anthropometric Measurements Comparison between Direct and Indirect Method using T-Test

Measured Items		Mean (SD) in mm	p-value
Hand length	D	169.21 ± 7.30	0.182
	I	168.93 ± 4.36	
Index finger Length	D	65.32 ± 3.61	0.655
	I	64.90 ± 1.61	
Medius finger length	D	72.75 ± 3.59	0.846
	I	72.54 ± 1.57	
Ring finger length	D	68.01 ± 3.88	0.246
	I	68.05 ± 2.14	
Little finger length	D	53.63 ± 3.98	0.54
	I	53.13 ± 1.28	
Palm length perpendicular	D	97.05 ± 5.09	0.854
	I	97.02 ± 3.15	
Hand breadth with thumb	D	76.91 ± 3.69	0.68
	I	75.84 ± 2.54	
Hand breadth with wrist	D	52.08 ± 3.16	0.15
	I	51.87 ± 2.58	
Hand thickness	D	26.29 ± 2.15	0.14
	I	26.14 ± 1.24	
Hand circumference	D	177.73 ± 9.0	0.94
	I	1776.24 ± 2.1	

D: Direct measurement method, I: Indirect measurement method.

Garrett, 1971 [9] performed the direct measurement using traditionally available tools to make the glove design and pattern development. However, the direct measurements are time consuming; the accuracy of the measurement depends on the person who is measuring those dimensions. Another important point need to be highlighted that using direct measurement methods there are limited number of hand dimensions can be measured. Nevertheless, the 3D hand scanned data contains numerous hand dimensions. From the 3D scanned data, many dimensions can be extracted using custom build software tools for example Rapidform. Also the repeatability of the indirect measurement is higher than the direct measurement method [4]. However, there are still in many developed countries both measurement methods are employed to construct national anthropometry database. The existence of an anthropometry database is essential in every society and this data should be up-to-date. As the size of the some body parts may alter during years [16]. With the indirect measurement methods it would be easier to update the anthropometry database.

4   Conclusion

The study performed Korean teenagers' hand anthropometric measurements by indirect measurement method using 3D hand scanner and compared the dimensions against the direct measurement method. The findings of this study imply that the average of hand dimensions has no significant difference in the two methods ($p > 0.05$). The statistical analyses showed that indirect measurement methods (using 3D scanner) can be replaced with direct measurement methods. It can provide an extended help to develop an anthropometric database for gloves manufactures and also to develop national anthropometric database.

References

1. Fraser, T.: Ergonomic Principles in the Design of Hand Tools. In Occupational Safety and Health Series No. 44. International Labour Office, Geneva (1980)
2. Freivalds, A.: The Ergonomics of Tools. International Reviews of Ergonomics 1, 43–75 (1987)
3. Nag, A., Nag, P.K., Desai, H.: Hand Anthropometry of Indian Women. Indian Journal of Medical Research 117, 260–269 (2003)
4. Yu, A., Yick, K.L., Ng, S.P., Yip, J.: 2D and 3D Anatomical Analyses of Hand Dimensions for Custom-Made Gloves. Applied Ergonomics 44, 381–392 (2013)
5. Leung, W.Y., Yuen, D.W., Ng, S.P., Shi, S.Q.: Pressure Prediction Model for Compression Garment Design. Journal of Burn Care & Research 31, 716–727 (2010)
6. Fricke, N.B., Omnell, M.L., Dutcher, K.A., Hollender, L.G., Odon, T., Engrav, L.H.: Skeletal and Dental Disturbances in Children after Facial Burns and Pressure Garment use: A 4-Year Follow-up. Journal of Burn Care & Research 20, 239–249 (1999)
7. Rappoport, K., Müller, R., Flores-Mir, C.: Dental and Skeletal Changes during Pressure Garment use in Facial Burns: A Systematic Review. Burns 34, 18–23 (2008)
8. Silfen, R., Amir, A., Hauben, D.J., Calderon, S.: Effect of Facial Pressure Garments for Burn Injury in Adult Patients after Orthodontic Rreatment. Burns 27, 409–412 (2001)
9. Garrett, J.W.: The Adult Human Hand: Some Anthropometric and Biomechanical Considerations. Human Factors: The Journal of the Human Factors and Ergonomics Society 13, 117–131 (1971)
10. Yu, C.Y., Tu, H.H.: Foot Surface Area Database and Estimation Formula. Applied Ergonomics 40, 767–774 (2009)
11. Yu, C.Y., Lo, Y.H., Chiou, W.K.: The 3D Scanner for Measuring Body Surface Area: A Simplified Calculation in the Chinese Adult. Applied Ergonomics 34, 273–278 (2003)
12. Lu, J.M., Wang, M.J.J., Mollard, R.: The Effect of Arm Posture on the Scan-derived Measurements. Applied Ergonomics 41, 236–241 (2010)
13. Hsu, Y.W., Yu, C.Y.: Hand Surface Area Estimation Formula using 3D Anthropometry. Journal of Occupational and Environmental Hygiene 7, 633–639 (2010)
14. Lu, J.M., Wang, M.J.J.: Automated Anthropometric Data Collection using 3D Whole Body Scanners. Expert Systems with Applications 35, 407–414 (2008)
15. Lin, Y.L., Wang, M.J.J.: Automated Body Feature Extraction from 2D images. Expert Systems with Applications 38, 2585–2591 (2011)
16. Habibi, E., Soury, S., Hasan Zadeh, A.: Evaluation of Accuracy and Precision of Two-Dimensional Image Processing Anthropometry Software of Hand in Comparison with Manual Method. Journal of Medical Signals and Sensors 3 (2013)

Development of an Awaking Behavior Detection System with Kinect

Hironobu Satoh[1]Kyoko Shibata[2] and Tomohito Masaki

[1] Kochi National College of Technology
Monobeotsu 200-1, Nangoku, Kochi, Japan
[2] Kochi University of Technology
Miyanokuchi 185, Tosayamada, Kami, Kochi, Japan
satoh@ee.kochi-ct.ac.jp, shibata.kyoko@kochi-tech.ac.jp
http://www.kochi-ct.ac.jp, http://www.kochi-tech.ac.jp

Abstract. The purpose of this study is detecting unsafe behavior of the person lying on the bed and warning caregivers that a person is falling down from the bed.

However, in the dark room at night, the detection ability of previous system is low, because the brightness adjustment processing of a Web camera is not able to adjust brightness of the dark room.

In this paper, we propose a new detection system using Kinect. Kinect has a depth sensor consisted of infrared leaser. And, Kinect is able to measure distance between Kinect and an object in the dark room. Moreover, the behavior of an old person is extracted from measured data by Kinect. By using Kinect, it is considered that the awakening behavior detection system is able to be used in the dark room at night.

In this paper, the awakening detection system using Kinect is shown. And, in experiment, the capability of the proposed system have been verified.

From the result of the experiment, the detection rate of the safe behavior have been 94%. And, the detection rate of the unsafe behavior have been 80%.

Keywords: Awaking behavior detection system, Neural network, Kinect.

1 Introduction

Old people, which need a nurse, sometime fall down from a bed and broke their thighbone. To avoid this accident, it is necessary to care for old people during a day by caregivers. However, to care during a day is a great burden for caregivers. Then, we have proposed an awakening behavior detection system that watches an old person during a day by artificial intelligence. And the awakening behavior detection system warns caregivers that an old people are falling down from the bed.

Our previous research, in the awaking behavior detection system, a Web camera is used for capturing the behavior of an old people. It is known that unsafe

C. Stephanidis (Ed.): HCII 2014 Posters, Part II, CCIS 435, pp. 496–500, 2014.
© Springer International Publishing Switzerland 2014

behavior is different between individual old people. Therefore, NN (Neural Network) detect unsafe behavior of old people using capturing images[1,2,3,4,5].

However, in the dark room at night, the detection ability of previous system is low, because the brightness adjustment processing of a Web camera is not able to adjust brightness of the dark room. It is a problem that the previous system is not able to use in the dark room at night.

In this paper, we propose a new detection system using Kinect, which is developed by Microsoft for human computer interface. Kinect has a depth sensor consisted of infrared leaser. And, Kinect is able to measure distance between Kinect and an object in the dark room. Moreover, the behavior of an old person is extracted from measured data by Kinect. By using Kinect, it is considered that the awakening behavior detection system is able to be used in the dark room at night.

In this paper, the awakening detection system using Kinect is shown. And, in experiment, the capability of the detecting unsafe behavior of the proposed system is verified.

2   Problem of the Previous Research

In the previous research, the detection algorithm is shown as follow. The person lying on the bed is captured by Web camera. Then, the captured image is transformed into the input data to NN as follows. The captured picture is transformed into the gray-scale picture. The picture is divided into 200 (20×10) blocks. Each block is transformed into a binary value, 0 or 1, depending whether the arithmetic mean of the values of the block is larger than a threshold or smaller. These binary values are used as the input data to NN[6]. By using NN, the system can learn each person's behavior easily and adapt user's peculiar behaviors.

The capability of the awakening behavior detection system is shown. Therefore, in the dark room, the capability of the proposed system is low. Because, the brightness adjustment included in Web camera is not able to adjust brightness of the dark room. So, the target subject is not able to be captured clearly. Then, the previous system is not able to detect the target behaviors in the dark room at night.

3   Proposed System

3.1   Kinect

Thereupon, in this paper, we propose new detection system using Kinect which is one of a human computer interface. In the proposed system, Kinect is placed near the ceiling and directly above the bed. Fig.1 shows the installation example of the Kinect. The proposed system using Kinect is able to measure the distance between Kinect and some objects in the dark room. The measured distance is used for determining the figure of the person lying on the bed.

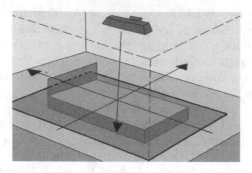

Fig. 1. Installation of Kinect

3.2 Preprocessing

The detection algorithm of the proposed system is shown as follow. First, the distance is measured between the bed and Kinect. And the measured distance is defined as threshold for detecting a person lying on the bed. As preprocessing, person's figure is detected using threshold. It is defined as a person's body each pixel of measured data by Kinect that the distance is closer than the threshold. Fig.2 illustrates the image of the person's body detection, when threshold value is changed. Fig.3 shows the detected figure of a person. As the figure shows, person's sharp is detected. By optimizing the threshold value, the shape of a human is able to be detected correctly. Pixels, which are detected as person's body, are converted to values as 0.98. And, other pixels are converted to values as 0.1(Fig.3).

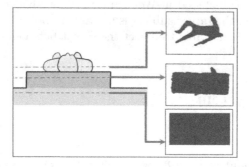

Fig. 2. Image of a human body detection

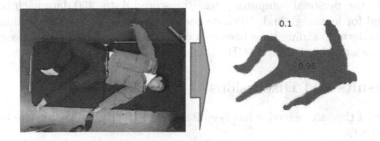

Fig. 3. Figure detection and converted values

3.3 Detection

Then, converted values are inputted to DBN (Deep belief networks)[7] beforehand executed learning. DBN is known as a one of the deep learning. In the
research field of speech recognition and image recognition, high recognition ability of DBN has been confirmed. DBN learn the safe behavior and unsafe behavior
using converted values. DBN recognize the behavior of the person lying on the
bed as safe behavior or unsafe behavior.

4 Experiment

In this section, the capability of the proposed system using Kinect is verified.
The purpose of this experiment is to verify the capability of the detection ability
of the proposed system. Thereupon, a coverlet was not putted on the subject.
A state of lying on the bed was defined as a safe behavior. Fig2 is an example
of safe behavior. A state of falling down was defined as an unsafe behavior.
Fig.4 summarizes an example of unsafe behavior. In the experiment, at the first,
safe behaviors and unsafe behaviors of the subject ware captured by Kinect and

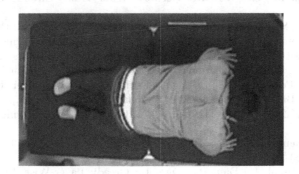

Fig. 4. Example of the unsafe behavior

stored on the personal computer. From the stored data, 250 data each behavior ware used for learning. And, 100 data each behavior ware used for evaluating as unknown data. Learning have been executed while 7days on personal computer, which consist of intel xeon 3.0GHz , 4core.

5   Results and Discussions

The rate of the safe behavior has been 94%. And the rate of the unsafe behavior has been 80%.

From the results, the capability of the proposed awaking detection system is practical. In this experiment, verification of the detection ability has been executed without the coverlet. The coverlet is usually put on the old person. In the feature, it is necessary that the experiment is executed, while the subject are put coverlet.

6   Conclusion

The detection ability of the awaking behavior detection system using Web camera is low in the dark room at night. Accordingly, we have proposed a new system using Kinect. In the experiment, it is confirmed that the proposed system is able to recognize the safe behavior and unsafe behavior of the subject lying on the bed.

References

1. Ikeda, R., Satoh, H., Takeda, F.: Development of Awaking Behavior Detection System Nursing Inside the House. In: International Conference on Intelligent Technology 2006, pp. 65–70 (2006)
2. Matubara, T., Satoh, H., Takeda, F.: Proposal of an Awaking Detection System Adopting Neural Network in Hospital Use. In: World Automation Congress 2008 (2008)
3. Satoh, H., Takeda, F., Shiraishi, Y., Ikeda, R.: Development of a Awaking Behavior Detection System Using a Neural Network. IEEJ Trans. EIS 128(11), 1649–1656 (2008)
4. Yamanaka, N., Satoh, H., Shiraishi, Y., Matsubara, T., Takeda, F.: Proposal of The Awakening Detection System Using Neural Network and It's Verification. In: The 52nd The Institute of Systems, Control and information Engineers (2008)
5. Satoh, H., Takeda, F.: Verification of the Effectiveness of the Online Tuning System for Unknown Person in the Awaking Behavior Detection System. In: Omatu, S., Rocha, M.P., Bravo, J., Fernández, F., Corchado, E., Bustillo, A., Corchado, J.M. (eds.) IWANN 2009, Part II. LNCS, vol. 5518, pp. 272–279. Springer, Heidelberg (2009)
6. Haykin, S.: Neural Networks a comprehensive foundation, New Jersey, USA, pp. 161–173 (1998)
7. Yoshua, B., Pascal, L., Dan, P., Hugo, L.: Greedy Layer-Wise Training of Deep Networks. In: Advances in Neural Information Processing Systems 19, pp. 153–160 (2006)

HCI in Business, Tourism and Trasport

Human Factors Engineering in Interactive Urban Planning Decision Support Systems

Reham Alabduljabbar[1] and Areej Al-Wabil[2]

[1] Information Technology Department, College of Computer and Information Sciences,
King Saud University, Riyadh, Saudi Arabia
ralabduljabbar@ksu.edu.sa
[2] Software Engineering Department, College of Computer and Information Sciences,
King Saud University, Riyadh, Saudi Arabia
aalwabil@ksu.edu.sa

Abstract. This paper presents a systematic review of technologies designed and developed for urban and architectural planning. The usability and user experiences of urban planning systems designed with mixed reality, virtual reality, tangible interaction, and direct manipulation tabletop interfaces are examined. Emphasis in this review is on the design implications of different interaction modalities in supporting decision making in applied scenarios of urban planning. The human factors engineering process for urban planning decision support systems takes into account the perceptive space, comfort, and productivity of planners and decision makers. Tactile fusion of human perception and action is examined in urban planning decision support systems that are designed with virtual and tangible interaction. Case studies describing applied scenarios of urban planning are reviewed with a critique of navigation design, human perception, collaboration support, and visualization of decision scenarios. The human factors for designing systems that support clear representations of urban planning states across all sensory modalities are reported.

Keywords: Urban planning, Virtual reality, Mixed reality, Augmented Reality, Tangible User Interface, Decision support system.

1 Introduction

Urban planning is a complex process that involves a systematic conception of a rational order on the basis of available relevant knowledge of the city's infrastructure and its inhabitants. Diverse stakeholders such as urban planners, national planning officials, investors and the general public are part of this process. Stakeholders have multiple points of views and developing a shared understanding of complex computational data presents a major challenge in the planning process. Therefore, collaboration between actors is a must in the urban planning process. Decision support systems are ideally suited for supporting urban planning decision-making process as they have been developed to in order to enable the creation of a shared vision, support a broad understanding and acceptance of final planning decisions. In addition to saving costs, time

C. Stephanidis (Ed.): HCII 2014 Posters, Part II, CCIS 435, pp. 503–507, 2014.

and improving the quality of decision making process [1]. The Human Factors (HF) in the design of interactive urban planning systems involve the physical, cognitive and ergonomic design dimensions. Interaction in these DSS contexts needs to exploit spatiality (i.e. innate ability to interact with virtual and tangible objects) by facilitating intuitive spatial skills that humans have with the objects they use in urban planning DSS interfaces.

Following is an overview of the state of the art of visualization methods, decision support tools that are used in urban planning.

2   Technologies for Urban Planning

A proliferation in research for designing urban planning systems has examined interaction with different visualization methods including virtual reality (VR), augmented reality (AR) and mixed reality (MR). Recent studies in this urban planning context are listed in Table 1.

Table 1. Visualization methods for some urban planning systems

Visualization Method	Reference No.
Virtual Reality (VR)	[2] ,[3],[4],[5],[6]
Augmented Reality (AR)	[7], [8] ,[9], [10]
Mixed Reality (MR)	[11], [12], [13], [14]

Interaction technologies vary from traditional ones such as mouse and pointers to head mounted and tactile hand held controls. For example, in [2] Stereo display, hand-held devices (PDA, tablet PC), optical tracking systems, touch sensitive surfaces, and speech were used. When designing an interface for a system that incorporates different stakeholders it is important to understand what the purpose of each interaction method is and how it fits into the context-of-use in urban planning.

Different Input/ Output modalities provide flexibility in manipulating objects and viewing the results in different ways to support understandings. However, there exists a trade-off between the number of modalities and the complexity of the system. Complexities in operating the system present more human factor design challenges. More recent research has tended to focus on tangible interaction and tangible user interfaces (TUIs) (e.g. [15-18]). The term TUI was coined by Ishii and Ulmerr and is used to describe objects that "give physical form to digital information," which in the context of an urban planning DSS, often provide intuitive physical controls for complex computational data [21]. The strengths of TUIs lie within their ability to provide a linkage between digital information and physical objects. The essence of TUIs is the direct mapping of physical interaction and direct manipulation with the computational data embodied in the system [19].

3   Human Factors of TUIs in Urban Planning Decision Support Systems

In urban planning decision support systems, it is important that users interact with the system based on their background and their interests. From that point of view, [20] noted that both human factors and system factors should be considered when designing the interface of a DSS for urban planning. For the purpose of this review, human-related factors will be considered.

The minimum requirements for the implementation of high-fidelity interactive urban planning systems are meaningful coupling of physical interaction with human perception and cognitive abilities. Most of the urban planning systems include navigation functionalities such as scenario generation, simulation and provides multiple levels of details (LOD) such as in [2] and [8]. In addition, user friendliness, engagement and utility are key usability objectives that need to be considered in designing the TUIs. Prior research has shown that complexity in the design of physical artifacts to represent computational data in TUIs often impacts the user experience in interacting with a DSS because of inefficiency in using the 'physical handles' to control and manipulate the urban planning DSS.

Tangible interaction can be used to provide better support for ergonomic and collaborative design in the complex urban planning projects while keeping the interaction simple as in ColorTable [18]. ColorTable is a TUI that was developed in an iterative process of design-evaluation-feedback-redesign in successive workshops with users in the domain of real urban planning projects. Users of ColorTable can move colored tokens of different colors and shapes to share their ideas. The tokens allow users to set urban components such as building, streets, etc. Developers of ColorTable share its story design in an attempt to highlight some general design issues related to TUIs in collaborative urban planning. The study in [18] highlights that round shaped tables with the possibility of rotation were highly favorable to users' interaction. Moreover, color objects were perceived as easy to understand and were found to be usable by experts and non-experts.

In recent years, several case studies of urban planning systems have that shown the potential for TUIs to benefit users in urban planning contexts because they exploit the visual, tactile and sensory cues [17, 21]. One case study is the Venice Unfolding: a Tangible User Interface for exploring architectural projects in Venice [17]. This TUI is a prototype developed collaboratively by architects, urban planners and interaction designers. A formative user study was conducted for gathering feedback from users on their experience of action-perception coupling. Findings of that study suggested that using TUIs reduces the boundary between the physical world in urban planning and virtual data. Another pilot study using protocol analysis was conducted in [19] which examined how designers' perception of spatial cognition is improved when using TUIs.

4   Conclusion

This review has investigated some of the available technologies and visualization methods for urban planning decision support systems. It is the first step towards a more detailed review of design activities in TUIs. More research is underway for examining personalization methods and adaptation in designing the TUIs for urban planning systems.

References

1. Kunze, A., Burkhard, R., Gebhardt, S., Tuncer, B.: Visualization and Decision Support Tools in Urban Planning. In: Arisona, S.M., Aschwanden, G., Halatsch, J., Wonka, P. (eds.) DUMS. CCIS, vol. 242, pp. 279–298. Springer, Heidelberg (2012)
2. Yao, J., Fernando, T., Tawfik, H., Armtiage, R., Billing, I.: A VR-centred workspace for supporting collaborative urban planning. In: 9th International Conference on Computer Supported Cooperative Work in Design Proceedings, vol. 1, pp. 564–569. IEEE Press (2005)
3. Chow, E., Hammad, A., Gauthier, P.: Multi-touch screens for navigating 3D virtual environments in participatory urban planning. In: Proceedings of CHI EA 2011 Extended Abstracts on Human Factors in Computing Systems, pp. 2395–2400. ACM Press (2011)
4. Chen, B., Huang, F., Fang, Y.: Integrating virtual environment and GIS for 3D virtual city development and urban planning. In: Geoscience and Remote Sensing Symposium (IGARAA 2011), pp. 4200–4203. IEEE Press, Vancouver (2011)
5. Calado, A.V.S., Soares, M.M., Campos, F., Correia, W.: Virtual Reality Applied to the Study of the Interaction between the User and the Built Space: A Literature Review. In: Marcus, A. (ed.) DUXU 2013, Part III. LNCS, vol. 8014, pp. 345–351. Springer, Heidelberg (2013)
6. Yan, X., Wan, W., Zhang, J.: 3D virtual city rendering and real-time interaction based on UC-win/Road. In: IET International Conference on Smart and Sustainable City 2013 (ICSSC 2013), pp. 56–60. IEEE Press, Shanghai (2013)
7. Kato, H., Billinghurst, M., Poupyrev, I., Imamoto, K., Tachibana, K.: Virtual object manipulation on a table-top AR environment. In: Proceedings of the IEEE and ACM International Symposium on Augmented Reality (ISAR 2000), Munich, pp. 111–119 (2000)
8. Broll, W., Lindt, I., Ohlenburg, J., Wittkämper, M.: Arthur: A collaborative augmented environment for architectural design and urban planning. Journal of Virtual Reality and Broadcasting (2004)
9. Allen, M., Regenbrecht, H., Abbott, M.: Smart-phone augmented reality for public participation in urban planning. In: Proceedings of the 23rd Australian Computer-Human Interaction Conference, OzCHI 2011, pp. 11–20. ACM Press, Canberra (2011)
10. Takeuchi, Y., Perlin, K.: ClayVision: the (elastic) image of the city. In: Proceedings of the SIGCHI Conference on Human Factors in Computing Systems, CHI 2012, pp. 2411–2420. ACM Press, Austin (2012)
11. Valérie, M., Markus, S., Dieter, S., Ina, W.: MR Tent: a place for co-constructing mixed realities in urban planning. In: Proceedings of Graphics Interface 2009, GI 2009, pp. 211–214. ACM Press, Canada (2009)

12. Sareika, M., Schmalstieg, D.: Bimanual handheld mixed reality interfaces for urban planning. In: Proceedings of the International Conference on Advanced Visual Interfaces, AVI 2010, pp. 189–196. ACM Press, New York (2010)
13. Wagner, I.: Building Urban Narratives: Collaborative Site-Seeing and Envisioning in the MR Tent. Computer Supported Cooperative Work (CSCW) Journal 21, 1–42 (2012)
14. Treyer, L., Koltsova, A., Georgakopoulou, S.: Visualizing Urban Anaylsis in Mixed Reality. In: 9th International Conference on Intelligent Environments, pp. 282–284. IEEE Press, Athens (2013)
15. Chen, T., Kratky, A.: Touching Buildings – A Tangible Interface for Architecture Visualization. In: Stephanidis, C., Antona, M. (eds.) UAHCI 2013, Part I. LNCS, vol. 8009, pp. 313–322. Springer, Heidelberg (2013)
16. Underkoffler, J., Ishii, H.: Urp: A luminous-tangible workbench for urban planning and design. In: Proceedings of the SIGCHI Conference on Human Factors in Computing Systems, CHI 1999, pp. 386–393. ACM Press, New York (1999)
17. Nagel, T., Heidmann, F.: Venice unfolding: a tangible user interface for exploring faceted data in a geographical context. In: Proceedings of the 6th Nordic Conference on Human-Computer Interaction: Extending Boundaries, NordiCHI 2010, pp. 743–746. ACM Press, New York (2010)
18. Maquil, V., Psik, T., Wagner, I.: The ColorTable: a design story. In: Proceedings of the Second International Conference on Tangible and Embedded Interaction (TEI 2008), pp. 97–104. ACM Press (2008)
19. Maher, M.L., Kim, M.J.: Do tangible user interfaces impact spatial cognition in collaborative design? In: Luo, Y. (ed.) CDVE 2005. LNCS, vol. 3675, pp. 30–41. Springer, Heidelberg (2005)
20. Valentini, P.P.: Enhancing User Role in Augmented Reality Interactive Simulations. In: Huang, W., Alem, L., Livingston, M.A. (eds.) Human Factors in Augmented Reality Environments, pp. 233–256. Springer, New York (2013)
21. Ullmer, B., Ishii, H.: Emerging Frameworks for Tangible User Interfaces. In: Carroll, J.M. (ed.) Human Computer Interaction in the New Millennium, pp. 579–601. Addison-Wesley (2001)

Interaction Design in a Tangible Collaborative Decision Support System: The City Schema DSS

Salma Aldawood[1], Faisal Aleissa[1], Riyadh Alnasser[1],
Anas Alfaris[1], and Areej Al-Wabil[2]

[1] Center for Complex Engineering System, King Abdulaziz City for Science and Technology
{saaldawood,fsaleissa,ralnasser,aalfaris}@kacst.edu.sa
[2] Software Engineering Department, College of Computer and Information Sciences,
King Saud University, Riyadh, Saudi Arabia
aalwabil@ksu.edu.sa

Abstract. In this paper, we introduce a decision support system (DSS) platform (City Schema) that is designed to connect a tangible interface within a 3D modeling environment (City Form) with a simulation engine for analyzing the data of the urban, transportation, energy and water systems of the city (City Analytics) to support collaborative city planning. This DSS connects two completely independent systems into one integrated system. The first system is a physical 3D model of a city with a tangible user interface that supports interactive and collaborative activities and provides users with direct manipulation interaction and intuitive interfaces. The second system is an urban modeling design tool which is a simulation engine that has several simulation modules such as operational energy, mobility, daylight, transportation and others. The DSS we present here can be used to describe a real world problem and identify possible solutions to the modeled problem through the computation of many scenarios/alternatives so that users of the DSS can evaluate, compare and select a potential solution. Our City Schema DSS consists of: database management component, simulation modules management component, and an interactive user interface with dynamic visualization and decision scenario simulations. Human factors for supporting multi-user co-located collaboration to assist decision makers in making better decisions are examined. Design implications of different interaction modalities for decision support systems and their impact on providing intuitive and engaging user experiences are discussed.

Keywords: DSS, HCI, Urban Planning.

1 Introduction

The world is experiencing a period of extreme urbanization. In the future, cities are expected to account for nearly 90% of global population growth, 80% of wealth creation, and 60% of total energy consumption [1]. The rapid economic and population growth occurring throughout Saudi Arabia is posing new challenges. In particular, problems related to planning and managing complex systems such as cities. Saudi Arabia's current growing population of 28 million is expected to double by 2032 [2].

C. Stephanidis (Ed.): HCII 2014 Posters, Part II, CCIS 435, pp. 508–512, 2014.
© Springer International Publishing Switzerland 2014

Therefore, developing better strategies for the creation of new "Smarter Cities" is a global imperative. Our need to improve our understanding of cities is pressed not only by the social relevance of urban environments, but also by the availability of new strategies for city-scale interventions that are enabled by emerging technologies.

Our proposition is that the livability and economic vitality of cities can be significantly improved while, at the same time, resource consumption is dramatically reduced. We believe that a new model for livable, high-performance, and resilient cities are achievable through the integrated application of next-generation design strategies, innovative technology, and enlightened public policy. This can be proven through a series of experiments using the City Schema Platform. The urban strategies to be tested using the City Schema platform will include designs that preserve and enhance the existing cultural fabric of the cities as well as new designs that capture the essence of the historic areas and bring new concepts in sustainable living/work, green transport, innovation hubs, and walkable neighborhoods.

2   Architecture of the City Schema Decision Support System

The Decision Support System (City Collaborative) component provides a way to synchronize and coordinate information and interactions between the two highly independent components City Scope and City Analytics. It provides decision support capabilities to the entire framework by collecting user input data from City Scope and feeding them into City Analytics for executing different simulations and analysis [4].

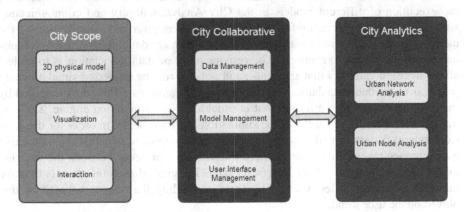

Fig. 1. Architecture of the City Schema Platform

The DSS we present here can be used to describe a real world problem and identify possible solutions to the modeled problem through the computation of many scenarios/alternatives so that users of the DSS can evaluate, compare and select a potential solution. Our City Schema DSS consists of: database management component, simulation modules management component, and an interactive user interface with dynamic visualization and decision scenario simulations.

The Database Management Component is responsible for data storage and manipulation as well as synchronization between different data stores. This functionality provides methods and techniques to manage different data sources and transform them into suitable format to be fed to the City Analytics models and coordinates between all the components within City Collaborative. It consists of multiple sub components including assigner, reporter, and conflict control manager. The assigner is the heart of the City Collaborative component where it is responsible for all the coordination between all the components as any request or change the user makes on the system and any communication between the different management components always passes through the assigner. The reporter allows users of the system to store the status of the running session including the values of the simulation's decision variables and the result of the simulation; it also allows users to conduct a comparative analysis between two simulation sessions where each session has a different input and output values. Since City Schema is a multi-user collaboration platform the system will need to control the conflict that different users might cause, for example two users entering different values for the same decision variable within a single session. This kind of conflict can be solved using different techniques. One is to take the change that is made last based on the date and time of the change. Another is to take the change of the user that has the higher priority on that decision variable, for example an energy planner has a higher priority on the decision variable of maximum energy consumption than a water planner. The third conflict control technique is to take the average of the two decision variable values entered by two users.

The simulation modules management component is responsible for coordinating the execution of different models in the City Analytics library and communicating with City Scope components for appropriate representation and visualization of the model outputs. It has three main functionalities which are data preparation, data translation and simulation execution. The responsibility of data association is to collect all the decision variables that are required in order to run the requested simulation and passes it to the data translator. The data translator translates all the data prepared by the data association into a format that is suitable for the simulation engine. The data translator also reads the results of the simulation and translates it in order for the decision support system to makes sense of it. The last component which is the interactive user interface takes care of the multiple interactions that occur between the decision makers and our Tangible User Interface (TUI). The goal of such interface is to make interaction intuitive, effective, and facilitate controlling the results that will be displayed on the user's end.

The user interface component takes care of two controlling factors in the TUI: First are the decision variables which maps to physical components such as Buildings, Roads, Parks, and Power Plants. Understanding the main physical components of a city is crucial when building the TUI of cities as it allows us to focus on the main characteristics of the city investigated when building its tangible user interface. The second factor is the Key Performance Indicators and this basically the behavioral components that infer and display crucial information regarding the city's degree of success in meeting its performance and economics objectives. These strategic goals and objectives involve (but not limited to) developing the city's economy, making the urban neighborhoods more resource efficient and reliable, enhancing transportation plans for future needs, and beautifying the city.

While the Listener part of the TUI monitors the interaction space for any triggers initiated by users, the Displayer projects the results of the requested simulation or query to the user on any interaction surface. Tracing this back to our controlling factors, the user interface for the Listener component will detect any selection or interaction that occurs with the decision variables described earlier. It will report these changes to the city collaborative component which will consequently deal with these changes by communicating with the City Analytics if needed; and the results will be sent back to the Displayer. The Displayer will visualize the corresponding information on the tangible objects or surface (e.g. touch screen surface) or surrounding walls. If the information is visualized as heat-maps or color-coded buildings, the result will be projected directly on the 3D physical model. Information such as scores, tables, and chart will be displayed on the digital interfaces for the experts to interpret and make decision.

3   Tangible User Interfaces in DSS

The interaction space in the City Schema DSS is comprised of three layers; namely, tangible objects, interactive surfaces (e.g. touchscreen), and the area surrounding the urban model and the nearby surfaces on the horizontal and vertical planes. City Schema utilizes innovative interaction modalities so that users can test alternative designs for large scale developments within the city by visualizing the implications of each design change in real time. For example, objects can be selected or activated for interaction by touch or hover; surfaces can be manipulated by touch or physical manipulation of detached or attached modes by an individual or multi-user interaction; gestures or presence of users are automatically detected to activate functionality. The urban strategies to be tested by our platform will include designs that preserve and enhance the existing cultural fabric of the cities as well as proposed designs that capture the essence of the historic areas and bring new concepts in sustainable living/work, green transport, innovation hubs, and walkable neighborhoods.

Different modes of direct manipulation will be utilized in our platform to deal with the interaction and visualization components in our platform. This include gesture recognition to interact with the system, touch screen with object detection capabilities to interact with different objects (e.g. buildings) within the system, and a TUI clock tool (e.g. position of the sun can be controlled by turning the physical hands of a clock tool) to give it a sense of reality [3].

For example, navigation gestures that can be used to interact with our system:

1. Start the Interaction mode: where actions are initiated by waving a hand with an open palm facing sensors, move the hand forearm left and right. Pointers for selection on the TUI will appear and the user can now use gestures to navigate through different objects.
2. Make a selection: Raising a hand with an open palm facing sensors and hovering over a specific object (e.g. building), and pushing it forward and then pulling it back to trigger the selection. The selected object will be visualized to confirm its selection.

3. Display an object information menu: Further layers of information can be projected by sustaining the gesture that was exhibited for selection or by a slight variation of the gesture to maintain an intuitive mode of interaction to view more from the TUI.

Interaction spaces will be implemented on the TUI surface surrounding the four sides of the physical model. Interacting with the DSS is via an interactive surface that offers a multi-user experience where multiple users can touch and share digital content simultaneously. One way of interacting with the DSS is via object recognition capabilities which captures and processes tagged physical objects that are placed on the screen (e.g. buildings) or movements that are within the range of detection (e.g. gesture recognition) by using cameras that operate in the near infrared light. Our goal is to create a collaborative and interactive interface that will help decision makers explore different scenarios with a responsive interface that provides intuitive and engaging user experiences.

4   Conclusion

In this poster, we describe a tangible collaborative decision support system that is designed to help urban planners in the context of large scale development areas. The DSS takes into consideration the complex systems of city infrastructures, to assist stakeholders in predicting future scenarios by utilizing different simulation and modeling techniques. The interaction interfaces are designed to provide urban planners with intuitive tools for manipulating data across spatial and temporal dimensions. Future work on this system involves developing the interaction modalities and evaluating them in real contexts of usage for case studies of urban developments in Saudi Arabia.

Acknowledgements. The authors extend their appreciation for King Abdulaziz City for Science and Technology (KACST) for funding this work and the Center for Complex Engineering Systems (CCES) at KACST and MIT for their support.

References

1. http://cities.media.mit.edu/about/cities
2. http://www.cdsi.gov.sa/english/
3. Ullmer, B., Ishii, H.: Emerging Frameworks for Tangible User Interfaces. In: Human-Computer Interaction in the New Millennium, pp. 579–601. Addison-Wesley (2001)
4. Reinhart, C., Dogan, T., Jakubiec, J.A., Rakha, T., Sang, A.: Umi - an urban simulation environment for building energy use, daylighting and walkability. In: 13th Conference of International Building Performance Simulation Association, Chambery, France (2013)

HCI Design of Technological Products for Eco-tourism

Chang-Franw Lee[1] and Chun Chang[2]

[1] Graduate School of Design, National Yunlin University of Science and Technology,
Yunlin, Taiwan R.O.C.
leecf@yuntech.edu.tw
[2] Graduate School of Industrial Design, National Yunlin University of Science and Technology,
Yunlin, Taiwan R.O.C.
rway12024@hotmail.com

Abstract. With the travel industry entering the experience economy era, improving tourism experience has become more important than ever. Technology is a good tool to improve traveling in ways such as weather predicting or tour guiding. However, the environment of eco-tourism is different from the general using environment of traditional tourism. Therefore, in order to apply technological products to eco-tourism, this paper proposes some HCI design suggestion from the perspective of UX like usability, information architecture and interaction design. We define two main design target groups as 'Normal tourists' and 'Narrators'. Expert system can be applied to the illustrating system for normal tourists while narrators need only a clear view of the system to make sure they find out the information of species they already know to give information to tourists.

Keywords: eco-tourism, expert system, the UX.

1 Introduction

With the advancement in technology, associated products have been gradually applied to tourism guiding, including eco-tourism. However, the using environment and requirements of eco-tourism guiding are quite different from those of normal tourism. Once we decide to apply technology products to the field of eco-tourism, the user experience (UX) about HCI like usability, information architecture, and interaction design should be re-designed to adapt to the user behavior in the particular environment of eco-tourism.

Therefore, proposing some HCI design suggestions from the perspective of UX to apply technological products (tablet computer, in the case of our research) to eco-tourism and improve traveling experience is the purpose of this research.

2 Tourism Trends and Technology Application

The management model of the traveling industry is inevitably modified by the revolution of technology. Technology such as GIS has been widely applied to tourism to

C. Stephanidis (Ed.): HCII 2014 Posters, Part II, CCIS 435, pp. 513–518, 2014.

improve traveling experience. However, users still have to interact with technology through hardware and software interface. Thus, it is necessary to realize how and when these technological products work before we use it.

2.1   Tourism Trends and Eco-tourism

Travel and tourism are among the world's fastest growing industries and are the major source of foreign exchange earnings for many developing countries. At the mean time, eco-tourism has been growing rapidly over the last decades(Wood, 2002). With the rise of individual traveling, travelers began to focus on personal feelings and travel experience, rather than simply travel. The structure of tourism, therefore, has been changed(Kelly, 1998; Yeoryios et al,2003). The term eco-tourism emerged in the late 1980s as a direct result of the world's acknowledgment and reaction to sustainable practices and global ecological practices. In these instances, the natural-based element of holiday activities together with the increased awareness to minimize the 'antagonistic' impacts of tourism on the environment (which is the boundless consumption of environmental resources) contributed to the demand for ecotourism holidays (Diamantis, 1999). This demand was also boosted by concrete evidence that consumers had shifted away from mass tourism towards experiences that were more individualistic and enriching. (Buhalis, 2003)

Besides the growing of eco-tourism, the travel industry is entering the experience economy era. Therefore, the issue of connecting and applying technology to create a wonderful tourism experience has become significant.

2.2   GIS and GPS Technologies Application

Information is the lifeblood of traveling, so the effective use of ITs(information technology) is pivotal. Unlike durable goods, intangible tourism services cannot be physically displayed or inspected at the point of sale before purchasing(Buhalis, 1998). Thus, to provide clear information before tourism and allow users to receive information they need immediately during their journey is very important for a tourism experience.

Widely applied to many fields, GIS(Graphic Information System) can be used in tourism as a decision supporting tool for sustainable tourism planning, impact assessment, visitor flow management, and tourism site selection(Rahman, 2010). In addition to GIS, GPS technology is also used in guiding. If we can apply these two technology to eco-tourism appropriately, it would become a good user experience for information searching.

2.3   Applications of Expert System

Expert Systems (ESs) are designed to support users in their decision making process. One of the most important features of an ES is the capability to make automated inference and reasoning.(Finnaca etc., 2014) An expert system is divided into two sub-systems: the inference engine and the knowledge base. The knowledge base represents facts and rules. The inference engine applies the rules to the known facts to deduce new facts. There are primarily two modes for an inference engine: forward chaining and backward chaining. The different approaches are dictated by whether the inference engine is being driven by the antecedent or the consequent of the rule(Wikipedia, 2014). For applying eco-tourism to a normal tourist, the system interface should be designed as simple as possible. The inference engine and interface design of Akinator the Genie, a popular application of smart phone, is a good example to refer to. Through a simple interface of five buttons (Yes/No/Don't know/Probably Yes/Probably not), the inference engine can lead users to the answer from asking only a few questions. If we can provide an expert system application like Akinator the Genie for self-guiding tourists of eco-tourism, chances are they can get information of species immediately once they meet that creature from describing its appearance to the system.

3   Methods

From the perspective of UX, this paper will investigate both human factors (usability) and user interface(information architecture and interaction design) with the 4D(Discover, Define, Develop and Deliver) service design procedure. The experiment was held in Sun-Link-Sea Natural Park in Taiwan, and divided into three stages.

During the first stage, a pair of researchers worked on participant observation for demand searching. One of them accosted tourists randomly and made conversation as a participant, and took notes of the conversation while the other one just observed and took pictures in the distance as an observer. After the process, group members shared the cases, analyzed and turned them into specific demands.

In the second stage we invited 6 participants to experience eco-tourism, and discuss the necessity of those demands we defined after they experienced in reality.

Finally by the last stage, we held a workshop, designed a prototype with focus group and proposed some HCI design suggestions.

4   Results

We defined two main design target groups as 'Normal tourists' and 'Narrators' according to the difference in using demands of tablet computers. From the interview with participants, we realize that on the human factors side, the portability and readability under bright light are important because the eco-tourism is an outdoor and dynamic activity. Subjects believe that 7'-8' inches screen size are best for carrying and still have enough size for visual experiences. Besides, normal tourists usually use their tablet computers on tourist sites or during way-finding only. Narrators, on the other hand need to operate their tablet computers frequently and turn it over to show information to tourists, so they prefer to have the hardware as wearable products.

5   Conclusions

On the operating interface side, the interaction design will be influenced by the dy-namic habitation of the living creature. Upon meeting a creature, well-trained narra-tors are capable of identifying it, so all they need is a reasonable path to search through the system and a clear view of information sectors to make sure that they can demonstrate the information immediately(Fig. 1.). Fig. 2. shows the interaction design and visual presentation of the system. Users can look up information of species with taxonomy or define their own custom way of searching. Besides, users can go back to any sector by touching the icon or nodes of the path shown on top of the block. In-formation of species that users usually use can be tagged as 'favorite', those informa-tion will be in a shortcut folder which users can open it immediately. Species that may occur will list on the right side of the screen through GPS.

For normal tourists, however, it is difficult to find the information through expert system when they meet an unfamiliar creature, so we recommend an illustration sys-tem combining ES and GPS technology for better and more accurate searching beha-vior(Fig. 3.). The system will ask questions about species characteristic that users meet on the block in Fig. 4., users can answer them through buttons under the block. After interaction with inference engine by few questions, users will be led to informa-tion of species which they meet. Progressing bar on the right side of the block can tell how close users are from the answer(information of species). Species that may occur will also list on the right side of the screen through GPS.

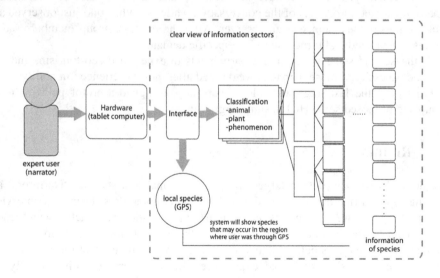

Fig. 1. Information architecture of the illustrating system for narrators

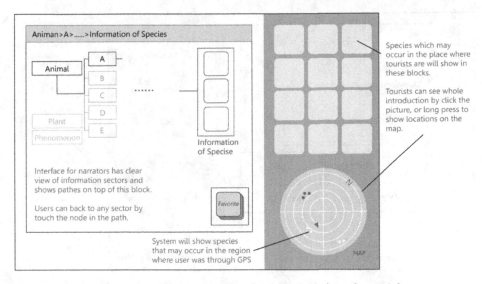

Fig. 2. Interaction design and visual presentation with clear view of sectors for narrators

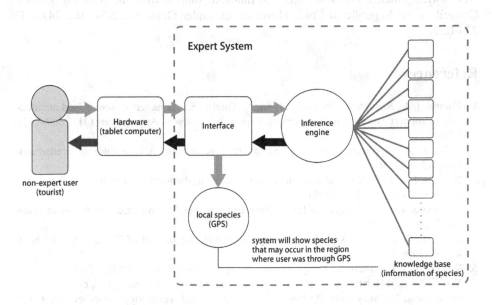

Fig. 3. Information architecture of the illustrating system with ES for normal tourists

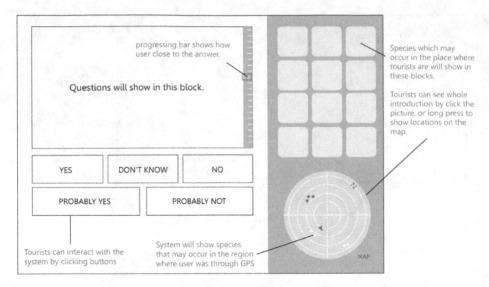

Fig. 4. Interaction design and visual presentation with ES for normal tourists

Acknowledgement. This study received financial support from the National Science Council of the Republic of China Government, under Grant No. NSC 102-2410-H-224-029.

References

1. Fiannaca, A., Rosa, M.L., Rizzo, R., Urso, A., Gaglio, S.: An expert system hybrid architecture to support experiment management. Expert Systems with Applications (41) 1609–1621 (2014)
2. Rahman, A.: Application of gis in ecotourism development: A case study in sundarbans, bangladesh (2010)
3. Buhalis, D.: Strategic use of information technology in the tourism industry. Tourism Management 19(5), 409–421 (1998)
4. Diamantis, D.: The Concept of Ecotourism: Evolution and Trends. Current Issues in Tourism 2(2&3) (1999)
5. Kelly, I.: Study tours: A model for benign tourism? The Journal of Tourism Studies 8(1), 42–51 (1998)
6. Wood, M.E.: Ecotourism: principles, practices & policies for sustainability (2002)
7. Wikipedia (2014), http://en.wikipedia.org/wiki/Expert_system
8. Stamboulis, Y., Skayannis, P.: Innovation strategies and technology for experience-based tourism. Tourism Management 24, 35–43 (2003)

Risk Management as Part of the Quality Management System According to ISO 9001

Hanna Gołaś

Poznań University of Technology, Department of Management Engineering,
ul. Strzelecka 11, 60-965 Poznań, Poland
hanna.golas@put.poznan.pl

Abstract. The top management staff of a company which applies a quality management system are interested in ensuring that the system safeguards a proper functioning of processes, achieves the objectives of these processes, and triggers perfecting mechanisms in a proper manner. Application of risk management in this system may provide some contribution to the fulfilling of the expectations of the management.

Keywords: risk, quality management system.

1 Introduction

Standard ISO 9001 specifies requirements for a quality management system. This system are the policies, procedures and rules of conduct that are carried out by employees of the organization on its behalf and its customers. It is therefore important to ensure that the risks which may render the established system ineffective and inefficient have been identified. The quality management system is important not only to ensure the quality of products but also the quality of the activities of each of the processes.

2 Quality Management System

2.1 The Notion of Management

In the literature, management is defined as [4]:

- a set of functionally discrete activities characteristic of organized projects involving more than one subject of action;
- a clear understanding of what is expected of people, and then ensuring that they do that in the best and cheapest way possible;
- a process of bringing certain things to a completion, efficiently and effectively;
- a process of planning, organizing, leading and controlling the work of the members of an organization and using all the available resources of the organization to achieve its objectives in an efficient and effective manner.

C. Stephanidis (Ed.): HCII 2014 Posters, Part II, CCIS 435, pp. 519–524, 2014.

Due to the complexity of the issue of management, it must be considered in a multidimensional way, through the prism of management itself (the management function), the scope of objectives and through the organisation in which management is conducted (management of units, processes/actions, and resources).

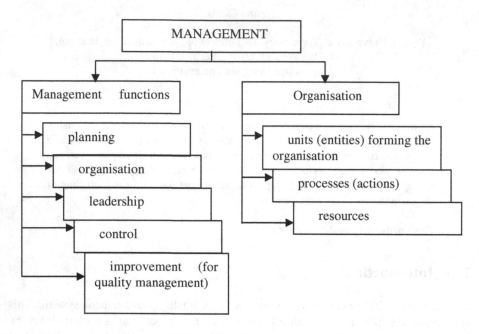

Fig. 1. Multidimensionality of management [4]

2.2   Quality Management

Quality management includes all management actions which determine the shape of the quality policy, the objectives and responsibilities as well as their implementation within a quality system, by such means as:

- quality planning,
- quality assurance,
- quality control (meeting the requirements)
- quality improvement [4].

Quality planning includes activities related to the establishment of quality objectives as well as all the resources, processes and responsibilities associated with the achievement of the quality objectives. Quality assurance is to ensure that quality requirements are met. Quality control is to prevent defects, shortcomings and incompatibilities, and to maintain an appropriate level of compliance while retaining an optimal level of costs. Quality improvement is to continuously improve the ability and capacity to maintain an appropriate level of the fulfilment of the requirements [4, 5,8].

A quality management system which complies with ISO 9001 is very popular these days and this is due in large part to the desire to streamline the operations related to the division of responsibilities, the flow of information within the company and the stimulation of an awareness of the quality of products or services among all employees [1,3]. A quality management system, although built on the same ISO 9001 standard, will function and look different from enterprise to enterprise. To a large extent it depends on their specificity, experience and qualifications of employees as well as on how the requirements are documented [1].

The underlying idea of ISO 9001 is the process approach, whose aim is to identify the processes taking place in the company and to manage the relationships between those processes. A model of a quality management system which is based on a process is shown in Figure 2.1.

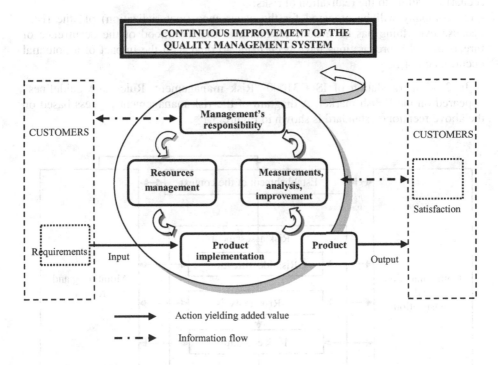

Fig. 2. A model of the quality management system based on a process [13]

3   Risk Management

Risk in management may be defined as the risk of making wrong decisions which prevent the achievement of objectives [11].

Implementation of the management system based on ISO 9001 is the first step to improve the functioning of an organization and to improve its management methods, which is evident in research on the causes of the implementation of quality management systems [6].

The main reasons for the implementation of risk management at the level of an organization include:

- it facilitates the monitoring of the company and the management and supervision over the key risks of the organization,
- it allows lower level managers to take risks in a controlled manner and in compliance with the objectives of the company,
- there will be common, transparent criteria for evaluation, comparison and procedures when handling risks relating to completely different areas of activity and functions of the company (e.g. the risk of losing the customer, the risk of an IT system failure),
- full awareness of all the risks facing the company, their consequences and possible scenarios leading to the realization of risks,
- the company will be prepared for the occurrence (materialization) of the risks, because everything has been done to minimize the likelihood of the occurrence of threats and also preparations have been made to deal with the impact of a potential occurrence [14].

In 2012 a translation of ISO 31000 "Risk management. Rules and guidelines" appeared on the Polish market. A diagram of the risk management process based on the above mentioned standard is shown in Figure 3.1.

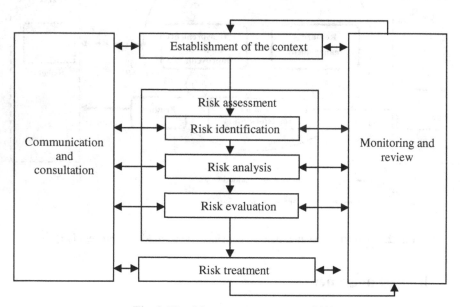

Fig. 3. The risk management process [12]

4   Risk Management in the Quality Management System

Table 1 shows the concept of the management system built on the basis of the ISO 9001 standard integrated with risk management for an organization [2,3,5,7,9,10].

Table 1. Risk management as an element of the management system according to ISO 9001

Elements of the management system according to ISO 9001	Risk management according to ISO 31000 integrated with ISO 9001
Management system	Determining the context of risk management Risk assessment for processes Handling of processes risk
Management responsibility	Business risk assessment Handling of business risk Strategy risk assessment Handling of strategy risk Policy of integrated management of risk and quality
Resources management	Personal risk assessment Handling of personal risk Assessment of infrastructure related risk Handling of infrastructure related risk Assessment of working environment risk Handling of working environment risk
Product implementation	Assessment of the client related process risk Handling of the client related process risk Assessment of the design process risk Handling of the design process risk Assessment of the purchases process risk Handling of the purchases process risk Assessment of the manufacturing process risk Handling of the manufacturing process risk Assessment of the measurement process risk Handling of the measurement process risk
Measurement, analysis and improvement	Monitoring and review of risks Communication and consultation in assessing and dealing with risks Identification and assessment of improvement actions

As one may see, the management system must take risk into account in order to ensure continuity of operations and achievement of its objectives.

5   Conclusions

Application of a systemic approach to risk management in such a way that each of the elements of the systemic approach to quality management is enriched by elements of risk assessment and management can contribute to a more efficient achievement of goals.

References

1. Gołaś, H., Mazur, A.: Zarządzanie jakością w małym przedsiębiorstwie produkcyjnym. In: Grudowskiego, P., Preihs, J., Waszczura, P. (eds.) Współczesne Nurty w Inżynierii Jakości, Gdańsk (2005)
2. Gołaś, H., Mazur, A.: Macroergonomic aspects of a quality management system. In: Jasiak, A. (ed.) Macroergonomic paradigms of Management, To Honour 40 Years Scientific Activity of Professor Leszek Pacholski, pp. 161–170. Poznan University of Technology Editorial Board (2008)
3. Gołaś, H., Mazur, A.: Wdrażanie systemów zarządzania jakością. Wydawnictwo Politechniki Poznańskiej, Poznań (2011)
4. Gołaś, H., Mazur, A.: Zarządzanie jakością, p. 163. Wydawnictwo Politechniki Poznańskiej, Poznań (2011)
5. Gołaś, H.: Personal risk management. In: Stephanidis, C. (ed.) HCII 2013, Part II. CCIS, vol. 374, pp. 489–493. Springer, Heidelberg (2013)
6. Mazur, A., Gołaś, H.: Zarządzanie jakością według normy ISO 9001:2000 a doskonalenie zarządzania przedsiębiorstwem, Organizacja i zarządzanie. Zeszyty Naukowe Politechniki Poznańskiej, vol. (47), Poznań (2007)
7. Mazur, A.: Application of fuzzy index to qualitative and quantitative evaluation of the quality level of working conditions. In: Stephanidis, C. (ed.) HCII 2013, Part II. CCIS, vol. 374, pp. 514–518. Springer, Heidelberg (2013)
8. Mazur, A., Gołaś, H.: Zasady, metody i techniki wykorzystywane w zarządzanie jakością, p. 113. Wydawnictwo Politechniki Poznańskiej, Poznań (2010)
9. Jasiulewicz-Kaczmarek, M., Drożyner, P.: Social dimension of sustainable development – safety and ergonomics in maintenance activities. In: Stephanidis, C., Antona, M. (eds.) UAHCI 2013, Part I. LNCS, vol. 8009, pp. 175–184. Springer, Heidelberg (2013)
10. Jasiulewicz-Kaczmarek, M., Drozyner, P.: Preventive and Pro-active Ergonomics Influence on Maintenance Excellence Level. In: Robertson, M.M. (ed.) EHAWC 2011 and HCII 2011. LNCS, vol. 6779, pp. 49–58. Springer, Heidelberg (2011)
11. Kaczmarek, T.T.: Zarządzanie ryzykiem. Ujęcie interdyscyplinarne. Difin, Warszawa (2010)
12. PN-ISO 31000:2012, Zarządzanie ryzykiem. Zasady i wytyczne. PKN, Warszawa (2012)
13. ISO 9001:2008, Quality management system – requirements (2008)
14. Szyksznia, W.: Prezentacja Zintegrowane zarządzanie ryzykiem. Gaz-System, Warszawa (2009)

Footprint of New Product in Mobile Market Using Diffusion Models

Zeyi He and Jing Kan

British Telecom, United Kingdom
zeyi.he@bt.com

Abstract. Facing any new product or new technology, a diffusion method, which can suggest exponential growth to some asymptote is important for both technical innovation and business decision. This paper produces the new study to examine and evaluate the diffusion models on mobile market. In order to evaluate two classic diffusion models, this paper chooses to use the existing 3G cellular mobile product data in UK as the sample data. This paper yields which diffusion model has the good prediction and good description features on different stage of product growth.

Keywords: Diffusion model, 3G, UK Mobile Market.

Mobile technology now becomes one of mainly methods to assist people access information, media and to generate their social life along with other communication methods. Although mobile telecommunication technology has been applied for public since 1960s, last two decades, the widespread diffusion of mobile technology has been at all speed. Interestingly, such speed appeared different level in different counts. According to the statistics at 2001, Luxembourg already has 96 mobile telecommunication services, whilst the US only has 44% on the same rates (Jang et al., 2005). As worldwide market generally share the same innovation of new technology, such difference of diffusion has been explained as government policy and regulation factors (Gruber and Verboven, 2001). Gruber and Verboven (2001) have pointed that governments' "regulatory delay in issuing first licenses, yet persisting initial cross-country differences also contribute to a lack of convergence". On the contrary, Jang et al.(2005) claimed that the network externality affecting the rate of diffusion of mobile telephones, such as market competition, the choice of fee payment. In their study, the diffusion of mobile telephone has been lead to the marketing relevant factors. Thanks to the convergence of diverse functionalities, mobile network has already shown great potential in terms of providing customized services to users regarding to their affordance, their demands and their preferences. Customers' preference and habits has been concerned as a significant factor to contribute the difference of diffusion of mobile telecommunications across countries (Park et al., 2010; Michalakelis et al., 2008; Karacuka et al., 2012). From previous researches, the common statement is that the pattern of diffusion of mobile telecommunications is characterized by countries based on various factors. So, what is the patter of diffusion of mobile telecommunications in UK?

C. Stephanidis (Ed.): HCII 2014 Posters, Part II, CCIS 435, pp. 525–529, 2014.

The UK has been one of the technological leaders over the last two centuries. The US and UK have been contributed the majority technology inventing over the last two centuries. Interestingly, UK has been identified as consistency of low uptake country on the diffusion of new technologies in the health area (Packer C et al., 2006). However, regarding to the Ofcom report, U.K. is the fast growth in subscribers to high-value smartphones such as the iPhone than any other nation in Europe. Specifically, the UK stands in the front of adoption of smartphone and uptake of mobile internet. The report also pointed out such high level adoption maybe caused by new generation. It is debate about how good UK performance on the adapting new technology from previous studies. Therefore, it is high interesting to understanding the diffusion of new mobile telecommunication in UK.

Facing a new product or new technology, a diffusion model, which can suggest exponential growth to some asymptote, is important for both technical innovation and business decision to understand the factors influencing further development of technology. As the methodological approach used to estimation, the diffusion model has been widely used to determine the adoption of technology or production innovations, by drawing the product's expected life cycle. It generally shows as the S-shaped growth pattern, which is the cumulative diffusion shape of innovation on sigmoid pattern.

In order to examine the diffusion of new mobile telecommunications in UK, this paper uses 3G mobile subscriber data as the example to display the diffusion model. 3G technology has been brought to UK mass commercial market at 2003 by O2. UK 3G mobile market is one of developed market in the world with the mature product and fully competitive marketing environment, which can help us to avoid any skew from unrealistic and monopolism influence. Also, after 4G launched in UK mobile market, 3G become the mature product in both business and technical perspective, which provides the authors more freedom to define different segments on their market data analysis. The data covered the period from 2003 to 2014, 15 years observation.

This paper produces the new study to examine and evaluate the diffusion models on UK 3G mobile subscribers by using two classic diffusion models: Logistic and Bass. The logistic model is a refinement of the demographic model published by Pierre Francois Verhulst in 1838. It has long been used to project cumulative output of new product (Mansfield, 1961). Bass model is produced 1969 by Frank Bass, specifically for sale forecasting in marketing.

- Logistics Model

The equation of Logistic model is shown as follows, where N is the number of individual adopters, K is the number of adopters in equilibrium in the diffusion study, and r is the intrinsic growth rate:

$$\frac{dN}{dt} = rN(1 - \frac{N}{K}) \quad \text{or} \quad \frac{\frac{dN}{dt}}{N} = r(1 - \frac{N}{K}) \tag{1}$$

In first order solution in terms of time t is shown as follows:

$$N(t) = \frac{K}{1 + e^{-r(t-m)}}$$

(2)

Where m is the system age of maximum changes in time period;

- Bass Model

In 1969, Bass suggested the diffusional equation for represent the time-dependent diffusion process, the distribution function is expressed as follows:

$$N(t) = K \left(\frac{1 - e^{-(p+q)t}}{1 + \frac{q}{p} e^{-(p+q)t}} \right)$$

(3)

Where N(t) is the number of individual adopters governed by time (t), K is the number of adopters in equilibrium in the diffusion study, p is the coefficient of innovation, and q is the coefficient of imitation;

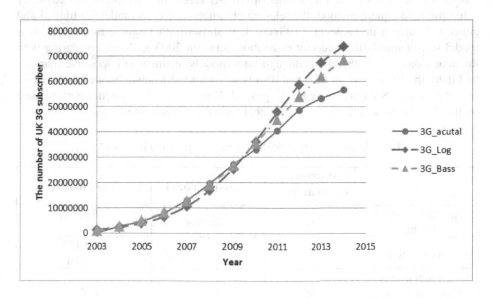

Fig. 1. The number of UK 3G subscribers from different models

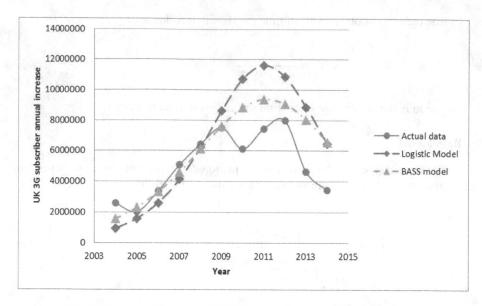

Fig. 2. The annual increase of UK 3G subscribers from different models

Applying Equation (2) and Equation (3) separately, the Logistic model and Bass model are used to estimate the number of UK 3G subscribers from 2003 to 2014. By using the least square method, the relevant parameters of each model are trained and generated (shown in Table 1). In Figure 1, it shows both Logistic model and Bass model shows small difference for estimation between 2003 to 2010, comparing with the actual data [1,2]. After 2010, although both models' estimation is positive than actual data, the increase peak of actual data is still near the Logistic model's estimation in 2012, around 8 million increase. In general, Bass model shows better performance on the data fitting with the actual data rather than the Logistic model.

Table 1. List of coefficients for Logistics model and Bass model

	Parameter estimation	Logistic model	Bass model
Adopters in equilibrium	K	0.85e+08	0.85e+08
Growth Rate	r	0.55	q=0.423 p=0.01
System age of maximum annual changes	m	8.55	9

---

[1] Analysis Mason 2014 Country report data annex: UK
[2] IDC: EMEA Telecom Services Database, 2Q13.

This paper uses two diffusion models—Logistic and Bass model on the UK 3G market data from 2003 to 2014. This paper yields which diffusion model has the good prediction and good description features on different stage of product growth. Additionally, this paper concludes that BASS model should be the better choice when applied to historical data based on the examination of veracity and accuracy through comparing the predictive results and actual marketing subscribe.

References

1. Satoh, D.: A discrete bass model and its parameter estimation. Journal of the Operations Research Society of Japan 44(1) (March 2001)
2. Jang, S.-L., et al.: The pattern and externality effect of diffusion of mobile telecommunications: the case of the OECD and Taiwan. Information Economics and Policy 17, 133–148 (2005)
3. Park, Y., et al.: An empirical analysis on consumer adoption of mobile phone and mobile content in Korea. Journal of Mobile Communications 8(6), 667–688 (2010)
4. Michalakelis, C., et al.: Diffusion models of mobile telephone in Greece. Telecommunications Policy 32, 234–245 (2008)
5. Karacuka, M., et al.: Network Effects in mobile telecommunications in Turkey, Discussion paper in dusseldorf Institete for Competition Economics
6. Gruber, H., Verboven, F.: The evolution of markets under entry and standards regulation—the case of global mobile telecommunications. International Journal of Industrial Organization 19(7) (2001)

A Service Design Framework for Manufacturing Enterprises toward Product Service System

Hyungmin Kim and Younghwan Pan

Graduate School of Techno Design, Kookmin University, Seoul, Korea
hm488.kim@gmail.com, peterpan@kookmin.ac.kr

Abstract. Manufacturing enterprises have been recently trying to create new value through a strategic alternative such as Product Service System because of the limitation of product growth, the keen competition of price and so on. Manufacturing enterprises have many risks to extend their business field over their core ability, with not enough the service domain knowledge, human resources and investment costs. This study suggested the framework that is needed for manufacturing enterprises to penetrate into a service business domain.

Keywords: service design, service framework, product service system.

1 Introduction

Manufacturing companies are creating a considerable portion of the added value on entire business from service, and the paradigm is changing into providing service rather than providing products. The Product Service System was introduced due to the factors of growth limit of manufacturing business, intensified price competition, and sudden rise of the late-starting nations of low production cost, including China. Due to such factors, the necessity of differentiating with a single solution of combined product and service is being magnified when providing a single product. This study intends to suggest a framework providing a strategic plan that can be selected in each step of the entire service process when manufacturing businesses are trying to carry forward a Product Service System when they are not equipped with core competence of the service business.

2 Service Design Framework

Manufacturing firms face strategic, developmental, and operational difficulties when they try to deliver differentiated value to customers through service and to secure competitive advantage. For manufacturing firms to penetrate the service market with limited resources and a limitation of so-called lack of capacity in the service business, they need to take full advantage of the external resources and capacities. There are 3 strategies that can be taken into an action in the service process for successful service management of the manufacturing firm, and they are Open Innovation, Outsourcing, and Internalization. Whereas securing various ideas, knowledge, and technology is

C. Stephanidis (Ed.): HCII 2014 Posters, Part II, CCIS 435, pp. 530–533, 2014.

possible for Open Innovation, the project management cost is high. The outsourcing promotes productivity and improves efficiency of a project by giving out functions that the manufacturing firm cannot carry out and can cut down the cost. Lastly, the advantage of internalization is in how manufacturing business can develop core ability of the service business, however, there is also a disadvantage that it takes a lot of resources to learn the capacity. As explained, each method has advantages and disadvantages. Manufacturing firms need to bear these advantages and disadvantages in mind when carrying their business forward by putting different importance on the 3 plans by each stage of the service process.

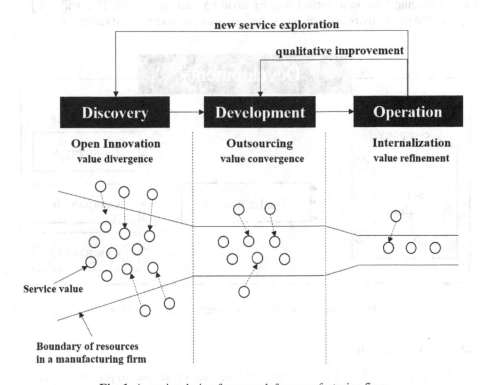

Fig. 1. A service design framework for manufacturing firms

2.1 Discovery Stage

For manufacturing firms to do service business of different domain from the existing manufacturing business, they need to establish a core value of the service first. It is because the absence of service value becomes the biggest obstacle when creating a new business. For this reason, collecting various ideas and knowledge seems appropriate at this stage by covering open innovation in depth. Specially, it is worth noting the crowd sourcing because various ideas and knowledge can be collected from many people at low cost. It would be necessary for the manufacturing business to distinctly establish value that the service intends to deliver to customers by linking their capacity that they accumulated in the existing manufacturing field based on such collected idea and knowledge.

2.2   Development Stage

It seems appropriate to approach the absence of competency for service development of manufacturing businesses through outsourcing. It is because establishing the internal service development organization and inputting human and material resources are very risky at wasting the cost. The entire service value for customers will be developed into the outsourcing form in a distinct way by dividing into sub values. This will not just improve the productivity and efficiency, but can also promote the cost reduction.

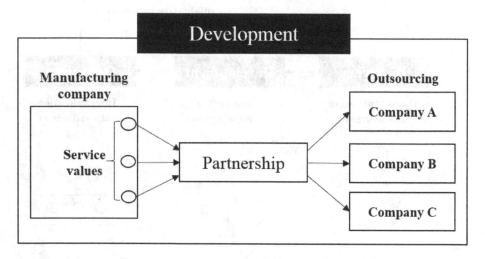

Fig. 2. Make partnerships among outsourcing companies

2.3   Operation Stage

The key point in service management is the service operation. Appropriate measure can also be developed rapidly because customer responses (satisfaction or dissatisfaction) that occur in the service encounter can be noticed quickly. Also, consistently improving the service quality through service operation can be expected as well. For a successful service operation, the organization capacity of various support organizations related to the customer relationship management and service operation acquires a great importance. Because manufacturing businesses do not have know-how's regarding the service operation at young stage of the service business, they can start trust management by sharing necessary systematic functions in the service operation in the outsourcing form with other businesses. However, as core competence in the service business is an empirical knowledge which is learned by operating the business, it seems necessary for manufacturing firms to internalize systematic functions regarding the service operation that were put on the outsourcing. In other words, it seems appropriate for the outsourcing to approach from the early service release and short operation perspective. In the end, learned empirical knowledge from the service operation will find new service business or will work as the driving force that can expect quality improvement of the newly released service.

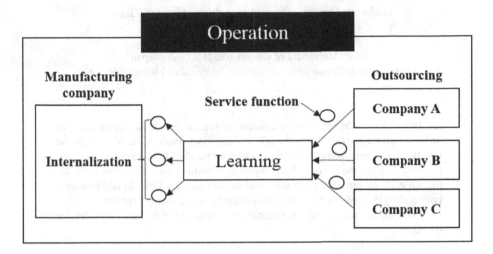

Fig. 3. Make learning process to internalize the operational ability

3   Conclusion

This study suggested a framework of an effective service management that can overcome relatively insufficient competencies in the service business compare to the manufacturing industry for manufacturing businesses to accomplish the product service system. The framework includes applicable strategic measures (open innovation, outsourcing, and internalization) in each stage of the service process, such as discovery, development, and operation. In future studies, the workers who are in charge of carrying forward the product service system in actual manufacturing firms will be interviewed to verify validity of the framework.

References

1. James, A.F., Mona, J.F.: Service Management: Operations, Strategy, and Information Technology. McGraw-Hill, New York (2013)
2. Martin, R.: Design of Business: Why Design Thinking Is the Next Competitive Advantage. Perseus, New York (2009)
3. Henry, W.C., John, S.B.: Open Innovation: The New Imperative for Creating and Profiting from Technology. Harvard Business, Cambridge (2006)
4. Jang, B.Y., Lee, Y.J., Lee, K.R.: Service R&D Strategy for the Integration of Product and Service. Science and Technology Policy Institute, Seoul (2010)
5. Christian, K.: The Service Function as a Holistic Management Concept. The Journal of Business & Industrial Marketing 26(7), 484–492 (2011)

Activity Models for Tourists of Medium and Long Term Stay in Japan

Toshinori Omura[*], Syotaro Hanabusa, Haojian Zhang,
Ryosuke Ogura, and Naotake Hirasawa

Otaru University of Commerce, Hokkaido, Japan
{omura,hanabusa,chou,ogura,hirasawa}@ouc-ux.org

Abstract. We conducted an investigation for the tourists at Niseko in Japan in order to build the as-is activity models of them. As a result, we could clarify the two types of tourist activities; one is to focus a steady life and another is to enhance a tourism experience. Both types of activities use often rent-a-car although each pattern of using transportation is different a little. In addition they collected by themselves the main information by using word of mouth.

Based on the results we are planning to envision the mobility services for them.

Keywords: Activity model, Tourist of medium and long term stay, mobility service.

1 Introduction

Niseko district is located in Hokkaido, in the northern area in Japan. The district is raising the brand awareness as ski resort. Especially in recent years, the populations of tourists of the medium-and-long term stay have been increasing rapidly there. With respect to their transportations, there are various types such as a privately-owned car, a route bus, a taxi, a train, a rent-a-car and so on. Although each service has its own feature, the existing services are said that these do not always meet the needs of the tourists during the on season in winter [1][2].

Our final objectives of the research project are to envision the mobility services for the tourists in order to satisfy the needs of them and to promote their new tourist experiences in the district. In this phase of the project we conducted an investigation to clarify the challenges of the means of transportation by building the as-is activity models of the tourists.

2 Investigation

Policy Bureau of MLIT (Ministry of Land, Infrastructure, Transport and Tourism) in Japan recommends to grasp the needs of the tourists by analyzing their actual

---

[*] Corresponding author.

C. Stephanidis (Ed.): HCII 2014 Posters, Part II, CCIS 435, pp. 534–538, 2014.
© Springer International Publishing Switzerland 2014

activities to develop tourism services for them [3]. In this study, we carried out an investigation to grasp their activities and information environment for supporting their activities in the district. Specifically we collected information related to the following;

— Stakeholders concerned with Niseko tourism,
— Tourists' activities and their knowledge,
— Available means of transportation,
— Tourist information.

Regarding the stakeholders concerned with the tourism, we explored the documents related to Niseko and the Web site of the Niseko administrative section and interviewed the persons concerned.

To reveal tourists' activities and their knowledge were main goal of the investigation. We planned and conducted the questionnaire survey for the tourists. For approximately 173 tourists, we could have done the survey in some area where the tourists took a break. We distributed the questionnaire directly to them and asked them to answer the questions. The investigation period was from January 2014 to March 2014.

About information of the available means of transportation, we collected the information by inquiring the tourist information centers in the district and checking the Web sites or the brochure related to the transportation.

In terms of the information the tourists can collect, we divided it into two types; "before coming" and "after coming". About "before coming" information, we investigated some Web sites that were assumed to be used by the tourists. About "after coming" information, we checked the Web site and collected the information which was located in the tourist information center, the train station, the road side station, hotels or restaurants etc. in the district.

3   The Problems about the Tourism at Niseko

After we analyzed the information collected by investigation, we could firstly clarify the following problems.

— Stakeholders concerned with Niseko tourism

• Some organizations provide the information about the tourism, however they do not necessarily cooperate to do it.
• No organization unifies the means of transportation based on the purpose of the tourist's activity.

— Tourists' activities and their knowledge

• It is difficult for the tourists who visited Niseko only several times to understand how to use the transportation and consequently their activities were very limited.
• Only tourist who uses a rent-a-car can go to a surrounding or nearby area.

— Available means of transportation

- Shuttle bus runs between only specific skiing areas.
- Some service offices providing a rent-a-car are scattered in the district.
- A bus to the adjacent town is difficult to use for the foreign tourists even for Japanese because of the difficulty of understanding of the timetable and the route map.
- In order to go to the adjacent big city, the tourist by himself or herself has to edit the timetable for the transit of the transportation.
- The number of the taxi is limited and the tourist may wait more than one hour even if he/she makes a reservation.

— Tourist information

- The information involved with playing ski could be available from various Web sites before visiting Niseko, however, the other information was difficult to collect except the word of mouth (e.g., [4]).
- There is no portal site that unifies all web sites related to the Niseko tourism.
- In tourist information centers there are various type of the tourist information such as a brochure, a magazine, a leaflet, a web site and so on, however they are not necessary organized for the tourists.

4   Discussion about the Tourist Activities

(1) Two patterns of tourist activities
We are analyzing the pattern of the tourist activities after basic statistical analysis. Although it is still in progress, by using the statistical method - Hayashi's quantification method, we could find two key factors that characterize the tourist activities.

One factor characterizes a tourist group who goes to a supermarket, a drugstore or a confectionery in the adjacent middle size town. We regarded the activities as a pattern for a stable and calm lifestyle and called "livelihood focus". On the other hand, another factor characterizes a tourist group who often visit tourism area that is adjacent to the skiing area at Niseko. The activities are regarded as a pattern for enjoying Hokkaido tourism except playing winter sports and called "tourism orientation".
(2) Means of transportation
We also found that each activity type we clarified above used different means of transportation.

Those who belong to "livelihood focus" type use a rent-a-car exceed seventy percent. On the other hand, although those who are in "tourism orientation" type use mainly a rent-a-car as well, they use the other transportation methods more than "livelihood focus" type (Figure 1). This leads us that it would be necessary to enhance rent-a-car services mainly. However, as we described above, the service offices for a rent-a-car are scattered at Niseko district, consequently it is very inconvenient to use the services. Considering many of tourists use the service actually, immediate improvement should be needed.

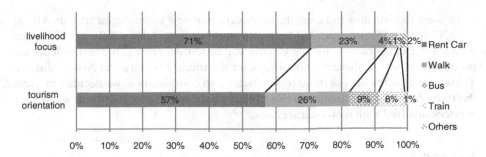

Fig. 1. The Means of Transportation

(3) Information environment

We also found main information resource for both of tourists was word of mouth. Both rate of collecting information exceeded fifty percent. Although many of web sites provided at Niseko are multilingualized, they do not always provide enough information to the tourists actually.

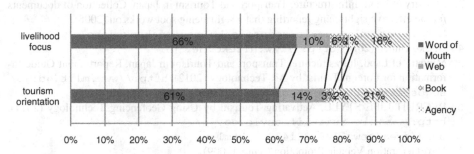

Fig. 2. The Means of Information Collection

Based on the analysis above, even in progress, we could understand that the typical tourists could manage to collect information while trial and error and try to achieve their goal of activities by using a rent-a-car.

5   Conclusion

We conducted an investigations for the tourists at Niseko in order to build the as-is activity models of them.

While we are still analyzing the results of the investigation, we could clarify the two types of tourist activities; one is to focus a steady life and another is to enhance a tourism experience. Both types of activities use often rent-a-car and collect the information by using word of mouth mainly. This shows that the as-is services at Niseko are not necessary enough for the tourist.   As the background that caused the situation, we presumed our country has not had little experience to support the tourist for medium-and-long term stay.

In some tourism area in Japan, the introduction of new technologies such as AR [5] or O2O service [6] are validated by a real-world testing. Additionally MLIT pushes forward the infrastructure for the electric car in tourism area [7]. These effects are promising, however, these are not always for the tourists we target at Niseko district. Taking the effectiveness of those technologies into consideration, we decided to focus the types of tourist we clarified in this project phase and to envision the new mobility services involved with rent-a-car services.

References

1. Hokkaido Bureau of Economy, Trade and Industry, Research report related to promote the globalization of tourism industry of Hokkaido (2009),
   http://www.hkd.meti.go.jp/hokiq/kanko_global/report.pdf
   (in Japanese)
2. Oshima, J., Nakagawa, M., Yamamoto, T., Sato, K.: Questionnaire surveys on Tourism in Niseko in winter (2005), http://www.gradus.net/new%20HP/
   kenkyuronbun/pdf/tokinoraido.pdf (in Japanese)
3. Ministry of Land, Infrastructure, Transport and Tourism in Japan, Collection of documents for the effective sightseeing reporting that a sightseeing spot works on (2008),
   http://www.mlit.go.jp/sogoseisaku/region/kankojoho/
4. Niseko United (2014), http://www.niseko.ne.jp/
5. Ministry of Land, Infrastructure, Transport and Tourism in Japan, Report about Guide Information for Foreign Tourist by AR Technology (2012), http://www.mlit.go.jp/
   sogoseisaku/region/sogoseisaku_region_tk_000008.html
6. RECRUIT LIFE STYLE, Activating Tourism by Using Geofencing Technology (2014),
   http://www.recruit-lifestyle.co.jp/
   news/area/news1140_20140217.html
7. Next Generation Vehicle Promotion Center (2009),
   http://www.cev-pc.or.jp/index.html

Research on Internal Dynamic in Interactive Development among Airport-Based Comprehensive Bonded Zones

Danyang Shen[1,2,3]

[1] School of Economics and Management, Civil Aviation University of China, Tianjin, PRC
[2] Aviation Transport Economics & Management Science Research Base, CAAC, Tianjin, PRC
[3] School of Civil Aviation, Nanjing University of Aeronautics and Astronautics, Nanjing, PRC
violetsdy@live.cn

Abstract. The intention of this paper is to investigate the interactive development among Free Trade Zones (FTZs). We take the ACBZs as an example type of FTZs. We adopt the System Dynamics Method to analyze the interactive development dynamic of ACBZs by using Vensim. We find that the increasing demand on efficiency of trading and producing are the two types of intrinsic motivation in the interaction. We also discuss the possible models from port, industry and customs aspects. The analyzing on causal relationship between each index, and drawing causal loop diagrams, and the establishing of flow diagram mode give a practicable study way on this kind of interactive development.

Keywords: Internal Dynamic, Airport-based Comprehensive Bonded Zone (ACBZ), FTZ, Systematic Analysis, Interactive Development Model.

1 Introduction

Airport-based Comprehensive Bonded Zone (ACBZ) is the Chinese name of a set special customs supervision areas (SCSAs), which feature and function are the closest to Free Trade Zone (FTZ). The ACBZs is playing an important role in reform and opening up, foreign trade development in China. And since 2008, along with the increasing of ACBZs, a serial of joint phenomenon emerged. For example, the air-ground joint in Suzhou Industrial Park CBZ, the bidirectional joint distribution of bonded Logistics between Beijing Lee Bridge Bonded Center and Shanghai Waigaoqiao FTZ, cooperation between Shenyang CBZ and bonded economic zone at the Parchim International Airport in Germany, and so on. This phenomenon can be named as the Interactive Development among ACBZs, which is a dynamic process of coordination, mutual promotion, and interactive development between ACBZs' administration, customs, enterprises, airports and other aspects.

Due to the "Enclave" nature, SCSAs' system components [1], operations, overflow effects [2], interaction between it and region, ports [3], [4] have been discussed most in recently academic and commercial literature. But the research on interaction among SCSAs has not yet been analyzed. In fact, benefiting from the smoothly policy

C. Stephanidis (Ed.): HCII 2014 Posters, Part II, CCIS 435, pp. 539–543, 2014.
© Springer International Publishing Switzerland 2014

flowing, and the similarity in businesses types, the interaction among SCSAs may be the best way to avoid the forming of "ISOLATED ISLAND". So this paper offers an insight into this issue.

2   Modeling on ACBZ System

ACBZ consists of three parts, Airport Functional Area (AFA), Airport-based Industry Area (AIA), and Customs Supervision Area (CSA). So ACBZ is economic complex with airport, bonded logistics, and export processing functions.

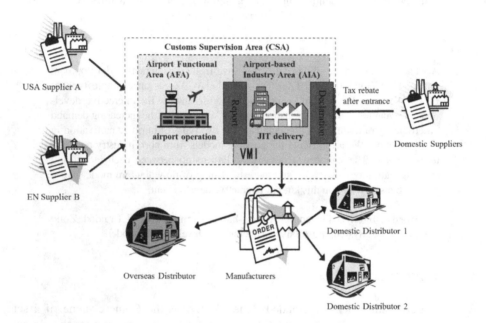

Fig. 1. The sub-system of ACBZ

According to the characteristics of ACBZ, we intend to adopt System Dynamics Method to analyze the internal joint dynamic of ACBZs. System Dynamics, first proposed by Professor Jay W. Forrester from MIT in 1956, [5] is mainly applied to solve the complex socio-economic issues, which are long-term and cyclical, with insufficient data, and less precision. The ACBZ is a complex social system, with all the characteristics of this kind of systems. And in the analysis, we use the professional system dynamics analysis software Vensim, which is developed by the U.S. Ventana Syestms Inc.

Firstly, we determined the purposes of ACBZ joint system modeling, secondly determined the system boundary and main indicators of the modeling, and then analyzed the causal relationship between each index, and draw causal loop diagrams, and ultimately establish the flow diagram model.

Based on the 9 business types of ACBZ approved by the State Council and the customs, we select 18 indexes as in table 1, with the consideration on the business type, system boundary, data availability and the comprehension of indexes.

We model the relationship of indexes in the whole interactive development system within a system causal relationship map with the setting of A & B for two ACBZs, as shown in figure 2.

Table 1. Indexes of ACBZs' system dynamics model

Sub-system	Index type	Specific indicators
Indexes of Economic & industry	whole status quo	GDP
		Investment in fixed assets
	2nd industry	Added value of the secondary industry
	3rd industry	Added value of the tertiary industry
	international business	Total import and export trade
	bonded inventory	Supply production
		Inventory of ACBZ
		Raw materials, semi-finished products capacity of ACBZ
Indexes of airport capability	international logistics airport	International transit throughput of ACBZ
		Incurred throughput of airport cargo
		Airport's handling pressure
		Port attraction
Indexes of interactive development	interactive development business	Other ACBZs' demand on cargo out transferring
		Own cargo out transferring demand
		Raw materials, semi-finished products transport from other ACBZs
		Raw materials, semi-finished products transport to other ACBZs
		Other ACBZs' demand on cargo transiting
		Own cargo transiting demand

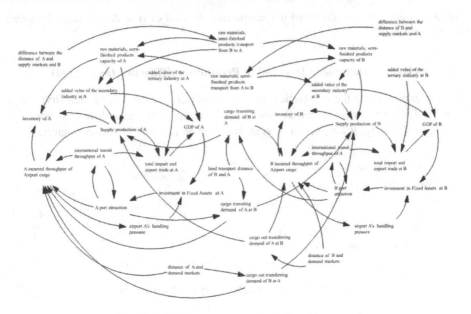

Fig. 2. A & B's system causal relationship map

3   Result and Discussion

Based on the systematic analysis, we find that there are two types of intrinsic motivation in the interactive development between ACBZs, which are the increasing demand on efficiency of trading and producing, and there are three levels of interactive development models according to the system configuration.

3.1   Driven by Increasing Demand of Trading Efficiency (as in Fig 3)

The distance of the A and the market determined the transfer of goods from A to B. If the distance between A and the market is shorter than that from B, the two ACBZs will be developing interactively with the driven of increasing demand on efficiency of trading.

On considering the logistics cost between A & B, the air networks and rights at A is rich than these at B, then B will transfer the cargos from A in its import and export process. So as the two ACBZs A & B can enhance their competitive strengths by developing interactively.

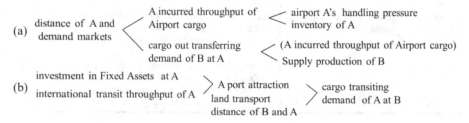

Fig. 3. Causality tree of (a) cargo out transferring demand of B at A, (b) cargo transiting demand of A at B

3.2   Driven by Increasing Demand of Producing Efficiency (as in Fig4)

ACBZs can enhance the companies' producing efficiency by deeply their division of work and the industries accumulation. Based on the seeking of low cost and high logistics efficiency, B may select A as its supplier on raw and processed materials.

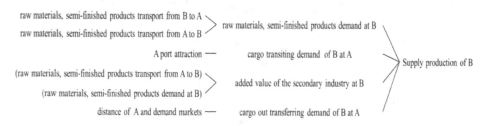

Fig. 4. Causality tree of supply production of B

In the developing of A & B, accompany with the free flow of productive factors, accumulation in spatial, work division, the reward of the regional economy increased. This is a reason and cause cumulative positive feedback process.

3.3   Interactive Development Models

Five types of interactive development models can be proposed from three levels, port, industry and customs. The first level is Port resources complementation model. This model relies on the differences of airport network connection, slots, flight schedule, by transforming between ACBZs under the whole processing supervision of customs. The second level is Industry vertical and horizontal interaction models. The vertical model is based on the vertical linkage on the same industrial chain. The horizontal model is the linkage between different industrial chains and it is an interactive development with both competition and cooperation. The third level is the Custom transfer or directly operation interaction models.

4   Conclusions

We discussed on the system dynamics model for the Interactive development of ACBZs, and we found that the increasing demand on efficiency of trading and producing are the two types of intrinsic motivation in the interaction. We also discussed possible models from port, industry and customs three levels. Although the analysis on this issue is limited by the data availability, and so does the qualitative model, we gave a practicable research idea.

Acknowledgments. The author would like to thank for the support by Fundamental Research Funds for the Central Universities (No. 3122013D024), and the Open Fund of Aviation Transport Economics & Management Science Research Base, CAAC (No. JGKF201304).

References

1. Zhen, Y.: The Research on the Joint Development Mode of Airport Logistics and Bonded Logistics. Civil Aviation university of China (2008)
2. Xu, H., Du, Y., Xiong, P.: Port-Bonded Zone Collaboration Information System Based on SOA. In: International Conference on Mechatronics and Automation, vol. 8, pp. 1099–1104. IEEE Press, New York (2010)
3. Jiang, W.: Research on System Dynamics of Bonded Port with Inland Port In-teraction Development Mechanism Model.Dalian Maritime University, Dalian (2011)
4. Zheng, H.: Research on Levels Selection Model of Interactive Development between Bonded Port and Inland Port. Dalian Maritime University, Dalian (2011)
5. Wang, Q.: System Dynamics (revised edition). Tsinghua University Press, Beijing (1994)

Missrail: A Platform Dedicated to Training and Research in Railway Systems

Frédéric Vanderhaegen[1,2,3] and Philippe Richard[1,2,3]

[1] Univ Lille Nord de France, F-59000 Lille, France
[2] UVHC, LAMIH, F-59313 Valenciennes, France
[3] CNRS, UMR 8201, F-59313 Valenciennes, France
{frederic.vanderhaegen,philippe.richard}@univ-valenciennes.fr

Abstract. Several railway simulators exist but none of them allow the design of rail infrastructure with the possibility to simulate other rail functions such as train driving, train supervision or train planning by using the designed infrastructure. The proposed tool consists in taking into account an existing physical platform called COR&GEST for rail driving and traffic supervision, and in developing supports to design any rail infrastructure in order to simulate driving, supervision or planning activity on predefined infrastructures. The resulting platform is called MissRail, a multimodal and multifunction simulation system for research and training in railway.

Keywords: rail simulation, training, research, sensemaking, reverse comic strip.

1   Introduction

The main simulators of transportation domains and more precisely on railway systems are usually limited to the simulation of an isolated function such as driving or supervision. Moreover, the associated interfaces are mainly based on digital supports and include a single mode. The paper proposes a new platform called MissRail dedicated for research and remote training in railway domain. MissRail is a multimodal and multifunction simulation system of a French IDEFI UTOP (French acronym for: Future Investment of Excellence for the development of a Pluri-Partner Open University of Technology) project.

This platform is dedicated to students at the Master Science level and is a support for specific remote training modules: it will be used for the design of rail infrastructures and of train routes, for the practice of driving and supervision of trains from different modes of interaction, and for a reverse engineering process to develop technological supports for achieving these railway functions. It is also used for enhancing research results and to applied research concepts developed at the University of Valenciennes such as: human error or risk assessment (Sedki et al., 2013; Vanderhaegen et al., 2004; Vanderhaegen, 2010a; Vanderhaegen et al., 2011), dissonance or resilience engineering (Ouedraogo et al., 2013; Zieba et al., 2010, 2011; Vanderhaegen, 2013a), human-machine cooperation and degrees of automation (Vanderhaegen,

C. Stephanidis (Ed.): HCII 2014 Posters, Part II, CCIS 435, pp. 544–549, 2014.

1977, 1999a, 1999b, 1999c, 2006, 2012a), learning from human errors (Polet et al., 2012), human behavior modeling (Aguirre et al., 2013; Richard et al., 2013; Vanderhaegen and Caulier, 2011; Vanderhaegen, 2010b). This paper details the MissRail modules and proposes a prospective module based on the so-called reverse comic strip to assess the difficulty of the sensemaking process or of understanding of the use of MissRail or of the control of events.

2   The MissRail Platform for Railway Research and Training

The MissRail platform is based on a physical platform called COR&GEST (Vanderhaegen, 2012b). COR&GEST includes a physical and fixed infrastructure on which miniature trains can move, Figure 1.

Fig. 1. The COR&GEST platform

Each train is equipped of a camera and the video of this camera is exported via a wireless connection to a screen. Around this screen, several interfaces are integrated to control the train, e.g. the control of the speed, the control of the braking system, etc. An interface to supervise trains on this infrastructure is also available. MissRail is an extended version of COR&GEST including several new advantages:

* The possibility to simulate any infrastructure
* The possibility to simulate several shared and real-time railway functions
* The possibility to take advantage of a database of short videos of train moving on the physical and fixed infrastructure of COR&GEST.

MissRail is based on Client/Server architecture and it is developed in Visual Basic, Figure 2. MissRail is dedicated to a French remote training program in order to familiarize students with railway operations by using different shared and real-time modules:

* A module to design rail infrastructures. It is based on a limited number of predefined objects such as straight line object, right turn object or left turn object. The designed infrastructures are on a database and students can select an infrastructure when they design train movement with the route train and planning module.

- A module to design route trains and planning. It is based on a classical space-time graph in order to prepare the routes of trains and to identify possible conflicts between trains. This support is a scenario editor that gives the possibility to design a specific scenario of train movement on a given infrastructure.
- The module to drive trains. It is based on sequences of short movies of straight and curved line moving taken on the COR&GEST platform. These sequences come from a database and a dedicated builder was developed to merge these views in order to obtain a continuous display and moving of a given train on the driving interface. Different modes of interaction can be used: the keyboard, the specific driving control support. A camera, a microphone and the keyboard can be used to communicate between students.
- A module to supervise trains on a given infrastructure. Different modes of interactions are integrated. A computerized interface gives a general view of the infrastructure where trains are moving with the possibility to act automatically on the signaling system and on the switching system. Another digital interface simulates a train signaling and switching workplace and aims at manipulating manually these systems.

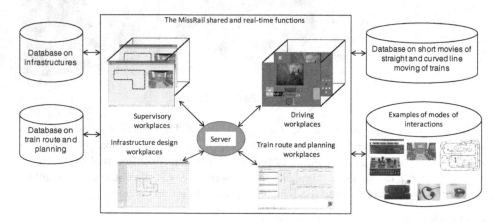

Fig. 2. The MissRail platform

3   The Reverse Comic Strip for Sensemaking Assessment

The MissRail platform is a support for research studies about the impact of a railway system configuration on human factors in terms of human-computer interactions, degrees of automation, etc... The use of such a MissRail platform implies the development of another support for diagnosing the users' emotional state related to misunderstanding, doubt or panic for instance. This research focuses on the feasibility of use of a facial recognition system and a sound recognition system in order to identify problems from the users during the sensemaking process related to two main problems: the use of the MissRail modules due to a lack of knowledge and the control of the events occurred during a given scenario due to a lack of vigilance for instance.

Then, the display based on the reverse comic strip concept is used. It consists in building a real-time comic strip based on the on-line data from facial and sound recognition systems, Figure 3.

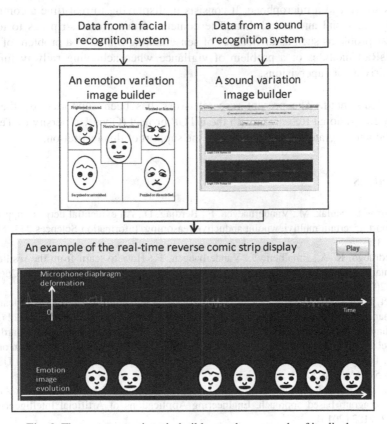

Fig. 3. The reverse comic strip builders and an example of its display

A degradation of the student's emotional state is then associated to the interpretation of the possible changes or sequences of changes of these facial and sound data. It is supposed to be link with a lack of knowledge or of vigilance that may affect the sensemaking process. This reverse comic strip process is developed in a JAVA platform.

4   Conclusion

This paper has presented the MissRail platform dedicated to research and remote training program of the University of Valenciennes. Developments are still going on to finalize the MissRail modules and the reverse comic strip builders and its display. The specifications of MissRail are original because they integrate different possible modes of interfaces and interactions between the system and their users for different shared and real-time railway functions such as the design of infrastructures, the design of train route and planning, the driving of trains and the supervision of train traffic flow. The reverse comic strip concept is integrated into MissRail by using the data from a camera and a microphone. It consists in displaying in real-time a comic strip by analyzing facial and sound data. The content of this comic strip has to identify particular problems such as difficulties of sensemaking linked to a problem of use of the MissRail modules or a problem of vigilance when achieving railway functions such as driving or supervisions.

Acknowledgement. The present research work has been supported by the ANR (Agency for National Research) with the UTOP project (Open University of Technology). The author gratefully acknowledges the support of this institution.

References

1. Aguirre, F., Sallak, M., Vanderhaegen, F., Berdjag, D.: An evidential network approach to support uncertain multiviewpoint abductive reasoning. Information Sciences 253, 110–125 (2013)
2. Ouedraogo, K.-A., Enjalbert, S., Vanderhaegen, F.: How to learn from the resilience of Human–Machine Systems? Engineering Applications of Artificial Intelligence 26(1), 24–34 (2013)
3. Polet, P., Vanderhaegen, F., Zieba, S.: Iterative learning control based tools to learn from human error. Engineering Applications of Artificial Intelligence 25(7), 1515–1522 (2012)
4. Richard, P., Vanderhaegen, F., Benard, V., Caulier, P.: Human Stability: Toward Multi-Level Control of Human Behaviour. In: 12th IFAC/IFIP/IFORS/IEA Symposium on Analysis, Design, and Evaluation of Human-Machine Systems, Las Vegas, Nevada, USA, pp. 513–519 (August 2013)
5. Sedki, K., Polet, P., Vanderhaegen, F.: Using the BCD model for risk analysis: An influence diagram based approach. Engineering Applications of Artificial Intelligence 26(9), 2172–2183 (2013)
6. Vanderhaegen, F.: Multilevel organization design: the case of the air traffic control. Control Engineering Practice 5(3), 391–399 (1997)
7. Vanderhaegen, F.: Cooperative system organisation and task allocation: illustration of task allocation in air traffic control. Le Travail Humain 63(3), 197–222 (1999a)
8. Vanderhaegen, F.: Multilevel allocation modes - Allocator control policies to share tasks between human and computer. System Analysis Modelling Simulation 35, 191–213 (1999b)
9. Vanderhaegen, F.: Toward a model of unreliability to study error prevention supports. Interacting With Computers 11, 575–595 (1999c)
10. Vanderhaegen, F.: Human-error-based design of barriers and analysis of their uses. Cognition Technology & Work 12, 133–142 (2010a)
11. Vanderhaegen, F.: Autonomy Control of Human-Machine Systems. In: 11th IFAC/IFIP/IFORS/IEA Symposium on Analysis, Design, and Evaluation of Human-Machine Systems, Valenciennes, France, pp. 398–403 (September 2010b)
12. Vanderhaegen, F.: Cooperation and learning to increase the autonomy of ADAS. Cognition, Technology & Work 14(1), 61–69 (2012a)

13. Vanderhaegen, F.: Rail simulations to study human reliability. In: Wilson, J.R., Mills, A., Clarke, T., Rajan, J., Dadashi (eds.) Rail Human Factors around the World - Impacts on and of People for Successful Rail Operations, pp. 126–135. CRC Press (2012b)
14. Vanderhaegen, F.: Toward a Reverse Comic Strip Based Approach to Analyse Human Knowledge. In: 12th IFAC/IFIP/IFORS/IEA Symposium on Analysis, Design, and Evaluation of Human-Machine Systems, Las Vegas, Nevada, USA, pp. 304–309 (August 2013a)
15. Vanderhaegen, F.: A Dissonance Management Model for Risk Analysis. In: 12th IFAC/IFIP/IFORS/IEA Symposium on Analysis, Design, and Evaluation of Human-Machine Systems, Las Vegas, Nevada, USA, pp. 395–401 (August 2013b)
16. Vanderhaegen, F., Caulier, P.: A multi-viewpoint system to support abductive reasoning. Information Sciences 181(24), 5349–5363 (2011)
17. Vanderhaegen, F., Chalmé, S., Anceaux, F., Millot, P.: Principles of cooperation and competition - Application to car driver behavior analysis. Cognition Technology & Work 8(3), 183–192 (2006)
18. Vanderhaegen, F., Jouglet, D., Piechowiak, S.: Human-reliability analysis of diagnosis support cooperative redundancy. IEEE Transactions on Reliability 53(4), 458–464 (2004)
19. Vanderhaegen, F., Zieba, S., Enjalbert, S., Polet, P.: A Benefit/Cost/Deficit (BCD) model for learning from human errors. Reliability Engineering & System Safety 96(7), 757–776 (2011)
20. Zieba, S., Polet, P., Vanderhaegen, F.: Using adjustable autonomy and human–machine cooperation to make a human–machine system resilient – Application to a ground robotic system. Information Sciences 181(3), 379–397 (2011)
21. Zieba, S., Polet, P., Vanderhaegen, F., Debernard, S.: Principles of adjustable autonomy: a framework for resilient human machine cooperation. Cognition, Technology and Work 12(3), 193–203 (2010)

Expanded Customer Journey Map: Interaction Mapping Framework Based on Scenario

Jaeyeon Yoo and Younghwan Pan

Graduate School of Techno Design, Kookmin University, Seoul, Korea
jyoodesigns@gmail.com, peterpan@kookmin.ac.kr

Abstract. This study proposed the mapping framework that was the intermediate layer between these two toolkits. The main attribute of mapping framework is that it is built up on the basis of scenario; thus, it plays the role of making the two toolkits correspond with the task based on a scenario as an output interaction as to the input of behaviors conducted by customers that are principle agents of the customer journey map and an output interaction as to the outcome actually conducted by the functions of system in the system map. It gives us an expectation that it would be usefully utilized for identifying problems later rather than merely visualizing intangible services.

Keywords: Service design, Service framework, Customer journey map, System map, Interaction.

1 Introduction

1.1 Background and Needs of Study

With the development of service industry and increased interest in service design in recent days, innovative service design based on design thinking is taking center stage as a new business solution. As the importance of customer-centric design UCD (User Centered Design) has been recently highlighted, the needs and inconveniences of customers are discovered and visualized through a variety of methods in order to deduct insights for service design. On that account, the customer journey map, the service blueprint, the system map, etc. have been utilized as a tool of visualizing intangible services. In particular, the customer journey map is to be utilized as one of "service experience modeling tools" that would summarize the temporal flow to be encountered by customers when experiencing a service and find improvements after analyzing the feelings of customers arising from each task. However, the customer journey map has the vulnerability of not including the perspective of providers as a tool to analyze the journeys from the perspective of customers; thus, it would be required to have a visual frame allowing for viewing the two harmoniously when determining the overall service flow.[1]

---

[1] Dongseok, Lee, Strategic Designing for Meaningful Experiences, p32, 2013.

C. Stephanidis (Ed.): HCII 2014 Posters, Part II, CCIS 435, pp. 550–555, 2014.

1.2   Purpose and Methods of Study

To achieve the objectives, this study aims to create the scenario-based mapping framework by selecting factors to be utilized as an intermediate bridge role that could effectively express and analyze the relationship between customers and system through further expanding the target from the existing customer-centric base in the customer journey map that was a tool of service experience modeling based on the underlying conceptual definitions and understanding as first conducting the theoretical review on the customer journey map and the system map.

2   Understanding of Customer Journey Map and System Map

2.1   Understanding of Customer Journey Map

The customer journey map for service design was first introduced through the Acela high-speed rail project of IDEO (1999). It has subsequently become one of the most widely used tools for service design. This project would allow us to confirm the fact that customers would encounter a service even before and after using it; thus, it has become an opportunity to sub-divide the scope of service into three phases (before use, use and after use).[2]

Definitions of Customer Journey Map. The customer journey map for service design could be considered to play the role of scenario in a movie. The customer journey map is to define the process in which customers would experience a service from the perspective of customers and be utilized in order to visualize customer experience generated during this process in a way that could allow for easy access to the feelings accompanied with service interaction.

Needs and Limitation of Customer Journey Map. The customer journey map is in use after being modified into various types by the nature of a project, creators and also research methods. And it could be used at the analysis phase by visualizing invisible intangible services in accordance with the temporal flow from the overall point of view. It has the advantage of gathering ideas for places where customers would feel uncomfortable and improvements based on tasks; however, it would be still necessary to materialize it since it has a difficulty of expressing the degree of satisfaction for specific features and several variables at the same time.

This study aims defined the customer journey map as the one that had visualized the process occurred in accordance with users' emotional satisfaction and experience and time step by step by identifying the flow between the overall service and interaction from the perspective of customers.

---

[2] Tim Brown, Change by design, p144 , 2009.

2.2   Definition of System Map

System map expresses the groups of various features related to a specific service in a visual and physical way. It is also expressed to allow for analyzing the relationship between staffs, consumers, partner organizations and several relevant stakeholders in a visual and physical way by displaying it in diagram form.

This study defined the system map as the one that listed up the features after organizing and visualizing a large quantity of intricate information as taking into account the technological environment as for service system.

2.3   Comparison between Customer Journey Map and System Map

To examine the differences between the customer journey map and system map, they were analyzed by using the pattern information of service users and providers as shown in Table 1.

Table 1. Customer Journey Map VS System Map

Pattern Information	Customer Journey Map	System Map
Main Agent	Customers	Service providers and system features
Task	User of service	Attributes of service
Behavior	Conducting directly to achieve requirements	Conducting inputted tasks
Prior Experience, Learning	Learning is required for initial use or case when not having a similar experience	Inputting in advance as to a assigned task
Components	Emotion, Needs, Satisfaction, Experience	System features

3   Interaction Mapping Framework

3.1   Definition of Framework

This framework plays an intermediate bridge role between the customer journey map and the system map and visualizes the interaction between services and customers.

3.2   Components of Framework

Input Interaction: Behavior Conducted by Customers for Tasks. This is an interaction process of customer behavior of encountering the service system and using a service at a task of the customer journey map. This was defined as an activity and contains the information as to how all the actions and reactions of customers would be implemented as focusing on the relationship between customers and system (or service and product).

Output Interaction: Outcomes Conducted by Features for Task. This is a list-up as to the outcomes of task performance inherent in the system that could be conducted by the features of system map for tasks.

3.3   Development of Framework

How the components of a frame would be expressed was defined as shown in the following table and the representation method is as follows.

First, it displays the service stage and then the tasks to experience the journey of customers in accordance with the temporal flow. Next, it creates a customer journey map. It states as to the needs, experiences and emotional state in accordance with the journey of customers in the customer journey map. Next, it creates a system map at the bottom. In the system map, it lists up the features suitable for the upper-level tasks among several features to be provided by the system. Finally, it creates a mapping framework between the customer journey map and the system map. At this point, an input interaction and output interaction must be created. At the input interaction layer, all the activities of customers in accordance with the tasks of customer journey map will be enumerated. The output interaction will list up the outputs of performance as to the features of system map as below. At this point, the customers and the service system will be interacted in a bidirectional way if the interactions of input and output correspond with each other. On the other hand, they will be interacted in a unidirectional way if the interactions of input and output do not correspond with each other.

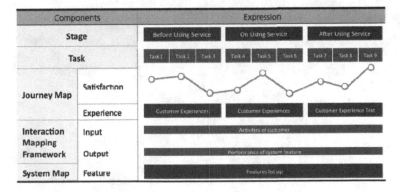

Fig. 1. Representation method of frame components

The features of frame that this study proposes based on such information are as follows. It is possible to view the journey of customers and the journey of overall service at the same time and also it is possible to identify which method each task would be connected and flowed by. The conventional customer journey map is focused on customers, whereas the extended customer journey map would allow us to view at a glance even the reactions of system as to customer behavior and the subsequent outcomes through the correspondence framework of input and output in addition to the information that has been already available to us. Moreover, it would be possible to find out whether customers and services would be interacted in a unidirectional or bidirectional way. Through this, it would be possible to further find pain-points that could be an issue for the service in the future.

4   Application Case of Frame

4.1   Process of Application Case

The case in which the frame proposed by this study had been applied was undertaken as an internal project of the laboratory and the theme was the improvement project for smart TV App Store UX. The purpose of this project is to propose improvement directions after identifying the problems occurred when entering App Store from the existing smart TV and the problems as to the operating method when using App Store. And the case was undertaken by applying the service design methodology and the extended customer journey map.

4.2   Application Case of Frame

The features were organized in a way that could allow us to conduct the minimal task while maintaining the features inherent in TV by deducting a specific target after identifying the overall problems of the existing smart TV App Store. Then, a persona was created, the target users were analyzed and the concept was determined. Based on this information, the overall flow of a service was identified by applying the extended customer journey map in order to resolve the present problems.

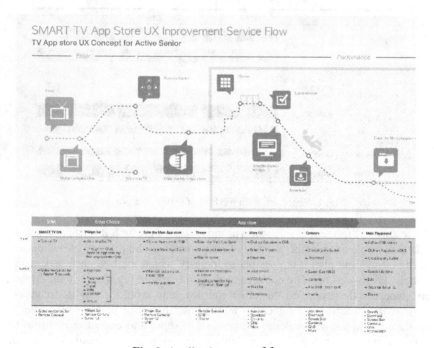

Fig. 2. Application case of frame

As a result of applying it to the frame, it was possible to view the journey of customers and the flow of the overall service system at the same time rather than looking at the service only from the perspective of customers by identifying the relationship structure for each task at a glance through the input and output framework. In addition, several problems of this frame were discovered through this case. First, the elements of customer journey map and the configuration of system map could vary flexibly depending on the nature of a service; thus, it might be unreasonable to define elements with a frame. Second, this only enumerates the essential tasks for the journey of customers; however, it has a limitation of representation for those services whose structure is complex with more features to be offered since the visualized frame would be so long horizontally.

5   Conclusion

This study is meaningful since it proposes a new framework to identify the overall interaction structure between customers and system by making the system features and the input and output interaction between the customers and system with the customer journey map in order to overcome the customer-centric limitation of existing customer journey map.

Based on such frame, this study conducted the case study for improvements of smart TV App Store UX and applied their effectiveness. Consequently, it is expected that it would be more effective for analyzing the customer journey map and it would be used conveniently when communicating based on customers' experience.

References

1. Dongseok, L.: Holistic, collaborative, ecological, and coevolutionary characteristics of service design process. Ergonomic Society of Korea 31(1) (2012)
2. Nakyung, L.: Spatio-temporal centered Evaluation model for service design (2012)
3. Sangyong, P.: Application of emotion words customer journey map (2013)
4. Seungju, K.: A study on the development of service experience frame according to the customer journey of ICT service with applied kano model (2013)
5. Moritz, S.: Service Design: Practical access to an evolving field (2005)
6. Brown, T.: Change by design. HarperCollins (2009)

Human-Human and Human-Agent Communication

Metacommunication through VLE Interfaces: Signs of Expression of the Teacher's Self

Luciana Espindola and Milene Selbach Silveira

Pontifícia Universidade Católica do Rio Grande do Sul – PUCRS,
Faculdade de Informática, Ipiranga 6681, Porto Alegre, Brazil
luciana.espindola@acad.pucrs.br, milene.silveira@pucrs.br

Abstract. This article fits in a broader context of a qualitative research seeking for traces or signs of expression, presence and representation of the self from the perspective of teachers as end-user developers of virtual learning environment interfaces. We chose Moodle as the environment to conduct this work and we counted with the voluntary participation of nine teachers with different profiles concerning the area, educational model and target audience. Questionnaire and interview were applied and testimonies were collected, uncovering three ways of self-expression and representation: expression through written language, interface customization and through the content. We focus this paper on the communication practiced via Moodle by means of written language.

Keywords: Computer-based learning, Metacommunication, Semiotic Engineering, Virtual Learning Environment.

1 Introduction

Recently we have witnessed the rise of a new educational paradigm, where the interaction between teacher and students happens through the Internet by the use of a Virtual Learning Environment (VLE). In this context, distance education has become a practical and attractive option for both students and teachers, mainly for those with displacement and time restrictions. Even the traditional (on-ground) classroom has adhered to this tendency by employing VLE to support extra-class activities.

The paradigm shift still preserves teacher's role as the knowledge mediator, but now there is an interface between him and his students, bringing new challenges to the teaching-learning context. From a broader perspective, this is a case of communication between humans, but it is also a subject of interest to the Human-Computer Interaction (HCI) research area, for this communication happens through the computer.

According to Monteiro et al. [1], most of the communication-centered investigations presented on formal HCI venues relies on social sciences such as psychology, but only a few of those study semiotic aspects of the communication through software interface, being these aspects key in our study. That said, this article is part of a research on how teachers express and represent themselves

C. Stephanidis (Ed.): HCII 2014 Posters, Part II, CCIS 435, pp. 559–564, 2014.

through a VLE from the perspective of Semiotic Engineering, a discipline that brings together concepts from HCI and semiotics.

Semiotic Engineering [2] is a theory of HCI based on semiotic aspects of communication. In this theory, HCI gains a new perspective where the system interface acts as the designer's deputy in his communication with the user. The idea is, every time the user interacts with the system he is engaging in a one-way conversation established by means of *one-shot message* directed from designer to user. This message is static and self-contained; it carries not only every information about how to use the system but also the designer's perception of who the user is, what he needs, and how user's interaction with the system is expected to be. Thus, one-shot message is a piece of *metacommunication* – communication of and about communication –, which is the foundation stone of the Semiotic Engineering theory.

In this research, teacher occupies the role of system designer, who manages and arranges the VLE for the best interest of his students, the system users. We counted with the voluntary participation of nine teachers which were asked about their perceptions on the way they express themselves via VLE. From testimonies we identified three ways of expressing the teacher's self: through content, interface customization and written language. Literature on End-User Programming (EUP, or EUD for End-User Development) [3,4,5,6] considers customization a special case of EUP, which places VLE configuration in a very particular kind of programming activity. Despite this study embraces aspects of customization and EUP, the lack of space forces us to focus this article on the metacommunication [1,2,7] practiced through written language.

Next section presents the methodology adopted during this qualitative research. It follows a section dedicated to data analysis, where the most significant testimonies concerning the written expression are presented. Last section concludes the paper with final considerations.

2 Methodology

Given the focus of this qualitative research – which is how the teacher expresses himself from the interfaces at his disposal –, among the virtual learning environments (VLEs) available, we chose Moodle [8] for conducting our work, since it is free, open-source and widely adopted.

We conducted this research as an exploratory case study divided into two stages: the first consisted on the application of a structured questionnaire; the second was conceived as a semi-structured interview. The strategy was to use the questionnaire to promote initial reflection on teacher's experience, and then deepen with open questions proposed during the interview. The results presented in this paper were obtained by means of qualitative analysis of data collected during the process.

The questionnaire consisted of four sections. The first gathered personal information such as the respondent's age, practice area, *etc*. The second was to foster early reflection on the teaching activity. Next section aimed to deepen reflection on the teacher-student relationship in the traditional classroom. The last was to prepare the teacher for the interview to come.

The interview was conducted in person, by video or by chat. It consisted of seven open questions about how teachers feel they express themselves via Moodle interface, giving the interviewee freedom to explore the subject and raise issues.

3   Data Analysis and Discussion

During this research, we have interviewed nine teachers (all Moodle users) whose profiles are available on Table 1. With exception to T3, a novice on both teaching and VLEs usage, all the others have long time experience on teaching and at least 5 years of experience with Moodle. With the interviews, we collected teachers' impressions in respect to the way they communicate with their students via Moodle. These testimonies highlight signs of self-expression and self-representation, characterizing the teachers' presence through the interface.

Table 1. Teachers' profile according to their overall experience with Moodle (current and past). Except to T3, all of them are currently using Moodle to deliver education through one or more of these educational models.

Teacher	Distance Education	Blended Learning	On-Ground Education	Time of Experience	Target Audience
T2	✓				
T6	✓			5 years	Corporative Education
T8	✓				
T4	✓		✓		
T5	✓		✓		
T1	✓	✓	✓	7 years	Higher Education
T9	✓	✓	✓		
T7		✓	✓		
T3			✓	1 year	
Note: teachers are numbered according to the order they were interviewed.					

According to them, educational model and target audience play important roles on the way teachers express themselves via Moodle. Unlike those teachers engaged with blended learning and on-ground education – which are completely in charge of every class-related thing –, teachers delivering distance education said they are usually assisted by an auxiliary staff responsible for technical issues related to configuration, use and customization of the virtual learning environment. Depending on the level of assistance due by the technical staff, teachers may have difficulty on expressing themselves via interface customization. This is the case for those in Table 1 delivering distance education classes whose audience consists of colleagues and associates of the corporation for which they work. Since the Moodle interface follows some corporative guidelines and the content is given by experts, unless they are part of the expert team, T2, T6, and T8 are tutors only and, as such, written language through forums, chats and messages are the only ways they may have some freedom to express their own selves. On the other hand, teachers engaged with higher education are responsible for producing the content for their classes, which add to the possible ways of expressing the teacher's self a third dimension: expression through the content, including personal interpretation in respect to the subject of study.

Given the overview, testimony analysis made it possible to distinguish three categories concerning the ways teachers express themselves: through interface customization, written language and through the content. The lack of room to go through all the aspects of this research made us choose to focus this article on metacommunication through written language. This kind of expression is mostly practiced via forums, the most important Moodle activity, according to teachers.

Interviewees were asked about how they feel in respect to self-expression through Moodle interface, what promotes and what hinders this expression. About the use of his own language, T3 said it is not difficult for him to express by writing in the same tone he uses to talk. Perhaps T3 feels so comfortable with that given the fact his is much familiar with technology, but for some it is a challenge. Teacher T7, for instance, is mostly concerned with the form of the expression. He said a teacher must be careful with the writing since it is subject to dual-interpretation, and a word out of context may end up discouraging the student in his journey to knowledge construction.

Teacher T2 said to be a trace of her personality being rather formal when writing. She believes this is why people find her extremely serious. This is an evidence of presence and self-representation according to teacher's perception about her receptiveness among students. According to her, distance education has the challenge to bring teacher and students together, and in this scenario too technical and formal language may be a problem. T2 said a teacher must ease the teacher-student relationship by being smooth on writing so that students feel close and assisted, and this is something for her to pursue.

In a similar way, the desire to be thorough made the text of teacher T4 too formal. In spite of this trace of personality, she realized it is worth to relax on formality so that students feel comfortable to interact and build knowledge together. According to her, it is important to ease on formality and reach for dialog when proposing activities, so that students feel invited to participate.

Teacher T8 is pragmatic, she values the need of closeness but also the importance of clarity. That is the reason why she prefers to communicate by using the same language of her students. However, closeness may be achieved not only by the use of a common language, but also by the presence, which she believes is perceived whenever she puts something in her writings to mark her personality. She said even a joke may break the ice and shorten distances, leaving students more comfortable to ask and to speak; to her, this is a way to be closer.

Following the same line, teacher T5 said she addresses her students as if she were talking to them. The idea seems to be: drop formality to promote clarity and closeness. However, closeness, presence and availability may be achieved by other means. For instance, T4 considers important that the teacher show he knows each student by name, notices his presence and concerns about his absence. It is, in fact, a personality trace of a caring teacher and also a way to be present. Even though T6 deals with restrictions of the corporative education, she agreed with T4 and called attention to the importance of ensuring that the same treatment of a face-to-face conversation be practiced via VLE, in order to narrow the relationship and foster the students' participation.

When asked about feeling present, T1 said his teaching style is reflected on Moodle but complaint about not feeling the students present, being more and more difficult to motivate them. According to T4, T5 and T9, students' lack of motivation may come from a methodological inadequacy. T1 uses to replicate classroom materials on Moodle, which is probably the cause of students' lack of interest. In the case of blended learning, T4 and T5 advise to avoid that the virtual area be a copy of the on-ground class. Teacher T9 believes that the ease to put things on Moodle gives the wrong idea that nothing more is necessary, but that content needs a pedagogical architecture for it to work.

But not only methodological issues hinder the expression via Moodle. Teachers complained about administration and the difficulty to keep plug-ins up-to-date. T4 said that Portfolio is an activity she would like it were part of the main package. According to her, Portfolio is meant to keep the student's record and should be configurable in a way the student could choose the mates with whom to share it. Teacher T7 believes knowledge is also constructed by interacting with peers, something he misses on Moodle. However, after saying that, he recalled of the Workshop (peer assessment) activity, which enables students to evaluate each others' works. Even so, teachers said Moodle is not prepared to work with students in group. Some of them workout this problem by using forums.

The most dissonant testimony about the adequacy of Moodle to express the teacher's self came from T9. She said Moodle is linear but herself is hypertextual; her discourse is congruent but not linear. Adding to this trace of personality, she said Moodle is not completely adequate for her since it is not graphical; it is not suitable to work with scientific computing. According to her, chat and forum are text-based, they were not meant to work with anything but text. One can use dollar sign to insert formulas on chat message, but she finds it too boring; she would like something different. It should also be possible to insert vector graphics, since static images, like a picture, don't fill her needs as teacher. Instead of being always worrying about the format and the logic of the content she makes available, she would like that Moodle were a place where you drop everything inside, classify with a tag, and the content were automatically rearranged. A place where each one finds his own way to read and construct knowledge.

4   Final Considerations

With this work we initiated a discussion on how teachers express and represent themselves through the use of virtual learning environments (VLEs) interfaces. Nine teachers were interviewed and the most significant testimonies were presented in this paper. We found signs of expression that highlight three ways of expressing oneself through the VLE interface: by means of written language, via interface customization and through content assembling.

These evidences of self-expression are considered in this work as a sign of self-representation, where the virtual learning environment acts as the teacher's deputy in the communication with his students. Most of all, we believe that the representation of the self impacts directly on teacher's perception about his own presence by the students, as we may observe by the testimonies.

We understand it is important to investigate different teacher profiles to better characterize the ways of self-expression via VLEs. Future work also includes executing the analogous research by interviewing the students, in order to collect the points of view of both interlocutors (teachers and students) of this communication between humans, mediated by Moodle.

This entire research, which includes also aspects of self-expression through interface customization and content creation, is expected to give insights on how to refactor the Moodle interface (and the interface of its tools) such that teachers can improve their expression through it. Some methodology guidelines about better practices when using a VLE may also be necessary.

References

1. Monteiro, I.T., de Souza, C.S., Leitão, C.F.: Metacommunication and semiotic engineering: Insights from a study with mediated HCI. In: Marcus, A. (ed.) DUXU 2013, Part I. LNCS, vol. 8012, pp. 115–124. Springer, Heidelberg (2013)
2. de Souza, C.S.: Semiotic engineering: bringing designers and users together at interaction time. Interacting with Computers 17(3), 317–341 (2005)
3. Blom, J.: Personalization: a taxonomy. In: CHI 2000 Conference on Human Factors in Computing Systems, pp. 313–314. ACM, New York (2000)
4. Fischer, G., Giaccardi, E., Ye, Y., Sutcliffe, A.G., Mehandjiev, N.: Meta-design: a manifesto for end-user development. Commun. ACM 47(9), 33–37 (2004)
5. Marathe, S.: Control and Agency in Customizable Video Games: A Theoretical Approach to Learning Outcomes. In: Annual Meeting of the International Communication Association, Montreal, Quebec, Canada (May 2008)
6. Wells, M.M.: Office Clutter or Meaningful Personal Displays: the Role of Office Personalization in Employee and Organizational Well-Being. Journal of Environmental Psychology 20(3), 239–255 (2000)
7. Monteiro, I.T., de Souza, C.S.: The representation of self in mediated interaction with computers. In: Proceedings of the 11th Brazilian Symposium on Human Factors in Computing Systems, IHC 2012, Porto Alegre, Brazil, Brazil, pp. 219–228. Brazilian Computer Society (2012)
8. Moodle.org: Moodle: community   driven,   globally   supported   (2013), https://moodle.org

Sign Language Recognition System Based on Prediction in Human-Computer Interaction

Maher Jebali, Patrice Dalle, and Mohamed Jemni

Research Lab. LaTICE - ESSTT University of Tunis, Tunisia,
Research Lab. IRIT Univ. of Toulouse3, France
maher.jbeli@gmail.com,
patrice.dalle@irit.fr,
mohamed.jemni@fst.rnu.tn

Abstract. While gesture recognition methods have been employed with success to real word applications, there are yet several issues that requires to be solved for larger Human-Computer Interaction (HCI) applications. one of such issues is the real time sign language recognition. The goal of this paper is to bring the HCI performance nearby the human-human interaction, by modeling a sign language resognition system based on prediction in the context of dialogue between the system (avatar) and the interlocutor, to make a ludic application. The main recognition method include an empirical tracking method which dynamically changed according to each stage of the dialogue.

Keywords: HCI, Sign language recognition, Object tracking, Sign language modeling.

1 Introduction

Incessantly, HCI is defining new communication modalities and new machines interacting ways. In fact, a gesture can transmit information for which other aspects are not suitable or efficient. In a spontaneous interaction, the gestures can be used as a single modality or in combination with multimodal interaction programs involving textual media, speech or facial expression. For instance, sign language has multi-aspects interactions where different manual or non-manual components may occur simultaneously. Moreover, SLR is an important application area of HCI that can be very useful to facilitate interaction between deaf person and technologies as well between deaf and hearing people [8]. SL is used by deaf and hearing-impaired communities, in order to establish a communication. It can be described as a visual language which characterized by the motion of certain parts of the body such as, the face, the mouth, eyes, trunck and hands. At the present time, we can admit that several researchers are meant to put the stress on the automatic analysis and recognition of signs, particularly automatic SL interpretation [6] [5]. This may help SL users to communicate without referring to human interpreter. To succeed in this achievement, video treatments and linguistic models are developped. Hands, face and other body parts are involved

C. Stephanidis (Ed.): HCII 2014 Posters, Part II, CCIS 435, pp. 565–570, 2014.

to create gestures. The most challenging task is that of hands and head tracking, regarding the semilarities of coloured objects. Additionally, what makes tracking much harder is the presence of occlusions, noise, background complexity and fast dynamic changes. Several tasks use special markers to overcome these problems [2], but this do not allows us to put in practice a real application used by all deaf persons, because of the difficulty in using these devices. To overcome these obstacles, many tracking algorithim has been suggested. We can chiefly refer to methods based on similarity cost function between the current image and a template and a dynamic model based method which estimates the posterior probability density function [1]. The particle filter [11] algorithm has become very common for non-linear or non-Gaussian problems. Popularly, colur features and contours are used by particle filter tracking algorithm [4] [10] [11]. The inconvenience of the colour based algorithms, is that the same model can be used for different object representation, for example, skin blobs represent hands and head, and further work is necessary to label each target. Next to this, it is not possible to handle occlusions between similarly coloured target because it disregard the spatial information. In previous works, data association, local features or body features is used to handle hands and head occlusions [4] [10] [12]. Giani et al. [4] suggested a particle filter based tracker using color cue. Their technique sees each target as a grouping of points, and to associate and interpret data in terms of various target, they use a probabilistic exclusion principle. it permit the directly handle of occlusion and this avoids filter to converge to the same object. However, the position of each object can not be precisely determined during occlusion, since the filters share the same skin blob. Several methods based on trajectories and motions have been suggested to recognize human gestures by motion information [15]. In the few last years, scalability was addressed by turning to sign linguistics to help classification. The initial work of Vogler and Metaxas [14] focused on a lexicon of 53 signs but later, a scalable solution using parallel hidden Markov models on both motion and hand shape to recognize a 22 sign, was reported. to overcome the problem of the vocabulary size or the complexity of modeling, many researchers shaped signs usings sub-units, such as cooper and all. [3] who linked the subunits resulted from 2D and 3D informations simultaneously, and they showed the efficiency of this approach with an independant signers (76%). These approaches have to be shown that they are able to be effective and extended to a wide range of vocabularies in terms of size. We must highlight that the majority of works do not contain a real time SLR system, through it is primordial aim. So that, the applications can be used by deaf community. In this work, we are exhibiting an orginal approach which allows us to recognize signs in a real timing and in a particular context. The proposed method of recognition is based on prediction, in a context of dialogue between interlocutors and the system. At this level, the recognition stage requires a tracking stage of different body parts. Our tracking method is in fact an emperic method and the recognition is adapted dynamically to different levels of dialogue by selecting the discriminant characteristics of signs.

2   Multiple Object Tracking

The multiple object tracking is very difficult because of the presence of occlusion between targets of same aspect, hand and face having a common colour of skin that depends on the signer. Several approaches focused on the skin segmentation [13]. Some of them tend to make a training step and create a model which depends on the colour of skin, lightening and conditions related to the environement in the training set. This work presents an explicit definition of skin regions for initialisation suggested by kovac and all. [9]. The main obstacle to achieve high recognition rate are the chrominance and luminance components which are not decoupled , which result in an inaccurate detection in the shadow area. However, the advantage side of this approach is that can ignore the training stage, in addition, it is easy to be applied. It also provides a rough skin region. The sample skin region pixels for the model are those which take part of the most important area connected component, hands or head depending on the frame. In the YcrCb color space, the skin colour is shaped as a bivariate normal distribution. Y component indicates the luminance and is rejected to find solutions to shadow problems, we note that the regions are better detected.

Fig. 1.   multiple object tracking

After dealing with the segmetation of the skin, we treat the issue of head and hands tracking. It is consisting of A) for each frame, we assign one or multiple labels for different bodyparts. B) the estimation of rectangles at region with multiple occluded labels. In this context, two cases are manifested. One or two objects in the occlusion case and three objects in the case of non-occlusion. the position of the face is determined by using the skin segmetation before occlusion (first frame). We consider that the connected region with the most significant area which is situated in the upper part of the frame corresponds to the face.

Not Occluded Objects: Concerning hand labeling, we applied a linear prediction of centroid position of each hand; considering the preceding frames; the predictor coefficient match to the model of constant velocity. Afterwards, we attribute the labels based on the minimum distances between the centroids of the objects and the prediction positions. On each object, we also adapt one rectangle assuming that a recatngle can rougly approximate the head or hand blob. We intend to use the suitable rectangles in case of occlusions.

Occluded Objects: the use of the bodypart rectangles parameters already computed from the last two preceding frames. Similarly to the previous case, we refer to the linear prediction for all parameters of rectangles of the current frame. When a number of consecutive occluded images is important, it can results in cases of ambiguity in the exit of occlusion. To overcome the uncertainty of two hypothesis (is the right hand on the right or on the left, and the same for the left one), we estimate the interim centroid of each party of the body corresponding to the skin model between consecutive frames. Add to this, we are repeting the prediction and the estimation of the correspondant model reculing faster through the sequence of the opposit frame, which is based on hand holding the ordinary position which is either the left or the right one of upper part of the body. Figure 1 illustrates the tracking result of the image sequences with and without occlusion. We notice that the system provides us a precise tracking even during occlusions.

3   Modeling of Sign Language Recognition System

We are using this algorithm of tracking to generate models of recognition. The signes are pre-analysed before being added to the basis which can be enriched in an incremental manner. there is no complilation of the whole basis ; it will be done during the interpretation, only on small groups of condidates signs. In fact, aiming to put in practice a fast and robust SLR system, we tend to exploit an approach of prediction-verification when possible. In an ascending classical approach, detection-tracking-measure-characterization-recognition, the presence of errors in the first levels will cause errors of recognition. Or, for the mentioned reasons, will risk to have frequent errors or inaccurance in these levels of image analaysis. At this stage, we can palliate this default through static approaches which directly link the signal aspect to the decision, as it has been used in vocal language treatement, but this fact can suppose important size corpus which are not available in SL, however the characteristics of SL (3D-2D projection, the least constraint of formulation of continous flow of signs in the space, can produce a great aspect variability) need opposingly more important corpus than vocal languages. We are studying a generic system of interaction in SL with a computing system in the context of scenario which can be changed from one application to another (Fig. 2). Apart a necessarily upward initial phase, the system exploit the scenario and the acquired information in the previous stages

Fig. 2. dialogue between the system (avatar) and the interlocutor

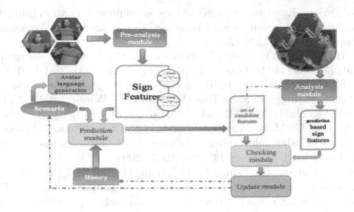

Fig. 3. modeling of sign language recognition system

to predict the content and th form of the statement in different levels. This allows it through a compilation in a real time of the predicted sign characteristic to substitue the signs description, least robust, regarding its labeling by checking the estimated characteristics which are not meant to be numerous and precise, and therefore, much more reliable. This coupling understanding recognition also exploit the specifity of SL, the narrow imbrication between the shape and meaning from the earlier stages, the given morphological data which are presented in the phonological component of the basis. Knowing that, the limit of this approach is presented in the possibility of being well predicted, but this can not be denied that it allows to achieve real applications, request system, pedagogical or playful application, where such scenario exist.

4   Conclusion

Gestural interfaces can help deaf people to have easy communication with computer. In this scope, we suggested an integrated framework for head and hand tracking in videos of SL, it is in fact employed in prediction based SLR. Concerning the detection of different components, a simple skin colour modeling is defined having results on fast and reliable segmentation. Additionally, the tracking resultson occlusion disambiguation in order to facilate feature extraction. The suggested prediction based recognition framework analyzed temporal visual signal obtained from the tracker which is changing dynamically in each level of dialogue, showing a system that allows a compilation in real time to be used by all the deaf with no exception.

References

1. Birchfield, S.: Elliptical head tracking using intensity gradients and color histograms. IEEE Computer Society Conference on Computer Vision and Pattern Recognition, 232–237 (1998)

2. Cem, K., Furkan, K., Yunus, E.K.: Real time hand pose estimation using depth sensors. In: 2011 IEEE International Conference Computer Vision Workshops (ICCV Workshops), pp. 1228–1234 (2011)

3. Cooper, H., Ong, E.J., Pugeault, N., Bowden, R.: Sign Language Recognition using Sub-Units. Journal of Machine Learning Research 13, 2205–2231 (2012)

4. Gianni, F., Collet, C., Dalle, P.: Robust tracking for processing of videos of communication's gestures. In: Sales Dias, M., Gibet, S., Wanderley, M.M., Bastos, R. (eds.) GW 2007. LNCS (LNAI), vol. 5085, pp. 93–101. Springer, Heidelberg (2009)

5. Habili, N., Lim, C., Moini, A.: Segmentation of the face and hands in sign language video sequences using color and motion cues. IEEE Transactions on Circuits and Systems for Video Technology 14, 1086–1097 (2004)

6. Imagawa, I., Matsuo, H., Taniguchi, R., Arita, D., Lu, S., Igi, S.: Recognition of local features for camera-based sign language recognition system. In: Proc. 15th International Conference on Pattern Recognition, vol. 4, pp. 849–853 (2000)

7. Isard, M., Blake, A.: Condensation-conditional density propagation for visual tracking. International journal of computer vision 29(1), 5–28 (1998)

8. Jaballah, K., Jemni, M.: Fuzzy Analysis of Classifier Handshapes from 3D Sign Language Data. In: Petrosino, A. (ed.) ICIAP 2013, Part II. LNCS, vol. 8157, pp. 621–630. Springer, Heidelberg (2013)

9. Kovac, J., Peer, P., Solina, F.: Human skin color clustering for face detection. In: EUROCON International Conference on Computer as a Tool, vol. 2, pp. 144–148 (2003)

10. Lefebvre-Albaret, F.: Traitement automatique de vidéos en LSF, modélisation et exploitation des contraintes phonologiques du mouvement. Phd thesis, University of Toulouse (2010)

11. Micilotta, A., Bowden, R.: View-based location and tracking of body parts for visual interaction. In: British Machine Vision Conference, vol. 2, pp. 849–858 (2004)

12. Tanibata, N., Shimada, N., Shirai, Y.: Extraction of hand features for recognition of sign language words. In: The 15th International Conference on Vision Interface, pp. 391–398 (2002)

13. Vassili, V.V., Sazonov, V., Andreeva, A.: A survey on pixel-based skin color detection techniques. In: Proc. Graphicon 2003, pp. 85–92 (2003)

14. Vogler, C., Metaxas, D.N.: Parallel Hiden Markov Models for American Sign Language Recognition. In: Proc. of International Conference on Computer Vision, pp. 116–122 (1999)

15. Zaman Khan, R., Adnan Ibraheem, N.: Hand Gesture Recognition: A Literature Review. International Journal of Artificial Intelligence and Applications, IJAIA (July 2012)

Investigating the Mutual Adaptation Process to Build up the Protocol of Communication

Youssef Khaoula, Takahiro Asano, Ravindra De Silva, and Michio Okada

Interactions and Communication Design Lab,
Toyohashi University of Technology, 441-8580, Japan
{youssef,asano}@icd.cs.tut.ac.jp, {ravi,okada}@tut.jp

Abstract. In our work, we are interested in exploring how people build a protocol of communication. We used the context of the SDT (Sociable Dining Table) to explore the emerging protocol. SDT integrates a dish robot put on the table and behaves according to the knocking emitted by the human. In a first experiment, we observe the protocol acquisition's process that occurs in the human-human interaction. By analyzing the latter experiment, we obtained implications that helped to understand how to facilitate the communication through knocking in the human-robot interaction and how to implement the SDT's model. In a human robot interaction (HRI), we validated our model and we showed that it allows the proliferation of a personalized protocol just like in the human-human interaction.

Keywords: human robot interaction, mutual adaptation, actor-critic algorithm.

1 Introduction

Child-caregiver interaction is most typically employed in robotics research as a source of inspiration. Many issues have been of interest to the robotics community such as how infants learn to grasp an object, to talk, to navigate unfamiliar places which may help them to create robust robots. We address the question of how a robot can build a protocol of communication when non technical users have no prior knowledge about the robot and the feedback is their only way to understand the interaction's meaning. In this vein, the child-caregiver interaction is our source of inspiration. In fact, children prefer to interchange signals and show better reactivity for human mediated behaviors [1]. An interaction that is reduced to a minimal number of cues but with an active joint attention of the child can bootstrap a basic common pattern of social relating with the caregiver. Consequently, the caregiver guess the meaning of the child's behavior by adapting to the infant's interaction. Piaget has elaborated many studies concerning child-caregiver interaction [2]. He argues that an organizational intelligence emerges incrementally through adaptive patterns. Those patterns represent the protocol of communication.

Our main goal is to explore the effectiveness of a minimalist architecture for building a protocol of communication. The robot and the human incrementally

C. Stephanidis (Ed.): HCII 2014 Posters, Part II, CCIS 435, pp. 571–576, 2014.
© Springer International Publishing Switzerland 2014

have to adapt to each other's assumptions during the interaction. We suppose that the SDT framework will give the primacy to the desires of trainers that had no programming skills to transfer their unique personalized proposed behaviors and also to adjust their assumptions about the robot's knowledge incrementally by watching the robot's behavior which may lead to a double sided adaptation.

First, we provide a brief description of the SDT's architecture, then we explain the human-human experimental setup and the results. Afterwards, we establish a computational model that guarantees to generate similar patterns of the human-human interaction's scenario. Finally, we validate our minimalist architecture with a human-robot interaction experiment.

2   Architecture of the Sociable Dining Table

The system consists of a web cam to verify the robot's position and its orientation angle. It uses four microphones to localize the knock's source using the locally weighted regression algorithm [3]. The robot can communicate with a host computer using a macro computer chip (AVR ATMEGA128) by wifi. A servomotor, battery and five reflectors are used for the motion. The photo reflector sensors are utilized to detect the boundaries of the table in order to avoid falling from the table (Fig.1).

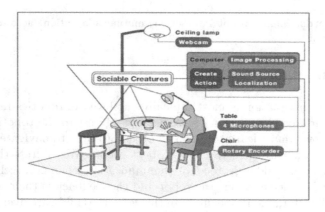

Fig. 1. The overall architecture of the SDT

3   Experiment 1: The Human-Human Experiment

3.1   Experiment Procedure

30 participants from 19 to 24 years old participated in this experiment. The participants were grouped into fifteen pairs. Each pair is formed by a controller that controls the robot and a user that emits the knocking patterns in order to lead the robot to the different checkpoints (Fig. 2). We intend to verify whether

the experiment's conditions help each pair to mutually adapt so as to build a protocol of communication and to detect through time-series the clues that lead to that. To avoid the distraction by other sensory channels, the controller is located in another room. Also, the controller ignores the goal, check points and refers only to the knocks. The user can see the different checkpoints and has to lead the robot through knocking to the final goal after passing by the other sub goals. There are 2 trials (each one lasts 20 minutes) where we have chosen several configurations to guarantee the diversity of the patterns proposed by the participants (Fig. 2).

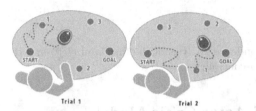

Fig. 2. In the first trial (*left*), each participant has to move the creature into 5 places (start, 1, 2, 3, goal) by knocking. In the second trial (*right*), we changed the place of the former points, and then the user has to guide the robot into the new points.

3.2 Results and Discussion

A questionnaire was conducted to see how people think they controlled the SDT. A matching between the controller and the subject answers' is applied to find the common points between the two beliefs of both parties. Four types of instructions emerged: command-like (for each behavior a different combination of knocks is attributed), switch the action (the knocker is constantly knocking in order to change the behavior very quickly), continuous-knocking (the knocker believes that continuously knocking keeps the robot moving), deny the action (the knocker stops knocking suddenly to inform the robot that it should stop immediately) (Table 1). To estimate the protocol that emerges, we apply the correspondence analysis that represents the associations between patterns of knocking and actions (Fig. 3). We notice that **Forward** is represented by (2 or 4 knocks) and **Left** corresponds (1 or 3 knocks) in the first trial. In the second trial,

Table 1. The emergent instructions in the human-human experiment

Marking instructions	Above 60 % of matching	No matching
Command Like	7 Pairs (7,5,6,9,12,13,15)	2 Pairs (10, 11)
Switch the Action	3 Pairs (1, 14,4	2 Pairs (10, 11)
Continuous Knocking	1 Pair (2)	2 Pairs (10, 11)
Deny the Action	2 Pairs (3, 8)	2 Pairs (10, 11)

Forward is represented by (2 knocks), **Left** corresponds to (1 knock) and **Right** is materialized by (3 knocks). We examined the other subjects' correspondence analysis where it was clear that each pair invent their own customized protocol with an ensemble of specific rules in the form of (pattern of knocking - meaning).

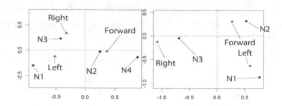

Fig. 3. The correspondence analysis of the first trial (*left*) and the second trial (*right*) of the pair 7 (human-controller)

4   The Social Actor-Critic Model

4.1   Insights from the First Experiment

Through the first experiment, we noticed that from time to time a personalized protocol is established and there are some features presented in Table 1 that people believe it controls the robot. People use in a trial-error process those features to disagree with the robot when there is a deviation from the intended direction and to agree if the robot's behavior is correct. We propose a social actor critic algorithm that helps to simulate such a behavior while interacting with the user. Initially, the robot observes the state S_t that is materialized by a knocking pattern after at least 2 seconds since the last agreement state and a new instruction meaning's decoding process starts.

4.2   Actor Learning

Each knocking pattern has its own distribution $X(S_t) \approx N(\mu_{X(S_t)}, \sigma_{X(S_t)})$ where $X(S_t)$ is defined as the number of knocks, $\mu_{X(S_t)}$ and $\sigma_{X(S_t)}$ are the mean value and the variance. Initially, the action is chosen according to the probabilistic policy $\Pi(s_t)_{nbknocks}$. The state of the interaction changes to the state S_{t+1} according to the user's knocking presence (disagreement)/ absence (agreement). After that, the actor updates the probabilistic policy $\Pi(s_t)_{nbknocks}$. If the human interrupted the robot's behavior execution before 2 seconds then we have a disagreement state about the current instruction's meaning, the action that is chosen based on the probabilistic distribution failed and the actor chooses the action henceforth (until we meet an agreement state as a closure for the current instruction meaning's decoding process) based on (1):

$$A(S_t) = \mu_{X(S_t)} + \sigma_{X(S_t)} * \sqrt{-2 * log(rnd_1)} * Sin(2\Pi * rnd_2) \qquad (1)$$

4.3 Critic Learning

The critic calculates the TD error δ_t as the reinforcement signal for the critic and the actor according to (2)

$$\delta_t = r_t + \gamma V(s_{t+1})V(s_t) \tag{2}$$

with γ is the discount rate and $0 \leq \gamma \leq 1$. According to the TD error, the critic updates the state value function $V(s_t)$ based on (3):

$$V(S_t) = V(S_t) + \alpha * \delta_t \tag{3}$$

where $0 \leq \alpha \leq 1$ is the learning rate. As long as the current instruction meaning's decoding is not achieved, the critic will each time it encounters a disagreement state updates δ_t, $V(S_t)$ and the distribution $N(\mu_{X(S_t)}, \sigma_{X(S_t)})$ according to (4) and (5).

$$\mu_{X(S_t)} = \frac{\mu_{X(S_t)} + A_{S_t}}{2} \tag{4}$$

$$\sigma_{X(S_t)} = \frac{\sigma_{X(S_t)} + |A_{S_t} - \mu_{X(S_t)}|}{2} \tag{5}$$

5 Experiment 2: The Human-Robot Experiment

5.1 Experiment Procedure

A second experiment HRI was conducted to show that our model learns on real time how to establish the protocol of communication based on the knocking patterns. In this experiment, 10 participants (20-24 years) accomplish the same task as in the first experiment with a different configuration per trial (Fig. 2).

5.2 Results and Discussion

Correspondence analysis showed that a personalized protocol is established for each participant. The discrimination between some behaviors was clear for some participants and as an example we expose the results of the participant 10. In the first trial, the **Back** was represented by 3 knocks, the **Right** by 1 knock, the **Left** by 4 knocks with some confusion for the **Forward** that is represented by 2 and 4 knocks (Fig. 4 on the left). In the second trial, the **Right** is maintained as 1 knock but with smaller euclidean distance between the knock and the behavior which supports our hypothesis of the capability of the human users to transfer their knowledge incrementally, **Forward** is represented by only 4 knocks while there is some confusion for the **Left** and the **Back** (Fig. 4 on the right). As a conclusion, to find out a common ground during an interaction when each one has his own assumptions we require a small amount of practice and then the mutual adaptation leads incrementally to the formation of the customized rules of communication.

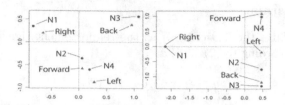

Fig. 4. The correspondence analysis of the participant 10 for the first trial (*left*) and the second trial (*right*)

6 Conclusion

We explored the conditions to meet incrementally a mutual sharing of rules. The SDT framework adapts with different humans' patterns of knocking which gives a preliminary idea about how the child and the caregiver (and then consequently the human and the robot) share a common ground even if they initially have different assumptions. In the beginning, one maintains an ensemble of assumptions about how to use the channel and how the other is thinking then he tries to transfer the meaning incrementally based on inferential rules. The rules emerge spontaneously and the interaction gets organized by the collaboration of both parts.

References

1. Trevarthen, C.: What Is It Like To Be a Person Who Knows Nothing? Inf. Child Develop. 20, 1522–7219 (2011)
2. Piaget, J.: The construction of reality in the child. Basic Books, New York (1954)
3. Vijayakumar, S., D'Souza, A., Schaal, S.: Incremental Online Learning in High Dimensions. Neural Computation 17(12), 2602–2634 (2005)

A Spoken Dialogue System
for Noisy Environment

Kazuki Kogure, Masahiro Yoshinaga, Hikaru Suzuki, and Tetsuro Kitahara

Nihon University
3-25-40, Sakurajosui, Setagaya-ku, Tokyo, Japan
{kogure,yoshinaga,hikaru,kitahara}@kthrlab.jp

Abstract. One of the important challenges for achieving a spoken dialogue system in noisy environments is to make the system's speech audible for the user. Although there have been many studies on speech recognition in noisy environments, very few attempts to improve the audibility of the system's speech. In this paper, we develop a spoken dialogue system that has three functions: real-time volume adjustment, utterance delay, and re-utterance. Experimental results have shown that these three functions improve the audibility of the system's utterances.

1 Introduction

Spoken dialogue systems are expected to play a role in reducing digital divides because speech is one of the most natural methods of human communication. In particular, this will be very helpful to blind people. In order to develop spoken dialogue systems that work in the real world, a robustness to environmental noise is required. To achieve this kind of robustness, we have to resolve two issues: one is to recognize the user's speech in noisy environments and the second is to make the system's speech audible for the user. Although many studies have attempted to tackle the first issue[1,2], only a small number have attempted to overcome the second issue.

In this paper, we develop a spoken dialogue system that has the following three functions: (1) real-time volume adjustment according to noise levels, (2) utterance delay for a particularly loud noise, and (3) re-utterance when asked by the user. Through these three functions, we reduce cases for which the user cannot follow the system's utterances due to loud noises.

2 Proposed System

We developed a spoken-dialogue-based railway route search system. This system is intended for installation on the platform of a rail station. To allow blind people to use this system, the system uses only auditory modality (speech inputs and outputs), and never uses a graphical display or a touchscreen. The system overview is shown in Figure 1 . Once detecting a user's face in the camera, the system asks the user to what station he/she is travelling. Given the response

C. Stephanidis (Ed.): HCII 2014 Posters, Part II, CCIS 435, pp. 577–582, 2014.

of the user, the system searches for the shortest route from the current station to the destination station using a railway route search API, called Expert Web API. The system then utters the search result. An example of the dialogues is shown below:

> **System:** Hi, this is a railway route guidance system. What station are you going to?
> **User:** Shinjuku Station.
> **System:** Shinjuku Station?
> **User:** Yes.
> **System:** First travel to Sasazuka Station via the Keio New Line.
> **System:** Then change to the Keio Line.
> **System:** It will take 15 minutes. The fare will be 150 yen.
> **System:** This guidance is now over. Thank you.

In this example, the departure is assumed to be the Sakurajosui Station. We use Julius [3] for speech recognition and OpenJTalk [4] for speech synthesis. To improve the system's robustness to environmetal noise, as described in the Introduction, we introduced the following three functions:

1. **Real-time volume adjustment:** to measure the noise level via a microphone array and control the volume of the system's voice according to the noise level;
2. **Utterance delay:** to delay the system's utterance when a particularly loud noise occurs;
3. **Re-utterance:** to utter again when the user utters a word requesting a re-utterance such as "eh?"

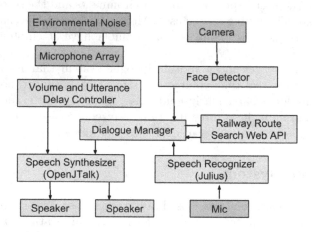

Fig. 1. System Overview

2.1   Real-Time Volume Adjustment

The environmental noise is observed by a 7-channel microphone array. For every second, the root mean square (RMS) of the audio signal of the environmental noise is calculated after the 7-channel signal is converted to monaural. The noise level is then estimated based on the RMS. If the sound pressure level of the system's utterances are lower than that of the noise, the system increases the volume setting of the system's utterances. If the sound pressure level of the system's utterances are higher than that of the noise, the system decreases the volume setting of the system's utterances.

2.2   Utterance Delay

If the noise level is higher than 64dB, the system delays the utterance as opposed to changing the volume because the noise is too loud. Specifically, the system stops the utterance and then restarts the utterance after the noise ends.

2.3   Re-utterance

When the user utters a word asking for a re-utterance, such as "eh?" and "*kikoe-nai*"(I can't hear it), the system utters the same sentence again. When the user utters "*kikoenai*", the system increases the volume setting as well as re-utters the reply.

3   Experiment 1

3.1   Experimental Method

The first experiment aimed to confirm improvements for the audibility of the system's utterances by two functions, volume adjustment and utterance delay. We installed a 6-channel speaker array around our system and virtually reproduced the noisy environment using a recording of noise from a Tokyo railway station platform. We asked 14 participants with normal hearing ability (Age: 21–24; 7 males and 7 females) to listen to the system's utterances under the noisy environment and rate the audibility, and choose from four options of what they believed the system uttered. As the aim of the experiment was to confirm the audibility of the system's utterances, face detection with a camera, users uttering a destination station, and producing an actual route were skipped. The system simply uttered pre-designed sentences. Examples of the sentences uttered include the following:

Type I
"*Aoto kara Aoi made no ryokin wa ni hyaku san ju en desu.*"
　　(The fare from Aoto Station to Aoi Station is 230 yen.)
"*Aoi kara Aoto made no ryokin wa ni hyaku san ju en desu.*"
　　(The fare from Aoi Station to Aoto Station is 230 yen.)

"*Aoto kara Aoi made no ryokin wa go hyaku san ju en desu.*"
  (The fare from Aoto Station to Aoi Station is 530 yen.)
"*Aoi kara Aoto made no ryokin wa go hyaku san ju en desu.*"
  (The fare from Aoi Station to Aono Station is 530 yen.)

Type II
"*Kameari kara Seibu Tamagawa-sen ni nori, Kameido e mukaimasu.*"
  (Get on the Seibu Tamagawa Line at Kameari Station, then get off at the
  Kameido Station.)
"*Kameido kara Seibu Tamagawa-sen ni nori, Kameari e mukaimasu.*"
  (Get on the Seibu Tamagawa Line at Kameido Station, then get off at the
  Kameari Station.)
"*Kameari kara Seibu Tamako-sen ni nori, Kameido e mukaimasu.*"
  (Get on the Seibu Tamako Line at Kameari Station, then get off at the
  Kameido Station.)

As above, phonologically similar confusing stations/lines were included. To avoid
issues resulting from the participants already knowing the station and/or lines,
untrue fares/routes were uttered. The subjective rating of audibility was based
on the following criteria:

1. Impossible to hear
2. Possible to hear but impossible to recognize the content
3. Possible to hear but difficult to recognize the content
4. Partly difficult to hear
5. Appropriate volume
6. Too loud
7. Much too loud

The experiment was conducted both with normal utterances (without volume
adjustments or utterance delays; our *baseline*) and with utterances of volume
adjustments and utterance delays (our *proposed*). For each condition, the experiment was repeated 21 times.

3.2   Experimental Results

The experimental results are shown in Figures 2 and 3. Figure 2 shows the
ratings of audibility for utterances using both methods. The system rarely failed
in picking up the utterances. Such cases have been removed from the results.
For the proposed method, the ratings of 1 and 2 were decreased by 6% and the
rating of 5 was increased by 14% when compared to the baseline method. Figure
3 shows the accuracy of the multiple-choice tests for listening to the system's
utterances. The accuracy for the proposed method was 8% higher than that of
the baseline method.

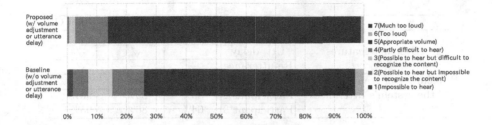

Fig. 2. Results of Experiment 1 (Audibility Ratings)

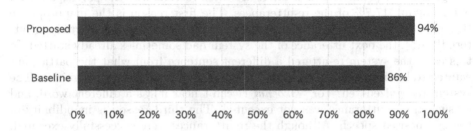

Fig. 3. Results of Experiment 2 (Accuracy of Listening)

4   Experiment 2

4.1   Experimental Method

The second experiment aimed to confirm the effectiveness of our system in actual dialogues. In the same environment as Experiment 1, we asked participants to search and write down a route (the name(s) of line(s) and transfer station(s), total fare) to a station. This was repeated 10 times for each of the following three systems:

System A: without any of the three functions
System B: with volume adjustment and utterance delay, without re-utterance
System C: with all three functions.

The experiment for the three systems was continuously conducted and the systems were chosen at random for each trial. The participants were not told which system was running. The participants were three people with normal hearing ability (Age: 21–24; two males and one female).

4.2   Experimental Results

The experimental results are shown in Table 1. From this table, it can be seen that the accuracy of the transcriptions of the system's utterances by the

Table 1. Results of Experiment 2

		System A	System B	System C
System's features	Vol. adj.	—	√	√
	Utt. delay	—	√	√
	Re-utterance	—	—	√
Accuracy of transcription of the system's utterances	Participant 1	65%	86%	96%
	Participant 2	80%	89%	96%
	Participant 3	64%	86%	95%

participant improved by the three functions. The three participants asked for re-utterance 17 times in total. Of the 17 re-utterances, 82.3% were successfully recognized by the participants. There are three reasons why the participants did not recognize 17.7% of the re-utterances. The first reason is the inappropriate timings of the participant uttering "eh?". At the exact time the participant uttered "eh?", the next utterance of the system had sometimes already started. In this case, the system re-uttered a different sentence from what the participant wanted to listen to again. The second reason is failure of speech recognition. The system recognized "eh?" or *"kikoenai"*(I can't hear it) as a different word, and as such the re-utterance was not executed. The third reason is inaudibility of the synthesized speech. Although the re-utterances were successfully executed, the synthesized speech was not of sufficient quality, so the participant did not understand it.

5   Conclusion

We illustrated the importance of making the system's utterances audible when developing a spoken dialogue system for a noisy environment, and thereafter proposed a system that has three functions: real-time volume adjustment, utterance delay, and re-utterance. Future work will include further experiments in various types of environments and when faced with different kinds of noise.

Acknowledgments. This research was supported by SCAT, Japan. We appreciate the VAL Laboratory Corporation for giving us permission to use Expert Web API.

References

1. Hinamoto, Y., Mino, K., Saruwatari, H., Shikano, K.: Interface for Barge-in Free Spoken Dialogue System Based on Sound Field Control and Microphone Array. IEEE Troc. ICASSP 2, 505–508 (2003)
2. Ishi, T., Matsuda, S., Kanda, T., Jitsuhiro, T., Ishiguro, H., Nakamura, S., Hagita, N.: A Robust Speech Recognition System for Communication Robots in Noisy Environments. IEEE Transactions on Robotics 3, 759–763 (2008)
3. Lee, A., Kawahara, T.: Recent Development of Open-Source Speech Recognition Engine Julius. In: APSIPA ASC 2009, pp. 131–137 (2009)
4. http://open-jtalk.sourceforge.net/

The Role of Physical Embodiment of Humanoid Robot Interaction: Focusing on Backchannel Head Nods in Danish First Meeting Encounters

Nicolaj Segato[1], Anders Krogsager[1], Daniel Grønkjær Jensen[1],
and Matthias Rehm[2]

[1] School of Information and Communication Technology,
Aalborg University, 9000 Aalborg, Denmark
{npeder09,akrogs09,dgje08}@student.aau.dk
[2] Faculty of Engineering and Science, Aalborg University, 9000 Aalborg, Denmark
matthias@create.aau.dk

Abstract. An important role for the communication management in human communication is head nods, e.g. as nonverbal feedback signal. Based on a Japanese study with virtual agents, have showed that the using head nods in virtual agents elicited more verbal output from the user, we look into the use of head nods in communications between user and a humanoid robot, Keepon robot and a virtual agent resembling a cat that the user encounters for the first time.

Keywords: Culture-aware robots, backchannels, feedback, physical embodiment.

1 Introduction

Robots have begun the migration from the factory floor and the restricted environments that have been designed for them, into the community and semi-public spaces where it is predicted they are to interact socially with users. Head nods have shown to be an integrate part of human communication and communication management, e.g. as a non-verbal feedback signal from the listening counterpart. Humans are skilled in casting judgment on the communication partner based in initial meetings and first time impressions. From cross-cultural studies it is known that using the wrong social signals in first encounters can easily lead to misunderstandings and breakdown in communication between humans. Backchannels feedback specifically head nods is one aspect of the many social signals humans use. Allwood and Cerrato [1] have shown that in dyadic conversations it is head movements that is the most common feedback signal, with nodding either single or rapeated head nods being the most frequent signal. In a follow-up analysis Boholm and Allwood [2] showed that a majority of repeated head movements (i.e. 74%) are accompanied by speech which contains expressed feedback information. A Japanese study with virtual agent [3] showed that using head nods aided in eliciting more verbal information from the users are stimulated with culture-specific head nod patterns, in their case Japanese culture in

C. Stephanidis (Ed.): HCII 2014 Posters, Part II, CCIS 435, pp. 583–587, 2014.

contrast to American head nod patterns. Based on these results we present a replication of this [3] study which changes two parameters:

(i) Cultural background of the users: Aiming at Danish users, we focus on Danish nodding patterns that is based on the analysis of a multimodal corpus of first meeting encounters (NOMCO) [5].
(ii) Embodiment of the agent: Instead of just using a virtual character, the experiment is replicated with a humanoid robot (Nao) and Keepon robot and assuming that the physical embodiment will have an effect on the results.

2   Approach

Users of robots need to be comfortable when interacting with the them. Additionally robots should be user-friendly systems in order to maintain a good relationship between the human counterpart and the robot. To ensure the good relationship between user and robot the idea of using backchannels can help users maintain a prolonged interaction with robots. Numerous studies on virtual agents have revealed that the paradigm of a listener agent has the potential to engage the user in prolonged interactions [4], [6], [7]. One important aspect is the production and recognition of suitable social signals to realize active interactions, which can be seen as a requirement for successfully founding rapport with the user and it can also be assumed that this is true for interactions with physically embodied agents, i.e. robots. Dittmann and Lewellyn [10] attribute backchannel head nods with two functions, as either feedback for the speaker or as a signal for the speaker that the listener aims to get the floor. Some parameters of the frequency of the head nods in dyadic conversations see to vary across cultures. Maynard [9] presents an in-depth analysis of Japanese dyadic interactions that centers on the frequency and distribution of head nods where listener is responsible for 44% of head nods where as the speaker is making 56% of the nods. His presented analysis revels that Americans make one head movement every 22.5 seconds on average (frequency of 2.7 movements/minute) in contrast to Japanese with a movement 5.75 seconds on average (frequency of 10.4 nods/minute). Research centred on head nods in robots mainly concern with recognizing and interpreting head nods created by users (e.g. [8]), yet not for employing head nods as means for the robot to arrange and maintain the dialogue with the user. Koda and her colleagues [3] conducted a experiment for analyzing cross-culture head nods for a virtual agent system. Their experiment showed that users spoke longer to an agent system that takes cultural differences in the effecting of head nods into account. Limitations of their experiment include the fact that they did not test on others than Japanese participants. Thus their reported results could be attributable to more nodding elicits more talking form the user. The same basic experimental setup will be used to test is Danish participants also would prefer to talk longer if a humanoid robot, Keepon robot or virtual cat exhibits the culturally adequate feedback signals in terms of head nods. In this paper we propose a wizard of Oz experiment that can investigate culturally specific head nods that affects the time a participant speaks to a robot.

3   Method

In order to investigate how head nods prolong user interaction with agents, the following wizard of Oz experiment was conducted. The experiments independent variable is the backchannel feedback of the Nao, Keepon and virtual cat. The dependent variable is the duration of time the participants speak to the robot. Before the experiment the participants were informed that they were going to talk to an intelligent robot that would listen to them, but otherwise remain passive. Participants are asked to talk to the robot about the chosen topic as long as they can. Participants were asked to talk to the listing robot about an open-ended, preselected topic from a list of 15 topics. Participants were randomly assigned to either a control group or one of two groups with backchannel feedback. The following types of backchannels were used; No Nod (NN), US nod (US) and Danish nod (DK). The participants go through each of the robot conditions, but only through one type of head nod. Each participant was left alone with the robot, while being observed by a test facilitator through a two way mirror and who heuristically triggered the head nods as the participant spoke. The session time the participant talked to the robot were recorded using a video camera, figure 1 displays the duration of time participants spoke to the robot in the three conditions.

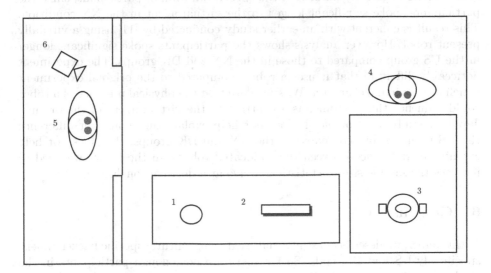

Fig. 1. Top-down sketch of the experiment setup: 1. Keepon, 2. cat agent on a screen, 3. Nao Robot, 4. Participant, 5. Test facilitator with laptopa and other equipment, 6. Recording camera.

4   Results

Analysis of speech duration for three groups of participants and three categories of agent embodiment show one combination of significant difference. When comparing the types of head nodding feedback, participant speaking with the cat agent had significantly longer duration of speech in the US condition (N = 4, mean = 132.5 s.) compared to NN (N = 5, mean = 56.6 s.) and DK (N = 6, mean = 68.6 s.).

A one-way independent ANOVA is calculated which showed significant difference between the three nodding groups $F(2, 12) = 4.013$, $p<0.05$. To determine which groups differ significantly Fisher's LSD post-hoc test is also calculated. It shows at $p<0.05$ significance that participants in the US group spoke longer than those in NN and DK groups to the cat.

5   Discussion and Limitations

The small sample size makes it hard to arrive at a decisive conclusion when analyze the results of the speech duration. Even so the result of this study seems to contradict the assumptions made from human communication and previous studies with virtual agents [3]. The head movement of the cat agent appear to some extend negatively influenced the speech duration of participant, since the participants spoke significant longer to the virtual agent in the NN condition. This result is coherent with an earlier study conducted by [11] using a virtually present robot. However analysis shows the participants spoke significant longer in the US group compared to those in the NN and DK groups. The experiment noticeably differs in that it uses a robot, compared to the original experiment which uses a virtual character. We speculate that the physical presence of a robot could influence this outcome, as a contrast to the virtual agent of the original Japanese study [3]. However it does not help explain the significant difference the US groupe spoke compared to the NN and DK groups. this does not help explain the difference between the co-located robots. In the future we need to increase the sample size to statistical arrive at a decisive conclusion.

6   Conclusion

In this paper, we described a study that used using cultural specific backchannels, specifically US and DK nods. So far there are not enough participants in the study to arrive at any significant conclusion. However, this work in progress paper reports the preliminary outcomes of the study. The study allows for further investigations to conduct future experiments that look into if a robot exhibits no visual feed back to a human speaker in fact elicits less speech duration from the participants. As it is not trivial to replicate human communication in interaction with robots. Nor is it a matter of simply reproducing communication signals in a robot to make users interact with it as if it were human.

Acknowledgements. The present work benefitted from the work of Constanza Navaretta and Patrizia Paggio researchers at "Center for Sprogteknologi" at Copenhagen University who provided the NOMCO data.

References

1. Allwood, J., Cerrato, L.: A study of gestural feedback expressions. In: Paggio, P., Jokinen, K., Jönsso, A. (eds.) First Nordic Symposium on Multimodal Communication, Copenhagen, pp. 7–22 (2003)
2. Boholm, M., Allwood, J.: Repeated head movements, their function and relation to speech. In: Kipp, M., Martin, J., Paggio, P., Heylen, D. (eds.) Proceedings of the Workshop on Multimodal Corpora: Advances in Capturing, Coding and Analyzing Multimodality, pp. 6–10. LREC (2010)
3. Koda, T., Kishi, H., Hamamoto, T., Suzuki, Y.: Cultural Study on Speech Duration and Perception of Virtual Agent's Nodding. In: Nakano, Y., Neff, M., Paiva, A., Walker, M. (eds.) IVA 2012. LNCS, vol. 7502, pp. 404–411. Springer, Heidelberg (2012)
4. Schröder, M., Bevacqua, E., Cowie, R., Eyben, F., Gunes, H., Heylen, D., ter Maat, M., McKeown, G., Pammi, S., Pantic, M., Pelachaud, C., Schuller, B., de Sevin, E., Valstar, M.: Building Autonomous Sensitive Artificial Listeners. IEEE Transactions on Affecite Computing 3, 165–183 (2012)
5. Paggio, P., Navaretta, C.: Feedback and gestural behaviour in a conversational corpus of Danish. In: Proceedings of the 3rd Nordic Symposium on Multimodal Communication, pp. 33–39. NEALT (2011)
6. Yoichi, S., Yuuko, N., Kiyoshi, Y., Yukiko, N.: Listener Agent for Elderly People with Dementia. In: Proceedings of the Seventh Annual ACM/IEEE International Conference on Human-Robot Interaction, pp. 199–200. ACM, New York (2012)
7. Meguro, T., Higashinaka, R., Dohsaka, K., Minami, Y., Isozaki, H.: Analysis of listening-oriented dialogue for building listening agents. In: Proceedings of the SIG-DIAL 2009 Conference, pp. 124–127. Association for Computational Linguistics, Stroudsburg (2009)
8. Riek, L.D., Paul, P.C., Robinson, P.: When my robot smiles at me Enabling human-robot rapport via real-time head gesture mimicry. Journal of Multimodal User Interfaces 3, 99–108 (2010)
9. Maynard, S.: Interactional functions of a nonverbal sign Head movement in japanese dyadic casual conversation. Journal of Pragmatics 11, 589–606 (1987)
10. Dittmann, A., Llewellyn, L.: Relationship between vocalizations and head nods as listener responses. Journal of Personality and Social Psychology 9, 79–84 (1968)
11. Krogsager, A., Segato, N., Rehm, M.: Backchannel Head Nods. In: Danish First Meeting Encounters with a Humanoid Robot: The Role of Physical Embodiment. Springer, Heidelberg (in press, 2014)

Controlling Switching Pause Using an AR Agent for Interactive CALL System

Naoto Suzuki[1], Takashi Nose[1], Yutaka Hiroi[2], and Akinori Ito[1]

[1] Graduate School of Engineering, Tohoku University, Sendai, Japan
{naoto_s@spcom.ecei,tnose@m,aito@spcom.ecei}tohoku.ac.jp
[2] Department of Robotics, Osaka Institute of Technology, Osaka, Japan
hiroi@med.oit.ac.jp

Abstract. We are developing a voice-interactive CALL (Computer-Assisted Language Learning) system to provide more opportunity for better English conversation exercise. There are several types of CALL system, we focus on a spoken dialogue system for dialogue practice. When the user makes an answer to the system's utterance, timing of making the answer utterance could be unnatural because the system usually does not make any reaction when the user keeps silence, and therefore the learner tends to take more time to make an answer to the system than that to the human counterpart. However, there is no framework to suppress the pause and practice an appropriate pause duration.

In this research, we did an experiment to investigate the effect of presence of the AR character to analyze the effect of character as a counterpart itself. In addition, we analyzed the pause between the two person's utterances (switching pause). The switching pause is related to the smoothness of its conversation. Moreover, we introduced a virtual character realized by AR (Augmented Reality) as a counterpart of the dialogue to control the switching pause. Here, we installed the character the behavior of "time pressure" to prevent the learner taking long time to consider the utterance.

To verify if the expression is effective for controlling switching pause, we designed an experiment. The experiment was conducted with or without the expression. Consequently, we found that the switching pause duration became significantly shorter when the agent made the time-pressure expression.

Keywords: Computer-assisted language learning, English learning, Spoken dialogue system, Switching pause, Augmented reality.

1 Introduction

With internationalization, learners of English conversation in the non-English-speaking world are increasing. Recently, language learning systems using a computer (Computer-Assisted Language Learning, CALL) have been used by many people [1].

There are several types of CALL systems, such as listening, grammar learning and dialogue practice [2]. In this paper, we focus on a spoken dialogue system for dialogue practice. Using the speech recognition technology, this kind of systems enable the

C. Stephanidis (Ed.): HCII 2014 Posters, Part II, CCIS 435, pp. 588–593, 2014.
© Springer International Publishing Switzerland 2014

learners to learn pronunciation and grammar by themselves [3,4]. Moreover, the learners can make conversation practices through making dialogues with the system. However, when the learner makes an answer to the system's utterance, timing of the answer utterance could be unnatural.

The pause between the two person's utterances (switching pause) is related to the type of the dialogue [5], and acoustic or linguistic cues [6]. Exercise of making utterances within a proper switching pause duration seems to be important to train a skill to make natural English conversation.

Speaking in the target foreign language (L2) requires more cognitive load than speaking in the speaker's mother tongue (L1) [7]. Therefore, a learner need to make more effort to react the utterance from the dialogue counterpart quickly. When talking with a computer, the system usually does not make any reaction when the user keeps silence, and therefore the learner tends to take more time (longer switching pause) to make an answer to the system than that to the human counterpart. To make the human-system dialogue more similar to the human-human one, shortening the switching pause seems to be useful for the English conversation learning.

The purpose of this study is to create an interactive CALL system that enables a learner to make a dialogue where the learner's utterances are controlled to have an appropriate pause duration.

To this end, two features were introduced to the system. First, an Augmented Reality (AR) character was introduced as a dialogue counterpart. It is known that a virtual agent makes the conversation more similar to a human-human dialogue [8]. Secondly, we made the AR character to express a "time pressure" to prevent the learner taking long time to consider the utterance.

In this paper, we report development of a spoken dialogue system with AR character, and discuss the results of the examination about investigating effects of the controlling by the expression of time pressure.

2   Related Works

For the temporal control method of user's speech, a method using entrainment in a conversation was proposed. Entrainment is a phenomenon that two (or more) persons who are making a conversation get adapted to each other at several levels such as lexical choices [9], prosodic feature [10], and even the physiological status [11]. Suzuki et al. [12] investigated how to change user's utterance and impression of the system using an eyeball CG character. They also changed speed of the system's utterance. In that study, they reported that the faster the system spoke, the slower users did. Observation from those works could be used to control properties of the learner's utterances, such as speaking speed and vocabulary.

However, we did not choose a method using entrainment, but chose the method using explicit expression of time pressure, where the AR character behaves to require the learner's quick response. Out target dialogues are supposed to have only a few utterances of the learner; therefore, it is difficult to exploit the effect of entrainment, which appears after several turns.

3   Experimental System

The spoken dialogue system is a kind of the Question-and-Answer-based systems [13], and learners are required for remembering the scenarios in advance [3]. Table. 1 shows the example scenarios. We used Julius [14] as a speech recognizer. The acoustic model was trained from the ERJ corpus [15], and the N-gram language model was trained from all sentences in the scenarios. Festival [16] was used as a speech synthesizer.

A dialogue management is simple. At first, the system waits for the learner's utterance. Then the system recognizes the learner's utterance and utter a reply sentence. To manage recognition errors and the learner's mistakes in the utterance, the system checks correspondence of recognized words and the words in the scenario without considering the word order. If ratio of the coincided words is high enough, the learner's utterance is accepted.

Table 1. An example of the dialogue scenario (Buying a hat)

System	User
Hello. May I help you?	Yes, I'm looking for a hat. Do you have one?
Yes, we do. What kind do you want?	A green one.
Like this?	Yes, like that one. Can I see it?
Yes. Here you are. Would you like to buy it?	I'm sorry. This isn't exactly what I wanted.
How about another product?	No, thank you.

Fig. 1. The AR character with the expression of time pressure

Fig. 1 shows the AR character used in the experiment with the expression of time pressure. The expression of time pressure is to turn the body red from the bottom of the character to the top every 1 second. When the learner makes an utterance, the expression stops. At the same time, the character changes its face from frown to smile. In a condition without time pressure, the character is always smiling. In both cases, the character continues nodding to provide the learners with human-like impression [17].

4   Experiment

4.1   Experimental Conditions and Procedure

We conducted an experiment to investigate the effect of the time pressure expression. The experiment was conducted inside a soundproof chamber, and the learner's behavior was recorded by a video camera. Procedure of the experiment is as follows:

1. The participants were asked to remember two scenarios in 20 minutes as the preliminary training.
2. The participants were asked to take an examination to confirm whether the subject remembered the scenarios correctly.
3. The participants were asked to talk with the dialogue system following the scenarios.
4. The participants filled a questionnaire after the dialogue.

A subject wore a head-mounted display (HMD, SONY HMZ-T2). A Web camera was attached on the HMD. The AR character was superimposed on the image from the Web camera and displayed on the HMD. The subject looked at the AR character and talked with that character. We instructed the participants that when the character expressed the time pressure, the participant should respond to the system before the character's head turned into red. In Step 2, we confirmed that all the participants remembered the scenarios correctly.

4.2   Effectiveness of the AR Character

In this experiment, we compared the impression of the learner to the dialogue with and without the AR agent to confirm the effectiveness of the agent. We employed four undergraduate students as the participants. After finishing all dialogues, the participants answered the enquiry for choosing one of the two conditions (with or without the AR character) from six points of view: (1) Which condition did you feel easy for making dialogue? (2) Which condition did you make a dialogue more smoothly? (3) Which condition did you enjoy talking? (4) Which condition did you able to have more motivation to learn? (5) Which condition did you have more feeling of making real practice? (6) Which condition did you feel being stressed?

The results are shown in Fig. 2. As we can see, the condition with the AR character was preferred by most of the participants, which suggests the usefulness of the AR character in the context of the dialogue for English learning.

4.3   Effect of the Time-Pressure Expression

We employed ten participants (5 graduate students and 5 undergraduate students) who have studied English for around 10 years without English conversation learning.

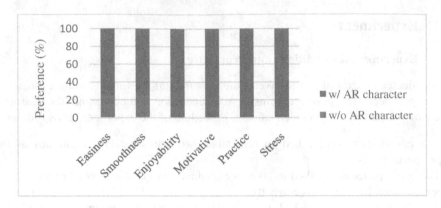

Fig. 2. Result of the preference enquiry

After the experiment, we measured the switching pauses of all the sessions from the recorded video data. Fig. 3 shows the average and standard deviation of the measured switching pauses in the two conditions. The standard deviation is indicated by the error bar. We conducted t-test and found a significant difference between the two conditions at the 1% level. As can be seen from Fig. 3, the switching pause became about 500 ms shorter by introducing the time pressure expression. This result suggested that we can control the timing of the learner's utterance by the AR character's behavior.

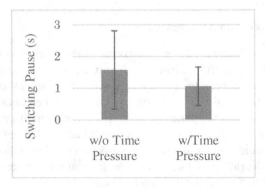

Fig. 3. Difference of the switching pause between with and without the time pressure

5   Conclusions

In this paper, we proposed a CALL system based on the spoken dialogue system and augmented reality. To control the timing of the learner's utterance when learning English conversation with AR character, we focused on the switching pause. We introduced an expression of the time pressure as a means of controlling the switching pause, and designed the experiment to investigate the effect of the expression. Consequently, we found significant difference of the switching pause duration between with and without the expression.

Acknowledgment. The present study was supported in part by a JSPS Grant-in-Aid for Challenging Exploratory Research 24652111.

References

1. Chujo, K., Nishigaki, C., Uchibori, A., Yamazaki, A.: Developing a beginning-level CALL system and its effect on college students' communicative proficiency. J. of the College of Industrial Technology, Nihon University 38, 1–16 (2005)
2. Eskenazi, M.: An overview of spoken language technology for education. Speech Communication 51(10), 832–844 (2009)
3. Kweon, O.-P., Ito, A., Suzuki, M., Makino, S.: A grammatical error detection method for dialog-based CALL system. J. of Natural Language Processing 12(4), 137–156 (2005)
4. Anzai, T., Ito, A.: Recognition of utterances with grammatical mistakes based on optimization of language model towards interactive CALL systems. In: Proc. APSIPA ASC (2012)
5. Trimboli, C., Walker, M.B.: Switching pauses in cooperative and competitive conversations. J. of Experimental Social Psychology 20(4), 297–311 (1984)
6. Miura, I.: Switching pauses in adult-adult and child-child turn takings: An initial study. J. of Psycholinguistic Research 22(3), 383–395 (1993)
7. Nation, P.: The role of the first language in foreign language learning. The Asian EFL J. 5(4) (2003)
8. Miyake, S., Ito, A.: A spoken dialogue system using virtual conversational agent with augmented reality. In: Proc. APSIPA ASC (2012)
9. Brennan, S.E.: Lexical Entrainment in Spoken Dialog. In: Proc. Int. Symp. on Spoken Dialog, pp. 41–44 (1996)
10. Levitan, R., Hirschberg, J.: Measuring Acoustic-Prosodic Entrainment with respect to Multiple Levels and Dimensions. In: Proc. Interspeech (2011)
11. Watanabe, T., Okubo, M.: Physiological analysis of entrainment in communication. J. of Information Processing 39(5), 1225–1231 (1998)
12. Suzuki, N., Kakei, K., Takeuchi, Y., Okada, M.: Effects of the speed of hummed sounds on human-computer interaction. J. of Human Interface Society 5(1), 113–122 (2003)
13. Nisimura, R., Lee, A., Saruwatari, H., Shikano, K.: Public speech-oriented guidance system with adult and child discrimination capability. In: Proc. Int. Conf. on Acoustics, Speech and Signal Processing, vol. I, pp. 433–436 (2004)
14. Lee, A., Kawahara, T., Shikano, K.: Julius — an open source real-time large vocabulary recognition engine. In: Proc. European Conf. on Speech Communication and Technology (EUROSPEECH), pp. 1691–1694 (2001)
15. Minematsu, N., Tomiyama, Y., Yoshimoto, K., Shimizu, K., Nakagawa, S., Dantsuji, M., Makino, S.: Development of English speech database read by Japanese to support CALL research. In: Proc. Int. Conf. Acoustics, pp. 557–560 (2004)
16. The Festival Speech Synthesis System, http://www.cstr.ed.ac.uk/projects/festival/
17. Hiroi, Y., Ito, A.: Evaluation of head size of an interactive robot using an augmented reality. In: Proc. World Automation Congress (2010)

Dereverberation for Speaker Identification in Meeting

Yi Yang and Jia Liu

Tsinghua University
Tsinghua National Laboratory for Information Science and Technology
Department of Electronic Engineering, Tsinghua University, Beijing, P.R. China
{yangyy,liuj}@mail.tsinghua.edu.cn

Abstract. Current state-of-the-art speaker identification is a well-established research problem but reverberation is still a major issue used in real meeting scenarios. Dereverberation is essential for many applications such as speaker identification and speech recognition to improve the quality and intelligibility of speech signal interrupted by real reverberation environments. The classical approaches were focused on estimating desired speech signal with de-reverberation by beamforming which is crucial for hands-free distant-speech interaction. Its performance degradation is caused when beamforming equipment is unable to comply with the restriction of being symmetric in time or synchronous in structure under real condition. In this paper, a new de-reverberated merging feature is presented for text-independent speaker identification issue applied as an important component of Multiple Distance Microphones (MDM) system used in real meeting scenario. This scenario poses new challenges: far-field, limited and short training and test data, and almost severe reverberation. To tackle this, we introduce a dimensionality reduction approach to extract informative low-dimension features from four kinds of MDM-based features. Experimental results on the MDM system processed reverberated signal show the effectiveness of the new approach and the presented performance evaluation demonstrates the robustness and effectiveness of the proposed approach with short test utterances.

Keywords: Speaker identification, multiple distance microphones, short utterances, severe reverberation, dimensionality reduction.

1   Introduction

Speaker identification (SID) [1] is a popular-studied research problem which deals with which one of the known voices best matches the input voice sample. It is also an important component of speaker diarization, which tries to know the speaker identity in the audio recordings. However, the existence of the reverberation severely degrades the performance of speaker identification in the meeting. The effectiveness of room reverberation is the major difficulty to overcome and lead to the performance degradation of speaker identification system in real meetings. Therefore, the suppression of reverberation, as known as deverberation in meeting environments, is an indispensable step to improve the performance of speaker identification and the following

C. Stephanidis (Ed.): HCII 2014 Posters, Part II, CCIS 435, pp. 594–599, 2014.

speaker diarization [2, 3]. In the last four decades, beamforming by Microphone Aar-
ray (MA), which consists of multiple microphones that are arranged in a specific pattern, has been proven effective in improving the performance of most speech-oriented
systems in reverberant environments. As an alternative to MA, Multiple Distant Microphones (MDM) [4, 5] is a speech signal capturing system composed of many
microphones whose elements have non-symmetric spatial intervals.

Therefore, we propose to combine the strength of acoustic observations and spatial
characteristics in both the feature-level and combination-level. The rest of this paper
is organized as follows. In Section 2, a new de-reverberation merged feature is
proposed followed by Section 3 that describes how to combine MFCC, TDOA and
proposed features by LDA. In Section 4 describe one real meeting MDM corpus and
show its applicability by conducting the speaker identification experiments. The experimental results are shown with the comparison to the traditional single and microphone array speaker identification system in Section 5 and this paper is concluded in
Section 6.

2   Acoustic Features

2.1   MFCC Features and MDM-Based Features

The feature set used in speaker identification typically is Mel-frequency cepstral coefficients (MFCC) which is a representation defined as the real cepstrum of a windowed
short-time signal derived from the FFT of that signal [6]. In speaker identification
with MDM redundant information is available (one signal per microphone) in comparison with single distant microphone. It has been demonstrated that the time delay
of arrival (TDOA) features between channels could be mixed with spectral features to
obtain improved performance over a base system that used only spectral features. The
shortcomings of TDOA methods are the result of distant microphones. There are
noises and reverberations in the recordings and the results are not free from errors.

2.2   MDM-Based De-reverberation Features

Reverberation denotes the multipath propagation of sound from an acoustic source to
the sensor [7]. The acoustic channel between a source and a microphone can be described by an Acoustic Impulse Response (AIR) shown in Eq.1. This is the signal that
is measured at the microphone in response to a source that produces a sound impulse.
The AIR can be divided into three segments [8], the direct path, early reflections, and
late reflections, as illustrated in Fig.2.

$$y(l) = \sum_{p=0}^{\infty} h_l(p)s(l-p) \tag{1}$$

where $s(l)$ is the source signal, $h_l(p)$ the acoustic impulse response (AIR), l is the
time variance and $p \in N_0$ is the lag index.

In [9], an inverse reverberation filter designed that does not make any a priori assumptions about the nature of the actual room reverberation filter. An All-pole IIR filter p is designed that operates on the reverberated signal x using a log-likelihood criterion with respect to the pdf of s to design the inverse filter parameters. Assuming that the all-pole IIR filter de-reverberating p is M taps long. The inverse filter $P[z] = \frac{1}{1+pz^{-1}}$ and the dereverberated signal y are of the form:

$$y(n) = x[n] - \sum_{m=1}^{M-1} p[m]y[n-m] \tag{2}$$

Where n indicates the feature frame index. The log-likelihood L for the compensated features y is:

$$L = \frac{1}{N_y}\sum_{j=1}^{N_y}\left(\log\left(\sum_i \frac{\omega_i}{\sqrt{2\pi\sigma^2}}\exp\left(-\frac{(y[j]-\mu_i)^2}{2\sigma_i^2}\right)\right)\right) \tag{3}$$

Using the above definitions we maximize Eq.3 by gradient ascent via its partial derivative with respect to the parameters in p.

$$\frac{\partial L}{\partial p[m]} = \frac{1}{N_y}\sum_{j=1}^{N_y}\sum_{i=1}^{N_\omega}\left(\frac{y_i^j}{y^j}\frac{(y[j]-\mu_i)y[j-m]}{\sigma_i^2}\right) \tag{4}$$

The parameters are iteratively obtained for p[m]:

$$p[m] = p[m] + \vartheta\frac{\partial L}{\partial p[m]} \tag{5}$$

Where υ is a small-valued learning-rate parameter.

3   Combinatorial Features by Dimensionality Reduction

Dimensions of aforementioned three kinds of features are essentially high due to their derivation procedures. To prevent the curse of dimensionality in the subsequent speaker pattern analysis or even classification system, it might be substantial to reduce the dimensionality of combinatorial feature space. In this study, LDA is adopted, which simultaneously maximizes the between-class separability and minimizes the intra-class variability. Suppose different features formulate one single feature vector $\vec{x}$. Training set contains n points associated with its speaker identity (totally C speakers), which are denoted by $(\vec{x}_i, y_i), i = 1, ..., n, y_i \in \{1, 2, ..., C\}$. Therefore, the intra-class variability and between-class separability could be measure by two scatter matrices:

$$B = \frac{1}{n}\sum_{c=1}^{C}(\vec{m}_c - \vec{m}_0)(\vec{m}_c - \vec{m}_0)^t \tag{6}$$

$$W = \sum_{c=1}^{C}\sum_{y_i=c}(\vec{x}_i - \vec{m}_c)(\vec{x}_i - \vec{m}_c)^t \tag{7}$$

Where $\vec{m}_i, i = 1, 2, ..., C$ refer to the mean vectors of each class and $\vec{m}_0$ the global mean of all training data. The combination is realized by a linear projection T: $\vec{z} = T\vec{x}$, in which T is derived by:

$$\hat{T} = \text{argmax}_T \frac{TBT^t}{TWT^t} \tag{8}$$

The output after dimensionality reduction $\vec{z}$ is generated for the subsequent classifier.

4   Data Collection

In our meeting scenario, five people put around one standard meeting table on 5 different locations speaking in turn and their voice is captured by a 64-element MDM device placed in front of the meeting room. A total of 50 speakers (20 female and 30 male) participated in this experiment. All data is sampled at 16kHz and 16-bit resolution.

4.1   Speech Recording Setup

Fig.1 is a multiple microphones device which we design as 64-channel elements and select part of asymmetric elements to compose one MDM system. The 64-channel digital signals are collected with PXI-4496 multi-channel collection board produced by National Instruments.

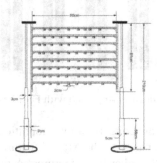

Fig. 1. MDM-based speaker identification device

4.2   Data Collection

In our meeting scenario, 5 people put around one standard meeting table on 5 different locations speaking in turn and their voice is captured by a 64-element MDM device placed in front of the meeting room. A total of 50 speakers (20 female and 30 male) participated in this experiment. All data is sampled at 16kHz and 16-bit resolution.

5 Experiment Setup and Result

Together with the proposed features, the concatenated feature vector and its low-dimensional representation are performed by Probabilistic Linear Discriminant Analysis (PLDA) [10], which is demonstrated as a comparative approach with our dimensional reduction approach. As a classification task, two different types of training/testing sets are generated by:

- Long-Long: 180-sec of training and 60-sec of test, 8,000 test trials in total;
- Short-Short: 60-sec of training and 20-sec of test, 8,000 test trials in total;

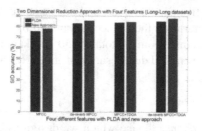

Fig. 2. Two Dimensional Reduction Approach with Four Features (Long-Long datasets)

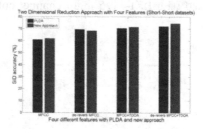

Fig. 3. Two Dimensional Reduction Approach with Four Features (Short-Short datasets)

The results under the Long-Long train-test condition are shown in Figure.3 by PLDA algorithm. The performance of the MFCC feature system alone is not comparable to the performance of the other three features. A relative improvement of more than 10% SID accuracy over the last de-reverberated merging features system is achieved and it is always beneficial in all systems. The results under the short-short train-test condition are shown in Figure.2 by PLDA and our approach. The new method achieve the 12% relative improvement of SID accuracy under the de-reverb MFCC+TDOA feature than classic MFCC on both speaker identification task. Figure.3 also indicates our new dimensional reduction approach has the better performance than PLDA except the second case which means PLDA performs better in de-reverberated acoustic feature vectors. Finally, compared to MFCC feature processing system, we note that the accuracy improved about 17% with the merged features processed by our approach.

6   Conclusion

In this paper we presented a new application of MDM speaker identification for meeting scenarios. We proposed a novel reverberation-robust feature and the use of dimensionality reduction to extract more distinctive information under the specific conditions of meeting applications which are limited training data and very short test utterances.

Acknowledgements. Thanks to NSFC (61105017) agency for funding.

References

1. Bhardwaj, S., Srivastava, S.: GFM-Based Methods for Speaker Identification. IEEE Trans. Systems, Man, and Cybernetics Society, 1–12 (2012)
2. Habets, E.A.P.: A Two-Stage Beamforming Approach for Noise Reduction and Dereverberation. IEEE Trans. Audio, Speech, and Language Processing 21(5), 945–958 (2003)
3. He, H., Wu, L., Lu, J., Qiu, X., Chen, J.: Time Difference of Arrival Estimation Exploiting Multichannel Spatio-Temporal Prediction. IEEE Trans. Audio, Speech, And Language Processing 21(3), 463–475 (2013)
4. Pardo, J.M., Anguera, X., Wooters, C.: Speaker Diarization for Multiple-Distant-Microphone Meetings Using Several Sources of Information. IEEE Trans. Computers 56(9), 1212–1224 (2007)
5. Anguera, X., Wooters, C., Hernando, J.: Speaker Diarization For Multi-Party Meetings Using Acoustic Fusion. In: IEEE Workshop on Automatic Speech Recognition and Understanding, pp. 426–431 (November 2005)
6. Davis, S.B., Mermelstein, P.: Comparison of parametric representations for monosyllabic word recognition in continuously spoken sentences. IEEE Trans. Acoust., Speech, and Signal Process. 28(4), 357–366 (1980)
7. Virtanen, T., Singh, R., Raj, B.: Techniques for Noise Robustness in Automatic Speech Recognition. John Wiley&Sons, United Kingdom (2013)
8. Habets, E.A.P.: Single- and Multi-Microphone Speech Dereverberation using Spectral Enhancement., Ph.D thesis, Technische Universiteit Eindhoven (2007)
9. Kumar, K., Stern, R.M.: Maximum-Likelihood-Based Cepstral Inverse Filtering for Blind Speech Dereverberation. In: International Conference on Acoustics Speech and Signal Processing (ICASSP 2010), pp. 4282–4285 (March 2010)
10. Prince, S.J.D., Elder, J.H.: Probabilistic linear discriminant analysis for inferences about identity. Computer Vision, 1–8 (2007)

Analysis of Factors that Affect the Understanding of Plain Japanese Sentence and Machine-Translated Sentence to Facilitate Cross-culture System Design

Takashi Yoshino[1] and Mai Miyabe[2]

[1] Faculty of Systems Engineering, Wakayama University, Japan
yoshino@center.wakayama-u.ac.jp
[2] Center for the Promotion of Interdisciplinary Education and Research,
Kyoto University, Japan
mai.miyabe@gmail.com

Abstract. A foreign resident of Japan can read and understand the contents of a sentence easily when shown native information in plain Japanese. However, a certain level of skill in Japanese is required to understand plain Japanese. A method is available for displaying native information by machine translation to allow communication with foreign residents. We investigate the difference in the ease of understanding plain Japanese and machine translations (Chinese sentences) for Japanese beginners whose native language is Chinese. Thus, we obtain the following findings: (1) Japanese beginners find machine translations easier than plain Japanese when it comes to understanding the meaning of a sentence. (2) The accuracy of a machine-translated sentence affects the understanding of the meaning of that sentence. However, we find that it is possible to understand the meanings of sentences with low evaluation accuracy in about 60% of cases.

Keywords: level of understanding, machine translation, plain Japanese.

1 Introduction

Plain Japanese is a language that can be understood by foreigners who are not good at Japanese in certain contexts, such as disasters[1]. Plain Japanese rewrites usual Japanese with a plain vocabulary and sentence structure. A foreign resident in Japan can read and understand the contents of a sentence easily when shown native information in plain Japanese. However, a certain level of skill in Japanese is required to understand plain Japanese. Furthermore, rewriting into plain Japanese has a relatively high cost, such as the use of intelligible words and paraphrasing.

A method is available that displays native information by machine translation to allow communication with foreign residents. The acquisition of skills in Japanese is not required because machine translation presents information in a

C. Stephanidis (Ed.): HCII 2014 Posters, Part II, CCIS 435, pp. 600–605, 2014.

native language. Machine translation from Japanese into a native language can be performed automatically and it has a low cost compared with rewriting into plain Japanese. If the translation accuracy is not good, however, this method may make it highly demanding to understand the meaning of a sentence, or it might not be possible to understand a sentence at all. Thus, these two support methods have advantages and disadvantages. However, no previous studies have compared the ease of the understanding using these two support methods.

Even when written in plain Japanese, it might not be easy to understand a machine-translated sentence, depending on the level of mastery of Japanese. In the present study, we investigated the ease of understanding a plain Japanese sentence and a machine-translated sentence for a Japanese beginner.

2   Related Work

Plain Japanese is studied as a language by foreigners who are not proficient in Japanese[1–4]. The aim of the present research was to help a foreigner to understand Japanese during disasters or emergencies. This study defines rules for simplifying a Japanese sentence: the use of a restricted vocabulary and use of subject-verb pair in a sentence.

NHK, Japan's national public broadcasting organization, provides a news service in plain Japanese for foreigners[5]. This service provides the main news from Japan in plain Japanese using Ruby characters[1].

It has been shown that plain Japanese is a language that is intelligible to foreigners[2]. The accuracy of plain Japanese is stable when manual rewriting is performed by native Japanese. Thus, a foreigner with any native language can understand the meaning of a sentence if they have some level of language skill in Japanese. However, plain Japanese is not in the native language of a foreigner. Thus, a foreigner needs to acquire a certain level of skill in the Japanese language. The accuracy of machine translation varies depending on each specific sentence. Machine translation can change Japanese sentences to his/her native-language sentence automatically, and enable a foreigner to obtain information by his/her native language.

No previous investigations have compared these two support methods to assess the ease of understanding.

3   Experimental Analysis to Compare the Understanding of Plain Japanese and Machine-Translated Sentences

We considered foreign residents in Japan who had Chinese as their native language. We investigated the degree of comprehension of plain Japanese sentences and machine-translated sentences (Chinese sentences).

---

[1] Ruby characters are small annotative glosses, which can be placed above or to the right of a Chinese character when writing languages that use logographic characters, such as Chinese or Japanese, to indicate pronunciation.

3.1   Evaluation Sentences

We used the following three types of text as evaluation sentences.

1. Plain Japanese sentences
2. Machine-translated sentences (Chinese)
3. Manually translated sentences (Chinese)

Three Japanese university students manually rewrote the sentences in plain Japanese. The plain Japanese used in the three sentence types was created from a single Japanese sentence because there are multiple methods of plain Japanese translation.

We used random test sentences to evaluate the machine translation system provided by NTT (Japan's major telecommunications company)[6][2]. In total, we produced 120 plain Japanese sentences.

We generated 40 machine-translated sentences in Chinese using the machine translation system[3] via Language Grid[4].

We evaluated the accuracy of the translated sentences using the adequacy evaluation method[5] developed by Walker et al.[7]. In this method, the following five-point scale was used to evaluate the accuracy of translation.

5: All (the same meaning)
4: Most (some grammar problems but roughly the same meaning)
3: Much (retained some of the meaning)
2: Little (the general idea remains but the actual meaning is not understood)
1: None (quite different meaning)

The evaluators were three Japanese-Chinese translators. We used manually translated sentences produced by a Japanese-Chinese translator. The manually translated sentences were produced after the ideal machine translations were generated.

In this experiment, one test sentence (Japanese) corresponded to one machine-translated sentence (Chinese), one manually translated sentence (Chinese), and three plain Japanese sentences. In total, 120 groups were used in the experiment.

3.2   Experimental Method

In this experiment, a foreign resident in Japan checked how many sentences they could understand when presented with plain Japanese sentences, machine-translated sentences, and manually translated sentences.

We investigated the level of comprehension in the following two types of experiments.

---

[2] We used a comparatively long sentence where the average number of characters in 40 sentences was 43.6 characters, the standard deviation was 14.3 characters, the shortest sentence contained 20 characters, and the longest sentence contained 90 characters.

[3] J-Server developed by KODENSHA: http://www.kodensha.jp/

[4] Language Grid Project, http://langrid.org/

[5] This evaluation was performed by more than two evaluators.

Experiment 1. Description of the contents after reading
Experiment 2. Evaluation of the sentence contents

Each experiment is described in detail in the following section.

Experiment 1: Description of the Contents After Reading. Experiment 1 was the first phase of the comprehension investigation. A foreign subject described the contents that they understood in each sentence produced in their native language (Chinese). The target sentences were plain Japanese sentences, machine-translated sentences, and manually translated sentences.

The foreign subjects comprised three Chinese foreign students who attended a Japanese class for beginners.

To eliminate any possible order effect, we presented the target sentences (plain Japanese sentences, machine-translated sentences, and manual translations) in a random order to each subject.

Experiment 2: Evaluation of the Sentence Contents. In experiment 2, we evaluated the descriptions obtained in experiment 1. We evaluated the meanings of the sentences described by the subjects (level of comprehension).

The evaluator determined: "How much of the meaning expressed in the original sentence was also expressed in the sentence description?"

5: All (the same meaning)
4: Most (some grammar problems but roughly the same meaning)
3: Much (retained some of the meaning)
2: Little (the general idea remains but the actual meaning is not understood)
1: None (quite different meaning)

The evaluators were three Japanese-Chinese translators. To eliminate any possible order effect, we presented the target sentences in a random order to each translator.

4   Experimental Results and Discussion

We verified whether the accuracy of the machine-translated sentences affected their understanding. Table 1 shows the results for the description evaluations of plain Japanese sentences. Table 2 shows the results for the accuracy evaluations and the evaluation values of machine-translated sentences for the descriptions. In Table 2, the sentence accuracy evaluations are the median values for three translators.

Table 1 shows that the foreign subjects did not understood the meaning of many sentences because of plain Japanese sentences. In total 360 plain Japanese sentences, we found that 162 sentences (45%) had an evaluation accuracy of 1 and 2, where 104 sentences (29%) had evaluations of 4 and 5, although the plain Japanese sentences had easy vocabulary and correct grammar. Table 2 shows

Table 1. Results of the description evaluations of plain Japanese sentences

Evaluation of the description contents					
1	2	3	4	5	Total
71	91	94	64	40	360
(20%)	(25%)	(26%)	(18%)	(11%)	(100%)

Table 2. Results of the accuracy evaluations and description evaluations of machine-translated sentences

		Evaluation of the description contents					
		1	2	3	4	5	Total
Accuracy of machine-translated sentences	1	1	3	4	4	9	21
		(5%)	(14%)	(19%)	(19%)	(43%)	(100%)
	2	3	4	14	21	9	51
		(6%)	(8%)	(27%)	(41%)	(18%)	(100%)
	3	0	0	4	18	17	39
		(0%)	(0%)	(10%)	(46%)	(44%)	(100%)
	4	0	0	0	4	5	9
		(0%)	(0%)	(0%)	(44%)	(56%)	(100%)
	5	1	2	7	40	70	120
		(1%)	(2%)	(6%)	(33%)	(58%)	(100%)
	Total	5	9	29	87	110	240
		(2%)	(4%)	(12%)	(36%)	(46%)	(100%)

that the foreign subjects understood the meaning of many sentences, although the machine-translated sentences had low accuracy. We found that 21 sentences had an evaluation accuracy of 1, where 13 sentences (62%) had evaluations of 4 and 5. In total, 51 sentences had an evaluation accuracy of 2, where 30 sentences (59%) had evaluations of 4 and 5.

Figure 1 shows the frequencies of the highly evaluated description values, i.e., evaluations of 4 and 5. Thus, the evaluation of the sentence contents tended to improve with the accuracy of the machine translation. We found that the accuracy of translation affected the ease of understanding. The accuracy of translation was quite low when sentences received an evaluation of 1. However, the subjects could understand the meanings of about 60% (evaluations of 4 and 5) of these sentences. We found that even if a sentence had a low translation accuracy in the native language, the subjects were still able to read the contents to some extent.

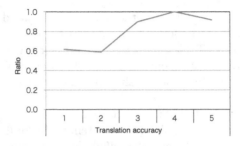

Fig. 1. Frequencies of the highly evaluated descriptions

Ten of 120 manually translated sentences with an evaluation accuracy of 5 received three or less evaluations. This was because the context was missing in these sentences.

5 Conclusion

In this study, we compared the ease of understanding plain Japanese and machine translations (Chinese) by beginners in Japanese who had Chinese as their native language. The main contributions of this study can be summarized as follows.

1. It was easier for Japanese beginners to understand the meaning of machine-translated sentences than plain Japanese.
2. The accuracy of a machine-translated sentence affected its understanding.

In future research, we aim to conduct further experiments and evaluations in other languages.

Acknowledgment. This study was supported partly by JSPS KAKENHI Grant Number 25242037 and an Original Research Support Project at Wakayama University during 2012–2013.

References

1. Iori, I., et al.: A preliminary study for the realization of the universal communication in a society using easy Japanese. Journal of Global Education 1, 31–46 (2010) (in Japanese)
2. Higashi, T., Miyabe, M., Yoshino, T.: Verification of Translation Repair Support using Plain Japanese, Technical Report of IEICE, Technical Group of Artificial Intelligence and Knowledge Information Processing (AI) 112 (435), 91–96 (2013) (in Japanese)
3. Iori, I.: From the Viewpoint of "Easy Japanese": What Can the Pedagogical Grammar of Japanese Say to "Grassroots" Japanese-Language Classrooms? Hitotsubashi Review of Arts and Sciences 3, 126–141 (2009) (in Japanese)
4. Moku, M., et al.: Investigation for Easy Japanese paraphrase dictionary creation to official documents. In: Proceedings of the Seventeenth Annual Meeting of the Association for Natural Language Processing, pp. 376–379 (2011) (in Japanese)
5. Science and Technology Research Laboratories of NHK: Journal of NHK STRL R&D, No. 130, p. 58 (2011) (in Japanese)
6. NTT Natural Language Research Group,
   http://www.kecl.ntt.co.jp/icl/mtg/resources/index.phpodensha.jp/
7. Walker, K., Bamba, M., Miller, D., Ma, X., Cieri, C., Doddington, G.: Multiple-Translation Arabic (MTA) Part 1, Linguistic Data Consortium (LDC), catalog number LDC2003T18 and ISBN 1-58563-276-7

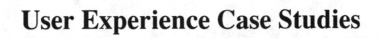

User Experience Case Studies

Advantages of Stereoscopic 3D Displays for Conflict Judgment Performance in Air-Traffic-Control: When and How to Use 3D

Andreas Baier and Alf C. Zimmer

Engineering Psychology Unit, University of Regensburg, Germany
andreas.baier@psychologie.uni-regensburg.de,
alf.zimmer@ur.de

Abstract. Three different stereoscopic 3D visualisations are compared with the 2D reference currently used at air traffic control (ATC) controller working positions. Using safety critical air traffic scenarios, air traffic controllers (ATCOs), pilots, and two groups of laypersons, one of which with an appropriate training, are asked to judge safety critical scenarios showing two converging aircraft. The cognitive demands that arising in peak-traffic situations are simulated by adding an additional auditory task that has to be conducted in parallel to judging potential conflicts. The results show that the 3D visualizations can enhance the efficiency of the ATCOs without compromising the safety. However, while the judgement certainty of all visualizations is virtually equal in cases of conflict, differences arise due to the dimension on which the aircraft miss each other in case of separation. While advantages of 3D arise when judging vertical distances, 2D better supports the judgment of horizontal distances.

Keywords: air-traffic-control, conflict detection, false alarm rate, judgment certainty, expertise, stereopsis.

1 Introduction

1.1 The Air-Traffic-Controller Task: Safety vs. Efficiency

According to the International Civil Aviation Organization (ICAO), the main task of an ATCO is to maintain a safe, orderly and expeditious flow of air traffic within the airspace he is responsible for. He guides them through his airspace and prevents conflicts between the aircraft. As a basis for this, the positions and movements of all aircraft in his airspace as well as of those that are about to enter it have to be considered. With exception for tower control workspaces, a two-dimensional (2D) visualization provides the required information. The lateral information, such as horizontal aircraft positions and distances between them, is presented graphically from a top view perspective onto the airspace. Altitudes are indicated numerically within a label attached

C. Stephanidis (Ed.): HCII 2014 Posters, Part II, CCIS 435, pp. 609–614, 2014.

to each object. Because of the multitude of information ATCOs have to process under time pressure in order to constantly assess all occurrences in their airspace, the decision about when and how to intervene often involves uncertainty. In each decision an ATCO has to deliberate about whether further observing the situation or intervening by instruction of a change. The former is accompanied by the risk of missing a conflicting situation and loosing time to plan and implement the required intervention, while with the latter may lead to producing a false alarm, which is an unnecessary and therewith inefficient intervention in the flight-path of two converging aircraft that would have continued to move safely separated. Hence, each decision features a trade-off between safety and efficiency. The level of safety can be expressed as the conflict detection rate, whereas the efficiency finds its expression in the rate of false alarms. Recent studies report conflict detection rates from over 99%, whereas the reported false alarm rates are about 70% and therewith showing a considerable potential for improving efficiency of the ATCOs' decisions (1).

1.2   Inconsistent Findings Regarding the Usefulness of 3D for Air-Traffic-Control

Since the late 1980s, researchers investigated with numerous studies the usefulness of 3D visualizations to support ATCOs' efficiency. Up to now, however, no consistent proof for or against the assumption that 3D can reduce the number of false alarms has been provided. Several factors could account for this; These are (i) differences in the research questions and therewith (ii) the study designs and tasks that are used to address them, (iii) the layout of the 3D visualizations that have been compared with 2D, (iv) the expertise with ATC tasks of the participants, (v) their spatial thinking abilities, and (vi) the methods used for data analysis. Since these factors have not been researched systematically within a single study before, we conducted an experimental study including these factors. This allowed us to derive an appropriate study design, and determine (a) if false alarms can be reduced with using a 3D visualization, and (b) to research the impact of each factor.

2   Theory

2.1   The Demands of the Air-Traffic-Control Task

Analyzing the ATCOs' task, the mental resources required for processing the information presented with todays' 2D visualization provides an explanation for the occurrence of false alarms, especially for those that are due to uncertainty about vertical separations; According to human-information-processing models, two tasks that required different mental resources to process them can be conducted in parallel, whereas tasks that share the same resources have to be processed sequentially (2). Since there are separate mental resources for processing visual-spatial and phonological information, the 2D visualization used today at air-traffic-controller workstations does not allow observing the movements of the aircraft independently and in parallel to the incoming radio-messages. The reason for this is that the numerical altitude information presented on the 2D airspace visualization competes for the same phonological resources than the radio-messages. The fact that the altitude information is presented visually while the radio-messages come in auditory does not influence the mental resources that are required for processing them. Only the lateral aircraft distances, which demand visual-spatial mental resources, can be processed at the same time, explaining the higher false alarm rates when judging vertical over lateral separations.

2.2   When 3D Promises to be better than 2D-and when not

Because observing the airspace with a 3D visualization theoretically only requires visual-spatial mental resources, judging aircraft separations and processing incoming auditory messages should be possible at the same time. As a result, and especially when both radio-messages and the airspace have to be observed in parallel, 3D promises to result in a reduced false alarm rate and an increased judgment certainty compared with today's 2D visualization. On the contrary, the use of a 2D visualization should result in a higher judgment certainty compared with 3D when judging lateral separations. The reason for this is line-of-sight ambiguities, which are inherit to all 3D visualizations, and reduce the precision with which distances can be perceived. Adding depth cues contributes to the precision with which distances can be judged, and therewith reduces the negative impact of ambiguities. Even though the more depth cues are added, the better distances can be judged, occlusions and display clutter limit the amount of depth cues that can be used. Motion parallax, binocular disparity, and interposition, however, are regarded as the most powerful aids for distance perception, and do not add further content to the visualization (3).

3   Methods

To research if the use of 3D visualizations for ATCO workstations facilitates judgment certainty and reduces the number of false alarms, a total of 48 participants has been recruited and asked to judge the outcome of a total of 108 representative and safety critical air-traffic-scenarios with each visualization. The scenarios were created by variation of the convergence angle between them ($0°$, $90°$ or $180°$) and vertical movement of none, one or both objects. In 54 of the 108 scenarios, the trajectories of the two objects were going to coincide in 45s after scenario start. The other 54 scenarios were duplications of the 54 conflicts that have been transferred into separations. To do so, the point where their trajectories were coinciding in 27 of the cases was separated vertically while in the other 27 cases the separation was done on the lateral plane. Therefore, separations on both the vertical and the lateral dimension existed. After displaying each scenario for exactly 10s, a six-point-rating scale masked the scenario with an entry mask for judging the outcome of the scenario with one of the following options: certainly conflict, probably conflict, maybe conflict, maybe no conflict, probably no conflict, and certainly no conflict. In order to simulate peak-traffic-situations, an additional auditory task had to be conducted in parallel to ¼ of the scenarios. To address the effect of training and spatial ability, the participants were equally divided into four groups consisting of ATCOs, pilots and two groups of laypersons, from which one received a conflict judgement training that has been derived from the well documented cognitive strategies controllers use to judge conflicts with the current 2D visualisation. The data analysis is based on signal-detection-theory and both conflict detection and false alarm rates are calculated. Figure 1 shows all four visualisations that have been compared with each other.

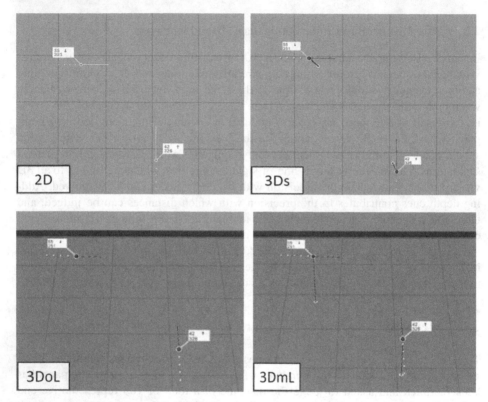

Fig. 1. Modes of visualisation that are compared with each other (4)

4   Results

4.1   Safety and Efficiency

Assuming that controllers only decide not to intervene when absolutely certain that no conflict will happen, all scenarios that show a conflict and being rated with of the five categories from 'certainly conflict' to 'probably no conflict' are considered as detected conflicts, for the operator would intervene in order to mitigate the risk of a collision. Conflicts that are judged with 'certainly no' constitute misses. An analysis of variance including the factors visualization, auditory task condition, and group membership indicates a significant advantage for 3D between the visualizations, when the numbers of false alarms is statistically controlled (p=0.022; F(3, 384)=3.244; η2=0.027). Since no significant interactions appear, this advantage also applies to the pilots and both groups of laypersons. Though not statistically significant (p=0.06; η2=0.021), the simulation of incoming radio messages results in a noteworthy interaction with the visualizations, indicating a higher negative impact on conflict detection performance with 2D compared with 3D. 3DmL results in the biggest advantage with a 4.5% higher conflict detection rate as 2D when the auditory task is added.

The false alarm rate is the percentage of separation situations which the operator erroneously treats as conflict. The corresponding false alarm rate for the conflict detection rate of 99% ATCOs achieve today with the 2D reference are calculated for the condition with the additional auditory task. The results show that the expected false alarm rates are on average 5.5% lower with any 3D visualization compared with the 2D reference. With 3DmL the biggest advantage results with a reduction of 8.7%.

4.2   Judgment Certainty and Line-of-Sight Ambiguity

The impact of the dimension on judgment certainty is analyzed by assigning values to each answer as follows: In the case of a conflict, the answer 'certainly no' equals a value of 0, whereas 'certainly yes' equals 1. For separations, the value 0 is assigned to 'certainly yes' and 1 for 'certainly no'. The values 0.2, 0.4, 0.6, and 0.8 are related to the other four categories accordingly. An analysis of variance including the factors dimension, additional auditory task condition, visualization, and group membership is conducted. An interaction between visualization and dimension (p=0.025; F(6, 43)=2.453; η2=0.054) points out that the differences regarding judgment certainty between the visualizations are independent from both the additional auditory task and group membership. Figure 2 illustrates this on the data of the ATCOs in the additional auditory task condition. The values resulting with 2D are adjusted to zero as baseline.

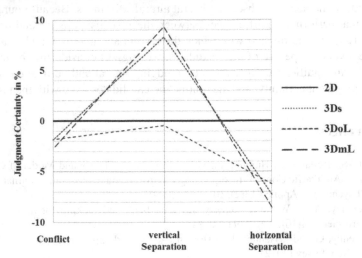

Fig. 2. Judgement certainty of the ATCOs in the additional auditory task condition. 2D serves as the baseline.

While no noteworthy differences with regard to judgement certainty appear for the conflicts, the uses of the 3D visualizations with drop-lines (3DmL and 3Ds) lead to a higher certainty than 2D in case of vertical separations, and disappear without the drop-lines. In cases of the horizontal separations, the 2D reference results in a higher judgement certainty than any 3D visualisation. These results can be explained with the characteristics of separations and conflicts: A conflict can be excluded by assessing the vertical information only in case of vertical separation, while the assessment of the horizontal information suffices therefore in case of a horizontal separation. Since 3D visualisations facilitate vertical separation judgements due to their additional analogous altitude representations, they result in a higher performance when vertical separations are to be judged. However, these advantages are counterbalanced by the line-of-sight ambiguities when horizontal separations are shown.

5   Conclusions

The results highlight that stereoscopic 3D visualizations can be beneficial for ATC, because they support a higher efficiency by promising a reduction of the number of false alarms compared with the 2D visualization currently used at air-traffic-controller workstations. Considering the fact that these advantages become particularly apparent in highly demanding situations, where incoming radio messages have to be processed together with the airspace information, further emphasises their potential. Also the gain in vertical distance judgment makes 3D a good ATC candidate for the future, specifically for airport areas, where approach and departure areas are characterised by a high number of vertical movements and therewith require the ATCOs to focus even more on vertical distances as elsewhere in the airspace. In these airspaces, procedures could further support the use of 3D visualizations by providing standardized routes that reduce the need for observing lateral aircraft distances. Because our analyses also proof that performance differences between the visualisations depend on various task characteristics, the method with which the results are analysed, and to a lesser extent on the level of expertise of the candidates, we suggest considering the impact of line-of-sight ambiguities and their impact on judging lateral and vertical distances, as well as the judgment certainty, and the routine the candidates have with the tasks.

References

1. Loft, S., Bolland, S., Humphreys, M.S., Neal, A.: A Theory and Model of Conflict Detection in Air Traffic Control: Incorporating Environmental Constraints. Journal of Experimental Psychology: Applied 15(2), 106–124 (2009)
2. Baddeley, A.D.: Working memory: Looking back and looking forward. Nature Reviews Neuroscience 4(10), 829–839 (2003)
3. Salvendy, G. (ed.): Handbook of Human Factors and Ergonomics, 4th edn. Wiley & Sons Inc., New Jersey (2012)
4. Baier, A.: Stereoskopische 3D Anzeigen für die Flugsicherung. Regensburg, Germany: Universität Regensburg (2013)

The Effect of Text Color and Background Color on Skim Reading Webpages in Thai

Sorachai Kamollimsakul[1,2], Helen Petrie[1], and Christopher Power[1]

[1] Human Computer Interaction Research Group, Department of Computer Science,
University of York, United Kingdom
{sk750,Helen.Petrie,Christopher.Power}@york.ac.uk
[2] School of Information Technology, Suranaree University of Technology, Thailand

Abstract. There are many sets of guidelines concerning the accessibility of the web for older adults, but little empirical evidence from studies with older people to support their recommendations. In addition, all the recommendations apply to text in languages using the Latin alphabet. This study investigated the effects of text color and background color on the performance and preferences of younger and older adults on webpages in the Thai language. There were 18 Thai younger participants (19 - 29 years) and 18 Thai older participants (59 - 70 years). There were three combinations of text color and color (black text on white background, white text on black background, and sepia text on off-white background). The text and background color combinations failed to have any significant effects on the performance measures of task completion rate or time spent skim reading webpages. However, for the preference measure, there was a significant difference between combinations of text and background color but no differences between the age groups. There was also a significant interaction between combinations of text and background color and age group. These results form an useful basis for web design guidelines for Thai websites for text and background color for both younger and older users.

Keywords: Web accessibility, older adults, web design guidelines, text color, background color, Thai language.

1   Introduction

An important issue for many societies at the moment is the aging of the population, with the number of older people (aged 60 years or over) rapidly increasing. In 2012, there were 841 million older people worldwide [12]. The United Nations estimates that by 2050 the proportion of older people will increase to 21 per cent of the total population or more than 2 billion people [11, 12]. If this prediction is born out, it will be the first time in history that the proportion of the population aged 60 years and over will be larger than the proportion of young people (aged under 15) [11]. In Thailand, in 2012 the proportion of older people (aged 60 or over) was 13 per cent and it is estimated to increase to 37.5 per cent by 2050 [12]. The United Nations Population Fund [13] reports that "Thailand is ageing faster than others in South-East Asia" (p2).

C. Stephanidis (Ed.): HCII 2014 Posters, Part II, CCIS 435, pp. 615–620, 2014.
© Springer International Publishing Switzerland 2014

The change in population demographics is also leading to an increase in the number of older web users. In Thailand, the current rate of web use by older adults is very low at 2%. However, the use of the web by older Thais is dramatically increasing, with a 33% increase from 2008 to 2010, and a 200% increase from 2010 to 2012. Nonetheless, older people face numerous barriers in using the web because of age-related physical, sensory, and cognitive disabilities [4] as well as the lack of familiarity with the computer technologies and the web amongst the current cohorts of older people. Therefore web accessibility and usability is an important topic for empowering and supporting older people to be able to use websites.

Although the Web Content Accessibility Guidelines (WCAG) [14] are well known, they do not cover the needs of older people, only those of people with disabilities. Petrie, Kamollimsakul and Power [7] found that many sets of web design guidelines for older people have been proposed, but most lack evidence-based research to support their recommendations. In addition, these different web design guidelines often make different recommendations on the same issue and the recommendations can be somewhat vague. An example is the recommendation about text color and background color for webpages: Holt [3] recommends "dark type or graphics against a light background (though sometimes the opposite can work fine with sufficient contrast)"; both AgeLight [1] and Zhao [9] recommend using dark type on light or white backgrounds; NIA/NLM [6] recommends using dark type against a light background, or white lettering on a black or dark-colored background. Some guidelines also recommend avoiding colored backgrounds: SilverWeb [5] recommends "Blue green tones should be avoided. Background screens should not be pure white or change rapidly in brightness between screens. Also, a high contrast between the foreground and background should exist". The Nielsen Norman Group [7] recommends "using highly contrasting text and background colors. For optimal legibility, use black text on a white (or a very, very light gray) background".

Kamollimsakul, Petrie, and Power [10] found that most web design guidelines for older people are in English and relate to the presentation of text on webpages in the Latin alphabet. Their research about font type found that Thai web users, both younger and older adults, preferred a Thai conservative font type which closely corresponds to a serif font type in the Latin alphabet in comparison to a Thai modern font which closely corresponds to a san serif font. This result is different from current web design guidelines for older people for the Latin alphabet which usually suggest a sans serif font type [2, 3, 5, 6, 7] or argue against the use of a serif font type [7]. Thus, investigating web design guideline related to other alphabets and languages is an interesting and important issue because there is evidence that web design guidelines for the Latin alphabet are not always appropriate for other alphabets.

This paper investigated the effect of text color and background color on skim reading webpages for Thai younger and older adults both using both performance and preference measures, with the aim of developing evidence-based recommendations for Thai language websites for both younger and older users.

2   Method

2.1   Design

A two way mixed design was used in this study. The between participants indepen-dent variable was age group with two levels: younger and older adults. The within participants independent variable was combinations of text and background color with three levels: black text on white background (black/white); white text on black back-ground (white/black); and sepia text on off-white background (sepia/off-white). The dependent variables included performance and preference measures. Two aspects of performance were measured: task completion rate and time spent reading per web-page. The preference measure was a five-point Likert item of liking for the three combinations of text and background color.

Each participant undertook six skim reading tasks, two tasks for each of the color combinations. The task was to skim read the page as quickly and accurately as possi-ble and to then answer four multiple choices questions about the page. Skim reading was chosen as the task as this is a very common reading task on websites. In an earlier study [8], we found that participants often used a mixture of scanning, skim reading and detailed reading, so for clearer results we set up the task as specifically skim read-ing. The order of presentation of color combinations was counterbalanced to avoid practice and fatigue effects.

2.2   Participants

There were 36 participants, 18 older and 18 younger Thai adults. The mean age of the older adults was 61.33 years (standard deviation 3.07, range 59 – 70 years), 3 were male and 15 were female. The mean age of the younger adults was 23.72 years (stan-dard deviation 3.06, range 19 – 29 years), 7 were male and 11 were female.

2.3   Equipment and Materials

Participants completed the study on a PC running Windows XP and Internet Explorer 9 with 21.5 inch LED Monitor, a standard keyboard, and 2-button mouse with a scroll-wheel.

A website with six pages about the Olympic Games was created for the study. Each page had four paragraphs and 354 words of text. There were four multiple choice questions for each page. The text and background colors in this study were black (#000000), white (#FFFFFF), sepia (#5E2612), and off-white (#F5EFDC).

2.4   Procedure

Participants were briefed about the study and completed an informed consent form and a short demographic questionnaire. They were then asked to make themselves familiar with the computer, monitor, mouse, and web browser. Participants were first given three practice tasks, one for each color combination. For each experimental trial, participants skim read the page with the appropriate color combination, pressed the spacebar when they had finished reading, and then answered the multiple choice questions. This process was repeated for the six tasks. After completing all the tasks, participants were asked to rate their preference for each color combination on a 5 point Likert item (1 = not at all preferred, 5 = very much preferred). As a reminder, examples of the combinations were provided.

3   Results

Analyses of Variance (ANOVA) on the task completion rate and time spent per web-page found that text/background color combinations had no significant effect on either performance measures. There was also no significant effect of age group and no interaction between the independent variables.   On the preference measure, there was a significant main effect for color combinations, $F (2, 68) = 30.01$, $p < .001$, but no main effect for age group. Fig. 1 illustrates the means for the three color combinations. An LSD post hoc analysis found that white/black was rated significantly lower in preference ($p < 0.05$) than either black/white and sepia/off-white. There was no significant difference between black/white and sepia/ off-white. In addition, t-tests were conducted to investigate whether ratings of preference were significantly above or below the mid-point of the rating scale, to investigate whether participants were positive or negative about each color combination. One sample t-tests against the neutral mid-point rating of 3 showed that the mean rating for white/black was significant lower than neutral ($t (35) = 4.66$, $p < 0.01$), but the mean ratings for black/ white and sepia/off-white were both significant higher than neutral (black/white: $t (35) = 6.35$, $p < .001$; sepia/off-white: $t (35) = 3.08$, $p < .01$).

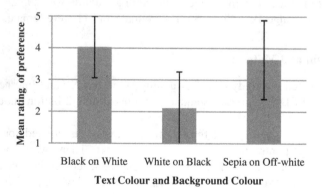

Fig. 1. Mean preference ratings for three combinations of text and background color (younger and older participants combined)

There was also a significant interaction between the color combinations and age group, $F (1, 34) = 17.44$, $p < 0.001$. Fig. 2 illustrates the means for the interaction.   A Scheffé post hoc analysis showed that for younger participants, white/black was significantly lower in preference rating ($p < 0.05$) than either black/white or sepia/off-white.

For younger participants there was no significant difference between sepia/off-white and black/ white. For older participants, there was a significant difference between black/white and either white/black or sepia/off-white (p < 0.05). There was no significant difference between the latter two combinations.

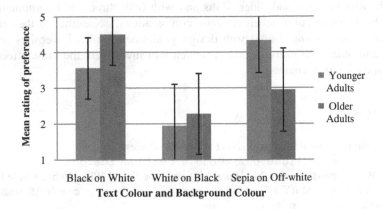

Fig. 2. Mean preference ratings for combinations of text color and background color for Younger and Older adults

One sample t-tests against the neutral mid-point of 3 showed that for younger adults, the mean rating for white/black background was significant lower than neutral (t = 3.86, df = 17, p < .005), but the mean rating for black/white and for sepia/off-white were both significantly higher than neutral (black/white: t = 2.76, df = 17, p < .05; sepia/off-white: t = 6.23, df = 17, p < .001). For older adults the mean rating for white/black was significantly lower than neutral (t= 2.72, df = 17, p < .05) and the mean rating of black/white was significantly higher than neutral (t = 7.42, df = 17, p < .001) but the mean rating for sepia/off-white was not significantly different from neutral (t= .20, df = 17, p > .05).

4   Discussion and Conclusions

This study found that three commonly mentioned combinations of text and background color had no effect on either younger or older participants' performance on task completion rate or time spent skim reading webpages. However, on the preference measure, there were significant differences between the combinations of text and background color and an interaction effect between the color combinations and age group.

Younger adults preferred black text on white background or sepia text on off-white background in comparison to white text on black background. Older adults preferred black text on white background the most and white text on black background the least and were neutral about the sepia on off-white.

Based on these results, proposing black text on white background is good for both younger and older Adults. Sepia text on off-line background is good for younger adults and acceptable for older adults. While White text on Black background should be avoided for all web users. This last point is interesting given that this currently seems quite a popular choice amongst web developers. These results represent only one study with younger and older adults and with only three color combinations of text and background color, albeit common combinations. Nonetheless they form an useful basis for evidence-based web design guidelines for Thai websites for both younger and older web users. Future research will investigate the same effects with English speaking participants.

References

1. AgeLight: Interface design guidelines for users of all ages, http://www.agelight.com/webdocs/designguide.pdf
2. Holt, B.J., Komlos-Weimer, M.: Older Adults and the World Wide Web: a Guide for Web Site Creators. SPRY Foundation, http://www.spry.org/pdf/website_creators_guide.pdf
3. Hanson, V.L.: Age and web access: the next generation. In: The 2009 International Cross-Disciplinary Conference on Web Accessibility (W4A). ACM (2009)
4. Holt, B.J.: Creating senior-friendly Web sites. Issue brief. Centre for Medicare Education 1(4) (2000)
5. Kurniawan, S., Zaphiris, P.: Research-Derived Web Design Guidelines for Older People. In: Proceeding of the 7th International ACM SIGACCESS Conference on Computers and Accessibility (ASSETS), Maryland, pp. 129–135 (2005)
6. National Institute on Aging/National Library of Medicine (NIA/NLM): Making your website senior friendly: A check list, http://www.nlm.nih.gov/pubs/checklist.pdf
7. Pernice, K., Estes, J., Nielsen, J.: Senior Citizens (Ages 65 and older) on the Web. Nielsen Norman Group (2013)
8. Petrie, H., Kamollimsakul, S., Power, C.: Web accessibility for older adults: effects of line spacing and text justification on reading web pages. In: Proceedings of the 15th International ACMSIGACCESS Conference on Computers and Accessibility (ASSETS). ACM (2013)
9. Zhao, H.: Universal Usability Web Design Guidelines for the Elderly (Age 65 and Older), http://www.co-bw.com/DMS_Web_the_elderly_on_the_web.htm
10. Kamollimsakul, S., Petrie, H., Power, C.: Web accessibility for older readers: Effect of Font Type and Font size on skim reading text on webpages in Thai. In: 14th International Conference on Computers Helping People with Special Needs. LNCS (in press)
11. United Nations. World Population Ageing: 1950-2050 (2002)
12. United Nations. World Population Prospects (2013)
13. United Nation Population Fund: Population Aging in Thailand: Prognosis and Policy Response, Bangkok (2006)
14. World Wide Web Consortium. Web Content Accessibility Guidelines 2.0., http://www.w3.org/TR/WCAG20

The Color and Blink Frequency of LED Notification Lights and Smartphone Users' Urgency Perception

Minsun Kim[1], Jiyeun Lee[1], Hyebeen Lee[1], Soyeon Kim[1],
Haemi Jung[2], and Kwanghee Han[1],[*]

[1] Cognitive Engineering Lab. Department of Psychology, Yonsei University, Korea
kimmin0414@hanmail.net, amethystljy@naver.com,
hblee27@gmail.com, england311@naver.com, khan@yonsei.ac.kr
[2] UX Lab, Mobile R&D Center, LG Electronics, Korea
hyemi.jung@lge.com

Abstract. LED notification lights are used in smartphones to deliver various information to users, such as missed calls, incoming calls, receiving a new text message, and low battery. This study explores whether the settings of the color and blink frequency of the LEDs notification lights affect smartphone users' urgency perception in two important information states, i.e., missed calls and incoming calls. We set the blink frequency of LED notification lights high and low, assuming that high frequency blink will be perceived as more urgent notification. As for color, we first set the color of LED indicators as White for both high and low blink frequencies. Then, we changed the color to Red for high frequency blink and Green for low frequency blink to examine whether color has any effect on smartphone users' urgency perception of the notification. We measured users' urgency perception by asking participants to evaluate how effective each setting of LED notification lights is in indicating the degree of urgency of the corresponding information state. In an experiment with 30 participants, we found that participants perceived high blink frequency as more intuitive and attractive and therefore more effective than low blink frequency in indicating high urgency in both information states. We also found that the use of color increases users' overall urgency perception. We further found that users' urgency perception—both intuitive and attentive—was highest when color was used and the blink rate of notification was high. That is, the urgency perception score was highest when the color was Red and the blink frequency was high. In the post-experiment interviews, participants chose red as the best color to indicate urgency. Given that, we conclude that the use of red color with high blink frequency of the LED notification light is most effective in conveying urgency information.

Keywords: LED notification light, smartphone, urgency perception, color, blink frequency.

---

[*] Corresponding author.

C. Stephanidis (Ed.): HCII 2014 Posters, Part II, CCIS 435, pp. 621–625, 2014.
© Springer International Publishing Switzerland 2014

1   Introduction

The smartphone LED notification lights help users to recognize various situations without activating the display. The LED notification lights use movement pattern and color to deliver various information states to users. For instance, movement pattern of lighting can deliver different information states to users such as warning or progressing by using different blink frequencies. Color is also useful in providing specific information because people have specific preconceived images of particular colors. Therefore, when a color is used in a way that does not match users' preconceived image of the color, intended information cannot be effectively delivered (Kang, 2006).

This study examines whether the use of movement pattern and color of smartphone LED notification lights can deliver intended information more effectively when they match users' mental model. This study focuses on two emergency situations, i.e., notification of missed calls and incoming calls, where LED notification is most frequently used. Specifically, we examine whether users perceive the urgency of the situations differently—in both cognitive and emotional aspects—as the blink frequency and color of LED lighting change. Perceived urgency leads individuals to take immediate actions or attentions to the situation (Suied, Susini, & McAdams, 2008) because individuals respond more appropriately and promptly to the situations when they perceive greater urgency of the situations (Guillaume et al., 2003; Bliss, Gilson, & Deaton, 1955).

Prior studies on colors found that long wavelength colors such as red have a greater arousing effect than short wavelength colors such as blue or green (Elliot, Maier, Moller, Friedman, & Meinhardt, 2007). Because colors with greater arousing effect can draw more attention from individuals, we predict that red color LED lighting will be more effective in generating perceived urgency among smartphone users. We also predict that smartphone users will perceive greater urgency when high blink frequency is used than when low blink frequency is used. We further predict that when both red color and high blink frequency are used together, smartphone users will perceive greater urgency than when they are separately used.

2   Experiment

2.1   Participants

30 undergraduate students participated in this study. All participants had normal vision and all of them were smartphone users.

2.2   Experimental Design

This study was conducted to verify the effect of blink frequency (speed) and pattern's color on perceived urgency. Blink frequency (high, low) and color (without color, color) were manipulated to compare the perceived urgency of Smartphone LED. It was 2 X 2 within factorial experimental design.

2.3   Experimental Tasks and Procedures

Before the experiment conducted, participants received Smartphone samples that would be used for the experiment. Then they turned on the several LED themselves in order to understand the experiment well. The LED which participants had to observe during the test was situated on the top of front of Smartphone. After simple instruction, participants took part in the experiment. The experiment was proceeded with the sample smartphone's display was covered. Participants were given two situations and there were four patterns in each situation. In a concrete aspect, the situations were consisted of incoming calls and notification of missed calls. Four smartphone LED patterns were presented from the combination of frequency (high, low) and color (without color, color) in each situation (table1).

Condition of frequency was consisted of high and low blinking conditions of LED light in identical time. Because the high frequency condition blinked more in the same amount of time, participants perceived the speed faster than low frequency one. We labeled the high blinking condition as urgent condition, and low blinking condition as normal condition. For the color condition, white color was presented as condition of without color (white). With color condition, normal condition was presented with green and urgent condition was presented with red to classify.

Table 1. Four LED types in each situation

Situation	1. Missed Call		2. Incoming Call	
	(Normal) Low Frequency	(Urgent) High Frequency	(Normal) Low Frequency	(Urgent) High Frequency
no color	Pattern 1 (White)	Pattern 2 (White)	Pattern 1 (White)	Pattern 2 (White)
color	Pattern 3 (Green)	Pattern 4 (Red)	Pattern 3 (Green)	Pattern 4 (Red)

The task for the participants was to assess how each pattern delivered urgent meaning effectively in cognitive and emotional aspects by comparing the conditions of changing frequency and changing both color and frequency. As for the questionnaire, intuitiveness (Current situation can be noticed through LED) and attentiveness (LED catches eyes and outstands) were presented for cognitive aspect of items, each item was measured with 7-point likert scale.

As for emotional aspect, emotional vocabularies which were related to urgency were selected. Participants measured how the given patterns match well with each vocabulary. In a detailed aspect, adjectives relate to urgency presented on two axes, and then participants had to situate the patterns on a spot on each axis. The adjectives related to urgency such as 'important', 'urgent' were chosen from the previous research. After finishing questionnaire for every situation and pattern, simple instruction of the experiment was presented and the experiment ended.

3   Result

The result is analyzed by comparing the measurement of intuitiveness and attentiveness in cognitive aspect, and by emotional words in the emotional aspect through SPSS 18.0 statistical program.

Firstly urgency perception depending on the frequency of pattern (urgent/normal) is analyzed by t-test, and there is a significant difference in cognitive aspect in without color condition, Missed call: t(29) =-2.576, p=.015(Intuitiveness), t(29) =-3.294, p=.003(Attentiveness); Incoming call: t (29)=-2.567, p=.016. In color condition, there is also a significant difference, Missed call: t(29) =-9.485, p=.001(Intuitiveness), t (29)   =-6.747,   p=.001(Attentiveness);   Incoming   call: t(29)   =-7.099, p=.001(Intuitiveness), t(29) =-4.878, p=.001(Attentiveness). It is higher score of attentiveness and intuitiveness in urgent condition than in normal condition. Also in emotional aspect urgent condition shows higher score than normal condition, in without color condition, Missed call: t(29)=-9.549, p=0.001(Urgent), t(29)=-10.476, p=.001(Important); Incoming call: t(29)=-9.492,   p=.001(Urgent), t(29)=-7.94, p=.001(Important). In color condition, there is also a significant difference, Missed call: t(29)=-4.36, p=.001(Urgent), t(29)=-2.677, p=.012(Important); Incoming call: t(29)=-2.904, p=.007(Urgent), t(29)=-3.188, p=.003(Important) .

In addition, urgency perception depending on color is analyzed by ANOVA. There is   a   significant   difference,   Missed   call: F(1,29)=20.39,   p<.001(Intuitiveness), F(1,29)=13.08, p<.001(Attentiveness); Incoming call: F(1, 29) =11.868, p<.05(Intuitiveness), F(1,29)=13.67,   p=.001(Attentiveness). Users' urgency perception-both intuitiveness and attentiveness- is the highest when color is used and the blink rate of notification is high. The urgency perception score is the highest when the color is Red and the blink frequency is high. There is similar result from emotional aspect. In the condition of with color, it is higher score than in the condition without color when measure of emotional   words   including   urgent   and   important, Missed   call: F(1,29)=33.143, p<.001(Urgent),   F(1,29)=29.876,   p<.001(Important); Incoming call: F(1, 29) =17.939, p<.001(Urgent), F(1,29)=11.744,   p<.05(Important).   Furthermore, it is similar with the result of cognitive aspect that in the emotional aspect, the conditions of red and high blink frequency makes the highest score.

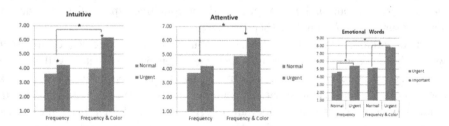

Fig. 1. Urgent perception score in Cognitive aspect (Left, Middle) and Emotional aspect (Right) of missed call

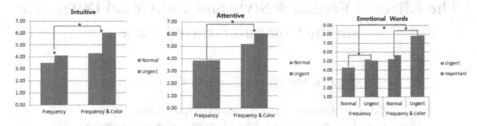

Fig. 2. Urgent Perception score in Cognitive aspect (Left, Middle) and Emotional aspect (Right) of incoming call

4   Conclusion

The present study showed that how the movement pattern and color of smartphone LED influenced users' urgency perception. As a result of measuring perceived urgency by manipulating LED blink frequency and color of smartphone, it is identified that high frequency pattern make meaningful higher score in cognitive aspect and emotional aspect and that the difference can be increased with using color. Also qualitative analysis of users through post-experiment interviews shows that most participants chose red as the best color to indicate urgency. Given that, we conclude that the use of red color with high blink frequency of the LED notification light is most effective in conveying urgency information. As stated earlier, people perceived urgency from red because a long wavelength color such as red has a greater arousing effect. To conclude, this study makes an important contribution by demonstrating that smartphone LED notification lights can be used to effectively deliver important messages to users when the movement pattern and color of LED lightings are properly designed.

Acknowledgement. This work has been supported by UX Lab, Mobile R&D Center, LG Electronics.

References

1. Bliss, J.P., Gilson, R.D., Deaton, J.E.: Human probability matching behavior in response to alarms of varying reliability. Ergonomics 38, 2300–2312 (1995)
2. Elliot, A.J., Maier, M.A., Moller, A.C., Friedman, R., Meinhardt, J.: Color and psychological functioning: the effect of red on performance attainment. Journal of Experimental Psychology: General 136, 154–168 (2007)
3. Guillaume, A., Pellieux, L., Chastres, V., Drake, C.: Judging the urgency of nonvocal auditory warning signals: Perceptual and cognitive processes. Journal of Experimental Psychology: Applied 9, 196–212 (2003)
4. Suied, C., Susini, P., McAdams, S.: Evaluating warning sound urgency with reaction times. Journal of Experimental Psychology: Applied 14, 201–212 (2008)
5. Kang, S.J.: The Functions of Color Based on Human Cognition in Information Design. Journal of Korean Society of Color Studies 20, 1–10 (2011)

The Effect of Feedback Style and Individual Difference on the Computer-Based Task

Jiyeun Lee, Minkyoung Shin, and Kwanghee Han

Cognitive Engineering Lab, Yonsei University, Seoul, Korea
{Amethystljy,gold7439}@gmail.com, khan@yonsei.ac.kr

Abstract. Although objectively same, feedback can be processed differently because of individual difference. The purpose of this study was to investigate how demographic factor (gender) and other individual difference (regulatory focus) influence afterward performances in computer-based situation. In the experiment, participants performed two phases of task with computer. Each task phase included two task types: cognitive task and creative task. After the first task phase, participants received feedback about their performance. Feedback was presented in two valence conditions: positive and negative. After the feedback, participants performed the second task phase. The participants' performance was measured by difference between the first and the second phase. As a result, the main effects of feedback valence were non-significant on both task types. However, in creative task, there was an interaction between valence and regulatory focus. Participants having prevention focus performed well after receiving negative feedback. On the other hand, people having promotion focus showed better performance after the positive feedback. Also, the interaction between valence of feedback and gender was marginally significant in creative task. Although, males' performances were almost same regardless of the feedback valence, females showed better performance after receiving negative feedback. No interaction effects were significant in cognitive task. This study was valuable in that we could reveal how individual differences and valence of feedback affect the performance of creative task on computers.

Keywords: feedback, valence, gender, regulatory focus.

1 Introduction

People often get a feedback such as a test result, a quiz result and GPA after their performance. These kinds of feedback are important not only as an outcome itself, but also as an objective assessment of current state. It also can be a trigger-point to lead a change in afterward performance. For these reasons, psychological, educational and industrial researchers continuously have paid attention to the feedback and its aftereffect.

Reviewing the literature about feedback studies, there were lots of studies about relationship between feedback style and performance. For instance, the absolute and relative feedback styles can make different effect on performer. Relative feedback has

C. Stephanidis (Ed.): HCII 2014 Posters, Part II, CCIS 435, pp. 626–631, 2014.
© Springer International Publishing Switzerland 2014

more strong impact on performers' subsequent behavior because people have a tendency to compare themselves with others and they are familiar with this comparison (Klein, 1997) [1]. Some researchers insist that valence of feedback is quite important. In other words, positive feedback and negative feedback have different effect on performer. Brett & Atwater (2001) showed that positive feedback is more easily accepted and regarded as desirable thing by performer than negative feedback [2]. Negative feedback, on the other hand, can decrease the intrinsic motivation and be regarded as an inaccurate result by feedback receiver (Anseel & Lievens, 2006) [3]. Sometimes, however, negative feedback can improve the fallowing performance by informing the gap between one's current performance and the goal (Carver & Scheier, 1998) [4].

In this context, we tested the feedback effect in computer using situation. Recently the prevalence of personal computer makes an online education and training more accessible. Also, feedback which comes from computer is generated frequently. But the scientific researches about computer-based feedback effect have been done little. In this article, we conducted experiment to investigate how feedback generated by computer influences the way people react.

In addition, we regarded that same information can be processed and remembered in different ways according to individual difference (Kelley & McLaughlin, 2012; Santesso et al., 2011) [5~6]. So, this study additionally investigates how individual differences influence performer's reaction when the feedback was presented. We focused on the two individual difference factors. One is gender. Male and female have different information processing style when facing emotional event (Hamann & Canli, 2004), so it makes sense that positive and negative feedback can be processed differently according to gender [7].

The other is regulatory focus. Regulatory focus is the cognitive style which refers to one's point of view toward positive and negative outcome. People who tend to promotion focus endeavor to achieve an ideal goal. So they are sensitive to presence or absence of positive outcomes. On the other hand, people who tend to have prevention focus want to avoid failure, so they are sensitive to presence or absence of negative outcomes (Higgins, 1998) [8]. So we thought that positive and negative feedback can be moderated by regulatory focus (promotion focus or prevention focus).

2   Experiment

2.1   Participants

78 undergraduate students in Yonsei University participated (mean age = 21.15 years; 42 males, 36 females). They took part in this experiment for their course credit. They didn't know the purpose and hypothesis of the experiment because we used deception to prevent demand characteristics. They knew the purpose of experiment is to find an average cognitive level of undergraduate student. They were randomly assigned to the positive feedback condition (n = 38) or the negative feedback condition (n = 41).

2.2   Stimuli and Procedure

The experiment was between-subject design. The external factor of this experiment was valence of feedback: positive and negative. After a first task phase, positive feedback condition was received high-score to their performance and negative feedback condition was received low-score to their performance. The inner factors factors were individual difference which is represented with gender and regulatory focus. The dependent variable was participants' performance of task.

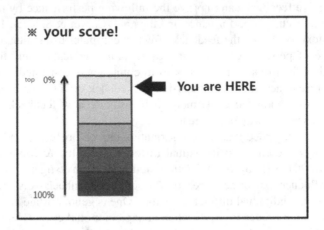

Fig. 1. The screen which positive feedback condition was received

In the experiment, participants answered some questionnaire and performed two task phases with online survey tool. First, they filled in the demographic information about their age and gender. Next, they completed a set of questionnaire measuring the level of regulatory focus (Elliot & Thrash, 2010) [9]. After that, participants met the two task phases. Each task phase consisted of two types of tasks: cognitive task and creative task. The reason we presented two different types of tasks was that the some kind of feedback can be more appropriate depending on task type [10].

After performing the first task phase (pre-feedback task phase), participants were given feedback on the computer screen. Positive and negative feedback were presented according to their predetermined condition. After feedback was presented, the second phase (post-feedback task phase) started. It was designed to have similar level of difficulty with the first task phase. The influence of feedback on participants was measured by calculating differences between pre-feedback and post-feedback task performance.

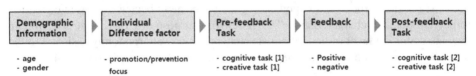

Fig. 2. Experiment procedure

2.3   Result

The effect of independent variables on participants' performance was analyzed by using SPSS. First of all, the main effect of external factor represented by feedback valence was confirmed. Then, individual differences which could influence the way of reaction were considered. Due to the limitation of online circumstance, we were not able to keep time people spent same. Especially, the time difference between pre and post-feedback tasks needed to be controlled. Therefore, we put the time difference as a covariate.

The Effect of Feedback Valence. To measure the difference between two feedback groups, we tried to find out the effect of the types of feedback valence (positive, negative). The influence of feedback on performance was measured by subtracting post-feedback score from pre-feedback score. As a result, the main effects of feedback valence on both creative, and cognitive tasks were not significant, $F (1, 75) = 2.93$, $p = .91$; $F (1, 75) = .51$, $p=.48$.   In other words, feedback valence did not affect the performance.

The Interaction Effects between Individual Differences and Feedback Valence. Although the effect caused by feedback valence was insignificant, it is hard to say that these two variables didn't have any influence on participants' performance. There could be other factors which influenced the way people reacted to the feedback, especially individual differences. The individual differences we focused were gender and regulatory focus. As a result, the interaction between individual difference and feedback valence was significant only in creative task condition.

Table 1. Interaction effect between regulatory focus and feedback valence

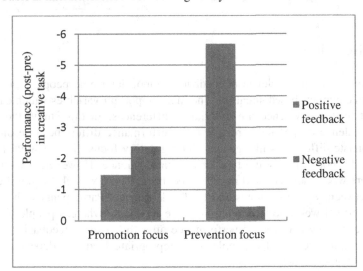

In creative task, there was an interaction between valence and regulatory focus, F (1, 69) = 7.28, $p < .05$. Participants having prevention focus performed well after receiving negative feedback ($M = -.45$, $SD = 6.49$) than positive feedback ($M = -5.68$, $SD = 4.44$), whereas people having promotion focus showed better performance after the positive feedback ($M = -1.47$, $SD = 5.33$) than negative feedback ($M = -2.39$, $SD = 4.20$).

In addition, the interaction between valence of feedback and gender in creative task was marginally significant, F (1, 69) = 3.19, $p = .078$. Although, males' performances were almost same regardless of the type of feedback valence, females showed better performance after receiving negative feedback ($M = .44$, $SD = 6.63$) than positive one ($M = -3.94$, $SD = 5.84$

Table 2. Interaction effect between gender and feedback valence (marginally significant)

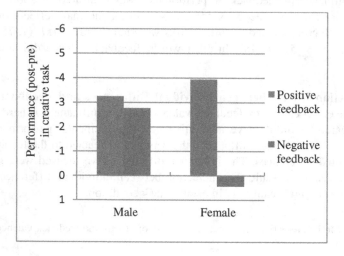

3   Discussion

This study reveals that valence of feedback cannot determine people's performance by itself in computer based situation. The more important variables which can change the effect feedback valence are individual differences. In this study, the effect of feedback valence on people's creative task performance differs because of the individual's innate differences like gender and regulatory focus. Specifically, men's performance did not differ by the type of feedback valence. However, women showed better score when they received negative feedback. There was also a significant interaction between regulatory focus and feedback valence. Participants with prevention focus performed well after receiving negative feedback, whereas people having promotion focus showed increased performance after the positive feedback. From these results, we can ascertain that people need appropriate feedback depending on their individual characteristics.

This study is distinct from former feedback studies in that the presented feedback was objective. There was no supervisor, so feedback didn't contain any emotional factor like face expression and voice tone. It means that how much people concentrate on task was totally dependent on each individual's ability. However, it is difficult to keep focusing on the given tasks. Therefore, it is more important to know individual differences when people learn through their computers, so that we can help people to keep optimal level of motivation.

Although this study is valuable when it comes to considering learning environment, still there are several problems. First, the creative task we provided was a word generation task which needs linguistic ability. Therefore, there is a possibility that only people who already knew a lot of words could get high scores. In the future study, it is necessary to verify whether the result is same even if the creative task does not contain linguistic ability. Second, people showed worse performance in post-feedback phase although it contained the same type of tasks with pre-feedback phase. The decline of performance can be explained by difficulty of concentrating. However, we did not check the concentration level in this study. Therefore, difference of concentration level should be considered to understand the reason in detail.

Nowadays, it is common to listen to online lectures. People also take examinations through computers. Therefore, understanding people's individual characteristics is getting significant to assist people when they study alone in the computer based situations.

References

1. Klein, W.M.: Objective standards are not enough: affective, self-evaluative, and behavioral responses to social comparison information. Journal of Personality and Social Psychology 72(4), 763–774 (1997)
2. Brett, J.F., Atwater, L.E.: 360° feedback: Accuracy, reactions, and perceptions of usefulness. Journal of Applied Psychology 86(5), 930–942 (2001)
3. Anseel, F., Lievens, F.: Certainty as a moderator of feedback reactions? A test of the strength of the self-verification motive. Journal of Occupational and Organizational Psychology 79, 533–551 (2006)
4. Carver, C.S., Scheier, M.F.: On the self-regulation of behavior. Cambridge University Press, New York (1998)
5. Kelley, C.M., McLaughlin, A.C.: Individual differences in the benefits of feedback for learning. Human Factors: The Journal of the Human Factors and Ergonomics Society 54(1), 26–35 (2012)
6. Santesso, D.L., Dzyundzyak, A., Segalowitz, S.J.: Age, sex and individual differences in punishment sensitivity: Factors influencing the feedback-related negativity. Psychophysiology 48(11), 1481–1489 (2011)
7. Hamann, S., Canli, T.: Individual differences in emotion processing. Current Opinion in Neurobiology 14(2), 233–238 (2004)
8. Higgins, E.T.: Promotion and prevention: Regulatory focus as a motivational principle. Advances in Experimental Social Psychology 30, 1–46 (1998)
9. Elliot, A.J., Thrash, T.M.: Approach and avoidance temperament as basic dimensions of personality. Journal of Personality 78(3), 865–906 (2010)
10. Shalley, C.E., Zhou, J., Oldham, G.R.: The effects of personal and contextual characteristics on creativity: Where should we go from here? Journal of Management 30(6), 933–958 (2004)

Won't It Please, Please Help Me?
The (Un)availability and (Lack of) Necessity
of Help Systems in Mobile Applications

Luana Müller, Lucio Cossio, and Milene Selbach Silveira

Faculdade de Informática — PUCRS
Avenida Ipiranga 6681, 90619-900, Porto Alegre - RS, Brazil
luana.muller,lucio.cossio{@acad.pucrs.br}
milene.silveira@pucrs.br

Abstract. The increasing dissemination of mobile devices has turned everybody into potential users of mobile applications. Due to the presumed ease of use of these applications along with the uncommon use of their help systems, most do not offer help systems within the applications and those that do are usually accessible only through Internet links. This double presumption that users do not need help because the application is easy to use and users have access to Internet everywhere - may negatively affect not only the use of the application in some (or various) situations, but even worse may cause users' to misunderstand their goals and possibilities. To explore this topic, we present a user study of 14 users about mobile applications and their (lack of) help systems.

Keywords: Help systems, mobile applications, user study.

1 Introduction

In countries such as the United States, Indonesia, Brazil, Russia, Japan and Germany it was estimated that there were more mobile subscriptions than the overall population in 2012 [6] (considering that some people have more than one mobile account). In this context, everybody is a potential user of mobile applications, including people with quite distinct digital literacy levels. For this reason, the majority of these applications must be easy to learn and use. Mobile application developers often assume that because it is easy to use an application, no help system is necessary. Therefore, they focus on creating a good design that users won't require help to use [1]. In addition to the fact that applications' ease of use "frees" them from built-in help systems, users lack of access of these help systems [2] [7] [9] seems to confirm the lack of necessity. As result, most mobile applications do not offer this function and those that do usually only offer hyperlinks to websites on the Internet.

But we should not assume that users always have access to mobile Internet, since it is not yet widespread in some countries. At the end of 2012, it was estimated that there was 23% 3G coverage globally. Countries such as Brazil, Indonesia and China had 35%, 19% and 16% coverage respectively [6]. Moreover, the

C. Stephanidis (Ed.): HCII 2014 Posters, Part II, CCIS 435, pp. 632–637, 2014.
© Springer International Publishing Switzerland 2014

user could also be temporarily disconnected or the service could be unavailable at a particular location. Simple tasks such as sending messages, configuring one's phone, or using an offline application such as video/music player/recorder/editor could be compromised by the lack of help available.

Moreover, solving a problem or answering a question is not the only reason for a help system. The help system is an essential component of an application. Designers can explicitly "speak" to the users through it, revealing how the application was built, how it can be used and what it can be used for. It is essential that users understand the designers' message so that they may better use and take advantage of the application [8].

As far as we know, there are few papers that present studies specifically regarding mobile help systems [2] [3] [5]. Previous studies refer to earlier types of help systems and take into account some of the new properties of these devices: the screen size is much smaller and the user's attention is frequently shifted away from the application to other tasks, generating a unique context when compared to other common computer paradigms. Despite this unique context, there has been little done in this field.

To better understand the impact of the availability, or lack thereof, of help systems in mobile applications, we performed a user study of distinct mobile applications and devices. We believe that the findings of this study can be used in the R&D of future mobile applications.

2   User Study

The motivation for the study came for an observation of a real usage scenario:

"John, a professional with more than 20 years of experience in the development of multi-platform software applications began to use a tablet. He realized he wasn't able to use some of an application's features. While searching for help, he noticed that this application and all of the other applications he needed to use did not provide any kind of help or only provided an Internet link to help information."

Based on this real scenario, we decided to conduct a user study, trying to better understand the way this (lack of) availability of help could affect users' interaction with mobile devices. We decided to use computer professionals in the study, considering the follow question: "If even professionals in the computer area are having problems using a mobile application, should we assume that these applications do not need a help system at all?"

Given that the more experience a user has with a system, the fewer usage issues he will have [4], these professionals thus represent a top boundary result in usability criteria. Hence, we conducted a user study, with 14 computer professional users that are all graduate students in Computer Science. A convenience sampling was used because of the ease and access to participants. They all also have had experience in research and/or experience in software development and have constant contact with customers and users of these systems. Thus, they were able to contribute good opinions about computer issues as professionals in the area.

The activities were performed on the authors' university campus in a computer laboratory. There were three observers to guide the experiment and observe the users while they executed the activities. The study will be described in detail in the next subsections.

2.1 Preliminary Study: Getting to Know Mobile Device Users

First of all, an online questionnaire was sent to the participants individually, to identify the mobile devices that they generally use and the tasks that they had difficulties performing at some time, in order to: (1) organize the participants in groups according to their device usage and (2) elaborate the possible tasks to be performed by them.

The questionnaire was composed of five questions. The first two questions were about the mobile devices that the participants were aware of and used and the last three, about their use of help systems and tasks that need them in their daily life.

The participants were asked about which devices they have some usage knowledge. Eleven participants mentioned the Android OS smartphone and 7 the Android OS tablet. The smartphone with iOS was mentioned by 8 participants and the tablet with iOS, was mentioned by 9.

2.2 Getting to Know the Users' Profile: Application of the Preliminary Questionnaire

This stage intended to identify the knowledge that participants had with smartphones and tablets and one of them did not have a daily contact with these kinds of devices. For the other 13 participants had the following characteristics:

- Age: the average age of this group was 30, ranging from 23 to 39;
- Current job: 5 work in the Information Technology area as developers, 1 as a test engineer, 1 a student, 1 a researcher, 3 as teachers and 2 did not specify.
- Professional experience: the average was 9.6 years of professional experience in computer science, ranging from one to 18 years. Three had one to five years, five had 6 to 10 years, three had 11 to 15 years and two participants had 16 to 20 years.

The use of mobile devices by the participants is described in Table 1. Of these, 11 participants reported that they have been using the device for more than one year, and only one does not use any type of mobile device such as a smartphone or tablet. Users reported performing activities as checking emails, accessing social networks, calendar, games, calls and SMSs, Internet access, photos and use of GPS. Of the 12 participants who have smartphones or tablets, 10 have daily access to the Internet through 3G or WAP. Participants were asked about how they usually learn about the functions of their devices. The answers are described in Table 2.

Table 1. The devices used by the participants

Devices	Number of participants
Smartphone iOS	3
Smartphone Android	8
Tablet iOS	2
Table Android	1

Table 2. How the participants usually learn about the functions of their devices

Learning method	Number of participants
Trial and error	12
Research on the Internet	8
Read the device's manual	2

Participants were also asked if they considered the existence of help systems unnecessary for these devices and their applications. Nine participants considered it necessary to have help systems in these devices. One of the participants described the help system in these devices as unnecessary because they are so easy to use and because of the abundance of information available on the Internet. Another participant reported that the help systems are necessary, because of lay users that need them. However he believes that younger users will probably not use this system.

In general, the participants reported that they don't use help systems (10 participants). To some of them, the help system is an option when they can't find the solution on the Internet. The participants also said that they believe that help systems need to be focused on the basic tasks of the software and the Internet should provide more complete information (other users that have/had the same problem and discussions about the subject). Most of them believe that some kind of software help is necessary to aid the user. They also believe that all applications must be prepared to address users' different knowledge levels and always work with the possibility that at some moment the user would have a question to be answered.

Grouping Users and Choice of Tasks. Participants were divided into four groups according to the mobile devices they had more affinity with/knowledge of (as stated by them in the first questionnaire). The four groups were characterized by the use of Smartphones with OS Android, Smartphones with OS iOS, Tablets with OS Android, Tablets with OS iOS.

Each group received a list of possible tasks to be performed on the related device. These tasks were based on the findings in the preliminary questionnaire and users' complaints discussed on social networks and discussion forums. The groups were asked to choose the task they thought to be the most complex to perform. They analyzed the possible tasks and tried to execute them on their own devices. After analysis, the tasks were selected: To modify the smartphone ringtone to a MP3 song available on the device (Android smartphone); to create a photo album using a app with some pictures available in the device (Android tablet); to turn on the flash when a call is received (iOS smartphone); to configure a printer on the device (iOS tablet). After the task selection, they were switched to another group. The group that usually uses smartphones with Android OS, had to perform the task chosen by the group that uses smartphones running iOS and vice versa. The group with Android OS tablets had to perform the task chosen by the group with iOS tablets and vice versa. The groups switched tasks and devices too.

Task Execution and Rationale Description. All of the four groups managed to accomplish the task they were assigned. After performing the tasks, each group was informed that they should describe the rationale they used to solve the problem (discussion, prior knowledge, trial and error, Google, help system, etc.). All the four groups used trial and error as first option in order to accomplish the task. Three of them had to research in Google to finish the task.

About the help systems of these devices, only the group with the Android OS smartphone found a help tutorial with little helpful information. On the Internet, help options were found on the device's web site.

Users Impressions: Application of the Post-testing Questionnaire. The participants were asked about how they understood the complexity of the task they received only by reading its description and how they understood the complexity of the task they received after executed it. The results are reported in Table 3.

Table 3. How the participants understood their tasks only reading and after executed it

	Simple	Intermediate	Complex
Only reading the description	10	3	1
After execute the task	2	10	2

They were also asked about the necessity of mobile applications providing help systems. Eleven of the 14 participants believe that they are necessary. According to them, the user may not be familiar with the device's OS or the app used. The three participants that said that the help isn't necessary justified this by saying they are used to finding help on the Internet or that in the case of the performed task the interface is the problem and needs to be redesigned.

3   Conclusions and Future Work

This work has presented a user study performed in order to explore the availability and necessity of help systems in mobile applications. Even experienced computer professionals found it difficult to execute some tasks without help. Based on this, we could predict that novice users would experience more acute problems in these situations [4].

At the end of the study, most of the participants changed their feelings about the complexity of the performed tasks, because they observed that without the help found through Internet searches they would not have been able to execute them. Based on this study and participants' reports, a good option would be a hybrid help system that allows users to access the main operational help on the device and redirects them to Internet content for more complex tasks and also allows them to get collaborative help from other users.

This work does not allow us to draw final conclusions for all situations, but we hope that future researchers and developers will think about how they will provide help to mobile application users.

References

1. Holtzblatt, K.: Customer-centered Design for Mobile Applications. Personal Ubiquitous Comput. 9(4), 227–237 (2005)
2. Inbar, O., Lavie, T., Meyer, J.: Acceptable Intrusiveness of Online Help in Mobile Devices. In: Proceedings of the 11th International Conference on Human-Computer Interaction with Mobile Devices and Services, MobileHCI 2009, pp. 26:1–26:4. ACM, New York (2009)
3. Jepsen, K., Glass, G., Englert, R.: When 'One Fits All' Does Not Fit: Study of Visualization Types for Mobile Help Systems. In: Proceedings of the 23rd British HCI Group Annual Conference on People and Computers: Celebrating People and Technology, BCS-HCI 2009, pp. 398–404. ACM, New York (2009)
4. Kjeldskov, J., Skov, M.B., Stage, J.: Does Time Heal?: A Longitudinal Study of Usability. In: Proceedings of the 17th Australia Conference on Computer-Human Interaction: Citizens Online: Considerations for Today and the Future, OZCHI 2005, pp. 1–10. ACM, New York (2005)
5. Leung, R., Tang, C., Haddad, S., Mcgrenere, J., Graf, P., Ingriany, V.: How Older Adults Learn to Use Mobile Devices: Survey and Field Investigations. ACM Trans. Access. Comput. 4(3), 11:1–11:33 (2012)
6. MobiThinking, Global Mobile Statistics 2012 Home (December 2012), http://mobithinking.com/mobile-marketing-tools/latest-mobile-stats
7. Novick, D.G., Ward, K.: Why Don'T People Read the Manual? In: Proceedings of the 24th Annual ACM International Conference on Design of Communication, SIGDOC 2006, pp. 11–18. ACM, New York (2006)
8. Silveira, M.S., Barbosa, S.D.J., Souza, C.S.: Designing online help systems for reflective users. Journal of the Brazilian Computer Society 9, 25–38 (2004)
9. Welty, C.J.: Usage of and Satisfaction with Online Help vs. Search Engines for Aid in Software Use. In: Proceedings of the 29th ACM International Conference on Design of Communication, SIGDOC 2011, pp. 203–210. ACM, New York (2011)

Classification of the Context of Use for Smart Phones

Ralf Reichmuth[1] and Sebastian Möller[2]

[1] Center of Human-Machine Systems, GRK prometei, TU Berlin, Germany
[2] Quality and Usability Lab, Telekom Innovation Laboratories, TU Berlin, Germany
rreichmuth@zmms.tu-berlin.de, sebastian.moeller@telekom.de

Abstract. Mobile devices like smart phones are used in various contexts of use. Hence we conducted an explorative field study to determine factors influencing smart phone interaction. The results of the study suggest that a smart phone is often used in a relaxed situation and a familiar environment. In contrast to this, few interactions take place in a stressful situation. In addition to that, the location and the activity of the test participant seem to have an impact on the smart phone interaction.

Keywords: classification of the context of use, mobile context of use, influence factors, mobile app.

1 Introduction

Smart phone applications are used in various contexts of use. With the intention to reduce the complexity of these applications for the user, the relevance of context-sensitive behavior increases. That is why it is essential to get a detailed description and classification of the context of use. Therefore we developed a native iPhone questionnaire app for a field study. Within this study we tracked the test participants' context of use while they were using their personal smart phones.

2 Method

We invited 16 test participants to the university to be briefed about the field study and to deploy the questionnaire app on their personal iPhone. For a period of two days test participants were asked to document the contexts of any use on their smart phones, where a *use* was determined by unlocking the display. To ensure a balance between work related and private usage, the test participants had to select one weekday (between Monday and Friday) and one day at the weekend (between Saturday and Sunday) for the record. Test participants should characterize their context of use with the help of the app each time before they normally interacted with their smart phones. They were also informed that sensor and user data would be recorded repeatedly in the background.

The handling of the questionnaire app was designed so that the participants could quickly and flexibly state their context and thus the regular interaction with the smart phone was influenced as little as possible. Furthermore, the opportunity was given to

C. Stephanidis (Ed.): HCII 2014 Posters, Part II, CCIS 435, pp. 638–642, 2014.

describe an interaction later in case they were under time pressure. For each use, answers to 15 questions (14 mandatory and 1 optional) had to be given. One question each was presented on one screen of the app. Care was taken that the questions cover each of the influence factors of Schmidt's [3] working model for context. This model refers to mobile computers and contains 6 influence factors which can be associated with 2 dimensions, namely *human factors* (information on the user, the user's tasks and social environment) and the *physical environment* (infrastructure, physical conditions and location). First, test participants were given the opportunity to skip the questionnaire in case they were unable to answer it in their current situation. Then, they had to provide the following information via the questionnaire: the perceived relevance of the interaction, their emotion, if and which other main tasks they had, their smart phone task, activity, social environment, location, environmental influences, other devices in the environment and whether or not they were influenced by something else. Finally, they had to state which of these potentially influencing factors was the most significant. To assess their emotion (pleasure, arousal and dominance) the 5-step Self-Assessment Manikin (SAM) [2] was used.

In addition to the manual entry of the context of use, the app ran in the background and recorded data about the participant's behavior. The selected answer options and the stored data were then sent to a server at TU Berlin for later analysis. After all test participants finished the study, the data were screened and usage instances outside the considered 2-day period were deleted. Two evaluators then sorted the free text responses into categories. For instance, the activity was classified into the categories *lying, sitting, standing, walking* and *other* and the location was classified into *home, mobile or outdoors, stationary and not a private apartment, work* and *other private apartment or garden*. The interval variables of the three dimensions of SAM and the perceived 5-step relevance of the interaction were normalized to the value 3 for each test participant.

3   Results

The study was conducted from August 12, to September 1, 2013. Sixteen test participants (7 male and 9 female, aged from 21 to 29 years) completed the questionnaire 736 times in total, with an average of 46 (min = 20, max = 86, sd = 21.4) interactions within the two days.

From the wealth of data collected in the study, in this paper we only present the findings which we can interpret by now. In 92.4% of the situations test participants were not affected by influences outside the model of context of use which was presented in Chapter 2. This indicates that the model covers most relevant factors of the context of use. The main influences which were added were tiredness and stress. The smart phone was mostly used in a stationary context, and especially a lot at home (62.9%). Furthermore, smart phones were used mainly for communication purposes (53.9%). The smart phone was no longer used primarily for making phone calls (9.4%), but a lot for written communication, especially for short messages (33% for chat and SMS).

We now present the influence factors *location* and *activity* in two contingency tables (Table 1 and 2) and their influence on the smart phone task. The percent values describe the distribution of all interactions in a row. The color is normalized in each column, which means the color white indicates the lowest value and the color green indicates the highest value in each column.

In a private apartment the smart phone was rarely used for phone calls (Table 1). Furthermore, test participants used the smart phone for short messages in the same distribution at all location except for *another private apartment or garden* (e.g. a friend's apartment). Games are used mainly at home and in a mobile or outdoor context. Not surprisingly, the smart phone was mostly used for navigation in a mobile context. In a stationary location, which was not a private apartment (e.g. cafe, concert) the smart phone was primarily used for communication (70.7%). Unfortunately, during the study only a few of the 16 test participants interacted with their smart phone in *other private apartment and garden* or at *work*.

Table 1. Contingency table of location and smart phone task

<table>
<tr><td rowspan="2"></td><td rowspan="2"></td><td colspan="10" align="center">Smart phone task</td><td rowspan="2">Total</td></tr>
<tr><td>Phone call</td><td>Short messages</td><td>E-mail</td><td>Social networks</td><td>Other mobile web</td><td>Games</td><td>Media consumption</td><td>Navigation</td><td>Basic smart phone functions</td><td>Other</td></tr>
<tr><td rowspan="5">Location</td><td>Home</td><td>7.6%</td><td>34.1%</td><td>10.4%</td><td>5.8%</td><td>18.6%</td><td>4.1%</td><td>4.1%</td><td>0.9%</td><td>13.4%</td><td>1.1%</td><td>463</td></tr>
<tr><td>Mobile or outdoors</td><td>13.3%</td><td>37.2%</td><td>10.6%</td><td>0.9%</td><td>13.3%</td><td>1.8%</td><td>7.1%</td><td>8.8%</td><td>6.2%</td><td>0.9%</td><td>113</td></tr>
<tr><td>Stationary, not a private apartment</td><td>15.5%</td><td>36.2%</td><td>19.0%</td><td>6.9%</td><td>5.2%</td><td>0.0%</td><td>5.2%</td><td>0.0%</td><td>12.1%</td><td>0.0%</td><td>58</td></tr>
<tr><td>Work</td><td>11.3%</td><td>34.0%</td><td>11.3%</td><td>1.9%</td><td>18.9%</td><td>0.0%</td><td>3.8%</td><td>0.0%</td><td>18.9%</td><td>0.0%</td><td>53</td></tr>
<tr><td>Other private apartment or garden</td><td>8.2%</td><td>8.2%</td><td>16.3%</td><td>16.3%</td><td>28.6%</td><td>0.0%</td><td>4.1%</td><td>0.0%</td><td>6.1%</td><td>12.2%</td><td>49</td></tr>
<tr><td>Total</td><td></td><td>69</td><td>243</td><td>85</td><td>41</td><td>128</td><td>21</td><td>34</td><td>14</td><td>89</td><td>12</td><td></td></tr>
</table>

Table 2. Contingency table of activity and smart phone task

<table>
<tr><td rowspan="2"></td><td rowspan="2"></td><td colspan="10" align="center">Smart phone task</td><td rowspan="2">Total</td></tr>
<tr><td>Phone call</td><td>Short messages</td><td>E-mail</td><td>Social networks</td><td>Other mobile web</td><td>Games</td><td>Media consumption</td><td>Navigation</td><td>Basic smart phone functions</td><td>Other</td></tr>
<tr><td rowspan="5">Activity</td><td>Sitting</td><td>10.2%</td><td>32.4%</td><td>11.1%</td><td>6.9%</td><td>18.2%</td><td>2.4%</td><td>3.8%</td><td>1.9%</td><td>11.1%</td><td>2.1%</td><td>423</td></tr>
<tr><td>Lying</td><td>2.3%</td><td>33.3%</td><td>11.7%</td><td>5.3%</td><td>18.7%</td><td>6.4%</td><td>6.4%</td><td>0.6%</td><td>14.0%</td><td>1.2%</td><td>171</td></tr>
<tr><td>Standing</td><td>11.4%</td><td>39.8%</td><td>12.5%</td><td>3.4%</td><td>14.8%</td><td>0.0%</td><td>1.1%</td><td>3.4%</td><td>13.6%</td><td>0.0%</td><td>88</td></tr>
<tr><td>Walking</td><td>24.4%</td><td>24.4%</td><td>13.3%</td><td>0.0%</td><td>13.3%</td><td>0.0%</td><td>8.9%</td><td>4.4%</td><td>11.1%</td><td>0.0%</td><td>45</td></tr>
<tr><td>Other</td><td>11.1%</td><td>33.3%</td><td>11.1%</td><td>0.0%</td><td>0.0%</td><td>0.0%</td><td>22.2%</td><td>0.0%</td><td>11.1%</td><td>11.1%</td><td>9</td></tr>
<tr><td>Total</td><td></td><td>69</td><td>243</td><td>85</td><td>41</td><td>128</td><td>21</td><td>34</td><td>14</td><td>89</td><td>12</td><td></td></tr>
</table>

While walking, the smart phone was used in 24.4% of all interactions for phone calls and less than usual for short messages (table 2). When the participants had a more relaxed body posture (lying or sitting), they used social networks and games more often compared to situations when they stood or walked.

In 80.7% of all cases test participants interacted with their smart phone while sitting or lying, 84.6% of the interactions took place in a stationary context and 64.8% with a low arousal level. The interactions which took place in a relaxed and stress-free situation (i.e. with low arousal, stationary and while sitting or lying all together) account for 48.8% of all interactions in this study. The data indicate that the participants often used their smart phones when they were in a relaxed body position, not on the move and in a relaxed situation. Furthermore, interactions which happened in a relaxed situation were perceived not to be very relevant for the test participant.

Looking at the most important 10% of all smart phone interactions compared to the least important 10% something stands out: communication is changing. With an above-average frequency the smart phone was used for phone calls (24.3%) and less often for e-mails (6.8%), if the interaction was perceived to be important. In contrast to that, the smart phone was never used for phone calls (0.0%) and more frequently for e-mailing (17.6%), if the interaction was perceived to be unimportant.

4   Discussion

In this study we detected some results which are consistent with other studies, for instance that the smart phone was mostly used at home [4] and primarily for communication [1]. In addition, the communication changed at different locations and when different activities were performed. Very often the smart phone was used for communication in a public location (e.g. cafe, concert). Possibly the smart phone was used to find each other in these cases. Furthermore, it could have been difficult to enter text for short messages while walking, so test participants took a break and stood or sat down. Unfortunately, because the study took place in the semester break and test participants were mostly students, the context *work* in the influence factor *location* may be underrepresented in this study.

5   Conclusion and Future Work

There is a large cluster that accounts for interactions which take place in a stress-free environment, and a small cluster that accounts for interactions, where the interaction is perceived to be important. The smart phone interaction and especially communication was changing in different locations and when the test participants performed different activities. So the smart phone was very often used for communication in a public location. Unfortunately, the sample is too small to make statements about more specific contexts. These initial findings can give a hint to describe the context of use better in further studies. We plan to distribute a questionnaire app to a higher number of test participants offering only multiple choice questions and no free text question and also to collect more dependent variables.

We hope these results will help us in further studies to classify the clusters for smart phones into more precise contexts. When available, sensors in the smart phone can automatically classify these meaningful contexts in the future, non-relevant information can be hidden, and relevant information can be shown to the end user, depending on the classified context of use.

References

1. Böhmer, M., Hecht, B., Schöning, J., Krüger, A., Bauer, G.: Falling asleep with angry birds, facebook and kindle: a large scale study on mobile application usage. In: Proc. MobileHCI 2011, pp. 47–56 (2011)
2. Lang, P.J., Bradley, M.M., Cuthbert, B.N.: International affective picture system (IAPS): Affective ratings of pictures and instruction manual. Technical Report A-6. University of Florida, Gainesville, FL (2005)
3. Schmidt, A., Beigl, M., Gellersen, H.-W.: There is more to context than location. Computers & Graphics 23(6), 893–901 (1999)
4. Verkasalo, H.: Contextual patterns in mobile service usage. Personal and Ubiquitous Computing 13(5), 331–342 (2008)

Usability Analyses of Interactive Children's iPad StoryBook

Pei-shiuan Tsai[1] and Lan-ling Huang[2]

[1] Department of Early Childhood Education University of Taipei, Taiwan
peishian@gmail.com
[2] Graduate School of Design National Yunlin University of Science & Technology, Taiwan
g9630806@yuntech.edu.tw

Abstract. The main purpose of the research is to understand the current situation of design and development of interactive children's iPad storybook and analyze the usability. The researcher used the ranking lists search and browsing in Apple Store for browsing various interactive children's iPad storybook in great number. We screened out six different models to be used in interactive children's iPad storybook and conducted the analyses of usability. We selected by purposive sampling 16 adults (including eight teachers, four mothers and four fathers) and four six-year-old children (2 boys and 2 girls) who had experiences of using iPad. The subjects at first browsed six interactive children's iPad storybooks. Then 16 adults filled out the questionnaires, four children were interviewed and their operations were observed to understand their preferences and the uses of the products. The recommendations for future publishers and designers were: a) increase the interactions of story content; b) increase traditional chinese subtitles and voice; c) integrate storybook platforms.

Keywords: e-Storybook, e-PictureBook, e-Book, iPad storybook, iPad picture-book, Usability.

1 Introduction

As 3C products are the favorite of youth groups, how to properly use the tools to become a very important issue. The 3C products such as tablet PC, iPad, smart phone and e-book reader are unknowing invade our daily life. For the new-generation of children, the time and opportunities for reading paper books hence become less and less while the time spending on 3C products are more and more. The contents provided by those tools become a focus point of concern. Even with new device, children do not necessarily love learning or reading, but undeniably, equipped by e-book reader and combined with multimedia elements, the reading contents have provided a different reading experience. When the iPad launched in May 2010, it was reported to be one of the most popular electronic devices [1][2]. iPad, combined a touch screen and multimedia, provides an experience of more intuitive operation than other device such as web pages and CD versions. The main purpose of the research is to understand the current situation of design and development of iPad electronic storybooks and analyze their usability.

C. Stephanidis (Ed.): HCII 2014 Posters, Part II, CCIS 435, pp. 643–648, 2014.
© Springer International Publishing Switzerland 2014

2   Literature Review

Electronic Book. The Chinese term "electronic book" is directly translated from English. In literature, Van Dam mentioned electronic books for the first time. In a broad sense, it means the media that stores and transmits the characters and pictures information through electronic channel [3]. Barker [4] argued that the electronic book was used to describe new type of books that was different from traditional paper books. But like paper books, they were composed of pages. The difference was that each page of an electronic book was designed and dynamic electronic information. Electronic book could be considered an aggregation of multi-pages, responsive and lively multi-media (includes information of characters, picture or voice). A storybook is an art form that combines visual and verbal narratives in a book format. A true storybook tells the story both with words and pictures. Electronic storybook (or e-Storybook, EPB) is to present storybooks in the electronic form including CD-ROM, WWW. The applied multi-media elements include characters, pictures, animations, voice, sound effects and music. It mainly operates through mouse and keyboard in user control (interactive operation pattern). The manipulation of mouse includes drag and click whereas the manipulation of the keyboard I include character enter and key enter. The source of story materials includes adaptation and creation. The E-book in the research means iPad e-Storybooks.

Usability. ISO defines usability as "The extent to which a product can be used by specified users to achieve specified goals with effectiveness, efficiency, and satisfaction in a specified context of use. Schneiderman [5] emphasizes consistency and predictability in interface design that provides for a high level of user control. Usability means that the people who use the product can do so quickly and easily to accomplish their own tasks. This definition rests on four points: (1) Usability means focusing on users; (2) people use products to be productive; (3) are busy people trying to accomplish tasks; and (4) users decide when a product is easy to use [6]. Lazar [7] highlights ease-of-use as an equally important usability consideration he also advocates for a balanced approach to Web design that allows for the appropriate use of media elements such as graphics, plug-ins, and animation. Usability is the quality of attribute that assesses how easy user interfaces are to use. The word "usability" also refers to methods for improving ease-of-use during the design process. Usability is defined by five quality components: Learnability, Efficiency, Memorability, Errors, Satisfaction. [8]

In conclusion, usability includes considerations such as: (1) Who are the users, what do they know, and what can they learn? (2) What do users want or need to do? (3) What is the general background of the users? (4) What is the context in which the user is working? (5) What has to be left on the machine? Usability is the ease of use and learnability of a human-made object.

3   Methodology

3.1   Procedure

1. In October 1 to October 31, 2013, the researchers searched for electronic story-books in the Books category of Apple App Store, and found over 100 production companies publishing electronic storybooks for iPad in total. According to the overall design, 6 more features free electronic storybooks were chosen by the researchers for further questionnaire, interviews and observation. The New iPad (Wi-Fi only) with 64GB memory and iOS 6.1.4 was selected for the study.
2. A questionnaire survey of five-point Likert items (1: strongly disagree, 2: disagree, 3: neither agree nor disagree, 4: agree, 5: strongly agree) and interviews were performed to adult users. The content of the questionnaire mainly included overall design, easy operation, story animation design, text design, and voice design. The interviews mainly involved questions about the operations of electronic story-books from different websites, and finding out the reasons of users' satisfaction or dissatisfaction.
3. Observations of child users' operations and interviews with those users were made. The researchers observed child users' behaviors in the operation process, and interviewed them about the issues they had encountered in their operations.

3.2   Study Subjects

1. 16 adults who had not used the iPad before (including eight teachers, four mothers and four fathers who had at least one child) randomly browsed the 6 electronic storybooks, then filled out the questionnaire. 8 of the adults had master's degrees, and 8 had bachelor's degrees. Every subject took about 1 hour to finish the process.
2. 4 children who had not used the iPad before (four 6-year-old, two boys and two girls) randomly browsed the 6 electronic storybooks, and were observed and interviewed by the researchers. Every time after finishing one electronic storybook, each child was asked if the rest was needed, and took rests when necessary. Every subject took about 1-1.5 hours to finish the process.

4   Results and Conclusions

The results of the questionnaire and interviews are summed up as follows:

Overall Design. Although the styles of the six electronic storybooks were different, users all had pretty good satisfaction to them. The scores the storybooks got on the questionnaires filled by the adults were all 4.1 and above. The children liked the storybooks as well. For example, C3 said "I hope Father and Mother will buy them for me, I like every one of them.", C5 said "It would be great if our textbooks were this interesting."

Operation Design. The user can operate the flip function of electronic storybooks. The storybooks that had left and right arrow marks on the screen were instantly understood by users. Children needed the researchers' reminding to roll over pages, but had no difficulties on operation either. Also, they became more skilled in operating auto and manual play, and text / voice switch, after they encountered them twice. Child users said that it was really convenient to click with fingers. "Snow White - 3D Pop-up Book" had the most different design among the six electronic storybooks, but could as well be smoothly operated with hints given. The recording function provided by some of the storybooks was very fresh to the subjects. For example, the child C2 said "It is fun that you can record the story you read."

Text Design. Taiwanese children's mother tongue is Chinese. E-storybooks that were presented only in English or non-Chinese were still difficult for the subjects. Adult subjects applauded that electronic storybooks provided versions of multiple languages for operators. For example, the teacher T4 said "Take Little Snail as an example. It provides many different text languages so that more people in the world can browse it. That is what present multimedia design can do." Only most adult subjects thought that the traditional Chinese version should be modified for Taiwan's readers.

Illustration Design. The six e-storybooks have different styles and each subject has his own preference. As a whole, the average scores of adult questionnaires were over 3.9. "I love all of them, but 'The Three Little Pigs' is the one I love most because the pig in the book can move; 'Snow White' is also very special and I have never seen such book."

Voice Design. Text and voice is mutually collocated that most of the adult subjects for the part of the Chinese voice proposed that it be appropriate to find native Taiwanese for dubbing to avoid the interference from an accent in listening. The adult subjects affirmed that the English text was helpful to the non-English speaking readers for the enhancement in learning English, but proposed to add the Chinese.

Animation Design. Most of the e-storybooks on the current iPad are presented without or with limited animation. The limited animation is dominated with the movement of leading characters or part of objects, or zoom-in and out and movement of camera shots. The child subjects showed high interest in the dynamic performance. When the researcher hinted that some figures or objects in the frame can be clicked with fingers. For children, it is a very new try and they will try to click to see if there is any reaction.

As a whole, there are two primary common points in the six e-storybooks: 1) single-line development of the story; 2) the contents of the story lacks of interactions that both adult and child users indicated that they wish to read more e-storybooks if they have a chance because there are many differences comparing to reading physical books.

5   Suggestions

This research evaluated the operation and uses of six selected e-storybooks and gave following suggestions for the reactions from the subjects. It is hoped that in future,

Table 1. The Basic Information of the Six Electronic Picturebooks

Story Name	The Little Snail	One Pizza, One Penny	Bedtime Monster	Just Grandma and Me	The Three Little Pigs	Snow White - 3D Pop-up Book
Publisher	Rye Studio	Apple Tree & Guru Bear	Siena Enter-tainment, LLC	Oceanhouse Media	Nosy Crow	lee hee suck
Illustration Design	2D	2D	2D	2D	3D	3D
Language (Text)	English, Traditional Chinese, Simplified Chinese, Japanese, French, German, Spanish	English, Traditional Chinese, Simplified Chinese	English Spanish	English	English	English
Language (Voice)	English, Chinese, Japanese, French, German, Spanish	English, Chinese	English Spanish	English	English	English
Sleeping Mode (voice only)	✓	✓	✗	✗	✗	✗
Record	✓	✓	✗	✗	✗	✗
Flip Mode	1.Auto 2.Manual (click on last/next page button to turn)	1. Auto 2.Manual (click on bottom left/right corner to turn)	1. Auto 2.Manual (click on last/next page button to turn)	1. Auto 2. Manual (roll over the page to turn)	1. Auto 2.Manual (click on last/next page button to turn)	1. Auto 2.Manual (click on last/next page button to turn)
Page Index	✗	✗	✓	✗	✗	✗
Bookmark	✗	✓	✓	✓	✗	✗
Operating Instructions	✓	✗	✓	✗	✓	✗
Story Scenes Content Clicking	✗	✗	✗	✓	✓	✓
Simple Animation	✗	✗	✗	✓	✓	✗
Extended Activities	✗	✓	✗	✗	✗	✓

more selected storybooks and subjects could be used for the usability evaluation that will prompt more concrete contributions to the designs of electronic storybooks.

Enhance the Interaction of the Story. Given the fact that many storybooks were adapted from printing storybooks in which the story is developed in single-line, the interaction of story contents is limited. The advantages of multi-media are that it could facilitate the increase of interaction. In the future, we could bring the characteristics into full play by increasing double-line or even multi-line developments of the story and the design of interaction with the contents of the story to enhance the interaction between readers and story contents.

Increase Traditional Chinese Subtitles and Voice. At the present time, only a few developers provide traditional subtitles and voice in their e-storybooks including Rye Studio、Apple Style、RYBooks Studio. Many other excellent electronic storybooks choose English as their only or primary language. But they can just add traditional Chinese subtitles and voice to meet the requirement from readers in Taiwan. So we suggest that the developers cooperate with foreign developers in adding traditional Chinese subtitles and voice for the readers in Taiwan that more children have a chance to read the rich contents of electronic storybooks.

Integrate Storybook Platforms. Although there is classification of books in Apple App Store, searching for specific e-storybooks is a time-consuming job. Therefore, we suggest that create a classification for the e-storybooks or design a browser search interface exclusively for the children.

In summary, from the angle of emotional interaction, operation interaction, cognition interaction and community interaction, the design of existing e-storybooks could strengthen the cognition interaction and community interaction that the visitors could interact with the contents of electronic storybooks through the characteristics of multimedia factors that are different from the printing books. Also, it could have meaningful community interactions with other readers through the linking of Internet. With the creativity and innovation of interactive technology, more and more excellent iPad storybook worthy of researchers continue to invest in research.

References

1. Anderson, H.: iPad: The savior of digital publishing. Journal of Internet Law 14(10), 15–20 (2011)
2. Murray, O., Olcese, N.: Teaching and learning with iPads, reading or not? Tech-Trends 55(5), 42–48 (2011)
3. Lwo, L.-S.: Electronic books and the new communication era. Instructional Technology and Media 21, 13–16 (1995) (Chinese)
4. Barker, P.: Electronic books and libraries of the future. The Electronic Library 10(3), 139–149 (1992)
5. Schneiderman, B.: Leonardo's laptop: Human needs and the new computing technologies. The MIT Press, Cambridge (2002)
6. Dumas, J.S., Redish, J.C.: A practical guide to usability testing. Intellectual Books, Portland (1999)
7. Lazar, J.: Web usability: A user-centered design approach. Pearson Education, Inc., Boston (2006)
8. Nielsen, J.: Usability 101: Introduction to Usability (2003), http://www.useit.com/alertbox/20030825.html (retrieved December 20, 2008)

Author Index

Printed in the United States
By Bookmasters